Studies in Church History

Subsidia

8

HUMANISM AND REFORM:
THE CHURCH IN EUROPE, ENGLAND, AND SCOTLAND, 1400-1643

James K. Cameron

HUMANISM AND REFORM: THE CHURCH IN EUROPE, ENGLAND, AND SCOTLAND, 1400-1643

Essays in Honour of James K. Cameron

EDITED BY

JAMES KIRK

PUBLISHED FOR

THE ECCLESIASTICAL HISTORY SOCIETY

BY

BLACKWELL PUBLISHERS

1991

© Ecclesiastical History Society 1991

First published 1991

Basil Blackwell Ltd
108 Cowley Road, Oxford OX4 1JF, UK

Basil Blackwell, Inc.
3 Cambridge Center,
Cambridge, Massachusetts 02142, USA

British Library Cataloguing in Publication Data

A CIP catalogue record for this book is available from the British Library

Library of Congress Cataloging in Publication Data
Humanism and reform: the Church in Europe, England, and Scotland, 1400–1643: essays in honour of James K. Cameron / edited by James Kirk.
   p.   cm.—(Studies in church history. Subsidia: 8)
Includes bibliographical references.
ISBN 0–631–17921–6
1. Reformation. 2. Church history—Middle Ages, 600–1500.
I. Cameron, James K. (James Kerr), 1924–   . II. Kirk, James.
III. Series.
BR309.H75   1991
274.05––dc20   91–672

Typeset by Joshua Associates Limited, Oxford
Printed in Great Britain by Billing and Sons Ltd, Worcester

CONTENTS

CONTENTS

CONTENTS

LIST OF CONTRIBUTORS

MATTHEW BLACK
Professor Emeritus of Divinity and Biblical Criticism and former
Principal of St Mary's College, University of St Andrews

EUAN CAMERON
Lecturer in History, University of Newcastle upon Tyne

CLAIRE CROSS
Professor of History, University of York

JANE E. A. DAWSON
Tutor in Modern History, University of St Andrews

A. G. DICKENS
Professor Emeritus of History, King's College, University of London

BRUCE GORDON
Post-doctoral Scholar, University of St Andrews

DENYS HAY
Professor Emeritus of Medieval History, University of Edinburgh

W. IAN P. HAZLETT
Senior Lecturer in Church History, University of Glasgow

JAMES KIRK
Reader in Scottish History, University of Glasgow

F. R. J. KNETSCH
Professor Emeritus of Dutch Church History, University of
Groningen

DAVID M. LOADES
Professor of History, University College of North Wales

I. D. McFARLANE
Professor Emeritus of French Literature, University of Oxford

JOHN MACQUEEN
Professor Emeritus of Scottish Literature and Oral Tradition and
former Director of the School of Scottish Studies, University of Edinburgh

JEAN-CLAUDE MARGOLIN
Professor at the Centre d'Études Supérieures de la Renaissance,
Université François Rabelais, Tours

CONTRIBUTORS

JOACHIM MEHLHAUSEN
Professor of Protestant Theology, Eberhard-Karls-Universität, Tübingen

G. H. M. POSTHUMUS MEYJES
Professor of Church History, University of Leiden

GERHARD MÜLLER
Professor Emeritus of Historical Theology (Modern Church History), University of Erlangen and Evangelical-Lutheran Bishop of Brunswick

WILLEM NIJENHUIS
Professor of Church History, University of Groningen

ANDREW PETTEGREE
Lecturer in Modern History, University of St Andrews

JILL RAITT
Professor of Religious Studies, University of Missouri-Columbia

R. W. SCRIBNER
Fellow of Clare College, Cambridge

GOTTFRIED SEEBASS
Professor of Historical Theology, Ruprecht-Karls-Universität, Heidelberg

W. J. SHEILS
Research Archivist, Borthwick Institute, and Provost of Goodricke College, University of York

FOREWORD

I am honoured by the editor's invitation to write this Foreword to the *Festschrift* for the Emeritus Professor of Ecclesiastical History in the University of St Andrews. I do so as a friend and former colleague over a period of more than thirty years (my chief qualification for the task), but also as an admirer of James Cameron's scholarly achievement as an ecclesiastical historian; for it has long been recognized by his peers that in J. K. Cameron we have a Church historian with an unrivalled knowledge of the Scottish Church, especially in the late medieval, Reformation, and post-Reformation periods. He is a widely-acknowledged authority on sixteenth-century Scottish history in an age when the heroes of the Reformation have not in all ways been loved and appreciated. His scholarly, critical edition of *The First Book of Discipline*, published by the Saint Andrew Press in 1972, has become a standard work on the subject.

A great deal of his research has been concerned with the ties between Scotland and continental Europe in that fateful century; and much of it has focused on his own College, St Mary's College, in the University of St Andrews. This is evident in his major work on *The Letters of John Johnston and Robert Howie*, both St Mary's men (published appropriately by St Andrews University); it was amply demonstrated in his opening College Lecture on 10 October 1988 on 'A Trilingual College for Scotland: the Founding of St Mary's College', a lecture timed to coincide with the commemoration of the 450th anniversary of the College on 7 March 1989. Thus, if James Cameron's painstaking scholarly research, as evidenced in his many studies, has contributed substantially to our knowledge of the Church of (and in) Scotland at a critical juncture in its history, it is St Mary's College which, for this among other reasons, is most deeply in his debt.

Born in Methven, Perthshire, on 3 March 1924, James Kerr Cameron was educated at Oban High School and St Andrews University, where he graduated as an M.A. in 1946, and proceeded to enrol in the Faculty of Divinity in St Mary's College, with a Carlow exhibition, in the same year. He graduated as a B.D. in 1949 with distinction in Ecclesiastical History, winning the James McGlashan Scott Memorial Prize in Church History and the Gray Prize in Hebrew. With a Pettigrew travelling scholarship and a Fulbright travel grant, he was admitted to Hartford Theological Seminary, Connecticut, to work under the supervision of Professor Matthew Spinka, the noted American Church historian, and graduated with a Ph.D. in 1952, *summa cum laude*, with a thesis on conciliarism. The thesis was of such quality that Dr Cameron was awarded a Hartford Jacobus fellowship. It will be of interest especially to St Andreans to know that one of his other teachers in Hartford was Professor George Johnston of Montreal, a former minister of Martyrs Church, St Andrews.

Thus, under J. H. Baxter, his teacher in Church History in St Mary's, and Matthew Spinka in Hartford, the foundations were laid for a future academic career. But at a time when divinity lectureships were virtually unknown, and, in any case, the Church of Scotland tended to look to the ordained ministry for its future professors, the next step for Dr Cameron was his licensing as a minister of the Church of Scotland, followed by his ordination as Assistant in the Church of the Holy Rude in Stirling, an assistantship (from 1953 to 1955) which was combined with that of Officiating Chaplain to HM Forces in Stirling. (By a singular coincidence, J. H. Baxter, as the last Regius Professor in Ecclesiastical History in St Andrews, was *ex officio* Dean of the Chapel Royal in Stirling Castle.)

In 1955, when the Professor of Church History in Aberdeen, Dr G. D. Henderson, was elected Moderator of the General Assembly, Cameron was appointed as his deputy and made a member of the Faculty of Divinity in King's College, Aberdeen. There, for the moderatorial year, he was in full charge of the Church History Department. In 1956, when the first lectureship in Ecclesiastical History was established in St Mary's College, St Andrews, J. K. Cameron was the obvious choice. Thereafter it was no secret that, with a growing and increasingly popular department, with undergraduate as well as postgraduate students, Cameron carried a heavy load of teaching and research for the next thirteen years. In 1969 he was promoted senior lecturer, and, on J. H. Baxter's retirement, he was elected in 1970 to the established Chair of Ecclesiastical History in St Andrews.

With his promotion to the Chair a second period of expansion in the Department followed, by the appointment in 1971 of Dr Sheridan W. Gilley and in 1973 of Dr James S. Alexander. When Gilley took up a lectureship in Durham University, he was replaced in 1978 by Dr Deryck W. Lovegrove. By these appointments the subject coverage of the Department was extended and now included specialists in the Early Church and patristics (James Alexander) and in the eighteenth century (Deryck Lovegrove). Following the St Andrews custom, the professor still continued to teach the general class, and Cameron gave courses on the medieval Church as well as on the sixteenth century. From the seventies into the eighties the Department has flourished, providing courses for B.D. and M.Theol., generally at honours level, and usually with a full quota of postgraduate and research students; Dr Cameron is himself a *Doktorvater* several times over.

James Cameron is a dedicated teacher as well as a productive scholar. With such a master of the elegant discourse as J. H. Baxter as his teacher, or such practitioners of the craft as Ronald Cant as his model, it is not surprising that his lectures, class lectures and public lectures, were always well structured, lucid as well as informative, laced with occasional touches of humour, and always with his own distinctive contribution, often drawn from his private research. He was a *paidagogos* in the best sense of the word, with a genuine pastoral concern for the progress and well-being of the students under his care. One of his staff has spoken warmly of 'his enviable approachability and genuine interest in others which helped to draw out the best in both colleagues and students.'

In 1978 Cameron was elected Dean of the Faculty of Divinity, and held office till 1983. It was a difficult time for the Faculty, for it was in those years that the full force of the 'cuts' was felt, and the Dean had the unenviable and delicate task of trying to steer a course between the Scylla of imposed financial restrictions and the Charybdis of unavoidable depletion in the academic provision for all students. It was the kind of situation where the only solutions had to be the least unsatisfactory ones, solutions which please no one: but it imposed a heavy burden of responsibility on the Dean. After his retirement as Dean he was appointed a member of the University Court.

If James Cameron was specially interested in the links between Erasmian Humanism and the Scottish Reformers in the sixteenth and seventeenth centuries, he himself has succeeded in fostering similar links in the twentieth century, especially between continental European Church historians and related bodies. Indeed, he has been an ambassador for his subject on both sides of the North Sea and the Atlantic. He is a member of the American Society of Church History, a past President of the Ecclesiastical History Society; in 1979 he was appointed Vice-President of the International Association for Neo-Latin Studies (the International Conference on George Buchanan was held in St Andrews in 1981); in 1980 he was President of the British Sub-Commission of the Commission Internationale d'Histoire Ecclésiastique Comparée: and in 1981 he was elected to the editorial board of the prestigious new *Theologische Realenzyklopädie*. More recently he has been appointed a member of the Grotius Commission by the Board of the Arts Division of the Royal Netherlands Academy of Arts and Sciences.

With our congratulations on this *Festschrift* go our warm good wishes for a happy—and equally active and productive—retirement.

MATTHEW BLACK

ABBREVIATIONS

Abbreviated titles are adopted within each paper after the first full citation. In addition, the following abbreviations are used throughout the volume.

AHR	*American Historical Review* (New York, 1895ff.)
APC	*Acts of the Privy Council of England, 1542–1629*, 44 vols (London, 1890–1958)
ARG	*Archiv für Reformationsgeschichte* (Berlin/Leipzig/Gütersloh, 1903ff.)
BHR	*Bibliothèque d'humanisme et renaissance* (Paris/Geneva, 1941ff.)
BL	British Library, London
BM	British Museum, London
BN	Bibliothèque Nationale, Paris
CalSPD	*Calendar of State Papers: Domestic* (London, 1856ff.)
CalSP, Spanish	*Calendar of State Papers: Spanish, 1485–1558*, ed. G. A. Bergenroth *et al.* (London, 1862–1954)
CPR	*Calendar of Patent Rolls preserved in the Public Record Office* (London, 1892ff.)
CR	*Corpus Reformatorum*, ed. C. G. Bretschneider *et al.* (Halle, etc., 1843ff.)
DNB	*Dictionary of National Biography* (London, 1885ff.)
EcHR	*Economic History Review* (London, 1927ff.)
EHD	*English Historical Documents* (London, 1953ff.)
EHR	*English Historical Review* (London, 1886ff.)
Foxe	*Acts and Monuments of John Foxe*, ed. G. Townshend and S. R. Cattley, 8 vols (London, 1837–41)
HThR	*Harvard Theological Review* (New York/Cambridge, Mass., 1908ff.)
InR	*Innes Review* (Glasgow, 1950ff.)
JEH	*Journal of Ecclesiastical History* (Cambridge, 1950ff.)
JMH	*Journal of Modern History* (Chicago, 1929ff.)
n.d.	no date
n.p.	no place
ns	new series
os	old series
PaP	*Past and Present. A Journal of Scientific History* (London, 1952ff.)
PBA	*Proceedings of the British Academy* (London, 1904ff.)
PCS	*Publications of the Camden Society*, os (London, 1938–72)
PRO	Public Record Office, London
PS	Parker Society (Cambridge, 1841–55)
RH	*Revue historique* (Paris, 1876ff.)
RS	*Rerum Brittanicarum medii aevi scriptores*, 99 vols (London, 1858–1911) = Rolls Series
RSCHS	*Records of the Scottish Church History Society* (Edinburgh, 1922/24ff.)
SCH	*Studies in Church History* (London/Oxford, 1964ff.)
ScHR	*Scottish Historical Review* (Edinburgh/Glasgow, 1904ff.)

ABBREVIATIONS

SCH.S	*Studies in Church History. Subsidia* (Oxford, 1978ff.)
SHS	Scottish History Society
STC	*A Short-title Catalogue of Books Printed in England, Scotland, and Ireland, and of English Books Printed Abroad, 1470–1640*, ed. A. W. Pollard and G. R. Redgrave (London, 1926, repr. 1945, 1950)
Strype, *Annals*	John Strype, *Annals of the Reformation and Establishment of Religion . . . during Queen Elizabeth's Happy Reign*, 4 vols in 7 (Oxford, 1840)
Strype, *Cranmer*	John Strype, *Memorials of . . . Thomas Cranmer*, 2 vols (Oxford, 1824)
Strype, *Memorials*	John Strype, *Ecclesiastical Memorials, Relating Chiefly to Religion and the Reformation of it . . . under King Henry VIII, King Edward VI and Queen Mary I*, 3 vols in 6 (Oxford, 1822)
THR	*Travaux d'Humanisme et Renaissance* (Geneva, 1950ff.)
TRE	*Theologische Realenzyklopädie*, ed. G. Krause, G. Müller, *et al.* (Berlin, 1974ff.)
VCH	*Victoria County History* (London, 1900ff.)
WA	D. Martin Luthers Werke, ed. J. C. F. Knaake (Weimar, 1883ff.) [*Weimarer Ausgabe*]
ZKG	*Zeitschrift für Kirchengeschichte* (Gotha/Stuttgart, 1878ff.)
ZRGG	*Zeitschrift für Religions- und Geistesgeschichte* (Cologne, etc., 1948ff.)
ZSRG.K	*Zeitschrift der Savigny-Stiftung für Rechtsgeschichte. Kanonistische Abt.* (Weimar, 1911ff.)
ZThK	*Zeitschrift für Theologie und Kirche*, ns (Tübingen, 1950ff.)

PART I THE CHURCH IN EUROPE

PAPAL COURTS AND COURTIERS IN THE RENAISSANCE

by DENYS HAY

THE cultural influence of Rome and the papacy during the late fifteenth and early sixteenth centuries has recently attracted much attention. At the same time, courts and courtiers have come under the scrutiny of a number of scholars anxious to define their function in the cultural sphere. This brief essay is an attempt to lean on such work collectively, so to speak, and it can make no claim to originality of source material or personal research. I should perhaps give the tone and indicate the level of my approach by explaining that the gist of what follows formed a lecture given in December 1986 to the Scottish branch of the Renaissance Society at a meeting in Glasgow. I should like to regard it as well as part of this tribute to James Cameron, also as an expression of my thanks to the late Judith Hook for her work for the Society; she herself wrote an important essay bearing on the topic, albeit at a later period, the pontificate of Urban VIII (1623–44), to which I shall refer later.

One must begin by making the obvious point that the papal court was in many ways unlike the princely courts found elsewhere in Europe. The court was the *curia Romana* and not the curia of a particular pontiff. Such a court indeed existed, but is not germane to this survey. Of course, the word 'court' is ambiguous everywhere. Even in northern Europe it was an institution as well as a mystique, and from it were derived a host of confusing terms in all European languages.

Modern interest has concentrated on the *courtier*, on which there was much contemporary writing, and not only the *Cortegiano* of Baldassare Castiglione, but on its derivatives and its critics.[1] But even the word 'courtier' is not free from complexity. It covered in some sense all the servants of a ruler, from the grandest, with honorific tasks, to the lowliest, whose services were menial. But the word can also mean a broker, a man who fiddles with dealings in exchange, and so is now often regarded as a dirty word; as is, I suppose, in certain refined circles the word 'courtesan', although, at any rate in Venice, we have been shown that the term

[1] Sydney Anglo, 'The Courtier. The Renaissance and changing ideals' in A. G. Dickens, ed., *The Courts of Europe* (London, 1977), pp. 33–53, 328–9. Two other recent works touch on the Roman curia: J. W. O'Malley, *Praise and Blame in Renaissance Rome* (Durham, N. Carolina, 1979); John F. D'Amico, *Renaissance Humanism in Papal Rome* (Baltimore and London, 1988).

involved social prestige and in some cases wealth high above that of the *meretrice* or *putana* in the hierarchy of the low pleasures offered by the City of the Lagoons.[2]

Even the adjective 'courtly' can be difficult. It can mean a collection of virtuous attitudes, rather like chivalrous or chivalric. Or it can suggest toadying, back-scratching flattery, insincere behaviour like Malvolio's. On the one hand, the courtier is the wise adviser of the prince; on the other, he is an ambitious and unscrupulous man on the make: I was pleased to notice recently in Balzac's *Le Cousin Pons* the society of the bourgeois Paris and France of the 1840s described as 'courtisane'. These antitheses have been sharply delineated and analysed in the essay by Sydney Anglo to which I have referred. In a British—or English— ambience they are illustrated in Thomas More's *Utopia*, books i and ii. In book i, the slick counsellor is displayed, the lickspittle with no conscience, aiming at his own promotion. In book ii, we are shown the virtuous Utopians, who regard wealth as contemptible and make their chamber-pots of gold. It is a shock to realize that book i was written second, and equally shocking that it was written just before More became what one might call a cabinet secretary himself. 'Economical with the truth' when dealing with his shameful master Henry VIII? 'A Man for all Seasons'?[3]

In theory, the *curia Romana* bore many striking resemblances to the princely pattern which is found elsewhere in Italy and in other parts of Europe. We can regard the cardinals collectively as a council. Nearly every cardinal by the early sixteenth century was behaving in a lordly manner, as a great aristocrat, with a palace and a *familia* and a life of pomp and protocol, himself a source of patronage and the route by which a client clerk could attain the pope's interest and support. Indeed, by this period many of the cardinals were indeed aristocrats, at any rate within the Italian context, which is to say families belonging to or allied with the greater houses—Gonzaga, Aragon, Medici—and even those with no such associations or antecedents rapidly emulated the buildings and other forms of display of those cardinals who behaved as to the manner born. Consider a nobody called Adriano Castellesi, who advanced irresistibly to the grandeur of cardinal, despite his obscure origins, and an imprudent marriage early on, which a complaisant pope dissolved. Cardinal Castellesi, bon viveur and spinner of wealth (and also of beautiful Latin),

[2] Cathy Santore, 'Julia Lombarda, Sumptuosa Meretrice. A portrait by Property', *Renaissance Quarterly*, 41 (1988), pp. 44–83.

[3] I have brooded more on this problem in my lecture to the Lincei, reprinted in *Renaissance Essays* (London 1983), pp. 249–63.

4

derived his income from procurations as a nuncio and then from holding successively two bishoprics in England (Hereford 1502, Bath and Wells 1504) besides many lesser benefices and curial pickings. Castellesi was also flamboyant in the sleazy Rome of his day and a great builder. His palace in Rome is now called Palazzo Giraud Torlonia, and still stands in the via della Conciliazione,[4] facing the Palazzo del Penitenzieri built by Cardinal della Rovere before it was appropriated for Vatican offices and later became a hotel. These palaces follow a pattern set earlier by the Palazzo Venezia, the grandest of the lot, which is in a sense paradoxical, since Venice itself had no princely tradition and, in these later fifteenth-century years, was frequently at odds with the papacy.

From Martin V (1417–31) onwards, Rome was slowly transformed. It is true that the papacy in the fifteenth century was poorer in revenue than it had been in the Avignon days. And it lacked the persistent pressure that a dynastic state had, the built-in need to demonstrate power and continuity. Such continuity was, indeed, not entirely absent. Two Borgia popes, two Piccolomini, two della Rovere, two Medici: but, though suggestive of the pressures of kin and the acceptance of the need to feather one's family nest, these pairs of popes do not constitute houses like the Tudors or the Valois or the Habsburgs. We should therefore turn to consider what groups the papal court aimed to impress, and ask why.

In some senses, they are comparable to those individuals and groups which were the object of the desire of princes to impress everywhere—the visiting grandees, ambassadors, increasingly of little diplomatic importance, but still worthy of much display. The pope sent some cardinals to meet them as they entered the city, and, as a cardinal moved with a large retinue, the visitor would be greeted by several cavalcades as he made his way to one of the gates—usually the Porta del Popolo, with its already large space for ceremonies.[5] In other courts the prince's table was the principal occasion for display—lavish food, lavish service, music and dancing. This form of public entertainment was not available to the prince of peace, the *servus servorum Dei*. He ate well, assuredly, but often

---

[4] Most of the details of Castellesi's rise and fall are to be found in the admirable article by Gigliola Fragnito, *Dizionario Biografico degli Italiani*, 21 (1978), pp. 565–71. His activities in the curia are displayed in many documents in the Vatican Registers: e.g. *Obligationes et Solutiones*, 86; *Formatori*, 9, with his own ordination to minor orders, fol. 108v. Castellesi wrote a beautiful *cancelleria corsiva* himself, unlike the hand of many of his brother curialists. His published work is elegant but insignificant.

[5] Pius II, *Commentaries*, ed. and tr. F. A. Gragg and L. C. Gabel = *Smith College Studies in History*, 22, 25, 30, 35, 43 (Northampton, Mass., 1937–57), pp. 426–7.

privately and equally often as the guest of a cardinal. Papal audiences were the equivalent, I suppose, and the pope's direction that a celebrated visitor should be given a privileged seat in the *capella* during a papal Mass, as when Sixtus IV placed Federigo of Urbino 'on the benches of the sacred college'. As for dancing, it was only Alexander VI who openly enjoyed such goings-on. The other courtly entertainment, the stately ballet called the joust, was indeed provided by popes in the great *Cortile del Belvedere*, in a specially-constructed tilting yard.

The end of the Great Schism, when only a legate was left to manage the papal territory round Avignon and Carpentras (the Comtat Venaissin), gradually, with a few hesitations, inaugurated the re-establishment of the papacy in Rome. The centuries of uncertainty after 1300 left a serious anxiety among the Romans, who viewed every occasion when the pope left the city with the fear that he would return to the fleshpots of the Rhône valley. Popes had only a precarious hold on Rome and Lazio until the mid-sixteenth century, and the occasions when they left the city were very limited in time and range. The *curia Romana* was thus unlike other princely courts in not being in perpetual perigrination. Pius II on one occasion felt the need to reassure the citizens that he was not going far.[6] It must have been a relief to the hundreds who worked in papal offices that they and their papers, so often ill-arranged and so liable to corrupt practice, did not have to trundle far on pack animals and handcarts. If Pius II was constrained to tell the Romans that he was to be regarded as a permanency, there were other ways in which he could comfort the innkeepers and the religious houses who relied on income from travellers and pilgrims.

This was public ceremony in Rome itself. The most ostentatious example of this was the *possesso*, when the pope with a vast retinue made his way from the Vatican, now his normal Roman residence, to the Lateran. The route followed what was known as the *via papalis*, across the Tiber and through the gradually refurbished quarters north of the Capitol, until the final scattering of coins, the attentions of the papal barber, and the return journey.[7] Gestures such as this were doubtless intended to secure a modicum of obedience from such unruly subjects as the slatternly Lateran canons, seculars of good family who bitterly and

---

[6] D. Hay, *The Church in Italy in the Fifteenth Century* (Cambridge, 1977), p. 47.
[7] On the *possesso* see Hay, *Church in Italy* (indexed under 'papal display'), and for Leo X's, L. Pastor, *History of the Popes*, ed. and tr. F. I. Antrobus *et al.*, 7 (London, 1908), pp. 36–42: 'The most magnificent spectacle which Rome had witnessed since the days of the Emperors.'

successfully resisted the pope's efforts to replace them with reformed Augustinian canons. The rumpus grew so inordinately that Eugenius had to send troops from Castel S. Angelo to restore order. The *possesso* and other public ceremonies may have rated as a distraction from the main activity of the curial clergy, getting and spending. And even for the citizens, some of whom actively participated in the fracas over the Lateran canons, so called although they failed to secure the Lateran.

Some of these processions, for example the *possesso* of Leo X, which, as noted above, is described by Pastor, wended their way through streets ornamented by triumph arches decorated by motifs, pagan, as Pastor laments, proclaiming Leo as a peacemaker. And so he was, one may suppose, after the bellicose Julius II (1503–13), who built the street named after him, the via Giulia; this runs straight for a kilometre from near the end of the bridge at S. Angelo to the Tiber beyond the Palazzo Farnese—another Cardinal's vast erection (1514) and still grand as the French embassy, and housing part of the French School at Rome. The via Giulia runs to the Tiber at the Ponte Sisto, so called after Sixtus IV (1417–84), who built it when the bridge at S. Angelo had collapsed under the press of pilgrims. A similar concern for the convenience of pilgrims lay behind the construction of the Lungara, the long straight road from the Vatican to one of the great pilgrim basilicas, Sta Maria in Trastevere. This concern for pilgrim traffic was also behind the simplification of the route to Sta Maria Maggiore. This began with the via Babuino from the Piazzo del Popolo, and then side-stepped, so to speak, the via Sistina (a 'systematization' of Sixtus V), and thence directly to the basilica. The other two exists from the Piazza del Popolo were the old Flaminian Way, renamed the Corso, which led down to the Campidoglio, and the via di Ripetta, which followed the Tiber to the small quayside which was all the unimportant river traffic of Rome needed. It is worth rehearsing the northern entrance to the city, and its three straight roads. This was to prove an influential pattern in baroque *urbanismo* and cast its spell for centuries—affecting, to name at random, Goethe and Burckhardt, who collected their letters at the Caffe Greco, still then in the via Condotti near the Spanish Steps, although now rather a tourist attraction.

It may be evident to the reader, as it is to the writer, that the magic of Rome is still posing a problem. To revisit the city, even in memory, is a distracting business. But it is not altogether irrelevant to my theme. The courtiers of the *curia Romana* were only responsible directly for a portion of the visual excitement which the place still arouses. But they lived amidst buildings erected by their direct employers, the pope and the cardinals, and it seemed to me when I first reflected on this theme that the buildings, palaces, streets, and fountains would demonstrate almost tangibly the contradiction between apostolic poverty and princely pomp, which was the milieu in which the curialist found himself, reflected in the title of the recent work of Paolo Prodi, *Il sovrano pontifice; un corpo e due anime* (1982).[8] It may, however, be doubted if this distinction or contrast is uniquely found in Rome. Given the poverty of many Italian dioceses, the riches of Rome seem dramatic; but the curialist who moved round Christendom, as many of them did, must have found Cologne, Paris, or Compostella equally imposing. Even a little bishopric like Wells houses its bishop in a moated palace and its canons in cosy houses; Castelesi may never have visited Wells, of which he was bishop, but his factotum, archdeacon Polydore Vergil, certainly did, and must have reported on its splendour to his master in Rome. These transalpine splendours were old-fashioned compared with the Rome growing up at the end of the fifteenth century and onwards, but no one working in the curia can have failed to realize that in the cameral registers only Aquileia was rated as wealthy as dozens of sees, not to mention other lesser consistorial benefices, outside Italy.[9]

We must not forget two relevant points. The pope, like sovereigns elsewhere, performed ritual acts of humility, washing the feet of poor men, the equivalent of the Maundy ceremonies in England, which all bishops and abbots were supposed to observe on the Thursday of Holy Week. Second, the pope was regularly harangued by preachers in the *capella* where, as noted earlier, distinguished visitors, princes, and their ambassadors were sometimes privileged to attend. These invited admonitions were the sermons *coram papa inter missarum solemmia* which have been studied by Father O'Malley.[10] He makes the point that the Roman liturgy was public and urban as in no other city. But the *capella* or *capelle pontificie* were not a public affair: it was the pope, cardinals, and senior curialists at prayer. The practice was old; the Renaissance saw it significantly modified by the introduction of a new type of oratory, corresponding to the needs of what O'Malley calls a private and courtly liturgy, which took place in the new building in the Sistine Chapel. At these solemn masses the pope

8 Tr. Susan Haskins, *The Papal Prince* (Cambridge, 1987).
9 H. Hoberg, *Taxae pro communibus servitiis . . . 1295–1455* (Vatican City, 1949). On p. 374 are listed the sees most heavily rated; this is admittedly a crude way of establishing the relative resources of various dioceses, but at least offers what papal officials in the later Middle Ages recognized as viable estimates.
10 O'Malley, *Praise and Blame*.

never himself preached, but it was the duty of his theologians to nominate the preachers for the nineteen or so occasions which followed a more-or-less fixed calendar. Care was taken not to coincide with occasions of great processions, which remained surely the most conspicuous evidence of the pope as prince. The choice of the Dominican theologian, who was master of the Sacred Palace, was somewhat limited by the convention that the four older orders of friars were to have a fixed part, into which the Servites successfully introduced themselves in 1508. For the rest, preachers seem to have been chosen in a very haphazard way. These sermons, in theory limited to fifteen minutes, could sometimes become excruciatingly boring.

But if the public, or even the clerical public, was not present at the *capella*, the Vatican palaces were adorned with pictures which the streams of impetrants had to pass to get the chits that had brought them to the throne of St Peter. Elsewhere the prince demonstrated his power and grandeur with great tapestries; in Rome it was displayed rather by the paintings in the splendid chambers we now visit to see some of the great Raphaels. The crowd of impetrants had time to be dazzled by these decorations as they arrived to do their business in these splendid saloons, hoping to get a return on their investment of time and money.

Of course the sermons *coram papa* were not the only exhortations to virtue heard by popes and cardinals. Before conclaves a sermon adjured the cardinals to think of the future. It does not seem to have weighed heavily on the cardinals who elected the pontiff, and to judge from what the pontiffs did, it does not seem to have weighed very heavily on them either. There were other occasions when rhetoric, the rhetoric of praise and blame, came to the pope's ears—a beatification or (more rarely, for popes did not usually attend them) a funeral. Exceptionally, Sixtus IV attended Bessarion's funeral in 1472. But the sermons before the pope were fitted into the heart of the liturgy of the Mass, and consequently more often they alluded to the text of the Mass and commented on its references to scriptural texts. The virtues of peace and joy were commonly elaborated, and attacks on corruption, which were never directed at the pope, were frequently directed at the curia—as they were in earlier reform proposals, such as those commissioned by Pius II and Alexander VI. But praise of the pope was excluded as a theme, and blame was not attributed to the reigning pontiff. That indeed would have smacked of conciliarism: and at the Fifth Lateran Council the same old generalized complaints about corruption in curial officials, and moral disorder in Rome, were repeated.

9

It is worth emphasizing how regularly the popes received good counsel (even if often wrapped up in the language of the newly cultivated *humanitas*), for the general view of Renaissance popes is highly critical of them. In fact, it is all too obvious that, in addition to their inability to control Rome itself and the administrative machinery, their belated and ineffectual attempts at so-called 'reform' would, if carried out, at best have made the great offices of the Camera, the Datary and so on, merely more efficient at gathering in revenue or plucking more fully the flocks who congregated in search of papal graces and the higher promotions that needed the approval of the consistory. All of this is well known and in many ways resembles the crowds who sought to importune a lay prince's favour. What then distinguishes the 'pope as prince' viewed in the ambience of the court?

(1) The impermanence of the pope's reign; and the dependence of his court (or cardinals) on his good will for their income. Unlike the countries in great secular principalities, the pope could make or break them, whereas the grandees of Castile or France were endowed with their own vast estates and a tradition of long-standing loyalty which they could counterpoise against the fancies of their sovereign. There were, it is true, a few cardinals who denied the pope, but their ultimate threat was a future council, and that, in effect, would have been to cut off their noses to spite their faces.

(2) The irregularity of papal magnificence. The great central displays of kings occurred at fairly set times unless they were interrupted by war, and, as mentioned, the desire for hunting, for entertainment at the expense of towns and nobility in royal territories, led to the perambulations which were more or less avoided by Renaissance popes. On the other hand, Rome was the centre of pilgrimage in western Europe, all the more so as Turkish dominance in the Middle East made the trip to Jerusalem both hazardous and expensive. The popes and clergy of Rome welcomed the pilgrims, if for no other reason than that they shared the alms laid on the altars of Roman churches. The stream of pilgrims was steady, though, of course, interrupted by pestilence and war; but it could, one might say, be turned on by the Jubilee. This, it will be recalled, was first begun by Boniface VIII in 1300. By the fifteenth century, it had long ceased to be the celebration of a centenary and had been reduced to thirty-three years; then Paul II in 1470 made the interval twenty-five. The indulgences poured out on the faithful ensured a vast response in person or in cash

in lieu, and, with its spiritual dividends, so to speak, had no parallel in secular courts. Moreover, it transcended political barriers in a way inconceivable in princely domains.

(3) Besides the swollen throng of pilgrims, many of whom, especially better educated Italians, were anxious to view the glories of old Rome—the Pantheon, the Colosseum, the Capitol, and the ambiguous Castel S. Angelo, as well as the obligatory services in the obligatory great churches—the curia itself transacted a vast amount of business, and clergy came, especially through the splendid chambers of the Vatican, with requests for documents which enabled them to acquire new rights in church revenue or legitimize old rights. And on top of that, the pope as the universal ordinary empowered bishops to deputize for him in ordinations on Ember days and other permitted occasions. These ordinations occasionally numbered very many clergy from all over the Roman obedience. They were advertised in important places in Rome, and theoretically the candidates needed to possess letters dismissory and a 'title', that is, a living. When one looks at the Vatican Register of these ordinations *apud sedem apostolicam* (the so-called *formatori*) it must strike the dispassionate reader that little or no real scrutiny can have been possible in the case of many of the candidates whose weird names are transcribed in the Register. One is left with the impression that for these Northerners (as most of the non-Italians seem to have been) their credentials, technical and moral, were unlikely to be scrutinized with any experience: how could they be? True, the majority seem to have been Italians, but just as likely for the same reasons; after all, few Italian sees had resident pastors.

(4) It was also the case that many of the artistic and verbal motifs used to decorate triumphal arches, banners hung out of windows and so on, using ancient visual or literary models (which must have puzzled the public which encountered them in England or France), would be more likely to be comprehended by at any rate a large number of curialists. There were some 2,000 of these by the early sixteenth century. Many of them had paid to be enrolled in one of the 'colleges' as a form of life insurance, but were more or less *literati*, or sufficiently so to admire the literary allusions. What of the weary queues parading through the Vatican to get the chits they hoped would give them livings or indulgences? One can be less sure whether Raphael's great frescos struck them as the stupendous works they have been regarded as since, and indeed from the beginning by a handful of *cognoscenti*.

(5) We may conclude, I believe, that it is fair to describe the papal Rome of the pre-Reformation era as indicating a future of recognizable courtly splendour: the Rome which is evoked and illustrated in Judith Hook's essay on the Rome of Urban VIII, the Barberini who reigned from 1623 to 1644. He it was who inherited the exploitation of the Rome elaborated by Sixtus V: the grandest backdrop in history, one might say. All it still lacked was the Bernini columns surrounding the piazza in front of St Peter's (1655–67). For the rest all was in place.

Judith Hook called her survey the 'paradox of papal monarchy'.[11] Did she expect to find the paradoxes greater than in fact she did? In essence, all she could offer by way of paradox was the antithesis between the pope's relative domestic simplicity and the grandeur of his environment. I, too, had expected, when I started my notes, to find a more startling contrast; but I did not really find it save in the murky ideologies displayed: the pope as the *servus servorum* and at the same time absolute ruler. Absolute ruler of what? Of the Papal States. If one looks at Prodi's book, where he deals with the time of Leo X and Clement VII, there were two papal representatives at Bologna, one in secular administration and one *in spiritualia*, as it was technically called. They were often at loggerheads. In Rome, as indicated, the pope depended on a quite undependable militia to make his will effective. I instanced earlier the Lateran canons, about whom Philip McNair has written so well.[12] I might have quoted the attempts by Leo X to reduce the *capella* to quiet, when it proved almost impossible to stop the gossiping of the spoilt brats of the curia even in the pope's presence. He ordered soldiers to enforce quiet, but having done it once they had later to be summoned to do it again.

And beyond the Papal States? Well, one is on the point of the Sack of Rome, which so greatly facilitated the further construction of a new Rome later in the sixteenth century—the anticipation of the Barberini Rome which we all enjoy today. And we are on the point of the collapse of the world claims of the pope, or at any rate of their validity. It is indeed a paradox that Luther on his first visit stayed in the Augustinian convent in the Piazza del Popolo, where Pius II so graphically describes the reception of St Andrew's head. A fiesta indeed, but not paid for by the pope.[13]

[11] Judith Hook, 'Urban VIII. The paradox of a spiritual monarchy', in Dickens, ed., *The Courts of Europe*, pp. 213–31.
[12] Philip McNair, *Peter Martyr in Italy: an Anatomy of Apostacy* (Oxford, 1967).
[13] Ruth Rubinstein, 'Pius II's Piazza S. Pietro and St. Andrew's Head' in *Essays in the History of Architecture Presented to Rudolf Wittkower* (London, 1967), pp. 22–33.

I have not mentioned the courtiers in Castiglione's book. Many of them were very familiar with Roman manners, not least Castiglione himself. How many were Roman courtiers? At least two were, or were to become, cardinals. But the barbaric soldiery of the Sack suspended this; and made the way for even more courtly developments in the future.

And how much more is there yet to explore! What about the Carnival? What about music, where we are back again in the *capella*? Kings had bands, but their choristers, if they were wise, migrated to Italy, and especially to Rome.[14]

University of Edinburgh

[14] These notes were completed before the appearance of *Renaissance Studies*, 2 (October 1988), which contains several contributions pertinent to the theme of this essay. The relevance of Alison Brown's 'Between curial Rome and convivial Florence', pp. 208–21, and Leslie J. Macfarlane, 'Precedence and protest at the Roman Curia', pp. 222–30, is particularly to be noted. I wish I could have referred to the recent work of Peter Partner, *The Pope's Men* (Oxford, 1990).

THE LATE RENAISSANCE AND THE UNFOLDING REFORMATION IN EUROPE

by EUAN CAMERON

Martin Luther, conducted no doubt by a higher providence, but in discourse of reason, finding what a province he had undertaken against the bishop of Rome, and the degenerate traditions of the church, and finding his own solitude, being no ways aided by the opinions of his own time, was enforced to awake all antiquity, and to call former times to his succour, to make a party against the present time. So that the ancient authors, both in divinity, and in humanity, which had long time slept in libraries, began generally to be read and revolved. This by consequence did draw on a necessity of a more exquisite travel in the languages original, wherein those authors did write, for the better understanding of those authors, and the better advantage of pressing and applying their words. And thereof grew again a delight in their manner of style and phrase, and an admiration of that kind of writing. . . .

Francis Bacon, *Of the Advancement of Learning* (1605) in *Works* (London, 1778).

I

IT is comparatively rare for two fundamental and unique episodes in the history of northern European thought to succeed each other within the space of a generation or so. Humanists and Protestant historians respectively defined their chosen causes, restoring *humanitas*,[1] and the 'renewal of the Gospel',[2] consciously and exclusively as unique, epoch-making events. Given that self-consciousness, and the closeness with which one followed upon the other in Europe north of the Alps, it is understandable that the relationship between them has continued to

---

[1] *Humanitas*, defined as a combination of moral generosity and scholarly learning, was a well-known ideal to the Renaissance, even if the term 'humanism' to describe a movement in ideas only dates from 1808. The *locus classicus* for *humanitas* was 'Aulus Gellius, *Noctes Atticae*, bk 13, ch. 16 (usually cited as 13: 15); see, for example, R. Estienne, *Dictionarium, seu latinae Linguae Thesaurus* (Lyons, 1543), s.v. 'humanus'.

[2] The formulation comes from Abraham Scultetus, *Annalium Evangelii passim per Europam . . . renovati decades duae*, 2 vols (Heidelberg, 1618–20).

fascinate. However, scholarly analysis of the links between the northern Renaissance and the Reformation has concentrated heavily on one *period* and on one *type* of relationship: on the dozen or so years *c*.1517–*c*.1530, between the indulgence quarrel and the defection of so many of the younger humanists to practical church reform; and on the causal, or sequential, connections between the two movements—how one led to, helped to protect, or learned from, the other.

A brief summary of the literature soon shows how many forms the 'Renaissance to Reformation' analyses can assume, even within that limited range. We have studies of the similarities and differences between the ideas and value systems of humanists and reformers, which tend to take particular issues, such as divine grace, human inadequacy, or free will, and compare them as they are found in otherwise dissimilar authors.[3] There is a monumental literature on the influence exerted by northern humanism on the teachings of the early Reformation: this can operate either at the level of theology pure and simple, or as part of the mental and spiritual biography of Luther.[4] In Germany especially, the humanists saw Luther at first as another protagonist against their common foes, reactionary and dogmatic theologians; the consequences of that 'fruitful misunderstanding' form another topos of early Reformation studies.[5] Many of those younger humanists, not so wedded either to literary pursuit or the old pieties, made the gradual transition from scholarly theory to practical churchmanship.[6] The clash of priorities and principles between humanists and reformers in the early 1520s is usually discussed in terms of the Erasmus–Luther debate, but could equally be seen in, say, Staupitz, Lefèvre d'Étaples, Willibald Pirckheimer, or Heinrich Loriti

---

[3] E.g., C. Trinkaus, *The Scope of Renaissance Humanism* (Michigan, 1983), esp. pp. 237–62: 'The religious thought of the Italian humanists: anticipation of the Reformers or autonomy', and pp. 263–73: 'The problem of free will in the Renaissance and the Reformation'.

[4] On the theological level, see, e.g., A. E. McGrath, 'Humanist elements in the early reformed doctrine of justification', *ARG*, 73 (1982), pp. 5–20; *Intellectual Origins of the European Reformation* (Oxford, 1987), pp. 32–68; *Reformation Thought: An Introduction* (Oxford, 1988), pp. 27–49; for the level of personal influences, see A. G. Dickens, 'Luther and the Humanists' in P. Mack and M. C. Jacob, eds, *Politics and Culture in Early Modern Europe; Essays in Honor of H. G. Koenigsberger* (Cambridge, 1987), pp. 199–213; H. Junghans, *Der junge Luther und die Humanisten* (Göttingen, 1985).

[5] B. Moeller, *Imperial Cities and the Reformation: Three Essays*, ed. and tr. H. C. E. Midelfort and M. U. Edwards (Philadelphia, 1972), pp. 19–38.

[6] For examples of this sort of biography see J. M. Kittelson, *Wolfgang Capito: From Humanist to Reformer* (Leiden, 1975); W. Maurer, *Der junge Melanchthon zwischen Humanismus und Reformation*, 2 vols (Göttingen, 1967–9); C. Bonorand, *Vadians Weg vom Humanismus zur Reformation* (St Gallen, 1962); G. Simon, *Humanismus und Konfession: T. Billican, Leben und Werk* (Berlin, 1980).

'Glareanus'.[7] Finally, 'humanism' is sometimes alleged to have generated a particular kind of Reformation, supposedly more concerned with ethics and less with scholastic dogma than Luther's; this distinctive 'humanist Reformation' can be held responsible, on the one hand, for the disputes between Swiss and German reformers, and, on the other, for the divisions among Lutherans after Luther's death.[8]

Vast as this family of scholarly studies is, it tends not to confront 'the Renaissance' in its essence—whatever that essence is—with 'the Reformation', however that may be defined. A great deal of such scholarship is concerned rather with personalities than ideas: how *humanists* responded to the events of *c.*1517–*c.*1530, rather than what became of their favourite themes and concerns. The prosopographical approach tends to boil down to why did this or that figure find Luther, Zwingli, or Matthäus Zell either compelling or repulsive, which inevitably entails considerations apart from ideas. Even the 'theological' approach to the same question usually concentrates on what 'the humanists', sometimes too readily homogenized, had to say on strictly religious questions; this method also tends to assume a clear line of demarcation between 'humanists' and 'reformers', which especially in the early 1520s is rather hard to justify.[9]

This preliminary sketch aspires to look at the question of the Renaissance and the Reformation in a somewhat different way. First, emphasis will be laid not on *humanists* as such, whether as individuals or as a class of intellectuals, but upon what one might call the elements of the humanist 'programme': those intellectual activities and priorities which were closely associated with those whom one calls 'humanists'. Identifying such a 'programme' is always controversial; however, there is ample evidence that such programmes for humanist intellectual reform existed. Secondly,

---

[7] On the Erasmus debate, see most recently Marjorie O'Rourke Boyle, *Rhetoric and Reform: Erasmus' Civil Dispute with Luther* (Cambridge, Mass., 1983); 'Erasmus and the "Modern" Question: Was he semi-Pelagian?' *ARG*, 75 (1984), pp. 59–72; on the German humanists, L. W. Spitz, *The Religious Renaissance of the German Humanists* (Cambridge, Mass., 1963).

[8] Particularly sharp forms of this distinction are found in Émile G. Léonard, *Histoire générale du Protestantisme*, I (Paris, 1961), ch. 4, pp. 118ff.; McGrath, *Reformation Thought*, pp. 41–5; for humanist influences as underlying some of Melanchthon's problems after Luther's death, see, for instance, C. L. Manschreck, ed., *Melanchthon on Christian Doctrine: Loci Communes 1555* (New York, 1965), pp. xix–xxiii.

[9] A number of figures in the early Reformation period wander somewhat confusingly along the border between humanism and reform: see, for instance, Johannes Sylvius Egranus of Zwickau, as in H. Kirchner, *Johannes Sylvius Egranus* (Berlin, 1961), and Susan C. Karant-Nunn, *Zwickau in Transition, 1500–1547: The Reformation as an Agent of Change* (Columbus, Ohio, 1987), pp. 100ff. Those who, in Germany or Switzerland, were humanists first, and involved with the 'Protestant' reform either as agents or opponents soon after, are too numerous and notorious to list.

it will not be the early, formative, inchoate period of the Reformation which will chiefly be considered, but the middle and later years of the sixteenth century, by which time no 'misunderstanding' about the respective priorities of the cause of Good Letters and the Gospel was any longer possible. The quest, in short, is to draw together a few of the strands of the northern humanists' aims and ideals, and then to see what became of those strands after the Reformation had overtaken, over-shadowed, and thoroughly transformed 'the Renaissance' as such.

II

There are two obvious difficulties involved in identifying a humanist 'programme' before one tries to track it down in the writings and practice of the established Reformation. First, 'Renaissance humanism' is a notoriously variable concept: no one 'humanist's' priorities need be exactly the same as any other's. More specifically, different case-studies have endowed humanism with contradictory properties: for instance 'Stoic' or 'Augustinian',[10] Platonist or Aristotelian,[11] republican or despotic (or both at once),[12] sympathetic or antagonistic towards the monastic order.[13] Faced with the threat of having to abandon such a convenient handle as 'humanism' altogether, scholars in search of a definition have insisted on one broad enough to include both the move-ment's variability, and its ability to combine with other idea systems.[14]

This last point—the Protean character of humanism—raises a second

---

[10] W. J. Bouwsma, 'The two faces of humanism: Stoicism and Augustinianism in Renaissance thought' in H. A. Oberman and T. A. Brady, eds, *Itinerarium Italicum* (Leiden, 1978), pp. 3–60.

[11] Compare, e.g., the figures discussed in P. O. Kristeller, *Eight Philosophers of the Italian Renais-sance* (Stanford, 1965), and in J. H. Randall Jr., 'Paduan Aristotelianism reconsidered', in E. P. Mahoney, ed., *Philosophy and Humanism: Renaissance Essays in honor of Paul Oskar Kristeller* (New York, 1976), pp. 275–82. C. Trinkaus, 'Renaissance Humanism, Its Formation and Develop-ment', in his *The Scope of Renaissance Humanism*, pp. 6–9, seems to deny the Paduan Aristotel-ians a place among the humanists. This is no doubt arguable in the case of 'scholastic' philosophers like Achillini, Vernia, or Pomponazzi, but much harder to sustain for their sixteenth-century followers like Francesco Vimercato, and impossible, say, for Jacques Lefèvre d'Étaples.

[12] See, for instance, the discussions of Machiavelli and the humanist traditions in Quentin Skinner, *The Foundations of Modern Political Thought*, 2 vols (Cambridge, 1978), 1, pp. 128ff., 180ff., and *Machiavelli* (Oxford, 1981), *passim*.

[13] Compare, for instance, the respective attitudes of Erasmus and Josse Clichtove to the reform of monasticism. See J. P. Massaut, *Josse Clichtove et la réforme du clergé*, 2 vols (Paris, 1968), 1, pp. 433–45.

[14] See, for instance, James D. Tracy, 'Humanism and the Reformation' in S. E. Ozment, ed., *Reformation Europe: A Guide to Research* (St Louis, 1982), p. 46.

problem. Towards the end of a phase in intellectual history, its ideas tend to be diffused both widely and thinly; in the 'Late Renaissance' it becomes difficult to find any figure of significance who was *completely immune* to the influence of humanism, but just as difficult to find one who was a humanist and nothing else. A similar diffusion can be observed among conciliar theorists on the eve of the Reformation; instead of conciliarism being concentrated in a small clique of committed enthusiasts, as in the decades *c.*1400, by the early sixteenth century all kinds of religious figures paid *some* lip-service, with varying seriousness, to the ideal of a council as the repository of supreme authority in the Church.[15]

This flattening out of the ripples generated by the outward spread of Renaissance ideas hinders the search for *humanists* as such; it does not, however, prevent one from identifying humanist *elements* in sixteenth-century thought, which can then be traced through the unfolding of the Reformation. Drawing up any sort of list is an imprecise exercise in selection: no sense of moral or intellectual priority is implied by the order in which these elements are described here.

Perhaps the most portentous trend in northern Renaissance thought was the application of the new philology—with its emphasis on restoring the integrity of the original text, rather than overlaying successive strata of selection and commentary—to the canon of Scripture. Its application required several mental disciplines: acquiring sufficient knowledge of the languages in which the earliest surviving texts were written; correcting texts against texts with reference only to philological, rather than legal or dogmatic, criteria; finally, editing and correcting the Vulgate text like any other translation. The achievements of this programme are well known: Pico della Mirandola's work on the Psalter; Reuchlin's composition of a usable Hebrew manual in 1506; Erasmus's publication of Valla's *Annotationes* in 1505, and of his *Novum Instrumentum* in 1516; Lefèvre d'Étaples's work on St Paul, and the compilation of the Alcalà Polyglot.[16] This programme had clear implications for the (various) concepts of *tradition*

---

[15] For late conciliarism, see Skinner, *Foundations*, 2, pp. 114–23; J. A. F. Thomson, *Popes and Princes 1417–1517: Politics and Polity in the Late Medieval Church* (London, 1980), pp. 17–28; and above all the detailed articles by Francis Oakley listed in Ozment, ed., *Reformation Europe*, pp. 27–8.

[16] See G. R. Evans, *The Language and Logic of the Bible: The Road to Reformation* (Cambridge, 1985), pp. 69–81; H. Holeczek, *Humanistische Bibelphilologie als Reformproblem bei Erasmus von Rotterdam, Thomas More und William Tyndale* (Leiden, 1975); J. H. Bentley, 'Erasmus' *Annotationes in Novum Testamentum* and the Textual Criticism of the gospels', *ARG*, 67 (1976), pp. 33–53; G. Bedouelle, *Lefèvre d'Étaples et l'intelligence des écritures* (Geneva, 1976).

within the Church, which must be considered.[17] A paradoxical consequence was the desire to promote *further* translations of the Scriptures into the vernacular. In this respect the humanist programme was only following an existing trend for printing vernacular Bibles; the style of the new translations, however, was bound to be different.[18]

The northern humanists' readiness to expose Scripture to both textual and popular scrutiny depended on another of their assumptions: that a structured, literate, 'liberal' educational technique would of itself produce moral rectitude in the pupil. A large part of humanist literary output, therefore, consisted of treatises on educational techniques; in the north, moreover, the emphasis seems to have been upon adding new educational approaches within the university system, rather than, as in the stereotype of Italian humanism, bypassing academic institutions altogether.[19] An enormous part of the humanist 'enterprise' was pedantic in character: a pedantry which was only saved from triviality by its intense ethical seriousness. Their reforms involved a revaluation of the respective status of rhetoric and logic, and a reform of both. Reformed Renaissance rhetoric comprised, notoriously, the cultivation of a pure, classical Latin style, usually not wholly subservient to classical models, but consciously avoiding the neologisms and vernacular word-order typical of medieval Latin. It affected both structure, for instance classically-inspired letters or speeches, and ornamentation, seen above all in the family of collections of sayings which clustered around Erasmus's *Adagia*.[20] 'Dialectic' or 'Logic' had a much more ambiguous treatment in the Renaissance. One enthusiast

[17] See especially Erasmus's *Letter to Martin Dorp* in *Erasmi Epistolae*, ed. P. S. and H. M. Allen (Oxford, 1906–58), 2, pp. 90ff.; for concepts of 'tradition' see the influential formulation of H. A. Oberman in *Forerunners of the Reformation*, 2nd edn (Philadelphia, 1981), pp. 51–120.

[18] Evans, *Language and Logic*, p. 81; for vernacular versions of the Bible before 1520, see J. Delumeau, *Naissance et affirmation de la réforme* (Paris, 1973), pp. 71–2; Erasmus's thoughts on translating the Bible are cited and discussed by A. G. Dickens, 'Luther and the humanists' in Mack and Jacob, eds, *Politics and Culture*, pp. 203ff.

[19] See works of Erasmus: *De ratione studii*; *De pueris statim ac liberaliter instituendis*; on educational reform see J. H. Overfield, *Humanism and Scholasticism in Late Medieval Germany* (Princeton, 1984); for rhetorical elements in Renaissance educational reform note the work of André de Gouvéa at the Collège de Guyenne in Bordeaux, as in Brian Vickers, *In Defence of Rhetoric* (Oxford, 1988), pp. 256ff., and 'Rhetorical and anti-rhetorical tropes: on writing the history of *elocutio*' in *Comparative Criticism: A Year Book*, 3 (1981), pp. 120ff.

[20] For Renaissance rhetorical theory see the essays in James J. Murphy, ed., *Renaissance Eloquence: Studies in the Theory and Practice of Renaissance Rhetoric* (Berkeley, 1983); Brian Vickers, *In Defence of Rhetoric* (Oxford, 1988), pp. 254–93; for 'ornamentation' see the list of additional compilers of 'adages' included in Erasmus, *Adagia* (Frankfurt, 1599, 1613, and numerous subsequent editions); M. M. Phillips, *The Adages of Erasmus: A Study with Translations* (Cambridge, 1964).

for the humanist programme could omit logic altogether from a proposed academic curriculum, presumably because of its association with essentially scholastic procedures.[21] Widespread reform of dialectical techniques does seem to have waited until the 1550s, when the alternative organizing methods of Peter Ramus came into vogue.[22]

'Humanist' ideas are sometimes associated with a particular approach to historical writing. It may well be premature to regard humanist scholars as precursors of a truth-for-truth's-sake kind of history, just as it is over simple to separate their philology from their ethics. However, some authors at least showed a conscious abandonment of medieval models, the adoption of classical style and rhetorical content, and the beginnings of a discriminating attitude to self-serving myths and legends associated with particular peoples or states.[23]

Two of the humanists' favourite themes touched in different ways upon social issues. First, the northern humanists called, more stridently than had been usual in the early fifteenth century, for some restraint to the excesses of cultic, mechanistic, 'magical', or, as they were called at the time, 'superstitious' forms of popular piety.[24] Since the drift of their religious propaganda was above all ethical, they criticized or simply ridiculed practices which replaced moral with ritual effort; this critique tended to eat away, however modestly, at the massive accretion of wholly orthodox rites—for instance, the almost infinite accumulation of

---

[21] Dialectic was omitted in a list of subjects proposed for a new college in the University of St Andrews by Archibald Hay, *Ad Reverendissimum . . . D. Iacobum Betoun . . . pro collegii erectione . . . oratio* (Paris, 1538), sig. D3v–D4r, and also omitted in the list of subjects proposed when the same college was refounded in 1553: *Evidence, Oral and Documentary . . . for visiting the Universities of Scotland*, 3: St Andrews (London, 1837), p. 362; see my 'Archibald Hay's "Elegantiae"' in *Actes du III⁰ congrès d'études néo-latines, Tours 1976* (Paris, 1980), pp. 282, 286, 294–5.

[22] Tracy, 'Humanism and the Reformation', p. 44; W. Ong, *Ramus, Method, and the Decay of Dialogue* (Cambridge, Mass., 1958); W. S. Howell, *Logic and Rhetoric in England 1500–1700* (Princeton, 1956), pp. 146ff.; N. Gilbert, *Renaissance Concepts of Method* (New York, 1970).

[23] For the Italians see Eric Cochrane, *Historians and Historiography in the Italian Renaissance* (Chicago, 1981); also D. Hay, *Polydore Vergil: Renaissance Historian and Man of Letters* (Oxford, 1952); P. Joachimsen, *Geschichtsauffassung und Geschichtsschreibung in Deutschland unter dem Einfluss des Humanismus* (Leipzig, 1910) and 'Humanism and the development of the German mind' in G. Strauss, ed., *Pre-Reformation Germany* (London, 1972), pp. 162–224; Dickens, *German Nation*, pp. 21ff., 35ff.

[24] For the content of this popular religiosity see K. Thomas, *Religion and the Decline of Magic* (London, 1971), pp. 27–57; E. W. Monter, *Ritual, Myth and Magic in early Modern Europe* (Brighton, 1983), pp. 6–22; Dickens, 'Luther and the Humanists', p. 205 and n. 8; contemporary evidence for popular practices, and the fifteenth-century Church's response to them, is found in the late medieval treatises on 'superstitions': see n. 75 below.

sacrificial masses for the soul, or of 'merit' through penitential exercises—which so characterized late fifteenth-century piety.[25]

A final aspect of the northern humanists' call for social reform concerned civic and State policy towards the poor. In the early sixteenth century some cities in heavily urbanized regions of Europe, whether Venice in northern Italy, or Ypres, Mons, or Lille in the Low Countries, found traditional, indiscriminate, and random private charity, usually in the form of pious bequests or foundations, unsuitable for the numbers and types of poor within their walls.[26] A structured programme of poor relief was gradually developed, comprising enclosure and care of the young and the disabled, enclosure and compulsory work for the able-bodied but un- or under-employed, and severe repression of public begging and vagrancy. This programme, which gradually took over most of urban Europe during the sixteenth century, coincided with the impact of that part of fifteenth-century Italian humanist thought which exalted the ideal of the busy, wealthy, layman and *paterfamilias* over against that of the monastic, contemplative, celibate, idle mendicant.[27] The two trends came together in the *De subventione pauperum*, published by Juan-Luis Vives at Bruges in March 1526, with its tirades against the idleness of the rich and the deceitfulness of the *picaresque* poor alike, and its call for existing charitable foundations to be so regulated as to supervise all categories of poor and make random charity redundant.[28]

These activities and projects—philological and textual scholarship,

---

[25] For the excesses of this piety see J. Toussaert, *Le Sentiment religieux en Flandre à la fin du moyen âge* (Paris, 1963); or more recently G. Audisio, *Les Vaudois du Luberon: une minorité en Provence (1460–1560)* (Mérindol, 1984), pp. 208–16, where 'Waldensian heresy' consisted in not accumulating Masses for the dead in the enormous numbers sought by even quite poor orthodox Catholic believers. Obviously Erasmus cannot be regarded as paradigmatic of the 'humanist' critique as a whole; he can be regarded as influential, if the cumulative effects of the *Enchiridion* after its third edition, the *Praise of Folly*, and some of the *Colloquies* are borne in mind. See also, for instance, Sebastian Brant's *Narrenschiff*; and the simplifications of religious worship in the Meaux circle, recently discussed by C. M. N. Eire, *War against the Idols: The Reformation of Worship from Erasmus to Calvin* (Cambridge, 1986), pp. 168–89.

[26] See J.-P. Gutton, *La société et les pauvres en Europe (xvie–xviiie siècles)* (Paris, 1974), pp. 97ff.; B. Pullan, *Rich and Poor in Renaissance Venice* (Oxford, 1971); P. Bonenfant, 'Les Origines et le caractère de la réforme de la bienfaisance publique aux Pays-Bas sous le règne de Charles Quint', *Revue Belge de Philologie et d'Histoire*, 5 (1926), pp. 887–904, and 6 (1927), pp. 207–30.

[27] This antithesis is, of course, a deliberate caricature; the *Nicomachean Ethics* justified the lay, active life, as did medieval authors like Guillaume de St-Amour of Jehan de Meung. However, thinkers like L.-B. Alberti may have made the active ideal more widespread, pervasive, and 'official', even if they did not invent it. See Gutton, *Société et les pauvres*, pp. 101–2; Skinner, *Foundations*, 1, pp. 98–9.

[28] Gutton, *Société et les pauvres*, pp. 104f.

especially of the Bible and the Fathers, education as a means to moral improvement, the reform of rhetoric and logic, historicism, the assault on popular superstition, and the moral reorganization of poor-relief—by no means exhaust even the most basic of the ideals of the Renaissance in those lands where the Reformation succeeded it. However, they are some of the most prominent and durable features of the programme. It is neither surprising nor even significant that they *survived* in those areas which became Protestant. The question is, rather, how far they survived in spite of, and how far as a part of, that series of social, political, intellectual, and religious processes known as 'the Reformation'. Were they simply part of the lumber left over from a previous period, or did they positively contribute to and shape the continuing history of the Protestant Reformation?

III

'Lutheranism and Calvinism were, in their doctrinal basis, an antihumanism.' This judgement, in fairness, referred strictly to the question of man's free will and moral abilities.[29] Nevertheless, even if such a judgement were overstated, one should still expect the reformers to entertain humanist ideas only to the extent that they helped rather than hindered 'the Gospel'. The 'programmes' envisaged by the generation of Erasmus, Wimpfeling, or Pirckheimer were necessarily downgraded, not to say degraded, to ancillary techniques in the service of dogmatic and confessional principles. However, those principles did not of themselves have answers to every question; in numerous areas the Reformers' concerns overlapped with, or had to draw from, previous intellectual trends.

The ambiguities are well illustrated in the history of the reformers' relationship with the Bible. Evidently, the scholarly priorities of the humanist critique of Scripture coincided at several vital points with the reformers' concerns. Erasmus advocated 'calling in the help of the grammarian', as the expert in language, to resolve textual problems in the Bible.[30] Consciously or not, his attitude clashed with those trends in late scholastic thought which regarded the text as part of a continuous tradition, where the text and the Church coinhered, and the text was

---

[29] Delumeau, *Naissance et affirmation*, p. 74. Delumeau's assumption that humanists in general believed in human free will is contested, at least for Valla and Pomponazzi, by Trinkaus, *Scope of Renaissance Humanism*, pp. 268–71.

[30] Erasmus to Martin Dorp, *Erasmi Epistolae*, 2, pp. 109ff.; Erasmus, *Praise of Folly and Letter to Martin Dorp* tr. B. Radice (Harmondsworth, 1971), pp. 244ff.

validated either by the papacy itself (for the cruder positivists) or by the continuous operation of the Holy Spirit within the Church (for subtler theorists like Gerson).[31] Once the *text* was taken out of the sphere of laws and institutions, the Gospel itself could be detached from the structure of the Church as the Reformers insisted.[32] Secondly, the Reformed exegete needed to have the full apparatus of humanist linguistic and philological expertise at his elbow: therefore he had to be a trained, expert, scholar. Thus the Bible was not emancipated from Roman tradition in order to be 'betrayed' to the sectarian, the spiritualist, or the amateur; it belonged to the expert custodian of the 'communal' priesthood of all believers.[33]

Approaches to interpreting Scripture suggest a further area of close coincidence between humanism and the ongoing Reformation. Lefèvre d'Étaples (following some late scholastic theorists) emphasized the 'twofold literal' sense of Scripture, the historical and the prophetic literal senses, in his *Psalms* in 1509, and seems profoundly to have influenced the early Luther.[34] Disputes later arose within the Protestant tradition over Calvin's application of the principle, where he to some extent rehabilitated the 'literal-historical' sense, the sense intended, for instance, by the prophets writing for their own times, as an 'accommodation' to the age in which it was written; later Lutherans denounced him for 'judaizing' for his pains.[35] Nevertheless, Lefèvre's rejection of elaborate allegories and the fourfold interpretation—even if it was by no means uniquely humanist—seems to have set out the ground-rules for the vast majority of Reformers.[36]

Thirdly, both Erasmus and Lefèvre were advocates, and the latter a practitioner, of translating the Bible into the vernacular.[37] On the face of

---

[31] For the issue of 'tradition' in interpreting the scriptures see H. A. Oberman, *The Harvest of Medieval Theology: Gabriel Biel and Late Medieval Nominalism* (Cambridge, Mass., 1963), pp. 361–422, and *Forerunners*, as above n. 17; F. Oakley, *The Western Church in the Later Middle Ages* (London, 1979), pp. 148ff.; McGrath, *Intellectual Origins*, pp. 149ff.

[32] See P. Althaus, *The Theology of Martin Luther* (Philadelphia, 1966), p. 75; G. W. Bromiley, ed., *Zwingli and Bullinger*, Library of Christian Classics, 24 (London, 1953), pp. 83–90; D. F. Wright, ed., *Common Places of Martin Bucer* (Abingdon, 1972), pp. 184ff., 215ff.; Calvin, *Institutes* (London, 1961), I, vii, 3.

[33] Althaus, *Theology of Martin Luther*, p. 323 and refs.

[34] Oberman, *Forerunners*, pp. 279–307; S. E. Ozment, *The Age of Reform* (New Haven, 1980), pp. 62–73; Bedouelle, *Lefèvre d'Étaples et l'intelligene des écritures*.

[35] Cf. *Institutes*, II, xi, 1–6.

[36] For Zwingli's use of allegorical exegesis see W. P. Stephens, *The Theology of Huldrych Zwingli* (Oxford, 1986), pp. 78–9; McGrath, *Intellectual Origins*, pp. 169–70.

[37] For Erasmus on translation see the *Paraclesis* of 1516, as cited by Dickens, 'Luther and the Humanists', pp. 203–4; on Lefèvre, Bedouelle, *Lefèvre d'Étaples*, and C. Pétavel-Olliff, *La Bible en France, ou les traductions françaises des Saintes Ecritures* (Paris, 1864).

it, no more conspicuous humanist legacy could be sought; Pierre Robert Olivétan's 'Waldensian' French Bible, produced by Farel's printer, Pierre de Wingle, at Neuchâtel in 1535, reproduced much of the language of Lefèvre d'Étaples's earlier translation (despite much-vaunted claims to draw on the original languages); it offers a particularly striking example of that legacy.[38] One might also cite the case of the publisher-printer Robert Estienne, drifting from humanist philology at Lyons to the service of the Genevan Reformation, who published Calvin's revision of Olivétan's Bible in the 1550s.[39]

However, at this point the ambiguities of the humanist contribution to the development of the Reformation begin to command attention. Behind the Erasmian wish for the Bible to be handled by everyone lay the belief—naïve as it seems with hindsight, and probably even in 1516—that the pious layman, with the *Enchiridion* in one hand and the Bible in the other, would use Scripture as a reservoir of moral examples and exhortations; and in dogmatics be content, like Erasmus himself in 1525, to 'believe what the Church taught whether he understood it or not.'[40] The Reformers were not naïve—or, at least, not after the experiences of popular enthusiasm in the early 1520s. The Reformed requirement of a *specialist* exegete who knew the Greek and Hebrew Bible (one humanist legacy) worked against the call for universal Bible-reading (another humanist legacy): the layman was meant to *follow* the interpretation prescribed by the expert.[41] Evidence is accumulating, controversial no doubt, that from the period of the *Kirchenordnungen*, and the constructive establishment of a new Reformed order, as opposed to the popular subversion of the old one, the Reformers used the Catechism,

---

[38] See my *The Reformation of the Heretics: The Waldenses of the Alps 1480–1580* (Oxford, 1984), pp. 208–9; Pétavel-Olliff, *La Bible en France*, pp. 89–117; J. Jalla, 'La Bible d'Olivétan', *Bulletin de la Société d'Histoire vaudoise*, 58 (1932), 76–92, and more recently, e.g., B. Roussel, 'La "Bible d'Olivétan": La traduction du livre du prophète Habaquq', in *Études théologiques et religieuses* 4 (1982), pp. 537–57.

[39] See E. Armstrong, *Robert Estienne, Royal Printer: An Historical Study of the Older Stephanus* (Cambridge, 1954), pp. 228–39.

[40] For this quotation see *Luther and Erasmus: Free Will and Salvation*, ed. E. G. Rupp and P. S. Watson: Library of Christian Classics, 17 (London, 1969), pp. 37–42.

[41] See, for instance, Heinrich Bullinger in 1549: 'the minister of the church doth expound the scriptures to the congregation ... we therefore, the interpreters of God's holy word, and faithful ministers of the church of Christ, must ... teach the people of Christ the word of God': *The Decades of Henry Bullinger*, ed. T. Harding, 4 vols, PS (1849–52), 1, pp. 70–5.

[42] See G. Strauss, 'Lutheranism and Literacy: A Reassessment', in K. von Greyerz, ed., *Religion and Society in Early Modern Europe 1500–1800* (London, 1984), pp. 109–23; R. Gawthrop and G. Strauss, 'Protestantism and Literacy in Early Modern Germany', *PaP*, 104 (1984), pp. 31–55.

structured, programmatic, and systematic, as a lengthy propaedeutic before the Bible was even touched.[42] Once the theological student reached higher education, he turned to Scripture with relief after years of systematics.[43]

The humanist belief in mass education as a means to moral improvement seems to contradict the pessimistic anthropology, the relentless emphasis on the weakness and instability of unaided human reason, which is usually stressed in comparisons of Renaissance and Reformation.[44] The antithesis may, in fact, be overplayed; *within* the congregation some, at least, would have been expected to enrich their understanding of religious doctrine as part of the work of 'sanctification'. A Reformed doctrine of grace could underlie a humanist educational theory without inevitable inconsistency. Moreover, the Reformed theological emphasis on *understanding* as the primary religious duty, rather than obedient participation in a cultic ritual, tended to subsume education within pastoral theology.[45] As far as laymen were concerned, the *Kirchenordnungen* of the middle of the sixteenth century laid continual stress on the obligation to set up an integrated system of education; the emphasis is common to Lutheran, south-German Reformed, and later Genevan-inspired traditions.[46] Not only was education required as such: the schooling process was systematized and made more rigorous by Johann Sturm at (Reformed) Strasburg. The Sturmian model replaced a process where time, money, and endurance would lead a student through the scale of honours, with one where a prescribed standard had to be attained before the student moved on to a higher level of study. The consequences of this reform reverberated through sixteenth-century education.[47]

Since the Protestant minister was the 'specialist' public interpreter of Scripture, his formation above all determined the character and identity of a Reformed church. The primary product of the Sturmian principle as applied to higher education was the series of *gymnasia* dedicated to

---

[43] B. Vogler, *Le Clergé protestant rhénan au siècle de la réforme* (*1556–1619*) (Paris, 1976), pp. 54–6; H. Meylan, *D'Érasme à Théodore de Bèze* (Geneva, 1976), p. 238.

[44] See, for example, *Institutes*, II, ii, 12–24.

[45] For the rationale behind educating sinful men see G. Strauss, *Luther's House of Learning: Indoctrination of the Young in the German Reformation* (Baltimore, 1978), pp. 173ff., 236ff.

[46] Strauss, *Luther's House*, pp. 4–24 and 'Lutheranism and Literacy', p. 121, n. 32; cf. J. K. Cameron, *The First Book of Discipline* (Edinburgh, 1972), pp. 54ff., 129ff. and nn.

[47] On Sturm and Strasburg see A. Schindling, *Humanistische Hochschule und freie Reichssadt: Gymnasium und Akademie in Strassbourg 1538–1621* (Wiesbaden, 1977); L. Junod and H. Meylan, *L'Académie de Lausanne au xvie siècle* (Lausanne, 1947), pp. 11–17; the influence of the humanist colleges is traced in Cameron, *First Book of Discipline*, p. 131, n. 13.

producing ministers first, and other graduates secondarily. The *confessional* aspect of these institutions represented, however, the least humanistic feature of this whole educational wave. The pre-Reformation humanists saw the aim of scriptural exposition, Bible translations, and mass education alike as fundamentally an ethical one. The Reformers taught and interpreted the Bible in the light of their systematic, catechetical, dogmatic principles; in just the same way they gave their institutions of education confessional orientation, whether in Philippist Wittenberg versus Gnesiolutheran Jena, or in the programmes espoused by the Johannea 'High School' at Herborn in Nassau-Dillenburg or the Casimirianum at Neustadt-an-der-Hardt in the Palatinate.[48]

Dogmatics, however, were not everything; within the Reformed educational tradition there is ample scope for tracing the fruits of humanist reform of other disciplines. The fortunes of the Renaissance approach to rhetoric and logic can be followed at two levels: first, their impact on the curriculum as taught in the universities and *gymnasia*; and secondly, how they affected the writings, ideas, and style of the later Reformers themselves. If one takes rhetoric first of all, the lessons from Reformed rhetoric are as ambiguous as those so far described. Several authors have analysed Luther's writings in terms of their rhetorical forms and characteristics; while discovering that in this area (as, one might add, in every other) the Lutheran concept of 'faith' redefines and transforms all other concepts.[49] Melanchthon, who produced three of the rhetorical textbooks most commonly used in sixteenth-century Germany, is credited with harmonizing and synthesizing the rhetorical, humanist, and Lutheran messages.[50] Several recent studies have emphasized how pervasive and important the rhetorical tradition became for all sixteenth-century schools influenced by Renaissance reforms; this trend would evidently have included the Protestant academies, not least through the

[48] On these last see G. Menk, *Die hohe Schule Herborn in ihrer Frühzeit (1584–1660): ein Beitrag zum Hochschulwesen des deutschen Kalvinismus im Zeitalter der Reformation* (Wiesbaden, 1981); V. Press, *Calvinismus und Territorialstaat: Regierung und Zentralbehörden der Kurpfalz 1559–1619* (Stuttgart, 1970), pp. 320–1.

[49] H. Schanze, 'Problems and Trends in the History of German Rhetoric to 1500' in Murphy, ed., *Renaissance Eloquence*, pp. 119–20, based esp. on B. Stolt, *Studien zu Luthers Freiheitstraktat* (Stockholm, 1969), and K. Dockhorn, 'Rhetorica Movet. Protestantischer Humanismus und karolingische Renaissance' in H. Schanze, ed., *Rhetorik: Beiträge zu ihrer Geschichte* (Frankfurt, 1974), pp. 17–42.

[50] The works were *De Rhetorica libri III* (1519), *Institutiones Rhetoricae* (1521), and *Elementorum Rhetorices libri II* (1531): see Schanze, 'Trends', p. 120, n. 27; Vickers, *In Defence of Rhetoric*, pp. 281–2.

EUAN CAMERON

influence of, for instance, André de Gouvea on Mathurin Cordier or George Buchanan.[51]

The practical side to rhetoric bulks even larger than the theoretical side in the unfolding Reformation. The Protestant emphasis on 'word' and 'faith' necessarily elevated the sermon into a permanent major feature of Reformed worship. It was the means by which the reforming message was most effectively promoted at first;[52] it was the main medium through which the didactic message of the Catechism was instilled into the congregation.[53] Protestant ministers, who needed to preach, therefore had a pressing need for oratorical skills; that need is reflected in their practical writings.[54] Melanchthon's own work on preaching, the *De officiis concionatoris* of 1529, like his rhetorical texts, absorbed Renaissance rhetorical principles more than its medieval predecessors. It inspired a genre of such works, for instance, by Veit Dietrich and Johannes Aepinus; and even influenced Catholic thought via unacknowledged quotations by the Spanish cleric Alfonso Zorilla.[55] While some writers on preaching, like Andreas Hyperius of Marburg, tried to adjust the classical *genera* of rhetoric to specifically Christian means and ends, strong classical motifs reappeared; the later theorist Bartholomaeus Keckermann likewise acknowledged his dependence on a humanistic, even cross-confessional tradition.[56]

Reformed writers were often as prolific in writing letters as they were in delivering sermons, if not more so.[57] Given the place which rhetoric and literary ornamentation played in their academic formation, and the status of the letter as a Renaissance literary form, their letters could hardly have remained immune from Renaissance influences. The self-conscious

---

[51] B. Vickers, 'Rhetorical and anti-rhetorical tropes', *Comparative Criticism: A Year Book*, ed. E. S. Shaffer (Cambridge, 1981), 3, pp. 120ff.; *In Defence of Rhetoric*, pp. 255ff.; cf. also L. W. B. Brockliss, *French Education in the Seventeenth and Eighteenth Centuries* (Oxford, 1987); I. D. McFarlane, *George Buchanan (1506–1582)* (London, 1980), pp. 78–83.
[52] See B. Moeller, 'Was wurde in der Frühzeit der Reformation in den deutschen städten gepredigt?', *Archiv für Reformationsgeschichte*, 75 (1984), pp. 176–93; R. W. Scribner, *For the Sake of Simple Folk: Popular Propaganda for the German Reformation* (Cambridge, 1981), pp. 244–5.
[53] See, for instance, Luther's prefaces to his 1529 *Larger Catechism*.
[54] Vickers, *In Defence of Rhetoric*, pp. 290ff.
[55] John W. O'Malley, 'Content and rhetorical forms in sixteenth-century treatises on preaching' in Murphy, ed., *Renaissance Eloquence*, pp. 241–6.
[56] O'Malley, 'Content and rhetorical forms', pp. 248ff.; P. Bayley, *French Pulpit Oratory 1598–1650* (Cambridge, 1980), pp. 61–3.
[57] Perhaps the most prolific letter-writer was Bullinger, from whom some 12,000 letters survive, rivalled by Melanchthon with 7,000, and Luther and Calvin with over 4,000 each: see Fritz Büsser, 'Bullinger et Calvin', *Études Théologiques et Religieuses*, 63 (1988), pp. 31–52.

allusiveness of Erasmus's *Adages* might have been eschewed, but the subtler literary cadences remained.[58] Nor should the letter be seen in isolation from the broader sense of community between scholars travelling around the Protestant world, to which itineraries and *alba amicorum*, the latter often replete with tokens of humanistic learning, bear witness.[59]

An even more striking instance of rhetorical impact on late Reformation writing arises with the fashion for allegorical 'emblems'. These images, combining picture, allegory, and abstruse allusion, gained popularity in Europe with the publication of Alciati's *Emblematum liber* in 1531.[60] Given the suspicion with which the Swiss Reformed tradition is supposed to have regarded iconography,[61] it may cause some surprise that Theodore Beza did not confine his *Icones* of 1580 to mere representational portraiture. The latter pages of the book comprise a series of allegorical emblems accompanied by Renaissance verse, all in the service of the Reformed cause. They were clearly noticed and copied elsewhere, as in the post-Reformation seal of St Mary's College, in the University of St Andrews.[62]

The fate of Renaissance logic is more problematical, inasmuch as there is significant disagreement as to what constituted a 'humanist' programme for university logic in the sixteenth century. If one takes the broadest definition of 'humanist', that favoured by such recent historians of English academic life as J. K. McConica and Margo Todd, one might conclude that there were, in fact, two schools of 'humanist' logic in the mid-sixteenth century: one, inspired by Ramus's *Dialecticae institutiones* of 1543, which was both empirical and willing to employ classical authorities (including, but not confined to, Aristotle); and another, drawing on such

[58] See, for example, *Letters of John Johnston c. 1565–1611 and Robert Howie c. 1565–c. 1645*, ed. J. K. Cameron (Edinburgh, 1963), esp. pp. 4–19.

[59] For studies of such contacts see J. K. Cameron, 'Some Continental Visitors to Scotland in the late sixteenth and early seventeenth centuries' in T. C. Smout, ed., *Scotland and Europe 1200–1850* (Edinburgh, 1986), pp. 45–61 and 'The British itinerary of Johann Peter Hainzel von Degerstein by Caspar Waser', *Zwingliana*, 15 (1980), pp. 259–95.

[60] For emblems see D. A. Larusso, 'Rhetoric in the Italian Renaissance' in Murphy, ed., *Renaissance Eloquence*, pp. 52–3 and refs; and the works of R. J. Clements, esp. *Picta Poesis: Literary and Humanistic Theory in Renaissance Emblem Books* (Rome, 1960); the massive reference work edited by A. Henkel and A. Schöne, *Emblemata: Handbuch zur Sinnbildkunst des xvi. und xvii Jahrhunderts* (Stuttgart, 1967), tabulates and illustrates a mass of such images.

[61] See, for instance, Eire, *War against the Idols*, pp. 73ff.; C. Garside, *Zwingli and the Arts* (New Haven, 1966).

[62] Theodore Beza, *Icones, id est, Verae Imagines . . .* (n.p., 1580); J. K.Cameron and R. N. Smart, 'A Scottish form of the Emblème de la Religion Réformée: the post-Reformation seal of St Mary's College in the University of St Andrews', *Proceedings of the Society of Antiquaries of Scotland*, 105 (1972–4), pp. 248–54; Henkel and Schöne, *Emblemata*, col. 1567.

texts as Melanchthon's *Dialectices* of 1527, vehemently anti-Ramus and much more respectful of Aristotle, but still inheriting humanistic rhetorical emphases.[63] One finds the Scots academic John Johnston engaging in just such a debate on behalf of the Ramists against the neo-Aristotelians at Heidelberg in the late 1580s.[64] Whether the 'neo-Aristotelian' school, as represented by John Case at Oxford, can be rigidly distinguished from so-called 'Protestant scholasticism' on the Continent remains uncertain; the debate may simply show how weak and diffuse a label 'humanist' had become.[65]

One practical impact of the Ramistic approach deserves, perhaps, more attention than it usually receives: its capacity for organizing any discipline, including theology, in a series of tables offering a schematic rather than linear approach. The *Tabulae analyticae* of the Magyar theologian István Szegedi Kis ('Stephanus Szegedinus', 1502–72) were less neglected in their own time than today, as at least one writer in the 1600s regarded them as one of the best available sources of theological commonplaces.[66] The militant Ramist John Johnston proposed publishing similar 'Theological tables' early in 1590.[67] It is noteworthy, though perhaps not too significant, that Szegedius adopted a 'Majoristic' approach to good works, often seen as a sign of humanist influence in a Reformed theologian.[68]

Historical writing was, of the humanists' favoured activities, the one most prone to suffer from the intrusion of ideology, propaganda, and apocalyptic. Even here, however, one can find Reformed historians who were humanistic in their tastes and judgements; though their search for

---

[63] The development of logic as a component in the English scholarly curriculum is discussed by Margo Todd, *Christian Humanism and the Puritan Social Order* (Cambridge, 1987), pp. 54–95, with reference to J. K. McConica, 'Humanism and Aristotelianism in Tudor Oxford', *EHR*, 94 (1979), pp. 291–317, and C. B. Schmitt, *John Case and Aristotelianism in the Renaissance* (Montreal, 1983); Ramism is discussed on pp. 67–72.

[64] *Letters of . . . Johnston . . . and . . . Howie*, pp. xxix–xxx.

[65] Todd, *Christian Humanism*, pp. 69–71; for 'Protestant scholasticism' see B. G. Armstrong, *Calvinism and the Amyraut Heresy; Protestant Scholasticism and Humanism in seventeenth century France* (Madison, 1969); O. Fatio, *Méthode et Théologie: Lambert Daneau et les débuts de la scholastique réformée* (Geneva, 1976).

[66] Stephanus Szegedinus, *Tabulae analyticae, quibus illud sanorum sermonum de Fide, Charitate, et Patientia . . . fideliter declaratur* (Schaffhausen, 1592); also his *Loci Communes* (Basel, 1599); Szegedinus is listed with Musculus and Peter Martyr as one of the best authors of common places by Richard Bernard, *The Faithful Shepherd* (London, 1607), p. 40. See Michael McGiffert, 'Grace and Works: the rise and division of Covenant Divinity in Elizabethan Puritanism', *HThR*, 75 (1982), p. 463.

[67] *Letters of . . . Johnston . . . and . . . Howie*, pp. xxxi, 58–60.

[68] Szegedinus, *Loci Communes*, pp. 273, 281.

balance, simple narrative, and secular, political analysis often militated against specifically confessional concerns. Philip Melanchthon and Kaspar Peucer successively worked to edit the *Cronica* of Johan Carion, but with the effect of contributing to the growth of a long-term religious and apocalyptic interpretation of human history, a tradition which was developed to its fullest in the works of Flacius Illyricus and James Ussher.[69] Two Reformed historians who *did* embrace some humanist ideals were both, in their way, swimming against the tide: Johannes Sleidan, whose *Commentaries* inspired few imitators by comparison with the more partisan martyrologies,[70] and Henri-Lancelot de la Popelinière, whose work was gravely censured by Protestant synods within France.[71] In this area the overwhelming verdict must be that humanist and Reformed values mixed very ill indeed.

On the face of it, the 'reform' of popular superstition suggests just the opposite conclusion. Erasmus and Sebastian Brant mocked the excesses of a cultic, mechanical piety which expected rewards for rituals observed, prayers said, or shrines visited; the reformers took that critique to its logical extent and not only abolished the Church's 'superstitious' rites, but also discouraged and condemned the popular superstitions which fed parasitically upon those rites, isolated as they were once the Church's own 'magic' was abolished.[72] Certainly, if one looks for Protestant ministers busily disparaging or dismantling popular customs, remedies, or entertainments, especially those which gathered around the sacred, they are not too hard to find.[73] In this respect the Protestant Reformation seems to show the most consistent embodiment of the humanists' criticisms, in

---

[69] A. G. Dickens and J. Tonkin with K. Powell, *The Reformation in Historical Thought* (Cambridge, Mass., 1985), pp. 8–9; for the 'apocalyptic' tradition in church history as it related to the exploitation of medieval heresy see my *Reformation of the Heretics*, pp. 243–52.

[70] Dickens and Tonkin, *Reformation*, pp. 10–19; see D. R. Kelley, 'Johann Sleidan and the Origins of History as a Profession', *JMH*, 52 (1980), pp. 573–98; an early imitator was Pierre de la Place, *Commentaires de l'estat de la religion et république* . . . (n.p., 1565).

[71] Dickens and Tonkin, *Reformation*, pp. 84–6; M. Yardeni, 'La Conception de l'histoire dans l'œuvre de La Popelinière', *Revue d'Histoire moderne et contemporaine*, 11 (1964), pp. 112–16; C.-G. Dubois, *La Conception de l'histoire en France au xvie siècle (1560–1610)* (Paris, 1977), pp. 124–53.

[72] See, above all, Thomas, *Religion and the Decline of Magic*, pp. 58–89; of this phenomenon A. G. Dickens remarks: 'Do we not come very clear to the nexus between Christian Humanism and the Reformation? Here we observe a momentous encounter between a would-be-Scriptural religion and a variegated host of cults, processed, mediated, or merely tolerated by ecclesiastical authority . . .': 'Luther and the Humanists', in Mack and Jacob, eds, *Politics and Culture*, p. 205.

[73] See, for instance, P. Collinson, *The Religion of Protestants: The Church in English Society 1559–1625* (Oxford, 1982), pp. 220–30; Cameron, *The Reformation of the Heretics*, pp. 179–80, 193–6.

that it abolished *all* mechanical forms of worship which did not rest on prayer and sanctification, in favour of a demanding ethical system; thus it avoided the uneasy compromises which accompanied the local Catholic reformations.[74]

However, this comparison raises a number of doubts and problems. The northern humanists were not the first writers to describe and criticize the extravagances of popular religious superstition. Credit for such criticism belongs, at the latest, to early fifteenth-century writers such as Jean Gerson, Nicolas de Clamanges, Johann Nider, or Henry of Gorinchem, or to Martín of Arles or Martin Plantsch in later decades. In fairness, such writers wrote specifically to define which *particular* superstitions ought to be reproved in penitents.[75] Nevertheless, the northern humanists, in criticizing the abuse or distortion of a particular cult, rather than recommending its abolition wholesale, were in some respects closer to their medieval forbears and Catholic successors than to the reformers.[76] A second, more profound difference between humanist and Reformed critiques of popular belief lay in the reasons behind them. The Erasmian call to eschew vulgar idolatry was meant to stimulate a sincere, ethical piety within the existing forms. The Reformed 'War against the Idols' attacked superstition as outrageous blasphemy against the all-sufficient sacrifice of Christ, and only as a part of a greater assault on official religion.[77]

A third objection is yet more surprising. If the Protestant campaign to 'reform' the culture of the people were an inherent consequence of the humanist input into their message, one would expect that popular manners and beliefs would be criticized from the very start of the movement. In fact, the early Protestant attitude to 'popular culture' was almost the exact opposite of the 'acculturation' process, as some social historians have called it.[78] In the early stages of publicizing the cause of the Reformation, the reformers readily turned to some elements of popular culture—

[74] On which see, above all, J. Delumeau, *Catholicism between Luther and Voltaire* (London, 1977).

[75] The work of Martín of Arles y Andosilla, *Tractatus insignis et exquisitissimus de superstitionibus contra maleficia seu sortilegia* (Paris, 1517ff.), collected some of its author's own experiences as a cleric near Pamplona, as well as writings by Gerson and Nider. The work of Henry of Gorinchem, *Tractatus de supersticiosis quibusdam casibus*, was printed twice at Esslingen in the 1470s and at Cologne in 1488.

[76] See Eire, *War Against the Idols*, pp. 45–53.

[77] Ibid., pp. 54–104.

[78] On 'acculturation', see R. Muchembled, 'Lay Judges and the Acculturation of the Masses (France and the Southern Low Countries, Sixteenth to Eighteenth Centuries)' in von Greyerz, ed., *Religion and Society*, pp. 56–65; also R. Muchembled, *Popular Culture and Elite Culture in France 1400–1750*, tr. L. Cochrane (Baton Rouge, La., 1985), *passim*.

especially carnival, parody, inversion, and forms of ritual insult—in order to denounce and degrade other such elements, for instance, the saint cults.[79] Religious plays could be a convenient medium of Reforming propaganda to one generation, and only to a later one a sinful distraction from the serious business of learning one's catechism.[80] At Nuremberg the *Schembart* Carnival processions of 1522 and 1523 contained popular, satirical anti-papal (and, implicitly, pro-Reform) displays which caused the magistrates some unease. Between 1524 and 1538 the procession was not held. In the 1539 procession the Lutheran preacher Osiander was represented on one of the floats surrounded by fools and devils.[81] The Reformers' response to popular modes of expression evolved slowly: from first riding on a wave of popular enthusiasm, to a 'new clericalism' attempting to repress and purge just these same popular high spirits, in Protestant and Catholic countries alike.[82] In view of this evolution, the humanist antecedents of their later response obviously require very subtle evaluation.

Humanist and Reformed attitudes to social responsibility and social control form a vast topic, surveyed for the English case in a recent monograph.[83] In the English case, the filiation between humanist and reforming motives for Poor Law reform can be made to seem fairly clear-cut: the ideas of Vives and the Netherlands towns were circulated in England in the 1530s and practically realized in the post-Reformation legislation of the Elizabethan period.[84] There seems little room for doubt that in the English case, humanist and Protestant impulses coincided and are indeed barely distinguishable. In Renaissance France and Italy similar moves were made (at Lyons, Venice, or Florence), this time without Protestant input.[85]

However, in the bulk of the Protestant regions of Europe the issue, to a non-specialist at least, seems less clear-cut. For central Germany perhaps the most influential text on this issue was the second part of Luther's

[79] Scribner., *Simple Folk*, pp. 59ff., 95ff.

[80] See, for instance, the propaganda value in the early Reformation of such plays as Nikolaus Manuel's *Die Totenfresser* and *Die Ablasskrämer*, or of John Bale's *King John*; Professor Patrick Collinson relates how one of the authors of the play *Gorboduc, or Ferrex and Porrex*, written by Thomas Sackville and Thomas Norton, became in later life a severe Puritan opponent of all theatre. The ambiguities are briefly discussed in Delumeau, *Naissance et Affirmation*, p. 358.

[81] R. W. Scribner, 'Reformation, Carnival, and the World turned upside-down', *Popular Culture and Popular Movements in Reformation Germany* (London, 1987), pp. 73–95.

[82] Scribner, 'Anticlericalism and the Reformation in Germany' in ibid., pp. 254–6.

[83] Todd, *Christian Humanism*.

[84] Ibid., pp. 137–47; P. Slack, *Poverty and Policy in Tudor and Stuart England* (London, 1988).

[85] Todd, *Christian Humanism*, p. 145, n. 107 and refs.

To the Christian Nobility, which combined both social and religious prescriptions. These included reducing feast-days to prevent idleness (no. 18); the abolition of all begging, with the imposition of systematic, prudent relief of the poor within each city (no. 21); restraints on luxuries and usury, and a ban on municipal brothels (no. 27).[86] Luther himself provided a more detailed blueprint in the Leisnig Common Chest Ordinance of 1523.[87] Meanwhile, cities merely teetering on the brink of the Reformation often adopted 'common chest' ordinances at the earliest opportunity: Nuremberg in 1522, Kitzingen in 1523, Windsheim and Magdeburg in 1524, and Zurich in January 1525.[88] Johannes Bugenhagen incorporated similar provisions into his north German Church Ordinances.[89]

In the first place, humanist influences are hard to discern here: several of the German Common Chest Orders were instituted well before either the Ypres scheme or the publication of Vives's *De subventione*. More importantly, however, historians of the Reformation city tend to attribute the haste with which many cities created common chests to very practical motives. Simply, such chests were used as a means to confiscate and bring under the city fathers' control the great disorderly mass of medieval charitable endowments—not to mention houses of mendicant friars— which formed substantial enclaves of clerical power and fiscal immunity. The Zwickau common chest became notorious as a fund from which the councillors could borrow to suit themselves.[90] The question may turn out to be not whether Protestantism or humanism was the ideological motor force behind systematic poor-relief; but rather why Luther, Vives, and the rest independently found ideological reasons to support developments upon which the late medieval bourgeoisie insisted (once the fear of treading upon clerical toes was removed) for economic reasons.

A similar debate hangs over the more sweeping 'reform' of attitudes towards social control in 'Puritan' England; some scholars find that the

[86] *WA*, 6, pp. 450ff., 465ff.
[87] Text in *WA*, 12, pp. 16–30, and in E. Sehling, ed., *Die evangelischen Kirchenordnungen des xvi. Jahrhunderts* (Leipzig, 1902ff.), 1, pt 1, pp. 598–604.
[88] Sehling, *Kirchenordnungen*, 2, pp. 449f.; 11, pp. 23ff., 72ff., 674ff.; Gutton, *La Société et les pauvres*, p. 103.
[89] B. J. Kidd, *Documents Illustrative of the Continental Reformation* (Oxford, 1911), pp. 231–2; Sehling, *Kirchenordnungen*, 5, pp. 359ff., 531ff.
[90] S. C. Karant-Nunn, *Zwickau in Transition 1500–1547: the Reformation as an Agent of change* (Columbus, Ohio, 1987), pp. 131–3; for the pressures for 'communalization' of the old Church in general see P. Blickle, *Gemeindereformation: Die Menschen des 16. Jahrhunderts auf dem Weg zum Heil* (Munich, 1985), pp. 179ff.

campaign to repress sexual irregularities leading to illegitimate births—
and a charge on the parish—goes hand in hand with more specifically
religious reforms, such as attacks on alehouses and popular festivities or
sabbatarianism.[91] Others find, in other places, that disorders leading to
poverty were much more severely dealt with than those leading simply to
ungodliness.[92] In view of this debate, scholars searching for the practical
impact of humanist social ideas have a complex task in respect both of
Protestantism *and* popular economics.

IV

It would be a tempting, easy, and mistaken response to the complexities of
the relationship between the humanist programme and the developing
Reformation to say that they show how vague and inadequate terms like
'humanist' or 'protestant' are, and that we need a new set of definitions. In
fact, the complexities lie not in the semantics but in the issues themselves.
Humanism and the Reformation are concepts with ill-defined edges, no
doubt, but a reasonably clear core, well founded in the sources of the
period; no other categories of equal usefulness have yet been devised.
Overlaps, inconsistencies, and contradictions in the adaptation of humanism by the reformers arose not because 'humanism', say, did not exist, but
rather because it so effectively (and diffusely) pervaded every area of
thought and life. On the other hand, humanism was not *so* universal that
one cannot easily find 'non-humanist' or 'anti-humanist' elements in later
sixteenth-century culture: one need only cite the neo-Thomist Aristotelianism of Bellarmine or Molina and Suarez, the attitudes of Domingo
Soto to Greek studies at the Council of Trent or to poor-relief and private
charity, or of Melchior Cano towards the Paduan Aristotelians. It is highly
interesting that militant anti-humanism is much more easy to detect in
Counter-Reformation Catholicism than in Protestant countries;
although, needless to add, many humanist features were found in

---

[91] These are approximately the findings of, for instance, K. Wrightson and D. Levine, *Poverty
and Piety in an English Village: Terling, 1525–1700* (London, 1979) and P. Collinson, 'Cranbrook
and the Fletchers: popular and unpopular religion in the Kentish Weald' in P. N. Brooks, ed.,
Reformation Principle and Practice: Essays in Honour of Arthur Geoffrey Dickens (London, 1980),
pp. 173–202.
[92] The case is put by M. Ingram, 'Religion, communities and moral discipline in late sixteenth-
and early seventeenth-century England: case studies' in von Greyerz, ed., *Religion and Society*,
pp. 177–93; and by his *Church Courts, Sex and Marriage in England 1570–1640* (Cambridge,
1988).

35

reformed Catholicism as well.[93] Yet in comparison to the attacks of Dominicans and neo-Thomists, Francis Bacon's reproofs that

> the exact study of languages, and the efficacy of preaching, did bring in an affected study of eloquence, and *copia* of speech ... the whole inclination and bent of those times was rather towards *copia*, than weight ... here therefore is the first distemper of learning, when men study words, and not matter[94]

seem mild criticism indeed.

University of Newcastle upon Tyne

[93] For some indications of common ground, see Delumeau, *Naissance et affirmation*, pp. 351ff.
[94] Bacon, *Works*, I (London, 1778), pp. 14–15.

LA NOTION DE DIGNITÉ HUMAINE
SELON ERASME DE ROTTERDAM*

by JEAN-CLAUDE MARGOLIN

L
E platonisme florentin, et surtout le fameux discours de Pic de la Mirandole *de dignitate hominis*[1] sont souvent considérés comme les manifestations primordiales de l'humanisme européen, pour peu que l'on accorde à ce dernier concept si controversé de par sa polysémie elle-même, le sens d'une philosophie ou, à tout le moins, d'une attitude mentale exaltant la grandeur ou la liberté de l'homme. La dignité de l'homme serait moins une valeur ajoutée à l'homme que l'expression même de son essence, ou sa définition spécifique: *homo loquens*, *homo rationalis*, *zôon politicon*, la notion de dignité subsumerait toutes les autres caractéristiques de l'homme, tant il est vrai que le don de la parole — qui distingue l'homme des animaux, capables seulement d'exprimer des sons (*sonitus*, mais non point *voces* ou *verba*)[2] — la puissance de la raison — qui le distingue également des bêtes brutes, mues par l'instinct — ou encore la volonté de former avec ses semblables une communauté civile — si différente des rassemblements de hordes ou de troupeaux de bêtes — constituent des aspects ou des modalités de la *dignitas*.

Ni Ficin ni Pic n'ont inventé ce concept, ils ne sont pas davantage les premiers à l'avoir exploité dans toutes ses dimensions. Mais il est sans doute exact de reconnaître dans le Quattrocento italien un vaste laboratoire où le mot et la chose ont été continuellement analysés, approfondis, lestés d'une substance philosophique telle que les générations suivantes ne pourront plus les manipuler à leur fantaisie: la dignité de l'homme continuera, hélas, d'être trop souvent piétinée, mais les deux termes 'dignité' et 'homme' (ou 'humanité') ne pourront plus être conceptuellement séparés. Cela est si vrai que des idéologies barbares (ou

---

* Cet article a fait d'abord l'objet d'une conférence à l'Université de Turin et a été publiée dans la *Studi Francesci*, 80 (1983), pp. 205–19.
[1] Sur ce discours, cf. Giovanni di Napoli, *Giovanni Pico della Mirandola e la problematica dottrinale del suo tempo* (Rome, 1965); H. de Lubac, *Pic de la Mirandole* (Paris, 1974); J. de Pina Martins, *Jean Pic de la Mirandole* (Paris, 1976); l'édition d'E. Garin, *De dignitate hominis* (Edizione Nazionale dei classici del pensiero italiano, Florence, 1942), pp. 102–64.
[2] Distinction classique: cf. notamment Erasme, dans son traité *De recta pronunciatione*, éd. J. Clericus, *Desiderius Erasmus. Opera omnia*, 10 vols (Lugduni Batavorum, 1703–6), [= *LB*], I, 913E–14B; éd. M. Cytowska, *Desiderius Erasmus. Opera omnia* (Amsterdam, 1969–) [= *ASD*], I-4 (1973), pp. 14–15. Voir aussi, *Lingua*, LB, 4, 661 et ASD, IV-1 (1974), pp. 243–4.

inhumaines), comme le nazisme — pour me limiter à cet exemple du XXᵉ siècle — ont été contraintes d'inventer ou de réinventer le concept de 'sous-homme' (*Untermensch*) pour justifier, si l'on peut dire, les abominables traitements qu'ils réservaient à des êtres que leurs particularismes ethniques ne faisaient pas accéder (à leurs yeux) à la dignité de l'homme véritable. Dès 1452 Giannozzo Manetti composait un ouvrage auquel il donnait le nom de *De dignitate et excellentia hominis*,[3] les deux termes caractérisant l'homme étant pratiquement synonymes, puisque l'idée de dignité implique celles de grandeur, de prestige, de qualités portées à leur plus haut degré d'expression; donc d'excellence, ou de 'précellence' — comme on disait volontiers au XVIᵉ siècle, ce dernier mot étant calqué sur le latin *praecellentia*[4] (que l'on trouve, par exemple dans le traité de Corneille Agrippa sur la 'dignité de la femme', ou plus précisément *De praecellentia feminei sexus*[5]). Autre expression, autre synonyme: le mot *praestantia*, que l'on trouve accolé à celui de *excellentia* dans le traité de Fazio, de quelques années antérieur, *De excellentia et praestantia hominis*.[6] Il n'est pas nécessaire de faire plus ample moisson de références, d'autant moins que la question a déjà été traitée — et de main de maître — il y a plus de quarante ans par celui auquel les études humanistes du XXᵉ siècle doivent tant, je veux parler du professeur Eugenio Garin dans un article célèbre (et toujours actuel) intitulé 'La *dignitas hominis* e la letteratura patristica'.[7] Il a en effet montré d'une manière définitive que l'une des sources vives — sinon la source essentielle — de la notion de dignité de l'homme, telle que les humanistes du Quattrocento l'ont comprise et analysée, c'était la littérature des Pères de l'Eglise, et d'une manière encore plus originelle, les textes bibliques. Nous avons abandonné depuis longtemps l'idée, encore si tenace au début de ce siècle, et au maintien de laquelle les travaux de

---

[3] Ouvrage imprimé à Bâle en 1532, et publié par les soins de J. Alex. Brassicano. Sur Giannozo Manetti, cf. H. W. Wittschier, *G. Manetti, das Corpus der Orationes* (Cologne-Graz, 1968).

[4] Expression qui n'est pas classique, mais que l'on trouve notamment dans Tertullien, *Apologeticus*, 23.

[5] Plus précisément encore: *De nobilitate et praecellentia foeminei sexus declamatio* (Anvers, 1529, in-8°). Dédiée à Marguerite d'Autriche. On pourrait faire remarquer que le terme de *declamatio*, qui désigne ordinairement un exercice oratoire par lequel on soutient une cause paradoxale, sinon absurde, laisse planer quelques doutes sur le degré de sincérité ou de profondeur de ce traité. Mais je pense que chez Agrippa, comme chez Erasme, le caractère 'extérieur' ou 'formel' de la *declamatio* est parfaitement compatible avec le sérieux et le caractère authentique des propos exprimés.

[6] Il porte aussi le titre de *De humanae vitae felicitate liber, seu summi boni fruitatione* et est dédié au roi Alphonse d'Aragon (il ne sera imprimé à Anvers, chez Plantin, qu'en 1556).

[7] *Humanisme et Renaissance* (1938), pp. 102–45.

Burkhardt[8] avaient si puissamment contribué, ainsi que l''esprit du temps', à savoir que la Renaissance et l'Humanisme avaient en quelque sorte détrôné Dieu au profit de l'Homme, Dieu qui règnait en maître exclusif au cours d'un Moyen Age dans lequel les hommes, plus ou moins anonymes, aliénant leur liberté individuelle, restaient soumis à la loi immuable de Dieu, comme aux lois instituées sur la terre par la Volonté du maître de l'Univers. Garin a montré à partir d'un grand nombre de textes d'une limpidité extrême[9] — textes de Lactance, d'Augustin, de Grégoire de Nysse, de Basile, d'Arnobe, de Jérôme, d'Ambroise, de Cyrille d'Alexandrie, et de bien d'autres — que la conception chrétienne de l'homme, c'est-à-dire d'un être créé à l'image et à la ressemblance de Dieu, était celle qui pouvait assurer sur une base solide et indestructible le maintien de cette dignité consubstantielle à l'homme. Loin d'opposer une dignité humaine, rien qu'humaine, mais totalement humaine, à la majesté, à l'omniscience ou à l'omnipotence divine, les humanistes, fidèles sur ce point à une tradition médiévale qui englobait les meilleurs penseurs et les théologiens les plus ouverts, voyaient dans la raison et le logos humains les reflets de la Raison et du Logos divins: d'où leur inaltérable valeur.

Mais le monothéisme judéo-chrétien et le fait chrétien de l'Incarnation et du dogme de l'Homme-Dieu ne sont pas davantage l'unique source de la notion de dignité humaine, même s'ils ont constitué pendant des siècles la nourriture spirituelle de la quasi-totalité de l'Europe. L'humanisme, chacun le sait, s'est abreuvé aussi largement aux sources païennes, essentiellement gréco-latines: Platon, Aristote, Plotin, Cicéron, Sènèque, Virgile constituent des références ou des *loci* d'une puissance et d'une force de rayonnement à peine inférieures aux références bibliques et patristiques, surtout quand, dans un remarquable syncrétisme, les humanistes les enrôlent plus ou moins métaphoriquement sous la bannière d'un christianisme élargi aux dimensions de l'humanité. On connait le mot d'un des personnages d'un colloque d'Erasme, jailli presque spontanément: 'Saint Socrate, priez pour nous!'[10] Et l'on sait que la

---

[8] Notamment *Die Kultur der Renaissance in Italien* (Bâle, 1860). Cf. trad. fr. *La Civilisation de la Renaissance en Italie* (Paris, 1958).

[9] L'affirmation d'un *regnum hominis* est une revendication de la spiritualité, car la *dignitas hominis* apparait dans tous ces textes — et jusqu'à Pic et à l'humanisme chrétien — contre toute interprétation physique du concept de microcosme.

[10] C'est Nephalius qui s'exprime ainsi dans le *Convivium religiosum*, ed. L.-E. Halkin, *ASD*, I–3 (1972), p. 253, line 710.

Theologia platonica[11] de Marsile Ficin, de par son titre même, mais surtout de par son contenu, constitue l'une des synthèses les plus admirables — je ne dis pas des moins incontestables, d'un point de vue philosophique ou théologique — du platonisme et du christianisme.

Ne pourrait-on pas, pour résumer en une proposition banale, ces quelques remarques préliminaires, affirmer que, par delà les diverses religions, mythologies ou philosophies qui traitent de l'homme, du monde et de Dieu (ou des dieux), dès que l'homme a pris conscience de lui-même, je veux dire de lui-même en tant qu'individu humain, sa conscience s'est scindée en une conscience de soi et en une conscience de l'autre: conscience de son identité dont l'unicité fait tout le prix, conscience de son appartenance à un monde créé dans lequel, parmi la multitude des espèces et des êtres plus ou moins différents de lui, il est des créatures avec lesquelles les nécessités naturelles mais surtout les impératifs moraux commandent que s'établissent des rapports privilégiés fondés sur la reconnaissance réciproque. C'est cette reconnaissance de l'homme par l'homme, sous le regard de Dieu (ou, dans une perspective évidemment aberrante pour les hommes du XVe ou du XVIe siècle, au nom d'une valeur ou d'un principe équivalent à Dieu), qui est le fondement de la dignité de l'homme.

*   *   *

Dans l'œuvre d'Erasme, lecteur, commentateur, traducteur ou éditeur de la Bible et d'un très grand nombre de Pères de l'Eglise, bon connaisseur de Ficin et plus encore de Pic, l'expression de *dignitas hominis* ne parait guère employée. En l'absence de tout index lemmatique complet établi sur les bases scientifiques que l'informatique permettrait pourtant de réaliser, nous sommes contraints à un travail artisanal. Nous disposons sans doute de l'index général établi par Le Clerc à la fin du tome X de son édition des *Opera omnia*,[12] et de quelques index incomplets ou partiels relatifs à telle œuvre de l'humaniste hollandais. Mais malgré leurs mérites, ils ont été conçus d'une manière à la fois si artisanale et subjective qu'on ne peut les utiliser qu'avec la plus grande prudence: quand on ne relève pas systématiquement tous les mots expresifs, on peut laisser passer des termes comme *dignitas* au profit de synonymes (comme *excellentia*, *praestantia*,

---

[11] *Theologiae Platonicae de immortalite animorum lib. XVIII* (1488). Cf. l'éd. trad. de l'Abbé R. Marcel (Paris, 1964, 1970) [= Classiques de l'humanisme].
[12] *LB* 10, *in fine*.

praecellentia, *virtus*, voire *ratio* ou *intellectus*, s'il est vrai que la dignité de l'homme est dans la raison, dans l'intelligence ou dans la pensée).

Ces réserves faites, et avec toute la prudence nécessaire, je reprends ma remarque: la dignité de l'homme est partout présente dans l'œuvre d'Erasme, mais le syntagme ne doit guère s'y trouver; en tout cas, pour ma part, je ne l'ai jamais rencontré.

N'essayons donc pas, par une lecture trop étroitement orientée, de traquer systématiquement, à défaut du terme *dignitas*, tel ou tel synonyme utilisé par Erasme. On sait que, s'il aime bien employer fréquemment les mêmes expressions pour désigner des réalités spirituelles ou morales précises — comme 'philosophia Christi', 'militia christiana', 'judaizare', 'virago', 'liberum arbitrium', 'affectus', etc. — le plus souvent il diversifie sa palette expressive pour des raisons qui tiennent peut-être autant à son idiosyncrasie qu'à des effets de style. Je ferais une exception pour son acribie des plus pertinentes en matière de traduction, et surtout de traduction biblique: car la Parole de Dieu ne doit rien laisser au hasard, et l'exégète est attentif aux moindres pulsations du texte sacré dont il veut rendre la 'vérité' (qu'elle soit hébraïque ou grecque).[13]

A défaut de rencontrer l'association de 'dignitas' et de 'homo', nous n'avons que l'embarras du choix dans les définitions et les analyses de l'homme lui-même. Et c'est de cette anthropologie d'Erasme qu'il nous sera facile de montrer ensuite en quoi la conception érasmienne de la 'dignitas hominis' diffère ou ne diffère pas de celle que la tradition antique, judéo-chrétienne et 'quatrocentesque' avait forgée avant lui.

* * *

L'une des formules les plus belles et les plus denses d'Erasme, sur laquelle j'ai eu l'occasion de m'exprimer plus d'une fois, se trouve au cœur de son traité pédagogique le plus important, le *De pueris statim ac liberaliter instituendis*,[14] publié au soir de sa vie (en 1529), mais conçu une trentaine d'années plus tôt, et constamment porté par son esprit: 'L'homme ne naît

---

[13] C'est-à-dire conforme au texte hébreu original (quand on en a connaissance et que l'on est hébraïsant), ou au texte grec (censé être resté fidèle au texte hébreu de l'Ancien Testament). A propos de la traduction latine du Nouveau Testament par Erasme et de ses références au texte grec (constitué à partir d'un certain nombre de manuscrits médiévaux), cf. H. J. De Jonge, '*Novum Testamentum a nobis versum*. De essentie van Erasmus' uitgave van het Nieuwe Testament', *Lampas*, 15 (1982), pp. 231–48.

[14] Cf. mes deux éditions: Genève, Droz, 1966 (avec trad. fr., étude critique et commentaire); *ASD*, I-2 (1971), pp. 1–78.

point homme, il le devient.'[15] Mieux vaudrait d'ailleurs traduire la
dernière partie de la proposition d'une manière un peu différente, pour
rendre exactement l'opposition des deux verbes latins utilisés par
Erasme: 'Homines, mihi crede, non *nascuntur*, sed *finguntur*' (Les
hommes, crois-moi, ne naissent point hommes, mais sont façonnés
hommes).[16] Le contexte immédiat ne laisse aucun doute sur cette
opposition hardie de la nature et de l'art, l'art étant fondamentalement
le travail du maître, façonnant en quelque sorte la matière malléable de
l'esprit du jeune enfant qui lui est confié; ce maître qui devient de la
sorte son second père, non pas son père *naturel*, son père par le sang,
mais son père spirituel, celui qui le fait véritablement accéder à l'état —
j'allais dire à la dignité — d'homme. Erasme venait d'écrire: 'Les arbres
naissent arbres, sans doute, même ceux qui ne portent aucun fruit ou
des fruits sauvages; les chevaux naissent chevaux, quand bien même ils
seraient inutilisables.'[17] Autrement dit, il y a une essence de l'arbre ou du
cheval qui se perpétue à travers chacune des espèces indéfiniment: les
soins ou le dressage — 'analogues' de l'éducation, mais d'une qualité
inférieure — peuvent améliorer la qualité ou le rendement d'un cheval
ou d'un arbre déterminé, mais ils n'en modifient pas l'essence. Au
contraire, des trois facteurs constitutifs de l'activité humaine, la nature
(*natura*), la raison (*ratio*) et l'exercice (*exercitatio*),[18] le premier ne
constitue en fait qu'une matière indéterminée, au sens aristotélicien,
susceptible d'une diversité de *formes* (toujours au sens d'Aristote);
autrement dit — même si la biologie moderne et notre connaissance des
facteurs de l'hérédité ne peuvent accepter pareille assertion — l'enfant, à
sa naissance, n'est pas encore un être véritablement individualisé, mais
une masse de chair, un système complexe d'instincts, un réceptacle
d'impressions. Au contraire, c'est la raison, mise en branle et en œuvre
par l'éducation qui sera seule en mesure d'informer cette matière brute
pour faire du petit enfant un être individualisé, pour lui faire conquérir
son identité, que nous assimilions tout à l'heure au le sentiment de la
dignité humaine. Le troisième facteur, l'exercice, est en fait une
application de la raison: à la raison enseignante (*ratio docendi*) du maître

---

[15] *LB*, 493B; Droz, p. 353; *ASD*, I–2, p. 31, line 21.
[16] A propos de ce passage, cf. S. Dresden, dans une conférence donnée à Rotterdam en avril
1969: 'Geloof me: mensen worden niet geboren.'
[17] *ASD*, I–2, p. 31: 'Arbores fortasse nascuntur, licet aut steriles aut agresti foetu; equi
nascuntur, licet inutiles; at homines, mihi crede, non nascuntur, sed finguntur.'
[18] Cf. mon article, 'Pédagogie et philosophie dans le *De pueris instituendis* de Erasme', *Paedagogica
Historica*, 4 (1965), pp. 370–91.

correspond dialectiquement une raison enseignée[19] (*ratio discendi*), toutes deux se reconnaissant dans une Raison transcendante, celle du Verbe incréé (comme aurait dit Malebranche). Erasme a beau avoir emprunté ses concepts à Quintilien et au pseudo-Plutarque, à Aristote et aux pédagogues italiens du Quattrocento, il les utilise avec une dextérité et une force de persuasion remarquables. Du topos de l'opposition de la nature et de l'art, ou des contradictions inhérentes à la nature elle-même, puisqu'elle est à la fois toute-puissante ('chassez le naturel, il revient au galop')[20] et susceptible d'être soumise aux lois de la raison, Erasme tire non seulement une pédagogie nouvelle, mais toute une philosophie de l'homme, s'il est vrai que l'éducation de l'homme commence à sa naissance et n'est jamais achevée. Philosophie aux puissantes racines psychologiques, également éloignée d'un naturalisme épicurien (au sens traditionnel) que d'un ascétisme ou d'un rationalisme abstrait. Erasme connait et met en pratique le précepte selon lequel pour commander à la nature, il faut commencer par lui obéir: on ne peut forcer certaines aversions, ni les menaces ni les coups ne feront aimer les mathématiques ou les sciences juridiques à un jeune homme qui n'éprouve pour elles aucune attirance; cependant la raison et une habile stratégie pédagogique peuvent affaiblir certaines résistances ou réticences; la prise de conscience d'intérêts bien compris peut vaincre partiellement l'agressivité instinctive.

On dira: l'utilisation du critère de la raison, ou de celui (équivalent) de la parole — *ratio* et *oratio*[21] ne constituent pas un vain jeu de mots — pour distinguer l'homme des autres créatures, et notamment des animaux, n'a rien d'original chez Erasme. Qui dirait le contraire? Mais ce topos, qu'il s'agisse de la traditon gréco-latine ou de la tradition judéo-chrétienne, est exploité par Erasme d'une manière personnelle car, s'il n'est pas aussi doué que certains humanistes de sa génération dans le traitement des abstractions métaphysiques, il n'a pas son pareil pour le sens de l'observation et la subtilité psychologique, le repérage des intentions patentes et de celles qui ne se découvrent qu'à la seconde perception ou par une réflexion latérale, et aussi pour l'esprit d'à propos et le goût de la polémique (qui l'a tellement servi dans sa vie). Toutes ces qualités donnent au dynamisme de la raison, moteur de l'activité humaine, ses traits spécifiques. Tout

---

[19] J'emprunte ces formules frappantes — qui correspondent d'ailleurs exactement au latin d'Erasme — au philosophe Gaston Bachelard, au demeurant maître-pédagogue.

[20] On connait le passage d'Horace, *Ep.* I, 10, 24: 'Naturam expellas furca, tamen usque recurrit', qui est à la source de ce topos.

[21] Sur les rapports dialectiques de *ratio* et d'*oratio*, cf. notamment M. O'Rourke Boyle, *Erasmus on Language and Method in Theology* (Toronto, 1977), notamment ch. 2 (*oratio*).

JEAN-CLAUDE MARGOLIN

d'abord, chez cet humaniste chrétien qui a accommodé à son usage le
concept patristique de 'philosophia Christi'[22] pour en faire un commentaire moral et religieux de l'enseignement du Christ, la raison est,
comme on l'a vu, l'expression de la vertu pédagogique par excellence:
enseignement du maître à l'élève, ou auto-enseignement — car nous
sommes tous à la fois maîtres et élèves, puisque l'éducation est un effort
constant et progressif d'élévation au-dessus de soi (*educere*), de dépasse-
ment du niveau intellectuel et affectif atteint, et aussi de mise en question
— parfois même de mise à la question — des évidences toute simples, ou
plutôt simplistes, fruits de la routine, des habitudes, des préjugés, de la
paresse mentale. D'où l'emploi si fréquent du paradoxe, non seulement
dans les exercices de style appelés (selon la formule antique) des 'déclama-
tions', généralement encomiastiques ('déclamation' ou éloge de la Folie,
'déclamation' ou éloge de la médecine, 'déclamation' ou éloge du mariage,
et aussi 'déclamation' ou éloge de l'éducation prématurée des enfants),[23]
mais dans la pratique pédagogique courante. En prenant le contre-pied des
idées courantes, en soutenant une thèse apparemment absurde ou en tout
cas choquante par rapport à l'étiage intellectuel ou socio-culturel moyen,
le maître érasmien, comme le maître socratique (dont il se recommande),
et comme le Pédagogue par excellence qu'est le Christ[24] (surtout dans son
incarnation paulinienne à travers les épîtres), se sert de la raison comme de
l'instrument dialectique fondamental. J'ai dit que les abstractions philo-
sophiques n'étaient pas le fait d'Erasme et que, soit par un sentiment
d'infériorité à leur égard, soit plutôt par une ironie agressive en leur
présence (attitude qui pourrait d'ailleurs être la conséquence de ce premier
sentiment), il en faisait généralement des 'flatus vocis', ou de vains songes
qu'il renvoyait aux méthodes de la scolastique décadente ou de la
grammaire médiévale, évocatrice d'essences auxquelles (selon lui) ne
correspondaient pas de référents réels: *verba sine rebus*.[25] Aussi faut-il
comprendre que cette dialectique est une dialectique concrète, vivante,

---

[22] Pour en avoir une idée claire, exposée rapidement mais substantiellement, cf. les deux brèves
monographies de L.-E. Halkin, *Erasme et l'humanisme chrétien* (Paris, 1969) [= Classiques du
XXe siècle) et de P. Mesnard, *Erasme et le christianisme critique* (Paris, 1969). Cf. aussi mon
Erasme (Editions du Seuil, Paris, 1965).

[23] Voir ma note sur *declamatio* dans mon édition du *De pueris* (Genève), p. 110.

[24] Ce Pédagogue mérite le nom de *Magister*: c'est le Christus *Magister*, plutôt que le Christus
Dominus (encore que ce dernier terme désigne, tout aussi bien, dans un cadre antique, le
maître par rapport à l'esclave, que, dans un cadre chrétien, le Seigneur dont la maîtrise ou la
domination est toute spirituelle).

[25] Cf. le colloque *De rebus ac vocabulis*, ed. Halkin, *ASD*, I-3, p. 566. C'est Luther qui reprochait
à Erasme de parler (*verba*) pour ne pas dire grand'chose de susbtantiel (*res*).

44

personnalisée par des êtres de chair et d'esprit: c'est bien pourquoi le genre dans lequel la raison humaine se déploie avec le plus d'aisance et d'efficacité est celui du dialogue. Dialogue que l'on rencontre d'ailleurs à peu près partout dans l'œuvre d'Erasme, sans parler de son immense correspondance, dialogue quasi-ininterrompu pendant un demi-siècle avec des centaines d'interlocuteurs, dont certains — privilégiés — constituent avec lui le second terme d'un binôme dont l'exploitation est enrichissante pour la connaissance de chacun des deux. A coté des dialogues proprement dits que constituent les colloques, les autres genres — même les traités de rhétorique, ou les commentaires, les manuels de civilité puérile ou de conduite chrétienne — prennent, à un moment ou à un autre (sous forme d'apostrophe, de répartie, de dialogue fictif et bref) l'allure de l'échange. Le soliloque n'est pas le fait d'Erasme. La prière[26] — il en a composé — est dialogue avec Dieu, le discours — profane ou sacré — est dialogue avec Dieu et les hommes.

Le dialogue implique le respect de l'interlocuteur, même si celui-ci n'atteint pas au même niveau intellectuel, ce qui est généralement le cas de l'orateur ou du prédicateur par rapport à la foule qui l'écoute, ou du maître par rapport à l'élève. Mais le pédagogue érasmien pratique, dans ses méthodes libérales, l'adage bien connu: 'maxima pueris debetur reverentia.' Le *De pueris* y revient souvent. Ce respect de l'autre, aussi bien dans la personne de l'enfant ou — il faut bien le dire — dans celle de la femme, dans celle de l'adversaire, du prisonnier, du croyant qui ne partage pas votre foi, de l'étranger, est l'une des grandes règles de l'anthropologie d'Erasme: elle a nom liberté ou, sous une certaine spécification, tolérance. Arrêtons-nous un moment à cette étape de l'analyse, car il ne faudrait pas attribuer à la conception érasmienne de la liberté, condition de la dignité de l'homme, des composantes qui seraient celles de la philosophie des lumières: le traité *De libero arbitrio*,[27] qui affirme hautement la liberté de choix de tout être humain, affirme non moins fortement la détermination métaphysique de l'homme par la Providence divine. Mais cette détermination lui ménage cependant une marge de liberté, et le redoutable pouvoir de dire non, de refuser l'enseignement de Dieu et la conduite axiologique qu'il implique. Cette liberté est le contraire même de la liberté d'indifférence. L'homme sait à quoi il s'expose en bravant Dieu. Quant à la

---

[26] *Precatio* est le terme ordinaire qui le *désigne* (cf. *Precatio dominica* d'Erasme, son commentaire du *Pater*), mais Erasme se sert parfois d'*oratio*; l'orateur pouvant exercer son éloquence aussi bien sur la place publique que dans une église (auquel cas il deviendra *ecclesiastes*, l'orateur 'sacré'). De toute façon, Erasme insiste sur le dialogue, l'échange (même muet).

[27] *Diatribe de libero arbitrio* (Froben, Bâle, sept. 1524).

tolérance, ou plutôt l'esprit de tolérance, il n'est pas davantage l'expression
d'un scepticisme à l'égard de la vérité, ou celle d'une incertitude quant au
choix du meilleur, du seul parti: il est fait d'indulgence ou de pitié à l'égard
du pécheur ou de celui qui est dans l'erreur (par rapport à la norme chrétienne qui est celle d'Erasme). Dans ces conditions il partage tout à fait le
point de vue qu'exprime dans un titre célèbre Sébastien Castellion, 'que les
hérétiques ne doivent pas être persécutés'.[28] L'hérésie, elle, doit être pour-
chassée et, dans toute la mesure du possible vaincue par la douceur et la
persuasion; mais l'homme de chair et d'esprit que l'on nomme hérétique,
doit être physiquement et moralement respecté. Respect héroïque quand
on songe à l'époque d'intolérance et de conflits de dogmatisme que fut en
grande partie le XVIᵉ siècle, sans parler des procès de sorcellerie (ou de pré-
tendue sorcellerie),[29] des tortures, des exécutions de créatures auxquelles
l'étiquette de sorcier ou d'hérétique semblait retirer le droit à la dignité,
cette dignité inhérente à l'homme, créature de Dieu. En fait Erasme lui-
même n'a pas toujours, dans sa vie, dans son comportement, dans ses
propos, appliqué parfaitement sa conception théorique de la liberté et du
respect de l'autre. On parlera peut-être de 'bavures' (selon un terme à la
mode, qui passe vite sur certaines inconséquences) ou de l'esprit du temps'.
Je prendrai l'exemple de ce que l'on pourrait appeler, avec un certain ana-
chronisme, les tendances antisémites d'Erasme. J'ai déjà eu l'occasion de
m'exprimer sur ce point dans un article paru dans les 'Temps Modernes',[30]
et surtout l'écrivain érasmisant soviétique Simon Markish a consacré à ce
problème de nombreuses pages de son livre sur *Erasme et les Juifs*.[31] Toute
proportion gardée, et en dépit de son militantisme chrétien qui peut
expliquer bien des choses, l'auteur du *Manuel du soldat chrétien* use parfois
d'expressions que je n'arrive pas à accorder avec sa philosophie de la
tolérance et de la liberté. Quand il écrit à un chanoine italien de Pérouse, un
certain Richard Bartholinus: 'Seule la France n'est infectée ni d'hérétiques,
ni de Bohémiens schismatiques, ni des Juifs, ni des Marranes demi-juifs, et
n'est pas influencée par la proximité des Turcs...'[32] on ne peut pas dire qu'il

---

[28] Cf. J. Lecler et M. F. Valkhoff, *Les premiers défenseurs de la liberté religieuse*, 1 (Paris, 1969). Sur Sébastien Castellion (1515–63), cf. pp. 95–131, et notamment la préface de son *Traité des hérétiques* (1554).
[29] *La Peur en Occident* (Paris, 1978), notamment ch. 11 et 12, pp. 346–88. Cf. aussi R. Muchembled, *La Sorcière au village* (Archives-Julliard, 1979).
[30] J.-C. Margolin, 'Antisémitisme d'hier et d'aujourd'hui: antisémitisme éternel?', *Temps modernes*, 410 (1980), pp. 429–43.
[31] Simon Markish, *Erasme et les Juifs* (Lausanne, 1979), lettera 'L'Age d'Homme'.
[32] *Erasmi opus epistolarum*, éd. P. S. and H. M. Allen, 12 vols (Oxford, 1906–58), 2, ep. 549 (10 mars 1517).

manifeste un respect exagéré à l'égard de ceux qui n'appartiennent pas à son univers socio-culturel et surtout éthico-religieux. Parlant de la présence des Juifs en Italie, et soupçonnant leur présence clandestine en Espagne, il stigmatise dans une autre lettre — lettre à l'hébraïsant chrétien Capiton[33] — cette 'épidémie', que l'on croyait 'jugulée', mais qui 'relève la tête'.[34] Ayant à se venger d'un ennemi, il se refuse à admettre que ce dernier soit un bon chrétien, et sa nature méfiante lui fait subodorer qu'il y a du Juif là-dessous (pour parler familièrement).[35] Je ne veux pas citer d'autres exemples — il y en a pourtant, et même de plus déplaisants encore pour notre mentalité moderne — et je ne voudrais pas manquer de rappeler que l'épithète 'Judaeus', comme le verbe 'judaìzare' peuvent s'appliquer, dans l'usage élargi qu'il en fait, à des non-Juifs qui vivent comme des Juifs, c'est-à-dire qui attachent beaucoup trop d'importance à la lettre sinon à des superstitions au détriment de l'esprit.[36] Mais cette extension du concept de 'judéité' entendu de cette manière ne va-t-elle pas dans le sens du mépris ou, à tout le moins, d'une incompréhension ou d'une volonté d'aveuglement à l'égard de tout ce qui fait la valeur et l'originalité de la religion et de la culture juives?

Ce commentaire un peu sévère à l'égard de l'homme Erasme est dû à la vérité des textes, à la vérité historique; il ne vise en aucune façon à opposer l'homme au penseur et encore moins à marquer les limites de sa conception de la dignité de l'homme. N'approuve-t-il, pas lui-même le fameux aphorisme: 'Amicus Plato, sed magis amica veritas'?

*   *   *

Laissons donc désormais ces passions ou ces faiblesses humaines que l'époque explique en grande partie, et qui seraient infiniment moins excusables de nos jours, où le concept de dignité s'est enrichi en compréhension comme en extension. Mais il nous faut maintenant examiner rapidement, dans l'axe de notre réflexion, l'attitude plus élaborée d'Erasme à l'égard des femmes ou de la femme. En théorie, la 'dignitas hominis' est la dignité de l'être humain, le concept de *homo* s'appliquant

---

[33] Ibid., 3, ep. 739 (15 mars 1518).
[34] Texte cité dans Margolin, 'Antisémitisme', p. 434.
[35] Par exemple à l'égard du moine espagnol Sepulveda, qui lutta de toutes ses forces contre l'influence d'Erasme et de l'érasmisme en Espagne (cf. à cet égard M. Bataillon, *Erasme et l'Espagne* [Paris, 1937], *passim*).
[36] Cf. à ce sujet quelques pages d'E.-V. Telle, *Erasme et le septième sacrement. Etude d'évangélisme matrimonial au XVIᵉ siècle* (Genève, 1954), pp. 84–5, 193–4.

aussi bien à l'homme (*vir*) qu'à la femme (*mulier*). Le problème de la femme — entendons, ici encore, la femme chrétienne — de la femme dans sa famille, dans ses divers états, célibataire, mariée, mère, veuve, de son enfance à sa mort, dans sa condition laïque ou religieuse, dans la société politique et économique, etc., est un de ceux que l'humaniste hollandais n'a cessé de reprendre, dans telle ou telle de ses œuvres.[37] Il a même consacré de nombreux colloques à des problèmes d'éthique sociale ou religieuse qui concernent plus particulièrement les femmes, comme celui des vocations religieuses forcées ou du mariage 'arrangé' par les parents sans l'aveu et sans aucune inclination de la part de la fille.[38] D'une manière assez générale, on peut dire que, surmontant bien des préjugés de son temps concernant l'infériorité physique, intellectuelle ou morale de la femme, triomphant d'une misogynie qui n'est pas seulement l'héritage d'une tradition médiévale populaire, mais qui peut aussi être rapportée à une fraction non négligeable de l'œuvre patristique, et à laquelle l'institution ecclésiale elle-même n'est pas étrangère, Erasme a lutté en faveur du respect et de la dignité de la femme. Il en appelle même aux autorités civiles et religieuses pour que cesse le scandale de ces mariages forcés, où des jeunes filles sont parfois contraintes d'épouser des vieillards malades ou tarés pour un titre, de l'argent, la vanité de leurs parents.[39] Et dans le colloque qu'il a intitulé *Abbas et erudita*, et que Léon Halkin a appelé en français 'Le Père Abbé et la femme instruite'[40] (pour éviter d'appeler cette dernière 'femme savante', ce qui eût pour effet d'évoquer Molière et de conduire à une interprétation parfaitement erronée de l'intention d'Erasme), le Rotterdamois met en parallèle deux types d'humanité, dont le premier, incarné par Magdalie, est un portrait de la femme selon son cœur: bourgeoise intelligente, fine, cultivée, pieuse, mariée, peut-être mère de famille, et pourquoi pas — mais ceci n'est pas dans le texte — jolie? Digne en tout point, respectée, respectable, damant le pion sans peine au sot et grossier personnage qu'est cet abbé, indigne (aux yeux d'Erasme) de la fonction ou du ministère qu'il remplit.

Il se sert même assez souvent, pour résumer d'un mot le caractère de ces femmes énergiques, intelligentes et pieuses devant lesquelles il s'incline,

[37] Cf. J.-C. Margolin, 'Erasme et le problème social' (conférence prononcée à Moscou, le 23 août 1970), *Rinascimento*, 13 (1973), pp. 85–112.
[38] Cf. en particulier les colloques philogamiques, et notamment *Agamos gamos sive Conjugium impar*, ASD, I-3, pp. 591–600.
[39] Cf. trad. fr. édit. du Pot Cassé, 4e Livre des *Colloques*, pp. 61–83.
[40] Cf. éd. crit. Halkin, ASD, I-3, pp. 403–8, et trad. fr. Halkin, *Les Colloques d'Erasme* (Bruxelles, 1971), pp. 90–6.

du terme de *virago*.[41] Mais ce compliment n'est-il pas ambigu? En effet, l'hommage rendu à la femme consiste à la considérer comme étant l'égale d'un homme (en se servant cette fois du mot *vir*, qui exalte la masculinité ou la virilité de l'homme, présenté comme le modèle achevé de l'humanité, comme dans la statuaire grecque où Apollon représentait un canon plus parfait de la beauté humaine que Vénus elle-même). Autrement dit, le plus beau compliment que l'on puisse adresser à la femme consisterait en quelque sorte... à nier sa féminité, ou à considérer celle-ci comme un accident ou une marque de la contingence de la nature, alors que son humanité ou sa 'virilité' d'emprunt serait le fruit de ses efforts, de son application, de son art. Réussite, certes, mais réussite plutôt exceptionnelle, si l'on suit encore Erasme (et d'une manière très générale, ses contemporains de sexe masculin), qui cite toujours les mêmes noms historiques: Cornélie, mère des Gracques, Porcia, la femme de Caton, Hortensia, la fille du grand orateur latin, et parmi les contemporaines, Isabelle la Catholique, la fille aînée de Thomas More, les sœurs de Willibald Pirckheimer, l'Italienne Cassandra Fidele, et quelques autres.[42] Tout naturellement, dès les premières lignes du *De pueris*, il félicite son interlocuteur fictif d'être devenu père, 'et surtout, ajoute-t-il, d'un garçon'![43] En dépit de ces femmes érudites qu'il admire, surtout quand leur savoir n'a pas aigri leur caractère ni affaibli leur foi religieuse, les préjugés de son temps le reprennent vite, et l'on peut lire sous sa plume des phrases de ce genre: 'Une femme maitresse d'école! Il est choquant qu'une femme puisse commander à des hommes' (entendons: à des garçons).[44] Ou encore, pour expliquer l'irritation d'une jeune mère à l'égard de sa fillette qui ne lui aurait pas rendu suffisamment de marques extérieures de respect: 'Ce sexe est prompt à la colère!'[45] Comme s'il ne connaissait pas lui-même un grand nombre d'hommes irascibles, ou en proie à des passions autrement funestes, dont il eut personnellement à souffrir.

---

[41] Cf. J.-C. Margolin, 'Une princesse d'inspiration érasmienne: Marguerite de France, duchesse de Berry, puis de Savoie' in *Culture et pouvoir au temps de l'Humanisme et de la Renaissance* = Actes du Congrès Marguerite de Savoie (Genève et Paris, 1978), pp. 155–83 (pour l'idéal de la *virago*, pp. 155–6); et 'Margaret More-Roper: l'idéal érasmien de la virago' (communication préparée pour le Colloque international de Lodz [Pologne] sur la Femme à l'époque de la Renaissance [oct. 1982]).

[42] *De pueris instituendis*, éd. Margolin (Genève), p. 587 et n. 832 (*LB*, 514C) et pp. 421 et 540 (note): cf. *LB* 503A.

[43] *LB*, 489D et *ASD*, p. 25, lignes 2–3, 'Audio te patrem esse factum, et quidem prole mascula.'

[44] *De pueris instituendis*, *LB*, 503C et *ASD*, p. 55, lignes 2–3: 'Praeter naturam est foeminam in masculos habere imperium.'

[45] *Inst. christ. matrim.*, *LB*, 1, 712E–F. Cf. aussi ce même passage du *De pueris*.

Quoi qu'il en soit, et sans faire appel ici aux progrès de la psychologie différentielle des·sexes, aux apports de la psychanalyse freudienne et post-freudienne, à ceux de la sociologie et surtout aux transformations sociales, économiques, politiques et culturelles qui sont intervenues depuis quatre ou cinq siècles (et singulièrement depuis quelques décennies) et qui ont modifié profondément la condition féminine, Erasme traite la femme, comme l'homme, en être autonome et responsable: à ce titre elle n'apporte aucun démenti à sa conception de la 'dignitas hominis'.

* * *

Parmi les situations collectives, sources d'innombrables drames individuels, il en est une, la guerre, qu'Erasme dénonce sans relâche, tout au long de son existence, à la fois par réflexion et conviction, et à la lumière des événements qui ont marqué l'Europe de tant de taches sanglantes.[46] Les arguments ne manquent pas pour la défense de la paix ou le procès de la guerre, mais l'un de ceux qui nous intéressent le plus, car il touche le fond de notre problème, c'est que le soldat est entraîné à commettre des actes qui lui font perdre, dans la personne de son adversaire comme dans sa propre personne, le sentiment élémentaire de sa dignité, et même le sentiment de son être, ce que nous appelons la conscience de soi. C'est cette dégradation de l'âme, cette dévalorisation de la personne humaine, cette perte du sens de la liberté et de la responsabilité, qui représente à ses yeux la tare suprême qu'aucune guerre — même celle que l'on prétend légitime ou juste — ne peut effacer. Cette idée apparait notamment dans le colloque intitulé *Militaria* sive *Confessio militis*[47] (Le métier des armes ou la Confession du soldat), où l'ancien combattant Thrasymaque confie à son interlocuteur Hannon quelques réflexions de ce genre:

J'ai vu et j'ai commis là-bas plus de crimes que je n'en avais vus et commis avant de partir pour la guerre ...

Mes rapines, je les ai rendues aux prostituées, aux cabaretiers, à ceux qui m'ont battu aux jeux de hasard ...

Les bouchers sont bien payés pour tuer des bœufs. Pourquoi nous reprocher de tuer des hommes? ...

[46] Cf. notre *Anthologie. Guerre et Paix dans la pensée d'Erasme de Rotterdam* (Paris, 1973).
[47] Ed. Halkin, *ASD*, I–3, pp. 154–8.

> J'irai chez les dominicains, et là je m'arrangerai vite avec les commissaires aux indulgences...
>
> Hélas! pourquoi t'ai-je rencontré, toi qui troubles la sérénité de ma conscience?[48]

Cet homme fruste et cynique, qui s'accommode des méfaits de la guerre, et qui se contente d'aller trouver un prêtre gagné par les vices du temps pour se faire absoudre de ses crimes sans demander son reste, commence par être troublé par le raisonnement de son interlocuteur et ses plus grandes exigences morales: c'est le début du retour à la conscience de soi, au sentiment de culpabilité et peut-être — Erasme le souhaite en tout cas — à une volonté de confession sincère, de rachat ou de rédemption. A la guerre, pense Erasme, on perd — le plus souvent irrémédiablement — son âme. Une idée qui revient souvent dans sa *Consultation sur la guerre contre les Turcs*[49] de 1530, c'est que le Chrétien, en s'imaginant combattre l'Infidèle pour le bon motif, en voulant peut-être sincèrement écarter la menace physique et spirituelle que la puissance ottomane fait peser sur la Chrétienté, est conduit par la force des choses à commettre lui-même des exactions et à se livrer à des actes de barbarie qui dépassent en horreur ceux que peuvent commettre les Turcs eux-mêmes. Autrement dit, le chrétien ne l'est plus que de nom, il a à la fois perdu le sens de sa dignité d'homme (en commettant des actions que réprouve même la loi naturelle) et celui de sa dignité de chrétien, en agissant au rebours de l'enseignement du Christ. C'est moins la guerre en soi qui est condamnée — car l'humaniste se rallie sans plaisir et non sans hésitation à la thèse de l''ultima ratio', quand un peuple défend par les armes l'intégrité de son territoire et ses raisons de vivre après qu'aient été épuisées vainement toutes les tentatives de conciliation — que la dégradation ou (si je puis dire) la 'bestialisation' de la conscience humaine, entraînée par les actes de guerre ou simplement par la propagande belliciste.[50] Le combattant chrétien peut-il préserver son âme et concilier les droits de la guerre et ses devoirs envers Dieu et envers les hommes? Tel est le dilemme que nous sommes conduits à poser avec lui, et dont il faut bien dire qu'il

---

[48] Trad. Halkin, *Les Colloques*, pp. 17–23.

[49] Texte complet dans *LB*, 4. De larges extraits traduits en français dans notre *Anthologie*, pp. 328 *et seq.* (cf. lettre à Johan Rinck, 17 mars 1530: Allen, 8, ep. 2285). Cf. aussi notre article 'Erasme et la guerre contre les Turcs', *Il Pensiero Politico* (1980), pp. 3–38.

[50] Cf. notamment *Confessio militis* et la *Querela pacis* (1517): notre *Anthologie*, p. 221.

l'embarrasse terriblement puisqu'il ne nous donne pas de réponse vraiment satisfaisante.

* * *

Droits et devoirs de l'homme: la réflexion d'Erasme est plus éthique que juridique, encore que sa fréquentation des Anciens — il commente longuement dans ses *Adages* la maxime 'Summum jus, summa injuria'[51] — sa connaissance d'Aristote et son analyse du concept d'équité naturelle (l'*epieikia*[52] de l'auteur de l'*Ethique à Nicomaque*) le conduisent à faire plus ou moins coïncider les deux domaines, en innervant sa conception éthique de la 'philosophia Christi' des principes juridiques du droit romain, et en humanisant ce que le juridisme peut avoir de raide et d'abstrait par l'observation attentive des cas individuels, des situations concrètes. Ce qu'il y a de certain, c'est que la dignité de l'homme ne peut devenir un objet de respect et une ligne de conduite authentique que si elle est liée à un ensemble de droits, à des dispositions légales — législation civile ou législation religieuse — qui puissent effectivement être respectées. Nous savons trop bien, même et peut-être surtout en cette fin de siècle, à quel point la proclamation des droits de l'homme et de la volonté de les défendre peut servir d'alibi au mépris effectif le plus total de ces droits, et que l'absence de contrôle ou de moyens de coercition à l'égard de ces pseudo-défenseurs est parfois pire qu'un vide juridique en la matière. Que dire de l'état des diverses législations, des sanctions pénales, de l'interaction du droit civil et du droit religieux, de la timide apparition de ce que l'on appellera plus tard le droit des peuples à disposer d'eux-mêmes, à l'époque où a vécu et réfléchi Erasme! Mais s'il a toujours existé — comment en serait-il autrement? — un écart sensible, et parfois considérable, entre l'idéal éthico-juridique (qui rejoint d'ailleurs souvent ce qu'on appelle le droit naturel et, par une autre voie, l'idéal de justice proclamé par les grandes religions à vocation universelle) et la pratique du droit institutionnel ou du droit pénal inscrits dans des lois progressivement acquises ou conquises au cours de l'histoire, nous ne devons pas nous étonner, et encore moins nous scandaliser de ce que la proclamation solennelle et sincère de la dignité de l'homme surplombe et anticipe sur les pratiques spontanées ou réglementées qui en assurent l'acualisation. Si

---

[51] *Adage* 925, *LB*, 2, 374D.
[52] Ce concept aristotélicien correspondant à l'*aequitas naturalis* a fait l'objet d'une étude appliquée aux humanistes et notamment à Erasme: G. Kisch, *Erasme und die Jurisprudenz seiner Zeit* (Bâle, 1960).

Sénèque n'avait pas lancé son cri d'alarme en forme de proclamation éthique, 'Les esclaves sont des hommes comme nous,' en un temps où la pratique de l'esclavage correspondait à un traitement des esclaves comme de simples objets animés, il est possible que cette même pratique ait duré encore davantage, et surtout sans cette mauvaise conscience, qui peut être le début d'une réflexions critique aboutissant à son abandon.

Cet examen de conscience, lié à une conscience éminemment critique — qui prend souvent un tour paradoxal pour scruter le problème jusqu'au fond — Erasme le pratique sans cesse. Tant et si bien que chez lui les lieux communs doivent toujours être examinés eux-mêmes avec une attention critique. Nous avons vu que le topos selon lequel l'homme, doué de la parole et de la raison, se distingue radicalement de l'animal, n'est pas purement répétitif. Il suffit de lire le texte du traité intitulé *Lingua* [53] pour que nous nous rendions compte qu'un mauvais usage de la parole, comme celui que pratique l'*homo loquax*[54] (le bavard) ne permet pas d'élever tout être à figure humaine au-dessus de la condition animale. Car si l'homme parle 'pour ne rien dire', si sa langue s'agite et ébranle les souffles aériens pour exprimer des 'non-paroles' — entendons une suite de mots privés de signification ou sans aucun rapport avec la vérité qu'ils sont censés exprimer — il renonce à sa fonction, c'est-à-dire à sa dignité d'homme, comme participant à un dialogue entre des esprits aimantés par une volonté commune de connaître une commune vérité. Qu'est-ce qui permettrait alors de le distinguer du perroquet, qui ne parle pas en vérité, même quand on reconnait dans ses émissions sonores des paroles qui pourraient avoir un sens . . . si le perroquet comprenait ce qui sort de son bec![55] Il ne faut sans doute pas pousser les choses trop loin et ne pas oublier qu'il y a toujours chez Erasme une dose d'ironie et que ses textes doivent faire l'objet d'une seconde lecture ou d'une lecture latérale. Il ne voudrait sans doute pas que son bavard fût traité indignement; il est même capable d'apprécier les futilités et les subtilités du langage, à condition toutefois qu'elles aient 'une idée de derrière'. Mais ce que je veux simplement souligner ici, c'est que, pour Erasme, il n'est pas de disposition innée, il n'est pas de qualité ou de fonction naturelle dont un être humain puisse se targuer s'il n'est pas décidé à les faire fructifier, c'est-à-dire à les actualiser

---

[53] *ASD*, IV–1 (1974), éd. F. Schalk, pp. 221–370.

[54] Par différentiation et même par opposition avec l'*homo loquens*, celui qui fait de la parole l'usage qui est inscrit dans son essence. Le bavard, c'est aussi le *garrulus*, celui qui ne dit que fadaises (*nugas*). Cf. *Lingua*, pp. 293–4.

[55] Les très jeune enfant, qui répète sans les comprendre les mots entendus, qui s'habitue à la voix humaine, fait de même (cf. *De recta pronuntiatione*, éd. M. Cytowska, *ASD*, I–4 [1973], p. 14).

par un effort conscient et finalisé, par la pratique de cette *exercitatio* dont sa pédagogie proclame la nécessité. Que la dignité de l'homme, pour Erasme comme pour Pascal, soit dans la pensée, cela ne fait aucun doute. Mais il faut immédiatement ajouter que cette pensée ne saurait être assimilée à une essence immobile mais au contraire à un principe d'action. Le volontarisme érasmien fait de la pensée humaine la source et le moteur de toute action authentique: en effet, si (comme on l'a vu), on peut parler pour ne rien dire, on peut aussi s'agiter sans rien faire et même souvent pour se dispenser de faire quoi que ce soit. La dignité humaine gît dans l'action individuelle qui prend ses risques et sa responsabilité: sur ce point, et malgré quelques faiblesses au cours d'une longue existence, Erasme a généralement été fidèle à ce principe. En revanche la fuite devant ses responsabilités et la facilité avec laquelle l'homme se dédouane souvent — comme on le voit dans le poème satirique d'Ulrich von Hutten, aboutissement humaniste d'une longue tradition médiévale, dont le titre *Nemo*[56] (Personne) et les multiples variations sur le pronom indéfini latin permettent toutes les échappatoires linguistico-existentielles — c'est pour lui une source de scandale, et au sens propre du terme, une attitude indigne de l'homme et de la place qui lui est assignée en ce bas-monde. La philosophie éthico-sociale qui se dégage d'un adage comme celui qu'il a intitulé 'Tu as obtenu Sparte: gouverne-la',[57] c'est celle qui fait appel à la plénitude du sens des responsabilités d'un homme, roi ou manant, prince d'un vaste royaume ou souverain d'une petite principauté. A la notion d'honneur ou de dignité extérieure, qui avait cours davantage à l'époque ou dans le système de la féodalité, Erasme oppose une conception de la dignité subjective ou intérieure, liée à l'examen de conscience. Pour le prince qui a 'obtenu Sparte', la dignité et le devoir impérieux, c'est de se limiter au gouvernement de sa cité, mais d'accomplir cette tâche avec le maximum de soin et d'efficacité, et non pas de conquérir des territoires, fût-ce sous le fallacieux prétexte de flatter l'orgueil ou l'amour-propre de son peuple. Entre cette 'dignitas hominis', subjective dont l'expression littérale, je le répète, ne se rencontre pas dans les textes d'Erasme que j'ai relus, et la dignité ou les dignités extérieures (*dignitas, dignitates*) pour lesquelles il n'éprouve qu'un respect lui-même très extérieur, il y a totale solution de continuité. Il suffirait de se reporter à l'un des premiers chapitres de son traité sur l'art d'écrire des lettres[58] (le *De conscribendis*

---

[56] Ed. E. Böcking des *Opera omnia*, 3 (Leipzig, 1866), pp. 106 *et seq.*
[57] *Adage* 1401, *LB*, 2, 551E. Cf. notre trad. in *Anthologie*, pp. 178–84.
[58] *ASD*, I–2 (1971), p. 266: 'De consuetudine unum multitudinis numero compellandi.'

epistolis de 1522), dans lequel il traite avec amusement de l'habitude, encore fort répandue de son temps, de donner à une personne, en matière de salutation orale ou écrite, des titres au pluriel, pour accroître son honorabilité, sa 'dignité': c'est ainsi que l'on qualifiera un noble personnage de 'vestrae dominationes' (formule héritée du Moyen Age féodal, et que l'on rencontre souvent dans des textes officiels des XIII e et XIV e siècles), un évêque de 'vos domini episcopi' (avec toutes les absurdités linguistiques qu'entraîne l'emploi du pluriel pour un individu singulier), sans compter les 'vestra pietas', les 'paternitates vestrae', les 'reverendissimae humanitates vestrae', ou les 'reverentiae humanissimae domini domini'![59] On sait qu'à la même époque et avec une verve semblable — car l'inspiration était la même, et le sens de l'humour assez voisin — Ulrich von Hutten, une fois de plus, s'était copieusement moqué de ces habitudes, à la fois d'un point de vue psycho-sociologique, et du point de vue d'un philologue, agacé par ces 'barbouilleurs de latin', dans ses *epistolae obscurorum virorum*.[60] Erasme, comme Hutten, faisait des gorges chaudes de ces 'magistri nostri' (et nos pas 'nostri magistri') de Louvain, qui attachaient plus d'importance à la place de l'adjectif possessif correspondant à leur titre, quand on leur adressait la parole, qu'au contenu philosophique ou théologique des propos entendus. Pour Erasme, critique social incisif et maître de la satire et de l'humour, ces titres pompeux — ces 'vocabula dignitatum', comme les résume d'un terme générique l'index de l'édition Le Clerc — étaient proprement ridicules, et n'ajoutaient pas plus — bien au contraire! — à la valeur humaine de leur détenteur qu'un blason armorié sur l'équipage d'un chevalier dont la conduite irait au rebours des principes d'honneur hérités de la chevalerie authentique: le colloque du 'Chevalier sans cheval'[61] nous renseigne suffisamment à ce sujet!

*   *   *

La dignité humaine ne serait-elle pas, par opposition à tous ces faux semblants et à toutes ces dignités d'emprunt, à toutes ces grandeurs d'établissement qui ressortissent à la catégorie de l'avoir, dans la prise de conscience de son être authentique, de son 'moi', profond, comme aurait dit Bergson?

---

[59] Ibid., pp. 272–3.
[60] 2 vols, repr. (O. Zeller, Osnabrück, 1966).
[61] *Hippeus anhippos, ASD*, I–3, pp. 612–19.

Nous sommes partis de la liberté de l'homme. Nous aboutissons à sa vérité. Mais ces deux concepts ne s'impliquent-ils pas l'un l'autre?[62] Peut-on être libre dans le mensonge? Peut-on exprimer ce que l'on croit être le vrai dans la servitude, servitude sociale, asservissement physique et surtout intellectuel? Nous avons essayé de montrer, à la lumière d'Erasme, que la dignité humaine n'est pas une propriété que nous devons gérer, mais un idéal que nous avons sans cesse à conquérit.

Ennemi des sectes qui divisent, Erasme s'avouait volontiers le libre serviteur de la vérité. Il avait également donné un sens nouveau à une formule ancienne dont il avait fait sa devise: 'Nulli concedo',[63] je ne cède à personne. C'est sur cette fière parole — que les actions de sa vie n'ont pas démentie, et qui rachète largement ses faiblesses humaines — que je prendrai congé de vous.

Centre d'Études Supérieures de la Renaissance,
Université François Rabelais,
Tours

[62] Ce que nous avons essayé de montrer dans notre article 'Erasme et la vérité', in *Colloquium Erasmianum* (Mons, 1968), pp. 135–69 (repris dans *Recherches érasmiennes* (Genève, 1969), pp. 45–69.

[63] Sur l'ambiguïté de la devise et de l'emblême de dieu Terminus qui en avait été la source, cf. E. Wind, 'Aenigma Termini: the emblem of Erasmus', *Journal of the Warburg and Courtauld Institutes*, 1 (1937), pp. 66–9.

FORMA CHRISTIANISMI: DIE THEOLOGISCHE BEWERTUNG EINES KLEINEN KATECHETISCHEN LEHRSTÜCKS DURCH LUTHER UND ERASMUS VON ROTTERDAM

by JOACHIM MEHLHAUSEN

I DAS PROBLEM

ERASMUS VON ROTTERDAM hat seine *Diatribe*[1] für einen weiteren Leserkreis bestimmt. Der *lector imperitior* soll angesprochen werden, also nicht nur der Theologe, sondern vor allem der Laie, denn — so betont Erasmus — *crassulis scribimus crassuli* (IIa 13; W 32,1). Schon durch eine klare und überschaubare Disposition des Werkes will Erasmus diesem Leser und seinen Verstehensmöglichkeiten entgegenkommen. So folgt auf eine zweiteilige Einleitung erst im Hauptteil die eigentliche *Diatribe sive collatio*, in der Erasmus zunächst jene Bibelstellen behandelt, die für, danach jene, die gegen den freien Willen sprechen. Durch den Widerstreit von Schriftstellen und Beweisen soll die Wahrheit einsichtiger gemacht werden ('hac collisione scripturarum et argumentorum fiat evidentior veritas': Ia 3; W 3,5f). Angesichts der bei diesem Arbeitsgang aufgedeckten Vielfalt der biblischen Stimmen stehen Autor und Leser dann vor einem hermeneutischen Problem, das Erasmus in die Worte faßt: 'Quoniam autem spiritus sanctus, quo auctore prodita sunt haec, non potest pugnare secum, cogimur velimus nolimus aliquam sententiae moderationem quaerere' (IV 1; W 77,5–7). Erasmus will bei der Behandlung dieser *Quaestio* den Disputator hervorkehren, er will nicht richten und entscheiden, sondern nur prüfen (Ia 6; W 5,10f); ihm geht es als Autor um den Vergleich, nicht um einen Streit (Ib 9; W 18,12). Diese *moderatio sententiae* wird dann im Schlußabschnitt des Werkes vorgetragen,

---

[1] Außer den üblichen Abkürzungen für die Editionen der Werke des Erasmus werden hier folgende *Sigel* verwendet: W = *De Libero Arbitrio ΔIATPIBH sive Collatio per Desiderium Erasmum Roterodamum = Quellenschriften zur Geschichte des Protestantismus H.8*, ed. Johannes von Walter (Leipzig, 1910); Le = Erasmus von Rotterdam, *Ausgewählte Schriften. Ausgabe in acht Bänden Lateinisch und Deutsch*, hg.v. Werner Welzig, Bd.4 (Übersetzt, eingeleitet und mit Anmerkungen versehen von Winfried Lesowsky) (Darmstadt, 1969); zur Erasmus-Bibliographie sei generell verwiesen auf: Cornelis Augustijn, *Erasmus von Rotterdam. Leben — Werk — Wirkung* (München, 1986), pp. 177–94.

der mit der berühmten Konklusionsformel endet: 'CONTULI, penes alios esto iudicium' (IV 17; W 92,8).

Der rhetorische Charakter des gesamten Textes ist evident und er wurde in der neueren Erasmus-Forschung wiederholt beschrieben.[2] Erasmus folgt mit seiner *Diatribe sive collatio* einer aus der Aristotelischen Rhetorik hervorgegangenen philosophisch-literarischen Gattung, deren Formprinzipien für sein eigenes Werk nicht bloß ornamental, sondern wesensbestimmend sind. 'While it could signify a discourse, ethical treatise, or lecture, an occasion for dwelling on a subject as in Aristotelian rhetoric, specifically a διατριβή was a classical mode of philosophical disputation, one with a tradition of literary adaptation. It was this precise meaning which Erasmus indicated with the Greek title.'[3] Solche Einsichten in die von Erasmus bewußt gestaltete formale Struktur seiner Schrift über die Willensfreiheit sind für die Interpretation des Werkes von großer Bedeutung. Sie verbieten es, die theologischen Einzelaussagen dieses Textes ohne Berücksichtigung ihrer jeweiligen rhetorischen Prägung zu lesen und zu deuten. Textimmanente semantische Relationen und Gliederungssignale müssen durch eine entsprechende Textanalyse[4] sichtbar gemacht werden und sind dann þei der Interpretation zu berücksichtigen.

Unter dem hiermit skizzierten Interpretationsaspekt wenden wir uns der zweiteiligen *Einleitung* der *Diatribe* zu. Sie enthält ein bisher nicht zureichend beachtetes kleines Textstück (Ia 8; W 6,11–22), auf das besondere analytische Sorgfalt angewendet werden sollte. Denn bei dieser Passage im Werk des Erasmus handelt es sich um jene Sätze, die den höchsten, fast atemlosen Zorn Luthers herausgefordert haben. Eine bloß inhaltsbezogene Analyse der theologischen Einzelaussagen dieses Textstückes vermag allein nicht zu erklären, warum es bei Luther zu dieser überaus heftigen Reaktion gekommen ist. Die reiche Literatur zum Streit zwischen Luther und Erasmus bietet hier bislang keine überzeugende Erklärung an. So ist es durchaus charakteristisch für die Forschungslage, daß man das kleine Textstück entweder beiläufig überging[5] oder zu

[2] Marjorie O'Rourke Boyle, *Rhetoric and Reform. Erasmus' Civil Dispute with Luther* (Cambridge, Mass. and London, 1983); Günter Bader, *Assertio. Drei fortlaufende Lektüren zu Skepsis, Narrheit und Sünde bei Erasmus und Luther* (Tübingen, 1985); James D. Tracy, 'Two Erasmuses, Two Luthers: Erasmus' Strategy in Defense of *De Libero Arbitrio*', *ARG*, 78 (1987), pp. 37–59.
[3] Marjorie O'Rourke Boyle, 'Erasmus and the "Modern" Question: Was he Semi-Pelagian?', *ARG*, 75 (1984), p. 60.
[4] Vgl. hierzu etwa Alex Stock, *Umgang mit theologischen Texten. Methoden — Analysen — Vorschläge* (Zürich/Einsiedeln/Köln, 1974).
[5] Hier nur wenige Beispiele: Oskar Joh. Mehl, 'Erasmus' Streitschrift gegen Luther:

einem bloß psychologischen Moment der Deutung Zuflucht nahm. Dies tat etwa der sonst so souveräne Kenner der Kontroverse, Karl Zickendraht, der schon vor achtzig Jahren die schwache Erklärung anbot, Luther habe sich an dieser Stelle 'von den über seinen Gegner umlaufenden Verleumdungen zur Unbilligkeit fortreißen lassen.'[6] Mit der nachfolgenden kleinen Studie, die von den formalen Eigentümlichkeiten des Textes ausgeht, hoffe ich zeigen zu können, daß es sich anders verhält — und warum es sich anders verhält.

II DER TEXT

Die Zweiteilung der *Einleitung* der *Diatribe* hat schon der aufmerksame Leser Martin Luther klar erkannt. Er bezeichnet die erste der beiden Einleitungen (Ia 1–Ia 11; W 1,4–11,21) als *praefatio*, die zweite (Ib 1–Ib 10; W 11,22–19,10) als *prooemium* (*WA* 18,638,12.18). Von der *praefatio* sagt Luther, sie umfasse fast schon die ganze Sache (*ferme totam causam*), und er fügt hinzu: 'magis pene quam sequens corpus libelli' (*WA* 18,638,13). In der Literatur zur *Diatribe* ist wiederholt versucht worden, für beide Einleitungen summierende und zugleich qualifizierende Inhaltsangaben zu machen. Hier seien nur zwei Beispiele angeführt: Otto Schumacher nennt das Thema der ersten Einleitung 'Wahrheit im Verhältnis zum erkennenden und handelnden Subjekt'; das der zweiten 'die Frage nach einem objektiven Kriterium der Wahrheit'.[7] Cornelis Augustijn sieht in den beiden Einleitungen folgende Fragen behandelt: (1) 'ist es sinnvoll, ein so tiefgreifendes Problem aufzugreifen?' (2) 'Wie kann man zu einer Antwort kommen, wenn Luther nur die Heilige Schrift als Norm anerkennen, aber bei deren Auslegung anderen nicht zuhören will?'[8]

Derartige auf den Inhalt bezogene Kurzbeschreibungen der beiden Einleitungen zur *Diatribe* können im Grunde nur der Information eines Lesers der Sekundärliteratur dienen; zur Interpretation des Textganzen tragen sie wenig aus. Berücksichtigt man jedoch den rhetorischen Charakter der *Diatribe*, dann wird folgendes deutlich: *Praefatio* und

---

Hyperaspistes', *ZRGG*, 12 (1960), p. 142; Jean Boisset, *Le Christianisme d'Erasme dans la Diatribe sur le libre arbitre = Colloquia Erasmiana Turonensia*, II (Paris, 1972), p. 660; Georges Chantraine, *Erasme et Luther libre et serf arbitre. Etude historique et théologique* (Paris, 1981), pp. 137f, 162f.
[6] Karl Zickendraht, *Der Streit zwischen Erasmus und Luther über die Willensfreiheit* (Leipzig, 1909), p. 66 (vgl. p. 29).
[7] Erasmus von Rotterdam, *Vom freien Willen. Verdeutscht von Otto Otto Schumacher* (Göttingen, 1956), p. 7.
[8] Augustijn, *Erasmus von Rotterdam*, p. 123.

prooemium geben dem Autor die Gelegenheit, vor der eigentlichen Behandlung des Themas mit einer gewissen subjektiven Unbefangenheit das zu sagen, was den Sachverhalt auszeichnet. Solche proömialen Bemerkungen dürfen periphrastisch sein und sie sind ein 'insinuatorisches Mittel der Erregung des Informationsbedürfnisses und der Aufmerksamkeit'.[9] Keinesfalls enthalten sie bereits abschließende Urteile. Sie wollen die später folgende Verhandlung — wie im römischen Gerichtsverfahren — nicht vorwegnehmen, sondern als *exordium* in Gang setzen. Der Richter wird sich nach Anhören des *prooemium* auf das argumentative Für und Wider der Verhandlung konzentrieren,und er ist bei seinem abschließenden Urteilsspruch nicht an diese, im *prooemium* geäußerte Sicht der Dinge gebunden. Überträgt man dieses forensisch-rhetorische Modell auf die *Diatribe* des Erasmus, so wird verständlich, warum der Autor ausdrücklich auf ein selbst gesprochenes Schlußurteil verzichtet: Erasmus trägt das Material in der diskursiven Verhandlung der *collatio* zusammen; anderen — dem Leser — überläßt er das Urteil. Im *prooemium* darf der Autor das Interesse seines Publikums wecken, indem er eigene Ansichten vorträgt. Diese exordialen Bemerkungen nehmen das Schlußurteil aber noch nicht vorweg! Diese formale Eigentümlichkeit im Aufbau der *Diatribe* wird auch durch den oft zitierten — und meist als 'Definition' mißverstandenen — Schlußsatz des Einleitungsteiles bestätigt. Er lautet: 'Porro hoc loco liberum arbitrium sentimus vim humanae voluntatis, qua se possit homo applicare ad ea, quae perducunt ad aeternam salutem, aut ab iisdem avertere' (Ib 10; W 19,7–10). Marjorie O'Rourke Boyle hat überzeugend nachweisen können, daß dieser Satz nicht im voraus — also schon vor dem dialogischen Arbeitsgang des *conferre*[10] — eine theologisch verbindliche 'Definition' aussprechen soll, mit deren Hilfe dann die biblischen Texte zu beleuchten wären.

> Erasmus' statement was no definition in the sense of a standard by which he would adjudicate the pericopes he was about to examine. It was simply a premise, a supposition, a conversational opener ... for that exercise of comparison.... It was rather a Socratic premise which would be inductively enlarged, clarified, and even altered in the very process of comparison.[11]

---

[9] Heinrich Lausberg, *Handbuch der literarischen Rhetorik. Eine Grundlegung der Literaturwissenschaft* (München, 1960), p. 156 (vgl. insgesamt pp. 150–63).

[10] O'Rourke Boyle, 'Erasmus and the "Modern" Question', p. 61.

[11] Ibid., pp. 64–6.

Der zitierte Schlußsatz des Einleitungsteiles der *Diatribe* sollte bei der Interpretation des gesamten Werkes künftig nicht mehr dazu verwendent werden, die vermeintlich semi-pelagianische Tendenz des Erasmus zu belegen. Der Satz ist 'Sokratische Prämisse', nicht These oder gar eine die eigene Meinung des Autors abschließend und verbindlich aussprechende Definition. Die rhetorische Gattung des *prooemium* erlaubt es dem Autor, vor der eigentlichen Verhandlung eine unvoreingenommene Ansicht, im besten Sinne ein 'Vor-Urteil',[12] auszusprechen, das den Dialog über die Sache hilfreich in Gang setzt. Erasmus bringt dies auch durch die offene, elliptische Einleitung des Satzes zum Ausdruck: 'Porro ... hoc loco sentimus' (Ib 10; W 19,7f). Jedes dieser Worte signalisiert Offenheit zum Diskurs hin; eine These oder 'Definition' hätte Erasmus mit anderen stilistischen Mittln in den Argumentationsgang eingebracht — gerade dies zeigt das Textstück, dem unser Hauptaugenmerk gilt.

Ziemlich genau in der Mitte der ersten der beiden Einleitungen der *Diatribe* gibt es ein auffälliges kleines Textstück, in dem Erasmus thetisch, affirmativ und urteilend spricht. An dieser Stelle wird — im Grunde dem gesamten Werk vorausgreifend — bereits ein Ergebnis des Schriftvergleichs, also der *collatio*, vorweggenommen. Mit unübersehbarer Deutlichkeit bezeichnet Erasmus die hier vorgelegte Sachaussage als ein eigenes Urteil, das er durch sein Schriftstudium gewonnen habe: 'Ergo meo quidem iudicio, quod ad liberum arbitrium attinet, quae didicimus e sacris litteris' (Ia 8; W 6,10f). Auf diese Präsentationsformel folgt die Sachaussage (W 6,11–22), dann wird die Affirmation wiederholt: 'haec, inquam, tenere meo iudicio satis erat ad Christianam pietatem' (Ia 8; W 6,22f). Durch die rhetorische Figur der Inklusion (zweimaliges *meo iudicio*; W 6,10.22) sind die dazwischen liegenden Sätze als in sich geschlossene besondere Einheit kenntlich gemacht. Das auf diese Weise deutlich hervorgehobene Textstück ist in sich selbst formal auffällig gestaltet. Vier jeweils mit *si* eingeleitete Kurzbeschreibungen religiöser bzw. allgemein-menschlicher Grundbefindlichkeiten werden durch einen oder mehrere *ut*-Sätze gedeutet, ja geradezu mit einer Antwort versehen. Das *si-ut*-Schema signalisiert eine dialogische Korrespondenz der einzelnen Aussageeinheiten. Zwei weitere, wiederum parallel zueinander angeordnete Textstücke wiederholen das gleiche, an Frage und Antwort erinnernde Formprinzip. Innerhalb des Textganzen gibt es mehrere Parallelismen und Chiasmen, Entsprechungen und Verschränkungen. So werden etwa

---

[12] Vgl. zu diesem Begriff Hans-Georg Gadamer, *Wahrheit und Methode. Grundzüge einer philosophischen Hermeneutik* (Tübingen, 1975), pp. 250–75.

die beiden letzten Aussageeinheiten ganz deutlich von zwei Gottesprädikaten her bestimmt; sie geben Auskunft, was der Mensch *a deo natura iusto* und *a deo natura clementissimo* zu gewärtigen habe (W 6,20.22). Diese Beobachtungen zur Form des Textes legen die Vermutung nahe, daß Erasmus an dieser Stelle mit einer bereits vorgeprägten Formel arbeitet, daß er also zumindest auszugsweise zitiert. Ein schon von Johannes von Walter bemerkter Konstruktionsbruch in der Rahmung des Textstückes (vgl. W 6, Anm.8) macht auf seine Weise darauf aufmerksam, daß innerhalb des Rahmens eine eigenständige Überlieferung zu Wort kommt, die sich mit ihrem eigenen Sprachduktus nicht ohne weiteres der hinzugesetzten Rahmung fügt. Man kann den Text nach den in ihm enthaltenen Gliederungssignalen in folgende Sinneinheiten oder Sequenzen aufteilen.

si in via pietatis sumus
 ut alacriter proficiamus ad meliora relictorum obliti
si peccatis involuti
 ut totis viribus enitamur
  adeamus remedium paenitentiae ac
  domini misericordiam modis omnibus ambiamus
   sine qua nec voluntas humana est efficax nec conatus
si quid mali est
 nobis imputemus
si quid boni
 totum ascribamus divinae benignitati
  cui debemus et hoc ipsum quod sumus
quicquid nobis accidit in hac vita sive laetum sive triste
 ad nostram salutem ab illo credamus immitti
  nec ulli posse fieri iniuriam
  a deo natura iusto
qua nobis videntur accidere indignis
 nemini desperandum esse veniam
 a deo natura clementissimo

Unter theologisch-inhaltlichen Gesichtspunkten betrachtet handelt es sich bei dieser Beschreibung der *via pietatis* um eine Zusammenstellung von Aussagen, wie sie im Werk des Erasmus vor 1524 vielfach anzutreffen sind. Das *via*-Motiv begegnet unter den Bezeichnungen 'via Christi, via virtutis, via pietatis, via perfectae vitae' oder 'via ad beatitudinem'.[13] Schon an zwei Stellen des *Enchiridion* bringt Erasmus den Heilsweg durch derartige Kurzformeln zur Sprache: Einmal wird ein zweistufiger Tugendweg beschrieben (H 46,22–24), an einer anderen Stelle werden drei Stationen aufgezählt, auf denen die trotz der Taufe verbleibenden Reste der Erbsünde (*ignorantia*, *caro* und *infirmitas*) zu überwinden sind (H 56,16–30). Die Aussage, daß der Christ alles, was er hat, *deo auctori ferat acceptum*, wird im *Enchiridion* als erstes der *veri Christianismi paradoxa* bezeichnet (H 99,14–17). Zusammenfassend kann von dem Heilsweg, den Erasmus mit immer neuen Formulierungen beschreibt, gesagt werden: 'Am Beginn und Ende des Heilsweges ... ist der Mensch ausschließlich auf Gottes Gnade angewiesen, im Verlauf des Heilsweges aber ist Gottes Gnade die erste Ursache, der menschliche Wille jedoch die zweite (LB IX 1244 AB).'[14] Eine unserem Textstück in den Einzelformulierungen besonders nah verwandte Aussage findet sich im Brief des Erasmus an Johann Slechta vom 1. November 1519, wo es heißt:

> Porro philosophiae Christianae summa in hoc sita est, vt intelligamus omnem spem nostram in Deo positam esse, qui gratis nobis largitur omnia per Filium suum Iesum. Huius morte nos esse redemptos, in huius corpus nos insitos esse per baptismum, vt mortui cupiditatibus huius mundi ad illius doctrinam et exemplum sic viuamus, vt non solum nihil admittamus mali verumetiam de omnibus bene mereamur; et, si quid inciderit aduersi, fortiter toleremus ... vt ita semper progrediamur a virtute in virtutem, vt nihil tamen nobis arrogemus, sed quicquid est boni Deo transscribamus (A IV,118,228–237).

Diese Briefstelle belegt, daß für Erasmus eine christologische Begründung des Heilsweges eine Selbstverständlichkeit ist; diese Begründung darf also — auch wenn sie in unserem Textstück nicht explizit vorgetragen wird — vorausgesetzt werden. Auch der Kontext spricht für eine solche Voraussetzung: Unmittelbar vor der Beschreibung der *via pietatis* zitiert Erasmus 1.Kor 13, 12 (Ia 7; W 6,8f), wie er auch im Slechta-Brief die *summa philosophiae Christianae* im Horizont der Wiederkunft Christi darstellt (A IV,118,235f). Was schließlich die Gliederung eines Frage- und Antwort-Schemas mit Hilfe von *si* und *ut* angeht, sei auf die *Dilucida et pia*

[13] Vgl. Manfred Hoffmann, *Erkenntnis und Verwirklichung der wahren Theologie nach Erasmus von Rotterdam* (Tübingen, 1972), pp. 211–20; wichtige Fundstellen für das *via*-Motiv: H 57,34; 60,8; 61,10.16; 69,3; 111,5; 135,35; ASD V/1, 342,51 (Anm.zu 51: *Viatores*).
[14] Augustijn, *Erasmus von Rotterdam*, p. 127; vgl. auch Friedhelm Krüger, *Humanistische Evangelienauslegung. Desiderius Erasmus von Rotterdam als Ausleger der Evangelien in seinen Paraphrasen* (Tübingen, 1986), pp. 185–98.

explanatio Symboli des Erasmus von 1533 verwiesen (ASD V/1,177–320), wo dieses Stilmittel für den katechetischen Dialog oft eingesetzt wird.[15]

Über derartige werkimmanente Verweise hinaus wäre zu fragen, ob in den katechetischen Traktaten des Spätmittelalters[16] und in der reichen vorreformatorischen *Speculum*-Literatur[17] formal und inhaltlich vergleichbare Beschreibungen einer solchen *via pietatis* zu finden sind. Johannes von Walter hat das kleine Textstück aus der Einleitung der *Diatribe* — das 'nicht so schlicht' sei, 'als es scheinen möchte' — der skotistischen Gnadenlehre zugeordnet (W 6, Anm.8). Diesem Hinweis müßte in einer umfassenderen Untersuchung weiter nachgegangen werden, wobei auch auf bernhardinische, franziskanische und quietistische Elemente in der Theologie dieser Formel zu achten wäre, die insgesamt das Verhältnis des Erasmus zur *Devotio moderna* auf eigene Weise wieder zur Frage macht.[18] Für unseren — auf bescheidenere Ziele ausgerichteten — Frageansatz bleibt festzuhalten: Seine Dialogstruktur und die Elementarisierung der theologischen Sachausagen kennzeichnen den hier hervorgehobenen Text als ein kleines katechetisches Lehrstück, bei dessen Niederschrift Erasmus mit einiger Wahrscheinlichkeit vorgegebene und literarisch bereits geprägte Traditionselemente verarbeitet hat. Innerhalb des Prooemiums zur *Diatribe* hat der Text die Funktion, vorab eine biblisch-theologische Aussage ('quae didicimus e sacris litteris': Ia 8; W 6,11) zum Problem der menschlichen Willensfreiheit bereitzustellen, die dem Leser einen Einblick in die Relevanz des Hauptthemas der Schrift vermitteln kann. Das im Hauptteil der *Diatribe* später folgende Verfahren des ausführlichen Schriftvergleichs wird durch diese proömiale oder exordiale Aussage nicht vorweggenommen und schon gar nicht überflüssig gemacht. Doch im Blick auf den Leser, für den Erasmus

---

[15] Schon die Definition des christlichen Glaubens setzt mit einer Vt-Formel ein: 'Vt tibi rudi definiam crassius ...' (ASD V/1,208,50); vgl. ferner: Rudolf Padberg, *Erasmus als Katechet* (Fribourg-en-B., 1956).

[16] Zum Forschungsstand vgl. Norbert Richard Wolf, ed., *Wissensorganisierende und wissensvermittelnde Literatur im Mittelalter. Perspektiven ihrer Erforschung* (Wiesbaden, 1987); darin insbesondere: Christoph Burger, 'Die Erwartung des richtenden Christus als Motiv für katechetisches Wirken, pp. 103–22 (als Definition für derartige katechetische Traktate: 'Sie müssen katechetische Stücke ausführlich darstellen und sie müssen durch eine erkennbare Disposition zu Einheiten zusammengeschlossen sein; vgl. Egino Weidenhiller, *Untersuchungen zur deutschsprachigen katechetischen Literatur des späten Mittelalters* (München, 1965), p. 101).'

[17] Vgl. die große Sammlung bei Petronella Bange, *Spiegels der Christenen. Zelfreflectie en ideaalbeeld in laat-middeleeuwse moralistisch-didactisch traktaten* (Proefschrift Nijmegen) (Nijmegen, 1986).

[18] Vgl. die Problemskizze bei Reinhold Mokrosch, '*Devotio moderna*. Verhältnis zu Humanismus und Reformation', *TRE*, 8 (1981), pp. 609–16, insbesondere p. 612.

schreiben will, enthält das hier hervorgehobene Textstück noch eine
zusätzliche Information, die über das bisher Gesagte hinausgeht: Ein
Mensch, der sich an das hält, was in diesen Frage- und Antwortsätzen
gesagt wird, tut — nach Ansicht des Erasmus — der christlichen Frömmigkeit bereits Genüge ('satis ad Christianam pietatem': Ia 8; W 6,23).
Was nun über die katechetische Lehraussage zur *via pietatis* hinausgeht,
lehnt Erasmus nicht etwa an sich ab, sondern er hält es für den von ihm
zuerst angesprochenen Leserkreis für unnötig. Durch den wohl exempla-
risch gemeinten Hinweis auf die fachtheologische Diskussion des Kon-
tingenzproblems (Ia 8; W 6,24–7,5) will Erasmus sichtbar machen, daß es
einen Trennstrich zwischen einer elementarisierbaren katechetischen
Theologie und einer wissenschaftlichen Theologie nicht nur gibt,
sondern im Interesse der *crassuli* auch geben muß. Wer als Laie für Laien
schreibt, sollte Auskunft über den Verlauf dieser Grenzlinie geben
können. Es ist der rhetorischen Struktur der *Diatribe* gemäß, daß Erasmus
diese für ihn wichtige Auskunft[19] im Prooemium seines Buches gibt und
sie nicht in die *collatio* hineinträgt. Es ist nahezu ein seelsorgerliches — in
jedem Falle aber zumindest ein pädagogisches — Anliegen, das Erasmus
dazu drängt, den Leser der *Diatribe* gleich zu Beginn des Werkes darüber
zu informieren, welche Bedeutung die zu verhandelnde Sache für dessen
eigene theologische Existenz habe.

III DIE KONTROVERSE

Martin Luther hat sofort mit Sicherheit erkannt, daß jenes kleine katechi-
tische Lehrstück in der ersten Einleitung zur *Diatribe* des Erasmus eine
besondere literarische Form besitzt. Luther war es, der diesem Textabschnitt einen eigenen Namen gab, den Erasmus später (im *Hyperaspistes I*)
ganz selbstverständlich und nur mit leicht variierenden Tonverschie-
bungen übernahm. Luther nannte jene Sätze zunächst eine *forma* (*WA*
18,609,17), dann eine *forma Christianismi* (*WA* 18,610,14; 611,1; 614,22;
656,3). Nach Ausweis des Tübinger Registers zur Weimarer Luther-
Ausgabe wird das lateinische Wort *forma* von Luther in drei verschiedenen Bedeutungsbereichen eingesetzt: (1) Gestalt, Schönheit; (2)
Form, Urbild (mit den Unterbereichen a. philosophisch, b. theologisch)

---

[19] Vgl. Alfons Auer, *Die vollkommene Frömmigkeit des Christen. Nach dem Enchiridion militis
Christiani des Erasmus von Rotterdam* (Düsseldorf, 1954), pp. 187–200; Robert Stupperich, *Das
Enchiridion militis christiani des Erasmus von Rotterdam nach seiner Entstehung, seinem Sinn und
Charakter*, ARG, 69 (1978), pp. 5–22; Heinz Holeczek, *Erasmus Deutsch*, Bd.1 (Stuttgart-Bad
Cannstatt, 1983), pp. 138; 169–81.

und (3) Ordnung.[20] Mit dem absolut gesetzten Begriff *forma* will Luther also offenkundig zum Ausdruck bringen, daß der kleine Textabschnitt in der *Diatribe* nach einer besonderen Ordnung gestaltet ist, daß es sich um eine geprägte, 'geformte' literarische Einheit handelt. Das von Luther recht oft benutzte lateinische Wort *Christianismus* (in WA 132 mal!)[21] stellt er nur in *De servo arbitrio* mit *forma* zu der Wortverbindung *forma Christianismi* zusammen. Zumindest durch Melanchthons *Loci communes* von 1521 mußte Luther dieser Begriff bekannt sein; denn Melanchthon schreibt im programmatischen Widmungsbrief an Tilemann Plettener: 'Fallitur, quisquis aliunde christianismi formam petit quam e scriptura canonica' (*CR* 21,82f; StA II/1,4,31f). Melanchthon bezeichnet mit den Worten *forma christianismi* das Gesamtvorhaben seiner *Loci communes*, nämlich die Darlegung 'der christlichen Hauptartikel'. Indem Luther diesen sehr weiten und generalisierenden Begriff auf das kleine Textstück bei Erasmus anwendet, setzt er für den eigenen Interpretationsansatz bereits einen folgenreichen Akzent: Er wird diese *forma Christianismi* daraufhin befragen, ob sie tatsächlich — wie Bruno Jordahn übersetzt hat[22] — das 'Wesen des Christentums' zulänglich zum Ausdruck bringt. Luther nimmt die Formulierung des Erasmus beim Wort, daß der kleine katechetische Lehrtext *satis ad Christianam pietatem* (Ia 8; W 6,23) sei. Und hier lautet nun Luthers erster, bereits sehr erregt vorgetragener Einwand: Der *forma Christianismi* des Erasmus fehle jeglicher christologische Bezug ('nam Christi ne uno quidem iota mentionem facis': *WA* 609,18f). Jeder Jude oder Heide könne in dieser Weise von dem *deus natura clementissimus* sprechen und einen ethischen Imperativ deklaratorisch über die Beschreibung des Heilsweges setzen. Es sei unfaßlich, wie ein Theologe und Lehrer der Kirche den Christen eine solche *forma Christianismi* vorschreiben könne, in der 'weder Gott noch Christus, noch Evangelium, noch Glaube, noch überhaupt etwas, nicht einmal vom Judentum, viel

---

[20] Der Verf. dankt an dieser Stelle den Mitarbeiterinnen und Mitarbeitern des 'Besonderen Arbeitsbereichs Spätmittelalter und Reformation' für die Erlaubnis, das noch nicht veröffentlichte Forschungsmaterial einsehen zu dürfen.

[21] Diese neue Zählung korrigiert frühere Schätzungen; vgl. Rolf Schäfer, 'Welchen Sinn hat es, nach einem Wesen des Christentums zu suchen?' *ZThK*, 65 (1968), p. 333: 'Viel seltener greift Luther zu dem nichtbiblischen Wort. Indessen kann auch er — falls man der Nachschrift der Jesaja-Vorlesung trauen darf — das Wesentliche am Glauben so beschreiben: "christianismus ... verissime est auditus verbi et ruminatio eius, ut semper nobis loquatur Christus" (*WA* 31/II,22,3)'; Hans Wagenhammer, *Das Wesen des Christentums. Eine begriffsgeschichtliche Untersuchung* (Mainz, 1973), pp. 40–9.

[22] Martin Luther, *Daß der freie Wille nichts sei. Antwort D. Martin Luthers an Erasmus von Rotterdam* (= Luther Deutsch E.R. Bd.1) (München, 1954), p. 19.

weniger vom Christentum übrig' bleibe (*WA* 18,610,17–19). Erasmus rede *more sceptico* und gegen sein eigenes *ingenium*, er gerate in Widersprüche und verrate mit diesen Worten eine völlige Unkenntnis der Heiligen Schrift und des Glaubens ('tantam ignorantiam scripturae et pietatis hic verbis tuis confiteris': *WA* 18,610,21f).

Nach diesem Ausbruch der Emotionen erklärt Luther, er wolle nun auf die Worte des Erasmus im einzelnen zu sprechen kommen. Tatsächlich bietet er dann seinen Lesern eine Paraphrase der *forma Christianismi* an, die deren Inhalt etwas gedrängt aber vollständig wiedergibt (*WA* 18,611, 1–4). Das kurze Referat zu den Sätzen des Erasmus erregt Luther jedoch erneut so sehr, daß er zunächst wieder nur mit einem Schwall von Vorwürfen argumentieren kann: Die *forma Christianismi* sei ohne Christus und ohne Geist, sie sei kälter als Eis ('Haec verba tua, sine Christo, sine spiritu, ipsa glacie frigidiora': *WA* 18,611,5); selbst der Glanz der Beredsamkeit des Erasmus nehme hier Schaden, und das Ganze sei wohl nur aus Furcht vor den 'Papisten und Tyrannen' niedergeschrieben worden, vor denen Erasmus nicht als völliger Atheist dastehen wolle ('ne prorsus Atheos videris': *WA* 18,611,7). Erst auf diesen unerhörten Vorwurf folgt die alles entscheidende argumentative Rückfrage: Die *forma Christianismi* des Erasmus setze voraus, daß die in ihr enthaltenen Sachaussagen dem Sprecher dieser Sätze in einem theologisch begründeten Sinne bewußt und gewiß sein. Was aber wolle Erasmus sagen und lehren, wenn dies nicht der Fall sei? Wenn der Nach-Sprecher des katechetischen Textes eben nicht wisse, 'was jene Kräfte sind, was sie vermögen, was ihnen widerfährt, was ihre Anstrengung ist, was ihre Wirksamkeit, was ihre Unwirksamkeit, was soll jener tun?' ('Si quis igitur ignoret ... quid tu illum facere docebis?' *WA* 18,611,10–12). Mit dieser Frage wird von Luther das theologische Zentrum der Kontroverse aufgedeckt. Es geht um das Problem, ob bei der katechetischen Vermittlung von Glaubenswissen die Einzelinhalte so weit elementarisiert werden dürfen, daß dem Verstehen dessen, was da geglaubt werden soll, unbeabsichtigt — und doch wirksam — Grenzen gesetzt werden. Gegen alle rhetorischen und didaktischen Bemühungen des Humanisten bringt Luther mit schroffer Einseitigkeit die Frage nach der Glaubensgewißheit in die Kontroverse ein.[23]

[23] 'Igitur non est irreligiosum, curiosum aut supervacaneum, sed imprimis salutare et necessarium Christiano, nosse, an voluntas aliquid vel nihil agat in iis, quae pertinent ad salutem. Imo ut scias, hic est cardo nostrae disputationis, hic versatur status causae huius. ... Haec si ignoraverimus, prorsus nihil Christianarum rerum noscemus, erimusque omnibus gentibus peiores. Qui hoc non sentit, fateatur sese non esse Christianum' (*WA* 18,614,1–8).

Luthers maßloser Angriff gegen die *forma Christianismi* ist an vielen Punkten schwach oder gar nicht begründet. Daß Erasmus die Christologie sowie die Soteriologie und die Lehre vom Heiligen Geist einfach ausklammere, kann nur behaupten, wer den Kontext, in dem die *forma* steht, bewußt überliest. Daß Erasmus diese katechetische Kurzformel irgendwelchen 'Papisten und Tyrannen' zuliebe in die *Diatribe* aufgenommen habe, ist eine verletzende Behauptung, der jeglicher Beweis fehlt. Und der böse Vorwurf der 'Gottlosigkeit' trifft Erasmus zunächst überhaupt nicht. Luther gibt sich gar nicht die Mühe, die Einzelaussagen der *forma Christianismi* theologisch-kritisch zu interpretieren. Seine Auseinandersetzung mit diesem Text stürmt auf ein einziges theologisches Argument zu, das allerdings hoch bedeutsam ist: Es ist die Frage, was der im Glauben zu unterrichtende Mensch lernen solle und was er wissen müsse. Genügen elementarisierte theologisch-ethische Basisinformationen, die dem Katechumenen eindeutige Verhaltensformen und überschaubare Handlungsanweisungen für die *via pietatis* vermitteln? Oder hat *jeder* zum Glauben zu führende Mensch einen Anspruch auf ein verstehendes Lernen, das bei kritischen Rückfragen (*si quis ignoret*) nie auf eine durch die katechetische Methode errichtete Schranke stoßen darf? Luther behauptet, die Lehrweise der *forma Christianismi* bleibe in einer gefährlichen und unzulässigen Weise oberflächlich, weil sie leere Räume im Glaubenswissen nicht nur hinnehme, sondern diese geradezu schaffe. Durch die pädagogische Reduktion der Lehraussage auf ein ganz einfaches System von Hauptsätzen werde der Katechumene gerade im Vollzug des Unterrichtens zu einem 'Unwissenden' gemacht. Luthers Vorwurf gegen Erasmus gipfelt in den Worten: 'Facturus ignaros ... eo ipso quo doces' (*WA* 18,611,20f).

Die Reaktion des Erasmus auf den Angriff Luthers bestätigt, daß die Kontroverse über die *forma Christianismi* in der Tat in der Frage nach dem Lernprozeß des Glaubens ihr substantielles Zentrum hat. Erasmus bezeichnet das umstrittene Textstück im *Hyperaspistes I* zunächst als *formula Christianae mentis* (LB X 1265 B; Le 288), dann nennt er es wiederholt bloß *forma*, gelegentlich *forma totius Christianismi* (LB X 1266 B; Le 294) und noch oft *formula*.[24] Erasmus erkennt somit die durch Luther erfolgte Qualifizierung des Textes als einer selbständigen Einheit an. Mit der zuerst vorgenommenen leisen Veränderung (*formula* statt *forma*; *Christianae mentis* statt *Christianismi*) will Erasmus wohl zum Ausdruck bringen, daß dieser kurze Text nicht verallgemeinernd verstanden werden

---

[24] LB X 1265 D; 1266 A; 1267 E; 1270 D.F; 1273 B; 1282 C.

dürfe und im Umfang seiner Lehraussagen auch nicht absolut gesetzt werden könne. Nicht von einem 'Wesen des Christentums' ist nach seiner Ansicht in der *formula Christianae mentis* die Rede, wohl aber von Mitteilungen zur Glaubenslehre, die zumindest partiell eine rechte 'christliche Gesinnung' (Le 289) zum Ausdruck bringen. Doch diese Abschwächung des inhaltlichen Geltungsanspruchs der *forma* ist für Erasmus keineswegs schon die Hauptsache seiner Erwiderung. Vielmehr betont er, nachdem er die Formel für die Leser des *Hyperaspistes I* noch einmal zitiert hat (LB X 1265 CD; Le 290), daß man auf die Adressaten des Textes achten müsse: 'haec forma datur idiotis Christianis' (LB X 1265 D; Le 290). Erasmus erinnert an den Leserkreis, für den die *Diatribe* verfaßt wurde: die Laien. Sodann wehrt er sich gegen Luthers Interpretation des zweimaligen *meo iudicio*, das nicht als Widerspruch zwischen erkenntnistheoretischer Skepsis und gleichzeitiger assertorischer Redeweise mißverstanden werden dürfe. Dieses *meo iudicio* war Gliederungselement in der proömialen Rede, nicht theologischer Programmsatz (LB X 1265 E; Le 292). Hier kommt erstmals die von Luther nicht gewürdigte rhetorische Struktur der *Diatribe* als Element der Kontroverse in den Blick. Wenig später beruft sich Erasmus dann ausdrücklich auf den rhetorischen Charakter des Einleitungsabschnitts der *Diatribe*: Die hier gemachten Aussagen zur Freiheit des menschlichen Willens gehören noch nicht in die eigentliche Disputation hinein; die Auseinandersetzung zum Thema wird erst noch folgen: 'sed haec occurrent suis locis. Nondum enim disputamus' (LB X 1266 A; Le 292). Luther verdrehe den Sinn der Worte, so als ob Erasmus an dieser Stelle eine Wesensbestimmung des *ganzen* Christentums für *alle* Menschen habe verbindlich vorschreiben wollen ('Tu huc torques mea verba quasi formam totius Christianismi praescripserim omnibus'; LB X 1266 AB; Le 294).Das sei nicht die Absicht der *forma*. Sie wolle sagen, was für 'einfache Leute' angesichts der strittigen und beinahe unerklärbaren Schwierigkeiten des Themas 'Willensfreiheit' zu wissen ausreichend sei ('quod satis esset simplicibus': LB X 1266 B; Le 294).

Die katechetische Elementarisierung des Stoffs wird im Blick auf den Leserkreis und auf den Schwierigkeitsgrad der theologischen Sachfragen von Erasmus verteidigt. Ausführlich geht Erasmus dann auf die einzelnen Vorwürfe Luthers ein — bis hin zu der schlimmen Unterstellung, er habe aus Furcht vor den 'Papisten und Tyrannen' die Formel in den Text der *Diatribe* eingefügt.[25] Doch so deutlich Erasmus erkennen läßt, daß ihn

---

[25] Zu diesem Argument und dem Vorwurf des 'Atheismus' vgl. James D. Tracy, *Erasmus. The Growth of a Mind* (Genf, 1972), pp. 200–2.

diese Vorwürfe verletzt haben, und so gründlich er sich Mühe gibt, sie zu entkräften, so kommt er doch zielstrebig auf das von Luther bezeichnete Zentrum der Kontroverse zu sprechen. Wie gut er Luther verstanden hat zeigt er dadurch, daß er den Differenzpunkt aus seiner Sicht präzise beschreibt. Luther hatte nach der Glaubensgewißheit gefragt und die Notwendigkeit absoluter Heilsgewißheit zum Maßstab und Ziel allen Lehrens gesetzt. Erasmus fragt demgegenüber — als Anwalt der Laien — nach dem 'katechetischen Minimum': Es müsse doch möglich sein, daß schwierige Fragen des christlichen Glaubens 'von einfachen Christen auch einfach geglaubt werden können' ('possunt a simpliciter Christianis simpliciter credi': LB X 1267 B; Le 300).

Noch zweimal verweist Erasmus auf den Stellenwert der *forma* innerhalb der rhetorischen Struktur der *Diatribe*. Sie sei keine Definition des menschlichen Willens und der göttlichen Barmherzigkeit; die Explikation dieser Begriffe erfolge erst im Hauptteil ('At in forma non definio . . . at explico satis, opinor, in ipsa disputatione': LB X 1267; Le 302. 'Sed non definio . . . in formula, quasi non satis fuerit in disputatione ubi oportebat id esse factum': LB X 1270 F; Le 320). Die *forma* ist kein Teil der fachtheologischen Auseinandersetzung, sondern sie ist als Hilfe für den 'einfachen Christen' gedacht ('doceat simplicem Christianum': LB X 1271 B; Le 322; vgl. LB X 1273 B; Le 332 u.ö.). Die Frage, die Erasmus schließlich geradezu beschwörend an Luther richtet, lautet: Wird das Wort Gottes gebunden, wenn man die katechetische Lehre (*doctrina*) in dieser Weise an das Verständnis und die Verstehensmöglichkeiten der Hörer (*ad utilitatem auditorum*) anpaßt? LB X 1280 D; Le 372). Unter Hinweis auf Hebr 6,1 betont Erasmus, daß man den Katechumenen zunächst die *rudimenta Philosophiae Christianae* mitteilen müsse, bis sie zu den verborgeneren Dingen fortschreiten können (LB X 1280 F-1281 A; Le 374). Oder wolle Luther den Katechumenen dasselbe lehren, wie den künftigen Bischof? ('Eadem docebis catechumenum, quae jam futurum Episcopum?' (LB X 1282 F; Le 386).

IV DIE THEOLOGISCHE DIFFERENZ

Erasmus hatte mit der *forma Christianismi* ein auf die Praxis bezogenes, undogmatisches Reden und Lehren über den Glauben als möglich erweisen wollen. Schon Hans Joachim Iwand hat dazu bemerkt: 'Erasmus formuliert hier sein in gewisser Weise überaus modernes Verständnis vom praktischen Christentum, wonach der christliche Glaube ein unentbehrliches Moment der praktischen, religiös-sittlichen Lebensgestaltung ist.'[26] Erasmus verfolgte das Ziel, den Anschluß zwischen der Theologie und der zeitgenössischen Kultur wieder herzustellen. Ein Text wie die schlichte *forma Christianismi* sollte dazu beitragen, 'Glauben und Erfahrungswelt wieder in Einklang zu bringen.'[27] Dogmatische Fragen und scholastische Distinktionen — zumal so schwierige wie die über die Freiheit des menschlichen Willens — sollten den Gelehrten überlassen bleiben. Der einfältige, nach der Einheit von Glaube und Erfahrung suchende Mensch, der Christ als *crassulus*, sollte in seiner schlichten Frömmigkeit nicht durch derartige Fragen belastet und verwirrt werden. Indem Erasmus diese Überlegungen und den Entwurf einer solchen überschaubaren katechetischen Kurzformel in den Einleitungsteil der *Diatribe* einbrachte, wollte er Sachkennern zu verstehen geben, daß es sich bei alledem noch nicht um die gelehrte Disputation zum Thema handelte, sondern um allgemeine, proömiale Vorausbemerkungen, die den notwendigen Diskurs und dessen Ergebnis nicht vorwegnehmen.

Luther hat die rhetorische Struktur der *Diatribe* und insbesondere die Funktion der beiden Vorreden im Gesamtaufbau des Werkes durchaus erkannt; er war aber nicht bereit, Konsequenzen aus dieser Einsicht zu ziehen. Gerade die Bemühung des Erasmus, die Glaubenslehre und die katechetische Formel 'an die verschiedenen Hörer anzupassen' ('variis auditoribus attemperare': *WA* 18,639,9), wird von ihm brüsk abgelehnt. Luther gibt ferner zu verstehen, daß er auch die rhetorischen Feinheiten der Darstellungsweise des Erasmus wohl sieht. Er will aber nicht über 'grammatische Figuren' verhandeln: 'Grammatica enim ista sunt et figuris verborum composita, quae etiam pueri norunt. Nos vero de dogmatibus, non de grammaticis figuris agimus in hac causa' (*WA* 18,639,10–12). Es sind also gerade diese grammatischen beziehungsweise rhetorischen Differenzierungsversuche des Erasmus, die Luthers Zorn provozieren. Weil Erasmus mit der zur Verhandlung anstehenden theologischen Sachfrage so distanziert und überlegen umgeht, spricht Luther von der 'Eiseskälte' der *forma Christianismi*. Luther weigert sich damit zugleich, das religiöse Anliegen anzuerkennen, das hinter den Akkommodationsversuchen und dem katechetisch-didaktischen Bemühen des Erasmus steht. Diese Weigerung, Erasmus dorthin zu folgen, wo dessen Theologie ihre

---

[26] Luther Deutsch, E.R. Bd.1, p. 274 (*Die theologische Einführung* in Luthers Schrift von Hans Joachim Iwand gehört immer noch zu den wichtigsten kommentierenden Beiträgen der Lutherforschung zu *De servo arbitrio*; a.a.O. pp. 253–315).

[27] Ich verweise hier auf die sehr erhellende kleine Studie von Cornelis Augustijn, *Erasmus und seine Theologie: Hatte Luther Recht?* = *Colloque Erasmien de Liège. Bibliothèque de la Faculté de Philosophie et Lettres de l'Université de Liège*, Fasc. 247 (Paris, 1987), pp. 49–68; 65.

wichtigste Aufgabe und Zielsetzung sieht, gibt der Art, wie Luther den Konflikt austrägt, ihre verletzende Schärfe.

Luther hält der Vorrede der *Diatribe* entgegen, sie sei sich über den Unterschied zwischen *verbum Dei* und *verbum hominum* nicht im Klaren. Denn wenn die Vorrede — und mit ihr die *forma Christianismi* — *de verbis hominum* handele, sei sie vergeblich geschrieben worden; sollte Erasmus die Absicht gehabt haben, in der Vorrede *de verbis Dei* zu handeln, dann müsse dieser Abschnitt der *Diatribe* 'völlig gottlos' genannt werden ('tota impia': WA 18,638,14). Es wäre sinnvoller gewesen, zunächst einmal eine Entscheidung darüber herbeizuführen, ob die gesamte Auseinandersetzung zur Frage der menschlichen Willensfreiheit über 'Gottes Worte oder über menschliche Worte' geführt werde ('an essent verba Dei vel hominum, de quibus disputamus': *WA* 18,638,17f). Erasmus hat Luther im *Hyperaspistes I* die geforderte Auskunft gegeben. Er unterscheidet gleich drei Sprachebenen bzw. Redeformen: Menschenwort, Gotteswort und Auslegungen des Wortes Gottes (LB X 1290 A; Le 424). Demgegenüber hat Luther nur zwischen Menschenwort und Gotteswort unterschieden, wobei er allerdings stets betonte, daß man im Wort Gottes Gesetz und Evangelium auseinanderhalten müsse, also zwischen Gebot und Forderung auf der einen Seite und Verheißung und Gnadenwort auf der anderen Seite sorgfältig unterscheiden müsse (vgl. *WA* 18,680,28–31).

Eine Unterscheidung zwischen Gott und Heiliger Schrift fällen beide, Luther wie Erasmus. Umstritten ist der Ort, an dem die Grenze zu ziehen ist. Erasmus unterscheidet innerhalb der Schrift und innerhalb der Sprache; Luther unterscheidet 'zwischen Schrift (= Sprache insgesamt) und Gott.'[28] An dieser Differenz scheidet sich Luthers assertorische Theologie von allem, was die erkenntnistheoretischen Voraussetzungen des Erasmus bestimmte. Eberhard Jüngel hat nachgewiesen, daß Luther mit der Unterscheidung von verborgenem Gott und offenbarem Gott verhindern will, 'daß über den offenbaren Gott geredet wird wie über einen gleichwohl verborgenen Gott, daß also der offenbare Gott in seiner Offenbarung nicht ernst genommen wird. Genau das ist ja nach seinem Urteil in der Diatribe der Fall.'[29] So läßt sich auch der Konflikt, der zwischen Luther und Erasmus wegen der *forma Christianismi* ausgebrochen ist, auf eben diese theologische Differenz zurückführen: Es geht

---

[28] Bader, *Assertio*, p. 155.

[29] Eberhard Jüngel, '*Quae supra nos, nihil ad nos.* Eine Kurzformel der Lehre vom verborgenen Gott — im Anschluß an Luther interpretiert', ZThK, 32 (1972), pp. 197–240; 220; ders., *Gott als Geheimnis der Welt. Zur Begründung der Theologie des Gekreuzigten im Streit zwischen Theismus und Atheismus* (Tübingen, 1977), pp. 262; 268.

auch hier um die unterschiedliche Grenzziehung zwischen 'Gott selbst', 'Gotteswort' und 'Menschenwort'. Erasmus konnte aufgrund seines Wort- und Sprachverständnisses den Versuch unternehmen, 'einfache Christen auf einfache Weise' über das Wort Gottes zu belehren. Nun schließt ein 'einfaches' Reden stets bestimmte Inhalte aus der Mitteilung aus. Zugleich muß die 'einfache' Redeweise Akkomodationen vornehmen. Erasmus erscheint sowohl die Reduktion wie die Akkomodation möglich. Fortfallende theologische Sachaussagen, die nach Ansicht des Erasmus in einem solchen Lehrtext für den Laien nur ein Hindernis für das Verstehen wären, werden dem Bereich der (stets strittigen) 'Auslegungen des Wortes Gottes' zugewiesen ('interpretationes verbi Dei'; LB X 1290 A; Le 424). Zugleich rücken sie aber — und das ist das Entscheidende! — dicht an jene Grenze heran, die Erasmus *innerhalb* des Offenbarungswortes der Heiligen Schrift zwischen dem *Deus revelatus* und dem *Deus absconditus* zu erkennen meint. Diese Grenzlinie will er in frommer theologischer Selbstbescheidung demütig achten und sie nicht bis ins einzelne ausforschen.[30] Zur Akkomodation der katechetischen Lehraussage fühlt sich Erasmus berechtigt, weil schon 'die göttliche Weisheit' selbst in der Heiligen Schrift 'ihre Redeweise an unsere Gefühle und unser Fassungsvermögen angepaßt' habe (LB X 1290 E; Le 428).

Für Luther ist ein solches ausgrenzendes und akkomodierendes 'einfaches' Reden über den Glauben unerträglich. Wer so lehrt, führe in die Unwissenheit hinein ('Facturus ignaros ... eo ipso, quo doces': *WA* 18,611,20f). Man könne aus dem einen Wort Gottes, der Offenbarung in Gesetz und Evangelium, keine Teile oder Einzelinhalte ausgrenzen, um 'einfach zu einfachen Menschen' zu sprechen. Der in seinem Wort offenbare Gott ist für Luther in eben diesem Wort ganz und unteilbar offenbar. Die Scheidewand zwischen dem verborgenen und dem offenbaren Gott sei nicht innerhalb der Heiligen Schrift aufgerichtet. Das der menschlichen Sprache und Rede anvertraute *verbum Dei* ist hell und klar; in seinem Wort hat Gott sich eindeutig für den Menschen definiert: 'Relinquendus est igitur Deus in maiestate et natura sua, sic enim nihil nos cum eo habemus agere, nec sic voluit a nobis agi cum eo. Sed quatenus

---

[30] 'Sunt enim in divinis literis adyta quaedam, in quae deus noluit nos altius penetrare, et si penetrare conemur, quo fuerimus altius ingressi, hoc *magis ac magis* caligamus, quo vel sic agnosceremus et divinae sapientiae maiestatem impervestigabilem et humanae mentis imbecillitatem. ... Multa servantur ei tempori, cum iam non videbimus per speculum et in aenigmate, sed revelata facie domini gloriam contemplabimur' (Ia 7; W 5,17–6,9). Die spezifische theologische Differenz zur Position Luthers besteht darin, daß Erasmus ausdrücklich von 'Dingen' spricht, die *in* der Heiligen Schrift enthalten sind!

indutus et proditus est verbo suo, quo nobis sese obtulit, cum eo agimus'
(*WA* 18,685,14–17). Auch gegenüber der vom Unglauben oder vom 'einfachen' Glauben gestellten Frage: 'wo ist Gott', 'gibt es keine doppelte,
sondern nur *eine* Antwort: Gott ist in Gottes Wort.'[31]

Erasmus hatte mit der *forma Christianismi* ein gemeindepädagogisches,
seelsorgerliches Ziel verfolgt, das gerade heute in den zahllosen Bemühungen um eine katechetische Elementarisierung und Aktualisierung
von Glaubensaussagen immer wieder angestrebt wird.[32] Luthers vehe-
menter Widerspruch gegen das kleine katechetische Lehrstück im
Eingangsteil der *Diatribe* macht auf die tiefgreifenden theologischen
Probleme aufmerksam, vor denen alle derartigen Versuche stehen. Hier
wäre auch an den schlichten Sachverhalt zu erinnern, daß Luther seine
eigenen Katechismen ausdrücklich für die Prediger, die Hausväter, die
Kinder und das Gesinde zugleich geschrieben hat.[33] Wer in der Art des
Erasmus in gemeindepädagogischer Absicht eine *forma Christianismi* für
den Laien verfaßt, der stellt das allgemeine Priestertum der Glaubenden
in Frage — auch wenn dem Autor diese Konsequenz seines Tuns völlig
fern liegt.

Luthers Zorn über die kleine *forma* mag auch dadurch angefacht und
verstärkt worden sein, daß er hinter den der Tradition verpflichteten
Einzelformulierungen dieses Textes jene alte kirchliche Lehre wahrnahm,
die zwischen 'Laien' und 'Priestern' in der Weise unterschied, daß sie diese
dem göttlichen Geheimnis näher sein ließ als jene.[34] Der Katechismus
einer Kirche der Reformation darf — wenn er sich zu Recht auf Luther
berufen will — diese Unterscheidung nicht einmal im leisesten Ansatz
treffen. Der Katechismus einer Kirche der Reformation muß für alle
Christen das Gleiche lehren, so wie es in dem von James K. Cameron so
meisterhaft edierten *First Book of Discipline* heißt:

> To wit, the knowledge of Gods Law and Commandments, the use
> and office of the same; the chiefe Articles of the beleefe, the right

[31] Vgl. Jüngel, *Gott als Geheimnis der Welt*, p. 268.

[32] Vgl. die Situationsbeschreibung der Fachdisziplin und die Skizze zur Aufgabe der Katechetik heute bei Christoph Bizer, 'Katechetik', *TRE*, 17 (1988), pp. 699–706, sowie Wolfgang Grünberg, 'Katechismus. Gegenwart', *TRE*, 17 (1988), pp. 723–28.

[33] *BSLK* 553,34–554,33; Vgl. auch *WA* 7,204,8–11; 30/1,27; Christoph Weismann, *Eine Kleine Biblia. Die Katechismen von Luther und Brenz* (Stuttgart, 1985) 2, pp. 19–24.

[34] Auf eine bedeutsame Sonderentwicklung verweist Knut Schäferdiek, 'Das Heilige in Laien-hand. Zur Entstehungsgeschichte der fränkischen Eigenkirche', in Henning Schröer / Gerhard Müller, eds, *Vom Amt des Laien in Kirche und Theologie. Festschrift für Gerhard Krause* (Berlin/New York, 1982), pp. 122–40.

forme to pray unto God; the number, use and effect of the Sacraments; the true knowledge of Christ Jesus, of his Office and Natures and such others, without the knowledge wherof *neither any man deserves to be called a Christian.*[35]

University of Tübingen

[35] *The First Book of Discipline. With Introduction and Commentary*, ed. James K. Cameron (Edinburgh, 1972), pp. 133f.

PASTORAL CARE AND THE REFORMATION IN GERMANY[1]

by R. W. SCRIBNER

I

O F the numerous criticisms and expressions of grievance directed at the Church in Germany on the eve of the Reformation, the most devastating was the charge of inadequate pastoral care. Reformers of all complexions bewailed the poor state of the parish clergy and the inadequate manner in which they provided for the spiritual needs of their flocks. At the very least, the parish clergy were ill-educated and ill-prepared for their pastoral tasks; at the very worst, they exploited those to whom they should have ministered, charging for their services, treating layfolk as merely a means of increasing their incomes, and, above all, resorting to the tyranny of the spiritual ban to uphold their position. The popular propaganda of the early Reformation fully exploited such deficiencies, exposing the decay in root and branch of a system of pastoral care depicted as no more than an empty shell, a façade of a genuine Christian cure of souls.[2] The attack on the traditional Church was highly successful, successful enough to provoke an ecclesiastical revolution, and almost a socio-political revolution as well. It was, indeed, so successful that generations of historians of the Reformation have seen the condition of the pre-Reformation Church largely through the eyes of its critics and opponents. This negative image was matched by an idealized view of what succeeded it: where the old Church had failed the Christian laity, indeed, so much that they had virtually fallen into the hands of the Devil, the new Church offered solutions, a new way forward, a new standard of pastoral care and concern that created a new ideal, the Lutheran pastor, who cared

---

[1] I wish to express my thanks to the British Academy and the British Council who made possible research visits to the archives of the German Democratic Republic to gather material on which this article is based.

[2] For Evangelical popular propaganda against the shepherds who have become ravening wolves, see R. W. Scribner, *For the Sake of Simple Folk. Popular Propaganda for the German Reformation* (Cambridge, 1981), pp. 52–7. The theme of pastoral care in the pre-Reformation Church has, however, been given little attention, except where it appears in studies such as Thomas N. Tentler, *Sin and Confession on the Eve of the Reformation* (Princeton, 1977). Much of the literature on 'the state of the Church' at the end of the Middle Ages concentrates too heavily on 'abuses' and ignores the efforts being made in successive diocesan synods to improve the quality of the clergy and their standards of pastoral care.

for his flock as a kindly father, a shepherd who would willingly give up his life for his sheep.[3]

That all was not quite as rosy as this idealized picture would have it is something Reformation historians have rather slowly begun to realize and accept. Numerous ecclesiastical visitations throughout the sixteenth and early seventeenth centuries seem to show that the Reformation was a failure in its primary purpose of turning the bulk of the population into devout, believing Christians. Visitation records have been regarded since the nineteenth century as an important source for understanding the state of the early modern Church, but modern church historians have been reluctant to make as much use of them as their nineteenth-century predecessors. Visitation evidence of the inadequacies of the new Church has been greeted by many with expressions of disbelief and a desire to reject such testimony as partial, unreliable, or distorted.[4] Whatever the merits of the subsequent debate on the 'success or failure' of the German Reformation, there is certainly enough evidence to show that all was not well in the Lutheran Church, even as it was being established in Germany from the late 1520s onwards. Moreover, the evidence provided by another substantial body of source material is that the new clergy, no more than the old, were less than adequate to the pastoral tasks facing them, indeed, were no better at the cure of souls than the discredited and dismantled pastoral system of the pre-Reformation Church. This essay presents only an initial discussion of a more extensive theme which has hitherto found too little attention in historical discussion, the relations between pastors and parish communities in Ernestine Saxony during the first two generations of the new Lutheran Church.[5] For reasons of space, I shall

[3] For the new image of the pastor, see the succinct statement by Heiko A. Oberman, *Masters of the Reformation* (Cambridge, 1981), p. 279.

[4] I refer here to the debate sparked off by Gerald Strauss's work on the 'success or failure' of the German Reformation, largely contained in his *Luther's House of Learning. Indoctrination of the Young in the German Reformation* (Baltimore, 1978). Critical views have been most strongly stated by James M. Kittelson, 'Successes and failures in the German Reformation. The Report from Strasbourg', *ARG*, pp. 75; and 'Visitations and Popular Religious Culture: Further Reports from Strasbourg' in Kyle C. Sessions and Phillip N. Bebb, eds, *Pietas et Societas. New Trends in Reformation Social History* (Kirksville, Miss., 1985), pp. 89–101. However, even sympathetic responses have raised similar critical comments: see Mark U. Edwards, 'Lutheran Pedagogy in Reformation Germany', *History of Education Quarterly*, 21 (1981), pp. 471–7.

[5] I have already touched some of these issues in a broader context in 'Anticlericalism and the German Reformation', *Popular Culture and Popular Movements in Reformation Germany* (London, 1987), pp. 243–56, esp. pp. 252–6, using source materials from Württenberg. Here I shall rely on archival material from Lutheran Saxony in the first two generations of the institutional-ization of the Reform. I have used from the Staatsarchiv Weimar, Ernestinisches Gesamtarchiv the inventories Reg. L1 (Pfarrbestallungen, Pfarrangelegenheiten), concerned

discuss this issue in terms of a few striking case-studies, although these were certainly not unrepresentative, nor by any means merely 'scandals' or isolated, unique events.

II

In April 1564, the entire parish community of Ringleben, north of Erfurt, addressed to the Duke of Saxony, Johann Friedrich II, a letter of complaint against their pastor, Phillip Schmidt. Schmidt had exercised the cure of souls in their parish for eight years, they wrote, and during that time had been so irascible and troublesome that their patience with him was finally at an end. He was negligent in the exercise of his office, he denied his parishioners access to the sacraments, subjected them to anger, scorn, and abuse (as did his wife), and showed little interest in whether he remained their pastor or not. He had held no weekday catechism classes for the past eight years, and when he did so on Sundays, he treated the children so coarsely and abusively that they were now afraid to attend. He prevented parishioners who presented children for baptism from making free choice of godparents. He gave preference to his own children and servants, for example, by giving them catechism lessons additional to those offered to other children and by always asking them to respond first, so making the other children feel inferior. Similarly, he allowed his daughter and his servants to go to confession at another parish, and allowed them to take Communion at home. He was unsympathetic in the confessional, easily moved to anger and reproof, and offered little by way of compassion or friendly instruction. Moreover, anyone wanting to confess outside the set times could approach him only through the churchwarden, with the result that they were often unable to confess in time to receive the Sacrament on the following Sunday and had to wait for eight days or more to receive it. Such matters deterred his parishioners from both confession and the Lord's Supper. He also insisted in putting unnecessary doctrinal questions during confession, demanding precise answers on five main articles of faith, confession, and the Lord's Supper before he would give absolution. Schmidt had even refused the Sacrament

---

with appointment and dismissals of pastors; Reg. Ii (Visitationsakten), concerned with special visitations and investigations of parish affairs apart from the more extensive general visitations; and some material from Reg. N (Religionssachen). A fuller discussion of this material will be presented in a chapter on the institutionalization of the Reformation in a wider work on the Reformation movements in Germany.

to a poor oil-miller, sending him away with the comment that he stank and that he could not bear his smell; indeed, when the oil-miller was ill, the pastor refused to take him the Sacrament, so that he died without consolation; and he had done the same to others. Finally, they listed a number of secular grievances: he refused to pay his share of grain to support the village cowherd, he used spiritual sanctions against those with whom he had secular disputes, and he left his tithe uncollected for several years, in order to demand payment in years when the prices rose. (It would seem that he thus acquired a considerable quantity of grain at times when he could most profit from rising prices, and correspondingly deprived the farmers of their own profits.)[6]

There are always two sides to every such story, and Phillip Schmidt spared no effort in defence of his office and the honour of his wife and children, covering some forty sides of paper with his reply. Much of his rebuttal of the charges against him pointed, as he saw it, to the religious laxity of his parishioners. It was impossible, he said, to hold weekday catechism classes, for he had tried it nine years before and found that the children would not attend — in fact, under the poor example of their parents, the children were simply lazy. He asked his own children questions on the catechism first in order to inspire the others by their example, but the village children lacked discipline, and when he questioned them on what they had learned, they merely fled from the church. Indeed, none of them had attended his lessons for the past three months. Their parents were over-sensitive to criticism of their children and had inculcated no discipline in their offspring. The matter of denying parishioners free choice of godparents arose, he claimed, because he would not allow persons to stand at baptism who had not confessed or taken Communion, and some of those he barred on these grounds had not done so for periods of between five and nine years. That his daughter and servants confessed outside the village was merely a matter of discretion, for both he and they did not want it to be thought that they were treated more leniently because they were members of his household. His behaviour in the confessional he explained in terms of the distinction he drew between repentant sinners and those unwilling to mend their ways, who deserved reproof. He had refused confession and the Lord's Supper to the oil-miller because he did not know the man, who mixed with Jews, so that it was unclear to Schmidt whether he was a Christian or a heathen. The man's death had occurred some considerable time after the pastor's

---

[6] Staatsarchiv (hereafter SA) Weimar Reg. L1 670, fols 1–3.

refusal of the sacraments, and he had then been living and mixing with Jews for some time, so that Schmidt felt justified in his assumption that he was no Christian. If his sermons were abusive and scolding, this was because he reproved his flock as a Christian preacher should. Other accusations he denied or dismissed as trivialities.

Schmidt did not omit to add his own list of grievances against the parish community. They insisted that he pay in grain for the services of the cowherd, but this was something completely new and unprecedented. On the other hand, his liturgical fees (*Opfergeld*) were never paid in full, and he virtually had to go around and beg for his tithes to be paid. His parish fields had been encroached upon, and the parish meadows almost halved in size. His parsonage was dilapidated, and he was desperately short of firewood. There was a disused vicarage belonging to the parish, for no vicar had been appointed for some time, but he was not allowed to make use of it, its garden, or its attached land. He had tried to obtain a copy of the parish register throughout the entire nine years of his incumbency, without success. Indeed, the real cause of the complaint against him, Schmidt claimed, was his demand for payment of arrears of tithes and *Opfergeld*. The hostility against him was caused by the old mayor, who had himself paid no *Opfergeld* for nine years. He also faced an extortionate demand by the community, which had given him on his arrival, as he thought, a free grant of three florins to help him settle in; now it was said that this was a loan, and the parish demanded repayment. Similarly, the demand that he pay the cowherd was a form of coercion, for they had prohibited him from having his cattle herded with the other parish cattle on pain of a five-schilling fine.[7]

If one were to read either document without being aware of the other, both sides would appear to have had valid grounds for complaint. The pastor apparently found himself confronted with religious laxity in a community unwilling to provide the necessary minimum for his upkeep. The community found themselves saddled with an irascible, scolding, almost tyrannical figure, who was far from the ideal pastor. We shall see later that both views were in some sense right, merely two sides of the same coin. However, we know enough about Phillip Schmidt's career to be able to say that the parish community may have had the better of the argument. Schmidt belonged to the first generation of Evangelical preachers, stating in 1564 that he had been preaching the Gospel for forty years, that is, since 1524.[8] He had been appointed to Rinkleben in 1555,

[7] SA Weimar Reg. L1 670, fols 5–25.
[8] Ibid., fol. 5r.

when the previous pastor became too infirm to continue with his duties. Prior to that he had been pastor in Leubingen, but had preached two trial sermons to the Rinkleben community, who found him pleasant enough to give their approval of the appointment.[9] That all might not go well was signalled only by the existence of a dispute between the pastor's son, who was a mercenary, and the son of a farmer in the district, which could have developed into a costly lawsuit or even a feud. Although they had been warned that any feud might also be directed against their new pastor and perhaps against themselves, and Schmidt himself called their attention to it, the community was not unduly worried by this fact, and merely sought assurances of adequate protection from the Duke of Saxony.[10]

They might have been more concerned had they known about the troubles Schmidt had experienced in a previous appointment, in 1541, when he was pastor to the small Thuringian town of Kahla. Throughout his appointment there, he had been almost continuously in dispute with the town council, and this had come to a head at the end of February that year, provoking the intervention of a visitation commission.[11] Two major issues emerged, one ecclesiastical, the other secular. A woman of the town had performed emergency baptism on her sickly child, as was permissible, and when she brought the child to church for a further baptism, Schmidt told the officiating clergyman of the emergency baptism, so that the child was only blessed to the accompaniment of prayers. This was wholly correct, although it clearly constituted a disappointment for the mother and perhaps the family. Baptism was a pre-eminently social occasion, on which the family displayed its status and connections through the choice of godparents, and through the extensive feasting that followed, sometimes lasting for several days. The refusal of the clergy to perform even a conditional baptismal ceremony may well have spoiled the occasion for the family concerned. Schmidt had complicated the matter, however, by casting a slur on the woman and implying that she had not baptized the child properly at all; indeed, he had demanded that she be gaoled. This aroused anger in the community, who saw the pastor as attempting to ease his own conscience by oppressing the unfortunate woman.[12] The secular dispute foreshadowed that of 1564 and concerned Schmidt's reluctance to pay his grain fees for the services of the community cowherd. When

[9] SA Weimar Reg. 671, fol. 1.
[10] Ibid.
[11] SA Weimar Reg. Ii 1499, fols 3–4.
[12] Ibid., fols 21–2, letter of complaint of Hans Glorius, citizen of Kahla, to the Elector John Frederick, 20 August 1541.

presenting his payment on 28 February of that year, he had turned up at the town council's measuring office bearing his own measure, with which he insisted on measuring out the grain, publicly asserting that the town council's official measure was too large and inaccurate.[13] This was an act of insubordination and potential sedition for which he was later to be imprisoned, but in the meantime the visitors recommended that he be dismissed from his post and transferred as far away as possible from the district, perhaps to the Saxon territories in Franconia or the Vogtland.[14]

How quickly Schmidt dissipated the goodwill with which he was greeted on his arrival in Rinkleben in 1555 is shown by a bitter dispute that arose in 1557 between him and the tax-official of Rinkleben, Johann Kunhold.[15] The dispute broke out in July that year, as Kunhold's cowherd was taken ill. After lying in a sick-bed in the tax-official's quarters for some days, the cowherd took a turn for the worse, and it was clear that he was dying. He was immediately carried home, and on Saturday 31 July the pastor was called upon to administer the Sacrament. Schmidt claimed that he was unable to do so, as the cowherd had already lost consciousness when he arrived, but when the tax-official then asked him to prepare the deceased for Christian burial on the Sunday, the pastor refused. Since the cowherd had died unshriven, and had not attended sermons regularly, nor received the Sacrament for many years before his death, Schmidt argued that he should be buried silently in the churchyard and that no public prayers be said for him from the pulpit.

The next day, as the bell tolled for the sermon, Kunhold had the cowherd's body carried outside and laid before the pastor's door. Schmidt preached that day on the *asinina sepultura* which the prophets threatened would befall the godless, but the body was allowed to lie there the entire day, until (as Schmidt put it) Kunhold thought he had revenged himself sufficiently, after which the village mayor had him buried quietly in the churchyard. This incident provoked the tax-official to an outburst of rage against the pastor, and he took further revenge on the Monday by riding repeatedly through the pastor's crops, and having his servants drive geese through his barley on the Tuesday. On Sunday 15 August Kunhold appeared drunk and armed before the pastor's house, accompanied by two cronies, and threatened him in life and limb. A few days later, he again appeared armed and drunk before the pastor's house and challenged him

---

[13] Ibid., fols 23ff.
[14] Ibid., fol. 4v.
[15] The following discussion of the dispute is based on SA Weimar Reg. Ll 669.

to come out or get a good hiding. By 21 August the pastor was so much in fear of his life that he went into hiding and sent off a petition to the Duke of Saxony seeking protection for himself, his family and property.

The enmity between pastor and tax-official had in fact been building up for some time, and the incident of the cowherd had merely caused a long-simmering conflict to boil over. The previous October Kunhold had abused Schmidt in an inn in the nearby village of Mittelhausen; on 8 March he had abused the pastor before all the guests at a dinner party; on Whit Sunday Kunhold had ordered the parish community that they should offer neither the pastor nor his cantor food or drink following the sermon, so that the pair were obliged to go around like beggars seeking a meal, and on Sunday 27 May the tax-official had actually locked the church, so that the pastor was unable to preach at all. Moreover, Kunhold had won the village officials over to his side, and expressly stated that his intention was to have Schmidt dismissed. Kunhold naturally denied all these accusations, and advanced a few of his own, accusing the pastor of drunken and violent behaviour, and of challenging the tax-official's authority by claiming that he had forged letters allegedly sent by Duke of Saxony.

The degree of bitterness in the dispute warranted a major intervention by the ecclesiastical and secular authorities, and the district superintendent and tax-official from Weimar were sent to hold a public hearing in Rinkleben on 16 September. This hearing caused a series of communal grievances against Schmidt to come tumbling out. It was said that he refused to hold sermons on days other than Sundays, he was surly with his parishioners, and sent many away without the Sacrament, telling them to come back when they knew their doctrine better and could give better replies. Several witnesses supported one of Kunhold's accusations, testifying that the pastor and his son had beaten a small boy. It is clear from the testimony of several witnesses that Kunhold had tried to intimidate Schmidt, but no evidence was offered to support some of the pastor's charges. The community supported the pastor against the claim that he was often drunk at baptisms and had abused the tax-official on such an occasion. Although testimony was given that he had abused Kunhold at a baptism, the community said that the pastor was not at baptism or in the tavern very often—a statement which could be read in a negative as much as a positive sense, for it showed Schmidt's refusal to join in village sociability.

The incident with the cowherd revealed an interesting divergence of viewpoint. Schmidt was convinced that the man was godless, because he had herded cattle on Sundays during the sermon and had not taken the Sacrament, offering these as the grounds for refusing him a proper burial. The community reported differently: the cowherd went regularly to sermons in winter, when he was not prevented by his work; he had not taken the Sacrament from the present pastor, who had been there scarcely six months before he developed his enmity against the cowherd, but he had received it from the previous pastor. More damagingly for Schmidt, the cowherd's wife testified that he had been conscious when Schmidt arrived, and when he was asked if he wished to confess and receive the Sacrament, he was silent at first, but then had answered weakly 'yes'. He died shortly thereafter, but according to her testimony, Schmidt had unchristianly refused him the Sacrament.

There is no evidence as to how the dispute of 1557 was resolved, although by 1564 Kunhold was no longer in office. Schmidt did not lose his post, as he had in 1541, but the seeds of the division between himself and the parish community had been sown and were sprouting even then, so that the dispute of 1564 was a culmination of long-standing ill will. Indeed, it seems in retrospect as though the pastor had been at loggerheads with his parishioners throughout the entire nine years of his incumbency. However, he was not so fortunate in his second major dispute at Rinkleben, for too much evidence had accumulated of unpastoral behaviour. Perhaps the most damning was that adduced by the investigating district superintendent and official of Weimar that Schmidt had applied spiritual coercion to those with whom he stood in personal dispute. He had refused the Sacrament to a man who threw a stone into his farmyard, as he did to another who had called him a thief, and he had rejected a baker as a fit godparent because the man had once spoiled Schmidt's bread. He had asked improper questions in the confessional, quizzing Lorenz Luckhart's wife so much about sorcery with milk that she refused to confess to him for a whole year out of fear. He had then impertinently asked her if the cause of her refraining from confession was perhaps that she had been pregnant (so implying either an illicit pregnancy or else that she had procured an abortion).[16]

That Schmidt stuck to his principles as he understood them is shown by the accusation that he refused the Sacrament to the cowherd Simon Weissleder for not knowing the Cathechism and for herding cattle when

---

[16] SA Weimar Reg. Ll 670, fols 29–34, report of the Superintendent of Weimar, Christoph Helmerich, and the tax-official of Weimar, Jorg Wolrab, 7 June 1564, esp. fols 29–31 on the cases mentioned.

he should have been in church.[17] In ecclesiastical terms, he was also probably correct when he refused the Sacrament to Paul Lamprecht because he would not reconcile his enmity with his son-in-law for secretly marrying Lamprecht's daughter. However, this appeared in the list of seventeen articles against him on which his dismissal hearing was based. The dismissal hearing seems to have been a foregone conclusion, for the two district officials wrote that they wished to stage a formal hearing such that the pastor could not claim that he had been improperly dismissed, and when it was held in June 1557, it was done in the presence of an eight-man deputation from the parish community. Schmidt wished to drag the affair out, by taking out a suit for unfair dismissal, but the district officials were determined that he had to go, and adduced as conclusive evidence that he had held only one sermon since Whitsun (almost certainly because he had been so heavily engaged in preparing a case for his defence!). The final decision was taken in the Saxon chancellery, where a secretary merely inscribed the laconic remark on the back of the file: 'On this basis the pastor is to be dismissed and another appointed in his place.'[18] There was a covert hint of old scores being settled in Phillip Schmidt's fate, for the district official of Weimar who conducted the investigation was Jorg Wolrab, who had been an assistant to Johann Kunhold in 1557, and who had given testimony on his behalf.[19]

III

Phillip Schmidt may have been an unusually difficult man, and he may have been involved in more bitter disputes during his long career than most Saxon pastors. However, many of the issues which arose in those disputes were certainly typical, and reveal the complex questions that have to be considered when assessing the problems of pastoral care. Some were structural problems inherent in the very nature, government, and financing of the Saxon Church. Rural pastors were poorly paid, for their incomes depended on the often meagre wealth of the parish lands and the

[17] SA Weimar Reg. Ll 670, fol. 30.
[18] Ibid., fols 40–2 (the 17 articles); fols 37–8 (Jorg Wolrab to Johann Rudloff, Secretary in the Saxon Chancellery, 16 June 1564); the dorsal note: 'dorauf soll den Pfarrer endturlauben und ein ander an sein stadt verordnent worden', fol. 38v.
[19] Sa Weimar Reg. Ll 669, fols 38–46 *passim*, for Wolrab's testimony, where he consistently backed Kunhold's version of events. It is also significant that Wolrab was related by marriage to Johann Rudloff, Saxon Chancellery Secretary, whom he addressed in correspondence as 'mein grosgunstiger Schwager': Reg. Ll 670, fol. 37r.

feudal dues assigned by pre-Reformation founders and donors. The restructuring of the old Church consequent on the removal of a system based on salvation by works — mass-priests, mass-foundations, pious foundations and annuities, monastic institutions and their investments and properties— merely reorganized existing fixed incomes. It thus removed traditional sources of extra income, without creating any new ones.[20]

Once the first few general visitations had redistributed monastic revenues and incomes for the support of the parishes and the parish clergy, the Saxon Church found itself squeezed between the iron pincers of fixed incomes and rising prices. Fixed capital assets, such as parish and church buildings, began to decay, falling quickly into such disrepair that the costs of maintaining them became almost prohibitive, for neither pastor nor parishioners had the surplus to devote to this purpose. Thus there were numerous complaints by pastors about the dilapidated condition of their dwellings, and they resented the apparent indifference of their flocks to their shabby living conditions. The new system of lay control of the church meant that the pastors regarded the upkeep of such buildings as the responsibility of the parish community or even of the prince, to whom numerous appeals were made for subsidies. Villages comprised largely of middling to small farmers were no more able than their pastors to raise such capital sums, and as a means to this end they tended to eye such assets as parish lands or properties, from which the pastor drew his incomes. The two sides of the problem can be seen as early as 1534, when the parish comprised of the three villages of Behlitz, Bressen, and Ochelnitz complained of the innovatory demands of their pastor, who insisted that they rebuild his residence and other buildings attached to it, repair his fences, and purchase the necessary timber. The pastor defended himself by pointing out that the residence and its outbuildings were dilapidated, and that cattle did great damage everywhere because of the status of the fences.[21] This explains much of the conflict in Rinkleben around the vacant vicar's residence. The parish could not afford to appoint a vicar alongside its pastor, and regarded the vicarage and its attached property as a source of revenue for the upkeep of

---

[20] On the problems of pastors' salaries see the pioneering study by Susan Karant-Nunn, *Luther's Pastors: the Reformation in the Ernestine Countryside* = *Transactions of the American Philosophical Society*, 69, pt 8 (Philadelphia, 1979), pp. 38–52.

[21] SA Weimar Reg. Ii 771. I have been unable to locate the precise position of these villages on a modern map; Bressen may be Bresen, south-west of Altenburg.

church fabric. For the pastor, it was a way of supplementing his meagre income.

Similar economic issues were involved in the vexed question of firewood. The sixteenth century faced a growing shortage of timber for fuel and building, aggravated by rising population and the extension in areas such as Thuringia of charcoaling and smelting for the booming fine-metal industry. Village pastors often had the use of a parish wood, from which they could cut timber for building or fuel, although there were occasions on which the pastors used this asset wastefully, cutting timber for sale to supplement their incomes, and so laying waste a natural resource of the parish. Often, however, pastors were without wood for fuel or building, and would certainly have severely depleted already thin incomes by having to purchase it on the open market. The princes of Saxony were aware of the problem and tried to alleviate it in two ways, by grants of timber from ducal forests, and by stipulating that parishioners should either provide fuel for their pastors, or at least transport it for them free of charge. Conflicts over such matters became a continual source of enmity between villagers and pastors, where both sides of the dispute felt aggrieved and cheated of a natural right.[22] The issue was succinctly summed up in 1551, when the pastor of Burkersdorf, in the district of Weida, petitioned Johann Friedrich II for a grant of timber, and was allowed to receive eight *Klafter* annually from woods belonging to the parish of Siefersdorf some three kilometres away.[23] The community of Siefersdorf protested that they needed this timber to repair their own village church, and the patch of trees was not so great that it could support such demands on it: in eight to ten years, it would be completely bare. They could not provide the timber necessary to repair the roof and windows of their church from their own properties, and were expected in addition to supply firewood to their own pastor.[24]

A similar source of conflict arose over the tithe, which had formed a major plank of peasant grievances during the Peasants' War of 1524–6. That massive rebellion achieved little by way of alleviation of the tithe,

---

[22] See, for example, SA Weimar Reg. Ll 547, two letters by the pastor of Mellingen, Christoph Etzell, complaining in very bitter terms about the false accusations of despoiling the parish woods levelled at him by his parishioners, 17 and 19 October 1568.

[23] The *Klafter* was originally a measure of length, roughly the length measured by an adult male with outstretched arms. It was first used as a square measure for a stack of wood in Augsburg in 1477: see J. and W. Grimm, *Deutsches Wörterbuch* (Leipzig, 1854–1954), 5, col. 903, although there were numerous local and regional variations in the quantity of timber encompassed by the term.

[24] SA Weimar Reg. Ii 2332.

88

which still contributed the greater part of clerical incomes. It continued as a rankling source of peasant grievance, and provided an ongoing occasion for conflict, with numerous disputes over the mode and manner of its collection. Pastors had to cope with the reluctance of their parishioners to supply it, or to supply it at times when it might be put to best use by realizing its market value. It is not surprising that someone such as Phillip Schmidt could be tempted into a piece of sharp practice, in which he perhaps sought to maximize his return. That so much of a pastor's income was supplied in *naturalia* was a source of ongoing anxiety in the struggle to maintain an adequate standard of living. When a community decided to spread its own costs, for example, by demanding that the pastor share the burden of paying the community cowherd by supplying a fixed amount of grain annually, it could fall as a hammer-blow to attempts to make ends meet. Similarly, it could lead to disputes about measuring out the grain, for the variation of measures in the Saxon-Thuringian area was considerable.[25]

A further feature of the economic situation of these first- and second-generation Lutheran clergymen, which Phillip Schmidt seems to exemplify as an extreme case, has also to be considered. That the parish clergy could marry and found families was a mixed blessing, for it added considerably to their economic woes. The sources do not tell us his age, but Schmidt must have been at least sixty by 1564, when he was still supporting children young enough to attend catechism classes. The desperation felt by men on small incomes providing for large families, many of them young children, communicates itself in the many petitions for subsidies and improvement of sources of income.[26] The visitors of 1555 in Ernestine Saxony were aware of this as a major problem; having investigated the incomes of all the pastors in the Duchy, they found that many were still inadequately provided for. The common income was fifty gulden per annum, or a little more, but with this amount it was not possible to support many children or to keep servants. Even with the arable land attached to many parishes, incomes were scarcely adequate, and the visitors signalled a new problem, in that many aged and infirm pastors would soon be forced to retire. It was just that they should receive a pension, but these could hardly be afforded from existing parish

---

[25] Cf. SA Weimar Reg. Ll 15, where the pastor of Auma complained in 1535 of several villages paying him his tithe according to the measure from Neustadt on the Orla rather than the Auma measure. On the general problems of disputes over measures and measuring see Witold Kula, *Measures and Men* (Princeton, 1986).

[26] These are preserved in SA Weimar Reg. Ii in very substantial numbers.

incomes. There was a similar problem with the widows and children of deceased pastors, who were often forced to leave the parish residence within four weeks of the pastor's death, and certainly before the arrival of a successor, although they may have had no store of supplies to see them through the remainder of the year. They too had a right to adequate support.[27]

To help overcome this problem, the Saxon visitors decided quite early to retain payment for liturgical services, in the form of a per capita fee—*Opfergeld*—of one new penny paid each quarter-day. Parish communities resented this charge bitterly, since payment for spiritual services had been a major grievance against the papal system. Yet many pastors still felt this was an inadequate supplement, and one senses an unbridgeable gulf which can only have soured pastoral relationships.[28] Stipends for baptisms and burials added to the sense of grievance, and the parallel with the demands of the papacy was certainly driven home when some communities began to regard it as virtually a tax for receiving the Lord's Supper.[29] The reorganization of the Church in the Ernestine lands, in consequence of the defeat of the Elector Johann Friedrich I in the Schmalkaldic War, probably made such fees indispensable, but they provoked a chorus of discontent from parish communities in the years following 1549.[30] Johann Friedrich II found himself forced into a defensive justification of the fees, pointing out how much had been paid out under the papacy to mass-priests and mendicants, insisting that it was perfectly right for communities to pay to support their pastors, and that this had been approved by numerous eminent theologians from Luther onwards.[31]

Villagers seemed little inclined to accept such arguments, particularly where they had to struggle themselves to maintain an adequate level of subsistence. The community of Neunhofen (near Neustadt, on the Orla) wrote in 1559 that they were unable to pay such fees (which were now euphemistically called 'parish dues' or *Pfarrecht*) because of their poverty.

---

[27] SA Weimar Reg. Ii 2487, Bericht der Visitatoren, 4 March 1555, fol. 4v.

[28] Both sides of the case were put in the 1534 conflict between the communities of Behlitz, Bressen, and Ochelnitz and their pastor: SA Weimar Reg. Ii 771.

[29] SA Weimar Reg. Ii 856, complaints of the village of Plotten against their pastor, 1534; see also the 1549 complaint of the town council of Creutzburg: 'von yder person die zum heilig hochwirdig Sacrament des altars gegangen oder gehen iii d. alle weichfasten zu geben': SA Weimar Reg. Ll 111, fol. 13.

[30] See, for example, the 1549 complaint of the town council of Creutzberg to Johann Friedich I, SA Weimar Reg. Ll 111, fols 13, 15, where it is condemned as an innovation.

[31] SA Weimar Reg. Ii 2334, Johann Friedrich II to the tax-official of Arnshaug, 5 May 1551, in reply to a complaint from the peasants of Zwakau.

They and their children had to work day and night at spinning and other forms of by-employment in order to make ends meet. Their children were being kept from the Sacrament because they could not pay the *Pfarrecht*, yet the pastor already had an adequate income from the sixty bushels (*Scheffel*) of grain he received annually.[32] This became a particularly sensitive grievance with villages incorporated into a larger parish as a means of providing an adequate overall income for the pastor, sometimes resulting in the loss of their parish autonomy. The community of Katherinen (on the Saale, near Rudolstadt) complained in 1551 about the unjust manner in which their pastor had appropriated grain grown on communal arable, but behind this complaint lay resentment at recent parish reorganization. In an earlier visitation Katherinen had lost full parish status and been annexed to the parish of Schada. The parish incomes from Katherinen were henceforth diverted to support the pastor of Schada, and the chaplain from Schada was given the former parish residence for his vicarage.[33] The loss of status and the affront to communal pride led the community of Katherinen to regard the arable from which the new pastor drew income as communal property to which he had no right. There were also anomalies in the amalgamation of parishes and parish incomes which further complicated this problem. Thus the community of Neuenhofen complained that the village of Lausnitz paid nothing for *Pfarrecht*, nor anything towards the repair of the parish buildings, while the village of Dobra complained that they had to pay *Opfergeld* to the pastor of Neuenhofen, although they received no cure of souls from him, and actually had their own pastor.[34]

Such villages were quick to complain about inadequate cure of souls, to withhold payment of the pastor's income, and finally to develop antipathy towards their pastor. A particularly difficult conflict developed in 1552–3 between two villages, Mennsdorf and Paitzdorf, not far from Ronneberg. In 1534 the visitors separated Mennsdorf from the parish of Nobdenitz, where the pastor was an irreconcilable papist, and attached it to the parish of Paitzdorf, the income previously paid to Nobdenitz being diverted to

---

[32] SA Weimar Reg. Ll 597.
[33] SA Weimar Reg. Ii 2325. Katherinen is today Catherinau, on the Saale, east of Rudolstadt, Schada is now Langenschade, just south of Catherinau.
[34] SA Weimar Reg. Ll 597 (Neuenhofen's complaint against Lausnitz, 1559); Reg. Ii 1458 (Dobra's complaint against the pastor of Neunhofen, 1540). I have been unable to locate on a modern map any village called Dobra in the vicinity of Neuenhofen and Lausnitz. It can hardly be the Dobra south-west of Altenburg but 45 km. to the north-east of Neunhofen. Dreba, which lies 8 km. to the south of Neuenhofen, is more likely.

the new pastor. By 1552 the pastor was complaining of non-payment of dues from Mennsdorf, and the parishioners of Paitzdorf backed him in his complaint. He was expected to preach in Mennsdorf once a week, and to hold a Sunday sermon and distribute the Sacrament there every third Sunday. This was a great burden to him and his home parish, since Mennsdorf contained only sixteen households, and he received from them only one new schock and nothing in grain. Both the pastor and the community of Paitzdorf regarded the villagers of Mennsdorf as free riders, who paid their dues from parish properties and contributed nothing themselves other than their meagre liturgical fees. The parish was poor, its residence dilapidated, its fences in poor repair, and its pastor received little for his support in grain or firewood. A ducal commission recognized the justice of the pastor's complaint—indeed, they mentioned that he had handed in his notice because he was unable to support himself and his family on the parish incomes, which amounted to only fifteen gulden from the Paitzdorf community. They also recognized that it would be impossible to find a competent successor willing to take on the incumbency at that level of pay. Their solution was to increase by one-third the fees paid by Mennsdorf, and to command them to share with Paitzdorf the cost of putting the pastor's residence into a state of good repair. It was then the turn of the villagers of Mennsdorf to plead poverty when they learned that their share of the rebuilding costs amounted to twenty-three gulden. They turned to the local nobility for support, to their immediate overlord, the lord of Wildenfels, and seem to have continued to withhold payment of dues to their pastor. The pastor retaliated by withholding religious services, and the situation remained deadlocked until late in 1555, when the Ernestine officials seemed to wash their hands of the whole problem by referring it to the lord of Wildenfels as holder of the lordship of Ronneberg, and telling him flatly that it should be settled by his territorial prince, Elector Moritz of Saxony![35]

Underlying these disputes was a contractual view of the supply of religious services. Parishioners provided for the upkeep of their pastor, and he provided the relevant cure of souls in a kind of tacit agreement that if he did not do so, he would not be paid. This tacit contract seems to have been regarded by villagers as a basic religious right, and could easily lead to conflicts of the kind that were experienced by Phillip Schmidt when a pastor chose for other reasons to withhold his spiritual services. This was rarely a blanket refusal, as happened in Mennsdorf and frequently under

[35] SA Weimar Reg. Ii 2353.

the old Church; it usually took the form of denying certain parishioners access to the Sacraments, often for moral or disciplinary reasons. Continual offenders, unrepentant sinners, those who stubbornly refused to attend Sunday sermons or who took the Sacrament infrequently were all likely candidates for exclusion from the Sacrament unless they showed genuine signs of amendment. However, it was often difficult to find a mean between what the pastor saw as the necessary firmness of a good shepherd anxious to inculcate spiritual discipline in his flock and what his parishioners perceived as their undeniable spiritual rights.

Conflicts arose in a number of well-defined circumstances: for example, when a parishioner feared he or she was in danger of death, as often occurred in times of plague, or when a woman was about to give birth. It was expected that the pastor should provide the Sacrament automatically on such occasions, as part of his duty in the cure of souls. As in the case of Phillip Schmidt, a pastor could be reluctant to do so if he thought the person desiring the Sacrament was not genuinely repentant. Thus in 1546 a dispute broke out between the Superintendent of Weida and the pastor of Veitsberg and Cronschwitz about how to treat those who had lived a dissolute life, but who wished to take the Sacrament in time of plague. It was accepted that they should renounce their vices, give plausible signs of their conversion, and provide testimony of prayer and adherence to the Christian faith. However, the pastor of Veitsberg and Cronschwitz believed that such persons should be allowed to receive only absolution after they had confessed their sins, but not to partake of the 'Sacrament of the Body and Blood of Christ'. The Superintendent asserted that this was unscriptural and would also give great scandal in the district.[36]

This seems an impeccable Lutheran judgement, but the matter was often not quite so simple. In 1559 Johann Friedrich II ordered an investigation into the behaviour of the pastor of Lobeda, a farm town south of Jena, who was suspended for refusing the Sacraments to a dying farm-hand. The pastor claimed that the man had not known the basics of the Christian faith, nor was he willing to learn them after repeated admonition by the pastor and others. He would not confess that he was a sinner according to the Ten Commandments, he did not know who his Saviour was, he denied both the resurrection of the dead and eternal life, and he showed no understanding of the Sacrament. He had been given an opportunity of instruction to remedy his unbelief, but chose not to avail

[36] SA Weimar Reg. N676, fol. 6.

himself of it. The churchwarden of Lobeda confirmed this account, and the Superintendent of Jena fully supported the pastor, requesting that his suspension from office be lifted.[37]

The testimony of the farm-hand's relatives revealed, however, that the issue was not quite so clear-cut. One brother, Michel Knabe, confirmed that the farm-hand had indeed wanted to have nothing to do with the pastor until he became ill; another, Anthonius, that he did not know the five principal articles of faith, nor keep the Ten Commandments nor accept that he was a sinner. However, a third brother, Ulrich, testified that when asked if he kept the Ten Commandments, he had replied 'yes'. When asked by the pastor where he was going when he died, and where he would finally end up, he had replied that he was going to the church-yard, but did not know where he would end up. If this hardly constituted a denial of eternal life, as the pastor claimed, the further testimony of Anthonius Knabe casts doubt on the pastor's assessment of the man's knowledge of the Sacrament. Anthonius testified that when he was asked about the Sacrament, his brother had said only that he wished to receive the Body of the Lord. As the pastor was about to leave, the farm-hand called him back and asked him to 'leave it there'; the pastor turned back towards him and asked what he should leave there, to which the man replied: 'Our Lord God, please' (*Ja, unsern Herrgott*). The old Catholic formulation *unserer Herrgott*, with its implication of the Real Presence, may have angered the pastor, who replied that 'he would not take Him away from him, but he could not administer the Sacrament to him.'[38]

There was much scope in such cases for divergence between the pastor's and the lay person's interpretation of the pastoral obligation to provide consolation, especially when it might revolve round understanding of doctrine. The same problem could arise about the admission of godparents to baptism. The pastor of Lobeda was again involved in 1558 in an investigation into his practice of interrogating intending godparents before allowing them to enter the church for the baptismal ceremony. He would explain to them the significance of baptism for personal salvation and tell them that it was his custom to admit no one who lived in discord or gave public scandal, for example, by adultery, whoring, theft, usury, greed, drunkenness, gluttony, and so on, asking them if they were guilty of such failings. In his explanation of this practice, the pastor commented that he found it necessary only with those whom he did not know, or who

---

[37] SA Weimar Reg. Ll 483, fols 1–2.
[38] Ibid., fol. 3.

attended sermons or the Sacraments irregularly, and cited Luther to justify quizzing such folk about doctrine as well as morals, for no one should be admitted as godparent who did not know Christian doctrine. He claimed that he did not go as far as he might had he followed Luther's injunctions to the letter, for he did not pursue the matter of doctrine too closely. None the less, he had certainly given offence to a local nobleman, who resented the aspersions against the sponsors chosen for his child's baptism by even the minimal enquiries about upright moral life.[39]

Even allowing that some pastors may have been as difficult as Phillip Schmidt, men of puritanical disposition or given to over-much scolding, there was still likely to have been a gap between lay expectations and clerical standards, which expressed itself through conflicts such as those in Lobeda or Rinkleben. The potential for conflict was complicated by a further matter, the extent to which the pastor's injunctions accorded with the example he himself set his parishioners. It is striking how often such disputes led to charges that the pastors themselves were drunkards, gamblers, or womanizers—in effect, they were accused of hypocrisy. In some cases these may have been slanderous attempts to deflect the pastor's justified criticisms of the failings of his flock, part of the way in which village power-games were fought out,[40] but in many cases the charges proved only too true. Parishioners were not only demanding that their pastors practise what they preached—there are sometimes traces of an older heretical view, from papal times, that a sinful priest could not validly perform his priestly duties. In a Lutheran context, this seemed to revolve round the demand that those persons in enmity be reconciled before they could be admitted to the Sacrament. Saxon pastors seemed so often to be in enmity with their parishioners, above all for economic reasons, that they scarcely seemed capable of performing their Evangelical role of reconciling hatred and administering the Sacrament of unity.

In such circumstances parish communities were also liable to fall back on the fundamentals of their Evangelical belief, to their right to elect their own pastors. When the community of Rinkleben reached the end of their tether with Phillip Schmidt they resorted to the claim that he had been

---

[39] SA Weimar Reg. Ii 2698.
[40] David Sabean, *Power in the Blood. Popular Culture and Village Discourse in Early Modern Germany* (Cambridge, 1984) has very usefully opened up new dimensions of such village power-games. I have provided a case-study of the complexity of the rules in 'Sorcery, Superstition and Society: the Witch of Urach 1529' in *Popular Culture and Popular Movements in Reformation Germany* (London, 1987), pp. 257–76.

forced upon them against their will.[41] They seemed to mean by this (unless they had conveniently forgotten Schmidt's two trial sermons and their approval of him) that the proposal to call him had not originated from them, but that they had merely been asked to give their approval to someone else's choice. They now decided to assert this right strictly and literally in choosing as Schmidt's successor their twenty-six-year-old schoolmaster. They encountered firm opposition from the tax-official of Rinkleben, Jorg Wolrab, and from their district Superintendent, and the resulting conflict revealed that it was by no means merely the in-adequacies of pastors that provoked ill will in a parish community. The tax-official had his own axe to grind, and this consisted of supporting another candidate and insisting that the stubborn peasants not be allowed to get their own way, for they were merely acting out of recalcitrance and self-interest. They sought an inexperienced man in order to overawe him in disputes about incomes, and to avoid having to pay adequately for a schoolmaster. The petition in the name of the community was deceptive and resulted from the machinations of only a few self-interested persons. His clinching argument, designed to squash any official sympathy for the community's demand, was the peasants wanted to use their free will like the free Swiss![42]

Whatever the conflicts between tax-official and pastor, Jorg Wolrab and Phillip Schmidt agreed at least on their assessment of the peasant claim to the right to elect their own pastors. In responding to the argument that he had not been called by the community of Rinkleben, Schmidt retorted that 'they want to have the right of electing, calling, confirming and deposing their spiritual shepherd just as they do with their cowherd and gooseherd', and if given their heads they would like nothing better than a good drinking companion or a pious, antinomian 'honey-preacher'.[43] The issues touched in such exchanges began to have implications beyond mere matters of pastoral care, and for reasons of

---

[41] See their initial complaint of 20 April 1564, SA Weimar Reg. Ll 670, fol. 1r: 'wie wol ohne vocation und willen verordnet'.

[42] The documents of the discussion are in SA Weimar Reg. Ll 671, fols 5–14, and include three petitions from the community of Rinkleben dated 8, 11, and 17 June, and two letters from Wolrab dated 16 and 18 June, addressed respectively to Bartholomeus Rosinus, the District Superintendent of Weimar and to his brother-in-law, Rudloff, the secretary to the Saxon Chancellery. The quip about 'freywillisch als die freyen schweitzer' on fol. 9r is addressed to Rosinus.

[43] SA Weimar Reg. Ll 670, fol. 7v: 'sie wollen das ius eligendi, vocandi, confirmandi und deponendi eines seelhirten gleich wie sie es mit Iren kue und genssehirtenn haben und behalten wollen.'

space cannot be discussed here in further detail. However, there were numerous other disputes besides those mentioned above, which raised important matters of principle: for example, clashes between pastors and secular officials,[44] between pastor and pastor, or between pastor and chaplain or churchwarden, and not least of all the conflict provoked by the wives of the new clergy, who seem to have been as little liked or respected as the old priests' concubines.[45]

It is a common feature of many such conflicts in rural parishes that a trivial disagreement or a minor complaint often let loose a deeper reservoir of resentment and set off a chain reaction of dissension and bitterness that seemed to subvert the very basis of the cure of souls. In pointing to such matters, we have but scratched the surface of the problem of pastoral care in the first two generations of the Reformation Church. Many of them were the result of structural problems beyond the control of individual pastors or layfolk. Many were the result of the new power structure in the Church and its interface with the secular structures of power. Many other conflicts arose from a clash of conflicting expectations, not least in the case of baptism, where the social dimension of the sacrament conflicted with its doctrinal aspects. We need not ascribe blame to either side in these disputes, even in the case of controversial figures such as Phillip Schmidt, but we can certainly discern how easily the seeds of a new anticlericalism were sown, and how the new Church came to confront its own intractable problems of pastoral care. It is, perhaps, to this area that we might look in order to understand why the Reformation could appear more as a failure than as the unqualified success it was once thought to have been.

Clare College,
Cambridge

---

[44] That Phillip Schmidt was not the only quarrelsome pastor in the district is shown by a dispute that arose between the tax-official of Rinkleben, Johann Kunhold, and the pastor of Mittel-hausen, Simon Kiswetter, who accused Kunhold of slandering him in 1556. Kunhold's low opinion of pastors was not confined to Schmidt; according to Kiswetter, Kunhold sneered that all pastors were made from churchwardens. Kiswetter, in a letter of 19 October 1556, reported the incident to Schmidt, who expressed solidarity with his colleague through copious underlinings in the letter and the notes he wrote on the case, see SA Weimar Reg. Ll 580. It is clear from this file that the two pastors saw themselves as comrades-in-arms in the struggle to bring good morals and doctrine to the district.

[45] I have cited some evidence from Württemberg sources in 'Anticlericalism and the German Reformation' (see n. 5 above), but there is also abundant evidence of the same phenomenon in the Saxon sources.

PROTESTANT VENERATION OF MARY: LUTHER'S INTERPRETATION OF THE *MAGNIFICAT*

by GERHARD MÜLLER

ACCORDING to Protestant understanding, veneration of Mary is only permissible when it is based on Scripture. When such scriptural proof is given, it should neither be used polemically against other churches nor be dismissed on account of unbiblical influences and pressures: the Bible is, and remains, the one foundation for all Evangelical Christians. In the New Testament, Mary is mentioned in particular in the birth stories of Jesus, recorded in the Gospels of Matthew and Luke.[1] Beyond this, she appears only incidentally in the accounts of Jesus' ministry. Here a certain detachment from the activities of Jesus can be discerned.[2] None the less, in the Gospel of John, Mary is seen as standing under the Cross.[3] This, in turn, helps to explain how the veneration of Mary originally arose. At the same time, however, veneration of Mary remains a part of the veneration of Jesus, as the Lord of the Anointed God.[4]

An essential text in favour of the veneration of Mary is found in the first chapter of the Gospel of Luke. Here Mary is depicted as having sung a hymn of praise, which begins in the Latin version with the word *Magnificat*. In this hymn of praise, Mary said of herself: 'Behold, henceforth all generations will call me blessed.'[5] This can be interpreted as an acknowledgement of legitimacy, and more, as an unavoidable summons. Martin Luther expounded on this hymn of praise by Mary, recorded in Luke 1. 46–55, in a short account which appeared in print in September 1521. His exposition has always been recognized as a particularly important witness of Lutheran veneration of Mary. The content of Luther's discussion will be explored in the following five sections: first by examining Luther's references to Mary as the mother of Jesus; then, by studying Mary's hymn of praise; thirdly, by examining Mary's place in a

---

[1] Cf. Matthew 1f.; Luke 1f.
[2] Cf. Mark 3. 31–5.
[3] Cf. John 19. 25–7.
[4] Cf. Walter Delius, *Geschichte der Marienverehrung* (Munich, 1963).
[5] Cf. Luke 1. 48.

Christian's faith; fourthly, by appreciating God's grace and action; and, finally, by discussing Luther's remarks on God's greatest work.[6]

I MARY, THE MOTHER OF JESUS

Luther presented the *Magnificat* in a German translation,[7] and then interpreted it word by word. He considered it a good custom to sing this hymn during the service of Vespers.[8] Indeed, this text belongs to the prayer at evening Vespers, which was sung in the monastery and used at hourly prayers. Luther called Mary 'the tender mother of Christ',[9] who lived like a 'maid', 'who does as she is told around the house'.[10] She belonged to the house of David, from which the Messiah was expected. Luther depicted Mary as 'the holy mother'[11] who praised God not only in speech, but with her total life, being, and senses and with all her might. The mother of Jesus had become the mother of God. When one speaks of her in that sense, 'no one can say anything greater of her or to her.'[12] One may also call her 'a queen of heaven', but dare not make 'an idol of her'.[13] Mary was 'no more than a cheerful guest-chamber and willing hostess to so great a Guest'.[14] Although she is 'the holy mother of God', Mary did nothing herself of her own accord; the work was entirely God's. Mary attributed all to God's grace, and not to her own merit. She gives nothing, for God gives all. In their prayers Christians 'ought to call upon her, that for her sake God may grant and do' what is requested. Indeed, all the holy saints may be invoked, but the work remains totally God's action alone.[15] Mary, the 'blessed Virgin', laid no claim to the work, the praise, or the glory which are God's alone. Yet Luther still assumed here that Mary and the saints are able to intercede for those who pray. Accordingly, his exposition

---

[6] Cf. *Luthers Werke* (Selected works), ed. Otto Clemen, 2 (Berlin, 1934), pp. 133–87. Page references for quotations from Luther are from this edition. (An English translation of Luther's exposition of the *Magnificat* is available in *Luther's Works*, 21, ed. J. Pelikan (St Louis, 1956), pp. 297–358.) See also Reinhard Schwarz, '"Die zarte Mutter Christi". Was uns Luther über Maria lehrt', *Zeitwende*, 57 (1986), pp. 204–16. Schwarz summarizes Luther's interpretation of the *Magnificat* with 'three essential characteristics of faith': 'acceptance of one's lowly estate', 'acceptance of God's promise', and 'entering in praise of God'.

[7] *Luthers Werke*, 2, p. 135, 14–31.

[8] Ibid., p. 131, 3–5.

[9] Ibid., p. 137, 39.

[10] Ibid., p. 138, 12–14.

[11] Ibid., p. 142, 32.

[12] Ibid., p. 159, 35f.

[13] Ibid., p. 160, 28–30.

[14] Ibid., p. 144, 5.

[15] Ibid., p. 161, 16, 28, 30.

on the *Magnificat* ended (before his epilogue to Johann Friedrich von Sachsen, to whom the work is dedicated) with the words: 'May Christ grant us this through the intercession and for the sake of His dear mother, Mary. Amen.' Later, Reformers felt that while it might be condoned, such an intercessory prayer had no support from Scripture and so could readily be discarded.[16]

Mary was, for Luther, the mother of Jesus, the mother of God, the Virgin who gave birth to a son who came from the will of God. All traditional references found in the New Testament and in the mainstream tradition for the veneration of Mary were used by Luther in his *Magnificat*. The uniqueness of Mary was that she became the mother of God.[17] The reformer also alluded briefly to the sinlessness of Mary, but emphasized how the grace of God in Mary was 'far too great for her to deserve it in any way'.[18] In his interpretation, Luther was not particularly interested in Mary, as the author of the hymn; nor was he primarily concerned here with God's son, whose mother Mary was; his attention was focused instead on God himself. This becomes even clearer from closer study.

II MARY'S 'HYMN OF PRAISE' TO GOD

The opening words in Mary's hymn, 'My soul magnifies the Lord', made Luther stress the glorification of God. He explained how Mary wanted to proclaim the great deeds and works of God to strengthen the faith of believers, to comfort all simple people, and to terrify the powerful on earth. Thus it was not just a hymn to be sung in particular circumstances, but to be sung generally by Christians.[19] For rulers in particular, 'this holy hymn of the blessed mother of God' was significant, more significant than many other biblical texts, for it taught the mighty to fear God, whose deeds are important for all people, regardless of their social standing.[20] The hymn teaches Christians not to believe that God intends to do great things only with others. Many with power do not fear God; others, lowly and resigned, can dare to lift up their heads.[21] Mary's hymn of praise for the great works and deeds of God was intended to awaken and strengthen

---

[16] Ibid., p. 157, 40; p. 185, 3; cf. Hans Düfel, *Luthers Stellung zur Marienverehrung* (Göttingen, 1968).

[17] *Luthers Werke*, 2, p. 159, 27–30.

[18] Ibid., pp. 159, 40–160, 2.

[19] Cf. ibid., p. 142, 2–6.

[20] Cf. Ibid., pp. 134, 31–135, 2.

[21] Cf. ibid., p. 142, 10–13.

faith by comforting the lowly and confronting the mighty, so that God's works are known and his divine love experienced, 'that man sees in God his greatness and appreciates his greatness.'[22]

Whoever acts in this way follows Mary in a direct line. Luther stated right at the start of his discussion that

> in order properly to understand this sacred hymn of praise, we need to bear in mind that the blessed Virgin Mary is speaking on the basis of her own experience, in which she was enlightened and instructed by the Holy Spirit. No one can correctly understand God or His Word unless he has received such understanding immediately from the Holy Spirit. But no one can receive it from the Holy Spirit without experiencing, proving and feeling it. In such experience the Holy Spirit instructs us as in His own school, outside which nothing is learned but empty words and prattle.[23]

Luther was sure that people were liable to praise God only when they felt he had done well by them, and at other times to think little about him. Others appropriated the good gifts of God to themselves. Those with such proud and complacent hearts, Luther believed, could not sing the *Magnificat* aright.[24] Mary, by contrast, praised God alone. Even though she experienced God's great work, she 'was ever minded not to exalt herself above the humblest people on earth.'[25] Because of her uniqueness, Mary might have seen fit to separate herself from other folk; but she did not do this: 'Mary's heart remains the same at all times; she lets God have his will with her and draws from it only good comfort, joy, and trust in God.'[26] For Luther, this thought was so important that he reiterated it several times. After all, Mary, who came from a humble background, was raised above all people, but she did not consider herself higher than the lowest servant-maid. By contrast, people are only too ready to assert themselves over others, even though in reality they have little power, honour, or beauty. Instead of acting so, they ought to do as Mary did, by allowing God to work within them and be of good comfort, cheer, and hope in him.[27]

Luther saw Mary as an example of a believing person who grasped the

[22] *Luthers Werke*, 2, p. 142, 16f., 25–8.
[23] Ibid., pp. 135, 33–136, 4.
[24] Ibid., p. 143, 10–15.
[25] Ibid., p. 143, 35f.
[26] Cf. ibid., p. 144, 6f.
[27] Ibid., p. 144, 11–16, 20–2.

incomprehensible through faith. This is necessary because God deals inscrutably. Mary appreciated the distance between herself and God, whom she first called her Lord and only thereafter her Saviour. Only then did she tell of his deeds.[28] This is the structure which Luther detected in the *Magnificat*. As an example of faith, Mary is regarded as one who truly loves. Whoever looks for his own gain in a loved one is a poor lover. This is also true of those who praise God only so long as he does well by them: they are more interested in salvation than in the Saviour, more interested in the gifts than in the giver, and think more about creatures than about the Creator.[29] Luther clarified this in his remark that 'such impure and false spirits defile all God's gifts',[30] and contrasted correct behaviour with the impure spirits when he wrote: 'that is the true bride, who says to Him: "I seek not Thine, but Thee; Thou art to me no dearer when it goes well with me, nor any less dear when it goes ill."'[31] Mary showed this by not seeking her own enjoyment, but by accepting God's goodness and love, and by being ready and willing to surrender what God might take from her.[32]

The reformer stressed how Mary had held on to God's goodness, which she could neither see nor feel, and let everything else go which she could feel: she rejoiced 'not in the good things of God that she felt, but only in God, whom she did not feel and who is her Salvation, known by her in faith alone.' It is for this reason that the pure goodness of God should be preached and known above all else. Just as God saves men out of goodness, without any merit of works, so they, in turn, should do the works without reward. An upright son serves his father willingly, for his father's sake, without thought of reward or gaining his inheritance. Whoever praises himself before God commits a sin. It is the goodness and grace of God which deserve praise, and in this Mary is the true example.[33]

Luther criticized some translations of the *Magnificat* which rendered Mary's 'low estate' as 'humility'. He was sure that this was wrong, for the truly humble are not aware of their humbleness: 'it is God alone who knows humility.' The *Magnificat* was concerned not with Mary's 'humility', but with her 'lowliness' before God.[34] Mary was neither proud

---

[28] Ibid., p. 144, 26f., 30–2.
[29] Cf. ibid., pp. 144, 38–145, 5; p. 145, 10–12.
[30] Ibid., p. 145, 20.
[31] Ibid., p. 146, 6–8.
[32] Cf. ibid., p. 146, 20–3.
[33] Cf. ibid., p. 146, 29–31; p. 147, 19f.; p. 147, 22–9.
[34] Cf. ibid., p. 148, 11f.; p. 148, 37f.

of the honour bestowed on her, nor did she glory in her 'worthiness nor yet in her unworthiness, but solely in the divine regard' that God had chosen her. For Luther, this is so important that he repeated it:

> True humility never knows that it is humble, for if it knew this, it would turn proud from contemplation of so fine a virtue. But it clings with all its heart and mind and senses to lowly things, sets them continually before its eyes, and ponders them in its thoughts. And because it sets them before its eyes, it cannot see itself nor become aware of itself, much less of lofty things. And therefore, when honour and elevation come, they must take it unawares and find it immersed in thoughts of other things.... False humility, on the other hand, never knows that it is proud; for if it knew this, it would soon grow humble from contemplation of that ugly vice. But it clings with heart and mind and senses to lofty things, sets them continually before its eyes, and ponders them in its thoughts. And because of this, it cannot see itself nor become aware of itself.[35]

In true humility, the heart remains the same, no matter how things change.[36] All this we can learn from Mary: even when we are put down and scorned, we should not give up as though God were angry with us; rather we should hope that he is gracious to us, for God comes to the lowly, as the *Magnificat* teaches.

III MARY'S FAITH AND A CHRISTIAN'S FAITH

Luther saw in Mary's hymn of praise that God comes to the lowly and despised. From such knowledge flows love and trust in God, 'by which we yield ourselves to Him and gladly obey Him.'[37] In this context, Luther observed how Mary was intent on teaching a twofold lesson: first, 'Every one of us should pay attention to what God does for him rather than all the works He does for others'; and, secondly, 'Everyone should strive to be foremost in praising God by showing forth the works He has done to him, and then by praising Him for the works He has done to others.'[38] To the first point, Luther added that it is not the deeds or clothes of others that are important; it is simply deception to trust merely in external works or to cover the dying with the cowl of a monk, as if one would thereby gain

[35] *Luthers Werke*, 2, p. 149, 9f.; p. 150, 18–35.
[36] Cf. ibid., p. 151, 18–20.
[37] Ibid., p. 152, 17–20.
[38] Ibid., p. 152, 35f.; cf. p. 153, 36–8.

salvation. God does not look at an individual's deeds, but at his heart and faith.[39] Each individual ought to concentrate on the works of God in himself, and to behave as if he and God were alone, as if God were dealing with no one else than with him. In the second place, Luther added that only the selfish become angry when they realize that they are not first and foremost in possessing the good gifts of God. The true believer is not selfish, but loves God and his neighbour; he appreciates God's gifts—'life, body, reason, goods, honour, friends, the ministration of the sun, and all created things'.[40] Life and all of creation should be considered as God's gift, and one should thank him for this gift. Luther felt that man could learn from the animals:

> A bird sings and is happy in the gifts it has; it does not grumble that it lacks the gift of speech. A dog frisks happily about, and is content even though it is without the gift of reason. All animals are satisfied with what they have and serve God with love and praise. Only the guile and selfish eye of man is never satisfied, nor can it ever be really satisfied because of his ingratitude and pride, wanting the best place at the feast as chief guest; it does not want to honour God, but would rather be honoured by God.[41]

Over against this, Mary is seen as one who knew that all that happened to her was based on the fact that God looked upon her and accepted her: where 'God turns his face toward one to regard him, there is nothing but grace and salvation, and all gifts and works must follow.' Because of this, Mary was blessed from generation to generation. Luther noted how Mary did not say 'men will speak all manner of good of her, praise her virtues, exalt her virginity or her humility, or sing of what she has done. But for this one thing alone, that God regarded her, men will call her blessed. That is to give all the glory to God as completely as it can be done.' When Mary is called 'blessed', the praise is directed not to Mary herself but to God's grace toward her 'that is to give all the glory to God as completely as it can be done.'[42]

Luther discussed all this in detail, for here in the *Magnificat* he discovered the proper way for venerating Mary. Here God's greatness is

[39] Cf. ibid., p. 153, 12–19; p. 153, 32–4.
[40] Ibid., p. 154, 7f.; p. 154, 15–17.
[41] Ibid., p. 154, 26–33.
[42] Ibid., p. 155, 18–27.

contrasted with Mary's low estate. Luther believed one ought to address Mary in this way:

> O Blessed Virgin, Mother of God, you were nothing and all despised; yet God in His grace regarded you and worked such great things in you. You were worthy of none of them, but the rich and abundant grace of God was upon you, far above any merit of yours. Hail to you! You are blessed from that hour to eternity, in finding such a God.[43]

Luther considered that Mary would not take it amiss when 'we call her unworthy of such grace'. What happened did not occur because of any merit in Mary, 'but out of God's pure grace'.[44] To ascribe merit and worthiness to Mary is to detract from the grace of God and to diminish the truth of the *Magnificat*.

To guard against the false veneration of Mary, Luther pointed out that

> Mary does not like to hear the useless babblers, who preach and write much about her merit, whereby they only want to show off their own skill and fail to see how they spoil the *Magnificat*, make the Mother of God a liar, and lessen the grace of God. For as much as we emphasize her merit and worthiness, we lessen the grace of God and the truth of the *Magnificat*.... For all those who heap much praise and honour on her are not far from making her an idol, as if she were concerned that men should honour her and look to her for good things, when in truth she rejects this and would have us honour God in her and come through her to trust in God's grace.[45]

The tendency towards a false veneration of the mother of God was, for Luther, to be detected in the piety focused on Mary in his own time. He considered this to be unbiblical and contrary to the *Magnificat* itself.

> Whoever, therefore, would show her the proper honour must not regard her alone and by herself, but set her in the presence of God and far beneath Him, must there strip her of all honour, and regard her low estate, as she says; he should then marvel at the exceedingly abundant grace of God, who regards, embraces, and blesses so poor and despised a mortal.[46]

[43] *Luthers Werke*, 2, p. 155, 32–8.
[44] Ibid., p. 155, 38f.; p. 156, 1.
[45] Ibid., p. 156, 3–15.
[46] Ibid., p. 156, 16–20.

Only because of this, we are moved

> to love and praise God for His grace, and drawn to look for all good
> things to Him, who does not reject but graciously regards poor and
> despised and lowly mortals. Thus your heart will be strengthened in
> faith and love and hope. What do you suppose would please her more
> than to have you come through her to God this way, and learn from
> her to put your hope and trust in Him, notwithstanding your
> despised and lowly estate, in life as well as in death? She does not want
> you to come to her, but through her to God.[47]

Luther spoke out strongly against those who made Mary an un-
approachable figure by 'contrasting us with her instead of her with God',
which, he was sure, was contrary to the biblical witness. In the *Magnificat*,
Mary was for him not a person of such importance that she could be
reached, but 'the best example of the grace of God'.[48] One only speaks to
her correctly when one says: 'O Blessed Virgin, Mother of God, what
great comfort God has shown us in you, by so graciously regarding your
unworthiness and low estate. This encourages us to believe that henceforth He will not despise us poor and lowly ones, but graciously regard us
also, according to your example.'[49] Yet, as Luther explained, 'now we find
those who come to her for help and comfort, as though she were a divine
being, so that I fear there is now more idolatry in the world than ever
before.'[50] Correct veneration of Mary, he was sure, did not result in
mistaken beliefs but in a strengthening of faith in God. Only then may
one correctly call her blessed 'when the heart, moved by her low estate and
God's gracious regard of her, rejoices in God.'[51]

Mary's hymn of praise was therefore a praise of God. To change it into
praise of Mary is to pursue a dangerous course. In all veneration of Mary,
the worship of God must remain central, for his grace lasts for ever.[52]
Mary is the best example of proper faith because she alone pointed to God
and recalled all the great things God has done for her: 'She teaches us here
that the greater devotion there is in the heart, the fewer words are
uttered.'[53] Her example of faith can strengthen man's faith in God, who
wishes to be worshipped in spirit and truth.

---

[47] Ibid., p. 156, 21–8.
[48] Ibid., p. 156, 38.
[49] Ibid., p. 157, 1–5.
[50] Ibid., p. 157, 17–19.
[51] Ibid., p. 157, 38f.
[52] Cf. ibid., p.158, 10.
[53] Cf. ibid., p. 158, 28f.

IV GOD'S GRACE AND DEEDS

For Luther, whoever praises God's grace, as Mary did, can also view his works. God's work for Mary was unique in making her the mother of God.[54] Yet Mary herself ascribed all to God's grace, not to her merit, and praised the works which God performs. She pointed out how God puts down the haughty and does away with the power of the mighty. Luther believed that with these words Mary made 'all the strong feeble, all the mighty weak, all the wise foolish, all the famous despised'; for Mary gave only 'God all power, works, wisdom, and honour'. To know God rightly, Luther explained, is the greatest achievement in heaven and earth. It is an art to recognize God's works.[55] The first of God's works is his mercy.[56] And the result of this work is 'justice', 'the precious and beautiful attribute of God'.[57] In this context, Luther also spoke of the responsibility of the State (which cannot be treated here). It is, however, essential, Luther believed, that mercy is given to the poor and weak. God is merciful to those who do not

> count their spiritual talents and are willing to be poor in spirit. These are the ones who truly fear God, who count themselves not worthy of anything, be it ever so small, and are glad to be naked and bare before God and man; who ascribe whatever they have to His pure grace, bestowed on the unworthy; who use it with praise and fear and thanksgiving, as though it belonged to another, and who seek not their own will, desire, or honour, but His alone to whom it belongs.

Mary also indicated how much more gladly God shows such mercy, his 'most valued work', than its counterpart, his strength.[58]

The second work of God which Mary mentioned is 'the breaking of spiritual pride'.[59] Luther considered 'wherever man's strength begins, God's strength ends.' Those who exalt themselves with their own power alone are forsaken by God. 'The mercy of God together with all His might is with those who fear Him, and the arm of God with all severity and power against the proud.'[60] This destruction occurs when the proud consider themselves to be 'the most clever and filled with their own

---

[54] Cf. *Luthers Werke*, 2, p. 159, 27–30.
[55] Ibid., p. 160, 35–8; p. 162, 37–40; p. 164, 2–7.
[56] Ibid., p. 165, 5.
[57] Cf. ibid., p. 168, 35.
[58] Cf. ibid., p. 170, 23–30.
[59] Ibid., p. 170, 36.
[60] Ibid., p. 172, 2; p. 170, 21–3.

wisdom'. The haughty and proud fall into three categories—the rich, the mighty, and the learned—all of whom are accounted enemies of God. The mighty are greater enemies of God than the rich; but the most dangerous are the learned, 'the most venomous and pernicious men on earth', for they turn men against God by extinguishing the truth.[61]

The third work of God, Luther explained, consisted in putting down the mighty. By understanding the first two works of God, Luther felt that the third work could be better appreciated. God does not destroy wisdom and justice, 'for if the world is to go on these things must remain'; but he does do away with the arrogant and proud, and at the same time exalts the lowly, whom he has chosen.[62] Luther found much truth in the phrase 'the learned, the perverted'.[63] What is important is the individual's inner attitude: the lowly submit to God; but the arrogant feel they can do without God's spirit and power. For Luther, Mary's words were spoken both for the comfort of the suffering and for the terror of tyrants: 'the Holy Spirit comforts truth and right by the mouth of this mother and bids them not to be deceived or afraid.' The lowly know God has not given them up, for as Mary has shown, salvation consists not in man's power and works, but in God's alone.[64]

God's fourth work which Mary mentioned is the lifting up of the lowly ('all those who are contemptible and altogether nothing in the eyes of the world'), the fifth is the feeding of the hungry, and the sixth deals with the rich who will be sent away empty. In his explanation of these biblical texts, Luther tried to show, for example, that by 'the hungry are not meant those who have little or nothing to eat, but those who gladly suffer want, especially when they are forced by others to do so for the sake of God or the truth.'[65] Outward wealth or physical hunger are not decisive. What is important is the individual's attitude to God: 'He judges not according to outward appearance, whether one is rich or poor, high or low, but according to the spirit and how it behaves itself within.' Whereas men are apt to judge according to outward appearances, God's works are performed in secret. For this reason 'a rich man does not realize how entirely empty and poor he is until he comes to die or in some other way is ruined. . . . On the other hand, the hungry and thirsty know not how filled with good things

---

[61] Ibid., p. 172, 36f.; p. 174, 5–7.
[62] Cf. ibid., p. 175, 9–14; p. 175, 34.
[63] Cf. ibid., p, 175, 38f.
[64] Cf. ibid., p. 176, 14–16.
[65] Ibid., p. 176, 23–6.

they are until their end has come.'[66] The hidden works of God need to be realized, and here the 'precious words of the mother of God' should be a help.[67] This, however, is only possible for those who do not make the present an idol, but listen to this comforting message.[68] Mary's hymn of praise did not indicate God's preference for certain human groups and the destruction of others, but it sought to open men's eyes to God and his deeds, also to comfort as well as to instil responsibility to God.

V GOD'S GREATEST WORK

Luther believed that the high point of the *Magnificat* is to be found at the very end. After enumerating God's various works, Mary finished by pointing to the greatest of all God's works, the Incarnation of the Son of God. She freely acknowledged that this work performed in her was not done for her sake alone, but for the sake of all Israel. The starting-point of this work is again the boundless mercy of God, who sent his son to redeem men, without any merit of worthiness on their part.[69] Even when men often think that God has forgotten them, God continually has them in mind to fulfil his promise.[70] God bound himself to men in Christ. Through Christ, the 'spiritual Israel' has come into being, placing all trust in God's son. For Luther, 'without Christ all the world is in sin, under damnation and cursed with all its work and knowledge.'[71] God's word and work do not demand the proof of reason, but were grasped through a free and pure faith.[72] The promised 'seed of Abraham' was not begotten by any of his sons, as the Jews had expected it would be, but was born of his daughter, Mary, the chosen tool for God's greatest work.[73] Everything depends on this. As Luther remarked, 'In the Bible everything has to do with Christ.'[74] As Christ came from the people of Israel, the Jews should be treated in a kindly manner, Luther urged, so that many might become converts to the Messiah.[75] Luther was certain that wherever Christ

---

[66] Cf. *Luthers Werke*, 2, p. 177, 9–15.
[67] Ibid., p. 179, 20–2.
[68] Cf. ibid., p. 178, 1–6.
[69] Cf. ibid., p. 180, 3–8; p. 180, 37–9.
[70] Cf. ibid., p. 181, 6f.
[71] Ibid., p. 181, 13; p. 181, 20–2.
[72] Ibid., p. 183, 12f.
[73] Ibid., p. 183, 25–7.
[74] Ibid., p. 183, 36–8.
[75] Ibid., p. 184, 29–33. In his writing 'That Jesus Christ was born a Jew' (1523), Luther argued to similar effect. Cf. Gerhard Müller, 'Tribut an den Geist der Zeit. Martin Luthers Stellung zu den Juden', *Evangelische Kommentare*, 16 (1983), pp. 306–8.

becomes known as God's greatest work, lives are changed as a consequence. A proper understanding of the *Magnificat* consists 'not merely in brilliant words but in glowing life in body and soul'.[76] This is the object of Mary's hymn of praise, that Christ takes hold in the believer.

On this note, Luther ended his discussion of Mary's hymn of praise. Above all, he saw it as praising God. This is emphasized by his explanation of the ideas and language which Mary used. Whoever wants rightly to know and honour God needs to look at the Scriptures, whose centre is Jesus. From this, Mary did not intend to move. She sought to serve by pointing to God and his work, in which she was allowed a humble part.

Even today Luther's view that Mary did not become the mother of God because of any personal qualities is still relevant. Mary did not become a distant figure: she was uniquely virgin and mother, a human being who believed. This faith was dependent neither on external works nor on God's good deeds, but focused on God himself and his impenetrable mysteries. Mary's hymn of praise remains as an important witness, pointing believers to proper trust in God. At the same time, the *Magnificat* is a text which both comforts and calls to penitence. Luther's point still remains valid: everything depends on faith and whether Mary's witness is accepted as true.[77]

University of Erlangen

[76] *Luthers Werke*, 2, p. 185, 3f.
[77] Cf. ibid., p. 176, 15.

THE IMPORTANCE OF THE IMPERIAL CITY OF NUREMBERG IN THE REFORMATION

by GOTTFRIED SEEBASS

T HE question of how a certain historical situation or event arises is doubtless one of the classical questions for any historian. It is true, however, that there can never be a final and exhaustive answer, because any question about origins can only be asked within a specific framework, and can therefore represent only a small section, and never the fulness of all the interwoven factors. Historical events are always based on much more than what we are able to get access to by analysis. Within this complex picture it is even more difficult to assess and determine the weight of individual factors in comparison with each other: only rarely can we produce or, indeed, find comparable situations without the factor in question. The question of the importance of one particular event or phenomenon can therefore only be answered in history by identifying the impulses coming from it.

In this sense, recent research has made a point, and sometimes stretched this point, of the importance of the German imperial cities for the Reformation. Among those, Nuremberg, if only for its size—next to Cologne and Erfurt it was most likely the largest city of the Empire—takes a special place. Its contemporaries were very much aware of this. In 1530 Martin Luther wrote from the Coburg: 'Nuremberg verily shines on the whole German land, like a sun among moon and stars, strongly moving other cities by what is going on there.' This certainly was not just typical praise of a city calculated to have a certain effect, but a realistic judgement. But is Luther's comment about Nuremberg also meant to include the Reformation? This is the question which is the subject of this paper. As far as I know, it has never been dealt with comprehensively in the rich literature on Reformation history in this Franconian imperial city. We try to arrive at an answer bearing in mind the introductory remarks, namely, by taking account in double perspective of the many-layered impulses coming from Nuremberg: in the first part we will seek the effects which the Reformation in Nuremberg had beyond the boundaries of the city and its territory. In the second part, we will try to clarify what the city council's politics on the religious question were, and what influence this had on the course of the Reformation in Germany.

I

(1) The imperial city on the river Pegnitz—cosmopolitan in its economic and cultural outlook, which was largely determined by craftsmanship, local and foreign trade—attained central importance for the Reformation mainly as a centre of communication.

We know that in the forefront of the Reformation proper, and during the early phase of the *causa Lutheri*, Luther became known in the council chambers of the cities and the princely chancelleries particularly by the correspondence of scholars, councillors, and councils of a humanistic frame of mind. Unfortunately, there is up to this day no comprehensive examination of the correspondence between German humanists for the years from 1516 to 1520. We do know, however, that Nuremberg, and not least the city councillor Christoph Scheurl II, contributed a great deal to make Luther known in humanist circles. Since 1516, an elite grouping, the *sodalitas Staupitziana*, had formed itself around the preachings of the Augustinian Vicar-General, Johann von Staupitz. It included not only humanist scholars, but also influential members of Nuremberg city council. Through Staupitz and his fellow monk Wenzel Linck, this circle became aware of Luther and was quickly won over by his theology, which had developed in the spirit of the Gospel and the writings of Augustine. And Scheurl did everything in his power to make the Wittenberg scholar known in the circle of the southern German humanists through his correspondence. The famous *Ninety-five Theses* were distributed from Nuremberg in written copies and in print. Scheurl sent them to the Augsburg city clerk, Conrad Peutinger, and Willibald Pirckheimer sent a copy to the Augsburg canon Adelmann von Adelmannsfelden. One of the leading men in the city, Caspar Nützel, made a German translation of the *Theses*. Soon the wider public got to know about Luther's connections with this Nuremberg circle: in the summer of 1518, after repeated requests from Scheurl, the Wittenberg professor, wrote an exegesis of Psalm 110 for the influential councillor Hieronymus Ebner, which was also printed, with a preface by the Saxon court theologian, Spalatin. And in the autumn of the same year, Luther passed Nuremberg on the way to being questioned by Cardinal Cajetan in Augsburg and, again, on the way back. If Scheurl had not been away travelling, the Nuremberg council would most probably have sent him to Augsburg to be Luther's legal adviser, as the Saxon Elector had asked them to do. These short stays in, and contacts with, the city were sufficient to make the humanist society want to change its name: from that time on it called itself *sodalitas*

Martiniana. It was not Luther's criticism of the Church, but a piety and a newly-formulated theology, which had grown from the knowledge of the justification of humankind through God's grace, which won over this circle. One should really study the correspondence of the members of this *sodalitas Martiniana* for the following years as well, at least until 1524. Only then would one be able to judge fully the importance of the circle for the spreading of early Reformation thought in the southern German cities. In this paper, we have to be content with mere suggestion.

Certainly it was thanks to the influence of the members of this circle that Nuremberg filled the posts of provost in the two parish churches of St Lorenz and St Sebald, as well as the preachers' posts in these churches, with young lawyers and theologians who had either spent part of their studies in Wittenberg with Luther, or who had been won over by his writings. In Nuremberg, as in other German cities, the Evangelical sermon was one of the main prerequisites for the early Reformation movement which finally provoked and led to the Reformation. We also know, however, that the sermons delivered by the Evangelical preachers in the cities had a huge following among the country population of the surrounding and remoter hinterland. It was not only the message of the grace of God who accepts the sinner, but also the criticism of financial exploitation by the Church which caught on, and established and reinforced an already existing anticlericalism. Thus, in the surroundings of cities where Evangelical preachers were working, a potential arose which was critical not only of the old Church, but also of existing structures of society. This became clear in various instances of unrest, mostly centred on the question of the payment of tithes, which arose in the forefront of the Peasants War from 1522 onwards in various places, also in the summer of 1524 in the surroundings of Nuremberg.

The Nuremberg preachers also made their impact felt over a far wider radius, for (particularly in the years when the *causa Lutheri* rapidly developed into the *causa religionis et fidei*) the Imperial Court and various Diets were sitting in the Franconian city. Even though during the first Diet in Nuremberg in 1522 the question of religion was not on the agenda, the princes, counts, and gentlemen, and their envoys, heard the sermons in the Nuremberg city churches, particularly, so it seems, those in St Lorenz, where Andreas Osiander was preaching from the pulpit. The report which the envoys of the Saxon Elector sent to him made Frederick the Wise ask for a sermon by the Lorenz church preacher via Spalatin. Osiander's sermons made a lasting impression on Graf Ludwig XV von Oettingen, and particularly on the head of the German Order of Knights,

Albrecht von Brandenburg. The later Duke of Prussia even many years later called the preacher of St Lorenz his 'spiritual father'. And when, towards the end of 1548, Osiander left Nuremberg because of the Interim, the Duke found him influential positions in the church and university of Königsberg. Most probably quite a few of the estates of the Empire and their representatives could agree with the judgement of Johann Hug, who reported back to his town, Hagenau, that the preacher of St Lorenz knew particularly well how to preach the Gospel and the teaching of Christ.

Particularly because of their sermons, the municipal theologians could make their influence felt much further than just in church services. Osiander especially was frequently asked to dinner at princely tables or with envoys. In the ensuing conversations, he courageously stood up for Evangelical teaching. 'Religious disputations' were also arranged frequently, where Osiander and an invited representative of the old Church discussed subjects and propositions which had been prepared beforehand. We know, for example, that thirteen Evangelical princes and gentlemen arranged a disputation of more than five hours length on the question of the authority of the Gospel and the pope between Johannes Cochläus and the preacher of the St Lorenz church. How far-reaching Osiander's influence was may be seen from the fact that in Holy Week of 1524 he even handed the Eucharist in both kinds to the sister of Charles V, Isabella of Denmark, in Nuremberg castle. These events have only been handed down to us in fragments of correspondence or in passing. But we can see what importance ought to be attached to the influence of the Nuremberg preachers for the spreading of Evangelical teaching during the Diets between 1522 and 1524. The opposition, in any case, was well aware of the weight and far-reaching consequences of sermons in Nuremberg and further afield: as early as 1523 the Emperor's representative Ferdinand together with the papal legate Chieregati attempted to have the Evangelical preachers arrested. But at this time the Evangelical movement in the population had already gathered so much momentum that the council refused to comply with this suggestion in unmistakable and crystal-clear tones.

Apart from the correspondence of the Nuremberg humanists and the influence of the spoken sermons of the municipal theologians, there was also a third factor—printing. Handbill and pamphlet had become a medium which, like the correspondence of the humanist circle and the Reformation sermon, which was directed at the general public, could overcome geographical boundaries even more easily and effectively. So far, there is no comprehensive study of what Evangelical pamphlets were printed in Nuremberg. But we know from some initial pilot studies that after Augsburg and Wittenberg, Nuremberg was one of the major centres which almost flooded the market with pamphlets in the years between 1520 and 1526. The City Council, particularly in the time of the Imperial Court's and the Diets' sittings in Nuremberg between 1522 and 1524, from time to time forbade the sale of Lutheran writings, in order to comply with the Edict of Worms, at least formally. It was, however, made clear that the Council intended to punish only very serious and obvious violations and would tolerate everything else. The secret printing of Thomas Müntzer's pamphlets in Nuremberg is proof of the fact that it was relatively easy to circumvent the censor in the first few years. It is also particularly remarkable that the very printer, who during the life of Lazarus Spengler got most of the official council printing contracts, also published the greatest number of Lutheran pamphlets. Altogether there were almost 400 different editions of Luther's writings published in Nuremberg up to the time of his death. This does not include the large number of Bible editions and individual books of the Bible. Here, too, Nuremberg takes fourth place after Wittenberg, Basle, and Augsburg. As was said before, this refers only to the works of Luther and not to the large number of other pamphlets and single-sheet prints. Luther himself, incidentally, was by no means overjoyed by the fast and mass reprinting of his writings in Nuremberg. Printers in Wittenberg referred to marketing problems and refused to take on any of Luther's larger manuscripts. This is an indication of the fact that Wittenberg, too, was relying on the southern German market. When, in 1525, even one part of the setting copy for Luther's *Postils* was stolen from a Wittenberg printer and appeared in Nuremberg a short time afterwards, Luther registered an official complaint with the City Council and obtained a ruling which prohibited printers from publishing reprints inside a certain time-span.

Apart from pamphlets and handbills—which were put on the market by the publishers for personal or business motives after the official transition of the city to being a Reformation one, following the Disputation of March 1525—there were also pro-Evangelical mass printing contracts from the neighbouring Ansbach margraves. So, for example, Margrave Kasimir had a sermon by the Ansbach preacher Johann Rurer printed and distributed to all parishes in his region which was directed against the peasants' uprising. Two years later Margrave George the Pious commissioned a Nuremberg printer to print a pamphlet against the Anabaptists, which likewise was distributed to all parishes. Incidentally, in both cases the Nuremberg City Council followed with a corresponding action for its own region with pamphlets by Osiander. This list of commissions could be easily expanded at will with reference to the Church Order of Palatine Neuburg of 1543. The print-shops of the city, which had been Evangelical since the twenties, thus could be effectively employed for the Reformation through commissions from outside, even for regions outside the city boundaries.

(2) Yet Nuremberg's commitment to the Reformation was by no means limited to language and communication as they were effective in the circles of scholars, sermons, and publishing: the city also achieved importance by the guiding and counselling intervention of individual Nuremberg personalities in adjoining areas. Quite frequently preachers were asked to take part in the introduction of the Reformation to other cities and territories, or to implement it.

This was the case with the introduction of the Reformation into Regensburg in 1542. The Nuremberg City Council on request from the Regensburg Council was prepared not only to help with the establishment of Reformation legislation in the city by sending a municipal lawyer, but it also sent to Regensburg Johann Forster, the then administrator of the provostship of St Lorenz, who had been expelled from Augsburg. He was sent in order to implement an Evangelical reform of the churches there. The guidelines for this were drawn up by Veit Dietrich, whom the Regensburg theologians and councillors had met during the Disputation the year before. Dietrich also defended the new order implemented in Regensburg when it was attacked by the Catholic party.

The following year Ottheinrich, Duke of Palatine-Neuburg, approached the Nuremberg City Council and asked them to grant leave to the preacher at St Lorenz, Osiander, in order to introduce the Reformation into his Duchy. Nuremberg did not want to decline the request by the Count Palatine, although he was asked to treat the matter confidentially. Thus, in 1542, and again in 1543, Osiander spent some time in the Duchy. He not only drafted the basic Reformation mandate for the Count Palatine, but he also worked out the Church Order for the area, modelled on the Electoral Brandenburg and the Brandenburg-Nuremberg Orders. We must in this context also single out the preacher Thomas Venatorius, who was 'loaned' to the city of Rothenburg on Tauber in 1544 and to the city of Donauwörth in the following year in order to introduce reformation there. In 1546 the City Council of Nuremberg allowed another preacher to travel to Ravensburg for a longer period of time to fulfil a similar task. Thus Nuremberg in this respect also became the vanguard of the Lutheran Reformation in the southern German area.

(3) The influence which Nuremberg had on the Reformation as a whole via the renewal of its church was rather less direct, but was decisively formative. This renewal and the restructuring of the legal sectors, which had become free of clerical jurisdiction, happened very gradually and slowly between the Nuremberg Disputation of March 1525 and the Church Visitation of 1528–9. It reached its conclusion in the Brandenburg-Nuremberg Church Order of 1533.

How far the Nuremberg renewal, developing along Wittenberg-Saxon lines or independently, became exemplary for other cities as well has not yet been examined in detail. It has to be taken into account, however, that there were hardly any official council publications. Not even the great Apology for the Reformation, which was worked out by Spengler, was published. Only a part of the Liturgical Order of Worship was distributed in print without, however, being used as a model beyond Nuremberg, even though Spalatin in Electoral Saxony had repeatedly written recommendations. Only the 'Eucharistic Exhortation' from the Order of Service of the parish churches of 1524, an extensive paraphrase of the Words of Institution, which were still sung in Latin, has almost become the common property of Lutheran Protestantism by numerous reprints and through the Church Orders. Additionally, the hospital mass had repercussions in the northeran German area.

The first and the last manifestation of the Nuremberg Reformation restructuring did, however, have far-reaching influence: the Poor Relief Order of 1522–3 and the Church Order of 1533. The Poor Relief Order, which reorganized the municipal provisions for the poor in the spirit of Protestantism, and which wanted to realize a comprehensive municipal welfare system, became exemplary for many cities, among them Strasburg and Ypres. It was not for nothing that the Leipzig edition of the Poor Relief Order stated on its title-page that it was 'a laudable order, which would be dignified and very useful for each and every country, town, and municipality to follow.' The Brandenburg-Nuremberg Church Order, which was largely written by Osiander, but published anonymously after long deliberations and delays in 1533, was to gain even more influence. With its threefold division of Reformation teaching, the renewal of the liturgy for church services, christenings, Communion, marriages, and funerals, and, finally, the catechetical sermons which at the end of each sermon merge into Luther's Small Catechism, this Church Order has been the basis of a group of Reformation Lutheran church orders besides those of Bugenhagen, Bucer, and Württemberg. If one wanted to enumerate the many towns, dominions, and territories in which it became officially acknowledged, this would be a long and maybe also long-winded list, which would increase in length if one were to include those church orders which were directly or indirectly influenced by it. It is not surprising that the Lutheran cities of the Empire in Franconia and several other southern German cities adopted the Church Order. But it was also adopted in Mecklenburg, and lastingly influenced the Church Orders in Electoral Brandenburg, Brunswick-Kalenberg, Palatine-Neuburg, and many others. The catechetical sermons have their own important history of influence; they were translated into Latin and from there into English, Polish, and even Icelandic. Their numerous reprints and translations indirectly promoted the distribution of the Lutheran Small Catechism.

II

So far we have examined the effect of the toleration and later implementation of the Reformation beyond the city boundaries and the territory. We shall now highlight Nuremberg's politics with reference to the religious question on various levels, in the context of the Swabian League, the imperial cities, and the Diets; and thereby we shall assess its importance for the Reformation in Germany. The city government was well aware early on that the religious question should not lead to a complete political isolation of the city. The neighbouring princes were still too much of a territorial threat for the city, which had established its territory only in the early sixteenth century at the cost of the neighbouring states; and local and foreign trade, the main sources of Nuremberg's wealth, could easily be affected. For these very reasons open and fundamental opposition to the Emperor was unthinkable; this did not mean, however, that Nuremberg committed itself to a political line of 'loyalty to the Emperor' in the crudest sense of the word. If the city's political existence were to continue, it was compelled in this climate of heightening tensions to try to defuse the potential for conflict inherent in the religious question by creating an agreed internal line which might be tolerated by potential opponents. Externally, on the level of the Empire, the aim was to keep the religious question open as long as possible and, if a decision were made, to prevent this religious question from becoming the all-important factor in the political activities of the Reich.

(1) The starting-point in this was that Nuremberg did not accept the condemnation of Luther and the new doctrine, as manifested as early as 1521 in the ban by the papal curia and in the Edict of Worms by the Emperor. One may doubt whether, even at this early stage, the City Council would have been in a position to impose the Edict on the population if it had wanted to do so. A 'popular movement', which would have to be taken into account by the Council, only developed after 1521-2 with the employment of Evangelical preachers and the backing of pamphlets. What must have been decisive at this time was those men in the council who saw in the actions against Luther only the machinations of the 'Romanists', which in Worms had recently been countered by the *gravamina*, or those councillors who themselves were already convinced of the truth of the Evangelical preaching, like the influential council clerk Lazarus Spengler. In any case, the city did not make any emhatic or serious attempt to implement the Edict of Worms. Nuremberg occasionally gave way to pressures in this direction when, between 1522 and 1524, the Imperial Court and the Diet were in session in the city, but at the same time people tried to annul the Edict in the sphere of the imperial cities and the Diets. In this context, they could point out, with increasing justification, that a strict implementation could not be enforced upon the population any longer. In addition, they asked for the consideration of the *gravamina*, which in their Nuremberg version did already show a distinct early Reformation influence. The cities, for various other reasons, did indeed protest against the recess of 1523, but they agreed to its conditions with reference to the religious question, and the corresponding mandate, since both did not expressly forbid Evangelical preaching. During the Diet of 1524 it was again Nuremberg which, urged by Spengler to use unambiguous language on the religious question, persuaded the cities to word their protest against recess and mandate; they asked for freedom of preaching based on the Gospel and corresponding actions until a free council was called. But the collapse of the united front of the cities on the religious question was already on the horizon: quite a few of them did not stand by that protest, but rather declared that they wanted to keep the Edict of Worms—as far as possible; and the Catholic cities of Upper Swabia did not appear at the next Diet of Imperial Cities. This why Nuremberg could have its way again: the cities stuck to their protest and commissioned particularly the Protestant towns—among them Nuremberg—to prepare the planned National Council in Speyer. The adoption of vindication by the Imperial Court was particularly in the interest of the city of Nuremberg where, in the meantime, the first Reformation

changes had been tolerated, after the threat of unrest spreading from the surrounding countryside to the city itself.

When the Emperor subsequently forbade the National Council in Speyer and a political solution of the religious problem had thus become impossible on the level of the Empire, it was Nuremberg which was particularly hard hit. The city immediately called a Diet of Imperial Cities which, in opposition to the Emperor's ban, had the religious question as its only topic. They passed a resolution to write to the Emperor not completely committing themselves to Luther's person, but in very decisive tones to Reformation teaching. They stated that it could not be the intention of papal or imperial mandates to take the Word of God away from the citizens. This is why they considered that the implementation of the Edict of Worms would lead to uproar. This very decisive language could not be supported by all the cities. Apart from the fact that a great number of them had not appeared at the Diet of Cities, others also distanced themselves from Nuremberg's attempt to commit all cities to a pro-Reformation line which at least tolerated the Reformation.

For Nuremberg's politics regarding religion, this Ulm Diet of Cities was a break. Up to this date the imperial cities, not least under the leadership of Nuremberg, had refused to implement the Edict of Worms, and thus allowed the Evangelical movement the space it needed for its emergence and development. From now on it was clear that the cities could not come to an agreement about a solution to the religious question. Thus, in principle, the resolution of the religious question at the level of territory and city was basically mapped out. And Nuremberg started on this path with the Disputation of March 1525 in the face of growing difficulties in the city and in the face of the Peasants' Revolt.

After the Peasants' War, the Protestant cities, and especially Nuremberg, which had pleaded with the Swabian League and the victorious princes for mild treatment of the neighbouring Franconian cities, found themselves under mounting pressure. Nevertheless, there was no general pact of the cities, nor did special negotiations with the large southern German cities lead to any success. On the other side, Nuremberg was not prepared to enter into a pact with the Protestant princes. In fact, the situation became less tense after the Diets of Augsburg and Speyer of 1525–6. Again headed by Nuremberg, the cities insisted on the treatment of the religious question and the *gravamina* and decided to send an envoy to the Emperor. Nuremberg could be content with the result of the Diet of Speyer which, in Evangelical interpretation, permitted a territorial and communal solution of the religious question. Thereafter, Nuremberg politics succeeded in keeping open also the religious problem within the Swabian League: the cities in the Swabian League decided not to permit decisions in religious matters to be taken by the League. Thus Nuremberg, together with the Margrave of Ansbach, through a visitation, managed to consolidate the Reformation. Furthermore, they succeeded in heeding the actions of the League against the Anabaptists of Franconia, actions which had also endangered the Evangelical movement.

Only the second Diet of Speyer changed this situation. When the Catholic cities renewed the Edict of Worms, Nuremberg and other cities joined the protestation by the Protestant princes and again urged a delegation to the Emperor. This situation forced the city to start negotiations with the Protestant princes about a possible pact. Nuremberg, however, always started from a double premise: the city, which since the start of the eucharistic controversy had suppressed all Zwinglian tendencies, and which had also tried to influence Strasburg in this sense, did not want to join a pact with the 'Sacramentarians'. On the other hand, any resistance to the Emperor was strictly rejected. Nuremberg also adhered to these principles after the Diet of Augsburg, when Nuremberg had adopted the *Confessio Augustana*, and subsequently undermined Melanchthon's negotiations for concord because it was feared that episcopal jurisdiction would be reinstated and thus the entire Reformation in the city and its environs would be endangered.

(2) Historians, and particularly church historians, have repreatedly voiced strong criticism of the religious politics of Nuremberg after the Diet of Augsburg in 1530; and even in the most recent work about the religious politics of the imperial cities we read that Lutheranism drove Nuremberg 'into complete political quietism'. Such a judgement, which only draws upon the position of the city in respect to the resistance against the Emperor is, however, entirely inadequate. Compared to this, Hans Baron, in his still very instructive contribution about 'Religion and Politics in the German Imperial Cities during the Reformation', had already given a much more balanced and understanding assessment of the situation. This has recently been taken up by Georg Schmidt. This, of course, presupposes that the assessment does not depend on what seems to be desirable to a modern historian—faithfulness to a confessional consistency, a readiness for resistance, or the promotion of the Reformation in the Reich, and so forth—but is based on what were the aims of Nuremberg's politics: to retain political independence and power and to secure the Evangelical confession within its own territory. Seen under this aspect,

Nuremberg's politics were altogether understandable and of an importance which went beyond the boundaries of the city.

In fact, the city did not feel threatened first and foremost for reasons of its faith or confession. Such a threat would have been directed not only against the city, but also against the neighbouring Margraves of Ansbach and against the other cities of the Empire and territories in the neighbourhood which had introduced the Reformation during the thirties and forties. Furthermore, it was possible to feel protected by the Nuremberg Agreement of 1532 and the ensuing peace promises of the Emperor to the protesting estates. What was not forgotten, however, was that the territorial princes were the real enemies of the city. And Nuremberg had repeatedly experienced how tense and unstable the political relation to the Margrave and the neighbouring palatine counts was. Not only because of this, but also because of the sensitive foreign trade, which was essential for the town and easily affected its politics, Nuremberg had to aim mainly at the maintenance and securing of peace in the country.

This explains why Nuremberg did not join the Smalcald League. This pact only offered protection in the case of an attack for reasons of faith; it could not give the desired general political security, and could not guarantee peace in the country. In addition, Lazarus Spengler saw that one would probably have had to come to the military succour of the supporters of the Upper German sacramental doctrine—that is, according to Nuremberg, of a wrong belief—and might have had to offer resistance to the Emperor, the ultimate sovereign of all imperial cities. This, in particular, seemed unthinkable in Nuremberg. People were well aware of the fact that the cities—particularly Nuremberg—depended on the Emperor's protection. In this situation, there was no reason for joining the Smalcald League. It was politically more prudent to stay on the lee side of the League, loosely associated as a signatory of the Augsburg Confession and pursuing one's own politics.

For the same reason, the city refused to let the question of faith and confession develop into an all-important factor in politics. This is why Nuremberg never entered into politics of obstruction against the Emperor, either at the election and coronation of Ferdinand as German king or in the question of the 'urgent Turkish help'. The council did not altogether dispute the competence of the imperial chancellery but only in respect of the religious question and the processes of jurisdiction and church property. For the same reason the city was not at all pleased to see the political formation of the Protestant estates in the Smalcald League develop again and again into politically explosive situations and even into wars. Nuremberg neither agreed with the repatriation of Duke Ulrich to Württemberg, nor with the widening of the right of Reformation in Augsburg or the military expeditions against the Duke of Brunswick by Hesse and Saxony; it also refused to intervene in favour of the Reformation in Cologne city council, for it was afraid that the Emperor might see this as a breach of his declaration. Thus Nuremberg was often in agreement with Luther who, also for the sake of peace, recommended that a further spreading of the Reformation should not be pushed.

This also explains why the council—unlike the members of the Smalcald League—supported the attempts of the Emperor to come to an agreement in matters of religion: they did not refuse to visit the church council, which had been planned and announced several times, and they really desired a positive result from the colloquies which the Emperor held in 1540–1 in Worms and Regensburg. As before, the city council was not averse to a solution of the religious question on a wider level than that of cities and territories.

On the other hand, Nuremberg had to try to find political allies. For this reason, the council was interested in a continuation of the Swabian League, which had served particularly as protection of the cities against the territorial princes since the beginning of the sixteenth century. Once it was foreseeable that the Swabian League would not be prolonged, Nuremberg was immediately prepared to enter into a pact for protection against a breach of the peace with Ulm and Augsburg, which was, however, not meant to be directed against emperor, king, and Swabian League. It did not shy away from such a pact with cities of a different confession either. Nuremberg would not have minded including even the king in the pact, but this attempt failed because of his lack of flexibility in the question of religion. This explains why, after the end of the Swabian League, Nuremberg and its allied towns, Windsheim and Weissenburg, entered the nine-year Imperial League, although it had mainly Catholic members, and although the religious question had not altogether been excluded. Only thus did the council think that they could secure the safety of the city against the pact of the Palatine Count and the Bishop of Bamberg (1534). And indeed, the Imperial League largely succeeded in keeping peace in the country. Only this alliance enabled the council to stay out of the Smalcald League for any length of time.

These 'seesaw politics', to which the council adhered even during the Smalcald Wars, and which were chiefly designed to serve the interests of the city, should not be underestimated in their consequences for the Empire and the course of the Reformation. On the one hand, they provided a stabilizing factor in the Franconian region where, at the end of the Swabian League, peace had been seriously at risk. On the other hand, it was doubtless of great importance that Nuremberg, together with its Franconian allied towns, as well as the Margrave of Ansbach, stayed away from the Protestant League. This certainly did weaken the unity of the Protestants. But it also prevented the emperor, the king, and the Catholic estates from seeing themselves confronted by a united Protestant front. Such a situation would probably have escalated the religious and political differences in the Empire even faster. One can only call the council's politics 'undynamic' if one considers as dynamic the spread of the Reformation by military means, as being desirable in principle. Nuremberg's politics made it an important link between the Protestant and the Catholic estate of the Empire. And, with at least the partial exclusion of the religious question, it followed a path which proved its worth for the cities in their assemblies in the forties. This succeeded in keeping peace in the German empire for another half-century after the Peace of Augsburg, although admittedly at great expense.

University of Heidelberg

Bibliography

Deutsche Reichstagsakten, Jüngere Reihe (Gotha and Stuttgart, 1893ff.; repr. Göttingen, 1962).

Martin Luther, *Eine Predigt, daß man Kinder zur Schulen halten solle* (*1530*), *WA*, 30, 2, pp. 517–88.

Andreas Osiander the Elder, *Gesamtausgabe*, vols 1–6, ed. Gerhard Müller, 7, ed. Gottfried Seebaß (Gütersloh, 1975–88).

Hans Baron, 'Religion and politics in the German imperial cities during the Reformation', *EHR*, 52 (1937), pp. 405–27; 614–33.

Martin Brecht, 'Die gemeinsame Politik der Reichsstädte und die Reformation', *ZSRG. K*, 94 (1977), pp. 181–263.

Adolf Engelhardt, *Die Reformation in Nürnberg*, 3 vols (Nuremberg, 1936–9).

Walter Friedensburg, *Der Reichstag zu Speyer 1525 im Zusammenhang der politischen und kirchlichen Entwicklung Deutschlands im Reformationszeitalter* (Berlin, 1887).

Harold J. Grimm, *Lazarus Spengler: A Lay Leader of the Reformation* (Columbus, Ohio, 1978).

Bernhard Klaus, *Veit Dietrich. Leben und Werk = Einzelarbeiten aus der Kirchengeschichte Bayerns*, 32 (Nuremberg, 1958).

Jürgen Lorz, *Das reformatorische Wirken Dr. Wenzeslaus Lincks in Altenburg und Nürnberg (1523–1547) = Nürnberger Werkstücke zur Stadt- und Landesgeschichte*, 25 (Nuremberg, 1978).

Gerhard Pfeiffer, 'Nürnberg und das Augsburger Bekenntnis 1530–1561', *Zeitschrift für bayerische Kirchengeschichte*, 49 (1980), pp. 2–19.

Georg Schmidt, 'Die Freien und Reichsstädte im Schmalkaldischen Bund' in Volker Press and Dieter Stievermann, eds, *Martin Luther. Probleme seiner Zeit = Spätmittelalter und Frühe Neuzeit*, 16 (Stuttgart, 1986), pp. 177–218.

——, 'Die Haltung des Städtecorpus zur Reformation und die Nürnberger Bündnispolitik', *ARG*, 75 (1984), pp. 194–233.

——, *Der Städtetag in der Reichsversassung. Eine Untersuchung zur korporativen Politik der Freien und Reichsstädte in der ersten Hälfe des 16. Jahrhunderts = Veröffentlichungen des Instituts für Europäische Geschichte Mainz*, 113, Abt. Universalgeschichte (Stuttgart, 1984).

Heinrich Richard Schmidt, *Reichsstädt, Reich und Reformation. Korporative Religionspolitik 1521–1529/30 = Veröffentlichungen des Instituts für Europäische Geschichte Mainz*, 122, Abt. Religionsgeschichte (Stuttgart, 1986).

Hans von Schubert, *Lazarus Spengler und die Reformation in Nürnberg*, ed. and intro. Hajo Holborn = *Quellen und Forschungen zur Reformationsgeschichte*, 17 (Leipzig, 1934).

Gottfried Seebaß, 'Andreas Osiander und seine Drucker' in Herbert G. Göpfert, Peter Vodosek, *et al.*, eds, *Beiträge zur Geschichte des Buchwesens im konfessionellen Zeitalter = Wolfenbütteler Schriften zur Geschichte des Buchwesens*, 11 (Wiesbaden, 1985), pp. 133–45.

——, 'Luther und Nürnberg', *Zeitschrift für bayerische Kirchengeschichte*, 53 (1984), pp. 1–18.

——, *Das reformatorische Werk des Andres Osiander = Einzelarbeiten aus der Kirchengeschichte Bayerns*, 44 (Nuremberg, 1967).

Gerald Strauss, *Nuremberg in the Sixteenth Century* (New York, 1966).

CALVIN'S LATIN PREFACE TO HIS PROPOSED FRENCH EDITION OF CHRYSOSTOM'S HOMILIES: TRANSLATION AND COMMENTARY

by W. IAN P. HAZLETT

Introduction

I

ONE of the traditional puzzles in Calvin studies has been Calvin's proposed and supposedly French edition of the sermons of the Greek Church Father, John Chrysostom.[1] The date, circumstances, and precise scope of this project have always been uncertain, chiefly because the only evidence for the plan is a substantial fragment of a prefatory introduction in Calvin's own hand. As yet, no mention of or allusion to it has been found in any other contemporary source. The fact that all we have is a preface, or the first draft of one, suggests that the scheme was abortive. At any rate, no such work was published by Calvin, though that does not prove that he never actually got round to translating the Homilies. It is just as conceivable that no publisher would take it on.[2] But it is likely that the combination of Calvin's other extensive literary commitments and the heavy demands and vexations of what was a pioneering local and cosmopolitan ministry simply hindered him from realizing his intention.

Whatever the problems surrounding this Calvin fragment, its contents

---

[1] Literature on Calvin and the Fathers in general, or on Calvin and Chrysostom in particular: A. N. S. Lane, 'Calvin's use of the Fathers and Medievals', *Calvin Theological Journal*, 16 (1981), pp. 149–205; H. O. Old, *The Patristic Roots of Reformed Worship* (Zurich, 1975), pp. 141–9; P. Polman, *L'Elément historique dans la controverse religieuse du XVIe siècle* (Gembloux, 1932), pp. 65–94; M. Réveillaud, 'L'autorité de la tradition chez Calvin', *La Revue réformée* (1958), pp. 24–45; J. Koopmans, *Das altkirchliche Dogma in der Reformation*, tr. H. Quistorp (Munich, 1955), pp. 36–41; A. Gancozy and K. Müller, *Calvins handschriftliche Annotationen zu Chrysostom* (Wiesbaden, 1981); J. R. Walchenbach, 'John Calvin as Biblical commentator. An investigation into Calvin's use of John Chrysostom as an exegetical tutor' (Pittsburgh, Ph.D. dissertation, 1974), pp. 23–35, 201–6; R. J. Mooi, *Het kerk-en dogmahistorisch element in de werken van Johannes Calvijn* (Wageningen, 1965), pp. 13–14, 30–8, 90–4, 273–80, 344–6; *Calvinus ecclesiae Genevensis custos*, ed. W. Neuser (Frankfurt, 1984), pp. 163–4.

[2] The publishers of the second edition of the *Institutes* (1539) had complained that it was not selling well: see *Correspondance des réformateurs dans le pays de langue française*, ed. A.-L. Herminjard (Geneva, 1866–97), 6, p. 156.

are a transparent testimony of the relationship between Christian human-ism and the Reformation; between the rediscovery of the sources of Christian (and Jewish) Antiquity by reform-minded Catholics, which accompanied the Renaissance, and the theological and religious revolu-tion initiated by Luther; and between patristic tradition and Scripture in the mind of a Reformer. Calvin's document is a miniature, embodying one of the most distinctive and potent amalgams of these forces.

II

At the head of the manuscript has been written by a sixteenth-century hand other than Calvin's: 'Praefatio in edition[em] Hom(i)liarum Chryso-stomi a D[octore] Calv[ino] medidatam q[uae] tam[en] n[on] extat. Inter-ponit aut[em] hic suu[m] tu[m] de Chrysostomo tu[m] de ali[qu]is quos illi comparat ecclesiae doctorib[us] iudicium appositum.' That is: 'The preface to an edition of Chrysostom's Homilies contemplated by Master Calvin, but which does not exist. Here however he puts forward his due opinion both on Chrysostom and on other doctors of the Church, whom he compares to him.' After the word *editionem* has been inserted above the line by a third hand the word *gall[icam]*, and then deleted. This is a reminder that Calvin does not state explicitly in the Preface that he intends to translate the Homilies into French. Further, it might seem strange that a preface to a popular edition should be in Latin. Yet it should also be borne in mind that even in those times, Latin could still be referred to as a vernacular.

Yet the case for believing that Calvin was envisaging a French transla-tion is very strong. He refers to his project as 'unconventional'. At a time when large quantities of new Latin translations of patristic literature were being published by Erasmus, Oecolampadius, Capito, Musculus, and many others,[3] Calvin would hardly have used the word 'unconventional' if he had been thinking of yet another Latin translation. And translations of the Fathers in the languages of the people were very rare, and in fact were to remain so for a long time. Anyway, in his text Calvin concedes that cultural reality means that not all pastors and teachers are competent in the classical languages, so that they too could benefit from a translation. As for the point about the Preface being in Latin, a look at the original manuscript shows that what we have is a first draft, with its errors, correc-

---

[3] Earlier humanists had had a special interest in Chrysostom; cf. C. L. Stinger, *The Renaissance in Rome* (Bloomington, 1985), pp. 226–34.

tions, deletions, interlinear and marginal insertions, sometimes minor, sometimes major, its extensive abbreviations, and so on. This would subsequently have been translated into French. Like most people from his background, and especially with his humanist training, the natural mode of Calvin's scholarly and theological written thought would be in Latin. Composing literary pieces in the less formally structured vernacular would not have come so easily. And so it can be neither a surprise nor a mystery that this first draft of Calvin's Preface is in Latin.

III

A justification for translating this Preface into English is necessary, since it was translated a quarter of a century ago by John H. McIndoe (published in the *Hartford Quarterly*, 5 (1965), pp. 19–26). An inter-library loan search in British libraries revealed that no copy of this was available, or known to be available. Fortunately access was gained to a copy in the Trinity College Collection of Glasgow University Library, where its location is almost certainly due to the fact that J. H. McIndoe was an alumnus of Trinity. Anyway, it seemed appropriate to make a translation of Calvin's Preface more readily available on this side of the Atlantic.

Further, while McIndoe's translation is perfectly reasonable and worthy, there seemed to me to be enough dubious and occasionally inexplicable renderings to warrant a fresh translation. Also, that translation is confined to a bare rendering of the Latin text in the *Corpus Reformatorum*. Variant readings in the various transcripts are not taken into account. And comparison of the *CR* text with the original shows that the former is not infallible either. None of the textual problems is of major or crucial significance. But some of them are problematical. Most of these textual discrepancies are indicated below in the first critical apparatus.

Lastly, the *Hartford Quarterly* text is completely devoid of an introduction and helpful footnotes. There are virtues in this, but there are also dangers. Many of the references, associations, and allusions in Calvin's text would remain arcane and cryptic. And so generous annotation of the text is provided below to illustrate fully the operations of Calvin's mind as he considered the dire problem of Christian and theological education among the people of the Church, whom he considered deprived of their inheritance.

IV

Dating: Estimations range from 1535 to 1559. That of 1559, proposed by Walchenbach, seems to be the least likely, as it is based on conjectures and assumptions which seem untenable. The first is that Calvin's reference to the 'generation of twenty years ago', when most people were ignorant of Christ, that is of the Bible, means before 1534 to 1535, when the French Bibles of Lefèvre and Olivétan appeared. That, however, would have been twenty-five or more years ago. Elsewhere in the document, however, Calvin refers to *our age*, when [Scripture] has *begun* once again to be circulated'. This must surely refer to the mid- to late thirties, when modern translations of the whole Bible became available. 'Twenty years ago' would then refer to before 1522, when Luther's German New Testament appeared. In addition, Calvin refers to protests raised when it was suggested that the Bible be read by the public. The most renowned expression of such a suggestion was that of Erasmus in 1516, the full positive consequence of which was there for all to see twenty years later.

Secondly, Walchenbach's dating also rests on the hypothesis that Calvin's familiarity with patristic commentaries implies that he was well advanced in writing his own commentaries, late in his career. But it is just as likely that he was familiar with patristic commentaries before he embarked upon writing his own, the first of which appeared in 1539.

Thirdly, Walchenbach adduces as circumstantial evidence Calvin's revised edition of his Isaiah commentary in 1559, and the preface to Edward VI of England. It is claimed that this contains themes similar to Calvin's Chrysostom Preface. I think this must be dismissed. Apart from the preface to Edward VI being a reprint of the one in the first edition of 1551, there are no thematic parallels suggesting a striking relationship with the Chrysostom Preface. There are echoes of basic concerns, such as the necessity of Scripture study for reforming and building up the Church, and of its dissemination among the people at large, but this can be found in many of Calvin's writings. Therefore, there is little convincing, and nothing decisive, in the case for 1559. And so internal evidence suggests the thirties.

Although he does not discuss the question, Mooi consistently cites 1535 when he refers to the Preface. This may derive from the editors of the text in the CR, who suggest as one possibility 1535, before Calvin left France. Their other suggestion is before Calvin embarked upon his New Testament commentaries, meaning before 1538 to 1539. They end up proposing 1540, which was before Calvin's return to Geneva. This corresponds to the note on the Zurich transcript in the *Simler-Sammlung*: *circa annum 1540*.

Palaeographic and forensic evidence corroborates this almost beyond doubt. In the handwriting of the Preface manuscript, distinctive is the visual dominance of Calvin's initial and medial long 's' in a word like 'sensus'. This is elongated, almost vertical, like a swan's neck, with a small, crescent-shaped crotchet at the top right. To make this 's', his quill has made two movements instead of one. This is typical of Calvin's handwriting until 1540. Thereafter, the idiosyncrasy no longer appears. Moreover, the watermark in the paper on which the Preface is written is a Basle crozier, a kind that first appeared there in 1538. Not only that; it is the same watermark which is found in Calvin's letters written from Basle and Strasburg in 1538 to 1540, but not in letters from 1541 onwards, when he had returned to Geneva.[4] While this is conclusive, another piece of circumstantial evidence supporting 1538 to 1540 may be cited. Ganoczy and Müller have produced a study of Calvin's personal copy of the 1536 Paris edition of Chrysostom's works, which contains his own marginal notes and underlinings and so on. These concentrate not so much on the exegetical as the didactic part of Chrysostom's Homilies, on the moral instruction elements relating to the Christian life of the individual and the ecclesial body.[5] It would seem that Calvin was using Chrysostom as a means of learning how to preach sermons with practical relevance. As a timid academic who found himself in the ministry with no pastoral or homiletic training, and whose first short ministry in Geneva had been a failure, it would have been perfectly natural for Calvin to seize on Chrysostom as a self-improving model to follow in the more benign atmosphere of Strasburg. Following his admiration of Chrysostom's exegesis and preaching, it is no wonder that Calvin would have the idea of translating him into French in the period 1538–40.

v

With regard to the content of Calvin's Preface, it is first and foremost a vindication of not just the propriety, but the desirability of circulating secondary aids to assist with the study and interpretation of Scripture.

[4] For decisive assistance in this matter I am grateful to friends and former colleagues at Geneva, Irena Backus, Alain Dufour, and Professor Pierre Fraenkel; and to Professor R. Lyall in Glasgow.
[5] See Ganoczy and Müller, *Annotationen*, p. 19, who refer to Calvin's 'paränetischaszetische Motiv'.

Secondary aids, in this case, means biblical commentaries. Just as Scripture itself is now available to ordinary people in their own languages, so also the best of biblical commentaries should be popularly accessible, and not confined to scholars who have the privilege of a classical education. Just as the Word of God belongs to the people of God, so, too, the tradition of interpretation guided by the Spirit is theirs as well. Those who are regrettably hindered because of linguistic limitations ought to be provided with translations. This is desirable not only for ordinary people, but also for similarly handicapped pastors and teachers in the Church; these in particular need access to the thought and practices of the Early Church, since the Church at that time was closer to the mind and will of Christ. The interpreter and presenter of the Word *par excellence* in Antiquity is John Chrysostom, whose Homilies and exegetical skill excel those of any other Church Father. And the fact that Chrysostom was clearly committed to communication with and instruction of the common people makes it important that his voice be transmitted again for the benefit of the Church at large.

Calvin admits, however, that Chrysostom is not as sound as he ought to have been in the matter of justification, that in the doctrines of election, free will, good works, grace, and so forth, he makes too much concession to human capacity and virtue. But this is no reason to ignore Chrysostom, who was no more infallible than any other teacher of the Church. Anyway, Chrysostom's position on these doctrines is largely explained by circumstances and pressures to which he was subject. (The matter of Chrysostom as an important patristic testimony to the spiritual supremacy of the see of Rome is ignored by Calvin.) The original manuscript shows how Calvin composed and drafted his thoughts; the most revealing feature of it is that his critique of Chrysostom, as well as the extenuating circumstances to which Calvin appeals, occurs to him as an extended afterthought. Textually, it has the form of an appended insertion.[6] For Calvin, then, his admiration for Chrysostom had priority over his criticism of him. Lastly, Chrysostom's writings can be read with profit because of their instructive historical value, the insight they offer into the life, worship, discipline, and organization of the Early Church—an example to be followed.

---

[6] Fols 161v–2v.

The Preface is a testimony to Reformation theology in Christian, more particularly Erasmian, humanist clothes. Calvin's belief that the reform of the Church as the people of God, in respect of right living (regeneration) as well as right thinking (justification by Christ alone), is dependent on two things: firstly, the restoration of original Christianity (*ad fontes!*), and, secondly, the liberation of the Word of God from the 'spiritual estate', that is, from the clergy and the theologians, and its restoration to its rightful heirs, the body of Christians as a whole and the common man. The latter must be made aware of and appropriate his inheritance by ways and means that he can understand. Even morons, idiots, and ignoramuses must somehow be brought to share in the gift of heavenly wisdom.

Related to this notion of the democratization of the Gospel is that of 'accommodation'.[7] At the theological level this is analogous to God's condescension to humanity in the Incarnation of Jesus Christ. In terms of the concepts and communication technology of humanism, the means of accommodation and getting through to all and sundry is provided by rhetoric, particularly erudition, persuasion, and decorum. Properly applied, these will help bring about change of behaviour and mental attitude more in line with the will of God. If in our times the meaning of 'decorum' has been contracted to refer to what is appropriate in polite society and solemn occasions, the Erasmian Christian humanists used it to mean what is appropriate for any sort or class of people on any occasion. As the essential function of rhetoric, 'decorum' is that which bridges the gap and alienation between humans. The language of teachers and preachers must be flexible enough to meet the needs of different individuals and societies; there must be 'accommodation' to one's audience for the sake of 'persuasion', and motivation to change. The learned textbook or general statements of doctrine are not effective among those who are educationally deprived, which in Calvin's time was the majority of people, including most women, as he notes in his preface to Olivétan's Bible.[8] Calvin may well also have been influenced by the popular rejection of the *Confession of Faith* in Geneva in 1537–8. The

---

[7] Especially illuminating on Calvin's application of this notion is W. J. Bouwsma, *John Calvin: a Sixteenth-Century Portrait* (New York, 1988), pp. 113–27; cf. R. Stauffer, *Dieu, la création et la providence dans la prédication de Calvin* (Berne, 1978), pp. 54–6.

[8] In John Calvin, *Institutes of the Christian Religion. 1536 edition*, ed. F. L. Battles, rev. edn (London, 1986), appendix IV, pp. 373–7.

person on the street was simply unmoved by it. Elsewhere Calvin pointed out that the failure of Job's friends to console him was due to their lack of decorum, that is, they were not on the same wavelength as he. And so it is no wonder that Calvin should turn to Chrysostom as a model to be learned from. 'He of the golden mouth' had been educated in classical rhetoric at Antioch, if not by the most noted pagan rhetorician of his day, Libanius, at least in his school.

The Preface is also a testimony to the Catholic Calvin, with his strongly ecclesial concern and sense of the communion of saints.[9] Strengthened rather than weakened by the Reformation doctrine of the priesthood of all believers, this way of thinking expresses itself in Calvin with his conviction that contemporary and earlier Christians have a mutual interest, namely the service of Christ in the common Christian and ecclesiastical ministry; that while the Word of God in Scripture is the sole authority, the tradition of interpretation or 'prophesying' among those guided by the Spirit in the past is for the edification of everyone in the Church in all ages. And so, following from this Catholic ecclesial thrust in his thought, Calvin is far removed from approving of individualist subjectivism, Scripture-unrelated spiritualism, and speculative theory of a human philosophical kind.

Calvin's characteristic hermeneutical and exegetical principles also manifest themselves in the Preface, especially when he assesses the biblical work of the various Fathers: Christ as the goal sought for in Scripture; paracletic exegesis, that is, the interpreter should be guided not so much by human canons and criteria as by the Spirit; the only valid exegesis is that which is profitable, useful, and edifying for the Church—in the sense of I Corinthians 4; the clarity and plain meaning of Scripture should not be departed from in pursuit of allegorical and mystical deep meanings, so that the genuine, straightforward, and authentic sense of the words prevail; lucidity and conciseness should be aimed for; the 'circumstances of the times' should enable elements of relativity to be identified and understood[10]—Calvin invokes these principles in the excuses he offers for Chrysostom's dogmatic unsoundness. On the whole, Calvin represents here the Antiochene tradition of exegesis, which was largely adopted by the Reformation. He is convinced that Chrysostom embodies these

---

[9] Cf. A. Ganoczy, *The Young Calvin*, tr. D. Foxgrover and W. Provo (Edinburgh, 1988), pp. 308ff.

[10] Cf. H.-J. Kraus, 'Calvins exegetische Prinzipien', *ZKG*, 79 (1968), pp. 329–41; A. Ganoczy and S. Scheld, *Die Hermeneutik Calvins. Geistesgeschichtliche Voraussetzungen und Grundzüge* (Wiesbaden, 1983), pp. 90ff.

principles—in contrast to Luther, who found Chrysostom to be a blether for whom he had little time, a writer of a 'chaotic heap of words without substance ... argumentative and garrulous', who sacrifices (dogmatic) substance to form and rhetoric.[11] It is striking how, in this respect, Calvin's opinion of Chrysostom is much more magnanimous and tolerant than that of Luther. As a fellow humanist, Calvin shared the views of Erasmus, Bucer,[12] and Zwingli[13] in this respect, whereas, again, Luther comments that everything he finds objectionable in Chrysostom pleases Erasmus, that loquaciousness and verbosity are the curse of Gentile theologians 'like Bucer and Chrysostom'.[14]

Calvin's Preface also clearly shows the issue over which Christian humanism and the Reformation went different ways, notably in anthropology and justification. Following the dispute between Luther and Erasmus in 1525 over free will, Christian humanists had to take sides. Calvin, of course, followed Luther, but he would not allow Chrysostom's semi-Pelagianism to dismiss him altogether. Further, while Calvin's Preface embodies his adhesion to basic Erasmian humanist principles in respect of the dissemination of religious knowledge, it also represents a break with an elitist form of humanism with which he had also experience in France. This is the kind represented by Budé and Sadolet.[15] They argued that the religious unrest which was among the ordinary people, and allegedly threatening the stability of society, was a consequence of theology falling into the hands of the ignorant and uneducated. Calvin turned this argument on its head: there was religious unrest and instability because the people were being denied that which was their right and inheritance, and only total exposure to Christian doctrine would solve the problem.

Lastly, the Preface shows incontestably that while Calvin learned the basic principles of humanism, Christian or otherwise, in France, and can hardly have been uninfluenced by the country's leading Catholic Evangelical humanist, Lefèvre d'Etaples;[16] the most immediate and identifiable

---

[11] See *Tischreden*, *WA*, 2, p. 516; 4, pp. 286, 652.

[12] Cf. F. Krüger, *Bucer und Erasmus. Eine Untersuchung zum Einfluss des Erasmus auf die Theologie Martin Bucers (bis zum Evangelienkommentar von 1530)* (Wiesbaden, 1970), pp. 3–68; Nicole Peremans, *Erasme et Bucer d'après leur correspondance* (Paris, 1970), pp. 28–33. On certain aspects of Calvin's indebtedness to Erasmian humanism see Marjorie O'Rourke Boyle, *Rhetoric and Reform: Erasmus's Civil Dispute with Luther* (Cambridge, Mass., 1983), pp. 43–6.

[13] Cf. A. Schindler, *Zwingli und die Kirchenväter* (Zurich, 1984), p. 61.

[14] Cf. n. 11.

[15] Cf. J. Bohatec, *Budé und Calvin. Studien zur Gedankenwelt des französischen Frühhumanismus* (Graz, 1950), pp. 127–30.

[16] Cf. Ganoczy, *The Young Calvin*, pp. 85, 178–81.

formative influences in this respect are those of Erasmus and Bucer. The footnotes to the text of the Preface illustrate the many obvious substantive parallels in those writers. Bucer, in particular, is Calvin's model for the wedding of Christian humanism and Reformation, with its characteristic notion of the reform of theology, Church, society, and the individual, as well as its concern for ethical amelioration. And since Calvin was working with Bucer in Strasburg when he composed this piece, his intimate relationship with, and relative dependence on, him as a Reformer who also held hands with humanism is hardly surprising. Further, Calvin had also sojourned in Basle, which had been effectively the city of Erasmus.

Preface to the Homilies of Chrysostom

MANUSCRIPTS

Autograph:

Geneva, Bibliothèque publique et universitaire, fr. 145, fols 160r–2v.

Transcripts:

Geneva, Bibliothèque publique et universitaire, fr. 145, fols 180r–1v.
Zurich, Zentralbibliothek, *Simler-Sammlung* V 48–1540, 183.
Bern, Staatsarchiv des Kantons, B III 62 (*Epistolae virorum clarorum*, vol. VII, 33 des Konvents-Archivs), pp. 12–25.

PRINTED EDITION

CR, *Calvini opera omnia*, 9, cols 831–8.

TRANSLATION

/col. 831/ Considering that this kind of work which I am now publishing is unconventional,[1] I think it will be worth my while to explain briefly the point of my project. For I am aware of what nearly always happens in the case of innovation, that there will be no lack of people who will not only condemn this work of mine as unnecessary, but also are of the opinion that it ought to be rejected out of hand as being of no particular benefit to

[1] Until then a patristic writing translated into the vernacular was extremely rare.

the Church.[2] I am optimistic that these very people will be sympathetic towards me, should they pay heed for a moment to my reasons.

We know what kind of protests were raised initially by backward people when it was suggested that the Gospel should be read by the public.[3] For they reckoned it to be an outrage that the mysteries of God, which had been concealed for so long by priests and monks, be made known to ordinary people.[4] Indeed, this just seemed to be sacrilegious profanation of the temple[5] of God.

[2] Cf. Martin Bucer in the Preface to his commentary on the Synoptic Gospels: 'One has to deplore the arrogance of those who disdain to read the writings of not only the holy Fathers but also of modern commentators which offer to explain the Word of God'; *Enarrationes perpetuae* (1530), fol. A 7b; see also Bucer's marginal comment in the same commentary (fol. 100b): 'They tempt the Lord who aspire to knowledge of scripture without a great deal of study.' A literalist application of the 'Scripture alone' principle gave rise to this anti-academic attitude. It was found among some of those committed to alternative Reformation, e.g. Thomas Müntzer and Andrew Carlstadt. The former referred to the Wittenberg theologians as 'mischievous Scripture thieves' (verschmitzte Schriftstehler) and 'spiteful biblical scholars' (gehässige Schriftgelehrten) who are the modern Pharisees. See his *Hochverursachte Schutzrede* in *Thomas Müntzer. Schriften und Briefe*, ed. G. Wehr (Gütersloh, 1978), pp. 108–9; cf. n. 46 below.

[3] The most influential call to have the Bible translated into modern languages had been that of Erasmus in 1516, in the *Paraclesis* of his *In Novum Testamentum Praefationes*: 'I disagree absolutely with those who are reluctant to have Holy Scripture, translated into the vernacular, read by the laity, as if Christ taught such complex doctrines that they could only be understood by a very few theologians, or as if the strength of the Christian religion consisted in people's ignorance of it . . . Christ wishes his mysteries to be published as openly as possible. . . . For it is not fitting that . . . doctrines alone should be reserved for those very few whom the crowd call theologians or monks . . . is he a theologian, let alone a Christian, who has not read the literature of Christ? Who loves me, Christ says, keeps my Word . . . Only a few can be learned, but all can be Christian, all can be devout, and, I shall boldly add, all can be theologians.' See *Erasmus von Rotterdam. Ausgewählte Schriften . . . Lateinisch und Deutsch*, 3, ed. G. Winkler (Darmstadt, 1967), pp. 15–23.

[4] Traditionally, the Church did not on principle ban the translation of the Bible, but she rarely encouraged such ventures for fear of facilitating heretical notions. But there were traditionalist individuals who openly opposed translations, and Calvin summarizes the debate with them in his Latin preface to Olivétan's French Bible in 1535: 'But the ungodly voices of some are head, shouting that it is a shameful thing to publish these divine mysteries among the simple common people. . . . "How then", they ask, "can these poor illiterates comprehend such things, untutored as they are in all liberal arts?" . . . Why don't these people at least imitate the example of the Fathers to whom they pretend to be so deferential? Jerome did not disdain mere women as partners in his studies. . . . Why is it that Chrysostom contends that the reading of Holy Scripture is more necessary for common people than for monks, [especially since the former] are tossed about by waves of care and business?' See *CR*, *Calvini opera*, 9, cols 787–8. English: *Institutes of the Christian Religion. 1536 edition*, ed. Battles, appendix IV, pp. 373ff.; cf. Bohatec, *Budé und Calvin*, pp. 129–30.

[5] That is, Scripture. Lat. *sacrarium*, meaning also sanctuary or shrine. *Oracula dei* is the phrase normally associated with Calvin, *Institutes*, 4. 9. 14, and before him Bucer, *Enarrationes*, fol. A 5b, 7b. The use of *sacrarium* illustrates that, for Calvin, Scripture as the Word of God is in a sense theophanic. But he was also to qualify this by saying that Scripture is no more than the *living image* of God; similitude, not identity. See also Stauffer, *Dieu, la création et la providence*, p. 54.

Yet even among those to whom this idea was so repugnant we now see that all such objections have been transformed into approval.[6] For it was obvious that the people of God had been deprived of the supreme repository[7] of their salvation—with Scripture lying hidden in the libraries of a select few, inaccessible to the general public. Accordingly, anyone nowadays with a modicum of religion recognizes that through the remarkable favour of God it came about that the sacred Word of God was restored to the entire Church. For in this way has Christ, *the sun of righteousness*,[8] shone upon his people—[the Christ] whom we only then truly take delight in after we have recognized his power, and embrace him when offered to us through the Gospel by God the Father.

And yet those who were in a position to observe the state of the world in the generation of twenty years ago[9] remember that, among the vast majority of people, there was almost nothing remaining of Christ except his name; any recollection of his power which did exist was both rare and scanty. This shocking situation, which is the worst possible, had undoubtedly occurred only because people—as if it were no business of theirs[a]—had left the reading of Scripture to the priests and monks. This is the reason /col. 832/ why we take pride in our age, when that repository, in which Christ is displayed to us with all the wealth of his benefits, has begun once again to be circulated among all the children of God;[10] that [namely, Scripture] is the specific means by which our heavenly inheritance[11] is authenticated, the very temple[12] where God exhibits to us the reality of his deity.

But just as it is of great concern to us not to be denied this wholesome

---

[a] *quum sit commune filiis Dei* + CR, but deleted in MS Geneva, fr. 145, fol. 160r.

[6] By this time a number of translations of the New Testament or the whole Bible by Catholic authors were available, e.g. in French by Lefèvre d'Etaples (1530), in German by Emser (1527), Dietenberger (1534), and Eck (1537), in Italian by Brucioli (1534) and Zacharia and Marmochino (1538). But that attitudes in the Old Church were slow to change is suggested by the fact that in his preaching, Calvin continued to denounce roundly the closed-shop treatment of scripture. See Stauffer, pp. 57–9.

[7] Lat. *thesaurus*, meaning also treasury or storehouse.

[8] Mal. 4. 2.

[9] That is, pre-1520.

[10] In German, there was Luther's Bible (1522–34), and the Zurich Bible (1529), in English, Tyndale's version (1525–31) and Coverdale's (1535), in French, Olivétan's Bible (1534). Modern translations were also available in Dutch, Low German, Danish, Swedish, Czech, and Hungarian before 1540.

[11] Cf. Eph. 1. 14, 18. Heb. 9. 15.

[12] Cf. n. 5.

140

knowledge, [b]by which[b] our souls are nourished for eternal life,[13] so once it is available to us, it is just as necessary to know what one ought to look for there, to have some sort of goal[14] towards which we may be guided. In the absence of this, we will[c] undoubtedly end up roaming aimlessly for a long time with little to show for it. And therefore it is my belief that the Spirit of God is certainly not only the best, but also the sole guide, since without him, there is not even a glimmer of light in our minds enabling us to appreciate heavenly wisdom;[15] yet as soon as the Spirit has shed his light, our minds are more than adequately prepared and equipped to grasp this very wisdom.

Since, however, the Lord, with the same consideration by which he illuminates us through his Spirit,[16] has, in addition, granted us aids, which he intends to be of assistance in our labour of investigating his truth, there is no reason for us either to neglect them as superfluous, or even to care less about them as if irrelevant.[17] For what Paul said ought to be borne in mind, that *though everything belongs to us, we however belong to Christ*.[18] Therefore, let those things which the Lord has provided for our use be of service to us.

The point is, if it is right that ordinary Christians be not deprived of the Word of their God, neither should they be denied prospective resources, which may be of use for its true understanding. Besides, [ordinary

---

[b] Retaining *CR* and Zurich *qua*, instead of MS Geneva, fr. 145, fol. 160r, and other copies, *quibus*.

[c] MS Geneva, fr. 145, fol. 160r and copies *continget*, instead of *CR*, *contingat*.

[13] Cf. John 6. 54ff.

[14] Lat. *scopus*—a nautical and astronomical term, which can refer either to the instrument by which a 'sighting' like a star is found, or the star itself. It was Erasmus, following his familiarity with the Greek Fathers, who had reintroduced this use of the word in his *Ratio seu compendium verae theologiae* (1518), ed. Winkler, pp. 200–1: 'We must not corrupt the heavenly philosophy of Christ.... May that goal remain intact.... May that north star never be darkened for us, may that sure sign never be missing by which we, tossed about in the waves of error, will find the right course again.' Cf. Marjorie O'Rourke Boyle, *Erasmus on Language and Method in Theology* (Toronto, 1977), pp. 4ff.

[15] Cf. I Cor. 2. 10–14. The expression 'heavenly wisdom' is characteristic of Calvin, and very much echoes Erasmian humanist usage; cf. J. Boisset, *Sagesse et sainteté dans la pensée de Calvin. Essai sur l'humanisme du réformateur français* (Paris, 1959).

[16] This section is an allusion to Calvin's doctrine of the 'internal testimony of the Holy Spirit'.

[17] Cf. Erasmus, *Prefationes: Methodus*, ed. Winkler, pp. 68–70: 'Someone may ask: "What? Do you regard the Holy Scripture as so straightforward that it could be understood without commentaries?" ... the work of the Ancients ought to relieve us of some of the labour.' Also *Prae-fationes: Apologia*, ed. Winkler, pp. 96–7, where Erasmus writes that 'The Holy Spirit is never absent, but he reveals his power in such a way that he leaves us with a share of the work [of interpretation].' Behind this way of thinking is the Pauline notion of 'prophesying' and the gift of interpretation. Cf. n. 2.

[18] I Cor. 3. 21, 23.

Christians] do not have the educational attainment. As this in itself is a considerable privilege, so it is not granted to everyone.[19] It is obvious, therefore, that they should be assisted by the work of interpreters, who have advanced in the knowledge of God to a level that they can guide others to as well. For what justice would there be in men of higher learning having that good fortune as well, whereas those deprived of all such resources /col. 833/ are lacking even that very [knowledge] which, out of everything, was their one entitlement? Because if it is a religious duty to help the weak, and to assist them all the more diligently the greater their need, let those who will censure this work of mine beware of being charged with an uncaring attitude. All I have had in mind with this is to facilitate the reading of Holy Scripture for those who are humble and uneducated.[20]

I am certainly well aware of what objection can be made to me in this business. This is what Chrysostom,[21] whom I am undertaking to make known to the public, aimed his studies at the intelligentsia only. But yet, unless both the title [of his work][22] and [its] style of language deceive, this man specialized in sermons which he delivered to a wide public. Accordingly, he plainly adjusts both [his] approach and language as if he had the instruction of the common people in mind.[23] This being the case, anyone maintaining that he ought to be kept in seclusion among the academics has got it wrong, seeing that he did go out of his way to cultivate a popular appeal.

That I share a common[d] concern with Chrysostom is unquestionably

---

[d] Reading *communem* with *CR*, Zurich, and Berne, instead of MS Geneva fr. 145, fol. 160v, and Geneva transcript, *coniunctam*.

[19] At this time, only about 5 per cent of the population of Europe was effectively literate.

[20] Cf. Calvin in his preface to Olivétan's Bible, ed. Battles, p. 374: 'I desire only this, that faithful people be permitted to hear their God speaking and to learn knowledge from [him]. ... When therefore we see that there are people from all classes who are making progress in God's school, we acknowledge His truth which promised a pouring forth of His Spirit on all flesh.'

[21] d. 407, successively bishop of Antioch and Constantinople.

[22] Calvin is alluding to the fact that the bulk of the exegetical material in known Chrysostom *opera* was presented in the form of homilies.

[23] The points made by Calvin here echo those made by Erasmus in the Preface to his Chrysostom edition of 1530, a preface which was republished in the Paris edition of 1536 used by Calvin, e.g., 'Among the various gifts of the Spirit [in Chrysostom], teaching ability is pre-eminent ... for who teaches more clearly? ... for all his great erudition and eloquence, there is in almost everything he wrote an incredible concern to be helpful; he adapted to the ears of the people, with the result that he brought the essence of a sermon down to the level of their comprehension, as if he were a schoolteacher speaking child-talk with an infant pupil'. *Chrysostomi omnia opera*, fols 9b E–10b G; cf. Stauffer, *Dieu, la création et la providence*, pp. 54–6, and Bouwsma, *John Calvin*, pp. 124ff.

more than adequate justification for me, because I am just imparting to ordinary people what he wrote specifically for ordinary people. Nor was he the only one to do this. As a matter of fact, others of the Ancients as well devoted the bulk of their studies to the people in this way when they composed homilies. For they rightly kept that guideline of Paul's, that all the endowments which God has conferred on his servants ought to be utilized for the edification of everyone.[24] They also knew that the more anyone was in need of their services, the greater the obligation on them. For in view of the fact that after Paul *had been caught up in the third heaven* and *had seen secrets unutterable to man*,[25] but yet still declared himself under an obligation to the simple and uneducated, how could [the Ancients] exempt themselves from that stipulation? Therefore, just as they would have very inadequately discharged what was their duty if they had not put to common use the skills they had received from God, so, too, woud we be invidious by failing to impart to the people of God what is theirs.[26] Likewise, the people themselves would be lacking in gratitude, were they not eager to take up the gift of God offered to them.

In addition to this point, there is a further consideration: among us it does not always happen that those charged with the ministry of the churches are sufficiently versed in Greek and Latin as to be able to understand the ancient writers in the original.[27] Yet I think it is widely recognized how important it is that a pastor of the Church knows what the nature of the ancient form of the Church was, and that he is equipped with at least some knowledge of Antiquity. And so in this respect, too, this work of mine could be fruitful, as everyone may admit; for no one denies that it is proper for all those responsible for Christian education to be familiar with this kind of writing. Yet there will maybe be some people around who will only manage this with the help of a translation. But to avoid /col. 834/ giving the impression of dragging on about such a sensitive issue, I will not press the point further.

---

[24] Cf. Eph. 4. 11f.

[25] II Cor. 12. 2–4.

[26] Cf. Bucer, *Enarrationes*, fol. 5a: 'My chief aim with this commentary has been to be of assistance to the very uneducated brethren, of whom you will find many . . . and to whom Christ our Lord is beginning to reveal himself again.'

[27] Cf. Erasmus, *Praefationes: Methodus*, ed. Winkler, pp. 42–3: 'Our first concern should be with the thorough learning of the three languages, Latin, Greek and Hebrew . . . to achieve a working knowledge, sufficient for exercising judgement.' Bucer, *Enarrationes*, fol. 3b, also regrets that 'there are a great number of those entrusted with the office of teaching in the Church who . . . bar many people from the Evangelists . . . due to linguistic incompetence.' See also Krüger, *Bucer und Erasmus*, pp. 95–6.

My reason for selecting Chrysostom as the most preferable needs likewise to be dealt with in passing.[28] From the outset, the reader ought to
bear in mind the kind of literary genre it is in which I prefer him to others.
Although homilies are something which consist of a variety of elements,
the interpretation of Scripture is, however, their priority.[29] In this area, no
one of sound judgement would deny that our Chrysostom excels all the
ancient writers currently extant.[30] This is especially true when he deals
with the New Testament. For the lack of Hebrew prevented him from
showing so much expertise in the Old Testament. And so to avoid giving
the impression of either making an ill-considered judgement on such an
important matter, or doing an injustice to other writers, I will summarize
my reasons for bestowing on him the praise he deserves.

Among the Greeks whose works are extant today, there was no one [of
distinction] before him or even in his own age, except Origen,[31]
Athanasius,[32] Basil,[33] and Gregory.[34] Yet Origen obscures very much the
plain meaning of Scripture with constant allegories. With the [other]
three there can be no comparison, because we do not possess any complete
commentaries of theirs which may be compared with those [of Chryso-
stom]. But from the fragments which do survive, one may suspect that the
latter two had more of an aptitude for oratory than for literary exposition.

Of those in the generation after that, the foremost is Cyril,[35] an
outstanding exegete indeed, and someone who among the Greeks can be
rated second to Chrysostom. He cannot, however, match him. Theo-
phylact[36] cannot be better assessed than with the observation that

---

[28] Bucer had stated that early Church exegetes had indulged far too much in allegorical and
mystical interpretations 'with the one exception of Chrysostom': *Enarrationes*, fol. 4a.
[29] Cf. T. H. L. Parker, *The Oracles of God. An Introduction to the Preaching of John Calvin* (London,
1947), pp. 13–21.
[30] A view still maintained in modern times, e.g. 'No Church Father expounded the sacred text so
thoroughly and at the same time in such a practical manner [as Chrysostom]': B. Altaner and
A. Stuiber, *Patrologie. Leben, Schriften und Lehre der Kirchenväter*. 8th edn (Freiburg, 1978),
p. 324. See also Frances Young, *From Nicaea to Chalcedon. A guide to the Literature and its Background* (London, 1983), pp. 154–9, and F. H. Chase, *Chrysostom, A Study in the History of Biblical
Interpretation* (Cambridge, 1887).
[31] d. 254, lay head of the famous Catechetical School in Alexandria.
[32] d. 373, Bishop of Alexandria.
[33] d. 379, Bishop of Caesarea.
[34] d. c.390, Bishop of Nazianzus.
[35] d. 444, Bishop of Alexandria.
[36] d. c.1108, more of a medieval Byzantine writer than a Church Father, Archbishop of Ochryda
(Bulgarian, Yugoslavia), his commentary on the Gospels was edited by the Basle Reformer,
Oecolampad, in 1524.

anything commendable he has he took from Chrysostom. There is no need to review more [writers], about whom there can be no dispute.

As regards the Latin writers, works by Tertullian[37] and Cyprian[38] of this kind have perished. Nor do we possess many of Hilary's works.[39] [His] commentaries on the Psalter do little towards an understanding of the mind of the prophet. [His] canons[40] on Matthew certainly contain more of consequence. But there too the most important faculty of an interpreter is missing: lucidity.

What Jerome[41] wrote on the Old Testament has deservedly very little reputation among scholars. For he is almost completely bogged down in allegories, by which he distorts Scripture with too much licence. [His] commentaries on the Gospel of Matthew and on two[42] Epistles of Paul are tolerable, except that they savour of a man not sufficiently experienced in church affairs.

Better and more profitable than him is Ambrose,[43] even if he is very laconic. There is no one after Chrysostom who comes closer to the plain sense of Scripture. /col. 835/ For if he had been equipped with a learning commensurate with his pre-eminence in natural acumen, judgement, and subtlety, he would perhaps be reckoned as the prime expositor of Scripture.

It is beyond dispute that Augustine[44] does surpass everyone in dogmatics. He is also a very scrupulous biblical commentator of the first rank. But he is far too ingenious. This results in him being less sound and reliable.

The chief merit of our Chrysostom is this: he took great pains everywhere not to deviate in the slightest from the genuine plain meaning of

---

[37] d. *c.*220, lay theologian in Carthage.

[38] d. 258, Bishop of Carthage.

[39] d. 367, Bishop of Poitiers.

[40] This unusual term in this context Calvin derives from Erasmus's Hilary edition—*Lucubrationes*—of 1523, in which the commentary on Matthew is entitled *In Evangelium Matthaei canones, seu commentarius.* The term's implausibility is discussed by Migne in his *Admonitio* preceding his edition of the commentary in *PL* 9, cols 912, XI—914, XIV. Cf. *Hilaire de Poitiers, Sur Matthieu* (ed. J. Doignon, *SC*, 254 (1978).

[41] d. 420, lay biblical scholar and translator, chief mediator of Origenist/Alexandrian allegorical exegesis to the Latin West.

[42] A slip by Calvin here, since Jerome commented not only Galatians and Ephesians, but also Philemon and Titus.

[43] d. 397, Bishop of Milan. It is more likely that Calvin had the Ambrosiaster (pseudo-Ambrose) in mind, rather than Ambrose himself, although Erasmus's edition in 1527 had distinguished between the two.

[44] d. 430, Bishop of Hippo.

Scripture, and not to indulge in any licence of twisting the straight-forward sense of the words.[45] I am only saying what will be acknowledged by those who are both in a position to make a correct assessment and who will not hesitate to state the fact.[46] I admit there are also things in him in which he is inferior to others and which deserve criticism, even if they are not compared with the writings of others.

But since we know that *while all things are ours, we belong to the one Christ*,[47] let us by all means make use of this favour of the Lord. I am saying: let us make a frank assessment of everything which has been written, but respectfully and impartially, and let us not accept anything unless it has been subjected to scrutiny.[48] For all the servants of Christ certainly did not intend what they wrote to be exempt from the rule which Paul fixes even for the very angels.[49] And to enable this work of Chrysostom to be read with less disfavour and more benefit, I will indicate in passing aspects with which I am not entirely happy, so that alerted readers may be more readily on their guard against them.

By being unrestrained in asserting human free will, and in claiming the merits of works, he obscures somewhat the grace of God in our election and calling, and thereby the gratuitous mercy which accompanies us from our calling right up to death.[50] Firstly, he attempts to link election to some

---

[45] In other words, Chrysostom is a representative of the anti-allegorical Antiochene exegetical tradition. Cf. J. N. D. Kelly, *Early Christian Doctrines*, 4th edn (London, 1968), pp. 75ff.

[46] Cf. n. 27.

[47] Cf. I Cor. 3. 21–3. Calvin writes in his Epistle to the King of France, at the beginning of the *Institutes*, ed. Battles and McNeill, *LCC* 20, 1, pp. 18–19 [*Calvini opera selecta*, ed. P. Barth and W. Niesel (Munich, 1926–36), 3, pp. 17–18]: 'We are so versed in the writings [of the Fathers] as to remember always that all things are ours, to serve us, not to lord it over us, and that we all belong to the one Christ, whom we must obey in all things without exception. He who does not observe this distinction will have nothing certain in religion.' Cf. Luther, *Operationes in Psalmos* (1519–21), *WA*, 5, pp. 280–1: 'Since Scripture and God's Word must have a single and unchangeable meaning, [we must] avoid turning the sacred text into a "wax nose" ... [we should] not accept something read in any of the famous Fathers as an oracle ... some make a habit of this, shredding Scripture with diverse meanings, so that we almost have as many opinions as there are syllables.'

[48] Cf. Erasmus, *Praefationes: Methodus*, ed. Winkler, pp. 68–70: 'One must of course read [the Ancients] critically and with discrimination. They were human beings, some things they did not know, and in some things they let their minds wander. Occasionally they were fast asleep.' And Bucer, *Enarrationes*, fols 7a–b: 'We are all human beings, and until now God has revealed that due to considerable lapses great men are mortal, lest honour should be given to them instead of him ... the blindness of those people is to be deplored who on reading something produced by a human being, treat it like oracles of God. It is the mode of the Holy Spirit that while one or the other prophesies, others make an assessment. We acknowledge this mode [at work] in some people, and they should acknowledge it in us.'

[49] Cf. I Cor. 6. 3.

[50] Calvin can do no other than to distance himself from Chrysostom's views on grace, works,

consideration of our works. Scripture, though, proclaims everywhere that there is nothing by which God may be moved to elect us except our pathetic condition, and that he does not base his decision to come to our aid on anything except his own goodness.[51] Secondly, to some extent [Chrysostom] divides the credit for our calling between God and ourselves, though scripture consistently ascribes the whole of it to God without qualification.

On free will he speaks in such a way as if it were of great importance for the pursuit of virtue and the keeping of the divine law.[52] Yet on the evidence of his Word, the Lord everywhere deprives us of all capacity for doing good, and leaves us with no virtue other than what he himself supplies through his Spirit. Therefore, he also ascribes more to works than is right, since he appears to base our righteousness in the eyes of God on them to some extent. Yet there is nothing which Scripture so strongly emphasizes as that one should ascribe to God the entire credit for justification, since our achievements and everything which is ours have been condemned as incapable of acceptance. Consequently, not only is he himself just, but by his gratuitous goodness he justifies his followers, not on account of any worth or merit belonging to works, rather by faith in Jesus Christ.[53]

Yet it is hard to believe that [Chrysostom] was so naïve about Christian teaching as not to be aware either of the afflicted condition of humanity /col. 836/ or of the grace of God, which is the sole remedy for its distress.[54] But the reasons which forced him into that position are clear: We

---

merit, election, justification, etc. Standing firmly within the Reformation version of the radical Pauline and Augustinian revival, he could have little sympathy with a theology which, in fact, represents the entire Greek patristic tradition. The latter proceeded on the basis of the semi-Pelagian notion of a mutual approximation between God and humanity, whereas the former posited a chasm and polarity between God and humanity, which can only be bridged by divine initiative and operation. In the 1559 *Institutes*, 2. 2. 4, Calvin writes: 'The Greeks above the rest—and Chrysostom especially among them—extol the ability of the human will.' And Bucer, in his *Romans Commentary* of 1536, ed. D. F. Wright, *Common Places of Martin Bucer* (Abingdon, 1972), p. 154: 'Chrysostom is most assiduous in championing man's will and capability for godly living.' See also Kelly, *Early Christian Doctrines*, p. 352. On the Augustinian revival see H. A. Oberman, *Masters of the Reformation: the Emergence of a New Intellectual Climate in Europe* (Cambridge, 1981), ch. 6; cf. A. E. McGrath, *Iustitia Dei: a History of the Christian Doctrine of Justification* (Cambridge, 1986).

[51] E.g., Gen. 3; Jer. 31. 18–20; Ezech. 36. 26–7; Joh. 8. 34–8; Rom. 4. 2ff., 8, 9, etc.

[52] E.g., as in Chrysostom's *De proditione Iudae homilia*, I, 3: *PG* 49, col. 377. Also his homilies on Genesis 19. 1; 53. 2; 25. 7: *PG* 53, col. 158; 54, col. 468; 53, col. 228.

[53] Calvin wrote *ex fide Iesu Christi*. The unusual form of this phrase, with Jesus Christ in a *genitivus objectivus*, appears only once in the Greek and Latin New Testaments, in Gal. 3. 22.

[54] Cf. Bucer, *Romans Commentary*, ed. Wright, p. 152: 'Scripture ascribes all the credit for salvation to the grace of God and universally condemns every part of our nature as utterly ungodly.'

are aware how the teaching handed down by the Scriptures about the blindness of human nature, the perversity of the heart, the impotence of the mind, and the corruption of the entire character accords little with common sense and the opinions of philosophers.[55] And there were philosophers at that time who used to censure that ᵉvery muchᵉ ᶠabout our religionᶠ with the aim of alienating some people from it.[56] Our Chrysostom considered it his duty to rebut their scoffing and crafty stratagems. But since no better method of answering them was available, he modified his own opinion in such a way as to avoid being at too great a variance with public opinion.[57]

This, therefore, seems to be the main reason why he both talked very vaguely about predestination, and conceded so much to our free will. The intention of this was undoubtedly to deny all opportunity for the Sophists'[58] slanders. Their explicit aim was to pour scorn on what were straightforward assertions on these matters in accordance with God's Word. That was not at all, I grant, a sufficiently good reason for him to depart from the plain meaning of Scripture. For it is certainly not right for

---

ᵉ⁻ᵉ Reading *miris modis* instead of MS Geneva fr. 145, fol. 162r and *CR*, *modis* only, and *modo* of copies.

ᶠ⁻ᶠ MS Geneva fr. 145, fol. 162v *in nostram religionem*, instead of *CR* and copies *in nostra religione*.

[55] Cf. Aristotle, *Nichomachean Ethics* III, 5, 2–3. Cicero, *On the Nature of the Gods* III, 36, 87–8. Seneca, Epistle 90 to Lucilius. See also Calvin, *Institutes* 2. 2. 2.

[56] Calvin's analysis of the situation recalls that of Bucer in an excursus on free will in his *Romans Commentary* (1536), ed. Wright, pp. 153–4. But there is an important difference of perception. Whereas Bucer explains the views of the Fathers, including Chrysostom, as a response to divergent interpretations of Scripture within the Church, Calvin understands the position of someone like Chrysostom as a response to pagan critiques of Christianity. There does not, however, seem to be much evidence in mainstream pagan anti-Christian polemics, as in Celsus or Porphyry, or in pagan apologetics as found in Saloustios or Libanius (under whom Chrysostom reputedly studied) that free will was an issue. Cf. P. de Labriolle, *La Réaction paienne: Etude sur la polémique antichrétienne du Ier au VIe siècle* (Paris, 1934). It is more likely that Chrysostom had Christian sects or heresies in mind which denied free will or its relevance, e.g. Marcionite Gnostics, Montanists, Manichaeans, etc. Anyway, the Neoplatonist philosopher Plotinus had long since refuted Stoic philosophical deterministic denial of free will.

[57] Cf. Calvin in his *Des Scandales* (1550), ed. O. Fatio, *Textes Littéraires Français* (Geneva, 1984), pp. 76–7: 'Would to God that the ancient teachers had not been so taken aback by the opposition of [the philosophers], since by taking the trouble to appease them, they have left us with a lifeless and counterfeit theology. To avoid annoying them, [Chrysostom *et al.*] have confused heaven and earth . . . they look for a way more in conformity with human opinion by selling out to free will, and allowing some natural virtue in men.' In a sense, then, Calvin's notion that Chrysostom embodies an accommodation to secular philosophy in the matter of free will adumbrated the 'Hellenization of Christianity' theory.

[58] A term of abuse to designate reputedly anti-Christian philosophers, usually employed by Calvin to describe the Scholastics.

God's truth to make way for human opinion. To the former, all human thinking ought to be subjected as if captive, and all minds ought to be made consciously obedient to it. But since it is true that [Chrysostom's] objective was simply to free himself from the enemies of the Cross of Christ, an undoubtedly good intention such as this, for all its lack of success, is still deserving of some sympathy.

But in another respect he was under even more pressure; for there were many people in the Church whose lives were shameful and licentious. When confronted by their pastors, they had a ready pretext for their slackness. This was that it could on no account be imputed to them that they lived in accordance with their carnal desires, since, in fact, they were compelled to sin necessarily by the defectiveness of their nature. As long as they were not assisted by the grace of God, it was not in their power [they argued], to surmount that relentless compulsion. In addition, with typical evasiveness, they had the irreligious and dishonourable habit of putting the blame for their sins, which lay within themselves, on to God—the author of all things good, and certainly not the cause of anything evil. There were also some individuals who used to prattle about 'fate'.[59]

This holy man [Chrysostom] had every reason to challenge shirkers of this kind. But since he was not very sure about the means of subduing them, whereby he might shake them out of their complacency and deprive them of every excuse, he had the habit of saying the following: that 'no person was prepared for spiritual benefit by the grace of God in such a way as to preclude some contribution of his own as well.'[60]

Such a formulation is not particularly consistent with the Holy Spirit's manner of speaking. But this is just what I indicated [g]initially[g]: that [this] trusty minister of Christ did deviate somewhat from the right way, although he had the best of intentions. /col. 837/ Yet just as lapses of this kind in such a great man are easily excused, so it is important that a devout

---

[g] MS Geneva fr. 145, fol. 162v and copies *principio*, instead of *CR*, *praecipio*.

[59] The reference here is to pseudo-Epicureans and fatalistic Stoics. The latter were forced into ethical indifference by a pessimistic determinist view of human nature. Cf. Bucer, *Romans Commentary*, ed. Wright, p. 153: 'The one thing the Fathers sought to guard against was a person's shifting the blame for his own ungodliness on to God's shoulders.' See also E. Osborn, *Ethical Patterns in Early Christian Thought* (Cambridge, 1976), pp. 134–5, who includes Manichaean and Marcionite dualists as Chrysostom's target.

[60] A fair summary of Chrysostom's position. Cf. Anthony Kenny, 'Was St. John Chrysostom a Semi-Pelagian?' *Irish Theological Quarterly* (1960), pp. 16–29. As a Reformation theologian, Calvin would find Chrysostom reminiscent of the doctrine of late medieval Nominalist theologians, against which the Reformers reacted so strongly, namely, 'God does not refuse grace to those who do what lies within them.' Cf. H. A. Oberman, *The Dawn of the Reformation* (Edinburgh, 1986), pp. 84–103.

reader is reminded not to be diverted from the plain truth by [Chryso-stom's] authority.

Furthermore, apart from that careful concern for straightforward and authentic interpretation which I have mentioned, you will find in those Homilies much historical material. From this you will gain insight into the kind of office and authority bishops had at that time, as well as the precepts by which the populace was kept duty bound; what sort of discipline there was among the clergy, and what kind among the people themselves; how responsible the former was, precluding an irresponsible abuse of the power entrusted to them; /col. 838/ how much respectfulness there was in the latter, avoiding the semblance of any degree of contempt for a regime so greatly commended by the Lord; what sanctity character-ized [their] meetings,[61] and how greatly they were frequented with the spread of religion; what kind of ceremonies there were, and to what end they were instituted; unquestionably [these are] things really worth knowing about.

In fact, if we want helpful discussion on the welfare of the Church, no more appropriate way is to be found, at least in my opinion, than to resort to the model from the early Church.[62] On the other hand, whenever both[h] in ecclesiastical. . . .[i]

University of Glasgow

[h] MS Geneva fr. 145, fol. 161v and copies *et*, omitted in *CR*.
[i] The rest is missing.

[61] Latin *quid habuerint sacri conventus*, taking *sacri* not as a nominative plural adjective, but as a partitive genitive noun.
[62] Typical Christian humanist idealization of the Early Church, corresponding to the Renais-sance view of Antiquity. For some modern studies on Calvin's relationship to humanism and tradition in general, see R. White, 'Fifteen Years of Calvin Studies in French (1965–1980)', *Journal of Religious History*, 12 (1982), pp. 140–61.

PROBABLY THEY ARE GOD'S CHILDREN: THEODORE BEZA'S DOCTRINE OF BAPTISM

by JILL RAITT

I THE CONTEXT

THE discussion that took place between Theodore Beza and Jacob Andreae during the Colloquy of Montbéliard in 1586 highlights the differences among the French Reformed doctrine, the doctrine derived from the Basle Reformation, and the Lutheran doctrine. It also makes very clear how consistently the Genevan Reformers related their sacramental theology, their understanding of the work of the Holy Spirit, and their doctrine of predestination.

The Colloquy of Montbéliard took place in a small French-speaking county belonging to the Lutheran Duke of Württemberg. The chief collocutors were Calvin's successor in Geneva, Theodore Beza, and Jacob Andreae, the Württemberg theologian, and one of the primary authors of the Formula of Concord. The two collocutors headed teams of Reformed and Lutheran theologians invited to Montbéliard by its count, Frederick, nephew and vassal of Ludwig, Duke of Württemberg. Frederick called the colloquy ostensibly to satisfy French refugees who wanted to practise the Calvinist form of Christianity for which they had been exiled by the French King, Francis III, in 1585.[1] Count Frederick, although sympathetic to the Reformed cause, was under pressure from his uncle, the very Lutheran Duke of Württemberg, to have all clergy sign the Formula of Concord. Although the colloquy was announced to be a debate about the doctrine of the Lord's Supper, the primary theological obstacle to Lutheran aid to the Huguenots during the French Wars of Religion, four other topics were added to the agenda: firstly, the two natures of Christ; secondly, the destruction of churches and images and music in the churches; thirdly, baptism; and, fourthly, predestination.[2] In this essay

---

[1] For the long history of the struggle between the Montbéliard Reformed and the Lutheran dukes of Württemberg, see John Viénot, *Histoire de la Reforme dans le Pays de Montbéliard depuis les origines jusqu'a la mort de P. Toussain, 1524–1573*, 2 vols (Paris, 1900); Jill Raitt, 'The Emperor and the Exiles: the clash of religion and politics in the sixteenth century', *Church History*, 52 (1983), pp. 145–56.

[2] The other topics will be handled *in extenso* in my forthcoming book *The Colloquy of Montbéliard, 1586* (New York, 1992).

I shall discuss two of these topics. The debate concerning the destruction of churches and the use of music and art in churches has heretofore been dismissed with the brief note that the collocutors agreed on these points.[3] While Andreae and Beza did agree in principle, the debate involved matters of considerable interest, and so I have included this debate as a brief prelude to the major issue in this essay, the discussion on baptism.

Andreae's *Acta* [4] describes the setting. The hall was filled with 'a great number of French exiles' and was presided over by Count Frederick. Two tables had been set a little apart from each other. At the first table sat Frederick with the Württemberg theologians. The Swiss collocutors sat at the second table. No comment was made by either party about the place of the Prince among the German theologians. In his welcoming address, the Superintendent of Montbéliard, Hector Vogelmann, set the tone of the colloquy. He explained that the French nobles had often asked for such a meeting concerning some articles of religion and the use of the French language in the liturgy. Out of compassion, Prince Frederick forwarded their petition to Duke Ludwig of Württemberg, who responded by sending his theologians and several politicians to participate in the colloquy.[5] As he closed his address, Vogelmann invited Beza to say whatever he had most on his mind. As the *Acta* reported it, Beza admitted that the colloquy had been called for the sake of the French exiles living in Montbéliard. He then requested that everything be taken down in writing to assure careful speech and fair play. Beza agreed to the format suggested by Andreae, that is, that written theses should serve as the basis of further discussion. Beza also agreed that the theses should be confirmed only from the Word of

[3] See, for example, P. Pfister, *Le Colloque de Montbéliard (1586): Etude historique* (Geneva, 1873); Armand Lods, 'Les Actes du Colloque de Montbéliard (1586): Une Polémique entre Théodore de Beze et Jacques Andreae', *Bulletin historique et littéraire de la Société de l'histoire du Protestantisme Français*, 46 (1897), p. 198. This article deals principally with the circumstances of the publication of the *Acta* of the colloquy.

[4] *Acta Colloquii Mon/tis Belligartensis: / Quod habitum est, Anno Christi 1586* (Tübingen, George Gruppenbach, 1587). Beza's published response to Andreae's *Acta* skips from the topic of the two natures of Christ to predestination. He does not respond to Andreae's marginalia on the topics of this essay. *Ad acta / colloquii / Montisbelgardensis / Tubingae edita, / Theodori Bezae / Responsio. / Genevae, / Excudebat Joannes le Preux. / M.D.LXXXVII.* The second part is: *Ad acta / Colloquii / Montisbelgardensis / Tubingae edita, / Theodori Bezae / Responsionis, Pars / Altera / Excudebat Joannes le Preux. / M.D.LXXXVIII.*

[5] The circumstances of the calling of the colloquy are much more complicated than this simple address indicates. Indeed, Henry of Navarre's agent, the Baron de Clervant, invited Andreae to participate, and encouraged Beza to accept Frederick's invitation. See my forthcoming book on the Colloquy of Montbéliard.

God, after which the dogma under dispute would be set forth.[6] Finally, Beza asked that the debate remain on one point until they agreed, or it became clear that they could not agree. After thanking God and the Prince profusely, Andreae responded. He reiterated that the sole norm was to be the Word of God. He objected to Beza's request that everything be written down. Andreae argued that it would delay proceedings and inhibit free discussion. He assured Beza that he need not fear foul play, since each side was committed to seeking the truth. Andreae then moved to the presentation of the Württemberg theses. The Swiss would be given time to respond to these in writing and then to draw up their own theses. When that had been done, the conversation concerning the theses could begin.[7] Before proceeding to the theses, the opening remarks require comment. Particularly important to this study, and indeed the principal problem of this period from the point of view of the history of theology, is the declared principle of *sola scriptura*.

Both collocutors claimed that the Word of God was to be the sole norm. Throughout this colloquy, the interpretation of that norm must be kept in mind. By 1586 the major confessions had been ratified. In 1566, the Second Helvetic Confession had been adopted by the Swiss, and also by the French at La Rochelle in 1571 as in harmony with their own French Confession of 1559. In 1580 the Lutheran *Book of Concord* was published. Each church considered its confessions both to be drawn from, and the correct interpretation of, the Word of God. Both groups of theologians accepted the ecumenical councils of the first five centuries as true to God's Word and appealed to these councils and to the Church Fathers in confirmation of an increasingly important claim: orthodoxy. Although no Protestant would admit that any of these secondary 'norms' had the unique priority of Scripture itself, in fact, the confessional positions of the churches were firmly entrenched.

Late in the morning of 26 March, at the conclusion of the long discussion of the Person of Christ, Andreae asked whether Beza had anything further he wished to say on the subject before they moved on to the topic of predestination. Beza took the opportunity to repeat that he and his colleagues had no wish to extend the colloquy to subjects they had not expected to discuss and for which they were not prepared.

When the collocutors met that afternoon, in the presence of Frederick

---

[6] That this condition was met by neither party is a matter of discussion below.
[7] It should be noted that Andreae kept at his table not only Count Frederick, but the initiative for formulating the theses.

and the persevering audience, Beza addressed them saying that he and his colleagues wished nothing so much as a resolution of the controversies between the churches. They had tried to come to such a resolution and thereby to satisfy Frederick's request. Now the Reformed team was asked to discuss predestination which, said Beza, is not a matter of an hour or even days or months. Beza therefore presented a written petition to Frederick asking that the colloquy conclude.

In response to Beza's request, Andreae said that the reason Frederick had not mentioned the remaining disputed topics in his letter to the councils of Geneva and Bern was probably because he had not realized that there were matters other than the Lord's Supper and the Person of Christ to discuss. But what good would it do, argued Andreae, if we were to agree on two points and there remained a third in dispute? Besides, the people need to understand the doctrine of predestination, and they are capable of understanding it. Nothing contained in Scripture should be kept from the faithful.[8] Andreae added to predestination the discussion of baptism and of music, statues, and paintings in churches.[9]

To Beza's objection that his side had not come prepared on these subjects nor were books available to them, Andreae chided that Beza was a veteran disputant who had no need of books. Indeed, the Württembergers had neither consulted nor needed to consult books on the remaining topics. He then assured the audience that he and his colleagues wanted only peace. But they had a duty to resist false doctrine, and so, in spite of their godly intentions, were dragged into controversy. Andreae had already declared that he was correct, had always taught the truth, and that Beza had only to admit his errors for there to be peace between them.[10] Andreae then turned to one of the problems lying behind the colloquy, namely, the plight of the French churches. He assured his hearers that the Württemberger theologians were deeply affected with the misery of the Huguenots, prayed for them, and exhorted their churches to pray for them. The peace that the churches seek, he added, can be found only in the Word of God, taken in its clear and obvious sense.

Picking up on the theme of the French churches, Beza appealed to Frederick on their behalf, reminding Frederick that Duke Christopher of Württemberg had helped them and that they had been favoured by

---

[8] There is irony in Andreae's argument. Calvin had argued that nothing in Scripture should be kept from the faithful, including predestination, difficult doctrine though it was: *Institutes of the Christian Religion*, 3. 21. 3.

[9] *Acta*, pp. 378–81 for Andreae's exhortation to Frederick.

[10] *Acta*, pp. 268–9.

Frederick's father, Count George. Beza thanked Frederick for the help he had sent to France and hoped that nothing would prevent future assistance. Beza ended with an appeal to end the bitterness and the sharp polemical publications that had marred past relations between the Württembergers and the Swiss.

There was no further debate on the continuation of the colloquy, since Andreae claimed that Count Frederick and the audience wanted it to continue. Andreae gave the Württemberg theses to Beza and his colleagues for study until the next day, 27 March, when they would begin with the easiest subject, namely, the destruction of Catholic churches and the place of art and music in church services. They would then turn to predestination and baptism.[11]

II THE DESTRUCTION OF CHURCHES: ART AND MUSIC IN SERVICES[12]

Andreae's four theses defended the retention of altars, statues, and paintings, even those that had been installed by 'papists', as long as they did not lead to idolatry. Music was not to be eliminated from church services. Andreae laid out the scriptural arguments to defend his theses. For example, he noted that although the Israelites were forbidden to make graven images, they nevertheless represented the cherubim on the Ark of the Covenant. The Psalms not only tolerated, but commanded, the use of musical instruments. Beza agreed with the theses, but modified them in the sense that while artistic representations need not be eliminated from churches, they could do more harm than good, given the tendency in human nature to fall into idolatry. In spite of his conciliatory tone and gentle representation of the Genevan preference for simplicity in church art and music, Andreae filled the margins with comments that could only be considered pugnacious. For example, when Beza deplored the destruction of churches, Andreae countered that the pulling down of churches in France and the Netherlands was not only wrong, it was done in the name of bad doctrine.[13] Beza responded that churches, statues, paintings, organs, and the like had been destroyed all over Protestant Europe by angry crowds. That did not mean that those crowds acted with

[11] Ibid., p. 388.
[12] *Acta*, pp. 389–427. Because there was general agreement on this topic, I shall discuss only those points that have historical or theological relevance, without presenting the complexities of the debate.
[13] *Acta*, p. 394.

ecclesiastical approval, and, in fact, the Genevan Church deprecated such behaviour. Andreae expressed relief to hear Beza say so, since he and his colleagues had supposed that the Reformed favoured pulling down Catholic churches.

In earlier treatments of the Montbéliard Colloquy, this section has been dismissed by remarking that Beza and Andreae agreed. That is too simple. They did agree that churches should not be destroyed, that altars used by 'papists' could be used by Protestants, that art and music in church services was a matter of prudent judgment. But it should be pointed out that while Andreae argued for organs, polyphony, painting, and sculpture, Beza preferred simple psalmody and felt that the Reformed churches were under no obligation to install organs. As for statues and paintings, Beza said that they were most useful in civil life, but the Reformed preferred not to put them in their churches. Both collocutors used Scripture to buttress their arguments. They agreed that Scripture gave no precise commands that must be obeyed on these matters, since even the specific commandment against graven images was obviously interpreted to allow for statues and other representations in ancient Israel. On the other hand, while the Psalms mentioned all sorts of musical instruments to praise the Lord, there was no specific command to use any particular instrument or any instruments at all. The final note sounded by both theologians was that in these matters the churches should exercise Christian liberty. At the same time, excess in either direction should be avoided so that there would be no cause for scandal.

III BAPTISM

After expressing the pious desire that the remaining points of controversy be concluded as agreeably, Andreae introduced the Württemberg theses on baptism. The pattern was the same as previously: points considered noncontroversial, doctrines the Lutherans considered contrary to Scripture, theses upheld by the Württemberg churches. It is intriguing to note that Andreae's marginalia became so extensive that they ran across the bottom of the pages as well as down the sides. Beza's responses appear in frames of editorial comment and contain fewer words than the marginal notes.[14] As before, Beza's remarks were much shorter than Andreae's perorations.

[14] It should be recalled that the marginalia were added at the time the *Acta* were edited by Andreae. In addition, Andreae's arguments at the colloquy form by far the larger part of the main text of Andreae's publication.

The noncontroversial points are simply summaried:[15]

(1) Baptism consists of water and the Word of God;
(2) It replaces circumcision;[16]
(3) It is to be administered to infants;
(4) Baptism is not just a sign and seal, but actually confers regeneration in the Holy Spirit;
(5) No one who is not regenerated can enter heaven;
(6) Regeneration is not earned by human works, but conferred by God's mercy;
(7) To be baptized is to put on Christ, to die, to be buried, and to rise with Christ to a new life.

The doctrines given as contrary to Scripture, and, by implication, ascribed to the Reformed, were:

(1) Baptism signifies, but does not necessarily effect what it signifies;
(2) Baptism is thereby reduced to an unnecessary sign of membership in the external Church;
(3) Baptism is effective only in the elect and, even in the case of the elect, not necessarily at the time it is administered;
(4) There is no need for midwives to provide emergency baptism.[17]

Andreae's theses, as was the case with regard to images and other things, presented positions that misrepresented Reformed theology. Beza's task was to set the record straight, at least for the audience at Montbéliard. He objected that the first thesis did not mention that baptism represented washing in the blood of Christ figured by the water.[18] The second and third theses, that baptism replaced circumcision and should be

---

[15] I have summarized the theses and responses which, if they were presented *in extenso*, would prove tedious, without providing greater understanding.

[16] There is no discussion of the necessary restriction of circumcision to boys and the extension of baptism to girls. Calvin discusses this point briefly, *Institutes*, 4. 16. 16.

[17] Since there had been no time for Beza's team to prepare written theses at this point in the *Acta* so that readers would have everything set out in an orderly fashion. In his Respose, pt 2, p. 41, Beza did not object to this arrangement.

[18] Calvin does not make so specific a relation between water and the blood of Christ, but Beza's development of this point may be based on Calvin's position as expressed in his Commentary on Acts 22. 16 in which Calvin says that Holy Spirit and the application of the blood of Christ are the constants in regeneration, while the means used by the Spirit to apply the blood of Christ vary. Among the means is the water of baptism, which signifies and offers washing in the blood of Christ, but 'the grace of God is not tied to the sacraments': *Calvin's New Testament Commentaries: The Acts of the Apostles*, 2, tr. John W. Fraser, ed. David W. and Thomas F. Torrance (Grand Rapids, Michigan, 1966), p. 218.

administered to infants, were not disputed. On these points, as in those remaining, Beza's answers were true to Calvin's theology of baptism.[19] All that is signified by baptism—remission of sins, regeneration, and adoption by God—is offered by God through the Holy Spirit to all the baptized. But not all are able to receive what is offered, since the external actions are effective only through the power of the Holy Spirit acting in concert with the gift of faith. In themselves, the Sacraments and their benefits are 'distinct but not separate', and so, said Beza, the signs are not 'nude',[20] since in them the benefits of baptism are truly offered. Beza affirmed also that his side approved all the scriptural citations dealing with the institution of baptism and its effects in those who do not repudiate its offered benefits.

In his marginalia, Andreae commented that the water does not signify the blood, but rather is a means through which, in the blood of Christ and the power of the Holy Spirit, the baptized are regenerated. Andreae also understood the implied parallel with the Lord's Supper, namely, that the benefits are offered to, but not conferred upon, all those who receive the sacrament externally. As in the case of the Lord's Supper, Andreae did not allow the principle of 'distinct but not separate', and claimed that Beza made two baptisms, one in water, the other in the Holy Spirit. With some relish, Andreae then picked up on Beza's sixth response on baptism and the elect. He interpreted Beza to mean that only the elect receive the benefits of baptism. It is horrible to hear, said Andreae, that thousands of baptized, whether children or adults, before they have done good or ill, are not regenerated, but damned, in spite of the Sacrament.

The discussion moved on to the points that the Württemberg theologians considered contrary to Scripture. Beza said that it is idolatrous to ascribe latent power to any water, even sacramental water. God does not transfer divine power absolutely to any created thing. Andreae responded that they were not talking about 'any water', but about water made effective through the power of the Holy Spirit. If there is no latent power in the sacramental sign, is it not a 'nude' sign? Once again the argument

---

[19] *Calvin's New Testament Commentaries: The Acts of the Apostles*, 2, p. 218. See also Jill Raitt, 'Three Inter-related principles in Calvin's unique doctrine of infant baptism', *The Sixteenth Century Journal*, 11 (1980), pp. 51–61.

[20] *Acta*, pp. 432–3: 'Neque nos Sacramenta docemus nuda esse signa, sed externae tamen actioni negamus tribuendum esse, quod est unius Spiritus sancti. Sicut a Ioanne, Matth. 3.v.11. & a Petro. I. Epist. 3.v.2. non separantur quidem, sed distinguuntur: dicente etiam Apostolo, de universo Ministerio; eum, qui plantat & rigat, nihil esse.' For the importance of the principle: 'not separate but distinct' in Calvin's theology, see Raitt, 'Three Inter-related Principles'.

was whether the sacramental sign is itself permanently changed by its cultic use or is an instrument through which God acts only during its application. In the first instance, the sign itself becomes an object of divine action; in the second instance, the sign is an instrument through which divine action passes to the believer, who alone is its object. Beza argued that salvation does not depend upon baptism, but upon one's faith; as for damnation, it is due to contempt for salvation and the instruments God uses to elicit faith.

To explain the way the signs are related to the reality they signify, Beza employed metonymy, a term already familiar in explanations of the Genevan theology of the Lord's Supper.[21] Simply put, sacramental metonymy takes the sign for the effect; baptism signifies the work of the Holy Spirit which, through the blood of Christ, cleanses interiorly. One can then say, by metonymy, that baptism is washing in Christ's blood. Andreae countered that baptism was not instituted by Christ *as a sign* of regeneration, but *to confer* regeneration. It is clear, from Andreae's argument that he, as well as Beza, understood the Sacraments of baptism and the Lord's Supper in tandem. Beza continued to insist that when children or adults are baptized, they receive the benefits of it only when the Holy Spirit gives them faith to receive those benefits. This gift, he explained, may be given at any time, the moment of baptism or at some later time. Nevertheless, infants should be baptized so that they are brought into the covenant to which they belong through their parents. At this point, Beza made a curious concession. He said that infants also probably receive remission of original sin and the fruits of adoption, as long as they do not repudiate these benefits as adults. This is a strange admission and seems to be an inconsistency in Beza's theology. If an infant receives remission of original sin and adoption, then is it not saved? And if it is saved, is it not regenerated? Surely it will not be doomed to hell if it is not guilty of original sin and is too undeveloped to be guilty of sins of its own. Was this concession made to try to win his hearers, who evidently shared Andreae's horror at the thought that, in spite of their baptism, infants might be reprobates and condemned to hell? But Beza added 'probably'. With this word, he retained his theological consistency, since he had always taught, as had Calvin, that the children of believers are *probably* elect.[22] Beza then added 'as long as they do not repudiate these effects as adults'. Were they

---

[21] See Jill Raitt, *The Eucharistic Theology of Theodore Beza* = *AAR Studies in Religion*, 4 (Chambersburg, Pennsylvania, 1972), pp. 55–6.
[22] See p. 164, below.

to repudiate their baptism, they would evidently be reprobate from the beginning. In that case, they did not receive any benefits from baptism, something that could not be known at the time since, in Reformed theology, the action of the Holy Spirit is God's secret and cannot be commanded by human actions, even sacramental actions. Beza insisted that it is absurd to say that infants are regenerated when they are baptized, since their understanding is not able to receive the Word of God and thereby to apprehend Christ through faith. Andreae, scandalized, said that baptism effects regeneration because God's promise is attached to it. As for children's faith, it is purer, less impeded by reason, than is the faith of adults. If these things were not true, how could baptism console? Doubt would overtake confidence in God's mercy, Andreae argued.

Beza could not concede Andreae's point without betraying a principle of Reformed theology, namely a determination to maintain the relation of natural faculties to supernatural gifts. Faith was not something dropped into a vacuum, but was given to a mind which, through grace, had understood the Word of God. Before understanding developed, there was nothing to respond to Grace, understand the Word, or receive faith.

The last point of the Montbéliard discussion of baptism was emergency baptism by midwives. It involved two concerns: the necessity of baptism for salvation, and the appropriateness of women's ministry or even laymen's ministry. Beza began by pointing out that baptism is part of the Church's public ministry. It is therefore not legitimate for private persons, whether men or women, to administer it. Nor is there any need for the laws of public ministry to be broken, since one can miss being baptized without being guilty of contempt for the Sacrament.[23] Beza had already said that damnation resulted only from contempt for salvation and the means God instituted to offer salvation.

Andreae's marginalium to this response is well worth noting, because Andreae did not seem to understand the full import of his own argument. Andreae objected that *the Scripture did not forbid any ministry to women*,[24] but only that they should not speak in church or when there are men present. But in a case of necessity, when there are no men present, women may not

---

[23] *Acta*, p. 435: 'Baptismus pars est Ministerii publici, quod est expresse Dei verbo mulieribus, imo etiam privatis personis interdictum: neque vel Baptismum videri potest contempsisse, qui nulla sua culpa excedens ex hac vita non baptizatur: neque necessitas ulla incidere potest, publici urgentis ministerii leges transgredi.'

[24] Emphasis mine.

only baptize, but also teach. Adreae invoked Galatians 3: 'In Christ there is no longer male nor female, but all are one in Christ Jesus.'[25]

The example provided here of proof-texting to support a doctrinal position involving unexamined assumptions is a telling one. Again and again in the history of theological development, theologians have failed to see the implications of their arguments. In this instance, the use of Galatians 3 ought to describe either a universal situation: men and women are equal in Christ, hence women may be called to minister as are men; or it could describe, as Andreae thought it did, an emergency situation. In the latter case, the inequality of men and women for ministry should have been recognized as a matter of human, not divine, law; of polity, not nature. Calvin had already come to the latter conclusion, but he did not foresee that ecclesiastical custom barring women from ministry would change. In fact, he found the idea that women might baptize horrifying. His theological basis was consistent, nevertheless, in that he rejected the idea that ecclesiastical order should be broken by the ministry of lay persons, male or female. Order (*police*) in the Church had to be maintained. Unless the whole order were changed, there could be no changes in this or that aspect of the order.[26] Nor were there any 'emergencies' that could justify such changes since God's election depends solely on God's good pleasure, not on human activity.

The next discussion revealed why Beza insisted, in reply to the first thesis, that the water signified Christ's blood. Beza asked Andreae in what baptism consists. Andreae answered that it includes all those things necessary for the substance (a word Andreae used frequently in this debate) of baptism: the external elements, the word of command, and the promise of God. Beza responded that in so far as Andreae was speaking of the external baptism, yes, it consists of the elements and word. So far they agreed. But if one speaks of the interior reason for baptism, the Reformed called Andreae's answer insufficient because baptism is not only the word and element or sign, but also the signified thing, the *res significatum*, that is to say, the blood of Christ, which is the most important thing in baptism. Beza then used the Lord's Supper as an example of a Sacrament which consists not only of external signs, but of the interior signification of the body and blood of Christ truly offered to faith. The same is true, he said, of baptism. The blood of Christ there signified washes the baptized from

---

[25] Apparently, there is neither male nor female in Christ, only in emergencies.

[26] For a detailed discussion of the relation of divine, natural, and ecclesiastical order with regard to the 'place' of women in Calvin's view, see Jane Dempsey Douglass, *Women, Freedom and Calvin* (Philadelphia, 1985).

all sin. Baptism also signifies, continued Beza, immersion in the death of Christ by which the old man, Adam, dies, and the new man rises spiritually from sin to justice and newness of life. All of these benefits are offered in the blood of Christ through their representation in the external application of water and the word. It is not correct, therefore, to say that the Sacrament of baptism consists only of water and the word, its external elements. It includes also the interior washing and rebirth effected by the blood of Christ through the power of the Holy Spirit. Beza concluded by saying that he was not speaking of a bare signification, but a representation by which, through external signs, an internal reality is offered.[27]

Andreae answered at length. He said that the Württembergers included in baptism the action of the Holy Spirit, who makes it the laver of regeneration and renovation. Baptism is not two things, one internal, the other external, argued Andreae. Rather, action and effect are so linked that they cannot be separated and always occur together. Andreae continued by denying similarity between baptism and the Lord's Supper. He failed to recognize that he had already made such a parallel by linking the content of the Sacraments to their sacramental elements and their application, regardless of the faith of the recipient. As the body and blood of Christ are substantially present and given to be eaten by worthy and unworthy alike, so the power of baptism effects what it signifies in the baptized infant. (Presumably the disposition of an unwilling adult would nullify the effects of baptism and render the adult guilty of condemnation, as in the case of the unworthy communicant who eats damnation.) But Andreae did not make such theological distinctions; he was more concerned, it seems, to refute Beza on every point rather than to find any basis for agreement. Andreae continued that baptism and the Lord's Supper differ in many ways: the elements, the actions, the words, their final causes. In baptism the final cause is regeneration; in the Lord's Supper, communicants are not reborn, but having been reborn by baptism, they are remade. Andreae conceded that in both Sacraments, the blood of Christ is applied, but for different ends. The discussion then disintegrated into long speeches by Andreae and very short lines from Beza while the two collocutors fruitlessly rehearsed the arguments already given.

The next exchange continued the comparison of baptism and the Lord's Supper. Beza emphasized that faith is necessary for the benefits of either Sacrament to be received. Thus those who are baptized without

[27] *Acta*, pp. 437–8.

appropriate interior dispositions are washed externally by the water, but not internally by the blood of Christ. They are offered baptism's benefits, but have no hand to grasp them, no receptivity. Andreae countered that both sacraments not only offer but confer what they signify. In both Sacraments, the word *est* means *is*, not *signifies*. Baptism *is* the laver of regeneration. The discussion here regarded infant baptism and its likeness to circumcision. Through baptism, as in circumcision, the child is made a child of God. There are no tropes in either Sacrament, insisted Andreae.[28]

No, responded Beza, since water has no latent power it is not, of itself, effective. Only the Holy Spirit can make a sinner a child of God, and the instruments the Holy spirit uses are external signs, water and words, and internal dispositions: in this instance, faith to receive the ablution of Christ's blood. Therefore the waters of baptism represent, but cannot be said to be, the laver of regeneration. For this reason, the effects of baptism may be activated whenever a person hears God's Word and is given faith, as happened before baptism in the case of the centurion, Cornelius, and after baptism in the case of one who lacks faith at the time and comes to it either during baptism or at some later time.

Unsurprisingly, Andreae refused to allow that a Sacrament is other than a 'bare sign' if it is not identified with the reality it signifies. Andreae would not allow that a relation between sign and signified is sufficient. Andreae therefore objected to distance between sign and signified, whether in time (baptism) or space (Lord's Supper). Andreae objected to Beza's doctrine on two more points: there is no need for the Holy Spirit to delay acting on someone who is baptized; there is no point in baptizing at all if the ritual makes no difference with regard to election and reprobation. Beza answered Andreae by repeating the Reformed defence of their sacramental doctrine, that baptism and the Lord's Supper are ordinances of Jesus Christ and, as such, must be obeyed. Not to obey Christ's commands would be to hold Christ in contempt, a sin meriting damnation. The Sacraments are also visible words and, as such, are instruments of the Holy Spirit, as is the preached Word. When they are received with faith, they communicate Christ and all his benefits.

Beza's next question elicited Andreae's answer with regard to the difference between adult and infant baptism. Was Cornelius adopted by

---

[28] Now while that argument may be made for the Lord's Supper, so that the unworthy receive the body and blood of Christ to their condemnation, i.e., without the vivifying fruits of their communion, can the same be said for adults dragged unwillingly to be baptized, or who pretend to desire baptism? Are the sins of such persons washed away, in spite of their resistance or duplicity? This point was not raised by Beza or Andreae, however obvious it may seem.

God prior to his actual baptism?[29] Andreae admitted that adults are capable of coming to faith through hearing, and hence of being justified, while infants lack that capability. But, Andreae continued, it is an Anabaptist error to say that without a developed intellect one cannot have faith. Faith is not dependent upon an active intellect; on the contrary, God can easily work faith in infants, as in John the Baptist, who leapt in his mother's womb when he heard Mary's voice. Baptism, Andreae argued, regenerates the infant in soul and body, so that it is no longer a child of hell but of God.

Beza responded that the Reformed teach that while the action of the Holy Spirit may not occur until the baptized person is able to hear and to respond to the Word of God, nevertheless children are to be baptized. It is done, he said, according to the formula of the covenant by which God said to Abraham and his posterity: 'I will be your God and the God of your seed after you.' It is enough, affirmed Beza, for the parents to have faith and to apprehend this promise for their children, and therefore it is proper that the children be baptized. Furthermore, that John the Baptist leapt in his mother's womb was a singular event. Scripture nowhere promises such an extraordinary response to all infants. Beza's last point was that although all children, like all people, are invited to hear and respond to God's Word, not all do or will respond in the course of their lifetime. Baptism is therefore a *probable, not a certain, sign* that baptized children receive the fruit of adoption. To say otherwise would be to make God's choice dependent upon human actions. Andreae objected that the sacraments would not be sources of comfort if they were merely sources of probability rather than certainty. Nor does the adoption of an infant depend upon the faith of the parents but upon the sacrament, just as inclusion in Israel's covenant did not depend upon the faith of the parents but upon circumcision.

If faith is not given until the Holy Spirit endows an individual with faith, is this action of God equivalent to election and hence without repentance? In other words, is faith admissible? The possibility of losing faith and adoption once these had been given by God became the subject of the next portion of the colloquy. Beza asked whether Simon Magus, who had been baptized as a believer, lost his adoption into the kingdom of God by his impiety. Andreae affirmed that grace could be so lost. Beza disagreed. Simon only pretended to believe, but he did not truly believe, and thus he was accursed.[30] Beza said that true faith, given by the Holy Spirit,

---

[29] *Acta*, p. 458.
[30] The discussion regarding Simon Magus occurs in the *Acta*, pp. 461–3.

is inadmissible. Andreae therefore asked whether faith and the Holy Spirit remained with David during his adulterous act with Bathsheba.[31] Yes, answered Beza, he retained them. Andreae included the audience in his expression of shock. (Andreae knew how to play his audience; according to the *Acta*, Beza never thus included the audience.) In spite of the buzz of disapproval, Beza insisted that even in the middle of his adultery, David retained faith and the Holy Spirit, illustrating his point by saying that a drunkard does not lose intellect and reason even though he may act contrary to both. In the same way, grace, faith, and the Holy Spirit remain in the elect who fall into sin, urging them to repentance.

Andreae protested that the faculties of intellect and reason that belong to persons because they are human beings are not the same as the divine gifts bestowed on baptized persons, so the example Beza used is inappropriate. What God has given can be lost, insisted Andreae. In fact, Scripture itself testifies to cases in which they were lost, for example, the Psalmist who prays, 'Do not take your holy spirit from me, but give me the joy of your salvation', and so on. As the argument continued, Andreae became indignant at the impiety of Beza's assertion that in the midst of perpetrating sins against conscience, sins of murder and adultery, the elect retain faith and the Holy Spirit. Beza challenged Andreae to show him anyone who is without sin, who is at the same time a human being of flesh and blood. There is a difference, answered Andreae, between human failings and manifest sins against God's law. The former are venial sins, that is, sins not imputed to believers and the elect, and into which the just person falls seven times a day and rises up through the Holy Spirit. But murder and adultery are, according to Paul, mortal sins which punish the flesh with eternal death.

Beza responded rather hotly that no sin is venial; all sins are mortal, that is, worthy of death. The papist distinctions among sins have no place in this discussion, he said. On the contrary, returned Andreae, Paul speaks of venial sin in Romans 7, when he says that he does not do what he wishes to do and performs what he does not wish to do because the habit of sin works in him. Beza said that the Reformed are far from teaching that all sins are equal, a stoic opinion, but that, nevertheless, all sins are mortal by their nature. Sin in the elect, although punishable by death and therefore mortal, is nevertheless venial, that is, pardoned except for the one sin of which John speaks that is against the Holy Spirit. When the elect sin,

---

[31] *Acta*, p. 463: 'Quaero igitur: num David adulterium perpetrans cum Bathsheba, uxore Uriae, fidem & Spiritum sanctum amiserit?'

however, faith and the Holy Spirit remain like fire under banked ashes. Andreae then asked what would have happened to David had he died before he repented? For Beza such a question made no sense, because David was elect; God would see to it that he repented before he died. No pun was surely intended when Andreae referred to God's gifts being without repentance. That means, said Andreae, not that the Holy Spirit is inadmissible, but rather that once baptized, even if one falls, there is no need to rebaptize. Andreae continued that although God's promise cannot fail, human beings can fail. In such an instance, God's promise remains valid and can be grasped anew by the repentant sinner. Beza protested, in the same terms as before, that election determines the permanence of faith and the Holy Spirit, that these may have their effect at any time in a person's life, and that baptism is of no avail to those who are reprobate.[32]

Andreae reminded Beza that they had agreed not to mix topics, and that it was not the time to introduce the subject of predestination.[33] At this point, Andreae preferred to continue the discussion of baptism and especially the problem of consolation in the face of doubt. He asked how one could be at peace if one's adoption as God's child remained uncertain. Beza answered that it is not God's fault if one baptized is not regenerated; rather, it is the fault of the impious person to whom God owes nothing as long as that person remains impious. The consolation of adoption into God's kingdom is to be prayed for as an effect of the Holy Spirit. So, for instance, one may feel the motion of the Holy Spirit testifying that one is truly regenerated and adopted as a child of God. Andreae failed to charge Beza with avoiding the question as he had posed it; it is not a matter of placing blame, but of assuring consciences. Beza's reply on that score was scarcely more helpful, since it reduced assurance to subjective feeling, a veritable Pandora's box of pastoral problems.

Andreae raised the pastoral issue when he asked how those being tempted and unaware of any motion of the Holy Spirit, in fact those whom Satan has inspired with contrary thoughts, can be kept from despair. Such persons might conclude that they are not elect. How can they have the consolation of knowing they are elect, if this knowledge is hidden in the eternal and secret decree of God? Andreae likened such a battle in conscience to David's battle with Goliath, in which he had a certain hope of victory because he relied on the fact that he had been

---

[32] *Acta*, pp. 469–70.
[33] The reader now as well as the audience then must be constantly aware that behind Beza's doctrine of baptism lay his certainty of double predestination.

circumcised in infancy. Who is this, he said, this uncircumcised Philistine? Andreae had raised the questions that were to plague Calvinists thereafter. How could one be certain of one's election; what were the signs? Calvin had said that such questions were inappropriate, since election did not depend upon the believer but upon the certainty of Christ's death and resurrection—in spite of one's feelings, doubts, and temptations. If one kept one's eyes on Christ and held on to God's promise, election was certain.[34] In addition, Beza denied that the Reformed teach that there is no consolation in the sacraments, but only that external baptism does not guarantee internal regeneration. Only when the elect hear the interior testimony of the Holy Spirit may they repose their confidence in the external baptism of water. Once they have been so confirmed, they should not return to that experience of external and internal baptism for comfort whenever they are tempted, in doubt, or disturbed.

At this point, the two theologians repeated arguments already heard. They adduced more scriptural examples, such as Saul, who was circumcised but not saved. Beza spoke of the circumcision of the flesh and the circumcision of the heart; clearly the two are not the same, he said.[35] Beza probably lost many of his hearers when he affirmed that many thousands of baptized children are never regenerated, but perish eternally.[36] Andreae's marginal note says simply: *Horrenda vox*.

In his summation, Andreae rehearsed the Württemberg arguments, leaning most heavily on the lack of assurance that the Reformed doctrine of baptism imposed on parents of baptized children and on all the baptized regarding the effectiveness of their baptism. There should be no doubt that when a child is baptized, it enters into God's adoption and love, said Andreae. There should be no 'probably', but rather assurance. Beza responded that no one who feels the Holy Spirit's motion should entertain any doubts about election. As for other people, continued Beza, no one can judge another or know for certain whether that person is reprobate or elect. Seemingly pious behaviour, like that of Simon Magus, may be hypocritical. Sinners may at the last moment be regenerated or called to repentance. The hearts of all are known to God, but they are not open to anyone else. The final resting place of one's assurance is not on behaviour, one's own or another's, but on God's grace, said Beza. Returning at last to

---

[34] *Institutes of the Christian Religion*, 3. 2. 17–25.

[35] *Acta*, p. 478.

[36] *Acta*, p. 479: 'Idem in Baptismo quoque fit, quem multa millia infantum accipiunt, qui tamen nunquam regenerantur, sed in aeternum pereunt.'

Calvin's theme, Beza said that faith is directed to Christ, not to one's self. To desire heaven, to desire to hold fast to Christ, is enough to assure a person that the Holy Spirit is moving in one's soul, and thereby to console and strengthen the Christian suffering from doubt and temptation. Thus Beza tried to turn his disturbing doctrine into a comfortable doctrine, but the majority of those listening to him at Montbéliard were not convinced. Andreae asked the pertinent question, 'What if one does not feel such a desire?' Then, answered Beza, one must be as a watcher waiting for the dawn. In the middle of the night there is no sign of dawn, all is dark; but one hopes, and that hope is not deceived, because the sun of justice will certainly rise. When it does, one will then feel its rays, the motion of the Holy Spirit.

Andreae remained unconvinced by this poetic metaphor. Consolation is needed in the night of doubt, he said. The nature of temptation at its worst is to question one's election and whether the sun will rise before one dies. Interior movements are too insecure; to rest assurance on such movements leads to despair and a miserable end. Andreae was right on this point. Beza's theological consistency had led him into a psychological morass. Andreae could well insist that the only basis for consolation in temptation is the reality conferred by the Word and the sacraments. The consolation Beza could hold out was that no matter how bad a person seemed during a lifetime, one could hope for a death-bed repentance and the activation of a dormant baptism. For the rest of the day, the two collocutors continued to debate these points without advancing the argument.

The next morning, Beza gave his best argument on the subject. If faith is an act of response to the Word, children cannot have such faith, since they are incapable of understanding preaching. But Paul says that faith comes by hearing the Word of God, for actual faith presupposes knowledge of what is preached, so that one can believe it. In extraordinary cases, like John the Baptist, God can bypass the normal course, but ordinarily faith comes through the external hearing of the Word of God (Rom. 10). Therefore the principal efficient cause and the instrumental cause are always joined. When faith is given or poured into a person the efficient cause is the Holy Spirit, and the instrumental cause is hearing the Word of God. So children do not have actual faith, but the seed or root of faith. Baptism is not, on that account, useless for children, but rather baptism is rendered efficacious when the child matures, hears the Word, even in memory, and believes. Further, baptism is a sign of the covenant to which the parents belong, and into which they therefore baptize their children, leaning on the faith of the Church. The faith of the Church supplements the faith of the parents, so that one can say that probably such children will be added to the number of the children of God.[37]

Andreae objected that children can have faith through the Holy Spirit. In fact, intellect is not at issue here, since reason sometimes impedes faith. Scripture says that the intellect must be brought into captivity in order to believe. It should be emphasized that Beza's argument is based on the instrumental causality of the human intellect actually working, whereas Andreae's argument says that faith is a gift which does not depend on the intellect, but may indeed be impeded by intellectual activity.

The section on baptism concluded with arguments about parental duties. The two collocutors agreed that parents show contempt for the Sacrament by not baptizing their children, and thereby sin. But the results for the children were differently presented. Andreae said that baptism is necessary, and emergency baptism can be supplied by women. Beza countered that if women can administer one Sacrament, they can administer the other and, on Andreae's ground, should be allowed to administer the Lord's Supper when no men ordained for the task were available. Andreae replied that the degree of necessity involved is quite different. In baptism, the eternal life of the infant is at stake. In the case of the Lord's Supper, a public ceremony is at issue. Beza did not pursue this last declaration of Andreae's, but argued that baptism is not necessary to the extent that non-ordained persons should be allowed to administer it. If a minister is not available, God's election suffices for salvation.

There were no concluding arguments, summaries of agreed-upon points or of points remaining in contention as there were at the conclusion of the discussion on the Lord's Supper. Rather, Andreae, playing well his psychological cards, appealed to the audience to judge between them. Throughout the colloquy, the philosophical differences between the two theologians were consistently maintained. Beza supported the integrity of created natures and of their instrumentality, whether these were sacramental elements, the humanity of Christ, or the operation of faith on the mind. For Beza, the Spirit worked through gifts that utilized human faculties. Andreae invoked the supernatural, bypassing natural operations, so that the sacramental elements were identified with the signified reality, regardless of the disposition of the human recipient of the sacrament. Therefore faith could be effective apart from human understanding.

During the first two discussions regarding the Lord's Supper and the

---

[37] *Acta*, pp. 490–1.

two natures of Christ, Beza had retained the sympathy of the French refugees and the bourgeois of Montbéliard. During the arguments about baptism, Beza lost the Montbéliardais, who equally rejected double predestination. The colloquy did not change their beliefs, and they continued to contend with Frederick concerning the doctrine of the Lord's Supper,[38] but while they tolerated the presence of the French Calvinists, they did not adopt their doctrine concerning baptism or the Genevan doctrine of predestination that lay behind it.

University of Missouri–Columbia

[38] See Raitt, 'The Emperor and the Exiles', pp. 55–6.

RELIGIOUS VERSE IN FRENCH NEO-LATIN POETRY UNTIL THE DEATH OF FRANCIS I AND MARGUERITE OF NAVARRE

by I. D. McFARLANE

I

RELIGIOUS poetry inevitably echoes the traditions and trends that are evident in the period. At first there are authors who followed paths that persisted well after the beginning of the sixteenth century, but pre-Reformation and Reformation attitudes were bound to mirror themselves among the writers, both in the vernacular and neo-Latin poetry. The ideas of the Reformation affect the neo-Latin poets especially during the 1530s, but they form, as it were, a bulge in the main current, modifying form and themes, but by the end of the period, conservative attitudes have re-established themselves. Neo-Latin may have benefited from the circumstances: Latin has some resonance beyond the frontiers as well as at home, and Protestant thinkers were not as hostile to the classics as may be assumed. There was perhaps a tendency—I will not say more—for censorship to be more lenient to a language that was not accessible to the *menu peuple*; and humanism, often associated with the new religious ideas, was open at an early stage to neo-classical and classical fashions. It is well known that the 'lyric' Horace, not popular at the closing of the Middle Ages, came first through the neo-Latin poets rather than through the *Pléiade* and its precursors. Horace was not unfamiliar to authors, even in the 1510s, though it was during the 1530s that his lyric poetry was familiar to poets, many of whom came to see what his metres could do for the psalm paraphrasts.[1] In the 1520s or early 1530s, when the Sorbonne's influence was mitigated, if not entirely reduced, this coincided with the growing interest in Erasmus and the themes he popularized. Regional centres acquired more vigour than Paris; in any case, pedagogic movement fostered the exchange of ideas. This does not mean a general trend towards Reformation in all neo-Latin circles; it is too simple to divide persons and attitudes by locations: many places had conservative attitudes and advanced views. Some Protestants

---

[1] R. Lebègue, 'Horace en France pendant la Renaissance', *Humanisme et Renaissance*, 3 (1936), pp. 141–64. We mention isolated examples from earlier writers.

fled to Geneva and beyond; here and there, authors did not publish all they had written in their lifetime; some were floaters whose thinking was affected by the passage of time or circumstance; for a few, discretion was the better part of valour, and one cannot trust literally what was said at any particular moment. And documents and printings suffered from the ravages of time and fortune.

II

In the early years of our period, the orthodox showed conservatism in their use of genres and themes. Many authors were ecclesiastics, several had ties with the court (or regional hierarchies) and acted as secretaries to high officials. Their poetic range was distinctly circumscribed: there are straightforward religious poems, often on the Blessed Virgin Mary, local saints, biblical figures; there are moralizing or satirical pieces—certain genres are acceptable to well-placed courtiers. Some poems, not merely didactic and pedagogic, are also polemic, when matters concern attitudes adopted by different orders. Printers often work under the aegis of the Sorbonne, though there is activity in Poitiers, Caen, or Toulouse. Royalty will soon come to see the political advantages of written propaganda. Some contemporary or recent events, such as the fall of Constantinople—Florentinus, *Carmen de destructione Constantinopolitana* (Paris, *c*.1491) [BN][2]—or the struggles against the Turks—Io. de Monte, a Parisian Minorite, *Incitamentum ad bellum in Turcas* (n.p., n.d.) [BN]. The influence of the Puys and the Jeux Floraux is felt, and we shall see the presence of Italians (like Beroaldo the Elder and Mantuan); and one must mention the appearance of numerous Flemish writers who publish or settle in France (like Petrus Burrus, Michael Anglicus, Petrus Caecus de Ponte). Some authors gravitate around Robert Gaguin, rector of Paris University and head of the Mathurin Order—*Ars versificatoria* (*c*.1478, with many following editions) [BL, OB]; *De puritate conceptionis beatae Mariae virginis* (Paris, 1492, 1500) [BL]. He had disciples in Petrus Burrus or N. Horius—*Opusculum de assumptione Mariae Virginis* (Paris, 1500) [BL]; *Opus in quin-*

[2] A number of the texts I mention will be found in the BL and/or the BN. However, as these titles are often rare, I have mentioned some holdings in other public libraries. Here is a list of abbreviations: Ars = Paris, Arsenal; AUL = Aberdeen University Library; BL = London, British Library (British Museum); BN = Paris, Bibliothèque Nationale; Brown = Brown University, Providence John Carter Library; CUL = Cambridge University Library; EUL = Edinburgh University Library; Maz. = Paris, Mazarine; MC = Manchester, Christie Library; MR = Manchester, John Rylands Library; NLS = National Library of Scotland; OB = Oxford, Bodleian Library; TCD = Dublin, Trinity College Library.

decim dispartitum libellos (Paris, 1507) [BL]; *Poemata nova in laudem fidei catholicae edita* (Paris, 1507) [BL, BN, OB]. After 1500 a slight thematic widening is visible: there is Guillaume de la Mare, rector of Caen—*De sancta eucharistica* (Paris, 1509) [CUL, NLS]; *Tripertitus in Chimaera conflictus* (Paris, 1511, 1513); *Sylvarumn libri quatuor* (Paris, 1511) [CUL]. Patriotism (not only local saints) accompanying religious themes is more aggressive, partly because the wars with Italy or England had flared up— G. Brixius, *Chordigerae navis conflagratio* (Paris, 1512) [BN, Maz.] (Strasburg, 1513) [OB]; Humbertus Mommoretanus, *Bellum Ravennae* (Paris, 1512) [BN]; *Duodecim silvae* (Paris, 1513) [BN]; *Herveis* (Paris, 1513) [BN]; *Parthenices Marianae* and *Christiados libri X* (Paris, 1513) [Maz.]. Most important is Valerandus Varanius, *De gestis Ioannae virginis . . . libri quatuor* Paris, ?1516) [BL]. Lesser works, but strongly religious, came out: a curious example is Guillaume du Bellay, *Peregrinatio humana* (Paris, 1509) [CUL], which is a versified, and shortened, rendering of Degulleville's *Pèlerinage de la vie humaine*, but has an *Ad Virginem Mariae oratio* with the capital letters opening and closing each line forming an acrostic of the first *carmen*. Thus do the games of the *rhétoriqueurs* find their way into Latin verse. Other writers include Olivier Conrad, whose *Epigrammata . . .* (Paris, 1510) [BN] incorporate one or two religious poems, but whose *Odae* (Paris, 1513) are about 'de praefiguratione conceptione nativitate, assumption Virginis Mariae una filii Jesu vitam complectentes'; Nicolas Chappusot, *Passionis Christi Iesu heroica elegansque deploratiuncula* belongs to about 1515 (but undated) [BN]; P. Corderius, *In Adami Protoplasti culpam Ode monocola* (Paris, 1517) [BN]; Denys Faber, *De purissima Mariae conceptu* (Troyes, n.d.) [BL]; anonymous, *Elegia funesta nephasii sceleris heretici* [BL]; C. de Seyssel, *Missus est angelus et cantici Divae Virginis* (Paris, 1514).

In this decade, and indeed earlier, printing has developed rapidly under the impetus of such men as Josse Bade, who prints not only home literature, but the works of foreigners, such as James Foulis (Follisius), 1513, and some of the Flemish authors already mentioned. But in the provinces interesting volumes appear: Julianus Pius, *Epigrammata necnon moralia opuscula* (Poitiers, 1509) [BN], in which we detect a nascent concern with Horace: he composes a prayer to the Virgin Mary (fol. 3r), a prayer of thanks (fol. 4r), a poem to Christ and Mary; Christ crucified is addressed (fol. 8r), so is St Ursula (fol. 20r). Numerical patterns with a medieval flavour come out in Burrus, but we find a series of nine vices expressed by Pierre d'Antravensis, *Aurea summa de fuga vitiorum nuncupata* (Paris, 1521) [BNJ]. J. Coquille, *Poemata* (Paris, 1510) [BN] contains several poems to saints (a vi to St Nicholas, v° to St Stephen, br° to St

Anthony), but he too is significant for the introduction of Horatian metres. This presence is no doubt due to the success of Perrotto's little manual, published some time back in Italy. We can note P. Belossus, *De laudibus Dei parae Virginis opusculum* (Avignon, 1512) [BN]. We find some poems in Ravisius Textor, *Officina* (Paris, 1502) (posthumus) and some poems in a *rhétoriqueur* printing of 1520, *Palinodz, Chantz royaulx, Ballades, Rondeaulx et Epigrammes à l'honneur de limmacule Conception de la toute belle mère de Dieu Marie ...* (Paris, 1520), where French and Latin mingle (lxv a *ballade latine* by Dom Nicole Lescarre; on fol. 99r we read an *Ode ad Divam Virginem* [stanza form, 12: 12: 12: 6], and on fol. 89v *In Mariae conceptus sincerissimi laudem heroicum epigramma*). Of little value, the bits and pieces show how the old themes and practices are maintained without much renovation, except perhaps in metrical experiments. The next decade, when Erasmus begins to assert his being, we see the stirring of new currents, however timid they may be.

III

Pierre Rosset is the first writer (except for Nicolas Barthélemy's *Momiae*, published c.1514 [BN]); he dies young in 1532, but his several volumes show that, conservative as he is, he is aware of 'modern' humanism, and his works are accessible to younger generations.[3] His first works are in the older tradition, but show the formal influence of Mantuan. The *De mirabili cultu hostie ... ad Christianam pietatem monitis divi Anthonii Paduani minorite converso* (Paris, 1515) [CUL] was accompanied by some poems by Nicole Dupuys; it narrates a hagiographic tale: St Anthony's sermon is given in Bourges: Guialduc's conversion is described. The poem is divided into rhetorical sections (*propositio*, *invocatio*, and so on) which suggests that it was a teaching model; a similar method is employed in the 1516 *Stephanis siue epos de beatissimi protomartyris Stephani agone*. The Preface, dated in the same year, says that the idea of the composition was inspired by the arrival of Count Sforza in Paris. The rhetorical layout of the first poem is repeated, the *narratio* is frequently interrupted by a series of *orationes*, which ends with a *cantus* (of twelve) *angelorum* by N. Dupuys. The text contains references to the evils of the time, and summarizes various passages from the Old Testament. Virgilian touches may be detected, as in all such examples of para-epic patterns. The year 1517 sees

---

[3] So far as I know there is no authoritative life of Pierre Rosset; but I have found a number of his books in the CUL, certainly more than in the BL or BN.

the appearance of the *Laurentias*, and in the same year we find the reprint of the three poems, published by Marnef, Paris [CUL, OB]. In 1522 Rosset publishes the first edition of his *Paulus*, through Josse Bade, Paris [BL, BN TCD, CUL]: this work is re-edited in 1537 by Hubert Sussannée, who had also brought out the *Christus* in 1534 [BL, BN]; there was another edition in 1543. These latter texts, written in a familiar formula, seem to have been popular with the *évangéliques*, though the epic genre is momentarily on the wane. Rosset had some following as a teacher, he probably gave instruction in Greek, he wrote liminary verse for Hector Boethius, *Scotorum historiae* (*libri XVIII*) [BL]. He was much admired by members of the Lyons *sodalitium*, and he was honoured, on his death in 1532, by a *Deploratio mortis Petri Rossetti* (Paris, Cyaneus) [2 copies in OB]. He was a vanguard humanist who had no problem in remaining orthodox.

Nicolas Barthélemy de Loches is known by references in his poetry: he was a priest, studied·at Orléans, taught at the Collège de Marmoutiers, and seems at one time to have been on the staff of the Collège du Cardinal Lemoine.[4] Later on he became a prior near Orléans. In 1521 he published his *Epithalamium Francisci Valesiae et Mariae Anglorum filiae* [BN]—somewhat prematurely, since the marriage did not take place; but the poem was complemented by the *Ennoea ad sospitalem Christum*, his *Hortulus*, and some epigrams. He follows the poetic paths of several humanists: epigram, epithalamium, school drama. In 1524 he brought out his *De vita activa et contemplativa liber unus*, together with a few epigrams, and some stricter religious verse in four poems addressed to friends or relatives: the two *ennoae*, a *monodia* on Christmas Day, and an ode addressed to the Virgin Mary [Maz.]. In 1529 his *Christus xylonicus*, a dramatic poem, had some success. The poems published in 1523 show the predomination of religious themes, but Horatian metres are brought into play. These pieces are reprinted in 1532 (in two separate editions), the year in which the *Ode dicolos* on Christ's birth also appears. Though he is virtually unknown nowadays, his work enjoyed some favour for a few years, but he was overtaken by better, more up-to-date talents. Even in his *Epigrammata* we note several religious poems (*Ad Deum*, *Ad divum Martinum*, fol. 36v); we find numerous epitaphs, and praise of humanists, some of whom are sympathetic to Erasmus. His verse is remembered in Léger Duchesne's anthology, but other scholar-poets neglect him.

---

[4] See R. Lebègue, *La Tragédie religieuse en France. Les Débuts* (*1514–1573*) (Paris, 1929), ch. 11, pp. 169–93). Lebègue found the rare *Dialogus*.
[5] Ibid., pp. 123–5.

The last of this generation (I omit writers not concerned with religious verse, or indeed verse) is **François Bonade**.[5] He is a fairly prolific character, but his main importance lies in the fact that he is the first one to have published a full set of Psalm paraphrases in verse form. In addition to his *Anacephaleoses genesum quinquaginta octo Francorum regum* (Paris, Gromorsus, 1543) [BL], which form a series of royal icons for teaching purposes, he writes many religious texts. He trained at Sainte-Barbe (where he was taught by Guy de Fontenay, who published his first poem in 1517), trained as a priest, and spent much of his career in western France. He was familiar with Greek and Latin; he may have taught for a time in Paris, but he does not seem to have been affected by the 'new' religious winds. He was a protégé of Marguerite de Navarre, and was in touch with various local humanists. He printed some verses to Eleanor of France (Paris, 1539) [BL, BN], two years before he published his *Divi Pauli Epistolae ad Orphicam lyram traductae* [BL, AUL] (a version later reprinted in Basle [AUL]). In 1537 also there came out the *Monodiae aliquot personarum* [BN, Maz.]. A rare *Dialogus passionis* was printed by Wechel in 1541;[6] and an early *Cruciatu beatae Mariae Virginis* [BN] completes our idea of his work which is late medieval in spirit, essentially pedagogic; nevertheless, his version of New Testament texts show him to be something of a back-woodsman, and yet he announces paraphrases that belong to the Counter-Reformation period.

IV

From 1528 a new spirit is abroad in the literary field: the *rhétoriqueurs* have died out as a vital force, Marot is in the ascendant, and Salmon Macrin, shortly to distinguish himself in religious verse, publishes experiments in Horatian and Catullan metres which mark the arrival of a fresh era. Another feature of this 'decade' is the collective activity of local centres. Orléans has its value: the University, unlike Paris, taught civil law: it attracted a number of humanists from abroad; it developed as a centre of Calvinist enthusiasm; and early on it seems to have taken an interest in the furtherance of Greek Studies: Aleander, important later for his part in the Counter-Reformation, taught Greek at Orléans, as well as at Paris. A first generation of humanists is linked with Orléans, where the daughter of de Loynes was to marry Jean de Morel, a habitué of the *Pléiade*, associated

[6] Lebègue, *La Tragédie religieuse en France. Les Débuts (1514–1573)* (Paris, 1929), ch. 11, pp. 125–8.

with Guillaume du Bellay; his interests were chiefly scholarly (rather than literary) and he moved towards Protestantism. The next generation was more concerned with poetry, though members were divided in religion. The most famous example is, of course, **Theodore Beza**, though his first collection of Latin poetry does not appear until 1548 (C. Badius, R. Stephanus, Paris) [BL, CUL, NLS]. However, a manuscript, recovered by the Orléans library from the Phillips collection, shows Beza's verse going back, in some measure, as far as the 1530s and early 1540s,[7] and is an expression of scholarship and Christianity. Later revised editions were more partisan, and published usually in Switzerland. Some poems were never printed, partly because the author did not care for them, partly because poetic considerations told against them. The majority of poems formed part of the 1548 edition, just before he left France for Calvinist pastures; and they give an idea of the company he kept in early life. However, there were humanist poets of talents who remained orthodox: the most prominent was **Jean Dampierre**, a Benedictine who had much influence over his friends, being known as the 'father' of the hendecasyllable.[8] Most of his verse remained in manuscript (except for what Gherus published in his *Delitiae poetarum gallorum*); there were poems written to and with Salmon Macrin and Denys Faucher de Lérins. His most important composition was *De regimine Virginum* (preserved in MS BN latin, 8349), which deals quite substantially with medical matters, and offers more than the title might suggest. Two other poets are worth noting: there is Jean Binet, the uncle of Ronsard's biographer; he was going to produce an edition of his verse which runs on to the reign of Charles IX (BM BN nouv. acq. lat. 2070). The letters and verse are of interest for his humanist connections (especially in Bordeaux), but the poems have little poetic appeal. Gentien Hervet, known for his activities during the Counter-Reformation, translated early in his career a version of the *Antigone*, which has a few slighter poems of no great value.

---

[7] F. Aubert, J. Boussard, and H. Meylan, 'Les premières poésies latines de Théodore de Bèze', *BHR*, 15 (1953), pp. 164–91, 257–94. See also P. Geisendorf, *Théodore de Bèze* (Geneva, n.d.); and F. Gardy, *Bibliographie des œuvres théologiques, historiques, littéraires et juridiques de Théodore de Bèze* (Geneva, 1960), *THR*, 41, esp. pp. 1–17.

[8] J. Boussard, 'Un poète latin, directeur spirituel au XVIe siècle, Jean Dampierre', *Bulletin philologique et historique* (1946–7; appeared in 1950), pp. 33–58, which has a list of Dampierre's writings.

V

Catholic poetry at this time was not very impressive, in so far as it was printed. One may note the *De passione Jesu Christi libri V* by Des Chausses (J. Calceatus, Paris, 1531) [Maz.], Le Mans, Bordeaux though the BN has copies of the 1538 edition and one s.l., n.d., which suggests that the epic formula still found readers at this time; one or two like M. Thierry or Nic. Marconville, were orthodox, but did not contribute to religious verse: on the other hand, P. Busseron, *Horae Sapphicae* (Lyons, 1538 [BN]), reveal a mixture of orthodoxy and Horatian metres, but include seven psalm paraphrases composed in pentameters! Denys Faucher de Lérins is known by one or two poem-letters to friends, such as Macrin and Visagier, but his *œuvre* was not published properly until 1613 [BN, BL, CUL, OB]. His poems are fully religious: he was concerned with reform of some houses,[9] he writes lines glorifying Christ, he has a few pieces against church abuses, he mentions Sannazar to his pupils, he composes religious or moralizing eclogues. His poems, known to a few friends no doubt around Tarascon, cannot have had a wide enough audience during his lifetime.

There is one area in which orthodox, *évangélique*, and Protestant held common ground: the **Psalm paraphrase**. There is a medieval tradition which is revived or continued, not necessarily in verse form. Two features are worth noting in our period: firstly, the paraphrases are frequently in verse; secondly, the genre benefits greatly from the development of Hebrew scholarship. Early practitioners do not break much ground. François Bonade's full set (1531) is composed in one metre and shows little familiarity with modern advances; and yet several scholarly names come to light. N. Clénard taught for a time in France before returning to Spain; Vatable established himself in the field as a teacher and as a writer; there were other figures such as A. Guidacerius, C. Campensis, and Santes Pagninus, whose writings were widely known. Some editions of Eobanus Hessus's paraphrases enjoyed some success, and were reprinted in France. It was the neo-Latin versions that came to the fore; in the vernacular, Protestant writers, such as Eustorg de Beaulieu, believed that the texts should be accessible to the common people (hence, no doubt, why he used old-fashioned genres); though many Calvinists were deeply suspicious of the classics, they were not unanimous in their hostility: a good number recognized the use of Latin as a pedagogic instrument and as a way of

---

[9] *Opera omnia R. Patris D. Dion. Faucherii Monachi Lerinensis et civis arelatensis*, ed. V. Barral = *Chronologia Sanctorum . . . Insulae Lerinensis . . .* (Lyons, P. Rigaud, 1613), 2, pp. 22–466.

crossing linguistic frontiers. Hebrew, through the advances of humanism, became more intelligible than it had been to previous generations; it was right that a proper understanding of the original texts should be achieved. Then, since the poetry of the original required more suitable expression, the full awareness of the lyric Horace was seen to have splendid advantages. A lead may perhaps have been given by Jean de Ga(g)nay (Gagnaeus), though his theories and practice did not reach publication until 1547—*Psalmi Dauidis septuaginta quinque . . .* (Paris) [BN, OB]; but he had been active for some time past, and he was thought to harbour Erasmian sympathies; he had close ties with many forward-looking humanists during the 1530s and early 1540s: his *Epitome paraphrastica enarrationum in epistolam Pauli ad Romanos* came out from Vascosan in 1533 [BL]. There are some sporadic Psalm paraphrases (in verse) appearing among members of the Lyons *sodalitium* during the 1530s; but **George Buchanan**[10] is more important, though the full set of paraphrases does not come out till *c.*1565. A few of his paraphrases may belong to the 1540s, some appeared in 1555, others were referred to by contemporaries. Now Buchanan may have kown Jean de Gagnay personally, he certainly was acquainted with Vatable, and he seems to have learned some Hebrew— one of his books—now held in Edinburgh University Library—Sebastian Munster, *Dictionarium Hebraicum* (Froben, Basle, 1531) is thus very relevant. In his Preface, Gagnay stressed the value of up-to-date scholarship, and pointed to the variety of Horatian metres—Prudentius will, of course, not be neglected. Buchanan's exercises enjoyed widespread popularity: Plantin despatched some copies of his edition(s) to Spain, and later we shall hear of his texts being adapted to Catholic purposes.

Now some other genres were acceptable to early Reformation and pre-Reformation poets: as we saw, the epic style would be modified to suit religious ends. Poems to saints did not lose popularity; and one should also mention the icon, which is first used as a mnemonic poem, and thus welcome to pedagogues. In due course, however, the genre followed the course of satiric verse (*pasquilli*); it was taken over by the Protestants, who saw in it a useful teaching weapon, but also a form of propaganda to spread the glory of figures associated with the cause (Beza). The epitaph underwent some modification, and flowers first in neo-Latin poetry— during the Middle Ages epitaphs were usually written in French. With the arrival of Robert Gaguin and his friends or disciples, it acquires literary status: on the one hand one notices a series of tributes (to royal or

---

[10] See I. D. McFarlane, *Buchanan* (London, 1981).

politically important characters) so that we have poems on Louis XII, Anne of Brittany, Louise of Savoy, the *vers vulgares* . . . for Henry the Dauphin (1536). There is a tendency for more than one language to be employed; collective authorship and greater proportions serve to celebrate the member of some profession, or offer homage to a religious leader. In due course, religious feelings show themselves on various sides; such tributes also promote the scholarly or poetic talents of those involved; and sometimes are on a very large scale (the death of Macrin's wife, the *tombeau*(x) of Marguerite de Navarre, the death of Bishop Viole).

VI

Now **Lyons** was really important. Without *parlement* or university, it thought itself relatively free from persecution, though vigilance was not absent. Lyons was the military 'railhead' of the Italian wars, and in consequence the royal court paid occasional visits; the town had local cultural activity (one thinks of Symphorien Champier, the development of interest in numismatics, and local archaeology). The Italian presence was far from insignificant; and printers had prospered over the years, while Paris was for a time something of a backwater. The *sodalitium* was loose enough, but Etienne Dolet had made attempts to hold it together. Its temporary nature was obvious, though there were members with local connections (the Scève cousins, Girinet, or Jean Raynier); others had links which brought them into touch with other groups. We tend to endow these men with Protestant or Reformist sympathies, but we must not overdo the association. Some inevitably floated; others were likely to stray from orthodoxy for only a short while; a few, whose sympathies were suspect, did not publish controversial works during their lives. However, one of the most consistent, from our point of view, is **Nicolas Bourbon**:[11] he remains a protégé of the court of Navarre, he becomes tutor to Jeanne d'Albret, he is safeguarded by Marguerite; he dies some time after 1551, when he makes his offering to her second *tombeau*. He starts as a vanguard Reformist: like others he objects to the way in which ultra-conservative religion stood out against modern humanism (which involved Greek and Hebrew as well as Latin); he was a fervent admirer of

---

[11] On Bourbon see G. Carré, *De vita et operibus Nicolaii Borbonii* (Paris, 1888); V.-L. Saulnier, 'Recherches sur Nicolas Bourbon l'Ancien', *BHR*, 16 (1954), pp. 172–91. On the *sodalitium* generally see F. Buisson, *Sébastien Castellion* (Paris, 1892), 1, ch. 2; R. Copley Christie, *Etienne Dolet, the Martyr of the Renaissance* (London, 1899); V.-L. Saulnier, *Maurice Scève* (Paris, 1948–9), 1, chs 5 and 6; Lucien Febvre, *Le problème de l'incroyance au XVIe siècle* (Paris, 1942).

Erasmus. Though he wrote a number of unpublished French poems in 1529, he is first noticed by the appearance of his *Nugae* in 1533 (Paris) [Basle, BL, BN, CUL, EUL, MC, MR, NLS, OB, TCD]: he attacks 'ignorant' scholars, he speaks in favour of advanced humanists, he is bitter against the monks, but, more significantly, he writes some religious poems which sail fairly close to the wind: *Fides christiana*, *Precatio Christianorum*, *Precatio Christiana*, *Vita aeterna piis exspectata*, *Ad Christum*, *Si Christus volet*, *Ad Christum crucifixum*, *Ad D. Jesum Christum*. One poem (omitted in the 1538 edition) caused some concern: the volume was certainly Erasmian in tone, and these matters helped to put him into prison. It seems that his release came through Marguerite's intervention: 'Le Roy (luy) commanda à la dicte court que l'on mist hors de prison Borbonius.' He was to confess to his error and to agree 'se contenir de plus faire tels mectres et de bien vivre en l'union de l'eglize sur quelques peines.' He went abroad, to England, where he was at the court of Anne Boleyn, who found him some noble pupils to tutor. He was thus out of circulation for a time: on his return he pointed to the dangers of religious persecution. In England he witnessed some brutality and was plagued by ill health. He was grateful to be put on Marguerite's civil list (1538), and in the same year he brought out the second edition of the *Nugae—Nugarum libri octo* (Lyons, 1538) [BL, BN, CUL, MC; 1540, Basle, EUL, OB]. The volume was augmented by his experiences in England, but he took care not to cause further nuisance. We hear little of him thereafter: poems on the death of Francis I [BL, EUL], an epithalamium for Antoine de Bourbon and Jeanne d'Albret (Paris, 1549) [AUL, BN], and the 1551 tribute to Marguerite de Navarre's second *tombeau*. He is undoubtedly the most explicitly 'evangelical' of all the contemporary poets we have seen.

Jean Visagier (Vulteius) is one to achieve reasonable fame; by his *Epigrams*—two books in 1536 [BL, Maz., MC] and four books in 1537 (Lyons, 1537) [BL, EUL]—his four books of Hendecasyllables (1538) [BL, BN, MC, OB], and two books of *Inscriptiones* (Paris, 1538) [BL, BN, CUL, OB] he combined scholarship and poetic talent: he was versed in Greek and was acquainted with Italian poets. He was thought to be *evangélique*: at one time he had links with Jean du Bellay and he knew Gérard Roussel, Briand de Vallée, Charles Fontaine, and Marguerite de Navarre. He makes the usual noises against monks and poor scholars; but in 1538 we see a change: he is connected with Périon, the orthodox translator of Aristotle, Scholastica Bectoz of Tarascon, and, especially, Denys Faucher de Lérins, who tells us that Visagier became a clear Catholic, and that he died in 1540 in the odour of sanctity; unfortunately he composed very little religious poetry. On Gilbert Ducher we are ill informed; he wrote an epitaph for Ravisius Textor (1520), which suggests that he was rather older than most members of the *sodalitium*; he published an edition (or anthology) of Martial in 1526; it was in 1538 that his *Epigrammatum libri duo* appeared. He does not write much religious verse, but we have a paraphrase of Psalm 127 and a prosopopoeia by Christ. He is in touch with humanists such as Florens Volusenus (Florence Wilson); he refers to Erasmus's religious ideals; but there is not much to go on, and he seems to have remained within the pale of orthodoxy.

Jean de Boyssonné,[12] in spite of pronounced attitudes, does not contribute much to the religious field, and in any case most of his verse and correspondence has remained in manuscript until recent times. He was anti-Toulouse, understandably; he knew Mathieu Pac, Briand de Vallée, and Visagier; and some of his friends went over to Geneva; the occasional religious references do not amount to anything significant. One cannot say much either about Etienne Dolet's poetry here: he avoids religious subjects in the *Carmina* (1534) [BL, BN, CUL; 1538, BL, BN, EUL, MR]—apart from some lines to the Virgin Mary; and his poem on the *Genethliacon* of his son Claude is, one might say, out of context.[13] Many have gone so far as to see in him a thoroughgoing atheist. He died an eccentric interpreter of a Greek passage.

Hubertus Sussannaeus[14]—there are various ways of spelling his name—is an odd humanist, unstable, peripatetic, much travelled, linked with innumerable scholars and teachers. He was born in Soissons in 1512, he distinguished himself in Latin, having learned Greek later. He sided with Dolet against Erasmus on scholarly points; he was a pupil of Pierre Rosset, whom he much admired. He is difficult to classify: Febvre and others thought of him as an *évangélique*; he married and had several children; he seems to have been addicted to drink and indisciplined in the class-room. Many of his works are devoted to teaching; nothing is known of him after 1551 when he wrote for Marguerite's second *tombeau*. His neo-Latin poems can be found all over the place: *plaquettes*, verse accompanying larger works, liminary compliments. In 1543 he composed a heroic poem in honour of Saints Prothasius and Gervasius, the patron

---

[12] Boyssonné's correspondence and poetry are in Toulouse, Bibliothèque Municipale, MSS 834 and 835. See F. Mugnier, *La Vie et les poésies de Jehan de Boyssonné. Mémoires et documents publiés par la Société savoisienne d'histoire et d'archéologie* (Paris, 1897).

[13] See n. 11 above for Etienne Dolet; and more recent works by H. Longeon.

[14] P. Renouard, 'Hubertus Sussannaeus. Hubert de Suzanne', *Revue des Livres Anciens*, 2 (1917), pp. 146–58 (with a bibliography).

saints of Soissons [CUL]. In his *Dictionarium Ciceronianum* (Paris, 1536) [BL, St John's, Cambridge, Glasgow, Hunter] there are several accompanying poems. His *Annotationes* appear in two separate editions (Paris, 1539 [St John's, Cambridge] and 1542 [BN]); like many humanists he attacks the obscurantist views of dyed-in-the-wool churchmen, but he honours Pierre Lizet, a bugbear of the Reformers, and he addresses the Virgin Mary: he strikes one as clearly orthodox. His *Ludorum libri IV* (Paris) [BL, BN, AUL] came out in 1538 and show him to be linked for a time with the *sodalitium*; he knew Rabelais, for whom he seems to have been a corrector, he knew Michel de l'Hôpital (and his father-in-law, Jean Morin) for whom he wrote an epithalamium. There is a little poem *Ad Virginem Mariam*; later (in 1543) he published a *De festo paschali carmen* (n.p.) [St John's, Cambridge] and there is a *De resurrectione Domini nostri Jesu Christi carmen*, Paris (Dijon). His religious poems are thus not very numerous, but they are clear enough to show that he is pretty orthodox for most of the time. The verse is fairly conservative so far as form and metre are concerned: one can hardly put him on the same pedestal as Bourbon. The only other figure worth a mention is Bishop Jean Olivier: he may have had Erasmian leanings, but little is known about him. He was a friend of Salmon Macrin, and he composed a poem *Pandora* (Dolet, 1541) [BL], which was translated into French on two occasions—1542, *La Pandore*, by G. Michel, and 1548, by P. Bouchet (Poitiers) [both BL]. The classical theme is associated with Eve and biblical themes and might be classed, very roughly as a religious poem.

VII

The most important writer, from our point of view, is **Salmon Macrin**. He is linked with the *sodalitium*, though more as a figurehead than as a colleague. He writes over a long period, and apart from an intermediate era, when he may have been tempted by Reformist ideas, he appears as a thoroughly orthodox poet.[15] He starts in a highly traditional way: he contributes liminary verse, in 1509 to the *Nova Corona Maria* [BN]; he performs a similar service for Valeran de Varanne's *De gestis Ioannae virginis Franciae egregie bellatricis libri quatuor* (Paris, ?1516). His first proper work is

---

[15] See I. D. McFarlane, 'Jean Salmon Macrin (1490–1557)', *BHR*, 21 (1959), pp. 55–84; 311–49; 22 (1960), pp. 73–89; Georges Soubeille, *Jean Salmon Macrin, Le Livre des Epithalames* (1528–31). *Les Odes de 1530* (*Livres I et II*) = Publications de l'Université de Toulouse-Le Mirail, Série A, tome 37 (Toulouse, 1978).

183

patriotic: *Elegiarum triumphalium liber* (1513) [BN], but it contains several religious poems on well known lines (*Ad Virginem . . .*; *De Christo natali*; *De incarnatione Dominica*; *Ad Virginem de Resurrectione*; *De domina ascensione*; *Peccator ad Virginem*). The poems are in elegiacs; they are therefore conservative in theme and form. The next collection shows more formal variety and, thematically, mixes the profane and religious. *De Christi superbenedicti assertoris ostri morte ἐφοδιον. Cui additur elegia de poetices abusu. Item duo hymni de Virgine Dei genitrice* (Paris, Gourmont, *c.*1514) [BN]. This was reprinted as *Elegia . . .* and belongs to 1515. Here the earliest Horatian experiment seems to be *De dominica incarnatione Ode Asclepiadea*, which is followed by *De purificatione Virginis Mariae Ode sapphica*. About the years 1515–16 Macrin published a text by Pontano— *De laudibus diuinis libellus optimus*, and accompanied it with his *Sylua cui titulus Soter* [BN]: this shows that Macrin, while remaining faithful to the accepted styles, has ventured out into Italian authors, and his relationship to Pontano will now remain until the end of his literary career. Between roughly 1516 and 1528, though some texts printed in the 1528 volume are composed rather earlier, the collection in the *Carminum libellus* (Paris, S. de Colines) [BL, BN, Brown, MC, MR] is valuable because Macrin owes much to Catullus and Horace for his inspiration: it is reprinted as the *Epithalamiorum liber* in 1531. In the previous year the *Carminum libri quatuor* (Paris, 1530) [BL, BN, Brown, EUL, MC, MR] tell us much about his relationships, but there is little religious poetry, apart from a poem to the Virgin Mary. The *Lyricorum libri duo* (Morrhy, Paris, 1531) contain a few religious poems (*Hymnus in Divae Caeciliae laudem*; *Ad divam Margaritam*, which honours the birth of his first child; the *Natali Christi . . .*; the *Ad Virginem Mariam*, in hendecasyllables, which shows Macrin's growing tendency to link his wife with the Virgin Mary); but we cannot talk of an essentially religious volume yet. During the 1530s, he becomes a court poet, having already contributed to a *tumulus* of Louise of Savoy (1531); but after the appearance of the *Elegiarum, Epigrammatum et Odarum libri tres* (Augereau, Paris, 1534) [EUL, OB], which were printed by a man who shortly went to the stake, the thematic orthodoxy becomes more marked: in 1537 the *Hymnorum libri VI* (Lyons, Brown) [BL, BN, AUL, CUL, Glasgow, NLS, MR, TCD] came out (dedicated to Jean du Bellay); they have much more Christian substance: *Precationis dominicae paraphrasi*, hymns to Christ and to various saints, a *Virginis Mariae apostrophe*, and paraphrases to Psalms 2, 119, 117, 127, 116, and 109. The *Odarum libri VI* (S. Gryphius, Lyons, 1537) had a paraphrase of Psalm 141, a sprinkling of poems to Christ, and a paraphrase of Isaiah 48 [BL, BN, CUL, OB,

Glasgow], but were less prominent than the Hymns. The increase of Psalm paraphrases is notable, and the Hymns have a poem from Cornelius Musius, a Dutch poet Macrin met in Poitiers—a staunch Catholic, he was later to suffer a gruesome death; in 1536 he had published at Poitiers his *Institutio christiana* (Marnef) [BL] with various poems including more paraphrases. I suspect that Macrin owes something to Musius's example, though the genre was becoming more widespread; for in 1538 Macrin published his *Septem Psalmi in lyricos . . . paraphrasticos versi*, together with *Paeanes*, which included paraphrases of Psalms 1 and 147 (Marnef, Poitiers) [BN, MR]. Here the religious elements are distinctly more important, with a corresponding reduction of poems to friends. In 1540 the Christian themes are in the ascendant (*Hymnorum selectorum libri III* (R. Stephanus, Paris) [BL, BN, MC, Winchester College]: they included Psalm Paraphrases 54, 113, 126, 127, 22, 23, 50, 64, and 99. By 1546, the *Odarum libri tres*, followed by Jean du Bellay's *Poematia* R. Stephanus, Paris) [BL, BN, MC] show that inspiration is waning: there are a few religious poems, but the courtier has regained the ascendant: the *Epigrammatum libri II* (Poitiers, Marnef) [BL, BN] show attempts to curry favour with the new luminaries at Henry II's court; the *Epitome vitae Domini nostri Jesu Christi* (M. David, Paris, 1549) is dedicated to Marguerite of Navarre, but is a rather humdrum exercise within orthodox lines. Something of a poetic *regain de jeunesse* shows in the *Naeniarum libri III* (Vascosan, Paris) [BL, BN, King's College, Cambridge, OB, MC], which is a *tumulus* to his wife, in which friends and colleagues took part. Lyric and elegiac metres are present, but what is of interest is that the *tumulus* was dedicated to his wife, who is the object of the whole volume: she is associated fully with the Virgin Mary, but, in honouring her, Macrin was following the steps of Pontano. He is also adding to the increasing enthusiasm for the collective *tumulus* by widening the formal and metrical qualities of the genre.

Macrin, in spite of Erasmian and Reformist 'temptations', does not really stray from the orthodox fold, however convinced many of his friends—and children—may have been. He is a good example of a poet whose orthodoxy is manifested by enriching traditional genres and topics through his living during the period of Erasmus, Lefèvre d'Etaples, the psalm theoreticians and paraphrasts, and of emerging Calvinism.

VIII

After the death of Francis I, in 1547, to give an approximate date, there is a definite harmonization of humanism, scholarship, and religious conservatism. Henry II's fanatical orthodoxy was an important cause; but confirmed Protestants were tending to leave the country; only some waverers, hoping that the Council of Trent might prove more lenient, were prepared to wait for a time. At first, a few commit themselves to print—G. Bigot, *Christ. Philosophiae libri IV*, where we find an *Ad Jesum Christum carmen* (Toulouse, 1549) [BN]; B. Faius, *Hymnus dominicus* (Paris, 1550) [Maz.]. Some manuscript poems (BN lat. 8497), thought to belong to the years 1545–50 are strictly Catholic. Only from 1552 or so does printing enter a golden age and neo-Latin verse enjoy much favour. The epic genre returns to success with the religious wars, and other genres re-establish themselves properly. The 1530s looked like a splendid episode, but though some authors showed themselves to have talent, and wrote poems that opened up religious themes, they did not succeed in breaking the traditional mould: consecrated practice, enriched by modern human-ist ventures, serves ultimately to confirm attitudes whose origins stretch back a long way into the past.

University of Oxford

CHURCH ORDINANCES AND REGULATIONS OF THE DUTCH SYNODS 'UNDER THE CROSS' (1563-1566) COMPARED WITH THE FRENCH (1559-1563)

by F. R. J. KNETSCH

INTRODUCTION

IN 1559 Philip II left the Netherlands for Spain, where, from then on, he was to rule his empire. The government of the Provinces united by his father, Charles V, was left to his bastard sister Margaret, Duchess of Parma. Although she faithfully followed the Habsburg line, which in religion meant opposing Protestantism, her reign was characterized by a certain lack of firmness, enabling opposing factions to assert themselves. Shortly before Philip's departure, Henry II, his French rival, had died in a tournament. His children and widow were as unable to quell the religious unrest in France as Margaret was in the Netherlands. In this situation, Calvinism grew irresistibly: from around 1555, it had already increased greatly in strength under Henry II, and in 1559 it had managed to hold a synod in Paris. That synod, as well as drawing up a Confession of Faith, produced its Discipline or Church Ordinance; and the best way of tracing the growth of Calvinism is to examine how rapidly the synods met, and to see how the Church Ordinances were adjusted to meet particular circumstances. That this development in the French Reformed Church had repercussions in the adjoining Netherlands, where the same language was spoken, at least in part, needs scarcely to be emphasized. Besides, during the reign of Elizabeth I, Calvinist refugee congregations were established in England, and these, in turn, could be used as bases for serving the Netherlands.

This present contribution aims at defining more clearly the influence exerted by French Calvinism on the Dutch Church Ordinances. The issue, of course, has been explored earlier: at the start of this century Hermann Edler von Hoffmann, an external lecturer at Göttingen University, produced a study of the subject.[1] Yet, curiously, later scholars,

---

[1] H. E. von Hoffmann, *Das Kirchenverfassungsrecht der niederländischen Reformierten bis zum Beginne der Dordrechter Nationalsynode von 1618/19* (Leipzig, 1902).

though honouring him in footnotes, have not adequately appreciated his discoveries. Neither Jan de Jong[2] nor Haitjema[3] or, again, Moreau[4] recognized the full significance of his pioneering work.

De Jong, in particular, can be faulted. Although he seems to have been familiar with two of the three editions[5] of the *acta* of the synods 'under the Cross', as well as the booklet by Hoffmann, De Jong did not explore the period before 1566 when preparing his thesis on the early polity of the Reformed Church in the Netherlands, written under the supervision of F. L. Rutgers: indeed, he devoted only thirteen lines of text, and two notes, to developments before 1566. In his notes (following Hooijer) he drew attention to the example of the French Church Ordinances, but failed to give further details, although these could easily have been found in Hoffmann's study. In any event, he needed more detailed evidence to substantiate his own theory that the meetings of the provincial synods were an integral part of the founding of the Reformed Church's organization in the Netherlands; and his own work concentrated entirely on the assembly of church ministers at Wesel. Having shown that this assembly was no more than a 'convent' (that is, an unofficial meeting of church ministers), De Jong ought to have recognized that the authority of the smallest provincial synod exceeded that of the largest 'convent' of the most powerful but unauthorized individual ministers.

What pattern, in any event, did the earliest provincial synods intend to follow? Without a doubt, they expected to introduce French Reformed practice, and a modified French Reformed Confession for the Netherlands. De Jong himself, who accepted all this, ought to have considered why provincial synods were held, whereas no general synod met, and he should have investigated how the various provinces were formed and to which body they considered themselves to belong. He would then have been faced with the question of why it was that these synods considered

---

[2] J. de Jong, 'De Voorbereiding en Constitueering van het Kerkverband der Nederlandsche Gereformeerde Kerken in de 16e eeuw. Historische Studien over het Convent te Wezel (1568) en [never published] de Synode van Emden (1572). 1st vol.' (Free University of Amsterdam, D.Theol. thesis, Groningen, 1911).

[3] Th. L. Haitjema, 'Calvijn en de oorsprongen van het Nederlandsche Gereformeerde Kerkrecht' in *Christendom en Historie* (Amsterdam, 1925), pp. 183–212.

[4] G. Moreau, 'Les synodes des églises wallonnes des Pays-Bas en 1563', *Nederlands Archief voor Kerkgeschiedenis*, ns 47 (1965), pp. 1–11.

[5] N. C. Kist, 'De Synoden der Nederlandsche Hervormde Kerken onder het Kruis, gedurende de jaren 1563–1577 gehouden in Brabant, Vlaanderen enz.', *Nederlandsch Archief voor Kerkelijke Geschiedenis*, 20, ns 9 (1849), pp. 113–210. C. Hooijer, *Oude Kerkenordeningen der Nederlandsche Hervormde Gemeenten (1563–1638)* (Zalt-Bommel, 1865), pp. 1–23; *Livre synodal contenant les articles résolus dans les Synodes des Eglises Wallonnes des Pays-Bas*, 1 (The Hague, 1896), pp. 1–13.

themselves competent to issue regulations of a rather general character. It might even have struck him that the regulations, though sounding rather French, displayed a structure of their own and so—anticipating my own conclusion—provide a constitutional analogy to the way in which the French Confession had been adapted by the Dutch.

While none of these discoveries can be found in De Jong, they are mentioned briefly by Moreau, even though he had no fresh information at his disposal and was not even aware of Hoffmann's study. What did Moreau find that De Jong missed? And where do these findings lead us? First, it is necessary to consider Moreau's argument, and then to trace the extent to which the French 'Discipline ecclésiastique' is quoted in the Dutch *acta*, and to determine which version the Dutch used; thirdly, to discover which parts of the 'Discipline' were borrowed and which were not; and, fourthly, to determine the distinctively Dutch contribution to the Church Ordinance established in 1564.

I GÉRARD MOREAU'S DISCOVERIES

In his article, Moreau came straight to the point by asking what was known about the synods of 1563. The answer is not to be found in the *acta* as printed in the *Livre Synodal*, nor, I might add, in former editions. These publications were all made from manuscripts which were not the original ones, but later seventeenth-century copies of the *acta*. It has to be kept in mind that not all the enactments of the synods have survived; those which have been preserved are quite incomplete. Indeed, closer inspection of the evidence raises further questions. Five synods are thought to have met within seven months; and according to the headings and order of the *acta*, possibly three synods met on the same day. Such a practice never happened afterwards, and it may be doubted whether it ever took place at all. If the acts of two synods supposedly held on the same day are set side by side, it becomes clear that for each of the sixteen articles making up the shortest enactment, a counterpart can be found in the acts of the other synod. This occurs not haphazardly, but in four sets of consecutive articles. Besides, if the eight articles of the undated synod acts are placed between those of the two synods already mentioned, the texts can all be related to corresponding articles in the acts of the synod which met on 24 June 1563. Are these synods to be regarded as identical in pairs? Alas, verbal similarities are few, but imagine the situation of these men, assembled secretly and making decisions quickly: each jotting down in his own words what might be important for him or his congregation, without further checking afterwards, and without any official *acta* being drawn up. According to Moreau, there was no chairman elected, although, in my view, this is going too far: it might be better to say that there was no scribe, for this is sufficient to explain the differences.

In the French *acta*, Moreau says, the same phenomenon of different versions of the same regulations can be found. Yet, in observing this, he does not do full justice to the complexities of the quick growth of the French 'Discipline ecclésiastique'. At the same time, he is quite correct in remarking that the reference to the 'synode Provincial', which occurs twice, has no meaning whatsoever, due to the fact that the name of the province has been omitted. His final argument, however, is most convincing: it is out of the question that assemblies could have been held in the towns defined by pseudonyms (except for Antwerp, rendered as 'La Vigne'), for there was simply no opportunity for such gatherings to meet in any of the places which might be identified as the mysterious 'Teur': Tournai, indicated by 'La Palme', had a military occupation within its walls, while in other places, Theux, Thourcoing, or Oudenarde ('Fleur de Lys'), as well as Armentières ('Le Bouton'), there was not yet a Reformed church in existence by 1563. Therefore Antwerp remains the only possibility, and it is here that Moreau assigns the meeting-place of the synods of 1563—which he reduces to three—together with those synods held earlier (such as the one held in 1562[6] under the chairmanship of Joris Wybo) as well as those held subsequently. According to Moreau, the pseudonyms in the headings are not to be understood to refer to the places where the synods were held, but to the places where the acts were kept later on. After this revealing remark, Moreau ends with the wish that a critical edition of the *acta* would be published. As I hope to execute this project within a few years, this present contribution can be taken as a kind of introduction to the planned publication.

To start with, Moreau's explanation points to some conclusions which he himself did not draw. If, in 1563, three synods were held in succession—and not simultaneously—they were clearly general, and certainly not 'provincial', synods. It should also be observed that these gatherings were held in Antwerp and were almost certainly not homogeneously Walloon. The very fact that Joris Wybo was chairman in 1562, together with the presence of other inhabitants of Antwerp, is sufficient proof of

---

[6] J. H. Hessels, *Ecclesiae Londino-Batavae Archivum II* (Canterbury, 1889), p. 357; A. A. van Schelven, *Kerkeraadsprotocollen der Nederduitsche vluchtelingenkerk te Londen 1560–1563* (Amsterdam, 1921), p. 320.

this. We know all this because ten years later those involved nearly came to blows in London over one particular decision taken in 1562, namely, permission to free the brethren then imprisoned by the civil authorities of Antwerp for their Protestant convictions.

The question of how the Dutch conceived the idea of holding synods can be answered very simply: they followed French example. The French Reformed leaders convened in Paris in May 1559, thereafter in Poitiers in March 1560, in Orléans in April 1562, and finally in Lyons in August 1563. These general synods assembled before provincial synods existed, or more exactly, the jurisdiction of the provincial synods was determined by the general synods, and this pattern was adopted in the Netherlands. That the French example was well known in the Low Countries is evident from the fact that the first article noted by Moreau in his synopsis (article 1 of 'Le Bouton'), is a literal quotation from the 'Discipline ecclésiastique', drawn up in Paris. Of the sixteen articles kept in Armentières/'Le Bouton', four appear to have been copied almost exactly from the French; twenty-five per cent is certainly not a bad harvest to start with.

Before exploring the issue more closely, we should note Hoffmann's findings, for he had been aware of the problem sixty years before Moreau. He discussed Dutch dependency on the French example, as well as the similarity of the Dutch and French articles, though he found fewer parallel regulations than Moreau did. Hoffmann attempted to explain the similarity of certain articles from the *acta* of the various synods in the following manner. He showed that the particular requirement which stipulated that those elected by the congregation to serve as elders and deacons should not be allowed to refuse office can be traced in the acts of four different synods, even though the wording differed somewhat.[7] He thought that this could not be explained by assuming that these regulations were drawn up by the same people at different times. His solution was that four different meetings of ministers, elders, and deacons must have taken place, and that these meetings were provincial synods. The occurrence in pairs of similar regulations in the *acta* strengthened this hypothesis. He, therefore, concluded, working from later data, that the provinces involved must have included Brabant, Hainault, and Flanders. In order to arrive at the required four meetings, he argued that the area from which the deputies to the fourth synod came covered either East and West Flanders separately or the whole of Flanders and Artois separately,

---

[7] Von Hoffmann, *Kirchenverfassungsrecht*, pp. 49ff. This concerns the first four synods, art. 12, art. 6, art. 2, and art. 1, respectively.

though he conceded that after 1563 no trace can be found of such a division. Yet all this did not prevent him from adhering to his thesis. In my view, however, the very fact that no trace for such a division can be found is sufficient ground for refuting his hypothesis. Besides, Moreau's synopsis is convincing. His whole explanation is preferable. Again, the proceedings of Hoffmann's four synods are more dissimilar than he thought: two by two, they are based on two different French articles.[8] Thus, it emerges that three synods did indeed meet in 1563, and they all assumed the characteristic features of general, rather than provincial, synods.

II. I QUOTATIONS FROM THE 'DISCIPLINE ECCLÉSIASTIQUE'

The above-mentioned synods authorized themselves—and from this, too, their general character is apparent—to draw up generally binding regulations. As a matter of fact, this was true of all 'ten' synods from the period of repression. In doing so, they followed uncritically the example given by the French, sometimes even adopting their regulations. In the course of time, this led to more than half the French regulations from 1559, as well as a number from later synods, being adopted by the Dutch synods. An interesting aspect is the question of which versions of the 'Discipline ecclésiastique' were known to the Dutch, for several variant texts have been handed down.[9] The answer may have more significance for French than for Dutch ecclesiastical history, but as Pannier did not solve all the problems here, it is worth while examining the issue. Hoffmann, however, did do explorative work on the subject, which Haitjema, though not De Jong, acknowledged.

The problem of the versions can be summarized as follows: except for some minor details, the texts rendered by La Place, 'Beza', Crespin, and

---

[8] Jean Aymon, *Tous les Synodes nationaux des Eglises Réformées de France*, I (La Haye, 1710), pp. 3, 5. Art. 13 of the French *Discipline Ecclésiastique*, is the basis of 'Teur' art. 12 and 'Le Bouton' art. 2; art. 26, on the other hand, is that of 'La Palme', art. 6, and 'La Vigne', art. 1.

[9] To be found in Jean Crespin, *Histoire des Martyrs* [according to Francois Méjan, *Discipline de l'Eglise Réformée de France* (Paris, 1947), p. 300, already in the 1562 edition; I used the 1582 edn, fol. 465]; Pierre de la Place, *Commentaires de l'estat de la religion et république soubs les roys Henry et François seconds et Charles neuviesme*, 1565 (Paris, 1836), pp. 14, 15; Henry de La Popelinière, *Histoire de France depuis 1550 iusques à ces temps* (La Rochelle, 1581) [copy at Utrecht University Library]; *Histoire ecclésiastique des églises réformées au royaume de France* ['Beza'] (Anvers, 1580), pp. 186–90. Also a different version in Jean Aymon, *Synodes nationaux*, and in the English translation by John Quick, *Synodikon in Gallia Reformata* (London, 1692). Besides Méjan, *Discipline*, see also J. Pannier, *Les origines de la Confession de Foi et de la Discipline* (Paris, 1936).

La Popelinière are identical. 'Beza' uses the word 'synod' more frequently, whereas the others speak of 'concile'. He also numbers the articles, and arrives at 40 articles, but Crespin, who does not number them, speaks of 42 articles. Besides this version, there is one by Jean Aymon. He, too, has 40 articles, but 6 of these cannot be found in 'Beza', and in Aymon's text 3 from 'Beza' are missing, namely, articles 23, 31, and 38. As these 3 articles are included in the Dutch *acta*, it is worthwhile consulting Quick's English translation, and, indeed, there we do find the 3 articles not mentioned by Aymon. Nevertheless, Quick also mentions the number 40, but when counting the articles he arrives at 41! For the rest, the words used by La Place, 'Beza', Crespin, and La Popelinière are rarely identical with those in Aymon's text: in the latter, most articles are more extensive, though he retains the same sequence, which means that structurally nothing has changed. It should be borne in mind, however, that although the 'Beza' text probably indicates the situation in 1559 (with Aymon and Quick wrongly suggesting that their text is that of the Paris synod), a process of change began in 1560 with the Synod of Poitiers, and by 1563 this clearly led to Aymon's text. This can be deduced with certainty from the words in the Dutch regulations, thereby demonstrating their importance for European ecclesiastical history. When, therefore, on the basis of Pannier's publication, it is more or less suggested that the text of Aymon is of a 'later' date, the qualification 'at most four years later' ought to be kept in mind.[10]

Hoffmann paid considerable attention to this process of development in the text of the 'Discipline ecclésiastique', but he also saw problems where none existed. The first occurred in the numbering. As mentioned, the Synod at Poitiers in 1560 made alterations and additions to the text of the 'Discipline ecclésiastique'. The articles altered, or added to, are given a number, and they are also quoted. None of the numbers, it appears, corresponds with those in Aymon, nor in most cases with those in 'Beza'. Moreover, two quotations do not fully agree with the version in 'Beza'. From this, Hoffmann concluded that the 'Beza' text is not a rendering of

---

[10] J. P. van Dooren, ed., *Classicale Acta 1573–1620. Particuliere Synode van Zuid-Holland I: Classis Dordrecht 1573–1600* = Rijks Geschiedkundige Publicatiën, small series, 49 (The Hague, 1980), pp. 7–8, with reference to a numbering problem. The solution lies not only in the 'extension' as can be seen in Aymon's version, but in the next stage, the systematization applied by the Synod of La Rochelle, 1571, which was widely known in this country, as evidenced by the extant manuscripts of the translation: *Kercken Discipline der Gereformeerder Gemeenten in Vranckenrijck vanden Jare 1559 tot int jaer 1571 Inden Nationalen Synodis des selven Ryckx besloten ende toegerichtet uyt der Fransoischer sprake trouwelyck overgeset*, which numbers the article counted by Beza and Quick as 7, and by Aymon as 8, as 13.

the 'Discipline' adopted in 1559, but only a draft plan. The real 'Discipline', Hoffmann thought, was missing, and we are left with Aymon's later standard version.

By not studying Crespin's text, Hoffmann, in my opinion, has merely made matters more difficult for himself. For a start, one finds in Crespin, in the article numbered 3 in 'Beza', as well as in the Synod of Poitiers, the words 'lesquels auront voix'. The omission in 'Beza' of this regulation on the rights of elders at synods may be considered merely to be a printing-error. The other deviation from the text in 'Beza' which Poitiers offers is more serious: the text of article 5 in 'Beza' mentions more frequent meetings of provincial synods than does the corresponding text of the Synod at Poitiers. The 'Beza' text may point here to preliminary plans and intentions. However, before this assumption can be applied to the entire text of the 'Discipline' found in the *Histoire ecclésiastique*, it ought first to be established that Hoffmann's remarks on the numbering of the articles are correct.

The answer is fairly straightforward, and can be found by looking at the differences which occur in the texts of Quick and Aymon. If one splits up article 10 in the 'Beza' text after the first full sentence—an alteration justified by later developments, as shown by Aymon, as well as by the way in which it is printed in Crespin—and then numbers the following four articles accordingly, one sees why the synod of Poitiers numbered as 12 the article which occurs in 'Beza' as 11, and likewise as 16, article 15 in 'Beza'. At the same time, the latter article gives rise to another problem: not only does Aymon combine, in his version, articles 15 and 16 as one, but Crespin does likewise, so that from this point on, the numbering by the Synod of Poitiers and by 'Beza' ought to be identical. Yet this is not the case: with articles 22 and 23 on Poitiers' counting, 'Beza' turns out to be too low. But here both Crespin and Aymon come to our aid: the last sentence of article 21 in 'Beza' can be separated, so that one arrives exactly at the article numbered as 22 in the Poitiers edition: 'L'office des Anciens ... n'est pas perpétuel.' In short, the numbering is of such secondary importance that nothing can really be proved from it. This, at any rate, rids us of the problem created by Hoffmann. Yet his theory that the 'Beza' text was no more than a preliminary plan remains difficult to refute, though it is still by no means proven.

II. 2 COPYING REGULATIONS FROM THE 'DISCIPLINE ECCLÉSIASTIQUE' IN THE NETHERLANDS

How quickly the text of the 'Discipline' evolved into the one rendered by Aymon and Quick becomes clear when one compares the regulations quoted in the Dutch *acta* with the French original: the similarity of the Dutch texts to Aymon is nearly always greater than to 'Beza'. There is one exception: on 1 May 1564, in article 25, the text of article 35 in the 'Beza' text is quoted, rather than its counterpart, article 36 in Aymon. But for the rest, all the additions to be found in Aymon, as compared with 'Beza', were known to the Dutch: articles 10, 18, 19, 20, and 27,[11] and the first and last of these were known as early as 1563. Only article 11 in Aymon escaped the Dutch. Even where the quotations are not copied word for word, it is obvious that the text which served as an example to the Dutch was more closely related to Aymon than to 'Beza'. An interesting testimony of this can be found in the way in which article 13 in Aymon has been transcribed:

> AYMON 13: Celui qui aura consenti d'être élú au Ministere, recevra la Charge qui lui sera denoncée: Et à son *refus* il sera sollicité par des exhortations convenables: toutesfois *on ne le pourra contraindre* en aucune autre maniere.

> 'BEZA' 10a: Celui qui aura été élu à quelque Ministere sera sollicité et exhorté de le prendre, et non toutefois contraint. . . .

> 'TEUR' 12: Que ceux qui sont esleus audit office, s'ils *refusent* de servir sans occasion legitime, qu'ils soyent admonestez, priez et menacez par le iugement de Dieu, s'ils ne s'emeuvent ne par prieres, ne par menaces *on ne les pourra contraindre*.

> 'LE BOUTON' 2: Ceux qui sont esleus audits offices, s'ils *refusent* de servir sans occasion legitime seront admonestez, priez et menacez par le iugement de Dieu, toutesfois s'ils perseverent *on ne les pourra contraindre*.

What strikes us here, apart from the fact that the decisive phrases refer to Aymon rather than to 'Beza', is the transposition of *ministère* to *office*. In other words, the Dutch have transferred the French regulation concerning the specific calling to the ministry of the Word to the vocation of elder or deacon. They often worked in this way: taking a French article as an example, they adapted it to a different situation. How free they felt to do this is shown by the transcription of article 10 in Aymon:

> Ceux qui s'ingéreront au Ministere dans les lieux où quelque Ministre de la Parole de Dieu seroit déja établi seront suffisamment avertis de

---

[11] For the last-mentioned article see Moreau, 'Les Synodes', p. 3; in 'Le Bouton' it is quoted almost literally as article 1.

s'en desister, et au cas qu'ils n'en veuillent rien faire ils seront declarés Schismatiques: et quant à ceux qui les suivront, on leur fera le même Avertissement; et s'ils sont contumaces et obstinés, ils seront aussi declarés Schismatiques.

'LA PALME' 9: A esté arresté que tous ceux qui sont du troupeau ne s'ingereront de faire assamblee illicite. Apres admonition a eux faite de s'en deporter, s'ils ne se deportent de ce faire, seront tenus pour schismatiques et par consequent, suspendus de l'assamblee; et aussi semblablement tous ceux qui estans rangez se trouveront au lieu où telles assemblees se feront, apres admonition à eux faite, de ne s'y plus trouver: et par consequent tous ceux qui s'adioignent avec les Anabaptistes pour ècouter leur doctrine.

'LA VIGNE', 24.6.1563, 4: Ceux qui escouteront les coureurs et s'adioindront aux Anabaptistes, apres les admonitions à eux faites seront retranchez, s'ils ne s'en deportent.

It is plain that the Dutch regulations have the same origin, but the person utilizing the version preserved in 'La Vigne' has briefly summarized the intention, whereas in the version preserved in 'La Palme', the French model can still be clearly distinguished; one should note such words as *ingereront* (a technical term for *intruding* into the ministry of the Word by *coureurs* in the other version), *faire*, and *schismatique*. Here a striking transposition has taken place. The French example refers to wandering preachers who considered synodal regulations as objectionable novelties to be ignored. The Dutch versions can be explained by the fact that the problem lay not in the few *coureurs*, but in the behaviour of Anabaptist competitors, with their considerable moral prestige. Thus we find this characteristic anti-Anabaptist sentiment expressed not only in the Confession, but also in the Church Ordinances. The French prohibition on socializing with wandering preachers is changed into a warning not to visit circles where Anabaptist doctrines were taught.

In attempting to classify the Dutch derivations from the French 'Discipline ecclésiastique', the following categories may be adopted:

(1) Regulations from the 'Discipline ecclésiastique' which have been borrowed almost literally. These are (by Aymon's counting) articles 1, 2, 12, 17, 18, 19, 20, 21, 25, 27, 29, 32; 'Beza': 31, 36, 40; 16 in all.

(2) Regulations adopted not literally but in spirit, occasionally with a special meaning: 10, 24; 'Beza': 24, 35, 38; 5 articles in all.

(3) Regulations in which, either freely or literally, only parts are borrowed: 5, 15, 16, 26, 28, 33, 34; 7 in all.

(4) Two articles, remarkably enough, which have been copied nearly literally, but nevertheless have acquired a totally different meaning: 13; and 'Beza', 38.

In all, thirteen articles have not been borrowed, namely, 3, 4, 6, 7, 8, 9, 11, 14, 22, 30, 31, and 39.

Summarizing, we may say that where texts have been quoted, it is nearly always from a version reminiscent of Aymon. The additional material found in 'Beza' has not been overlooked, but the fact that the items are also available in Quick shows that their omission in Aymon is incidental. Evidently, up-to-date texts of the French 'Discipline ecclésiastique' had been available to the Dutch from the start, though they were freely interpreted. The longest sequence of successive articles quoted is four.

III WHAT WAS COPIED AND WHAT WAS NOT

Having analysed the sources and the way in which texts were quoted, we come to the question of the content of the copied material. To solve the question, we can indicate the subjects dealt with by the French and see whether or not the articles were taken over by the Dutch.[12]

Articles 1–3, the basic regulation of the 'non-dominatio', applicable to the functioning of the chairman of the synod, were borrowed.

Articles 4–6, on the composition of synods, were not adopted.

Articles 7–9, on the functioning of the Church on a provincial or even a national basis, were not taken over.

Articles 10–12, on the exclusion of wandering preachers, were only utilized in a very limited way, in so far as the issue lay within the competence of local congregations.

Articles 13–16, on the duties of ministers, were only taken over in part, in so far as the matter could be kept under the control of local congregations.

Articles 17–18, on the possibility of ministers changing places, were adopted in such a way that, for the first time, a specifically regional church organization can be distinguished.

Articles 19–21, on the exclusion of ministers whose doctrine was suspect or worse, were copied word for word.

Articles 22–3, on supervising the lives of ministers, were not adopted.

[12] Cf. Appendix I for a condensed survey of these data.

Articles 24–8, including 'Beza' 24, on the election and duties of elders and deacons, were utilized, except for article 26, in which the deacons were deprived of their function as catechists. The formulations concerning the supervision of moral behaviour were worded in more moderate terms.

Article 29, on censoring books, was adopted with an even broader meaning to include every book written by a church member.

Articles 30–1, on excommunication for obdurate offenders, were not taken over.

Articles 32–3, on the other hand, on absolving and readmitting excommunicated persons, were adopted.

Article 35, on registering baptisms and marriages, was utilized merely in part: the section on baptism was used only in adapted form.

Articles 34, 36, 38; and 'Beza' 38, regulating the marriage contract, were not completely taken over; and on the question of the absolutely binding character of the marriage vows, the Dutch regulation differed entirely.

Article 37, allowing divorce after adultery, was borrowed.

Article 39, forbidding local congregations to settle important matters independently, was not adopted.

Article 40, on the possibility of altering church ordinances, was borrowed, but in a less strongly-worded form.

Briefly summarizing, we may conclude that those regulations relating to the structure of the Church were not borrowed by the Dutch; those relating to the function of local congregations were adopted, with the understanding that regulations on general behaviour should be left out, whereas those concerning the supervision of doctrine were couched in somewhat stronger terms.

IV THE STRUCTURE OF THE DUTCH CHURCH ORDINANCE OF 1564 COMPARED WITH THE FRENCH

Before drawing any conclusions, we should apply a further test to find an answer not only to the question of which part of the 'Discipline ecclésiastique' came to be in the Netherlands, but also how the Dutch dealt with the French material when, for the first time, they drew up their own Church Ordinance. This, after all, was what they undertook to do on 1 May 1564, at Antwerp—'La Vigne'. To this end, we will not only examine the quotations from the 'Discipline ecclésiastique' proper, but also investigate what was quoted from the French *acta* of the time, namely, from the acts of the Synods of Paris (1559), Poitiers (1560), Orléans (1562), and Lyons (1563).

It appears that the *acta* were well known: the entire harvest of quotations is extremely rich: nearly 70 per cent of the regulations consist of derivations or, at least, of obvious allusions, and nearly half of these, more than 45 per cent, came from the 'Discipline ecclésiastique', the remainder from other *acta*. There is no need to dwell further on the nature of these quotations. But a pressing question now arises: were the Dutch completely dependent on the French? The answer which emerges is that they were not: here, too, appearances can be deceptive. To put it more precisely, the synod assembled at Antwerp, in formulating the regulations it decided to include, was willing to use the French example; but in the regulations themselves, the Dutch were fairly independent. To demonstrate this point, we will summarize the 48 articles of the synod which met at Antwerp on 1 May 1564, covering a number of the subjects it determined,[13] to which some comments may be added.

Articles 1–3 are all quotations and even fairly literal ones; but read in their context and taking into account their slight deviation from the source, their purpose becomes clear: their intention was to regulate the functioning of local congregations and church councils.

Article 4 does not continue in the same vein, for it deals with meetings of the synod. Yet nothing is said about the synod's functioning; only the role of its 'president' is discussed; and he is understood to act merely as chairman, and not as a higher church official.

Articles 5–10, turning away from higher meetings of the Church, focus on congregational matters. Here the relationship between minister and congregation is discussed, along with the supervision of the minister. It is very striking how the separate article in the 'Discipline' on censoring books finds its proper place here (in article 10). Curiously enough, the duties of the minister of the Word are not described. Evidently, existing practice on this point had begun to follow a set pattern.

Article 11 shows that this was not yet true of the elder, whose duties are described in even greater detail and differently from the 'Discipline'; in addition to his pastoral and administrative functions, the elder must uncover cases of hidden poverty.

Articles 12–21 describe the deacon's work, with a surprising number of detailed regulations for which no French examples can be traced. Only

---

[13] Cf. Appendix II for a schematic outline of the derivations.

article 12 was copied from the French; the rest seems to reflect the particular ideas of the Dutch. More than anything else, these regulations prove that the Dutch had a different structure in mind from the French. They looked not to an organization and network of numerous assemblies of ministers, but to the local community, where the brethren and sisters lived, and where the heart of Christ's body was seen to beat. The meeting of the true believers in Christ, to which more exalted words were devoted in the *Confessio Belgica* than in the *Gallicana*, is to be found in the individual congregations. This digression ought not to suggest that the regulations on the care of the poor were not worded in level-headed terms; in fact, they are particularly 'down to earth' in their listing of the various kinds of poor (who are classified not by the degree of their poverty, but by the extent of their involvement within their congregation) and the support for which they were eligible. At the end, they even refer to the 'worldly' support, the 'hospitaux', where the Reformed poor, it was considered, ought also to receive their share, provided they were not forced to commit 'idolatry' in the process.

Article 22, an abbreviated quotation, ends the series of regulations on the three ministries (Calvin's 'doctor' being totally omitted), with a hint of the 'propositions', semi-official divine services in which students supervised by a professor or an established minister delivered a sermon (from old French *proposer*), as occasions to train people for the ministry of the Word. Logically this should be followed by regulations on the administration of the Sacraments and on the marriage ceremony; but still, no word is said about the Lord's Supper, or about baptism as such.

Articles 22–4. Here two points are made about baptism: only men (the father or godfather) are allowed to present a child for baptism, and no pagan names, names of idols, or those reserved only for God should be used. Here the French exxamples pointed the way for the Dutch.

Articles 25–31. Not surprisingly, there are many precise regulations for the contracting of marriage and all that goes with it, including divorce and the grounds for it, as well as pre-marital intercourse and bigamy. Great importance was attached to a proper definition of these matters, which, despite diverging Reformed opinions, were still considered to lie within the Church's domain. During the Synod, the French *acta* had been carefully studied on this point in selecting regulations which could be taken over and systematized.

Up to this point, the Dutch Church Ordinance of 1564 is so well constructed that it might be assumed that a prepared draft had been presented to the synod meeting at Antwerp. But thereafter the Ordinance continues, without any warning, with a much looser series of regulations on a variety of subjects, which the French would discuss under the heading of 'Faits généraux' or even 'particuliers'. The most remarkable feature of this is that we find ethical prescriptions in between institutional regulations without much coherence.

Article 32 marks the transition to particular issues by mentioning, quite unexpectedly, the care of the records and proceedings of church courts, and even more unexpectedly by suddenly recognizing the provincial synod as the proper organ for receiving the *memoires* from local congregations, a duty which the French, more fruitfully, had imposed on Geneva.

Article 33 makes a start on certain ethical issues by prescribing the need for conformity with the king's edicts in receiving interest payments and for acting in the spirit of mutual love and understanding. The French, too, had repeatedly broached this subject; it is remarkable that the Dutch took the least obvious example in the French *acta* from the regulations of the Synod of Lyons in 1563.

Articles 34–42 describe the enforcing of discipline in a curious mixture of rules aimed at obstinate drunkards, the rejection of funeral liturgies, and prohibiting printers and pictorial artists from associating with papistical superstitions. They end with an article authorizing church councils to hear the faithful, called before them, under oath. The majority of these regulations have no French counterpart, except for the one forbidding artists from serving 'les superstitions de l'Eglise Romaine'.

Article 43, which advised against holding discussions with Anabaptists, was also unknown to the French, and the rule prohibiting the introduction of strangers to the meetings without the foreknowledge of at least one elder (article 44) had a very distant parallel in the French model.

Article 45, on the other hand, with its injunction to be simple in dress did not spring from the desire to avert a specifically Flemish or Brabant abuse, as Kist states,[14] but is an almost literal derivation from the proceedings of the Synod of Orléans in 1562.

Articles 46–8. Curiously, article 46, on how to alter church ordinances, was not actually the final one; it was followed by article 47, allowing the consistory to elevate a deacon to the office of elder, without discussion—a curious step after all the regulations devoted to the former—and, then, by article 48, permitting the proclamation of marriages 'au temple des papistes', which is explained by one of the French sources on the ground that this was a purely 'political' or civil matter.

[14] Kist, 'De Synoden', note to article 45 of 'La Vigne', 1 May 1564.

Surveying these articles, it can be stated that the *acta* of 1 May 1564 up to article 31 have all the qualities of an elaborate and thorough piece of work. From that point onward, the remainder have been either partly lost at a later date or, perhaps due to lack of time, were rushed through at the synod. This had its effect on the articles dealing with moral conduct, which contain a number of regulations which, though strict, are hardly discussed in an orderly fashion. This tendency is particularly evident at the end, where the closing article is followed by some inconsequential phrases.

None the less, on the basis of the text as we read it, it can safely be concluded that the Dutch church model was different from that of the French 'Discipline'. Apart from the mysterious mention of the provincial synod as the general custodian of the records, the Dutch emphasis was on the local congregation. Synodal assemblies exist for the benefit of local churches; special needs are discussed at synods in so far as they can be conveniently resolved at that level.

In trying to explain the differences between the French and Dutch churches, one has to recognize the very different circumstances which prevailed in France and the Netherlands. In due course, the French Reformed had managed to build up a solid position in more-or-less connected regions. Their Dutch co-religionists were not so fortunate. They had only two options: to set up clandestine churches in a few towns or refugee churches elsewhere. They lacked the possibility—even had it occured to them—of building up a structure at the higher levels. The creation of local congregations was plainly their primary objective. This they saw as a top priority in the teaching and practice of Calvin, whose death occurred in the same month as the Antwerp synod drew up its Church Ordinance. Moreover, in its relevant articles, the Dutch Confession of Faith shows how deeply committed they were to this priority. Yet, with changing circumstances, priorities also shifted. If J. P. van Dooren was right in his hypothesis (which is tempting but unproven) that the so-called 'Convent' (meeting) of Wesel was not held there at all, nor in 1568, but in Antwerp at the beginning of 1567, as a true synod, we can see that the new situation had quickly persuaded the brethren to accept the French model, a model which was to dominate completely in the Synod of Emden, held 1–3 October, 1571.[15]

This would suggest that 'Wesel' can be seen as marking the end of the

[15] J. P. van Dooren, 'Der Weseler Konvent 1568; neue Forschungsergebnisse', *Monatshefte für Evangelische Kirchengeschichte des Rheinlandes*, 31 (1982), pp. 412–55.

period in which the Dutch Church lay 'under the Cross'. It remained merely a fleeting episode, and later synods never referred to it, despite the fact that delegates to the later synods had already attended the 1567 synod as well as earlier ones. Had they felt, looking back, that the group they represented (and certainly the group which they themselves had formed into a 'synod') was too small to be accorded any authority, or did they feel that compared with their French brethren, with their developed infra-structure, they were perhaps rather insignificant? At present, as matters stand, this cannot be established. One thing is certain, however: the men who assembled 'under the Cross', that is, during the repression, in Antwerp should be credited with having quietly gone their own way, charting the road ahead for the Reformed churches in the Netherlands.

University of Groningen

Appendix I

Survey of the Articles from the *Discipline ecclésiastique* as they are quoted in the Deeds of the Dutch Synods under the Cross

	A	B	N		A	B	N
article	1+	1	2+N6	article	24	{ 20 / 21ᵃ	11~N6
	2+	2ᵃ	4+N6		25	{ 21ᵇ / 22	12 N6
	3	2ᵇ	—		26	23	{ 1 N4 / 6 N2
	4+	3	—		—	24	{ 14 N1 / 4~N3
	5+	4	4~N7		27	—	{ 1 N3 / 11 N1
	6~	5	—		28	25	2~N4
	7~	6	—		29~	26	10~N6
	8+	7	—		30+	27	—
	9	8	—		31	{ 28 / 29	—
	10	—	4~N4; 9 N2		32	30	34 N6
	11	—	—		—	31	36 N6
	12+	9	6 N6		33	32	3~N2
	13~	10ᵃ	12 N1		34+	33	11~N8
			2 N3		35	34	2~N7
	14	10ᵇ	—		36~	35	27 N6
	15	11	25~N1		37	36	28 N6
	16+	{ 12 / 13	—		38	37	{ 2~N1 / 8 N2
	17	14	6 N3		—	38	4×N2
			23~N1		39	39	—
	18	—	6 N6		40	40	46~N6
	19	—	7 N6				
	20	—	8 N6				
	21+	15	9 N6				
		16					
	22+	17	—				
	23+	{ 18 / 19	—				

+ extra   ~ deviations   × contradictions

Legenda

A = the version of the *Discipline* from Jean Aymon, *Tous les Synodes*

B = the version of the *Discipline* from the *Histoire ecclésiastique des Eglises Réformées* ascribed to Beza

N = Deeds of the synods held in the Netherlands

N1 = Deeds of the synod of Teur(s), 26 April 1563

N2 = Deeds of the synod of 'La Palme' (24 June) 1563

N3 = Deeds of the synod of 'Le Bouton' 26 April 1563

Appendix II

Survey of the Articles from the Deeds of the first French Synods, quoted in the Synod of Antwerp/La Vigne, 1 May 1564

	N6	French deeds		N6	French deeds
article	1	7 Poitiers F.G.	article	28	37 A
	2	1A		29	9 Orléans F.G.
	3	6 Orléans F.G.		30	10 Orléans F.G. ~
	4	2~A		31	10 Lyon F.P.
	5	12 A		32	1 Lyon Mém.
	6	18 A		33	{ 8 Lyon F.P.
	7	19 A			1 Lyon F.G.
	8	20 A			17 Orléans F.G.
	9	21 A		34	32 A
	10	{ 29 A ~		35	3 Poitiers F.G.
		26 B ~		36	31 B
	11	{ 24 A ~		37	—
		21 B ~		38	—
	12	25 A ~		39	—
	13	—		40	15 Orléans F.G. ~
	⎮	—		41	20 Orléans F.G.
	21	—		42	25 Orléans F.G.
	22	5 Poitiers F.G.		43	—
	23	25 Poitiers F.P.		44	21 Paris F.S. ~
	24	21 Orléans F.G.		45	12 Orléans F.G.
	25	{ 15 Lyon F.P.		46	40 A
		19 Lyon Observ.		47	—
	26	{ 20 Lyon Observ.		48	{ 11 Lyon F.P.
		23 Lyon F.P.			24 Paris F.S.
	27	35 B ~			21 Lyon Observ.

Legenda

A = Paris, 1559, *Disc. Eccl.*, version Jean Aymon   F.P. = Faits Spéciaux
B = Id. 'Beza'   Mém. = Mémoire
F.G. = Faits Généraux   Observ. = Observations etc.

N4 = Deeds of the synod of 'La Vigne' 24 June 1563
N5 = Deeds of the synod of 'La Vigne' 15 October 1563
N6 = Deeds of the synod of 'La Vigne' 1 May 1564
N7 = Deeds of the synod of 'La Vigne' 21 November 1564
N8 = Deeds of the synod of 'La Vigne' 11 June 1565
N9 = Deeds of the synod of 'La Vigne' 3 December 1565
N10 = Deeds of the synod of 'La Vigne' 16 April 1566

ZURICH AND THE SCOTTISH REFORMATION: RUDOLF GWALTHER'S *HOMILIES ON GALATIANS* OF 1576

by BRUCE GORDON

THE conjunction of humanism with reform is a familiar aspect of the Zurich Reformation.[1] Zwingli's own eschatological sense of impending divine judgement upon the nations of the world led him towards a more radical understanding of Erasmian humanism, a humanism in which the corporate life of the State expressed the inner relationship between God and man. For Zwingli, the Scriptures, when approached through the proper humanist exegetical methods, revealed the principles necessary to the founding of the true *Corpus Christianum*. The effective transformation of human communities into reflections of Christ's universal Church through the co-operation of the evangelical faith with political authority was the urgent agenda of the Zurich reforms in the 1520s. Zwingli conceived of a confessional confederation of Swiss and German territories for which his theology and the reforming process in the Limmat city would serve as the basis and model. The appeal of his humanist conceptions of doctrine and Church was extensive, and Zwingli used his wide range of personal connections with leading theologians and humanists in his evangelism to the European courts.

The defeat of Zurich at Kappel and the terms of the treaty imposed by the Catholic cantons curtailed the evangelism of the Zwinglians in Germany, and succeeded in isolating the Swiss Reformers for much of the 1530s.[2] Outside the Swiss Confederation, Zurich exercised virtually no political influence. Heinrich Bullinger, Zwingli's successor, understood

---

[1] I am extremely grateful to Herr Kurt Jakob Rüetschi of the Bullinger Briefwechsel in Zurich for drawing my attention to Gwalther's *Homilies on Galatians*, and for his willingness to share his own extensive research on Gwalther's life and work. I would also like to thank Dr Andrew Pettegree, in the Department of Modern History, and Mr Peter Woodward, in the Department of Humanity, both of the University of St Andrews, for their generous assistance.
[2] For the political situation after the war, see Helmut Meyer, *Der Zweite Kappeler Krieg* (Zurich, 1976), pp. 173–8; Hans Ulrich Bächtold, 'Bullinger und die Krise der Zuercher Reformation im Jahre 1532' in Ulrich Gäbler and Erland Herkenrath, eds, *Heinrich Bullinger 1504–1575 Gesammelte Aufsätze zum 400. Todestag* (Zurich, 1975), I, pp. 269–89. Bächtold demonstrates the extent to which political pragmatism dominated events in Zurich after the war. Also J. Wayne Baker, 'Church, State and Dissent: The Crisis of the Swiss Reformation, 1531–1536', *Church History*, 57 (1988), pp. 135–52.

that it was humanism, which stood at the centre of Zurich theology and provided the necessary connections with other Reformers, which offered the basis for the continuance of the Zwinglian faith as a vital reforming force. Bullinger's position as leader of the Reformed cause after Kappel in the decades before the emergence of Calvin has recently received wider recognition among English-speaking scholars. Bullinger restored Zurich as the pre-eminent Reformed city by two means: by making confessional unity with other Protestants possible by refining Zwingli's theology, and by promoting his theological and ecclesiological positions through his correspondence with his wide circle of reforming and humanist friends and his printed works.[3] Consistency and thoroughness were the hallmarks of Bullinger's reforming career, for he considered nothing to be more dangerous than theological innovation. His method in preaching, in doctrinal works, and in his correspondence was to restate continuously positions he had worked out during his early years as head of the Zurich church.

Rudolf Gwalther, Bullinger's pupil and friend, was in every way a suitable candidate to succeed his master in 1575. Trained in the best Reformed humanist traditions, he spent a life in service to the Zurich church, first between 1542 and 1575 as a minister in St Peter's Church and as Bullinger's theological lieutenant in the city, and then as *antistes*, or head of the church. Gwalther's authority derived less from his work as a theologian, although he was a respected and prolific, if not highly original, defender of Zurich positions, than from the extensive network of personal connections he developed through his travels as a student and later as Bullinger's assistant. The importance of Gwalther's travels should not be underestimated for their role in establishing relations between Zurich and foreign courts, particularly in the case of England.[4]

Gwalther's travels to England put him in touch with the leading figures of the Elizabethan Church, particularly Grindal and Parkhurst, with

[3] Walther Hollweg, *Heinrich Bullingers Hausbuch* (Neukirchen, 1956); H. Fast, *Heinrich Bullinger und die Taüfer* (Weierhof, 1959). Hollweg and Fast have traced the theological and historical background to Bullinger's *Decades* and anti-Anabaptist writings, and, further, have provided through their research a clear picture of the widespread readership of these works and the extensive use made of them in the sixteenth century. On Bullinger's correspondence see F. Büsser, 'Bullinger et Calvin', *Études Théologiques et Religieuses*, 63 (1988), pp. 31–52. Professor Büsser offers a comparative study of the surviving correspondence of Bullinger and Calvin with Reformers in Switzerland and other European countries.
[4] Helmut Kressner, *Schweizer Ursprünge des anglikanischen Staatskirchentums* (Gütersloh, 1953), esp. pp. 73–98, concerning Gwalther's influence in England.

whom he corresponded during the vestment controversy.[5] The surviving correspondence between England and Zurich reveals that the English bishops esteemed Gwalther as a trusted friend and adviser in much the same way they did Bullinger. It was Gwalther's knowledge of the situation in the English Church that inspired him to dedicate his *Homilies on the Epistle to the Corinthians* in 1566 to the English bishops.[6] These English contacts were also the means by which Gwalther and Bullinger were kept informed of events north of the border in Scotland. Gwalther never travelled to Scotland, but the importance of the debates taking place there after 1560 were not lost on Zurich. Bullinger and Gwalther frequently consulted with Calvin and Beza over Scottish developments, though there are no surviving letters between Scotland and Zurich in the corpus of the Bullinger *Briefwechsel*.

The lack of documentary evidence has thwarted attempts to trace systematically Zwinglian influences in the Scottish Reformation, with the resulting tendency to look to Geneva alone.[7] In this context, Gwalther's correspondence with George Buchanan, former Principal of St Leonard's College at St Andrews University, and tutor to the young King James VI, are of added interest.[8] The exchange of letters between 1576 and 1579 are of little doctrinal or political interest of themselves, but they are suggestive both of the active interest taken by Zurich in Scottish affairs and of the existence of an audience receptive to Zwinglian ideas in the northern kingdom.[9] It was Buchanan who, in the light of the favourable reception accorded the *Second Helvetic Confession* (1566) by the Scots, and

---

[5] Gwalther to Bishop Parkhurst, 11 Sept. 1566 in H. Robinson, ed., *Zurich Letters 1508–1602*, PS (1842–5), 2, pp. 140–6.

[6] Kressner interprets Gwalther's *Homilies on Corinthians* as a specific attack on Genevan presbyterianism. He writes: 'Gualthers Homilien enthalten die klassische Antwort auf Tendenzen solcher Art, eine Antwort, die zugleich der von Zwingli geformten politischen Theorie die prägnanteste und schroffste Formulierung gab': *Schweizer Ursprüng*, p. 81.

[7] Two scholars recently have taken up the question of Zurich–Scottish relations and have shown both the problems bedevilling attempts to establish the extent of Zwinglian influence in Scotland and the challenging questions open to further research. Professor G. M. Locher, 'Zwingli's Influence in England and Scotland' in *Zwingli's Theology: New Perspectives* (Leiden, 1981), pp. 367–83, and D. Shaw, 'Zwinglischen Einflüsse in der Schottischen Reformation', *Zwingliana*, 17 (1988), pp. 375–400.

[8] On Buchanan's role as tutor to the King and his cultivation of James's interest in *bonae litterae*, see I. D. McFarlane, *Buchanan* (London, 1981), pp. 446–9.

[9] Professor McFarlane argues that Buchanan was considered one of the most formidable humanist opponents of Catholicism and that the exchange between Gwalther and Buchanan must be seen from this perspective. While this is certainly true, Professor McFarlane's summation of the exchange as 'little more than an episode among colleagues committed to a similar cause' requires some revision. *Buchanan*, p. 456.

the context of the debates surrounding the drawing up of the *Second Book of Discipline*, encouraged Gwalther to dedicate his *Homilies on Galatians*[10] to the King of the Scots. This was a shrewd move, since it provided Gwalther with the opportunity to lend support to the Regent Morton's attempts to mould the new Reformed Scottish Kirk along the lines of the Tudor doctrine of Royal Supremacy, which placed the sovereign in complete control of the Church. It is within the context of this formative period for the Scottish Reformed polity in the 1570s, during the drafting of the *Second Book of Discipline*, that Gwalther's Preface should be considered as part of the debate.[11]

The dedicatory Preface is structured to lay out the essential argument of the text: the king must control the religious affairs of his State through the proper ordering of the Church. Accordingly, Gwalther began with a celebration of James's piety and an outline of the characteristics of a monarch. From kingship, Gwalther then defined the Church, both in its universal and its local manifestations. It is, in fact, with the external

---

[10] *In D. Pauli Apostoli/ Epistolam ad Galatas/ Homiliae LXI./ Authore/ Rodolpho Gualthe-/ ro Tigurino// Accessit operi Praefatio ad Sereniss. Scotorum Regem,/ Iacobum VI. de Regum et Principium in Ecclesia recte con/stituenda et gubernande officio. INDICES item duo rerum et/ locorum Scripturae, quae toto hoc libro explicantur.// Tiguri/ Excudebat Christophorus Froschoverus/ Anno M.D. LXXVI//*, fol. col. a6 b8 A–Z, Aa–B. Known copies of the first edition: Zurich, Zentralbibliothek (4×); Basle, Universitätsbibliothek; Lausanne, Bibliothèque Cantonale et Universitaire; Winterthur, Stadtbibl.; Augsburg, Staats- and Stadtbibl.; Bretten, Melanchthonhaus; Erlangen, Universitätsbibl.; Esslingen, Evangelische Pfarrbibl.; Marburg, Universitätsbibl.; Nuremberg, Stadtbibl.; and Landeskirchliches Archiv; Halle, Hauptbibl. der Franckenschen Stiftungen; Aberdeen, UL; Cambridge, UL; Cambridge, Peterhouse College; Carlisle, Cathedral Library; Edinburgh, UL; Newcastle-on-Tyne, UL; Norwich, Colman and Rye Libraries; St Andrews, UL; Oxford, Christ Church College, Merton College, Magdalen College, Wadham College; Shrewsbury, Shropshire Public Library; Windsor, St George's Chapter Library; Bordeaux, Bibl. Municipale; Colmar, Bibl. du Consistoire (en Bibl. de la Ville); Vatican City, Bibliotheca Palatino-Vaticana; Graz, Univ. Bibl.; Budapest, Univ. Bibl.; Sibiu–Hermannstadt (Rumania) Brukenthal-Museum; Breslau-Wroclav (Poland), Ossliñskich Biblioteka, Danzig-Gdańsk (Poland), Biblioteka Polskiej Akademia Nauk; Yale, UL. A manuscript of Peter Young's catalogue of James's library from 1573 to 1583 contains the entry 'Rudolphi qualtheri Homiliae in galatas, fol. Ex dono ipsius auctoris': G. F. Warner, 'The Library of James VI, 1573–1583', *Scottish History Society Miscellany* (Edinburgh, 1893), p. xli. (I am grateful to Dr Roger Mason, University of St Andrews, for this reference.) See also Kurt Jakob Rüetschi, *Rudolf Gwalther (1519–1586), Leben und Werk* (in preparation): Index W71.1.

[11] Gwalther's hope that the Elizabethan Settlement might have been applied to the Scots is evident from his letter to Grindal of 24 Aug. 1576, concerning events in Germany, in which he wrote: 'She [Elizabeth] will therefore perform the part of the pious nursing mother of the church, if she will consider this business; nor will there be wanting reasons for drawing the king of Scotland into co-operation with her, the accession of whom may be of great advantage to the cause at hand. But I understand that the Scottish churches are on the friendliest terms with us, and I think they would be wanting in no service which ought to be required from Christian men': *Zurich Letters*, p. 275.

Church that Gwalther was primarily concerned, and he treated its distinguishing points. This was followed by a return to the responsibilities of the king in bringing the State into conformity with divine laws. Failure to accomplish this placed the State in danger of tyranny, and was a departure from the ideal of Christian magistracy as seen in the reigns of Constantine and Justinian. Gwalther's arguments on kingship and the Church led to his principal concern of recommending the clerical synod, as practised in Zurich, as the means by which the Scottish king should control his Church.

Gwalther's greetings to James in the opening of the Preface made much of the Reformer's concern for the King's education. While professing the greatest respect for James's tutors, Gwalther remarked that it was always useful in matters of religion for a monarch to receive instruction from abroad, which confirmed his lessons at home.[12] This was Gwalther's pretext for writing, and he established himself immediately in the prophetic role as adviser to the king: a role instituted by Zwingli in Zurich for the senior clergy and carefully moulded by Bullinger in his relationships with both his own and foreign governments.[13] Gwalther saw the prophet as an important figure, as adviser to the ruler, but it was the king who was supreme, for God had raised up certain men to the office of king, and all others were his servants. The divine nature of kingship was based upon its continuity with the kingship established by God amongst the Israelites. The coming of Christ had in no way diminished the responsibilities of the monarch before God to establish and maintain the Church and State according to divine laws: all that Scripture said of David applied to the young King of the Scots.[14] Gwalther described those who denied the king's authority over religious matters as either liars or followers of the inventions of the popes, false prophets who subjugated kings to themselves through oaths that these rulers might act on their behalf rather than 'kissing the feet of Christ'.[15]

---

[12] Fol. a2.
[13] F. Büsser, 'De Prophetae Officio eine Gedenkenrede Bullingers auf Zwingli', *Wurzeln der Reformation in Zürich* (Leiden, 1985), pp. 60–71; Hans Ulrich Bächtold, *Heinrich Bullinger vor dem Rat* (Bern, 1982), especially the chapter 'Der Prediger: Prophet oder Diener am Staat?', pp. 37–46.
[14] 'Quae et si Iudaeorum Regibus olim dicta sint, ad eos tamen qui Christia/no nomine censentur, et hominibus christianis imperant, illa non minus pertine/re, David Rex potentia et victoriis clarissimus testatur': fol. a2. See the discussion of Bullinger's understanding of the connection between the Christian and the Old Testament in the continuance of God's covenant in J. W. Baker, *Heinrich Bullinger and the Covenant* (Athens, Ohio, 1980), pp. 55ff.
[15] Gwalther, *Homiliae*, fol. a2.

Gwalther's starting-point was that all authority, both religious and political, flowed from God; therefore, any argument which distinguished between the source of human and divine jurisdiction was false. Human authority was legitimate only in so far as it conformed with the divine ideal as expressed in Scripture. Gwalther argued that since Scripture described how God had placed the Church in the hands of kings and magistrates to act as guardians or custodians, Christian rulers had, by virtue of their office, a reflected divinity which demanded the obedience of all members of the State.[16] Gwalther politely reminded James of how God's blessing upon the King's rule had borne fruit in the existing harmony between the Scots and the English, and in the manner in which Scotland had reformed its churches while maintaining its ancient laws and customs.[17] To his humanist concern for concord, Gwalther added the reminder that the Scottish and Swiss churches were united through a common Confession, and it was in the name of that unity that he asked his *Homilies on Galatians* to appear under James's patronage.[18]

Gwalther passed from kingship to the Church, which he understood in both its universal (or catholic) form, which is the unity of all believers throughout time,[19] and as the visible institution in the world, which he identified with the political State. Both are the body of Christ, but whereas the universal Church is unerring, the visible Church, consisting of both the elect and the reprobate, is prone to error. This does not mean that God's requirements of the earthly church are any less than those of the eternal body, for both must make a perfect confession and exist at one with the divine will. Gwalther enumerated the marks (*noti*) of the true Church as the preaching of the Word, a true confession of faith, the invocation of the one God through Jesus Christ, and the proper administration of the Sacraments.[20] These are well-known Reformed criteria

---

[16] Gwalther, *Homiliae*, fol. a2v: 'Ex eo enim apparet, Reges atque Magistratus omnes non solùm ut pacis def/ensores, et iuris publici executores, in precio habendos esse, sed in iisdem dignita/tem humana maiorem agnosci debere, neque illos in scripturis temere Deos dici,/ quando aeternus ille et solus versus Deus illorum opera et ministerio in iis uti/tur, sine quibus neque ipsius gloria neque sponsa sua incolumitas consistere potest.'

[17] Ibid., fol. a2v–a3.

[18] Ibid., fol. a3.

[19] Ibid., 'Ecclesiam in Symbolo Apostolico definimus esse communionem sive societatem/ sanctorum, id est, eorum qui per Iesu Christi sanguinem et spiritum san/ctificati et filii Dei facti sunt.'

[20] Ibid., fol. a3v. Gwalther follows the order set out by Bullinger in the Fifth Decade, where he writes: 'The Chief and principal points of godliness of the church of God are, the sincere teaching of the law and the prophets, of Christ and the apostles: faithful prayer offered unto her only God through Christ alone; a religious and lawful administration and receiving of the

of the Church, and Gwalther's interest in the Preface was not to debate what they meant. His argument centred on his belief that where political rule was brought into accord with scriptural teachings both the individual and the community became liberated as 'sons of God' and the true Church.[21]

The king, for Gwalther, did not simply rule over the community or Church, but was the active means through which the State was brought into a proper relationship with faith.[22] The ruler was the instrument of God and therefore must have a guiding hand in the political and religious affairs of his domain. Zwingli and Bullinger both identified the State with the Church, and Gwalther followed this principle in arguing that the *res publica* could not exist outside true religion.[23] True religion is the Christian faith, though Gwalther looked to Antiquity to cite examples of foolish rulers neglecting religion to show how this truth was prefigured in pagan societies.[24] Such an understanding of Antiquity reinforced Gwalther's identification of Christian duty with civic virtue, a concept which developed from the meeting of humanist ideas with established thinking in the Swiss city. He told James that where a ruler's decrees were seen to flow from Scripture and the preaching of the Gospel was freely allowed, there could be no questioning of the ruler's authority.[25] The other side of this coin, which Gwalther passed over, is the argument promulgated by the Zurich divines that where a ruler acts against the faith he can legitimately be removed.

Since Gwalther believed that the visible Church could err to the point of ceasing to be the true Church, the king should be privately pious and publicly willing to act in religious matters. The king, he argued, must be

---

Christ's sacraments': *Decades*, ed. T. Harding, *PS* (1849–52), V, 10, p. 479; cf. Calvin, *Institutes*, ed. J. T. McNeill and F. L. Battles (London, 1961), IV, i, 7, and Bucer, *De regno Christi*, ed. F. Wendel (Paris, 1954), pp. 50, 54–6. Interestingly, the *Second Book of Discipline* contains no treatment of these *noti* of the true Church.

21 Gwalther, *Homiliae*, fol. a4: 'Ita nimirum innuens, ve/rbi Evangelici ministerium in hunc finem esse institutum, ut per illud in Ec/clesia communionem vocati, in eadem adolescamus in perfectos Dei filios,/ et Christo conformes facti in eodem ad caelestium bonorum haereditatem ac/cedamus.'

22 Ibid., fol. a4v: 'At hic sui officii Reges admonentur, ut Ecclesiis, quarum nutritii à Deo/ constituti sunt, in primis hoc parte prospiciant, ut verbi praecones habeant/ fidos et idoneos, qui salutis doctrinam ex puris scriptura sacra fontibus fi/deliter depromant, et Dei verbum rectè secando novos quotidie discipulos/ christo faciant, ut iam factos adificent, inqué officio contineant, ne vel ad/ superstitiones, vel ad prophanam morum licentiam relabantur.'

23 Ibid.

24 Ibid.

25 Ibid., fol. a5.

able to protect the Church from doctrinal errors and control the means to remove false prophets. This identification of State with Church was at the heart of the Zurich Reformation; the citizens were all outwardly members of the same confessing body, whether they were of the elect or not. As God's elect, who constitute his eternal Church, are known to him only, all men must subject themselves to a human jurisdiction which can only be based upon external righteousness. Hence the Word of God, when it is proclaimed in the churches, is heard by both the elect and the reprobate to different ends.[26] To the faithful it is the saving power of God which proclaims Christ and serves as a moral guide, while to non-believers it is merely a set of moral constraints restraining them from carrying out the evil desires of their unregenerate hearts. Consequently, it is crucial that the king ensure the Word of God is properly and freely preached in his land by men of adequate training and good character.

As the ministry is the chief medium through which the truths of the Gospel are interpreted to men, Gwalther argues that it is particularly full of wolves who wish to make use of its authority for their own ends.[27] He draws upon the image of a father ruling his house to explain how a church without a rigorous discipline will inevitably collapse. A Church lacking discipline parallels the State which falls into tyranny through the usurption of legitimate political authority.[28] Although Christ's kingdom is not of this world, God delegated authority to Moses and Aaron to establish purity of worship amongst the people; this authority has passed to all succeeding generations of rulers within the covenant, and it is the basis for a Christian political jurisdiction.[29]

Gwalther avoided any specific reference to Zurich or Switzerland in touching upon these matters of authority, and his comments upon the ruler's duty to eradicate error from the Church cautioned that laws and customs varied from country to country, with no one State serving as a

[26] Galther, Homiliae, fol. a5v.
[27] Ibid.
[28] Ibid., fol. a6.
[29] Ibid.: 'Ut enim regnum Christi non est ex hoc mundo, ita Evangelii doctrina/ magistratibus politicis, sive illi Reges sive Optimates sint, suum ius integrum/ et illibatum relinquit. Et tunc demum disciplinae executio efficax et fructuo/sa erit, si hic operas suas coniungant qui in Repub. praesident, et qui in Ecclesia/ docent. Ideo Deus in suo populo olim duos fratres germanos, Mosem et Aaro/nem, delegit, ex quibus hunc quidem sacris, illum verò religioni praefecit, ut doc/eret, perpetuum inter politicum et Ecclesiaticum ordinem consensum esse de/bere, et tunc demum Rempub. cum Ecclesia florituram, si isti coniunctis stu/diis atque consiliis ea agant, quae ad publicam pacem et honestatem propagan/dam atque conservandam faciunt.'

complete model for another.[30] Gwalther had warned bishop Parkhurst earlier in the English vestment debate of the danger of identifying the Gospel with customs and habits; unity of confession did not mean uniformity of practice. Each Church must find what was best for it through submission to the guidance of the Holy Spirit. Gwalther's argument echoed Zwingli's optimism that where men were open to the Gospel they would arrive at the practical laws necessary for Christian society. It is the Holy Spirit, he believed, who must lead in all matters of discipline. For as Christians must be tolerant of practices not contrary to the faith, so also must they be mindful of the individual person in the administration of discipline.[31] Discipline pertains only to the visible Church because of its capacity for error, hence its purpose is in reconciling and not breaking the body of Christ by driving sinners out of the community.[32]

Gwalther argued that the best means by which the ruler can bring about peace and unity within his church is through the institution of the clerical synod.[33] This body is sanctioned by the Scriptures, specifically by the work of St Paul, who in his travels through Jerusalem, Ephesus, and Asia held public meetings of all the local prebyters in order to resolve questions concerning the faith and to rebuke those in error.[34] That these apostolic gatherings were intended as models for future Christian societies to resolve publicly matters of discipline and doctrine was understood by the Zurich divines from the adoption of synods by Constantine, when Christianity was reconciled with the Empire. The Zurich reformers interpreted the period of Constantine as the commencement of a sort of golden age when the Church sought harmony and doctrinal purity under the leadership of the Emperor, which lasted until the pontificate of Gregory the Great. Gwalther quoted Eusebius' description of how

---

[30] Ibid., fols a6–a6v.

[31] Ibid., fol. a6v: 'Itaque disciplinae publicae praefici oportet viros graves quidem et seve/ros, sed non minus moderatos et prudentes, qui quid unoquoque loco et tem/pore facto opus sit, videant, et non tam quid quisque meruerit spectent, quàm/ quid ipsos deceat, quidue sit è re totius Ecclesiae.'

[32] Bullinger, following Zwingli, would not allow that discipline could be the basis for distinguishing between the righteous and the unrighteous in society; discipline pertained solely to outward actions. Its primary function within the Church was to restore harmony. For Bullinger's fight with the Anabaptists over *Kirchenzucht*, see Fast, *Bullinger und die Täufer*, pp. 140–5. Bullinger's dispute with Geneva over the tying of discipline to the Lord's Supper is well explained in J. W. Baker, 'In Defence of Magisterial Discipline: Bullinger's *Tractatus de Excommunicatione* of 1566', *Heinrich Bullinger 1504–1575 Gesammelte Aufsätze zum 400. Todestag*, 1, pp. 141–59. Baker outlines the struggle between the Zurich and Genevan traditions of discipline at the court of Frederick III in Heidelberg during the 1560s.

[33] Gwalther, *Homiliae*, fol. a6v.

[34] Ibid.

Constantine called synods of the clergy to establish unity and to drive out the Arian heretics. The Emperors Gratian, Theodosius, and Martianus similarly are recalled for their use of synods to deal with the Eudoxian and Euthycian heresies.[35]

In addressing the problem of how an individual synod might speak on behalf of the whole Church, as the Zurich Synod did, Gwalther looked to the provincial synods set out in the *Imperial Constitutions* of Justinian for support. Zwingli had pointed to this text when defending the authority of the Zurich Disputations, and Bullinger made reference to it in his *Decades*.[36] The *Imperial Constitutions* was a crucial work for the Zurich Reformers because it clearly stated that the holding of clerical synods was a most ancient practice. Further synods were understood as giving unequivocal support to the idea that from the earliest days of the acceptance of Christianity within the Empire the political rulers assumed control over the affairs of the Church. Gwalther quoted Justinian's commandment to the provincial lieutenants that where the bishops were negligent in holding synods the rulers must take the matters into their own hands to ensure that the synods were held; and those responsible for the delays were corrected. The *Constitutions* gave to those synods duly called by the ruler competence in matters of faith, canonical questions, the administration of ecclesiastical affairs, the amendment of lives and of all other things in error.

Gwalther concluded his treatment of synodal government by distinguishing between a true synod, or council, and a false one. This was a particularly sensitive point for Zurich in the light of the claims of the Council of Trent. The distinction was made that only rulers could call a meeting of all the clergy, for God gave them alone power over the Church in their lands.[37] The papacy, from the time of Gregory the Great, assumed unto itself a false authority when Rome was allowed to assert its primacy over other ecclesiastical provinces. The bishop of Rome, who ought not to be a secular prince, could not legitimately convene a council consisting of clergy outside his province and coerce rulers to obey its decrees. As the visible Church was no longer united, the king alone was responsible for the calling of synods, and Gwalther ended with a final commendation of this order to the Scots.[38]

---

[35] Gwalther, *Homiliae*, fol. b2.

[36] Bullinger, *Decades*, V, 10, pp. 505–7.

[37] Gwalther, *Homiliae*, fol. b2v.

[38] Ibid.: 'Synodus autem tum Provinciales tum/ Generales in suis regnis cogi curent locis idoneis pro temporum et negotiorum, quae incidunt, ratione: in quibus de doctrinaa puritate

The biannual synods of the clergy in Zurich, from their resumption in 1532 after Kappel, were crucial in the establishing of the Reformation in the canton.[39] The whole *modus operandi* of the synod was an expression of the Zurich polity: it was neither a legislative body nor strictly a church court, rather its function lay formally in teaching and admonishing. In practice, though, its importance stemmed from its usefulness as a forum for the exchange of information between the city and the *Landschaft*. The clergy, who were required by their oath of office to attend the sessions, brought to the council invaluable information concerning all manner of activities in the rural areas, while in return they received instruction from the civic leaders on council mandates, which they were required both to announce from their pulpits and to ensure correct adherence to in their community. The clergy were in every sense servants of the State, entrusted with the promulgation of the Gospel and civil laws, and this relationship with the government is expressed in the oath of office which they swore in the synod.

Rudolf Gwalther's dedicatory Preface both brings out the strength of the Zurich position and suggests something of its weakness. The Reformation in Zurich grew from a situation in the fifteenth century where ecclesiastical and civil jurisdiction stood in opposition to each other; the exemption of clergy from taxation and civil punishment precluded any formulation of a true civic unity along the lines envisaged by late mediaeval guild-based Swiss thinking. Zwingli's reforms in the 1520s, effected through the authority of the magistracy, grounded the freedom of the individual and the community in a complete subordination to sovereign power, as found in divinely established institutions. What made this possible, as Gwalther reasserted, is firstly the establishing of Scripture through the service of humanist-based exegesis, and then of a publicly debated common doctrine, first formulated through the ecumenical Councils of the Early Church, and continued through such institutions as properly-convened national synods under the control of the magistrate. These foundations of Scripture, doctrine, and legitimate authority are the basis for participation in the *res publica*; for the Zurich

---

servanda, de morum/ disciplina exercenda et Ecclesiarum incolumitate, sententis liberis et ex Dei/ verbo depromptis statuatur. Quod cum hactenus apud Scotos tuos Rex Se/reniss. non absque luculenta fructus et magna cum laude factum sit, ut idem/ porrò fiat, Maiestas tua, pro suo erga puriorem Dei cultum studio, etiam/ atque etiam curabit.'

[39] See F. Büsser, 'Synode — gestern und heute. Vortrag', *Wurzeln der Reformation in Zürich* (Leiden, 1985), pp. 231–5; K. Maeder 'Bullinger und die Synode', *Bullinger — Tagung 1975*, ed. Ulrich Gäbler and Endre Zsindely (Zurich, 1975), pp. 69–76.

BRUCE GORDON

divines there never could be a distinction between Church and State or even between civil and ecclesiastical laws. The common faith of the community is the basis for any legislation concerning the moral and spiritual obligations of citizens, whether clerical or lay. Hence, as exemplified by the functioning of the Zurich synod, the rules governing admission to, participation in, and removal from the church are civil laws.

The weakness of Gwalther's position is exposed in the Preface by the extent to which his thinking, even late in his career, is determined by a conception of the Christian State as an urban phenomenon. This was the problem for Bullinger in the reforming of the Zurich *Landschaft*, where the peasants and ministers had difficulty grasping the new evangelical faith precisely because of its urban orientation. Further, Gwalther's understanding of the whole Reformation process is limited by his experiences of the situation in Switzerland and England, where reforms were brought about by the ruling authorities.[40] The Zurich position was less capable of embracing a revolutionary situation such as existed in Scotland, where the Reformed Church emerged in opposition to the Crown, and the first church courts came into existence without royal authority.[41] The radical line of thought taken by the Scottish Reformers tended not to see the 'godly prince', James VI, as the instrument through which reform was to be established, and consequently the Genevan presbyterian polity, with its built-in independence of ecclesiastical jurisdiction was favoured.[42] The sixteenth-century struggle between Genevan and Zurich conceptions of church authority manifested itself in Scotland in the attempts by Regent Morton to follow the lead of the English Tudors in bringing the Church under Royal Supremacy, and the resistance of Reformers such as Knox and Melville to such an idea, which they saw as differing little from papal subjugation.[43] Morton's defeat on the issue and acceptance of the competence of the General Assembly to draw up 'a constant form of church policy' was as much a reversal for Zurich as the outcome of events in the German Palatinate had been less than ten years previously. Nevertheless, Gwalther's contact with the Scottish court argues both for the

[40] Kressner, *Schweizer Ursprünge*.
[41] On the background of the Reformed church courts in Scotland, see Dr J. Kirk's introduction to his *Records of the Synod of Lothian and Tweeddale* (Edinburgh, 1977).
[42] J. Kirk, ed., *The Second Book of Discipline* (Edinburgh, 1980), p. 9.
[43] Dr Kirk, ibid., p. 41, writes: 'The accuracy of the description by one critic of Morton's "purpose to restrean the fridome of application in preaching, and authoritie of the Generall Assemblies, and bring in a conformitie with Eingland in governing of the Kirk be Bischopes and injunctiones" is wholly supported by English diplomatic reports in 1575.'

continued vitality of Zurich as an expositor of Reform and a wider appreciation of its influence amongst the young Reformed churches emerging in Europe in the latter half of the sixteenth century.

University of St Andrews

CHARLES PERROT (1541-1608):
HIS OPINION ON A WRITING OF
GEORG CASSANDER

by G. H. M. POSTHUMUS MEYJES

I INTRODUCTION

CHARLES PERROT, a contemporary and colleague of Theodore Beza, came from a well-known French family belonging to the *noblesse de robe*. He was born in Paris in 1541, and seems to have spent a number of years as a monk, before joining the Reformation movement. In 1564, at twenty-three years old, he enrolled in the Academy of Geneva. That same year saw him called to the ministry in Moëns and Genthoz, not far from Geneva. Having acquired the citizenship of Geneva in 1567, he was appointed minister in this city a year later, a position he was to hold for forty years, until his death in 1608, his delicate health notwithstanding. In addition, he occasionally deputized for Beza as professor at the Academy, where during two periods (1570–2 and 1588–92) he acted as rector.[1]

Perrot, like other Genevan ministers (such as Jacqemot, Rotan, and Du Faye), was during his active lifetime overshadowed by Beza, who reigned supreme in this bulwark of Calvinism. Only in the nineteenth century did Perrot get the limelight he deserved when he and his work were treated in their own right. His biography was written by the Genevan Old Testament scholar J.-E. Cellérier,[2] who between 1857 and 1861 published three excellent articles on Perrot, which to this day have not been surpassed.[3] No new information worth mentioning about Perrot has come

---

[1] For the bibliography of Perrot, see the list in Suzanne Stelling-Michaud, *Le Livre du Recteur de l'Académie de Genève* (1559–1878), 5, ns (Geneva, 1976), 132; H[erman] de Vries [van Heekelingen], *Genève, pépinière du Calvinisme Hollandais*, 2 vols (Fribourg, 1918; La Haye, 1924); Corrado Vivanti, *Lotta politica e pace religiosa in Francia fra Cinque e Seicento* (Turin, 1963; repr. 1964). For the Perrot family, see the fine contribution by R. Zuber, 'Humanistes parisiens en Champagne (1560–1610). Les origines familiales de Perrot d'Ablancourt', *Mémoires de la société d'agriculture, commerce, sciences et arts du département de la Marne*, 89 (1974), pp. 125–48, esp. pp. 135–8 on Charles Perrot.

[2] On Cellérier, see J. Courvoisier in *Die Religion in Geschichte und Gegenart*, ser. 3, I (Tübingen, 1956), 1630.

[3] J.-E. Cellérier, 'Trois hommes de paix au 16e siècle', *La seule chose nécessaire. Receuil mensuel d'édification Chrétienne* (Harlem, 1856–7), 'Charles Perrot, pasteur genevois au seizième siècle. Notice biographique', *Mémoires et documents publ. par la société d'histoire et d'archéologie de Genève*,

to light since then, so that the picture Cellérier sketched still stands. The only criticism one could possibly level at Cellérier is that he almost exclusively concentrated on Perrot's psychology, without paying any attention whatever to Perrot as a theologian.

In recent literature on Perrot one aspect particularly highlighted is his pursuit of peace and reconciliation.[4] It has often been pointed out that he was responsible for the abolition in 1576 of the need for Genevan students to adhere to the Confession of Faith.[5] Although this decision required the consent of the entire *Compagnie des pasteurs*, Perrot is often given the credit here, and this, in turn, is seen as an indication of his tolerant mentality. This attitude also seems to be confirmed by the much-quoted utterances of the Dutchman Uytenbogaert who, like Arminius,[6] a pupil of Perrot, was later to eulogize Perrot's irenical leanings. If we add the opinion of someone like Casaubon, who praised Perrot for having once said that enough had been preached on justification by faith alone, and that attention should now be paid to good works,[7] the picture seems complete enough to enable us to determine the sort of person Perrot was. The portrait which emerges is that of an irenicist, an angel of peace, a lamb in the lion's den.

It may well be asked, however, whether this picture is consistent with historical reality. What sort of a man was Perrot? Should he be regarded as an irenicist? And, if so, how does he relate to the Erasmian tradition of Wicel, for instance, or Cassander, Baudouin, Hotman, and, later on, Hugo Grotius? The existence of a review in his hand of a booklet by Georg Cassander (1513–63) does at least serve as a guide in the quest for an answer. But first of all an examination is called for of Perrot as a person and as a theological writer.

---

11 (1859), pp. 1–68 [= *Notice biogr.*], and 'Charles Perrot, son histoire et ses lettres', [Extrait des] *Entrennes Religieuses pour 1861* (Genèva, 1861) [= *Perrot*].

[4] This opinion can be found, among other places, in the work of Maronier mentioned in n. 6 below.

[5] Charles Borgeaud, *Histoire de l'Université de Genève. L'Académie de Calvin, 1559–1798*, I (Geneva, 1900), p. 140. For the same reason the University of Leiden took a similar decision on 11 March 1578. Cf. P. C. Molhuysen, *Bronnen tot de geschiedenis der Leidsche Universiteit* ('s-Gravenhage, 1913), pp. 55–7.

[6] Cf. J. H. Maronier, *Jacobus Arminius* (Amsterdam, 1905), pp. 39ff.; Carl Bangs, *Arminius. A Study in the Dutch Reformation* (Nashville and New York, 1971), pp. 76ff.

[7] The discussion between Uytenbogaart and Casaubon from 1610 in *Praestantium ac eruditorum virorum epistolae ecclesiasticae* (Amsterdam, 1660), p. 324 [= ed. 1704, p. 250]: quoted by G. Brandt, *Historie der Reformatie*, 11 (Amsterdam, 1674), pp. 121ff. See also Mark Pattison, *Isaac Casaubon 1559–1614* (Oxford, 1892; repr. Geneva, 1970), pp. 222–5.

His personality, as his contemporaries and his later biographers agree, was veiled in mystery. In Cellérier's words:

> His manners were awkward and shy. Outwardly, he was of a quaint mansuetude. He bore—and accepted—the nickname 'peccator', a name so widely known that in the margin of the official registers of the city council he was invariably indicated as such. It was assumed that in his younger years he had been a monk, and he was reproached for having preserved his austerity, his oddness even, partly from that time.[8]

His character was curiously contradictory. He was capable of erupting in impetuous, if not reckless, activity; there again he was apt to be overcome with a distrustful shyness that bereft him of all energy. He was precise, with an inclination to perfection, but at the same time he could prattle on like a child. He could be remarkably independent in his thinking and his actions, but when called to account, he countered by keeping silent. After his death, the *Compagnie des pasteurs* declared to the city council that 'it was in his nature to counter rebukes with resignation and silence, while retaining his "méditations particulières".'[9]

This eccentric man, seemingly devoid of laughter, and whose motto *gemere et silere* testified to his demureness and contrition, was a much sought after and honoured preacher, emphasizing in his sermons humility and love and repeatedly stressing the value of the inner life. It has been affirmed more than once that he himself displayed the virtues he so strongly commended: with unwavering loyalty he would visit the poor, and with great courage he rendered assistance when Geneva was in the grip of the plague. All his life he was an assiduous student and writer. He excelled in the knowledge of Antiquity and the Church Fathers: Ambrose, Chrysostom, and, above all, Augustine. He was involved in the publication of Calvin's Letters (Geneva, 1575; Lausanne, 1576), but besides that he also composed theological writings independently, in which he must have given expression to the results of his 'méditations particulières'.

The caution with which this assumption is made is justified, for so little of his work has been preserved that it barely provides a foundation for verification. Regardless of whether his modesty or some other factor was responsible, the fact is that not one of Perrot's writings appeared in print during his lifetime. And when he died, in 1608, the opportunity to publish

[8] Cellérier, *Perrot*, p. 6.
[9] Ibid., p. 8.

his work was lost: the powerful Genevan syndic Jean Lect, who was no friend of Perrot, and a critic of his allegedly liberal ideas, had all his papers confiscated. This resulted in the destruction or loss of the greater part of his literary legacy. As much as could be gathered from the official papers about this confiscation and censorship has been painstakingly described by Cellérier. It is a sad story indeed, a reminder of the not so elevating *faits et gestes* of Genevan notables in the early seventeenth century.[10]

Hopeless as the situation may seem, not all traces of Perrot's theological works have been lost. By other means, at least the titles of his writings have been preserved. Apart from that, a part, though a very modest part, of his output eluded the itchy fingers of Jean Lect and the city council. This was because some of Perrot's writings had ended up outside Geneva during his lifetime, and beyond the council's reach. Such, for instance, is the case with the document relating to Cassander, and with a number of letters and other writings which came into the hands of his friend Nicolas Pithou, and were later included in the famous 'collection Dupuy', now in the Bibliothèque Nationale in Paris.[11] Cellérier did not draw exhaustively from this material: he merely consulted some of Perrot's letters in the 'collection Dupuy', and disregarded *inter alia* an autobiographical writing entitled *Principiorum aliquot theologicorum ad usum pietatis subnotatio*.[12] Nor, it seems, has anyone since then taken a good look at this material.

II JEAN HOTMAN

The work at issue emerged from the archives of Jean Hotman (1552–1635),[13] the eldest son of the well-known François Hotman, jurist, pamphleteer, and diplomat, friend of Calvin and Beza.[14] The son followed in his father's footsteps. He read law at Orléans, found himself at Oxford in the eighties, and, within a short time of having found his way to the court, was engaged as a diplomat by Queen Elizabeth. Assigned as secretary to Robert Dudley, Earl of Leicester, he soon followed Leicester

---

[10] Cellérier, *Notice*, pp. 44–68; see also Borgeaud, *Histoire*, pp. 306, 337.

[11] Cf. L. Dorez, *Catalogue de la collection Dupuy*, Table alphabétique (Paris, 1928).

[12] MS Paris, BN Dupuy 139; see also Vivanti, *Lotta politica*, p. 382, n. 1.

[13] For J. Hotman's biography see F. Schickler, 'Hotman de Villiers et son temps', *Bulletin de la société de l'histoire du protestantisme français*, 2, ser. 3 (1868), pp. 89–111, 145–61, 464–76, 513–33; David B. Smith, 'Jean de Villiers Hotman', *ScHR*, 14 (1917), pp. 147–66; Vivanti, *Lotta politica*, pp. 189–245.

[14] An excellent biographical survey is given by F. Dareste, 'Francois Hotman d'après sa correspondance inédite', *RH*, 2 (1876), pp. 1ff., 367ff.

to the Netherlands, and from then on was active in the diplomatic service for the greater part of his life.

The English interlude was of decisive importance for Hotman, not only because it was the starting-point of his career, but also because in this period his Calvinism developed into irenicism as a result of his experiences with the English Church. After returning to his native France, he continued his diplomatic career by entering the service of Henry IV, who sent him as his envoy to the German Protestant princes.

Apart from his diplomatic activities, Hotman dedicated himself to the reunion of the churches. With the benefit of his father's renown in Calvinist circles, it was especially his Reformed compatriots he tried to win over in seeking a solution in irenical fashion to the religious quarrels. In concrete terms, this meant that he endeavoured to initiate a French Established Church, a church, in other words, that would be both French and national, with the king as its natural head, a French counterpart to the Church of England.[15]

With this ideal in mind, Hotman composed well-documented writings on ecclesiastical politics, got in touch with kindred spirits in the Republic of Letters, and also turned to influential Calvinists, in particular to Beza. But his most important contribution to theology and church history was the preparation of a list of assorted printed and unprinted writings from the sixteenth and early seventeenth centuries, suitable for serving and furthering the cause of irenicism.[16]

This list, the first version of which (1607) was repeatedly reprinted (= Syllabus I), later to be published anew in a greatly enlarged edition in 1628 (= Syllabus II), and again a few years later (= III), also contains the name of Charles Perrot as author of two writings. Although the lists for 1607 and 1628 have a different order, the writings they contain are the same.

Syllabus I (1607)[17]

(a) Advis d'un Théologien de G. sur le livret susdict de Cassander, de officio pij viri, non imprimé.

(b) De extremis in Ecclesia vitandis, pij cuiusdam Theologi liber, nondum editus.

---

[15] Cf. G. H. M. Posthumus Meyjes, 'Jean Hotman en het calvinisme in Frankrijk', *Ned. Archief voor Kerkgeschiedenis*, 64 (1984), pp. 42–77.

[16] G. H. M. Posthumus Meyjes, 'Jean Hotman's *Syllabus* of eirenical literature', *Reform and Reformation. England and the Continent c.1500–c.1750* (Oxford, 1975), pp. 175–94.

[17] *Syllabus I* was added to the reissue by Hotman of Cassander's anonymously edited *De officio pii ac publicae tranquillitatis vere amanti viri, in hoc Religionis dissidio* (Paris, 1607), pp. 38–48. (For Perrot, p. 42.)

Syllabus II (1628)[18]

(b) De extremis in Ecclesia vitandis. Caroli Perroti, pii & moderati Theologi liber: nondum, quod sciam, editus.

(a) Eiusdem observatio in libellum Georgii Cassandri, de officio pii viri.

While the name of Perrot does not appear in the first version of the list (presumably for reasons of safety, so as not to add to his troubles, and he is only guardedly described as 'un Théologien de G(enève)', Hotman finally removed the mystery in Syllabus II; by that time Perrot has been dead for twenty years, though Hotman omitted to record the 'non imprimé'.

However that may be, the *Advis* which now concerns us is to be found in the rich collection *Hotmanniana*. This collection was originally in Dutch ownership, but after being sold by auction in the nineteenth century it came into the hands of the well-known Tractarian and Hebraist Dr Edward Bouverie Pusey, who then donated it in 1867 to the recently founded *Bibliothèque de la Société pour l'Histoire du Protestantisme* in Paris in the course of his goodwill journeys through France, on the eve of the first Vatican Council. The manuscript under discussion, an autograph, is very legible and runs to six pages.[19]

Cassander's writing, which Perrot commented upon, is the well-known *De officio pii ac publicae tranquillitatis vere amantis viri, in hoc religionis dissidio*, published anonymously for the first time in 1561, and afterwards reprinted frequently under its author's name. Its content has been discussed so frequently that no further amplification is needed.[20] More recently, several studies have been devoted to it, specifically by the late Richard Stauffer, who in a very lucid article confronted Cassander's argument with Calvin's viciously barbed criticism of it.[21]

That Hotman was one of Cassander's staunchest admirers is evidenced by his own letters and writings, as well as the fact that he published a reprint of *De officio pii viri* in 1607.[22] Moreover, he prepared a French

---

[18] (Theodosius Irenaeus), *Syllabus aliquot synodorum* . . . (Aureliae [= Strasbourg], 1628), p. (C4).

[19] *Hotmanniana*, 2, no. 52, fols 121r–3v. The 'Advis sur le livre de Cassandre intitulé *De officio pii ac publicae tranquillitatis vere amantis viri*' in MS BN Dupuy 477, fol. 144, is a late copy erroneously ascribed to N. Pithou; cf. Vivanti, *Lotta politica*, p. 240, n. 4.

[20] See, e.g., F. W. Kantzenbach, *Das Ringen um die Einheit der Kirche im Jahrhundert der Reformation*. Vertreter, Quellen und Motive des 'ökumenischen' Gedankens von Erasmus von Rotterdam bis Georg Calixt (Stuttgart, 1957), pp. 207ff. and the literature mentioned there.

[21] Richard Stauffer, 'Autour de Colloque de Poissy: Calvin et le "De officio pii viri ac publicae tranquillitatis vere amantis viri"', *Actes du Colloque l'Amiral de Coligny et son temps* (*Paris 24–20 oct. 1972*) (Paris, 1974), pp. 135–54; A. Stegmann, 'G. Cassander, victime des orthodoxies', *Aspects du Libertinisme au XVIe siècle* (Paris, 1974), pp. 199–214.

[22] See n. 17 above.

translation of this booklet, which, in the event, was never published, and now forms part of the Paris collection *Hotmanniana*.[23] He also co-operated assiduously but unobtrusively in the edition of Cassander's *Opera omnia*, edited in 1616 by Jules Descors (Cordesius). And, finally, he passed on information about Cassander to J. A. De Thou in aid of the latter's famous *Historia sui Temporis*.[24]

It may be assumed that Hotman, inspired as he was by Cassander's message, would have sent his treatise to Perrot about 1592, along with a request for Perrot's thoughts on it. It is not clear whether there had been any previous contact between the two men. It is known, however, that Hotman, when he addressed Perrot, was in Basle in connection with the winding up of his father's chaotic estate. It may well be that it was only then that he became aware of Perrot existence and his irenical reputation, and decided to write to him in the hope of gaining his support for his own activities in church politics—a strategy not unusual when some writing or other had caught his attention. With similar intent, he sent Henry Constable's *Examen Pacifique* to the ministers Pierre Loyseleur de Villiers and Merlin;[25] it is striking, too, that he did not refrain from incorporating even their strongly negative reactions into his Syllabus, and he also did this with Perrot's *Advis* concerning Cassander's writing.

III PERROT'S *ADVIS*

It is preferable to paraphrase the content of the *Advis*, rather than to reproduce the entire text. This permits a fuller discussion of Cassander's argument than Perrot undertook. After all, Perrot could keep his own reaction succinct and to the point, because Hotman knew the treatise in question and had a copy close at hand. Perrot, therefore, had no need to reiterate the substance of Cassander's writing: a mere reference to the pages and passages sufficed in formulating his criticism. Modern readers, however, need some introduction outlining Cassander's position before a summary of Perrot's relevant remarks is made.

Perrot began his criticism of Cassander's work by claiming that someone with good intentions who lacked the gift of prophecy clearly had

---

[23] *Hotmanniana*, 1, no. 7, entitled 'Le Debvoir de l'homme de bien et désireux du repos public en ce différent de religion', fols 41–50.

[24] The present author is preparing an article on the relationship between Hotman and Cassander.

[25] G. H. M. Posthumus Meyjes, 'L'Examen Pacifique de la doctrine des Huguenots et son auteur (1589). Henry Constable et la Critique', *LIAS* 14 (1987), pp. 1–14.

no vocation, and would do better to keep silent and remain strictly within the bounds of his calling as a private person. He unbraided Cassander for being so naïve as to have ignored this rule.[26] Apart from this shortcoming, which was a subjective one, there was also, Perrot pointed out, an objective one. He considered that Cassander's writing might have been useful had it been written at the beginning of the religious quarrels, but now that the strife had to come to a head it could no longer serve any useful purpose. He regarded the contemporary situation as fully comparable with that in Hosea's time, when iniquities had come into the open, and the Lord had struck his people with judgement and punishment in order that they would return to him (Hosea 7. 1; 13. 9). Accordingly, people should return to him now, honour him, and confess that the present confusion was caused by the sins of both this generation and the preceding ones. Rather than delight in the title 'church', men would do better to lament its decay due to sin. Instead of wounding one another like wild beasts and continually deepening the wounds, people had better investigate whether Gilead still had balm to offer, and look out for healers willing to blame themselves rather than others.

Having given his reaction to Cassander's writing in general terms, Perrot proceeded to a detailed criticism. His first objection against *De officio pii viri* concerned the use of the term 'tradition'. In his view, Cassander's definition was too wide for a concept that could only be applied legitimately when limited to the apostolic tradition, which ended around Irenaeus' time. By then all disciples of the Apostles had died, and thereafter Scripture alone could be used as the source of doctrine.

Cassander had indicated as its foundation, firstly, the canonical writings, and, secondly, the Catholic tradition, which, following in Vincentius van Lerinum's footsteps, he defined in terms of *antiquitas*, *universitas*, and *consensio*. Although Perrot was willing to agree to this, he immediately emphasized that tradition had no claim to an independent role next to Scripture. The only function tradition had was ancillary, serving to articulate Scripture. He thus clearly dissociated himself from Cassander, who had posited that Scripture and tradition were in line: indeed, that their interrelation should be seen in terms of potency and act,

---

[26] This was a frequently recurring issue at that time, the implications of which are not fully clear to me. It is my impression that the argument was used mainly by advocates of a strong government authority *in sacris*, arguing that the Church was a public institution in which only the public body had the right of decision-making. For this reason, only those officially appointed were competent to reform the Church.

in the sense that he had defined Scripture as implied tradition, and tradition as Scripture made explicit.[27]

The divergence was further enhanced by Perrot's total rejection of all the gradations and distinctions Cassander had brought to his concept of tradition. In particular, there could be no room in the Church for those traditions that consisted in non-scriptural customs and practices, because all that was no more than 'human tradition'. On this point Perrot was exceptionally vehement. 'Le sens pervers des prétendus Catholiques', he observed, comes out revealingly clearly when one sees how especially Jesuits, like Bellarmine, make the durability of customs, practices, or opinions the hallmark of truth. Cassander, Perrot continued, avoided this issue; whereupon he himself adduced, by way of example, the doctrine of transubstantiation (which had taken the place of the generally accepted concept of the 'sacramental truth' in Antiquity), the invocation of saints, and idolatry.

Proceeding from *doctrina* to *disciplina*, Perrot argued that Cassander had put church ceremonies under the sacrosanct authority of Christ. But here again something resembling the concept of tradition was at issue: Cassander had also put all later additions of a ceremonial nature under the same unimpeachable authority. Perrot called this an insufferable absurdity, a reversal or order, substituting the Church's regulations for divine truth. He appealed to St Augustine, who so many centuries ago had lamented that all those ceremonies had made the Church sick. And now, Perrot affirmed, the Church lay buried in a grave of meaningless rites, diametrically opposed to the true spiritual Kingdom of Christ.

Another criticism he brought to the fore concerns the distinction Cassander made between the responsibility for the church of 'private' persons—the laity or congregation of believers—on the one hand, and of 'public' persons—ministers and priests—on the other. Perrot blamed Cassander for leaving the laymen in the Church 'confined in the prison of their consciences' when he advised them to steer clear of contamination if faced with abuses in the Church. In fact, said Perrot, what this amounted to was no cure for the sick body as the medication prescribed for the Church was purely superficial.

On the responsibility of office-holders in the Church, Cassander had

---

[27] Cassander, *De officio pii viri*, in *Opera omnia* (Paris, 1616), p. 783: 'Cum haec traditio nihil aliud sit, quam scripturae ipsius explicatio et interpretatio: ita ut non inepta dici posset, scripturam esse implicatam quandam et obsignatam traditionem, traditionem vero esse scripturam explicatam et resignatam.'

said that it was their task to contradict erroneous opinions, and to denounce transgressions of God's law candidly and without fear. Following the example of the prophet Zechariah, who had had to pay for his devotion to God's house by being stoned, they, too, should offer resistance in a prophetic spirit and not evade martyrdom. Perrot, in turn, bitterly objected that not one of the (Roman Catholic) servants of the Church had ever set such an example. Nor had anyone shown any awareness of the fact that the time of the prophet Ezekiel had returned, and that the Lord himself was looking for the lost sheep for want of dedicated shepherds (Ezekiel 34. 11ff.).

Cassander had recommended communion with the Church of Rome as one of the most important members of the Universal Church, if not the mother of all churches. Perrot, dissociating himself from these pretensious claims, argued that it is far more sensible to distinguish two communities: one divinely-ordained inner community of the conscience, based on the fundamental truth of baptism, symbol, and Scripture, and an external community in the sense of the Church as an institution. He posited that God had not permitted his truth to sink into perdition, altogether in Christianity, but the point was that this truth—as proclaimed by Scripture—was no longer safe in the church. 'How the faithful city has become a harlot', he quoted from Isaiah 1. 21, and so, for those whom God had intended to bless there was nothing for it but to break away from the community of the Church and weep over Zion.

Cassander had argued that the Church of Rome confessed Christ truly in her articles of faith. Perrot upbraided Cassander for having treated this doctrinal point in a very scholastic and pharisaical manner in total disregard of the insight, evoked and given by God in this century, into the abyss of human depravity, on the one hand, and the power of divine grace, on the other. But, alas, due to the prevalence of sin, men had not taken full advantage of this magnificent gift. The religious quarrels had prevented people from profiting from it to the extent that was needed.

Cassander had conceded that some churches had devoted themselves to the cause of the Reformation, and done so after careful consideration, in a spirit of reconciliation, and fraught with sorrow over the dissension it had engendered. What he had in mind was probably a reform akin to the one implemented by Hermann von Wied in his diocese: an attempt to bring about a reform along Erasmian lines, which in all probability would appeal to Cassander. Be that as it may, Perrot immediately raised the objection that no such renewal had been effective, that very few people had displayed such noble feelings, and that no real conversion had taken place. One should, moreover, bear in mind that the 'schismatic party' of Rome threatened all those who refused to obey her with extinction.

Perrot also maintained that Cassander was far too optimitic in his expectations of *rapprochement* of the parties. Cassander had indicated a third road between the idolizers of the pope, on the one hand, and the followers of Luther and Calvin, on the other. In Perrot's eyes, the impracticability of this *via media* had been proved by its lack of success. The situation was rather that, all around, people stuck to their guns and were so deeply entrenched in their attitudes that it was impossible for them even to understand one another. Nor did a *rapprochement* in love, as suggested by Cassander, offer a solution, for if this love were not sincere and deeply rooted nothing could be expected of it. This, therefore, left only one solution, namely 'to sigh'; people should point one another to God's promise and confess their sins before the Eternal One.

Finally, Cassander had mentioned the shortcomings of the bishop of Rome only in passing. Yet that was the very starting-point and continuing breeding-ground of evil. Perrot adduced several witnesses, including Adrian IV, to substantiate this thesis; and then abruptly ended with the biblical passage: 'What is impossible with men is possible with God' (Luke 18. 27).

IV INTERPRETATION

It is, of course, extremely hazardous to make sweeping pronouncements on an author's range of thought purely on the basis of such meagre evidence. But so little is known about Perrot, a conspicuous enough figure (though subordinate to Beza) in Geneva and its Academy, that it is tempting to make the most of what is available in the hope of solving at least part of the riddle surrounding him.

What is immediately striking in his *Advis* are the very frequent references to the Old Testament, especially to the Prophets. In contrast to a mere seven references to the New Testament, there are thirteen to the Old Testament, nine of which refer to the Prophets. Again, when it comes to determining the importance of the biblical passages to the argument, it is the Prophets who tip the balance; their pronouncements virtually dominate the discussion. Apparently Perrot felt that an appeal to the Prophets was the best way of promoting his own ideas.

Perrot emerges from his comments as one who draws an exact parallel between the current situation of the Church and Christianity in his time, and that of Israel in the Prophets' time, and he radically appropriates the

Prophets' judgement on the state of the Covenant and the temple service, yet without arrogating to himself the Prophets' cloak, which to him, the *peccator*, would have been tantamount to self-exaltation. In other words, all around he found depravity, apostasy, infidelity, an interchange of divine truth and human untruth, and the poor, ordinary people wandering aimlessly about because of clerical betrayal. In short, he detected a dead-end and hopeless situation, were it not for the promise, the support, and the mercy of heaven. What is remarkable in all of this is that Perrot, in contrast to Beza, Goulard, and other Genevan authorities, was so deeply convinced of the sinfulness and unworthiness of everyone that he looked askance at over-confident know-alls, the self-assured and thoroughgoing temple purgers, not out of a sense of detached scepticism or any wish for toleration, but simply because he shrank from being confronted time and again with human, sinful arrogance and the besmirching of all that is holy. Perrot's attitude, in other words, was suffused with quietism and resignation, if not with pious despondency, which makes it extremely difficult to indicate his place in the confessional diversity of his time. Where did he belong?

To start with, his sharp repudiation of the Church of Rome is striking. He was full of indignation and passionate protest against that Church, her loss of initial purity and subsequent total degeneration. Her ministers and teachers—above all, the pope—had violated what was holy, betrayed the Sacraments, and abandoned or led astray their flock. Scripture had been strangled by tradition; human inventions and rules had been substituted for divine truth. In short, 'How the faithful city has become a harlot' (Isaiah 1. 21). All connection with the Church of Rome must be severed, for in this house God could no longer be served appropriately.

This criticism of the Church of Rome, particularly noteworthy in confessional terms, had, for Perrot, a positive outcome in his conviction that the Reformation had been a salutary new start. He spoke of 'the light that God in his mercy has caused to shine anew in the past century', and he had no doubt that this new insight concerned the doctrine of justification: in other words, an awareness of the abyss of human despondency and guilt, and of the overwhelming mercy and absolution on offer as a remedy. All the same, he felt deeply distressed by the fact that, due to sin and dissension, this magnificent gift was not fully grasped, and, by the same token, that the prospect of renewal had not been fully achieved in the strict sense.

Taking both observations together—his aversion to Rome, on the one hand, and his gratitude for the insight of justification, on the other—

Perrot cannot but be placed in the Reformation camp. Yet Perrot's remarkable emphasis on the inner life cannot be explained simply by identifying him as a spiritualist. In spiritualist circles, the Church of Rome would not have been regarded merely as 'schismatic', as Perrot called it. Nor would spiritualists have been as panegyrical as he was about justification by faith alone.

Is this meagre result all that can be achieved, or is there a more specific way of defining Perrot's theological position? He was reputed to be a peace-loving man, and was highly praised by irenicists, such as Casaubon, Pierre de l'Estoile, and Hotman, whose irenicism was unmistakably that of a Christian humanist, closely tied to Erasmus. The question is how exactly Perrot should be related to this tradition on the basis of his opinions on Cassander's *De officio pii viri*, one of the finest products of this very tradition.

Perusal of his *Avis* reveals the little sympathy Perrot could muster for Cassander's message. Basically he considered Cassander superficial in his judgement on Rome and too gullible in his expectations of the will to achieve renewal in the Church. Cassander had had no inkling of the apostasy Rome was guilty of, nor of the extent of betrayal by its leaders, and so on. And yet, however strongly opposed to Cassander's peace programme Perrot may have been, he may still be considered as a follower of that very tradition, with the qualification that for him 'Erasmian Reform' and 'Calvinist Reformation' amounted to virtually the same thing; he felt that both movements were deeply committed to bringing about an ethical renewal of the Church. There can be little doubt that in his younger years (about which so little is known) Perrot was inspired by this kind of Reform. He emerges as someone who had dreamed his dreams of a renewal in Church and faith in his youth, and who later was disappointed when everything turned out so very differently from what initially had been hoped for.

All this may be no more than a hypothesis, yet evidence is not wholly lacking. Particularly revealing is his statement that had Cassander's writing appeared at the start of the religious quarrels, it might have served its purpose, but that now that the quarrels had reached their height, the work could no longer serve any useful purpose. It is very unlikely that anyone wholly rejecting the Erasmian tradition would have expressed himself in this way. In any case, it would be very difficult to find a comparable utterance in any Calvinist response to Cassander's *De officio*.

A further indication that Perrot belonged to the evangelical Reform tradition is to be found in the noticeable absence of the names of the great

Reformers in the *Advis*. Luther, Melanchthon, Calvin, and Beza are all conspicuous by their absence.[28] The few names he did mention at the end of his *Avis* are those of persons highly esteemed in the evangelical tradition. This is especially true of Claude d'Espence and the Cardinal of Lorraine, both frequently cited by irenicists in Perrot's day and afterwards.

Mention of these few 'Reform theologians' is not purely coincidental; it is indicative of Perrot's deep roots in evangelical thought. This is borne out by Perrot's letters, extant in the Dupuy collection (Paris, BN). From these highly interesting and very confidential letters, Perrot emerges as a 'Hieronymus im Gehäuse'.[29] This Hieronymus, too, read, meditated, turned things over in his mind, and delved into the mysteries of Scripture. Yet he preferred the company of the early Fathers and of those contemporaries who dealt with the tradition in a kindred way. All this ties in with the Erasmian context, which to him (as to others in magisterial circles who had their decisive experiences in the 1560s)[30] had not yet broken away from the 'Reformation' line of thought. This, perhaps, might also be the reason why later irenicists sought his company, whereas Calvinists kept him at arm's length.

For Perrot himself, the secret underlying his life, and his motto— *gemere et silere*—might well be found in his despair that nowhere could he see any sign that the new ideas had really borne fruit anywhere in Christendom, neither in the Church of Rome after the Council of Trent,

---

[28] What is particularly remarkable is that Perrot did not mention Calvin's refutation of Cassander's writing at all, and probably did not even know it.

[29] In spite of Cellérier's article (*Perrot*) mentioned above (n. 2), Perrot's 45 letters in the Dupuy collection (MSS BN Dupuy 103, fol. 127; 699, fols 104–7; 700, fols 161–200; 806, fol. 107, 108) and one in MS BN fr. nouv. acq. 22740 (cf. M. L. Dorez in *Bulletin d'histoire du comité des travaux historiques* (1916), pp. 276ff.) are too little known and insufficiently examined. They date back to the years 1590–1606 and, with a very few exceptions (e.g. MS BN Dupuy 806, fols 107 and 108, to J. A. de Thou) are addressed to his friend Nicolas Pithou de Changobert in Basle. They are interesting witnesses, providing evidence of his concerns and poignantly revealing his anguish over the age he lived in. Apart from the fathers of the Early Church, and Bernard, Luther, Erasmus, Melanchthon, Claude d'Espence, Jean du Tillet, Ponet (*Dialecticon*), Lambert Daneau ('mon singulier ami'), Stapleton, and Bellarmine are mentioned.

[30] Biographically interesting is Perrot's letter to N. Pithou, 10 June (1601) (MS BN Dupuy 700, fol. 185). Speaking about certain brotherhood, and parish, festivals, participation in what he strongly advised against because of their superstitious character, he then continued: 'Nostre Seigneur me pardone de ne l'avoir autrefois apréhendé en l'occasion au banquet de feu monsieur DuDrac en la confrairie des jeunes advocatz au palais l'an [15]63.' Presumably he was referring to Adrien II du Drac. Cf. Édouard Maugis, *Histoire du Parlement de Paris de l'avènement des rois Valois à la mort d'Henri IV* (Paris, 1916), p. 175. The wording confirms Perrot's close connection with the Parliament and magistracy in Paris in his youth.

nor in the 'purified' Church in which he himself served.[31] Certainly his Church had cherished the new insight afforded by the doctrine of justification by faith alone, but it was less than clear whether this, in turn, had contributed to a more profound understanding or to an abundance of love.

Perrot saw no noticeable change, and blamed this on the fact that the new faith had become moulded into scholastic doctrine. Correct formulations were held in higher esteem, it seemed, than correct conduct. On all sides, people had become entrenched in their own beliefs, which they called orthodoxy. But repentance and love—'orthopraxy', 'orthovie'—had been altogether banished.[32]

This, then, was the limbo, the impasse, in which Perrot had to live: resigned and silent, waiting for the judgement, distressed by current conditions, reaching out falteringly towards heaven in disappointment, yet constantly searching for the meaning of Providence.[33] Rilke immediately springs to mind.

[31] The admiration for 'the light' that God had granted to the world in the sixteenth century, expressed in his *Advis* (I. 141ff.), is confirmed by statements in the letters to Pithou. For instance, 15 May 1593 (MS BN Dupuy 700, fol. 198 bis): 'Je suis après à passer le troisième tome de Bellarminus ... auquel il me donne tant plus à admirer *l'œuvre que nostre Seigneur a monstré en ce dernier siecle* [my italics] ...'; 30 Oct. 1597 (fol. 162): 'Je desirois que nostre siecle eust peu profiter selon *les œuvres qui s'en sont presentées du commencement* [my ital.]'; 'Ce qui n'a succedé en la plus part, et s'en retire plus que ci devant, partie pour ne nous estre asssez humiliez envers celui qui estait voulu entrer au jugement par sa propre maison pour le grand bien d'icelle, partie pour avoir estimé, avoir tout fait *quand on a bien dit, mais tant moins fait* [my ital.]'; 'et avoir trop fondé sur l'importunité et de l'appui et support du monde ...'; 23 Aug. 1601 (fol. 179): 'Mais il [*scil.* Stapleton] m'a fait penser combien il y a à adviser de bien orthotomiser la vérité (II Tim. 2. 15), comme en parle St. Paul, y ayant à requerir en cet esgard en ceux qui au demeurant ont enseigné la verité par *le singulier don et support de nostre Seigneur en ce siecle dernier* [my ital.].'

[32] To N. Pithou, 23 Aug. 1601 (MS BN Dupuy 700, fol. 179): 'Les medecins sont les plus malades et ne le pensent nullement. On tomba là après le premier calme exterieur à la chrestienté sous Constantin. On a recherché l'orthodoxie, et à bon droit, *l'orthovie est demeurée en arriere* [my ital.].' See also n. 31 above.

[33] To N. Pithou, 6 Aug. 1593 (MS BN Dupuy 700, fol. 198): 'Nostre siecle m'a semblé quelque fois nous promettre quelqu'enfantement mais ce qu'Erasme en escrivoit ... n'est que trop vray: *Mundus jampridem abortit et nescio an umquam vivum erit pariturus*. C'est le temps de la retraite, en tant qu'un chascun y pense pour soy, puisqu'en gros et en commun on se pert par les montagnes'; 22 April 1569 (fol. 197): 'C'est le tems de la revue et de la recherche du Seigneur, lequel est caché de devant nos yeux, afin que son jugement nous surprenne et nous soyons sans excuse ...'; 23 Feb. 1598 (fol. 182): 'Nostre siecle est plus charnel que jamais, pourtant faut-il qu'il sente comme le Seigneur abrege son terme pour le bien des siens'; 28 Apr. 1597 (fol. 200): 'Nostre siecle a besoin de patience et de gemissement. *Tempus orandi, non inquirendi*'; 30 Oct. 1597 (fol. 162): 'Nostre siecle est sujet a des paroxysmes dont il ne fait son profit come il serait a desirer. L'Eglise apostolique a eu de telz assaultz, mais l'esprit du Seigneur a toujours tiré sa lumiere des ténèbres'; 5 Dec. 1597 (fol. 180): 'Je ne voy en nostre siecle qu'un accroissement et continuation de banquerotte de bien ...'; 30 Jan. 1595

Wer jetzt kein Haus hat, baut sich keines mehr,
Wer jetzt allein ist, wird es lange bleiben.

Herbsttag

University of Leiden

(fol. 181): 'Je ne voy ni près ni loin rien plus expres pour nostre siecle que *memores estote uxoris Lot* (Luke 17. 32) et me semble que nous devrons trop plus prier interieurement.'

A DISPUTED LETTER: RELATIONS BETWEEN THE CHURCH OF SCOTLAND AND THE REFORMED CHURCH IN THE PROVINCE OF ZEELAND IN THE YEAR OF THE SOLEMN LEAGUE AND COVENANT

by WILLEM NIJENHUIS

I 1643

IN the year 1643 the Dutch revolt against Spain was dragging gradually to an end. Repeated attempts by Stadtholder Frederick Henry to take Antwerp had failed. Since 1640 only minor military operations had been undertaken. The demand for peace was growing, but this, at the same time, led to divisions of opinion.[1] During this period of domestic tension the United Provinces became involved in events in England leading to the Civil War.[2]

On 12 May 1641 the wedding between the Stadtholder's son, the future William III, and Mary, the eldest daughter of Charles I, had taken place at Westminster. The English and the Dutch had various aims. The British King, faced with deteriorating relations with Parliament and with the Scots, hoped for Dutch assistance. Orange, in turn, wanted to detach England from Spain, and so strengthen his own monarchical ambitions.

Consequently Frederick Henry embraced the Stuart cause and one of the preoccupations of his later years was to make the republic support the English Royalists. But the province of Holland was not prepared to let itself be drawn into a war which only could be a maritime war against the Parliamentary party including London, the merchant fleet and the navy. In 1643 the States of various provinces, among them those of Holland, refused further to collaborate in the government by the standing committee[3] of the States General. It was

---

[1] J. Presser, *De tachtigjarige oorlog* (Amsterdam and Brussels, 1963), pp. 228–33; J. J. Poelhekke, *Frederik Hendrik Prins van Oranje. Een biografisch Drieluik* (Zutphen, 1978), pp. 503–6; G. Parker, 'Why did the Dutch revolt last so long?' in *Spain and the Netherlands, 1559–1659. Ten Studies* (Glasgow, 1979), pp. 45–63.

[2] The present author hopes to publish in the near future a more comprehensive contribution on Dutch–Scottish political and ecclesiastical relations in the first half of the seventeenth century.

[3] The so-called 'secret besogne', a committee of the States General, which, compounded by

therefore matters of foreign policy which undermined Frederick Henry's so carefully built up semi-monarchical position.[4]

Besides the royalist Stadtholder and his party, supported by such Roman Catholics as the great poet Joost van den Vondel, the States General was pursuing a policy of neutrality, and made some vain mediatory attempts in the English conflict. A third party in the United provinces, namely the Reformed part of the population (almost half of the northern Netherlanders), was on the side of the English Parliament.

In the country as a whole there was great interest in the political and ecclesiastical events overseas. Numerous official statements by all parties in Britain—King, Parliament, English, and Scots—were translated into Dutch. Such documents as the National Covenant (1638) and the Solemn League and Covenant (1643) were published as pamphlets in Dutch translations in the very years of their signing.[5] In the same way, part of the ecclesiastical correspondence was brought to the notice of the Dutch.[6]

II THE INTERMEDIARIES AND THEIR AIMS

The Scottish theologians Robert Baillie and William Sprang acted as intermediaries between the Kirk of Scotland and the Reformed churches in the northern Netherlands. Baillie's correspondence reveals a great deal of the background to the composition of these documents.[7] The Covenanter Baillie, minister at Kilwinning, and from 1642 professor at Glasgow,[8] was one of the Scottish commissioners at the Westminster Assembly.[9] In this capacity he shared the effort to create a confessional

---

supporters of the Prince of Orange, settled vital questions of foreign policy. Gradually, as an almost almighty camarilla, it assumed a considerable degree of independence. See Poelhekke, *Frederik Hendrik*, pp. 324–8, 536f.; S. Groenveld, *Verlopend getij. De Nederlandse Republiek en de Engelse Burgeroorlog 1640–1646* (Dieren, 1984), pp. 82–7.

[4] E. H. Kossman, 'The Low Countries', *The New Cambridge Modern History*, ed. J. P. Cooper (Cambridge, 1970), 4, p. 375. On Orange and Stuart, see P. Geyl, *Oranje en Stuart* (Zeist, Arnhem, and Antwerp, 1963), pp. 16–34; S. Groenveld and H. L. P. Leeuwenberg, *De bruid in de schuit. De consolidatie van de Republiek 1609–1650* (Zutphen, 1985), pp. 112–14.

[5] W. P. C. Knuttel, ed., *Catalogus van de pamflettenverzameling berustende in de Koninklijke Bibliotheek*, 9 vols (The Hague, 1889–1920), nos 4561, 4948, 4949.

[6] Ibid., nos 4980, 4992, 4993, 5062, 5153.

[7] *The Letters and Journals of Robet Baillie*, ed. D. Laing, 3 vols (Edinburgh, 1841–2).

[8] Ibid., nos XXI–LXXIV; J. Howie, *The Scots Worthies* (Edinburgh, 1870), pp. 413–15; H. M. B. Reid, *The Divinity Professors in the University of Glasgow 1640–1903* (Glasgow, 1923), pp. 75–126; F. N. McCoy, *Robert Baillie and the Second Scots Reformation* (Berkeley, Los Angeles, and London, 1974); *DNB*, 1, pp. 892–4.

[9] On the role of the Scots at Westminster see J. Bartlett Rogers, *Scripture in the Westminster*

and disciplinary unity for the 'Three Kingdoms'—England, Scotland, and Ireland—in the spirit of the Solemn League and Covenant: in fact, an attempt to presbyterianize England. To achieve this, he looked for support from his Dutch co-religionists.

In March 1645 Baillie was able to see The Netherlands for himself when he and the Edinburgh minister George Gillespie, on their way from Scotland to London by ship, were driven off course by the wind and ended in Dutch waters. He therefore had an unexpected opportunity to visit Middelburg and Rotterdam.[10] As is apparent from the acts of the Consistory of the Scots Kirk in Rotterdam, both ministers attended the session of 5 April. At this meeting they assisted and counselled the Scots minister Alexander Petrie in a disciplinary procedure and in his action against 'so many inordinate and stubborne persons of our nation in this land'.[11] Later on, during the spring of 1649, Baillie stayed in The Hague for more than two months as a commissioner of the General Assembly, in order to discuss with Charles II the religious conditions for his accession to the Scottish throne.[12]

Baillie was well informed about the works of Dutch Reformed theologians, and tried as far as possible to make them known in Scotland. In doing so, he often used the mediation of his cousin, William Spang, who from 1630 to 1652 was minister of the Scottish Staple at Veere,[13] in former times known as Camphere[14] (in British documents, mostly 'Campheir' or 'Camphire'). During his lengthy stay on the island of

---

Confession. A Problem of Historical Interpretation for American Presbyterianism (Kampen, 1966), pp. 138–54, 193–200.

[10] W. Steven, *The History of the Scots Church, Rotterdam* (Edinburgh, 1832), pp. 15f.

[11] Archives of the Scots Church Rotterdam, Inv. no. A 1.

[12] A. F. Mitchell and J. Christie, eds, *The Records of the Commission of the General Assemblies of the Church of Scotland holden in Edinburgh the years 1648 and 1649* (Edinburgh, 1896), pp. 236, 242–8.

[13] A. L. Drummond, *The Kirk and the Continent* (Edinburgh, 1956), pp. 51, 71, 82f., 126, 132–6; D. Nauta, A. de Groot, *et al.*, eds, *Biografisch Lexicon voor de geschiedenis van het Nederlandse Protestantisme* [hereafter *BLGNP*], 5 vols (Kampen, 1978ff.), 2, pp. 409f. with bibliography; McCoy, *Baillie*, p. 8, n. 14; on the staple and its church see 'Documents relative to the Scottish Colony and Church at Veere', MS Edinburgh, University Library, X15/63/2; J. Davidson and A. Gray, *The Scottish Staple at Veere. A Study in the Economic History of Scotland* (London, 1909); M. P. Rooseboom, *The Scottish Staple in the Netherlands. An Account of the Trade Relations between Scotland and the Low Countries from 1292 till 1676, with a Calendar of Illustrative Documents* (The Hague, 1910); K. L. Sprunger, *Dutch Puritanism. A History of English and Scottish Churches of the Netherlands in the Sixteenth and Seventeen Centuries* (Leiden, 1982), pp. 28, 176, 195, 206–11, 446–9; on Spang see also *BLGNP*, 2, pp. 409f.

[14] Thus called because in the town there was a ferry ('veer') to the village of Campen on the island of Noord-Beveland. This village was flooded in 1532.

Walcheren,[15] Spang had built up many relations with Dutch colleagues, especially with Gideon van Deijnse, Reformed minister at Veere, and with William (Guilelmus) Apollonius, minister at Middelburg.[16] The latter was highly esteemed by Baillie for his theological abilities.[17] Both divines enjoyed great authority in Zeeland. They often represented the classis of Walcheren in the 'Ecclesiastical Assembly of the Churches of Zeeland'. Apollonius wrote several drafts of letters to the British churches. Van Deijnse represented his classis in the plenary session of the States General, requesting them in the name of the Zeelanders to direct a national day of prayer and fasting for Ireland and England. The seventeenth-century historian Lieuwe van Aitzema gathered from this evidence that 'in that time the affection of the people of Zeeland was directed toward the parliament, and against the king.'[18] The Reformed Church in the United Provinces indeed nourished warm feelings toward the Presbyterian party in England. When, on 3 July 1645, the Westminster Assembly had finished its draft of a Presbyterian church government to be submitted to the English Parliament, the Provincial Synod of South Holland (Woerden, 4 July–5 August 1645) expressed its approval of the document as 'in most points sufficiently in conformity with the government of the Reformed Church in this land'.[19]

Yet although public statements expressed a sense of fellowship with the English Presbyterians and approval of Scottish attempts to institute a Presbyterian system *à l'écossaise* in the Church of England, such

---

[15] From 1653 to 1664, the year of his death, Spang was a minister of the English Church at Middelburg, whose congregation was in fact a mixture of English and Scots and was called by him the 'British Church'.

[16] J. P. de Bie, J. Loosjes, *et al.*, eds, *Biografisch woordenboek van Protestantsche godgeleerden in Nederland* [hereafter *BWPGN*] 6 vols (The Hague, 1903–49), 1, pp. 199–206; P. C. Molhuysen, P. J. Blok, *et al.*, eds, 10 vols (Leiden, 1911–37), 6, p. 48; *BLGNP*, 2, pp. 30–2.

[17] Baillie, *Letters*, 2, p. 197. Through Spang, Baillie expressed the hope on 28 June 1644 that Apollonius would continue his writing. In 1642 the Middelburg divine in his *Jus majestatis circa sacra* had defended the original Calvinist viewpoint on relations between Church and State against the Reformed theologian Nicolaus Videlius, who advocated a greater measure of State authority over the Church. On behalf of the Walcheren classis (State Record Office of the Province of Zeeland [hereafter RAZ]: *Acts of Classis Walcheren* [hereafter *ACW*], 20 vols, 1, no. 3 [1 Dec. 1639–13 Feb. 1653], 18 Aug., 1 Sept., 15 Sept., 6 Oct. 1644), he wrote his *Consideratio quarundam controversiarum* against the Independent's pamphlet *Apologetical Narration*. See D. Nauta, *De Nederlandsche Gereformeerden en hat Independentisme in de zeventiende eeuw* (Amsterdam, 1936), pp. 15–17: Extracts from the Acts of the Classis Walcheren, 1643–1644: ibid., pp. 37–49.

[18] Lieuwe van Aitzema, *Saken van Staat en Oorlogh. In, ende omtrent de Vereenigde Nederlanden*, 6 vols (The Hague, 1669–72), 2, p. 521.

[19] W. P. C. Knuttel, ed., *Acta der particuliere synoden van Zuid-Holland 1621–1700*, 6 vols (The Hague, 1908–16), 2, p. 505.

communications, as mentioned above,[20] did not come about quite spontaneously. Time and again, William Spang was urged by Baillie to encourage his Dutch colleagues to support by letters the ecclesiastical aims of their countrymen at Westminster. Sometimes he went even so far as almost to dictate in detail what the Dutchmen should write in support of the Solemn League and Covenant.[21] Baillie, however, underestimated the difficulties which the Dutch churches would meet by entering into a correspondence with foreign churches on such delicate issues without the knowledge and permission of their political authorities. The churches in the Low Countries, mostly those in Zeeland, were more strictly subordinated to the States than a Scottish Calvinist could imagine. The States of Zeeland had not approved the discipline of the great Synod of Dordrecht, but instead had adhered to their own ecclesiastical discipline of 1591.[22] Only on six occasions since 1591 had they given permission for calling a provincial synod, and the last time was in 1638. From 1638 no provincial synod met.[23] Irregularly, the representatives of the four classes in the province (Walcheren, Zuid-Beveland, Schouwen, and Tholen) did hold meetings, called 'coetus synodales', authorized by the States and attended by their deputies, 'Gecommitteerde Raden', a kind of executive committee.[24] Sometimes there was talk about 'Co-operation of the four

---

[20] See note 6 above.

[21] Baillie, *Letters*, 2, p. 115: 'It is my earnest desyre, if by some of the eminent brethren there, yow can obtain, in their answers, which I hope will come, some clauses to be insert, of the churches of Holland and Zeeland [their] grave counsell, and earnest desyre, that, according to our profession in our late Covenant, taken now by both the Assemblies of Scotland and England, we would be carefull in our reformation, after the word, to have an eye to that Discipline wherein all the Reformed churches doe agree; and that we be verie diligent to eschew that democratick anarchy and independence of particular congregations, which they know to be opposite to the word of God, and destructive whollie of that Discipline, wherby they, and the whole Reformed churches do stand. If by your dealing, such clauses could be gotten put into your letters unto us, and in the letters of the churches of France, Switze, Geneva, and others, by the means of your good friends Dr Rivett and Spanheim, or some others, it might doe us much good.'

[22] C. Hooyer, *Oude kerkordeningen der Nederlandsche Hervormde gemeenten (1563–1638)* (Zaltbommel, 1865), pp. 306–23; Resolutions of the States of Zeeland (hereafter RSZ), 13 Nov. 1643.

[23] L. W. A. M. Lazonder, 'Acta der Zeeuwsche synode van 1638', *Archief vroegere en latere mededeelingen voornamelijk in betrekking tot Zeeland, uitgegeven door het Zeeuwsch Genootschap der Wetenschappen 1909* (Middelburg, 1909), pp. 97ff.

[24] Acts of the coetus of 10–31 Dec. 1626, RAZ, MS 241, fol. 63. The 'Gecommitteerde Raden' consisted of delegates from the States. On their position in the administrative machinery of the province, see K. Heeringa, ed., *Rijksarchief in Zeeland. Het Archief van de Staten van Zeeland en hun Gecommitteerde Raden 1574 (1578)–1795 (1799)* ('s-Gravenhage, 1922), XIII–XIX; S. J. Fockema Andreae, *De Nederlandse Staat onder de Republiek = Verhandelingen der Koninklijke Nederlandse Akademie van Wetenschappen*, Afd. Letterkunde, no. LXVIII, no. 3 (Amsterdam, 1961), p. 52.

respective classes of Zeeland'.[25] Obviously this 'coetus' was also supervised
by the States. These did not allow the classes to enter into a correspondence with their English fellow believers so long as the conflict between
King and Parliament was dragging on. Apollonius's writing, *Jus majestatis
circa sacra*, which was very much admired by Baillie, caused a dispute
about the authority of the State over the Church which lasted for years
and years.[26] Such a ban on ecclesiastical correspondence with England and
Scotland also applied to Holland,[27] and was characteristic of relations
between Church and State in the United Provinces.[28]

<h2 style="text-align:center">III GENESIS OF THE LETTER</h2>

Tracing the origin of the letter from the classes of Zeeland to the Scottish
Kirk, dated 18 July 1643, is quite straightforward. On 9 August 1641 the
General Assembly in Edinburgh had decided 'that it seemed expedient for
correspondence that might be from foreign parts, for the weal of this
Kirk, that the Scots Kirk at Campheir were joyned to the Kirk of Scotland,
as a member thereof.' Baillie was charged to ask the Scots consistory at
Veere to send their minister, together with an elder, to the next General
Assembly, which would meet at St Andrews in July 1642. There they
would be enrolled as representatives of their Church.[29]

It is obvious from the correspondence between the English Paliament
and the Assembly[30] that the Scottish desire for a 'uniformity of government' and for 'a common confession of faith, catechism, and directory of

---

[25] Thus the coetus at Tholen of 25–6 July 1634, RAZ, MS 241, fol. 142.

[26] The so-called 'Grallenstrijd' because of the anonymous writing *Grallae seu vere puerilis cothurnus sapientiae, quo se iactat apud imperitos Guilelmi Apollonii* (1646). See P. J. Meertens, *Letterkundig leven in Zeeland in de zestiende en de eerste helft der zeventiende eeuw = Verhandelingen der Nederlandse Akademie van Wetenschappen*, Afd. Letterkunde no. XLVIII (Amsterdam, 1943), pp. 190f., 213; *Archief Zeeuws Genootschap der Wetenschappen*, I, 5 (1863), pp. 80–6.

[27] When the Reformed ministers of The Hague, after the execution of Charles I, sent a letter of condolence to his son, Charles, containing a strong condemnation of this 'particie', the States of Holland summoned them to tell them to abstain henceforth from such statements to foreign princes and from any correspondence with Englishmen (Resolutions of the States of Holland and Westfriesland [hereafter RSH], 26–7 Feb., 1–3 Mar. 1649).

[28] When the 'Grote Vergadering' (great assembly), a kind of constituency, of 1651 discussed the maintenance of the Reformed religion, the five deputies of the provincial synods had to stand. Van Aitzema scorningly observed: 'For the ministers of secular princes, chairs are wait-ing and they have permission to keep their heads covered. Ought the ambassadors on behalf of Christ (II Cor. 5. 20) to stand bareheaded?' (Van Aitzema, *Saken*, 3, p. 505.)

[29] *A True Copy of the Whole Printed Acts of the Generall Assemblies of the Church of Scotland, 1638–1649* (n.p., 1682), p. 110.

[30] Ibid., pp. 124–31.

worship' was an important subject of discussion, and that for this purpose 'a hearty conjunction with all the Reformed Kirks' was thought necessary.[31] It is easily appreciated that Baillie brought this 'conjunction with all the Reformed Churches' with forceful arguments to the notice of his cousin, who was welcomed in the Assembly on 27 July 1642.[32] First of all, of course, the Scots minister at Veere made an appeal to his relations on the island of Walcheren. The classis decided that letters should be dispatched to the churches of England, Scotland, and Switzerland. To England they would send an expression of their sympathy and support, to the Scots an exhortation to do their duty 'on behalf of the freedom and the salvation of their brethren'. The same should be required from the Swiss. From the beginning Walcheren tried to have the other classes in Zeeland involved in their initiative.[33] In the next session, and in the meeting of the coetus on 19 March, a request to the States to call a day of prayer and fasting was discussed.[34] Shortly afterwards Deÿnsius could state that all the classes had decided jointly to send the three letters.[35]

But then the troubles ensued, resulting from the civil government's supervision of the churches. Already, after asking the churches to pray in their worship for the suspension of hostilities and for 'the conservation of the Reformed religion' in England, the authorities had warned the ministers 'to abstain from mentioning anything referring to politics both in England and in this country'.[36] This order was prompted by the wish to maintain 'a complete neutrality between His Majesty of Great Britain and the Parliament of England'.[37] Being very well aware of the sympathy of the Reformed believers for the parliamentary party, and for their co-religionists in England and Scotland, the States had good reasons for distrusting the classes. That is why they required inspection of the letters to the churches overseas before they were sent. The classes, however, refused to comply with the demand of the State.[38] The latter, in vain, repeated its claim;[39] the classical deputies, however, in a discussion with the pensionary of the province, reiterated their refusal. They were only

---

[31] Ibid., p. 130.
[32] Baillie, *Letters*, 2, p. 46.
[33] *ACW*, 5 Mar. 1643.
[34] Ibid., 19 Mar., 26 Mar. 1643.
[35] Ibid., 26 Apr. 1643.
[36] RSZ, 23 Mar., 18 Apr. 1643.
[37] Ibid., 29 Jan. 1643. On this unsuccessful policy of neutrality, see Groenveld, *Verlopend getij*, pp. 104–20.
[38] *ACW*, 4 Jun., 18 Jun., 1643.
[39] Ibid., 9 Jun. 1643.

prepared to give a verbal summary of the substance of the letter, and to deliver 'a copy of the English letters as soon as they were printed'. So the Church was determined to confront the authorities with a *fait accompli*. They could scarcely have acted more provocatively. The conflict escalated when the States reminded the divines that holding a coetus meeting without their prior permission was not allowed.[40] After spending three sessions on the affair, the States delegated the final settlement to the Gecommitteerde Raden, asking them to use 'gentle and proper means'.[41] But this measure was just as ineffective. However gentle the deputies of the States might have been in their consultations, the ministers adhered to their refusal to deliver copies of their letters. The Gecommitteerde Raden also spent four sessions on the conflict.[42] But on 1 July the representatives of the four classes announced that they had revised and confirmed their letter to the Swiss without considering the States' demand. The terms 'revision' and 'consideration' make it likely that, although they were not prepared to deliver a copy of the letter, the churches did not overlook the comments of the States made during the oral discussions. It may be that in the end the States were satisfied with an oral reading of the letters. At any rate, the resolutions of the Gecommitteerde Raden do not mention the conflict after that date.

The letter to the Scots, dated 18 July 1643, was addressed to their commissioners in Westminster. The document, written in Latin, was translated at once, first into English, then from English into Dutch. In England, the original Latin text, together with the English translation, was published in a pamphlet of eighteen pages.[43] In The Netherlands the letter was published as a pamphlet, under the title *Letter from the Synod of Zeeland*![44] Unfortunately, because of typographical shortcomings, both the English and Dutch translations have been handed down in defective

---

[40] *ACW*, 11 Jun. 1643.

[41] Ibid., 12 Jun. 1643.

[42] RAZ, no. 499, Resolutions Gecommitteerde Raden, 15 Jun., 18 Jun., 29 Jun., 1 July 1643.

[43] *A Letter from the Synod of Zeland to the Commissioners of the Generall Assembly of the Kirk of Scotland: Written by them in Latin, and now faithfully translated into English: expressing, 1. Their fellow feeling of the present condition of the Kirks of Ireland and England, & exciting us to the like. 2. Their respects and affection to the Kirk of Scotland. 3. Their zeal to the Reformation of the Kirk of England, in Government and Ceremonies, and to the preservation of Religion there, Against the pride of Popery at this time. 4. And their desire of Unitie in Religion, and Uniformity of Kirk-government in his Majesties Dominions* (Edinburgh, 1643).

[44] *Een Brief Van de Synode van Zeelant, Aan de Gecommitteerde van de Generale Vergaderinge der Kercke in Schotlandt. Eerst by hun den 18 July 1643 in 't Latijn beschreven, ende uyt het Latijn in 't Engelsch, ende nu uyt het Engelsch in 't Nederlants getrouwelijck vertaelt. . . . Eerst ghedruckt tot Edinburgh. Anno 1643.* Knuttel, *Pamflettern*, no. 4991.

form.[45] We do not know if the undated letter to the English was also published as a pamphlet in The Netherlands. In England the original Latin version was printed in the same year, without the word 'synod' in the title, as an appeal of 'the Zeeland classes and churches to the English churches'.[46] The letter is a testimony of fraternal solidarity with fellow believers overseas,[47] an appeal for perseverance in the struggle, particularly against Rome, and an assurance of the support of the Dutch churches. Although its authors did not refer to the political situation in England, one can easily read between the lines which party had gained their sympathies.

IV THE SUBSTANCE

The classes opened their letter with a testimony of their 'anxiety and sorrow arising from the lamentable condition of the Kirk in Ireland, and troubled Estate of the Kirk in England'.[48] Evidently they aimed to point out the responsibility of the Scots for the English Presbyterians, for they saw the lot of the other European Reformed churches as depending on the events in England. Behind royalist efforts to restore episcopacy, they suspected there lurked the Romanist pursuit of the Counter-Reformation:

> If they be able to prevail over the Kirks of the flourishing and potent Kingdome of England, they are hopefull without difficultie to over-turn the Kirks of Scotland; as also to bring easily the Reformed Kirks of the Netherlands to the same desolation. And that there is no Reformed Kirk in Europe which shall be able to withstand their formidable power.[49]

The argument was frequently repeated, not unreasonably, given the Roman influence in the royal army and the disastrous massacres of Protestants by Catholics in the Irish Rebellion.

The Church of Scotland, according to the Zeeland coetus, was the

---

[45] In the English translation, the text between page 7, line 8 to page 9, line 5, is missing; and in the Dutch translation, the content between page 5, line 21, and page 10, line 12, is also missing. A complete Latin text is to be found in the edition cited in note 43 above. A complete Dutch translation is available in Van Aitzema, *Saken*, 2, pp. 929–31.

[46] *ΠΡΟΣΦΩΝΗΣΙΣ classium et ecclesiarum Zelandicarum ad ecclesias Anglicanas Intestino bello perturbatas* (London, 1643).

[47] Ibid., p. 12: 'In eadem familia estis, unum communem habetis Dominum, Christum in ecclesia, Regem in Regno, qui in una domo morantur, concordes par est.'

[48] We are quoting the English translation so far as it is available.

[49] Ibid., p. 13.

nearest neighbour to the *Ecclesia Anglicana*. The realms were joined 'under the government of one king, who is resolved to live and die in the Reformed religion, as in his public Declarations plainly he has professed.' This sentence probably refers to Charles I's letters to the General Assembly, dated 23 July 1642, intimating that he would rule his kingdoms 'by their own lawes, and the Kirks in them by their own Canons and Constitutions', and that 'where a Reformation is settled, we resolve . . .' to maintain and defend it in peace and libertie against all trouble that can come from without, and against all Heresies, Sects and Schismes, which may arise from within.'[50]

Apollonius, who was involved in drafting the letter, had become acquainted, doubtless through Spang, with the substance of this declaration, which was read twice in the General Assembly at St Andrews.[51] The Scots were urged to make every effort to heal the rift between King and Parliament. If the Church of England were left to its own devices, the danger which threatened was that the popish forces would win through 'and the times of Queen Mary would return; yea much more cruell than these.'[52] The Scots therefore ought to join their English fellow believers in their fight against the 'intolerable tyrannie of Episcopall government . . . lest they come again . . . under that tyrannicall yoke; but rather that they may stand courageously for the maintenance of their libertie (yet so, that they fall not on the other extreame, Anarchy, a more dangerous evill.)'[53] The latter warning aimed at the growing influence of Independency both in Parliament and in the Westminster Assembly. The phrases quoted are very much in the spirit of Baillie, who again and again warned of this danger. The coetus's letter said exactly what he wanted to hear from a European church.

The letter dealt largely with what it called 'idolatrous rites and ceremonies',[54] such as liturgical vestments, celebration of holy days, iconolatry, and 'one fermentum pontificium'.[55] It opposed particularly the Catholic and Anglican forms of celebrating the Eucharist by kneeling at the altar rail instead of sitting at the table.[56]

Finally, the classes of Zeeland suggested that the Scots should refute the

---

[50] *Copy of Acts*, pp. 111f.
[51] Baillie, *Letters*, 2, pp. 46f.
[52] *Letter Synod*, p. 14.
[53] Ibid., p. 15.
[54] Ibid.
[55] Ibid., pp. 7–9 in the Latin text. This portion is missing in the English and Dutch translations.
[56] Ibid., pp. 9f.

calumny of their being adversaries of the King. The King should be well aware

> that He has not any more loyall Subjects, than these who are devoted to the Reformed Religion: He knoweth that there is nothing that can establish more His Throne, that can enlarge his Royall Honour and Magnificence more, or can better preserve His Royall Person, than if with the whole Power He defend the reformed Religion, against all the adversaries therof.[57]

Here we hear a theme well known from the beginning of the Dutch Revolt against Habsburg, and reiterated in the Dutch national anthem: resistance is not to be directed against the king.[58]

V RECEPTION OF THE LETTER IN SCOTLAND

Did the letter from the Zeeland classes meet the expectations of the Scottish commissioners at the Westminster Assembly to whom it was addressed? On 26 July Baillie acknowledged receipt of the document, 'which we caused to translate and print in Latin and English'. He had learned from Spang to his satisfaction that the classes would try to move the churches of the other provinces in the Low Countries to write a similar letter. But at the same time he reported that 'some few did except a little at some expressions which they thought not so opposit to the English government and ceremonies as the tymes required.'[59] Probably Baillie himself belonged to these 'few'. He had hoped that the continental Reformed churches would join the Church of Scotland on its way to accepting the Solemn League and Covenant (17 August 1643).[60] As a Scottish Calvinist, interpreting this document primarily from a religious viewpoint, Baillie underestimated the troubles which would be caused by an involvement of the Zeeland coetus in the English political conflict, for in the Civil War political and ecclesiastical motives were so inextricably connected[61] that the States of Zeeland would never have allowed the

---

[57] Ibid., p. 18.
[58] '... den koning van Hispanje heb ik altijd geëerd.'
[59] Baillie, *Letters*, 2, p. 75.
[60] *Copy of Acts*, pp. 185–7.
[61] 'Those who denied that the people should have a voice in the government of the church ... increasingly ceased to have any alternative but to support the King and the existing episcopalian church, and this became a main reason for supporting the royalists. Those who were prepared to agree that the people should have some voice in the government of the church were bound to accept that this involved radical changes in the government of the

ministers to go further than they had done in their first writing. The divines were fully aware of this restriction, as became clear at the Provincial Synod of South Holland (Brill, 6–25 July 1643). Here they proposed that the synod should ask permission from the States General that all provincial synods—for after the great Synod of Dordrecht (1618–19) the authorities had forbidden the holding of general synods—should send similar letters to the Reformed Churches of England, Scotland, and Ireland. On this occasion they stated repeatedly that such letters should not deal with political matters, neither might they express 'any partiality against His Majesty of Great Britain or his Parliament . . . as ecclesiastical and political affairs should be distinguished.' Referring to letters of recommendation from the States of Zeeland, the deputies of the classes defended themselves strongly against the rumour that their own political authorities did not approve their action.[62]

In other respects, too, the strict supervision of the State was slowing down ecclesiastical activities in the international field. An exception was the days of prayer and fasting on behalf of England, which could be organized without any difficulties. With regard to this tradition, the initiative of the States General had been accepted since 1572.[63] The preparation for a national fast on 24 June 1643 took less than three months.[64] Later in the same year, requests for making a church collection on behalf of the Protestants in Ireland[65] were readily granted. But difficulties arose about the way the money should be sent to Ireland and how it should be spent. The States wanted to have control over these

---

church, possibly the establishment of some form of presbyterianism or congregationalism, and this meant supporting Parliament in the Civil War': B. Manning, 'Puritanism and Democracy 1640–1642' in D. Pennington and K. Thomas, eds, *Puritans and Revolutionaries. Essays in Seventeenth-Century History presented to Christopher Hill* (Oxford, 1978), p. 153.

[62] Perhaps the States having heard an oral reading of the coetus's letter had given up their objections and, being of the opinion that political partiality was out of the question, had decided to support their ministers' action. (Knuttel, *Acta*, 2, pp. 399–402.) It is remarkable that in the further acts there is talk of England and Ireland (ibid., pp. 465f.), but we do not hear any more of Scotland. At a later stage, the Provincial Synod of South Holland (The Hague, 4–28 July 1644) responded to the letter of the Committee at the Westminster Assembly (ibid., pp. 476–9). The English letter was translated into Dutch and published as a pamphlet together with a reprint of the English theologians' plea for Ireland. (Knutel, *Pamfletten* no. 5044.)

[63] W. Nijenhuis, 'Vastenopvattingen en vastenpraktijken in de Reformatie, bepaaldelijk bij de Gereformeerden', *Nederlands Theologisch Tijdschrift*, 36 (1982), pp. 12–28.

[64] *ACW*, 19 Mar., 26 Mar. 1643; RSZ, 20 Mar., 23 Mar., 18 Apr., 14 May, 8 June, 14 June 1643; Knuttel, *Acta*, 2, pp. 399, 425, 465.

[65] Sources concerning this collection in Groenveld, *Verlopend getij*, pp. 296f. and n. 11.

activities and they ordered remittance of the money to the Bank of Middelburg. The classes objected to this procedure.[66] The English Parliament recognized that it could not ignore the Dutch political authorities. That is why it twice addressed itself through written communications to the States.[67] Members of Parliament discussed the use of the collection.[68] On 24 March 1644 they submitted a list of the goods bought,[69] and in June and July they expressed their thanks to the States and to the Gecommitteerde Raden.[70]

Before the General Assembly formally replied to the letter of the Zeeland classes, according to an order of the English Parliament of 22 November 1643, a letter was written and directed from the Assembly of Divines in Westminster and the Commissioners of the Church of Scotland at this Assembly to the churches of Zeeland,

> earnestly intreating them (1) to judge aright of the afflicted condition of England, of the innocency and integrity in their just defence to acquit them in their hearts, and make their apologie for them in all their Churches, (2) to sympathize with them as brethren who suffer in and for the same cause wherein [they] themselves had bene oppressed, (3) that they would embrace the Church of Englands condition as their owne cause and contribute every way to their helpe etc. . . .

Neither the manuscript nor a printed copy of this letter, mentioned by Thomas Cunningham, conservator of the Scots Staple at Veere,[71] has been preserved.

On 4 June 1644 the Church of Scotland sent to the Dutch Reformed churches a letter of thanks for 'the liberal collection'. At the same time they repeated their appeal to them to consider joining the Solemn League and Covenant.[72] In their answer, however, the classes informed the Scots that they considered such a move a matter not only for all the Dutch provinces together, but also for all European countries holding the Reformed religion as the religion of the State.[73]

---

[66] *ACW*, 24 Sept., 12 Nov., 3 Dec., 1643; RSZ, 13 Nov., 23 Nov., 25 Nov. 1643.
[67] 27 July, 7 Nov. 1643, RAZ, MS no. 949.
[68] 29 Dec. 1643, RAZ, MS no. 499.
[69] RAZ, MS no. 500.
[70] Ibid., nos 500, 950.
[71] *The Journal of Thomas Cunningham of Campvere 1640–1653. With his ThrisselsBanner and Explication thereof*, ed. E. Courthope (Edinburgh, 1928), pp. 71f.
[72] Knuttel, *Pamfletten* no. 5062.
[73] RAZ, MS 241 p. 237.

Not until 4 June 1644 did the General Assembly send a formal answer to the classes' letter of 18 July 1643. Sir Archibald Johnston of Wariston, a lawyer, one of the framers of the National Covenant of 1638, and Scottish commissioner at the Westminster Assembly, had informed the assembly about its content. Remarkably enough, the Scots praised the coetus for its readiness in helping to achieve a unity of all British churches. In the last paragraph of their letter, directed to all Reformed churches in the United Provinces, and published as a pamphlet in a Dutch translation in the same year,[74] they again urged the Dutch to join the Solemn League and Covenant. Such a union, it was thought, would be of major importance to both the British and Dutch churches in their common struggle against the Roman danger, heresies and schisms.[75]

VI CONCLUSION

On the one hand, the correspondence between the Church of Scotland and the classes of Zeeland in 1643 and afterwards showed a deep spiritual kinship and an obvious desire to strengthen their communion. In this respect, to use a modern term, one could consider this correspondence an indication of an 'ecumenical persuasion'. On the other hand, it is evident that both churches had different aims. The Dutch were urging the Scots to support their Presbyterian fellow believers in England. The Scots, however, wanted to go further, and tried to make the Dutch and other European churches join the Solemn League and Covenant. If the classes of Zeeland had given in to this desire, they would have come into conflict with their political authorities at home. In two respects they would have acted contrary to the policies of neutrality pursued by the States. They would openly have sided with Parliament in the English Civil War, and perhaps they would also have been involved in discussions about the interpretation of the Solemn League and Covenant: whether it was primarily a political agreement, as the English saw it, or whether it was an ecclesiastical alliance, as the Scots tended to see it.[76] Apart from discussions of the meaning of the term 'according to the Word of God',[77] they would openly have declared themselves 'opposite to the English government'. But the political authorities of the United provinces and the States of Zeeland would never have allowed such a fulfilment of Baillie's wish.

[74] Knuttel, *Pamfletten*, no. 5062.
[75] *Copy of Acts*, pp. 239–43.
[76] R. Ashton, *The English Civil War* (London, 1978), pp. 200–3.
[77] W. Makey, *Church of the covenant* (Edinburgh, 1979), pp. 71ff.

The public Church in The Netherlands was both a privileged and yet an unfree church at one and the same time.[78] Although in 1651 the Reformed religion was formally acknowledged as the religion of the State, in practice, everyday life did not accord with this fundamental statement. In fact, as far as relations between Church and State were concerned, the model of Zurich prevailed over the theocratic principle of the Calvinist *Confessio Belgica*.[79]

University of Groningen

---

[78] W. Nijenhuis, 'De publieke kerk veelkleurig en verdeeld, bevoorrecht en onvrij', D. P. Block *et al.*, eds, *Algemene Geschiedenis der Nederlanden*, 15 vols (Haarlem, 1977–83), 6, pp. 325–43; W. Nijenhuis, 'Religiegeschiedenis 1621–1648: Kerk in meervoud', *Algemene Geschiedenis der Nederlanden*, 6, pp. 377–411.

[79] The *Confessio Belgica* (1561) says in its 36th article, 'Of Magistrates': '. . . And their office is not only to have regard unto and watch for the welfare of the civil state, but also that they protect the sacred ministry, and thus may remove and prevent all idolatry and false worship; that the kingdom of antichrist may be thus destroyed, and the kingdom of Christ promoted. They must, therefore, countenance the preaching of the Word of the gospel everywhere, that God may be honoured and worshipped by every one, as he commands in his Word: P. Schaff, *The Creeds of the Evangelical Protestant Churches*, 3 (London, 1877), p. 432. In fact, the governing bodies, often themselves religiously mixed, were tolerant of people of other beliefs and turned a blind eye to their practices.

PART II   THE CHURCH IN ENGLAND

MONASTIC LEARNING AND LIBRARIES IN SIXTEENTH-CENTURY YORKSHIRE

by CLAIRE CROSS

I N July 1565 Edmund Skelton, clerk, left to the curate of Egton to remain in the parish for ever a book called *Postella Cassiodorus*, a *Catholicon*, and a Latin Bible, works distinctly at odds with the Protestant ethos which the new generation of bishops was striving to introduce into the Elizabethan Church. This bequest in itself singles Skelton out from the usual run of priests serving in Yorkshire villages at this time. In fact, until his prior surrendered the house on 31 August 1539 he had been a monk of Grosmont Priory, and then, at the Dissolution, at the age of thirty-six, with a pension of £3 6s. 8d, he had apparently settled in the adjoining parish of Egton. In his will he also gave a gown, tippet, and hat to Nicholas Morley, almost certainly the former prior of Whitby Abbey, and 20d. and certain other unspecified books to a former fellow canon, Robert Holland. Both the books destined for Egton church and those intended for Robert Holland may once have formed part of Grosmont monastic library. Although the evidence can only be re-assembled with difficulty, sufficient records have survived to suggest that a significant number of erstwhile monks and friars were similarly re-distributing medieval books around Yorkshire in the generation after the Henrician Reformation. An examination of the religious known to have attended the two English universities in the reigns of Henry VII and Henry VIII, a survey of monastic schools and, in particular, an assessment of monastic libraries and books can together provide at least an impression of the state of learning within Yorkshire monasteries and friaries, and of the contribution they may still have been making to northern intellectual life at the close of the Middle Ages.[1]

In the early sixteenth century, Yorkshire reflected in microcosm the successive developments which had taken place in medieval monasticism in England as a whole. The Benedictines had planted five houses in the county, St Mary's Abbey in York, Selby Abbey, Whitby Abbey, and the smaller priories of Holy Trinity, York, and Monk Bretton. In their turn,

---

[1] Borthwick Intitute, York, Prob. Reg. 17, pt ii, fol. 474v (Skelton); *LP*, 15, p. 555; *Miscellanea III*, *Yorkshire Archaeological Society Record Series* [hereafter *YAS RS*], 80 (1931), pp. 106–7. The spelling in all quotations has been modernized.

the Cistercians possessed no less than eight abbeys, Byland, Fountains, Jervaulx, Kirkstall, Meaux, Rievaulx, Roche, and Sawley. The Augustinian canons had established priories at Bolton, Bridlington, Drax, Guisborough, Haltemprice, Kirkham, Healaugh, Newbrugh, Nostell, Warter, and North Ferriby. The Carthusians had made two foundations at Hull and Mount Grace, while the Cluniacs had a priory at Pontefract; the Gilbertines four houses at Ellerton, Malton, Watton, and York; the Grandimontines a house at Grosmont, and the Premonstratensians three small priories at Coverham, Easby, and Egglestone. The friars, moreover, had proved just as prolific as the monastic orders. The Austin friars maintained convents at Hull, Tickhill, and York; the Franciscans friaries also at York and Beverley, Doncaster, Richmond, and Scarborough; the Dominicans houses at Pontefract, Scarborough, Beverley, York, and Yarm; the Carmelites priories at York, Scarborough, Doncaster, Hull, and Northallerton, and there was a single convent of Trinitarian friars at Knaresborough. Although some of these foundations were very small and poorly endowed, they all continued into the 1530s, when there may well have been a total of some 900 male religious in the county, approximately 750 monks and 150 friars.[2]

Some years ago, Dr Emden drew attention to the number of monks and friars studying at the two English universities in the first forty years of the sixteenth century. He did not make precise calculations for Cambridge, but at Oxford he uncovered some 750 religious, 366 monks, and 383 friars. To set against this national picture, 33 Yorkshire religious are known to have studied at Oxford and Cambridge during the same period, 15 monks, and 18 friars, a total which, because of the inadequacy of sixteenth-century academic records, is almost certainly an underestimate of those who had had some connection with a university. By the 1520s, the accountant of St Mary's, York, as a matter of course was making allowances for monks of the abbey studying at Cambridge, and other evidence indicates that probably most of the larger Yorkshire monasteries, and even more the Yorkshire friaries, had forged links with the two chief centres of learning in England. The subsequent careers of Yorkshire monastic graduates to a greater or lesser extent demonstrate the influence of this education.[3]

---

[2] This figure is compiled from a count of religious known to have been in the county at the Dissolution: it is likely to be an underestimate since the King's commissioners failed to list the members of some monasteries and friaries.

[3] A. B. Emden, *A Biographical Register of the University of Oxford 1501–1540* (Oxford, 1974), p. xxi; C. Wellbeloved, 'The Compotus ... of Thomas Syngleton, monk ... of the

As might have been anticipated, their sojourn at the university merely confirmed most of the monks in their adherence to late medieval scholasticism. This seems certainly to have been the case with Thomas Clynte, a Bachelor of Theology, probably from Oxford, and sub-prior of St Mary's. After the surrender of his abbey he settled with a pension of £10 a year in the parish of St Martin's, Micklegate, in York, where he received a bequest to perform Masses for the soul of a dead colleague. His relative economic prosperity enabled him to perform numerous acts of generosity to the local poor both during his lifetime and at his death. Other Benedictine graduates, such as Robert Kirkby, of Monk Bretton, and Nicholas Morley, of Whitby, seem to have shared Clynte's conservative piety, but also acquiesced in the closure of their houses without open opposition. Two Cistercian graduates, however, dared to voice their defiance. Edward Kirkby, alias Cowper, who in 1523, after eleven years' study of logic, philosophy and theology had successfully supplicated for the degree of Bachelor of Theology at Oxford, had become abbot of Rievaulx in 1530. Only three years later he lost his office at Cromwell's insistence, but against the wishes of his brethren, because of his hostility towards recent changes in the Church. His academic senior, William Thirsk of Fountains, who had supplicated for a Doctorate in Theology at Oxford in 1528, fared even worse. Having reluctantly retired to Jervaulx after ten years at Fountains, he very unwisely involved himself with the rebels during the Pilgrimage of Grace, and was executed for treason on 25 May 1537.[4]

Robert Pursglove, the Augustinian prior of Guisborough, seems to have been more conscious of new academic trends than these Yorkshire Cistercian graduates, though he, too, remained conservative in religion. He had entered Corpus Christi College, Oxford, at the early age of fourteen, though there is no record of his having taken a degree. After the surrender of Guisborough he had been rewarded with the provostship of Jesus College, Rotherham, until it, in its turn, was abolished in 1548. Pursglove welcomed the restoration of Catholicism by Mary and refused to take the oath of supremacy on Elizabeth's accession, retreating 'very wealthy and stiff in papistry' to his native village of Tideswell, in Derbyshire, where he founded a grammar school in 1560. The twenty-five

---

Monastery of St Mary, York', *Proceedings of the Yorkshire Philosophical Society*, 1 (1855), p. 129.
[4] Emden, *Oxford 1501–1540*, pp. 335, 567, 669; Borthwick Archbp. Reg. 29 fols 73v–4r (Ketland); Prob. Reg. 13 fol. 683r (Clynte).

books he presented to the school included pagan classical authors, such as Horace, Juvenal, Ovid, Sallust, and Cicero, Greek dictionaries, and the *Colloquia* of Erasmus, as well as a biblical concordance, expositions of the Psalter, and Augustine's *De civitate dei* and *De vita christiana*. At all events, by the time of his death he had quite clearly espoused the 'new learning', though not Protestantism.[5]

In his intellectual development John Elmer of St Mary's, who proceeded to a Doctorate of Divinity at Cambridge in 1536, closely resembled Pursglove. When he was being considered for the post of abbot in 1530 Anne Boleyn, a notable patron of humanists, intervened to ensure that if he was not elected, he might be allowed to continue his studies. He succeeded in evading high office on this occasion, but some years later the Queen again felt moved to protest that his superiors had recalled Elmer, 'a man ... of good learning, sad demeanor and virtuous governance' from the university, and loaded him with administrative responsibilities which prevented him continuing his academic work. It is just possible that these duties involved some connection with teaching in the Minster grammar school.[6]

In contrast to Pursglove and Elmer, an interest in humanism led two Yorkshire canons to adopt the 'new religion'. Thomas Cromwell imposed Robert Holgate—a Gilbertine canon, and previously the head of the Gilbertine priory of St Catherine at Lincoln—as prior upon the Gilbertine double house at Watton, precisely because of his Reformist sympathies, which he seems to have acquired at Cambridge. Despite the violent opposition of his brethren, which came to a head during the Pilgrimage of Grace, he weathered the crisis to surrender the house in 1539. After the Dissolution, he became first Bishop of Llandaff and later Archbishop of York, while simultaneously acting as President of the Council in the North. Though of a very different religious persuasion, like Pursglove he founded grammar schools, in this case at York and at his birthplace of Hemsworth. Because he had married, Holgate was deprived of his see when Mary came to the throne, though he subsequently renounced Protestantism and was reconciled to the Catholic Church. Robert Ferrar, the last prior of Nostell, suffered a very different fate. A native of Halifax, he went to Oxford as an Augustinian canon, where, as early as 1528, he

[5] Emden, *Oxford 1501–1540*, pp. 467–8, 735.
[6] J. and J. A. Venn, *Alumni Cantabrigienses* (Cambridge, 1922), pt i, 2, p. 99; M. Dowling, *Humanism in the Age of Henry VIII* (London, 1986), p. 90; C. Cross, 'York Clerical Piety and St Peter's School on the Eve of the Reformation', *York Historian* (1978), pp. 17–20.

was suspected of Lutheran tendencies. Cromwell, too, promoted his election as prior of Nostell in 1538. Once installed, he attempted to obtain the government's consent to the conversion of the priory into a college 'for the nourishment of youth in virtue and learning to the increase and advancement of the lively word of God, diligently, sincerely and truly to be preached to God's people and the king's in these parts.' Not surprisingly he found a scant welcome among his canons for so radical a plan. After the surrender of Nostell he received the bishopric of St David's in 1548, but failed to win over his Welsh prebendaries to his religious views. In 1554 he was deprived of his see, tried for a breach of his monastic vows, and burnt for heresy at Carmarthen on 30 March 1555.[7]

The graduates among the Yorkshire friars at the Dissolution appear to have been just as divided in their intellectual and theological allegiance as the university monks. William Vavasour, a member of the gentry family from Copmanthorpe, seems to have been entirely traditional in his interests. He had attended the Oxford Franciscan convent in the 1490s, taking his Doctorate in Theology in 1500, and being made warden of the Oxford convent about this time. While studying at the university he transcribed the works of Duns Scotus and Antonius Andreas. He had moved on to become warden of the York Franciscan Friary by 1524, which he surrendered to the Crown in 1538. When he died, in 1544, he bestowed twenty-six unnamed books upon legatees before leaving the remainder of the books in his study to one of his former brethren, Ralph Clayton. John Pickering's career followed a similar pattern to that of Vavasour. A Dominican friar, he took his B.D. at Cambridge in 1525, before being elected first prior of his house in Cambridge, and then prior of the Dominicans in York. At the time of the Northern Rebellion he committed himself with deliberation to the Pilgrims' cause, openly joining with Robert Aske in his discussions, and in the aftermath of the rebellion was sent to the Tower, condemned for high treason and put to death at Tyburn on 25 May 1537.[8]

Yet Vavasour and Pickering did not have things all their own way, and at least one Yorkshire graduate friar came to adopt views as radical as

---

[7] Venn, *Alumni Cantabrigienses* pt i, 2, p. 392; A. G. Dickens, *Robert Holgate, Archbishop of York and President of the Council in the North* Borthwick Publications, 8 (York, 1955); Emden, *Oxford 1501–1540*, pp. 202–3; *LP.*, 13, pt i, nos 1195, 1518.

[8] A. B . Emden, *Biographical Dictionary of the University of Oxford to 1500* (Oxford, 1959), 3, p. 1843; York Minster Libary D and C Prob. Reg. 5 fols 6r–7r (Vavasour); Venn, *Alumni Cantabrigienses*, pt i, 3, p. 359; C. F. R. Palmer, 'The Friars Preachers or Black Friars of York', *Yorkshire Archaeological Journal*, 6, pp. 417–19.

theirs were conservative. In August 1535 William Broman confessed that 'one Bale, a White Friar, some time Prior of Doncaster, taught him about four years ago that Christ would dwell in no church of lime and stone made by man's hands, but only in heaven above, and in man's heart in earth.' Having taken the degree of B.D. at Cambridge in 1529, John Bale had abandoned his Order some time before the Dissolution, and married. He fled to Switzerland with his family on Cromwell's fall, and spent the following eight years in exile. In the reign of Edward VI he held several pastoral cures before his consecration as Bishop of Ossory, at Dublin, in 1553. When Mary came to the throne he went again into exile, publishing in Basle his *Scriptorum illustrium catalogus*. On Elizabeth's accession, he returned once again to England, and received a prebend at Canterbury, where he died in 1563.[9]

Simon Clerkson, prior of the York Carmelite convent at the time of its surrender in November 1538, contrived to tread more of a middle path. After nine years of study, he had supplicated for the B.D. degree at Oxford in 1533. Very soon after the loss of his house, he acquired the vicarage of Rotheram, being licensed by the Crown to be absent for ten years, so that he might preach the Gospel throughout the realm in Latin or English, as might be most convenient for his auditory. The intellectual horizons of Brian Godson, the last prior of the York Dominicans, seem to have been much narrower. Even though he had lived in his Order's house at Oxford in 1505, when he made his will in 1541 he failed to refer to any books, though he did bequeath vestments to Sir Edward Smyth, probably the former cellarer of St Leonard's Hospital in York, and to William Bradfurth, one of his former friars, as well as to the church of Newton on Ouse, all of which may have previously belonged to his convent.[10]

So far as it is possible to judge from the meagre fragments of personal information, Brian Godson seems to have lost touch with his university connections, in any case forged some forty years previously, and by the time he died to have identified himself with the humbler world of York city clergy, very different from the more elevated Minister circle. In his own person he raises the wider question of the extent to which individual monks and friars who had studied at the university succeeded in mediating that culture to the more insular world of the north. Schools proved to

[9] Venn, *Alumni Cantabrigienses*, pt i, 1, p. 75; *DNB*, 3, pp. 41–2; *LP*, 9, no. 230; C. Garrett, *The Marian Exiles* (Cambridge, 1938), pp. 77–8.
[10] Emden, *Oxford 1501–1540*, pp. 123, 236; *LP*, 16, no. 1308 (38); Minster Lib. D and C Prob. Reg. 2, fols 198v–9r (Godson).

be the most immediate vehicle for conveying academic developments to society at large, and, despite the reservations of some earlier historians of education, there can be no doubt that some Yorkshire monasteries and friaries were still making a contribution to secular education. In York, St Mary's Abbey kept a boarding-house, called the Clee, by the outer gate of the monastery, from which fifty boys in 1535 went to study grammar at the Minster school. In John Elmer it seems that the monks may themselves have had somewhat closer connections with teaching in the city than has previously been thought. When, in 1535, Richard Oliver, the vicar of All Saints', North Street, was making preparations for his funeral, he asked that the usher of the Minster school should obtain 'Master Amler's' leave to bring his scholars to his burial at Holy Trinity Priory. Since Oliver owned a Calepinus, the most modern Latin and Greek dictionary, as well as copies of Erasmus's *Adages*, and the *Epistles* and *Offices* of Cicero, he may probably himself have augmented his stipend by instructing boys in grammar.[11]

Dr Jo Ann Moran has found a remarkable number of informal parish schools being conducted in York in the late middle ages, and shown that the city had no real need to turn to its monasteries and friaries for secular teaching. The situation in the Yorkshire countryside, however, seems to have been rather different. There religious houses may have made more deliberate provision for the education of boys in their immediate neighbourhood. Once again the evidence remains tantalizingly incomplete. In an ecclesiastical case over the rights of the inhabitants of Wistow to have their children baptized in Kirkham church, Roger Bell of Langton casually disclosed in 1496 that for five years he had gone to the school 'of Dom John Kyllam', an Augustinian canon of Kirkham Priory, and remembered in his childish games throwing stones at the top of the old font, which was shaped like a steeple. Particularly because of their parochial obligations, it seems very likely that other Yorkshire Augustinian houses were also teaching children in their local churches.[12]

At Tickhill on the eve of the Reformation the Austin Friars were apparently performing a similar function to that of the monks of St Mary's in York. Although in Thomas Hancoke they had a scholar who had

[11] A. F. Leach, *Early Yorkshire Schools*, I, *YAS RS*, 27 (1899), pp. xxvii–xxxi, 30–2; A. F. Leach, 'Schools', *VCH, The County of York*, I, (1907), p. 421; C. Cross, 'York Clerical Piety and St Peter's School on the Eve of the Reformation', *York Historian* (1978), pp. 17–20.
[12] J. A. Hoeppner Moran, *The Growth of English Schooling 1340–1548; Learning, Literacy and Laicization in Pre-Reformation York Diocese* (Princeton, 1985), esp. pp. 92–122; Borthwick CP F 307; J. S. Purvis, *Educational Records* (York, 1959), pp. 10–11.

attended Oxford University in the mid-1530s, and so was well qualified to teach, the friars seem merely to have offered premises where a school could be held. In a tithe case of 1569 Nicholas Storres, yeoman, and a native of Tickhill for the first eighteen years of his life, recollected how 'he learned at school in the friarage or religious house of Tickhill by the space of seven years together, viz from the eighth year of his age until the end of his fifteenth year, . . . with one Sir John Raynolde, chaplain to the Lady Harrisonne, a sojourner in the said friarage.' A Tickhill husbandman, John Gaunte, deposed in the same case that he had also 'learned at the school in the friars of Tickhill from the fourth year of his age until he was fifteen years of age.' Again it is plausible to suggest that schools may have been being held in other Yorkshire friaries.[13]

Although equally episodic, considerably more information survives in the early sixteenth century about the libraries of Yorkshire religious houses than about their schools. Adherents of the 'new learning' understandably had little use for medieval books at the time of the dissolution of the monasteries, and such works seem to have commanded very low prices on the open market. The fourteen great Latin books, for example, which had belonged to Mr Thomas Stockes, in 1556 parson of Treeton, but previously prior of Worksop, were appraised at a mere 20s. in a total estate worth over £240. Consequently the government's commissioners, anxious to preserve valuable monastic fixtures like lead, stone, or timber for the Crown, seem to have allowed many religious to take their books away with them when they left their monasteries. Certainly in June 1538 the abbot of Roche, Henry Cundall, in addition to his pension of £33 6s. 8d., received permission to remove 'his books, and the fourth part of the plate, the cattle, the household stuff, a chalice, a vestment and £30 in money at his departure, with a convenient portion of corn at his discretion'. Unfortunately, when he drew up his will some sixteen years later, he did not provide any details of these books.[14]

One group of monks, the Benedictines of Monk Bretton, made an heroic attempt to prevent the dispersal of their library. At least three if not more of the monks had settled at Worsborough near Monk Bretton around their former prior, William Brown. At his own expense Brown had acquired thirty-one books from the priory which included the Vulgate, several sermon-collections, the *Preceptorium* of Johannes Nider,

---

[13] Emden, *Oxford 1501–1540*, p. 263; Borthwick CP G 1384/12.
[14] *LP*, 13, pt ii, app. 25; Borthwick Chancery wills 1556 (Stockes); Prob. Reg. 14 fols 78v–9r (Cundall).

commentaries of Aquinas, the *Revelations of St Bridget*, Gerson, *De imitatione Christi*, and two or three English books, *The Golden Legend*, the *Flowr of Comawndments*, and *Ye pylgramage of perfeccyon* by William Bonde. When he died in 1557, Brown expressly instructed his executors to return these books, together with vestments, his house, and various closes to Monk Bretton Priory, if it should ever be restored. As well as William Brown's books, in 1558 Thomas Wilkinson and Richard Hinchcliff, both former Monk Bretton monks, had twenty-eight volumes in their chambers, which were 'of the gift and at the expense of Thomas Frobyscer, formerly subprior of the aforesaid monastery'. These again consisted chiefly of theological works: Nicholas of Lyra on the *Old Testament* in four volumes, the complete works of Chrysostom; Augustine, *De civitate dei*; Nicholas of Gorran on St Paul's *Epistles*; Boethius, *De consolatione philosophie*, together with one English book, *Schepard Kalendare*. Some, if not all, of these books must have been in manuscript like 'Alius liber introductorius pro novitiis de ritu et ceremoniis Religionis collectore Thoma Frobiscer scriptus R. Tyckyll.' Thomas Wilkinson, alias Bolton, had himself brought together a further fifteen books, once more almost entirely medieval and theological, such as the *Postilla* of Hugh the Cardinal, otherwise known as Hugo de St Charo, Robert Holcot on the *Proverbs of Solomon*, the *Quodlibetales questiones* of Aquinas. He did, however, have two Renaissance books, *Novum testamentum Erasmo translatore* and *Colloquia Erasmi*. Richard Hincliff, alias Wolley, had assembled the greatest number of books, no less than fifty-four, and again they were very much of the same genre, the *Homilies* of Pope Gregory the Great; the *Sermones* of Nicholas de Blonis; *Commentaries* of Dionisius Carthusianus; Sanctus Thomas de Aquino, *Super Magistrum Sententiarum*, but again he had one or two more recent books including Ambrosius Calepinus's Latin and Greek dictionary. Hinchcliff may indeed have been teaching boys either before, or more probably after, he left his monastery, since, in addition to a dozen or so medieval books, he also possessed a little collection of more recent grammar books; '*Roberti Whitintoni editio*, *Johannis de Garlandia*, *Tam Synonima et Equivoca*; *Epitole et oratii*; *Colloquium Erasmi*; *Elegantie terminorum*; et *Cato cum commentario*; et *Seneca moralissimus cum commentario*; etcetera plurimis.'[15]

Despite their best efforts, this little band of former Monk Bretton monks did not succeed in keeping their library together, and their books

[15] J. W. Walker, ed., *Chartularies of the Priory of Monk Bretton*, YAS RS, 66 (1924), pp. vi–vii, 5–9; Borthwick Prob. Reg. 15, pt iii, fols 151r–2r (Brown).

came to be dispersed as death took its toll. In his will of 1579, Robert Scoleye, vicar of Brodsworth and a former member of the community, made what may have been a final reference to the collection when he consigned all his books to his godson, Robert Helum, if he should decide to become a priest; if, however, he determined upon a different career, he wished Robert's father to sell them and to give the proceeds to the poor of South Kirkby, where he had been born.[16]

Other former monks besides those from Monk Bretton tried to preserve their monastic libraries. Although he named no specific books, apart from the *Sermones discipuli* of Johannes Herolt, destined for Leeds parish church, when he drew up his will in 1558, Edward Heptonstall, a former Kirkstall monk, solemnly charged his executors to safeguard the books in a chest at the foot of his bed and others in his custody elsewhere, which had once belonged to the abbey, and restore them to Kirkstall if it ever went up again.[17]

At least one other Yorkshire monastic library seems to have been kept together until late in the sixteenth century. In 1581 Robert Barker, the namesake and successor as vicar of Driffield of Robert Barker, the former prior of Byland, bequeathed in trust 'until such time some one or more of my natural blood be able to understand them' ninety-nine named books, together with 'forty other old written books' of small value. These closely resemble volumes contained in the libraries of two other Yorkshire Cistercian houses, Meaux and Rievaulx, in the fourteenth century, and which may well also have survived until the Dissolution. The Cistercian constitutions did not encourage the study of canon law, and the books in Robert Barker's collection were almost exclusively theological: the *Commentaries* of Dionysius the Carthusian, Hugh of St Victor's *Didascalicon*, the works of Jerome, Ambrose, Augustine, St Gregory, St Bernard, St Bonaventure, and St Thomas Aquinas. Unlike the Monk Bretton books, this collection contained nothing published as late as the sixteenth century, and, with the exception of Aeneas Silvii Senensis, *Poete epistolae*, very little showing the influence of the Italian Renaissance. If the library can on these circumstantial grounds be attributed to Byland Abbey, then it would seem that the monks until the end had shunned legal, historical, and new grammatical works, and continued to concentrate upon theology as their statutes prescribed.[18]

---

[16] Borthwick Archbp Reg. 31 fols 80v–11 (Scolaye).
[17] Borthwick Prob. Reg. 15 pt iii, fol 59v (Heptonstall).
[18] E. A. Bond, ed., *Chronica Monasterii de Melsa*, *RS*, 43, pt iii (1868), pp. lxxxii–c; A. Hoste, ed.,

The academic interests of the friars, who from the beginning had fostered far closer links with the universities than the Cistercians, appear to have been far less exclusively theological. In the late fourteenth century, the convent of the Austin Friars at York owned a library of 646 books, a third of which had been gathered together by a single friar, John Erghame. As well as the expected emphasis upon Bible commentaries and theological works, the Austin Friars owned books on grammar, rhetoric, and the arts (including numerous pagan classical authors), canon law, history, astronomy, arithmetic, music, and medicine apparently not available in the other Yorkshire libraries. The catalogue of the York Austin friars' library survived into the sixteenth century to be later incorporated into the library of Henry Saville of Banke and then that of Archbishop Ussher, and it seems reasonable to suppose that the Austin Friars had also retained their books until the surrender of their convent. If the Carmelite, Dominican and Franciscan houses in York had built up collections of even half this size, then the city at the beginning of the sixteenth century must have possessed an impressive number of medieval libraries which all seem to have been lost at the Reformation.[19]

Because of the poverty of their convents, few Yorkshire friars, apart from some priors, received pensions on the closure of their houses. The majority of friars in consequence had not much of importance to leave when they died. Of those whose goods are known, none mentioned specific books. Former monks, on the other hand, generally emerged into the secular world better provided for, and more information about their books can be gleaned from their wills. In the diocese of York there are around a hundred wills made by priests who had formerly been religious, although only about a quarter of these refer to books. Particularly for those former monks who died within twenty years of the Dissolution, it seems reasonable to assume that they had derived most if not all of their books from their former monastic libraries.

The books which may once have belonged to St Mary's Abbey in York appear to have been very traditional. In 1542, only three years after the surrender of his house, Richard Barwike bequeathed to the parish church of Escrick, the village to which he had retired, the *Vita Christi*, probably

---

Bibliotheca Aelrediana (Steenburg, 1962), pp. 149–76; C. R. Cheney, *Medieval Texts and Studies* (Oxford, 1973), pp. 328–45; Borthwick Peculiar wills, Driffield 1581 (Barker); cf., C. Cross, 'A Medieval Yorkshire Library', *Northern History*, 25 (1989).

[19] M. R. James, 'The Catalogue of the Library of the Augustinian Friars at York', *Fasciculus J. W. Clark dicatus* (Cambridge, 1909), pp. 2–96.

by Ludolphus, the Master of Stories (Peter Comestor), and the *Legenda sanctorum*, giving John Pott, a former fellow monk, a *Catholicon* and *Summa angelica*, and the *Chronicles of England* to Robert Brawshay. Six years later Thomas Singleton, who had gone on to become rector of Foston, assigned the oversight of his books, which he did not name, to the rector of Bulmer. Very much later, in 1573, Thomas Marse, who ended his life as vicar of East Markham, in Nottinghamshire, passed on to the vicar of Tuxford his five books of the 'Bible called Lyre', of which one was a concordance, works which almost certainly would have found a place in his former monastic library.[20]

Monk Bretton and St Mary's apart, the wills reveal little further about Benedictine libraries, but do contain rather more about possible Cistercian book collections. In addition to Edward Heptonstall's attempt to preserve the Kirkstall Abbey books as a whole, in 1565 Richard Hall, once of Rievaulx but then serving the cure of Lathom, left the vicar of Pocklington a fair great book called *Speculum morale Vincentii*, a medieval dictionary, *Ortus vocabularum*, Erasmus's *New Testament* in Latin, and a *New Testament* in English to Robert Riche, and seven of his best books to a priest, Sir John Brigham, before sharing the residue between the parson of Elvington, Sir Christopher Hustler, and Sir John Thompson, priest of Wheldrake. Four years later, in 1569, William Watson, alias Hyrde, then curate of High Melton, but once a monk of Meaux, assigned the residue of his books to his nephews after he had bequeathed Dionisius Carthusianus to the Dean of Doncaster, Mr Hudson, an unnamed modern work by Judocus Clicthoveus to his cousin, Sir Thomas Robinson, a Latin Bible to Sir Richard Furnes, two books of Haymo to the vicar of Brodsworth, and the *Constitutiones Provinciales* to William Motte.[21]

Books probably from Augustinian priories, about whose collections otherwise virtually nothing is known, feature fairly prominently in the wills of their former members. In 1550 Richard Lynne, once a canon of Kirkham, who remained to minister in the parish after the dissolution of his house, gave Erasmus's *New Testament* and 3s. 4d. to John, son of Robert Bulmer of Bulmer, whom he may have been teaching, a side gown, a tippet and Calepyne to a former fellow canon, James Parkinson, and a black silk hat, a book called Theophilactus (a writer of numerous biblical commentaries), and another book called Titilman (probably

[20] Borthwick Prob. Reg. 11, fol. 640r (Barwike); Prob. Reg. 13 pt i, fol. 443v (Singleton); Chancery wills 1573 (Marse).
[21] Borthwick Prob. Reg. 17, pt. iii, fols 538v–9r (Hall); Prob. Reg. 19 pt i, fols 52v–3r (Watson).

Titelmann's work on the Psalms) to a second former canon, James Blackett. Two years later Robert Collinson, who had previously been the prior of Haltemprice, but then described himself as a priest of Cottingham, set aside 'to them that will study to remain in the parish church of Cottingham for ever, one Latin Bible, the works of Origen, the *Morralles* of St Gregory, *Vita Christi afer Lodolphus*, the Master of the Sentences, the Master of Histories, *Sermones parati*, *Rationale divinorum* with other', requiring his executors to have made a little stand with shelves, and to place it under the vault where the Holy Cross stood, where there was a fair window and good light. This selection did not contain a single recent book, and must surely have come from the former priory. John Clarkson, a former canon of Guisborough, who stayed on as a curate in the parish after his priory's surrender, in 1556 left to a former fellow canon, Sir Richard Starre, various antiphoners, psalters, and a grayle, and 'such other that be of our use and service'. He returned to Sir John Steele three books, *Tractatus sacerdotalis*, *Aureum opus*, and *Speculum mortalium*, which he had borrowed and, in addition, gave him two of his own little books containing the New Testament. He intended George Tocottes to have a book of Haymo, which treated of the Epistles of St Paul, and any other book which his father, Mr Roger Tocottes, might 'think good and profitable and for the learning of the said George, his son.' Clarkson seems to have been teaching other boys in addition to George, for he required other unspecified books to be given to Robert and Rowland Rokebie before arranging for the residue of his books to be distributed by Roger Tocottes, Mr Oliver Grayson, another former canon of Guisborough, and Sir Richard Starre.[22]

Richard Hinchcliff included among the many books he had acquired from Monk Bretton 'musica monarchorum Johannis Norton Prior de Monte Gratie'. Otherwise very little can be deduced from wills about the contents of the libraries of Yorkshire Carthusian houses. As a 'clerk and sometime a professed brother of the monastery of Mount Grace and now abiding at Newcastle upon Tyne', Sir William Bee made his testament in March 1551, and as well as giving 'the father of Mount Grace' (presumably the former prior, John Wilson) two pairs of silver spectacles, he conferred upon another brother of the house, Leonard Hall, his cloak, his

[22] Borthwick Prob. Reg. 13, pt i, fol 724r–v (Lynne); Prob. Reg. 13, pt ii, fols 951v–2r (Collinson); Prob. Reg. 15, pt i, fols 242v–3r (Clarkson); a Psalter from Guisborough Priory is now in the Bodleian Library, while Douai Abbey possesses a breviary and missal from the same house, N. R. Ker, *Medieval Libraries of Great Britain* (London, 1964), p. 94.

tawny tippet, and all his books, both at Newcastle and Wakefield, without mentioning their titles. Ralph Maleverer, the erstwhile prior of Hull, revealed slightly more about his library when he composed his will in 1551. Maleverer seems to have studied at Cambridge in 1517 before he joined his Order. At his death he left his servant, Richard Baker, 40s. 'to help him to his learning', 5s. to Sir William Browne, 'late one of my breder', one of his books called *Cronica Cronicarum* to the parson of Everingham, his law books to his cousin, Thomas Thweng, and all the rest of his books, not specified, to young William Robinson and to William Remington, another former Hull Carthusian.[23]

These bequests create an overwhelming impression of intellectual conservatism. Apart from a sprinkling of widely disseminated Renaissance textbooks and dictionaries, which former monks and friars may in any case have bought after the Dissolution in order to earn a living by teaching, neither they nor, it seems, their monasteries appear to have made any great effort to obtain recent theological books, even less works of a controversial nature, and this at a time when, in 1528, the library of the Chancellor of York Minster, in addition to all its medieval books, contained Erasmus, *Paraphrases in libros Novi Testamenti*, Thomas More, *Utopia*, and three tracts of John Fisher, Bishop of Rochester, confuting Luther. Although some of the larger Yorkshire foundations may have been dispatching some of their young monks to the universities, unlike Evesham Abbey, which in Robert Joseph could boast a humanist of some distinction, they do not seem to have been exerting themselves to keep abreast of Renaissance scholarship.[24]

Based as it needs must be on very tenuous evidence, any evaluation of the quality of learning among the religious in sixteenth-century Yorkshire must be tentative in the extreme. Since in the 1530s some of the monks and friars themselves were merely in the process of taking sides for or against Reformation innovations, it is unfair to make a judgement upon the contents of their libraries before these changes had come fully into effect. Had some of the monasteries been permitted to continue, then they might well have updated their books, if only because of the require-

[23] 'Chartularies of Monk Bretton', *YAS RS*, 66, p. 7; J. Raine, ed., *Wills and Inventories I*, Surtees Society, 2 (1835), pp. 134–6; Borthwick Prob. Reg. 13, pt ii, fols 720v–1r (Maleverer); C. B. Rowntree, 'Studies in Carthusian History in later Medieval England' (York D.Phil. thesis, 1981), pp. 153, 520.
[24] *York Clergy Wills 1520–1600: I The Minster Clergy*, Borthwick Texts and Calendars (York, 1984), pp. 17–22; H. Aveling and W. A. Pantin, eds, *The Letter Book of Robert Joseph*, Oxford Historical Society, new series 19 (1967).

ments of theological debate. Nor should it be assumed that all Yorkshire houses would have rallied to the defence of the old religion, though it seems likely that most would have taken the conservative side. Despite the hostility of his canons, had he been given his head, Robert Ferrar would have converted Nostell into a bastion of Protestantism, and Robert Holgate might well have tried to follow his lead at Watton. What, however, united Yorkshire religious of very different shades of belief was their respect for their books. When they departed from their abbey, the Cistercians of Roche may have accidentally left manuals lying around in the church, which the local people then took away to repair their wagons, but neither they nor any other northern monks seem to have dreamt of staging a deliberate rejection of scholasticism, such as occurred at New College, in Oxford. Whatever their political sympathies, in Yorkshire the monks and friars retained a more balanced appreciation of their medieval heritage.[25]

University of York

[25] A. G. Dickens, ed., *Tudor Treatises*, *YAS RS*, 125 (1959), pp. 123–5; *LP*, 9, no. 350.

THE BATTLE OF FINSBURY FIELD
AND ITS WIDER CONTEXT

by A. G. DICKENS

ON 4 March 1554 some hundreds of London schoolboys fought a mock battle on Finsbury Field outside the northern wall of the city. Boys have always gratified their innate romanticism by playing at war, yet this incident, organized between several schools, was overtly political and implicitly religious in character. It almost resulted in tragedy, and, though scarcely noticed by historians,[1] it does not fail to throw light upon London society and opinion during a major crisis of Tudor history. The present essay aims to discuss the factual evidence and its sources; thereafter to clarify the broader context and significance of the affair by briefer reference to a few comparable events which marked the Reformation struggle elsewhere. The London battle relates closely to two events in the reign of Mary Tudor: her marriage with Philip of Spain and the dangerous Kentish rebellion led by the younger Sir Thomas Wyatt. The latter's objectives were to seize the government, prevent the marriage, and, in all probability, to place the Princess Elizabeth on the throne as the figurehead of a Protestant regime in Church and State. While Wyatt himself showed few signs of evangelical piety, the notion of a merely political revolt can no longer be maintained. Professor Malcolm R. Thorp has recently examined in detail the lives of all the numerous known leaders, and has proved that in almost every case they display clear records of Protestant conviction.[2] It is, moreover, common knowledge that Kent, with its exceptionally large Protestant population, provided at this moment the best possible recruiting-area in England for an attack upon the Catholic government.[3] Though the London militia treasonably went over to Wyatt, the magnates with their retinues and associates rallied around the legal sovereign. Denied boats and bridges near the capital, Wyatt finally crossed the Thames at Kingston, but then

---

[1] It was in fact mentioned by J. A. Froude, *History of England* (London, 1870), 6, pp. 375–6, as well as by P. F. Tytler, *England under the Reigns of Edward VI and Mary* (London, 1839), p. 330.

[2] M. R. Thorp, 'Religion and the Wyatt Rebellion of 1554', *Church History*, 47 (1978), pp. 363–80.

[3] P. Clark, *English Provincial Society . . . Religion, Politics and Society in Kent, 1500–1640* (Hassocks, 1977), esp. pp. 34–107.

failed to enter London from the west. By 8 February 1554 his movement had collapsed, though his execution did not occur until 11 April.

Our chief narrator of the sequel at Finsbury was the French diplomat François de Noailles, an attractive clerical diplomat, soon to become Bishop of Dax and to serve as French ambassador at Venice and with the Sultan. In 1554, being then thirty-five years of age, he was present in London, assisting his elder brother Antoine, ambassador of France to the Court of St James. Unlike Antoine, François found England tolerably pleasant, but in 1554 neither of them could remain an objective spectator of the English political scene. In sharp rivalry with the able imperial ambassador Simon Renard—a confidant of Queen Mary, and her main link with the Emperor Charles and his son Philip—the brothers Noailles saw the interests of France gravely threatened by the proposed entry of England into the ever-expanding Habsburg confederacy. This classic confrontation in London has been admirably described by E. Harris Harbison in his work *Rival Ambassadors at the Court of Queen Mary*.[4] On 12 March François sent—by a Scottish gentleman—a report to Anne, Duc de Montmonrency, Constable of France, in which the following passage occurs. Here I translate it rather freely, the French text being readily available as printed in 1763 by the Abbé Vertot from the Noailles family archives.

> You have learned how the Estates of this country, having heard of the extreme desire of their Queen to call a foreigner to the government of this kingdom, have not ceased to try all means of hindering this design, well foreseeing that it would be the total ruin of their freedoms and liberties. On that account they have made several remonstrances and requests, both particular and general, not forgetting to allege the ancient custom of the country, the will of the late King Henry her Father, and even the oath and promise she made to them when they went to the farthest parts of Norfolk, in order to give her the crown. All this has not availed to change her from her first opinions, and has been the reason why those with the boldest hearts, fearing this tyranny, have sought their remedy by force. Nevertheless, this has not succeeded as they hoped, God having perhaps reserved it for other times and other methods.
>
> Thence she has become so exalted and proud, that she has attributed this victory [over Wyatt] only to her own prudence,

---

[4] (Princeton, 1940; repr., Freeport, NY, 1970.) On François de Noailles, see pp. 306–8, 334–5.

without giving the glory to whom it belongs. And on this occasion it has happened that, since she has scorned and rejected the advice of the wisest and best advised, God has caused her to be warned by the children, who, being last Monday assembled from several schools to the number of two or three hundred, divided themselves into two sides [*en deulx troupes*], one of which they called the army of the King and of M. Wiat, the other that of the Prince of Spain and the Queen of England. These immediately fought one another with such hatred and fury that the battle was long and far too cruel for their age, in such a manner that it could come to an end only with the capture of the Prince of Spain, who was suddenly led to the gibbet by those on the side of the King and M. Wiat. And unless some men had prov-identially [*tout à propoz*] run up, they would have strangled him. This can be clearly ascertained by the marks which he has—and will have for a long time to come—on his neck.

This has so displeased the Queen that the youngest [boys] of this gathering could not be spared the whip, or the bigger [ones] from being put in prison, where she has under guard a goodly number. It is said that she wishes that one of them shoud be sacrificed for all the people [*sacrifié pour tout le peuple*]. By this you can see how welcome the Prince of Spain will be to this country, since the children place him on the gibbet.[5]

What of the other sources? As might be anticipated, one of these occurs in a despatch to the Emperor from the indefatigable Simon Renard. On this matter he is for once brief. Writing on 9 March, he relates that 300 children gathered together in a field, divided into two bands and fought out the quarrel of the Queen against Wyatt. Several on both sides were wounded, and most of them have been arrested and shut up in the Guild-hall.[6] As a Marian partisan, Renard cannot draw the same critical moral as that of Noailles. He adds cheerfully that a certain alderman of London has just made in the Guildhall such an able, vehement, and convincing speech, persuading men to obey God, religion, justice, and the Queen, that several persons who had strayed from the right path have been rescued from their errors and heresies.

A third informant is the diarist—apparently an official of the Royal Mint—who compiled the so-called *Chronicle of Queen Jane and Two Years of*

---

[5] Translated from *Ambassades de Messieurs de Noailles en Angleterre*, ed. A. Vertot and C. Villaret, 5 vols (Leiden, 1763), 3, pp. 128–30.
[6] *CalSP, Spanish*, 12, p. 146. Cf. Tytler, *Reigns of Edward VI and Mary*, p. 331.

Queen Mary. Mistaking the date of the battle, he wrote: 'the vjth of Marche certayn boyes, some toke Wyates parte and some the Queenes, and made a combacte [*sic*] in the feldes, &c.'[7] In justice to this often useful reporter, one should not fail to obseve that on an earlier page of his diary he provides another graphic instance of the hostility of the Londoners, including the schoolboys, toward the preparations for the Queen's proposed marriage. He had in fact written that on the previous 2 January, when Count Egmont and other representatives of Philip arrived in London, 'the people, nothing rejoysing, held downe their heddes sorrowfully', adding that 'the day before his [Egmont's] coming in [that is, 1 January], as his retynew and harbengers came ryding through London, the boyes pelted at theym with snowballes, so hatfull was the sight of their coming in to theym.'[8] Thus it would appear that even before the end of 1553 popular resentment in the capital had fully communicated itself to many of the young.

Having read the above passages, the present writer felt that these events should have left some traces in the manuscript archives of the city, and he was not disappointed. At the Corporation of London Record Office the voluminous Repositories of the Court of Alderman (301 volumes from 1495 to 1948) yielded two relevant entries, each with the marginal heading 'Boyes'. The first of these, dated 5 March, 1 Mary, reads:

> Item yt was agryed that Mr Alderman Hynde should cause certayne of the boyes that foughte yesterday in Fynnesbery felde to be apprehendid if he coulde and to be broughte hyther to morowe, that further knowledge maye be had of the number of theym.[9]

Hence this entry is the one which authoritatively provides the correct date of the event itself: 4 March. The second entry is dated 6 March:

> Item the ponyshmente and correccyon of the lewde boyes that lately made certayne unlawfull assembles and conflyctes in Fynnesbery felde and other places withoute the Cytie was holy referred to my m[aste]rs thalderman of the wardes where they do dwell.[10]

It is not made clear how many offenders had been rounded up, or whether—as would seem unlikely—that within twenty-four hours or less

---

[7] *Chronicle of Queen Jane*, ed. J. G. Nichols, *PCS*, os, 48 (1850), p. 67.

[8] Ibid., p. 34.

[9] Corporation of London Record Office, Court of Aldermen, Rep. 13, fol. 131.

[10] Ibid., fol. 132b.

Alderman Hynde had accomplished the feat alone. Whatever Renard supposed, there were no prisons at Guildhall, and the boys were presumably incarcerated at the sheriffs' counters or in some other city gaol. Augustine Hynde, Master of the Clothworkers' Company in 1545, and Sheriff in 1550, is a familiar figure to historians of mid-Tudor London. In 1546 he had been elected as Alderman for Farringdon Ward Without, and had then served for Cripplegate Ward from 1547.[11] His ward was the nearest to Finsbury Field; hence, no doubt, the task was assigned to him. We might well suppose that he may have been glad to display his conformity and zeal on this occasion. In 1550, along with two partners, he had purchased former monastic lands with the immense value of £18,744,[12] and like many others, he must have sensed a probability that the pious Queen might resume at least a part of such lands in order to restore and re-endow some of the monasteries. In the event, on the following 10 August death relieved him of such anxieties, this date having been inscribed on his monument in the church of St Peter Cheap, since destroyed.[13] Indeed, anxiety must to some extent have affected most of the city magistrates, since the Queen and the Catholic party had become well aware of the extent to which they had hitherto favoured the Protestant cause. When, in 1557, Cardinal Pole preached to them, he bluntly recalled their former heresy and anti-clericalism, adjuring them to take example from Sir Thomas More, Bishop Fisher, and the Carthusians, and henceforth to atone by service and loyalty to the Church.[14]

At this point, we may leave the unfortunate boys as they receive their beating probably under the stern eyes of their ward-aldermen, and conceivably at the hands of professional experts in the art of flagellation: their own schoolmasters. Yet before proceeding to general conclusions, several more circumstantial aspects need some clarification. Regarding the actual site of the battle, we are fortunate to have available a good contemporary bird's-eye view of what might be called the 'north London' of Tudor times. There have survived two copper plates, which have been

[11] J. J. Baddeley, *The Aldermen of Cripplegate Ward* (London, 1900), p. 45; A. B. Beaven, *Aldermen of the City of London*, 2 (London, 1913), p. 32. Concerning this passage I am grateful for the expert advice of Dr Caroline Barron.

[12] T. H. Swales, 'The redistribution of the monastic lands in Norfolk at the Dissolution', *Norfolk Archaeology*, 34 (1966), p. 40.

[13] Baddeley, *Aldermen*. *The Diary of Henry Machyn*, ed. J. G. Nichols, PCS, os, 42 (1848), p. 67, describes his lavish funeral, noting his proximity to the office of Mayor.

[14] Strype, *Memorials*, 3, pt ii, pp. 482–510.

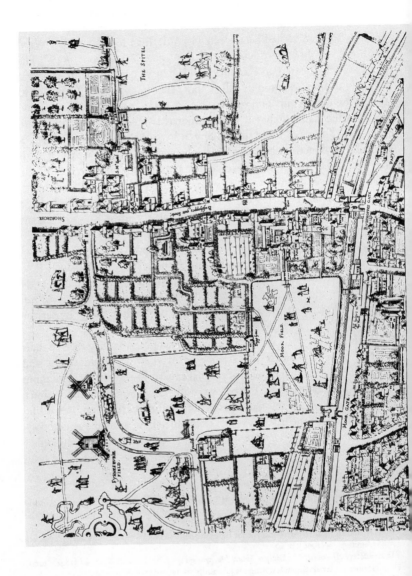

dated as neither later than 1559 nor earlier than 1547.[15] One of these enables us to set the scene with unusual accuracy, being furnished with human figures and the appropriate place-names (see plate 1). Easily may we envisage the boys leaving the walled city by 'Moor Gate' and walking northward by a fenced road along the western edge of 'Moor Field', where our view shows cloth-workers pegging and stretching (tenting) their cloths upon the grass. Passing the manor house 'Fynnesbury Courte', the boys would diverge leftward from the road and enter 'Fynnesburie Field', where we see men, women, children, and animals. Several men are carrying bows or actually shooting, while another man appears to be waving a flag. The field is dominated by two wooden windmills, though in fact there appear to have been four, and later as many as six.[16] A path crosses the grass from east to west, bridging a small stream. Here, then, was a large open space favoured for field sports, and doubtless very familiar to the boys, who would readily choose it as the nearest suitable area on which to stage a mock battle. Already in the twelfth century, the young men of London had been accustomed to engage in warlike exercises, violent games, and winter sports within this same area.[17]

The boys' homes and schools lay not far away within the close-packed square mile of the city. Within easy walking distance of Finsbury were Christ's Hospital in Newgate Street, St Anthony's in Threadneedle Street, St Peter's in Cornhill, St Thomas Acon in West Cheap, and, of course, St Paul's in the Cathedral Close.[18] Participation from Westminster School would seem less likely, though a Tudor boy would have thought little of walking even that distance. The Merchant Taylors' School cannot, however, figure on our list, since it was founded seven years later. Yet how did hundreds of boys escape from their masters and abscond to Finsbury for an organized event? For once, the answer proves surprisingly simple,

[15] Reproduced by S. P. Marks, *The Map of Mid-Sixteenth Century London*, London Topographical Society Publication, 100 (1964), plate I.
[16] On the windmills see *A Survey of London by John Stow*, ed. C. L. Kingsford, 2 vols (Oxford, 1908), 2, p. 370.
[17] William fitz Stephen, *Description of the City of London* (1170–83): the passage is translated, e.g., D. C. Douglas and G. W. Greenaway, eds, *EHD*, 2, 2nd edn (1981), pp. 1027–9.
[18] Ibid., 1, pp. 71–5, together with the references to individual schools given in Index II.

Plate 1 (*opposite*) Copper-engraved Large-scale Map of Sixteenth-century London. Two of the original copper plates have survived, of which this is the northern one, extending from Finsbury Field to south of Moorgate. It is not later than 1559, and not earlier than 1547. This plate is in the London Museum; the other is in private possession. (Stephen Powys Marks, *The Map of Mid-Sixteenth Century London* [London Topographical Society, 1966])

when we recall that the correct date is 4 March, and that the calendar for 1554 shows this date as falling on a Sunday, the one day in the week when the boys must have been free from school and—presumably after noon—free also from church attendance.

Topography apart, a more intricate problem arises from one sentence of the report by Noailles. To whom did he refer when he wrote that the party opposed to Philip and Mary was led by a boy representing 'the King', in addition to the impersonator of Wyatt? Rumours to the effect that Edward VI was still alive circulated in London at this time, and obviously attracted Protestant and anti-Spanish partisans. From time to time the story revived even during the reign of Elizabeth. On 12 November 1553 three men came before the Privy Council on the charge that they had spread such 'lewde reportes'. Again, on 12 January 1554, a man employed at the Wardrobe of Robes was sent by the Council for the same offence to the Fleet Prison, pending further inquiries.[19] It is likely enough that even boys who doubted the truth of these rumours would have been prepared to accept them for the purposes of this exercise. That someone else was invested with the royal part seems not quite impossible. This could hardly have been Guilford Dudley, Queen Jane's husband—to whom she had, in fact, denied the title of king—since on 12 February his execution had undeniably occurred. Yet still very much alive, there remained in the Tower a more possible candidate. This was Edward Courtenay, the still youthful Earl of Devonshire, whose grandmother had been Catherine, younger daughter of Edward IV, and sister-in-law of Henry VII.[20] In consequence of his father's conviction and execution for treason in 1538, this potential claimant to the throne had spent most of his short life in prison, but his Devon and Cornwall adherents had endeavoured to support Wyatt, while he himself had started to make regal gestures, even obliging visitors to kneel in his presence. More important, he had been suggested as a possible husband for Queen Mary, and later for the Princess Elizabeth, in which latter case London might readily have envisaged the pair as future Protestant monarchs. In 1555 Courtenay was to receive permission to leave the Tower and travel abroad, only to die at Padua the following year. Those of the disloyal populace who did not accept the survival of Edward VI in 1554 might conceivably have adopted Courtenay as an anti-

19 Margaret E. Cornford, 'A Legend Concerning Edward VI', *EHR*, 23 (1908), pp. 286–90; *APC*, 1552–4, pp. 363, 383–4.
20 On this theme see A. F. Pollard, *Political History of England*, 6 (London, 1929), pp. 105–7, 115–17, 161; *DNB*, 4, pp. 1260–7. On Wyatt's personal relations with Courtenay, see *DNB*, 21, pp. 1102–4.

Marian 'king', though this would seem by far the less convincing explanation of the passage.

Another sentence of Noailles may deserve a brief glance, though hardly more. Did the Queen seriously express a wish that one of the miscreants should be 'sacrificed for all the people'? By this odd phrase it was presumably meant that the execution of a young leader might serve the community by deterring further disastrous activities. It seems very credible that the insult offered by proxy to Philip aroused her deep anger. Moreover, the execution of a boy did not mean then what it would mean today. The executions which followed the Evil May Day riots in 1517 included 'some men, some laddes, some chyldren of xiij yere', and were accompanied by 'great mournyng of fathers and frendes', especially as the Knight Marshal, Lord Edmund Howard, 'showed no mercy but extreme cruelty to the poore youngelinges in their execution.'[21] Even so, the Queen and her advisers would scarcely have been so imprudent as to stage the execution of a representative schoolboy in the politically unstable London of those days. The evidence of Noailles on this point is second-hand and not to be cited as evidence of Mary's inhumanity. In her wrath, she may well have uttered incautiously a thought which she had no settled intention to translate into a deed.

As Dr Brigden has shown in her highly important article 'Youth and the English Reformation',[22] many apprentices and young serving-men had long been virulently anticlerical, directing gross ridicule and even physical attacks upon inoffensive clergy. As early as 1543, a priest walking in London 'was lewdely sett uppon and evell entreted' by a party of 'pretenses and mennes servantes which had played at fute ball.'[23] Nevertheless, the Finsbury 'battle' does not bear the marks of an apprentice riot. Here we seem to encounter a different mentality. Apprentices commonly came from the provinces in their late teens, and a high proportion must have reached their mid-twenties by the time they completed their seven-year apprenticeships.[24] All accounts of the Finsbury affair mention 'boyes'

---

[21] *Edward Hall's Chronicle* (1809), p. 590. In the second edn of 1550 (*The Union of the Two Noble Families*, etc.) see the section on Henry VIII, fol. lxii. On such executions, see Keith Thomas, 'Age and Authority in Early Modern England', *PBA*, 62 (1976), pp. 219–20.
[22] Susan Brigden, 'Youth and the English Reformation', *PaP*, 95 (1982), pp. 37–67.
[23] Ibid., p. 56.
[24] G. D. Ramsay, 'The Recruitment and Fortunes of Some London Freemen in the Mid-Sixteenth Century', *EcHR*, ser. 2, 31 (1978), pp. 526–40. On the geographical origins of London apprentices, see J. Wareing in *Journal of Historical Geography*, 6 (1980), pp. 241–8. For biographies of Protestant apprentices, see J. Fines, *A Biographical Register of Early English Protestants* (1981), s.v. Beale, Boggens, Cornet, Davis, Gough, Hinshaw, Hodgesby, Hover,

or 'children', and never refer to apprentices. Moreover, they came from 'several schools' and included both older and younger pupils, though none is likely to have exceeded seventeen or eighteen years of age.[25] Perhaps inspired by their intensively Latin education, including the inevitable military passages of Caesar and Livy, they had (in our terminology) divided themselves into supranational Catholics, and patriotic Protestants aware of the martial achievements of their own countrymen. The latter faction, judging by its victory and capture of 'the Prince of Spain', and by the London evidence in general, was probably the more numerous. That many were hurt shows that the animosity went well beyond that of mere horseplay, as indeed Noailles clearly records. Planning a mock battle, with commanders drawn from contemporary politics, was not, as we shall observe, limited to England. We are here encountering a metropolitan group of grammar schools, uniquely placed, and familiar to us from some graphic passages of John Stow's *Survey of London*. In an idiom more sophisticated than those of xenophobic apprentices and anticlerical football gangs, London schoolboys could also be aggressive, competitive, and moved by inter-school rivalries. That such rivalries were involved would seem inevitable, and the evidence gives more than a hint to that effect. Stow describes their grammatical disputations, witnessed by him in St Bartholomew's churchyard, Smithfield. Though scholastic disputation had been discontinued, 'the arguing of the Schoole boyes about the principles of Grammer [had] beene continued even till our time.' In these formal contests, the boys of St Anthony's, Thomas More's old school, were regarded as the best scholars and won most prizes. Nevertheless, adds our informant:

> the schollers of Paules, meeting with them of St Anthonies, would call them Antonie pigs and they againe would call the other[s] pigeons of Paules, because many pigions were bred in Paules Church, and Saint Anthonie was always figured with a pigge following him: and mindfull of the former usage [boys] did for a long season disorderly in the open streets provoke one another with *Salve tu quoque, placet tibi mecum disputare, placet?* and so proceeding from this to questions in Grammar, they usually fall from wordes, to blowes, with

---

Hunter, Leaf, Lincoln, Smith, Tudson, Vivian, Wilmost. Of similar age were the 54 Protestant exiles classed as 'students' and listed in Christina H. Garrett, *The Marian Exiles* (Cambridge, 1938).

[25] Jo Ann H. Moran, *The Growth of English Schooling 1340–1548* (Princeton, 1985), pp. 64–70; N. Orme, *English Schools in the Middle Ages* (London, 1973), p. 134.

their Satchels full of bookes, many times in great heaps that they troubled the streets, and passengers: so that finally they were restrained with the decay of Saint Anthonies schoole.[26]

In such passages as this we see a likely mental background of the battle of Finsbury, even though tempers finally got out of control, having been from the first enmeshed in those religious and political issues which at this time were vividly engaging the emotions of Londoners. Another obvious link about to occur in the careers of many of these boys was the one existing between their schools and the numerous law students not far distant at the Inns of Court. These students formed a notable Protestant group in mid-Tudor London, and Stow specifically states that many had come up directly from grammar schools.

Here then we witness a special configuration of youth; but did it then have English parallels in the provincial schools? The present writer is at present aware of only one provincial example, and of all unexpected places at Bodmin, in Cornwall, over 230 miles from London. Nevertheless, similar events on a smaller scale may have been common, yet unrecorded. After all, the absence of newspapers dooms us to a relative ignorance of innumerable minor events in Tudor local history! This Bodmin affair occurred in the year 1548, amid a half-Celtic Cornish society, some members of which in the rebellion of 1549 protested that they did not understand English, and hence rejected Archbishop Cranmer's First Prayer Book. Yet it would now seem misleading to name the western rising of 1549 by its traditional label, the 'Prayer Book Rebellion', since the trouble was in large part aroused and enhanced by social and economic grievances, not to mention a host of family feuds and local rivalries.[27] At Bodmin the townsmen's long tradition of struggle against their overlords, the priors, attained an ugly climax during the last decade of the priory, when the town submitted petitions to Henry VIII and Thomas Cromwell, protesting most bitterly against the misdeeds of Prior Vivian and his violent henchmen.[28] These people had little reason to love the old ecclesiastical regime! Regarding the youth problem at Bodmin, our sole source of information is that readable Cornish

---

[26] Stow, ed. Kingsford, 1, p. 75. Bale uses 'pigeons' to mean the courtesans who could be encountered inside St Pauls!

[27] Joyce Youings, 'The South-Western Rebellion of 1549', *Southern History*, 1 (1979), pp. 92–122; A. L. Rowse, *Tudor Cornwall* (London, 1941), chs 11, 12, 15; R. Whiting, *The Reformation in the South-West of England* (Exeter Ph.D. thesis, 1977), esp. pp. 293–8.

[28] For surviving documents from the town archives, see J. Wallis, *The Bodmin Register* (Bodmin, 1827–38), pp. 293–312.

antiquary, Richard Carew of Antony (1555–1620), whose *Survey of Cornwall* (1602) serves that county as Stow serves London. In recalling the major revolt of 1549, Carew points out that a presage ('afore-halsening') of the trouble had occurred in the previous year in the conflicts of the boys of the grammar school at Bodmin. He had heard the story long afterwards, and directly from some of the participants.

> I should perhaps have forgotten the free schools here, maintayned by her Maiesty's liberalitie, were I not put in mind thereof through afore-halsening of this rebellion, by an action of the schollers, which I will report from some of their owne mouthes. About a yeare before this sturre was raysed, the schollers, who accustomably divide themselves for better exploiting their pastimes, grewe therethrough into two factions; the one whereof, they called the olde religion; the other the new. This once begunne was prosecuted amongst them in all exercises, and, now and then, handled with some eagernesse and roughnes, each partie knowing, and still keeping the same companions and Captaine. At last one of the boyes converted the spill of an old candelsticke to a gunne, charged it with powder and a stone, and (through mischance, or ungraciousnesse) therewith killed a calfe; whereupon the owner complayned, the master whipped, and the division ended. By such tokens, sometimes wonderfull, sometimes ridiculous, doth God at his pleasure foreshewe future accidents: as in the Planets, before the battel at Thrasimenus, between Hannibal and the Romans, by the fighting together of the Sunne and Moone.[29]

At this point Carew develops his presage theory by a wealth of classical allusions; but then, in a passage unhappily omitted from the modern edition, he produces some parallel events far more closely related to our present subject. The two of most interest are drawn from the French Wars of Religion. From his study of French history in the pages of the Portuguese Dominican José Teixeira (d. 1604), who had spent many years in France, Carew derived a comparable incident, which had become linked with the death of Louis, Prince of Condé, the famous Huguenot leader. Saintes, a cathedral city and pilgrimage-centre, diverged from the

[29] Richard Carew, *The Survey of Cornwall* (London, 1602), fols 124–5. The chantry certificates of 1548 give Nicholas Tapsell (57) as schoolmaster, also chantry priest in the parish church. They call the people of Bodmin (2,000 communicants) 'very ignorant'. They do not praise Tapsell's ability to teach Latin (though so doing in regard to the master at Launceston) and give no detail on the academic status or size of the school. Cf. L. S. Snell, *Documents towards a History of the Reformation in Cornwall*, no. 1, *The Chantry Certificates* (Exeter, 1953), pp. 10–12.

neighbouring merchant cities of La Rochelle and Saint Jean by remaining Catholic when they embraced Protestantism. It did, however, experience a brief but very destructive Huguenot occupation in 1568. The following year the young people of Saintes, from nine to twenty-two years of age, assembled and chose from their ranks impersonators of the rival leaders about to fight the Battle of Jarnac—Louis, Prince of Condé, and 'Monsieur', by which title the French designated the eldest brother of a reigning monarch. In 1569 this was the brother of Charles IX: Henry, Duke of Anjou, later Henry III, who gained the victory even as his Hugenot rival Condé was fatally shot. Meanwhile, between the divided and embattled young people at Saintes there had arisen a struggle more deadly than those of London or Bodmin.

> For three dayes space, they violently assaulted each other, with stones, clubs, and other weapons, until at last it grewe to Pistoles: by one of which, the imaginary Prince received a quelling wound in his head, about 10 a clock in the morning: the very howre (saith this Portugall Confessour) that the Prince himselfe, by a like shot was slaughtered.

In the same source, and from a nearby historical background, Carew was to discover

> a semblance chaunce, somewhat before the siege of Rochell, 1572, where, some of the boyes banded themselves, as for the Maior, and others for the King; who after 6 dayes skirmishing, at last made a composition, and departed: even as that siege endured six moneths, and finally brake up in a peace.[30]

Father Teixeira acquired most fame as a patriotic champion of Portugal against its forcible acquisition by Philip II in 1580, but in addition to these writings he occupied much of his long exile in France in compiling several genealogical-historical works centred upon the great families of that country. Apart from mentioning his name, Richard Carew gave no references; but after a rather tedious perusal of Teixeira's French books, the present writer located the source of the above quotations in a chapter concerning Louis, Prince of Condé, which occurs in a minor work (dated 1598) on the family of Bourbon.[31] These stories about Saintes and La

---

[30] Ibid., fols 125–6.
[31] *Rerum ab Henrici Borbonii Franciae Protoprincipis Majoribus Gestarum Epitome* ... (Paris, 1598), pp. 107–10. The British Library has a copy: 521 a 36(1).

Rochelle Carew took with fair exactitude from Teixeira, who incidentally claims that he himself got this information from an honest eye-witness: 'Haec mihi narravit vir quidem probus et verus: quique mihi ipsi se hujusce rei occulatum testem fuisse multis verbis confirmavit.' It emerges that Carew took even his beliefs in the supposed historical omens from 'this Portugall confessour', who, in fact, appears the marginally less super-stitious of the pair. At all events, Teixeira freely admits that some people did not swallow the story that the youth died at exactly the same time as the Prince whom he impersonated. Indeed, these same sceptics main-tained that he was shot six days before the Prince encountered a similar fate!

Richard Carew's third modern 'parallel' to the Bodmin affair seems less appropriate, even though it also relates to a politico-religious conflict. This story concerns an eccentric Turkish governor in Greece, who in 1594 assembled about 500 Turkish boys between eleven and fourteen years of age. These he divided into two troops, terming the one Christian, the other Turkish, and ordering the former to call upon Jesus, the latter upon Allah. In the end the 'Turks' fled, and what Carew called 'the Jesus party' won the victory.

These remarkable parallels by no means exhausted the erudition of the Cornish antiquary. From Dion Cassius he had already recalled that the Roman boys divided themselves between Pompey and Caesar, spontaneously fighting in unarmed combat; and so did their successors between Octavius and Mark Antony. Again Carew relates how the Samnite youths fought among themselves under leaders playing the parts of Justinian's general Belisarius and that of his adversary Vitiges, King of the Goths. All these passages help us to establish a pattern, showing how the notion of ritual combat between young people, sometimes organized under individual leaders impersonating con-temporary or historical figures, was far from strange to sixteenth-cen-tury students of the classics. Because it seems impossible that the French examples of 1569 and 1572 could have been imitations of our English examples of 1548 and 1554, we seem bound to relate all four to some more widely diffuse models, possibly owing much to these three exam-ples adduced by Carew from the histories of Rome and Byzantium. Doubting nevertheless whether these passages would have figured in the normal programmes of grammar-school boys, one begins to wonder whether our young English combatants had been deliberately inspired by partisan schoolmasters, a considerable number of whom are known to have been embroiled in the struggles of the English Reformation, and mostly on the Protestant side.[32] On this issue a definitive answer seems unlikely to emerge, even though robust partisanships may often have arisen elsewhere in England, but with negligible chances of surviving in records still available. Such activities could quite possibly have tempted teachers who wanted to stage public demonstrations, while avoiding the dire penalties likely to be incurred by adult participation. All in all, the several parallels, ancient and contemporary, added by Teixeira and Carew are of major significance for our enquiry, since they establish a wider, Continental contest for the events in London and Bodmin.

It also becomes apparent that the London boys passionately reflected the political and religious convictions of their elders. Even at anticlerical Bodmin, this juvenile contest could not have occurred, had the vast majority of Cornish parents really adhered to the ultra-conservative stereotype imposed upon Cornwall by most historians (though not by Dr Rowse!) until fairly recent years. Nevertheless, for us, the mid-Tudor youth should not remain mere reflectors, since collectively they exercised a special function in our national history. Though by no means among the pioneers of the English Reformation, they belonged to that generation of Londoners which—by action or inaction—decided the Protestant preponderance beyond serious doubt. The child was father to the man: a mere decade later the boys who fought at Finsbury had become Elizabethans of the capital city, and had in most cases already adapted themselves to the Elizabethan Settlement in Church and State.

Finally, where should we locate these half-symbolic battles amid the complex currents of sixteenth-century mental history? What aspects of the period do they represent, over and above the juvenile yet timeless theme of cowboys versus Indians? As we have seen, they clearly relate to the contemporary religious and political conflicts of the adult world. Conversely, they also reflect that clash between age-groups already documented as an important theme in Reformation England and in France during the Wars of Religion.[33] Yet again, we have tentatively noticed the possible influence exerted by such models as those observed

[32] On mid-Tudor Protestant schoolmasters in London and elsewhere, see Brigden, 'Youth', pp. 59–60; Fines, *Biographical Register*, 2, s.v. Bland, Cobbe, Cole, Cox, Forde, Henshaw, Hopkins, Lome, Marsh, Nowell, Palmer, Patenson, Radcliffe, Senes, Talbot, Traheron, Tyndale, Twyne, Udall.

[33] For a summary of youth-participation in France see N. Z. Davis, 'The rites of violence: religious riot in sixteenth century France', *PaP*, 59 (1973), pp. 87–8. For several anti-Spanish 'games' by 'children' in the Netherlands, c.1565–81, see G. Parker, *The Dutch Revolt* (London, edn 1988), pp. 80, 130, 189, 303, n. 18.

by Richard Carew in ancient history, models possibly cultivated by partisan schoolmasters. These factors may not tell the whole story, and imaginative social historians may well seek to probe further in the light of recent emphases. For example, several explorers of *mentalités* have stressed that temporary relaxation of ecclesiastical pressures, that remarkable licence allowed—especially to the young—by the medieval Church during certain feasts and periods of carnival. Even more prominently in Germany than in France or England, the youth savoured with relish the ephemeral joys of a world temporarily turned upside-down. Amid this international farrago of mock-monarchs, boy-bishops, and carnivalesque cardinals, can we reserve a modest place for mock-battles with juvenile generals?

As with the religious drama, the satirical idioms and the spirit of carnival certainly overflowed from late medieval society into that of the Reformation. With regard to war-torn France, this situation has been discussed in erudite detail by Janine Estebe and Natalie Zemon Davis.[34] Meanwhile, R. W. Scribner has co-ordinated and expanded a tradition of research on the theatrical representation of religion, the anticlerical masquerade, the near-blasphemous satire, which all continued to bulk large in Luther's Germany.[35] Throughout western Europe there survived an imaginative populace with a marked tendency to dramatization and other forms of symbolic action based mainly upon medieval religion. To employ modish jargon, the psychodynamics of the sixteenth century were very complicated: they are inadequately comprehended within the traditional concepts labelled 'Renaissance' and 'Reformation'. To this broad complex all the varied demonstrations waged by children and young people are obviously interrelated, yet the battles appear to maintain little connection with medieval religion or with the licence of carnival. In England, by far the strongest tribute of the Church to youth had been the boy-bishop, long permitted to reign in several dioceses during certain seasons of the year.[36] Abolished by Henry VIII, he was halfheartedly revived by Queen Mary, yet nevertheless he seems unrelated to the youth demonstrations of mid-Tudor England. In England, as in France, the young combatants were obviously far more

[34] J. Estebe, *Tocsin pour un massacre. Le saison des Saint-Barthélemy* (Paris, 1968); N. Z. Davis, *Society and Culture in Early Modern France* (Stanford, Calif., 1975). The latter reprints some, but not all, of her articles in *PaP* from 1971 to 1981. Another article is in *ARG*, 56 (1965), pp. 48–64.
[35] R. W. Scribner, *Popular Culture and Popular Movements in Reformation Germany* (London, 1987), esp. ch. 4.
[36] H. Maynard Smith, *Pre-Reformation England* (London, 1938), pp. 137–41.

The Battle of Finsbury Field

conscious of the politico-religious present than of the ecclesiastical past. To say much more, we need additional facts rather than imaginative interpretations.

Institute of Historical Research,
University of London

THE PIETY OF THE CATHOLIC
RESTORATION IN ENGLAND, 1553–1558

by DAVID M. LOADES

> Of the observation of ceremonies begynnthe the very educatyon of the chylderne of God; as the olde lawe doythe shewe, that was full of ceremonyes, whiche St. Paule callythe *Pedagogiam in Christum* . . .
>
> Reginald Pole[1]

THERE was very little in Reginald Pole's previous record as a scholar, confessor, or ecclesiastical statesman to suggest that he attached great importance to the externals of traditional worship. However, in his task of restoring the Church in England to the Catholic fold, he felt constrained to use whatever methods and materials were available to his hands. Ceremonies, as Miles Huggarde rightly observed, were 'curious toyes',[2] not only to the Protestants, but also to those semi-evangelical Reformers of the 1530s whose exact doctrinal standpoints are so hard to determine. Along with the papal jurisdiction had gone the great pilgrimage shrines, not only St Thomas of Canterbury—that monument to the triumph of the *sacerdotium* over the *regnum*—but also Our Lady of Walsingham and a host of others. Down, too, had gone the religious houses, lesser and greater, with their elaborate liturgical practices, and many familiar saints' days had disappeared from the calendar before the austere simplifications of 1552.[3] Such changes had provoked much opposition and disquiet, but they had left intact the ceremonial core of the old faith, the Mass in all its multitude of forms, and the innumerable little sacramental and liturgical pieties which constituted the faith of ordinary people. The recent researches of Professor Scarisbrick, Dr Haigh, Dr Susan Brigden, and others have reminded us just how lively these pieties were before—and during—the Reformation, even in places heavily

---

[1] Cardinal Pole's speech to the citizens of London, in Strype, *Memorials*, III, 2, p. 502.
[2] *The Displaying of the Protestants* (London, 1556) [*STC*, 13557], preface: Prelacy is popishe pompe / Vertuous vowews are vaine / Ceremonies curious toyes / Priesthood popery plaine.
[3] The Royal Injunctions and proclamation of 1538 had caused some saints, such as Thomas of Canterbury, to be removed from the calendar. By the time the official primer was published in 1545, a very substantial reduction had taken place. H. C. White, *Tudor Books of Private Devotion* (Wisconsin, 1951), pp. 108–9; C. H. Butterworth, *The English Primers* (New York, 1971), pp. 168–70.

infiltrated by the New Learning, such as London.[4] It was at this level that traditional religion seems to have been at its most flourishing; in the small fraternities and guilds attached to parish churches; in the ornamentation and equipment of the churches themselves; and in the provision of gifts and bequests for obits, lights, and charitable doles.

Consequently, it was the Chantries Act of 1547 and the Uniformity Act of 1549 which were really felt at the popular level, not the legislation of 1533–40, but popular piety was ill equipped to defend itself. Considering the short time which it had at its disposal, the achievement of the Edwardian government in suppressing such piety was remarkable. Despite the disturbances of 1548–9, by the time that the Protestant campaign culminated in the Commission for Church Goods in 1552, a very high outward level of conformity had been reached.[5] Altars and rood-screens had disappeared from the great majority of churches, along with the traditional service-books and liturgical equipment. It was, as Martin Bucer pointed out at the time, a negative achievement.[6] Much of the banished equipment was quietly hidden, and there was little sign of enthusiasm for attendance at Protestant sermons—even where these could be provided. The stream of gifts and bequests to parish churches virtually ceased, and secular charities did not gain to anything like a proportionate extent. Vocations to the priesthood fell away dramatically.[7] However, before the Commission for Church Goods could even complete its work, King Edward was dead, and within a month of her accession his successor, Mary, had made it clear that she intended to pursue a very different policy.

By the end of August 1553, sometimes through the initiative of 'Lords and Knights catholic', as Robert Parkyn tells us, and sometimes through the spontaneous actions of clergy or parishioners, the Mass was again being widely celebrated.[8] Service-books and vestments came out of

[4] J. J. Scarisbrick, *The Reformation and the English People* (Oxford, 1984); C. Haigh, 'From monopoly to minority: catholicism in early modern England', *TRHS*, ser. 5, 31 (1981), pp. 129–47; S. Brigden, 'Youth and the Reformation in London', *PaP*, 95 (1982), pp. 37–67.

[5] The evidence for this statement is to be found mainly in the activities of Mary's council to secure the return of church goods in the hands of the commissioners, and in the returns of such Marian visitations as those of Cardinal Pole *sede vacante* at Lincoln (1556) (Strype, III, 2, pp. 389–413) and Archdeacon Harpesfield at Canterbury (1557): Catholic Record Society, 45–6 (1950–1).

[6] Bucer to Brentius, 15 May 1550: *Original Letters relative to the English Reformation*, PS (1847), 2, p. 542.

[7] W. H. Frere, *The Marian Reaction* (London, 1896), pp. 101, 266; C. Haigh, *Reformation and Reaction in Tudor Lancashire* (Cambridge, 1975), pp. 154–5.

[8] 'Robert Parkyn's narrative of the English reformation', ed. A. G. Dickens, *EHR*, 62 (1947), 2; D. M. Loades, *The Reign of Mary Tudor* (London, 1979), p. 153.

hiding, and All Saints Day provided the occasion for the reappearance of many traditional ceremonies and practices. Indeed, considering the brief duration and undoubted unpopularity of the Edwardian Protestant regime, it is the patchy and hesitant nature of the restoration, rather than its speed and enthusiasm, which is surprising.[9] Both Robert Parkyn and Henry Machyn testify with some indignation to the existence of those who 'would not away' with the new order until they were commanded by public authority.[10] However, this may well have been the result of suspicious caution rather than Protestant zeal, and the general picture is one of a happy willingness to go back to the religious practices of the recent past. It was this popular piety, therefore, which formed the raw material out of which the Catholic Church in England had to be refashioned, but it was recalcitrant matter, and, paradoxically, it probably distorted the Marian Church into which it had to be absorbed, more than the Edwardian Church, which had rejected it.

At first this problem seems scarcely to have been perceived. Both the Queen and Stephen Gardiner, the Bishop of Winchester and Lord Chancellor, acted as though the only procedures necessary to restore the Church to its pristine state was a proclamation of the government's intention and the repeal of heretical laws.[11] Several chronicles bear witness to the conservative euphoria of these early days:

> Item, in August was the alter in Pawles set up againe . . .

> The 5th of August at seven at night, came home Edmond Bonner, bishop, from the Marshalsea, like a bishop, that all the people by the way bade him welcome home, both man and woman, and as many of the women as might be kissed him . . .

> Item, 17th September, the Bishop of London, Bonner, sange masse in Pawles . . .[12]

> The xxiii day of August . . . begane the masse at sant Nicolas Colaby, goodly song in Laten, and tapurs, and (set on) the owtter, and a crosse, in old Fysstrett.[13]

---

[9] As late as June 1556 the ecclesiastical authorities in London were still trying to make participation in procession compulsory for at least one representative of each household 'on peyne of forfettynge xii d every time', but as the conservative author of the *Greyfriars Chronicle* noted, 'it was lyttyll lokyd upon, and the more pytte': *Chronicle of the Grey friars of London*, ed. J. G. Nichols, PCS, os, 53 (1852), p. 97.

[10] 'Robert Parkyn's narrative': *The Diary of Henry Machyn*, ed. J. G. Nichols, PCS, os, 42 (1848).

[11] D. M. Loades, *The Oxford Martyrs* (London, 1970), pp. 109–12.

[12] *Grey friars Chronicle*, pp. 82, 84.

[13] *Machyn's Diary*, p. 42.

There were warning signs that some Protestants would fight the new order, but for a variety of reasons the dispossessed hierarchy confined itself to passive resistance, and by the end of the year it seems that official optimism had been largely vindicated. 'In this newe and miraculous reign of mercifull Marye', wrote the enthusiastic John Procter, 'wherein [we] see so many good olde orders newely restored, and so many new and erronious novelties antiquated and made olde ... ʼ.[14] A few heretics were not going to be allowed to spoil the party.

The Council's first big push in the direction of Catholic conformity, which began with the royal Articles of March 1554, revealed increasing anxiety about sacramentaries and 'persons ... infected or damned with any notable kind of heresy', but in other respects encouraged established opinions and traditional practices to reassert themselves.[15] This was particularly the case in the treatment of the erstwhile married clergy, who seem to have been especially unpopular with the rank and file laity, whose sentiments echoed the Queen's own. The unremitting pursuit of these men and of their former wives is one of the most curious and revealing features of the Marian Church. At the very end of the reign, in Bishop Bonner's *Interrogatories* for Churchwardens of 1558, articles 2, 3, and 4 relate to this issue, 'heresye and unlawfull doctryne' only making an appearance in number 5.[16] Clerical marriage seems to have been regarded by the conservative of all shades of opinion as symbolic of that moral laxity and disorderly behaviour which they claimed to be the characteristic of all Reformers.[17] Ironically, marriage was a poor test of Protestant opinions. Perhaps a substantial proportion of the 243 who were deprived for that reason in the diocese of Norwich did hold the views of Luther or Zwingli, but that was certainly not the case with the 16 'clerici coniugati' detected in the remote rural diocese of Bangor, where protestantism had barely pierced the skin.[18] Clerical celibacy, like the familiar ritual of the

---

[14] J. Procter, *The waie home to Christ and truth leadinge from Antichrist and errour* (London, 1556) [STC 2455], preface.

[15] E.g. item 13 '... the laudable and honest ceremonies which were wont to be used, frequented and observed in the church, be also hereafter frequented and observed.' W. H. Frere and W. M. Kennedy, *Visitation Articles and Injunctions* (London, 1910), 2, p. 328.

[16] *Interrogatories upon which churchwardens shall be charged* (London, 1558) [STC 10117].

[17] The bitter comment of the layman Miles Huggard, is typical of this sentiment: 'A just plague of God upon such dissolute priestes, who cared not what women they married, common or other, so they might get them wyves ...': *Displaying*, fol. 73v.

[18] G. Baskerville, 'Married clergy and pensioned religious in Norwich diocese, 1555', *EHR*, 68 (1933), pp. 43–64; A. I. Pryce, *The Diocese of Bangor in the Sixteenth Century* (Bangor, 1923), pp. 12–14. These deprivations created 30 per cent of the vacancies during the reign.

Mass, and the liturgical processions which marked out the Church's year, was a part of the 'right order' of things—an order at once comforting and propitiatory, which was disrupted only at the peril of the whole social and natural order. 'There was never such unthriftiness in servants, such unnaturalness in children, such unruliness in subjects, such fierceness in enemies, such unfaithfulness in friends, such beastliness of mind' as under a Protestant regime.[19] The remedies were obedience to the 'Godly author-ity' of 'miraculous Marye', and a return to the good old ways: 'Come home, come home, gentle brethren, to youre lovynge and tender mother's lap . . .'.[20]

Up to a point this was both a straightforward and appealing message, but as the restoration began to gather pace, it began to develop problems of its own, which had nothing to do with the defiance of genuine and committed Protestants. It was easy to call for a return to the 'good old order', but less easy to say exactly what that order had been, or to agree that all aspects of it had been good. The Queen herself made it clear at an early date that she intended to restore the papal jurisdiction, but amid all the popular rejoicing, and the numerous displays of Catholic zeal in the autumn of 1553, the general silence on that subject was palpable. I have discussed the problems which attended the actual restoration of the Roman obedience on many occasions, and I do not intend to do so again.[21] It is, however, worth remembering that both Gian Francesco Com-mendone, who came secretly from Julius III, and Henry Penning, who was Cardinal Pole's personal envoy, recognized the difficulties, and reported that there was little enthusiasm for the papacy.[22] This was not simply a question of apprehensive 'possessioners' concerned for their monastic lands; it was a reflection of the fact that Rome had never occupied more than a peripheral place in the religious consciousness of Englishmen, and that twenty years of constant anti-papal propaganda had also had its effect. The author of the *Greyfriars Chronicle* considered it to be worthy of especial note that the pope was prayed for at the opening of Parliament November 1554[23]—the Parliament which was actually to

---

[19] Procter, *The waie home*, preface.
[20] Ibid.
[21] Loades, *Oxford Martyrs*, pp. 138–49; *Reign of Mary*, pp. 321–30.
[22] Giacomo Soranzo to the Doge and Senate, 11 September 1553, *CalSP, Venetian*, pp. 410–11. Penning's report is calendared in ibid., pp. 429–32. The imperial ambassador, Simon Renard, was even more pessimistic. In May 1554 he reported that the name of the pope was 'odious', even among those who favoured the old religion, and that there was scarcely such a thing as a true Catholic in the country: *CalSP, Spanish*, 12, p. 243.
[23] Ibid., p. 92.

revoke the Royal Supremacy. John Proctor's fulsome *The waie home to Christe*, based upon St Vincent of Lerins and published in 1554, despite its praise of Mary, and constant emphasis upon the unity of Holy Mother Church, makes no specific mention of either the pope or his office. Nor was any such mention inserted when the work was reissued in 1556.[24] On the whole, after 1555 references to the papacy in official works, like Bonner's *A profitable and necessary doctrine*, are careful and correct. In expounding the creed, he points out that the unity of the Church is preserved by its having one single head and governor, appointed by Christ as the successor of St Peter, and that anyone who rejects the authority of that head cannot be a member of the Church Universal. Nevertheless, when it came to awakening the laity to an awareness of that authority, the priority accorded was a low one.[25] It was not until the forty-fourth article (out of forty-nine) addressed to the Churchwardens of London that they were finally asked to identify any who 'deprave or condemn the authority of the Pope'.[26] No one could have been more dutiful in his deference to the Holy See than Reginald Pole, but the role which King Philip played in negotiating the settlement, and his subsequent quarrel with Pope Paul IV, left the Cardinal stranded in a political wilderness, and effectively destroyed any chance that there might have been for the papacy to recover real prestige and influence in England.[27]

English Catholics consequently always felt that they owed far more to Mary than they did to the pope, and with their constant emphasis upon 'the Queen's Godly proceedings', reinforced the paradox of a Catholic Church by law established. No one could have been less insular than Cardinal Pole, who had spent most of his adult life in Italy, and who had brought with him to England a papal commission to negotiate peace between the King of France and the Emperor, yet by 1555 he was completely out of sympathy with current thinking in the curia. As Dermot Fenlon has pointed out, his experiences over the *Beneficio di Cristo* and the Tridentine decree on Justification had exhausted him physically and

---

[24] STC 24754, 24755. James Canceller in *The pathe of Obedience* (London, 1556) [STC 4565] makes frequent reference to 'the churche of Rome', but not to the pope. As far as I can discover, the only work specifically defending the papal authority was John Standish's *The triall of the Supremacy* (London, 1556) [STC 23211].

[25] See, for example, Bishop Brooke's Injunctions for Gloucester diocese (1556), where the only mention of the pope comes in article 16, in which the clergy are instructed to ensure that the pope's name is restored to the intercessions. The seventeen articles addressed to the laity make no reference to him. Frere and Kennedy, 2, pp. 401–8.

[26] *Interrogatories*.

[27] For a full examination of the effects of this quarrel see Loades, *Reign of Mary*, pp. 428–52.

mentally.[28] His friends and allies had either died, like Contarini, or lost influence, like Morone. The death, in March 1555, of Pope Julius III, who had sent him to England, was a further heavy blow. Significantly, when Pole was looking abroad for help in revitalizing the English Church, it was to the reformed congregation of Monte Cassino that his eyes turned, while the assistance offered by Ignatius Loyola was rejected.[29] In the event, the Cassinese did not come, and there was very little direct Continental influence on the restored English Church. Pole modelled his legatine synod of 1556 on the Council of Florence rather than that of Trent,[30] and the only foreign divines to be active and to hold preferments in England were Philip's Spanish confessors, Pedro de Soto and Juan de Villa Garcia.[31] The Spanish scholar Tellechea Idigoras has recently argued that Pole was greatly influenced by Bartolomé Carranza, but those who were subsequently responsible for Carranza's protracted misfortunes clearly believed that the influence had worked the other way.[32] Worst of all, in April 1557 Pole's legatine commission was withdrawn, and from then until his death he controlled the *Ecclesia Anglicana* by virtue of his primatial office and the unwavering confidence of the Queen, whose own relations with the Holy See varied from the chilly to the downright hostile.

Pole's lack of theological self-confidence, and his profound distress and disillusionment at the actions of Paul IV go a long way towards explaining his attitude towards his mission in England. He had become a reluctant preacher, believing that sermons merely stirred up controversy. When the Queen set out her priorities for the Church in January 1555, immediately after the question of church property, she wrote '. . . touching good preaching, I wish that may supply and overcome the evil preaching in time past.'[33] The Cardinal never openly demurred, but he seldom preached himself, and when his synod came to draft its decrees, sermons were accorded a much lower priority, as they were in most of the visitation articles of the reign.[34] For Pole, sound doctrine could only be

---

[28] Dermot Fenlon, *Heresy and Obedience in Tridentine Italy* (Cambridge, 1972), pp. 116–36.

[29] D. Knowles, *The Religious Orders in England* (Cambridge, 1959), 3, pp. 424–5; J. H. Crehan, 'St. Ignatius and Cardinal Pole', *Archivum historicum Societatis Iesu*, 25 (1956), pp. 72–98.

[30] J. P. Marmion, 'The London Synod of Cardinal Pole' (Keele University M.A. thesis, 1974).

[31] Appointed to the chairs of Hebrew and Divinity at Oxford.

[32] J. I. Tellechea Idigoras, 'Bartolome Carranza y la restauración católica inglesa (1553–1558)', *Anthologia Annua*, 12 (1964), pp. 159–282.

[33] MS BL Cotton Titus C VII, fol. 120.

[34] *Reformatio Angliae ex decretis Reginaldi Pole* (1565): Bodleian MS film 33 (Vat. Lat. 5968); Frere and Kennedy, 2, pp. 330–414. The shortage of competent preachers was also recognized to be a problem, although much less emphasized than by the Protestants, 'There be not in half a

inculcated by good habits. He was profoundly convinced that ordinary Christians were incapable of comprehending their faith, except in the most simple visual and ceremonial terms. In the address quoted above, in praise of ceremonies, he went on to declare:

> But this I dare saye, whereunto scrypture doth alsoe agree, that the observatyon of ceremonyes for obedyence sake, wyll gyve more light than all the readynge of Scrypture can doe, yf the reader have never so good a wytt to understand what he readythe.[35]

Obedience was a key concept. The laity were 'lytle chyldern', and the images of the nursery and the school-room came readily to his lips. In spite of his earlier humanist record, and his continuing belief in the importance of education for the clergy, Pole's view of his flock as a whole was both paternalistic and negative. The function of the layman was to perform his sacramental and ceremonial duties, to pay honour (and tithe) to the clergy, and to restore the battered material fabric of his parish church.[36]

Up to a point, this was a sound, common-sense approach. The need for order and stability was desperate, and in supporting ceremonies the Cardinal was, as we have seen, appealing to the mainstream of popular religious consciousness. It was, however, significant that he should have chosen to urge ceremonies in preference to the reading of Scripture. In spite of its Lollard and Protestant associations, there was nothing specifically heretical about reading the English Bible, and it seems to have been a habit which had grown upon Englishmen over the previous fifteen years. Moreover, the English primers, which had gradually replaced the Latin books of hours after 1529, and which had come to contain substantial portions of Scripture as well as prayers and devotional verses, had become generally popular, and some of them had run to many editions.[37] During Mary's reign thirty-nine primers were published in England. Of

---

shyre scarcely two hable men to showe their faces in the pulpitt': M. Glasier, *A Notable and very fruictfull sermon made at Paules Crose* (London, 1555) [*STC* 11916.5].

[35] Strype, III, 2, p. 503.

[36] Ibid., p. 483: 'yet there be other churches, that are nowe fryste to be helpen, and these be your parryshe-chyrches; which albeyt they have not byn cast downe by coulore of authoyte, as the abbayes were, yet have they byn sufferede to fawle downe of themselves.'

[37] Books of hours and primers together (the distinction was not always clear cut) accounted for 50 titles during the 1520s, and 60 during the 1530s, when they began to reflect the struggle between conservative and reforming churchmen. Alison F. Bartholomew, 'Lay Piety in the reign of Mary Tudor' (Manchester M.A. thesis, 1979), pp. 16–18; White, *Tudor Books of Private Devotion*, pp. 53ff.

these, sixteen were in both Latin and English, five in English alone, and eighteen in Latin alone. Although this last group clearly represents a deliberate return to an earlier practice, the official primer, issued in 1555, was in both Latin and English, and reflected the influence, not only of the official Henrician primer of 1545, but also of the Protestant formularies of Edward's reign. As Helen White wrote several years ago, 'The fact remains that there is . . . striking evidence of regard to opposing points of view even in the restoration of the old primer in this book of Philip and Mary.'[38]

More remarkable still, the Great Bible was never withdrawn, nor was its use prohibited, although it was forbidden for any lay person to 'expound or declare any portion or part of Scripture in any church or elsewhere, or put the same to printing of writing'.[39] Orthodox writers repeatedly inveighed against the 'fantasies' of those who interpreted the Scriptures 'after their own wit', but the habit of Bible reading seems to have spread well beyond the narrow circles of the explicitly Protestant, and to have become too widespread to be easily suppressed, no matter how suspicious to the ecclesiastical authorities.[40] Perhaps, also, Pole's humanist conscience was at odds with his pastoral and disciplinary instincts, and he deliberately confined himself to making discouraging noises. John Standish published two editions (in 1554 and 1555) of *A discourse wherein is debated whether it be expedient that the scripture should be in English for al men to reade that wyll*, but his forceful condemnation was never translated into action.[41]

The reading habits of pious laymen had also changed in other respects since the 1520s. That one-time bestseller the *Legenda Aurea* disappeared from the publishers' catalogues after 1527, and the lives of the saints in general had obviously gone out of fashion by the mid-1520s. Only a handful were published during Mary's reign, in spite of official insistence upon the worthiness of praying to saints, and explicit orders to restore their images and calendar festivals.[42] Richard Brereton of Middlewich, dying in 1558, left a total of fifty-seven books, which were inventoried in

---

[38] Ibid., p. 122.
[39] Bonner's Articles for London Diocese; Frere and Kennedy, 2, p. 324.
[40] An authorized Catholic translation of the Bible was promised at the legatine synod, but never produced: *Reformatio Angliae*.
[41] *STC* 23207, 23208.
[42] Royal Articles of 1554; arts 12 and 13. Frere and Kennedy, 2, p. 328. One example of this small output was *This is the boke of the wais of God . . . unto Elizabeth* (R. Caly? 1557?) [*STC* 7605.5].

his will. His collection included many traditional liturgical works, and an English translation of the *Imitatio Christi*, published in 1556; but it also contained several English Bibles and parts of Bibles, and no controversial theology from either side.[43] Sir William More of Loseley's collection, inventoried in 1556, although much larger shows a similar profile. Neither of these can be described as a 'typical layman', but there is no reason to suppose that they were unrepresentative of the literate gentry. Clerical reading, too, had changed since the early days of the Reformation. Mirc's *Festiall* had long since got out of fashion as a handy *vade mecum*, and when Edmund Bonner decided in 1554 to provide some help for overworked or inadequate clergy, the model which he followed was Cranmer's *Homilies* of 1549.[44] In contrast to the laity, the clergy were encouraged to read the Bible, both in Latin and English, not least to avoid the embarrassment of having their ignorance exposed by such Protestants as still ventured to challenge them. Bonner's *Profitable and Necessary Doctrine*, the classic statement of Marian orthodoxy, was not based upon any pre-1529 formulation but upon the *Necessary Doctrine and Erudition* of 1543.

The reactionary nature of Marian Catholicism can therefore easily be overestimated. The Queen herself may have hankered after the pious days of her childhood, but Pole and Bonner, and indeed Gardiner, knew that too much water had passed under the bridges, both in England and in Rome, for such a simple policy to be feasible. No serious attempt was made to revive even the most important of the pre-Reformation shrines. Images of St Thomas of Canterbury reappeared, and were promptly subjected to Protestant vandalism, but the shrine itself was not rebuilt. When Mary wished to give thanks to God for her victories over Northumberland and Wyatt, she made grants to the University of Oxford and to Trinity College, Cambridge.[45] Amid all her numerous and substantial benefactions to pious uses, none went to the old cult-centres, and Mary never undertook a pilgrimage as Queen, a fact which her mother would certainly have found surprising. Nor is there much evidence of spontaneous popular attempts to revive these cults. There were a few small bequests to St Richard of Chichester after 1556,[46] and no doubt

---

[43] Bartholomew, 'Lay piety', p. 40; *Archaeologia*, 36 (1856), pp. 284–93.
[44] These homilies were published as an adjunct to the *Profitable and Necessary Doctrine*, and went through ten editions [STC 3285.1–3285.10].
[45] *CPR*, *Mary*, 1, pp. 165–6, 203. Abbot Feckenham of Westminster solemnly reinterred the body of Edward the Confessor in 1558, and seems to have intended to re-erect the shrine, but without any official encouragement.
[46] Bartholomew, 'Lay piety', p. 105.

a detailed examination of wills would reveal similar examples elsewhere, but without royal or aristocratic patronage they could make no impact on the religious life of the wider community.

A serious attempt was made, as is well known, to re-establish the regular religious life, an endeavour in which both Pole and the Queen were very active.[47] These were new foundations, not revivals, as all the erstwhile religious houses had been canonically extinguished in 1555.[48] They were six in number, and their endowment of rather more than £2,000 a year came almost entirely from the Crown. Only Westminster, with an income of £1,460 and an ultimate strength of over 30, was on a significant scale. Two of these communities, at Sheen and Syon, were made up mainly of returning exiles, and of the estimated 1,500 or so surviving ex-religious in England, only about 100 elected to return to the cloister. This is not surprising, given the lapse of time, and we have no means of knowing whether lay generosity would have been rekindled, given a longer opportunity. Small bequests to monasteries do begin to appear in lay wills, although the caution of Margaret Sutton of Stafford in July 1556 was probably typical: '... my fyne kercher [to] be made a corporas and geven to the freres if go up againe, or if not then to some other chirche.'[49] Certainly there was no immediate surge of lay sympathy or support, and at least two of the communities were subjected to hostile demonstrations.[50] We know virtually nothing about the quality of life in these briefly revived houses, beyond an impression of Westminster, recorded long after by Fr Augustine Baker, who wrote that the monks 'sett up there a discipline muche like that ... observed in cathedral churches, as for the Divine Office', and in other respects followed the 'laws and customs of colledges and innes of court'[51]—a sober and dignified life, but not a strenuous or ascetic one. Perhaps that is why Pole wanted to bring in the Cassinese. The number of new vocations attracted was small, but given that the whole experiment lasted only about three years, nothing can be deduced from that.

[47] For a full account of these restorations, see Knowles, *Religious Orders*, 3, pp. 421–33. Pole, like More, had been greatly influenced by the Carthusians in his youth, and this affected his personal piety deeply. Fenlon, *Heresy*, pp. 27–8; W. Schenk, *Reginald Pole, Cardinal of England* (London, 1950).

[48] By the Bull, *Praeclara*, 20 June 1555. This was a direct result of the terms upon which the English settlement had been negotiated. Knowles, *Religious Orders*, 3, p. 423.

[49] Bartholomew, 'Lay piety', p. 158.

[50] The Franciscans at Greenwich and the Dominicans at Smithfield', *APC*, 5, p. 169.

[51] 'Life of Father Baker' in *Memorials of Father Augustine Baker*, ed. J. MacCann and R. M. Connolly, *Catholic Record Society*, 33 (1933), pp. 95–6.

Collegiate churches, hospitals, and perpetual chantries also began to reappear; the first two mainly on the initiative of the Crown, but the latter through the private benefactions of conservative royal servants, such as Sir William Petre and Sir Robert Rochester.[52] Here, too, the effect of changing times and fashions can be seen, and most of Mary's pious subjects—or those who wished their piety to be noticed—either endowed educational foundations or returned impropriated livings to the Church.[53] The pious instincts were not dead—it would have been remarkable indeed if four years of Protestantism had succeeded in killing them off—and they were flowing in channels already dug before the Reformation, but into learning, charity, and parish uses rather than large-scale or permanent liturgical foundations. A similar generalization can, I think, be applied to religious vocations. The regular life had been in the doldrums since the later fifteenth century, and only the Carthusians enjoyed much prestige in the 1520s.[54] Vocations to the secular priesthood, on the other hand, were high, and continued so until the Protestant innovations of 1548–9. It is therefore not surprising to find only a handful of regular vocations, but a positive flood of ordinations. Bonner alone ordained 257 priests and 272 deacons in 63 separate ceremonies over the five and a half years of the reign.[55] There could be no more convincing demonstration of the appeal of traditional religion than these figures, which can be paralleled on a smaller scale in other dioceses. Such striking success, however, was not without its hazards, and it was not only Protestants who began to mutter in alarm that 'the priests are coming back to take their revenge', an alarm which was reflected in both Houses of Parliament.[56]

Apart from the crucial matters of money and jurisdiction, which I do not intend to discuss here, Pole and his bishops gave the highest priority to the restoration of parochial life, and the sharp rise in ordinations was both a cause and an effect of that priority. This meant not only a revival of

---

[52] CPR, Mary, 1, p. 230 (Collegiate church of Wolverhampton); 3, p. 513 (Manchester College); 3, p. 543 (Savoy Hospital); 3, p. 542 (Petre at Ingatestone); 3, pp. 363–4 (Rochester at Terling).

[53] For example: Sir Thomas White (St John's College, Oxford); CPR, 2, p. 322; Sir Thomas Pope (Trinity College, Oxford); CPR, 3, p. 90; and numerous schools. Viscount Montague returned a number of impropriated livings, and others followed his example; CPR, 3, p. 290; CPR, 4, p. 91.

[54] Knowles, Religious Orders, 3, pp. 222ff. John Colet was also among those deeply influenced by the Carthusians.

[55] Bartholomew, 'Lay piety', p. 152.

[56] Examinations of John Danyell. PRO SP 46, 8, 35. Both the Commons and the Lords expressed unease over the return of ecclesiastical jurisdiction. Loades, Reign of Mary; J. Loach, Parliament and the Crown in the Reign of Queen Mary (Oxford, 1985).

processions and other ceremonies, the repair of fabric, and the replace-
ment of equipment, but also, and above all, the revival of the sacraments,
particularly those of the Altar and of penance. These were, *par excellence*,
the sacraments upon which the authority of the priestly order depended,
but Marian writers, unlike their Protestant opponents, placed little
emphasis upon this fact. The Sacrament of the Altar was the acid test of
orthodoxy, but the way in which it was regarded varied considerably from
one author to another. In popular works, such as James Cancellar's *The
pathe of obedience*, the emphasis was social and collective; presence at the
Mass, and veneration of the Elements, were what mattered, actions seen
in a whole context of ritual acts.

> Dyd not our late pretensed bishops, as Lucifer before had done,
> presume to sytte in Goddes seate, proudly speaking against God ...
> and to set up the abhominable desolaccion, whiche was the ceasinge
> of the veneration of the Body and Blood of Christ in the blessed
> sacrament of the alter, and the taking away of oure holye fastynges,
> holye feastes and holye prayinge to saints.[57]

To the learned Thomas Watson, on the other hand, worthy reception was
the critical factor, and mere presence was passed over in silence. In the
first of three sermons on the subject in his *Holesome and catholyke doctryne
concerninge the seven sacraments*, he wrote: 'And because a man doth dayley
offende, and so decayethe in his spiritual lyfe, therefore ought he often to
receive this spiritual medecine, whiche is called our dayly bread.'[58]
Continuing this line of thought in the next sermon, he came remarkably
close to echoing the phraseology of Cranmer's Prayer Book: 'For he that
eatethe and drinketh the body and blood of oure Lorde unworthely,
eateth and drinketh judgement and damnation to himselfe.' Preparation,
therefore, was of great importance, and preparation consisted not only of
prayer and abstinence, but of confession to the parish priest and the
performance of due penance.

Both Watson and Bonner were very careful in their discussion of the
sacrament of penance. The mere performance of ritual gestures, whether
of penance or of almsgiving, was not sufficient: genuine and inward
contrition was needed. But contrition could not be assessed by inquisitive
archdeacons, and there was always strict insistence upon auricular

---

[57] Cancellar, *Pathe of Obedience*, Sig. A. iii.
[58] Thomas Watson, *Holesome and catholyke doctryne concerning the seven sacraments* (London, 1558),
sermon 9, fol. 48.

confession.[59] Nevertheless, it was here, in these official manuals of Catholic instruction, that the Marian Church came closest to that individual and contemplative piety which was to be fostered by the Counter Reformation. Watson's sermons 17, 20, 21, and 23 provide step-by-step guidance in self-examination, designed to convince the sinner of the indissoluble bond between faith and works. Salvation, he argues in a specific attack upon justification by faith alone, is never impossible to the penitent. 'The successe of the worke brygneth sweetness, and the encreae of virtue newe repayred bringeth gladnes to our myndes.'[60] Despite the strong emphasis upon the visible and liturgical expression of all the sacraments, here was no crude quantification of the kind which had so angered the early reformers, but thoughtful and sensitive spiritual counselling. Pole's bishops were, for the most part, men of this calibre and turn of mind, and they represented an indigenous strain of intellect and spirituality running back through Richard Whitford and Thomas More to Colet and Linacre. In 1559 the survivors among them rejected the return of Protestantism, and the Royal Supremacy, and were deprived. Their pupils and heirs, fostered in the universities by the Cardinal's careful oversight, formed the first generation of English Catholic exiles, and the basis for the later recusant movement.

At its best, therefore, as represented by these writers and a few others like them, such as John Christopherson and John Feckenham, Marian piety was intelligent and persuasive, recognizing the importance of an informed laity, and accepting many of the changes of emphasis and practice which had occurred between 1520 and 1540. What it lacked at this level was the kind of passion and commitment which was to be found at the same time among the Theatines and the early Jesuits. Pole was significantly described by one of his Spanish critics as 'lukewarm'—a Laodician.[61] It was an unfair criticism of a man who worked so hard, and under such difficult circumstances, to restore the Catholic Church in England, but it had a point: the same point that Professor Dickens was to make when he said that Mary 'never discovered the Counter Reforma-

---

[59] Thomas Watson, *Holesome and catholique doctryne concerning the seven saacraments* (London, 1558), sermon 9, fol. 66. Bonner, *Profitable and Necessary Doctrine*, 'On the sacrament of penance', sig. D vi, wrote 'When I do say a declaration or uttering, I do use the same to exclude mental confession, which though it may and at times ought to be made unto God, yet that is not the sacramental confession of which we heare speake.' These Marian guides have nothing of the systematic intensity of the later Catholic manuals on confession.

[60] Watson, *Seven sacraments*, sermon 15, 'Against desperation', fol. 86.

[61] Don Gomez Saurez de Figueroa, Count of Feria, to Fr Ribadeneyra, S.J., 22 March 1558: *CalSP, Spanish*, 13, pp. 370–1.

tion'. No doubt, had the restoration lasted, English piety would have assimilated more Continental features, but this had not even begun to happen by the time that Cardinal Pole died. There were no meditations on the rosary, no modern hagiography, no cult of the Sacred Heart or the Holy Name; and none of the recently established orders recruited or established cells in England.[62] There was passion, but much of it was channelled into persecution, and into the unmeasured denunciations of popular polemic: 'What fylthy frute buddeth out of this frantike franternitie and synfull synagogue of Sathan', wrote William Barlow, in a mood not to be outmatched by John Bale himself.[63] There can be no doubt that some middle and lower ranking clergy, and some laity as well, were outraged by Edwardian Protestantism, but that was not the prevailing sentiment.

Many aspects of the old faith had been greatly weakened and undermined, not so much by heretical doctrine as by the pressures applied by royal policy between 1530 and 1547. Changing fashions of piety had been visible before that, and had helped to make some parts of that policy acceptable. The enthusiasm for the Mass, and for traditional ceremonies, which was clearly visible at the beginning of Mary's reign, was certainly a reaction against the Prayer Book, and the brief Protestant austerity of 1550–3. It did not signify a general desire to put the clock back to 1529, even if anyone had known exactly what that meant. Pole and Mary almost certainly realized this, and in spite of their determination to restore the Roman jurisdiction, were not excessively reactionary in the conformity which they endeavoured to impose. What they were trying to do was to re-establish a distinctively English type of reformed Catholicism, under the papal jurisdiction; a regiment of the kind which would have appealed to Colet or the young More. Unfortunately for them, such a policy required not only time, but also freedom from theological controversy. It was an ideal of order, discipline, and peace, which Protestant resistance, papal intransigence, and Mary's own political entanglement with Spain conspired to make unrealistic. Evidence for the actual achievement is conflicting. Apathy drifts into conformity quickly under pressure, so between these who wanted the old order restored and those who did not

[62] There was a beginning of a hagiography of Fisher and More, the latter mainly promoted by the More family, and associated with Rastell's edition of his collected works, published in 1557.
[63] *A dialogue describing the originall grounde of these Lutheran faccions* (London, 1553) [STC 1462]: preface.

much care, a high level of outward conformity was achieved by 1558.[64] Anxious clergy and gentlemen were requesting all sorts of minor dispensations from Pole, even before he returned to England,[65] and bequests for pious purposes were picking up noticeably by the end of the reign. Episcopal authority was strengthened, and a worthy state had been made with the intractable problems of poor livings and ruined churches. Nevertheless, there was little sign that Protestant dissent had been either suppressed or silenced, and for that purpose weapons were needed of a kind which the Marian Church did not seem anxious to acquire. Judicial persecution on its own was not enough, and neither the habit-forming ceremonialism upon which Pole was so keen, nor the sensible humanist theology of Watson and Bonner could provide adequate support. Paradoxically, it was the insularity of the Marian Church, not its ultramontanism, or even its association with Spain, which was its fundamental weakness.

University College of North Wales

---

[64] The main deficiencies revealed by visitations in the last year of the reign are concerned with the dilapidation of churches. Churchwardens' accounts, where these have been studied, almost invariably record substantial payments for liturgical restorations. Scarisbrick, *Reformation*, pp. 136–61.

[65] These were mostly for eating meat in Lent, or having a consecrated super altar for a private chapel: Pole's Legatine Register, Douai Municipal Archives, MS 292 (microfilm in Lambeth Palace Library).

THE LATIN POLEMIC OF THE
MARIAN EXILES

by ANDREW PETTEGREE

N a recent number of the *English Historical Review* Dr Jennifer Loach
argued for a more positive view of the relationship between the
government of Mary Tudor and the printing-press. Against a historical tradition which has been persistently critical of the regime's failure to
understand the importance of printing, Dr Loach has argued that Mary's
government in fact had a very real understanding of the value of printed
propaganda, and took positive measures to promote abroad a favourable
view of the restoration of Catholic worship in England.[1] The key events of
the reign, the Queen's accession and marriage and the ending of the
schism, were all marked by the publication abroad of pamphlets in Latin
or foreign vernacular languages promoting the government's viewpoint.
The speed with which such accounts appeared suggest an official version
of events, usually in Latin, was sometimes deliberately circulated to
sympathetic printers to ensure wide publicity.[2]

The point is well made, and Dr Loach has certainly identified a
substantial body of literature to set alongside the well-known polemical
efforts of the Protestant Marian exiles. But her article prompts in turn a
further question: how aware were the Protestant exiles of this same international audience? Studies of the exile literature have thus far concentrated almost exclusively on vernacular works, published abroad for
clandestine importation and distribution in England. The exiles were
extremely diligent in this task, publishing during the six years of the exile
more than 120 tracts and pamphlets which found their way back to
England.[3] But this vernacular literature, important and influential though

---

[1] J. Loach, 'The Marian Establishment and the printing press', *EHR*, 101 (1986), pp. 135–48.
J. W. Martin, 'The Marian regime's failure to understand the importance of printing',
Huntington Library Quarterly, 44 (1980–1), pp. 231–47. I wish to thank Dr Jane Dawson for her
help and valuable suggestions which went towards the writing of this paper, and Geoffrey
Hargreaves, Bruce Gordon, Scott Dixon, and Robert Peberdy for their help with biblio-
graphical references.

[2] Loach, 'Marian Establishment', pp. 143–7.

[3] E. Baskerville *A Chronological Bibliography of Propaganda and Polemic Published in English between
1553 and 1558* = Publication of the American Philosophical Society (Philadelphia, 1979);
'Some lost works of propaganda from the Marian period', *The Library*, ser. 6, 8 (Oxford, 1985),
pp. 47–52.

it undoubtedly was at home, would obviously not have had the same impact abroad. To carry their case to an international and scholarly audience the exiles would have to employ a different medium.

It is with this in mind that the appended list of the Marian exiles' Latin works has been compiled. Latin was by and large the only language which the exiles had in common with their hosts: it was a necessary medium if they were to address a wider court of popular opinion.[4] And, on the evidence of this list, this was a more important aspect of the exiles' literary activities than has hitherto been recognized: the forty different works and fifty editions detailed here represent a considerable body of work. The introduction which follows is intended to do no more than present a brief outline of the works and suggest some of the major issues which the exiles addresssed, together with some broad general conclusions as to the scope and purposes of the literature.

The exiles' earliest publications were inevitably largely a reaction to the traumatic events of 1553. These included one very curious work, a Latin narrative of the events surrounding Edward's death and the abortive attempt to set up Jane Grey in his stead.[5] The unknown author is more likely to have been one of the foreign merchants than a theologian, but his hostility towards Northumberland was widely shared among the religious exiles. This little tract has more in common with the popular 'sensation' books than the bulk of the exile writings.[6] More important by far was the account published early in 1554 of the disputation in Convocation the previous autumn, prior to the restoration of the Mass, where the Reformers present had made an eloquent last-ditch defence of the Edwardian Settlement.[7] The account, penned by John Philpot after his arrest, was carried abroad by Valérand Poullain, one of the foreign

---

[4] Grindal taught himself German, but he seems to have been unusual in this. P. Collinson, *Archbishop Grindal* (London, 1979), p. 69. See the letter from Aylmer to Foxe, quoted in J. F. Mozley, *John Foxe and his Book* (London, 1940), p. 57.

[5] No 1. Modern edition and translation, *Historical Narration of certain events which took place in the Kingdom of Great Britain . . . Written by P. V.* (London, 1865).

[6] Not least in giving currency to the rumour that Northumberland had brought about the King's death by poisoning him. There were also two vernacular German editions of this tract: *Warhafftige beschreibung deren ding, die sich in dem loblichen konigreich Engelland, im hew monat dies gegenwertigen 1553. Jars, zugetragen haben; Von kleglichem unzeitigen Tod Edwardi des sechsten, konigs zu Engelland etc. Warhafftiger grundlicher Bericht. . .* (Leipzig, 1554). Copies of both in the British Library.

[7] Appendix 1, no. 3, English edition *True report of the disputation . . .* [STC 19890]. The revised *STC* suggests Emden, Mierdman and Gailliart? as printer, but on typographical grounds this seems improbable. Reprinted in Foxe (London, 1858), 6, pp. 395–411 and *Examinations and Writings of John Philpot*, PS (1842), pp. 173–214 (with Poullain's preface).

ministers employed in England in Edward's reign. Poullain rendered it into Latin and published it along with a translation of Archbishop Cranmer's declaration in defence of the Eucharist, publication of which (in September 1553) had effectively sealed his fate.[8] Through Poullain's agency this was now made available to a Continental audience.

Valérand Poullain was one of a number of foreign ministers and theologians who had found employment in England during Edward's reign, and who were now forced to return to the Continent. Their writings made a significant contribution to the literature of the exile. In addition to his translation of Philpot, Poullain was responsible for the publication of two editions of the liturgy used by the Frankfurt exile community. Based on the church order of his former church in Glastonbury, and intended primarily for the use of the small French congregation, Poullain's liturgy was endorsed also by representatives of the English congregation.[9] In the same vein, the distinguished Polish reformer John a Lasco published in 1555 a Latin version of the church order of the foreign church in London, of which he had been the first superintendent. This model church would exercise a considerable influence in Reformed Protestant circles. Lasco, an able polemicist, also involved himself in the defence of the troubled Frankfurt community.[10] But the figure of greatest stature among the exiled foreign theologians was undoubtedly Peter Martyr Vermigli, friend of Cranmer and former Professor of Divinity at Oxford. Martyr's continuing commitment to defend and elaborate the doctrine of the English Church was reflected in several important works. Most influential was the *Defensio ... de Eucharistiae* against Stephen Gardiner, a response to Gardiner's final salvo against Cranmer in their prolonged controversy over sacramental theology.[11] Writing to Martyr from prison, in 1555, Cranmer expressed his regret that no one had yet answered the book. This task was by common consent resigned to

---

[8] 'Purgatio ... adversus infames rumores a quibusdam sparsos de missa restituta' in J. Strype, *Memorials of Archbishop Cranmer* (Oxford, 1854), 3, pp. 453–9. Jasper Ridley, *Thomas Cranmer* (Oxford, 1962), pp. 351–3.

[9] Appendix 1, nos 4 and 9. 'Subscripsit etiam Angli ob Evangelium profugi totius Ecclesiae sua nomine' (with five names): *Liturgia Sacra* (Frankfurt, 1554), fol. f7. Modern edition *Valerandus Pollanus, Liturgia Sacra*, ed. A. C. Honders (Leiden, 1970).

[10] Appendix 1, nos 10, 18, and 19. On Lasco see Basil Hall, *John a Lasco. A Pole in Reformation England* = Friends of Dr Williams's Library, 25th Lecture (London, 1971).

[11] Appendix 1, no. 46. Marvin Anderson, *Peter Martyr. A Reformer in Exile* (Nieuwkoop, 1975), 'Rhetoric and Reality: Peter Martyr and the English Reformation', *Sixteenth Century Journal*, 19 (1988), pp. 451–69. Gardiner's *Confutio Cavillationem* was published in Paris in 1552 and reprinted in 1554 at Louvain: see M. A. Shaaber, *Checklist of Works of British Authors Printed Abroad in Languages other than English* (New York, 1975), p. 76.

Martyr, who was working on it during his time in Strasburg, although the book appeared finally only after his removal from Strasburg to Zurich in 1556.[12] Two other publications also date from this Zurich period: a reply to Richard Smith, who had written against his teaching on clerical celibacy and monastic vows, and an edition of his Oxford lectures on Romans. This latter work Martyr had prepared for publication before he left England, but it was only in 1558 that he had time to see it through the press; Martyr now took the opportunity to add a dedication to Sir Anthony Cooke, in which he expressed the prophetic hope that the Church of England might one day be restored.[13] Martyr's continuing commitment to the English Church earned him a position of special respect among the English exiles, many of whom attended his lectures in Strasburg. His stature and reputation ensured that he would be one of the most formidable defenders of the English Protestant settlement during the exile. The foreign theologians' writings in exile served to underline their continuing commitment to the English Protestant polity established with their assistance during Edward's reign. The death of Martin Bucer had deprived the English Church of another eloquent advocate, but he, too, was represented in the publications of the exile, notably with a posthumous edition of his *De regno Christi*, his final considered proposal for the organization of a Christian state.[14]

It would be wrong, however, to give the impression that the English exiles were prepared to leave the defence of their Church entirely to their distinguished foreign guests. Several of the English exiles contributed effectively to the doctrinal debate, including John Ponet, former Bishop of Winchester and the senior churchman among the exiles.[15] Ponet is best known for his *Short Treatise of Politic Power*, a discussion of the right of resistance which played an influential role in directing the exiles' thoughts

[12] *Original Letters relative to the English Reformation*, PS (1846), 1, pp. 29–30. Anderson, 'Rhetoric and Reality', pp. 464–7.
[13] Appendix 1, nos 37 and 47. Anderson, *Reformer in Exile*, pp. 328–55, 497–507. See also nos 27 and 28, both new editions of works first published during Edward's reign.
[14] Appendix 1, nos 7 (including the Commentary on Judges) and 26 (*De Regno Christi*). On the Judges Commentary and its influence on the development on Protestant political thought see Hans Baron, 'Calvinist Republicanism and its political roots', *Church History*, 8 (1939), p. 37. On *De Regno Christi*, see C. Hopf, *Martin Bucer and the English Reformation* (Oxford, 1946), pp. 99–126. Bucer's Lectures on Ephesians at Cambridge were also later published, edited by Tremellius. *Praelectiones Doctiss. in Epistolam ad Ephesios* (Pernam, Basle, 1562).
[15] Winthrop S. Hudson, *John Ponet, 1516–1556. Advocate of Limited Monarchy* (Chicago, 1942). C. Garrett, *The Marian Exiles* (Cambridge, 1938), pp. 253–8 is useful, though speculative and unsympathetic. See also E. J. Baskerville, 'John Ponet in Exile: a Ponet Letter to John Bale', *JEH*, 37 (1986), pp. 442–7.

into more radical paths, but he also wrote a number of works in Latin including the *Diallacticon*, a cogent and effective statement of the position of the English Church on Eucharistic doctrine. Although not published until after Ponet's death, the work enjoyed considerable success, with several reprints during Elizabeth's reign.[16] Thomas Becon was another exile who, alongside his English tracts, wrote works aimed at a more scholarly audience, most notably his *Coenae sacrosanctae dominae*, a comparison between the Lord's Supper and the Mass.[17]

The most prolific of the English authors were John Bale and John Foxe, two men whose paths became increasingly intertwined during the years of the exile. Bale, a veteran of the Henrician exile and an energetic pamphleteer since the 1540s, had made his way to the Continent from Ireland, whither he had been despatched as Bishop of Ossory in the last year of Edward's reign.[18] At Frankfurt he met up with Foxe, before the troubles which afflicted the English congregation in that town caused both men to move on to Basle. Here Foxe (and possibly Bale also) found employment as a proof-reader for the printer Oporinus, while both men shared quarters provided by the town for the English exiles in the former *Klarakloster*.[19] The association proved a happy one: over the next three years the two men published more than a dozen Latin works on Oporinus's presses, including arguably the two most important books of the whole exile, Bale's *Scriptorum illustrium maioris Britanniae* and Foxe's *Rerum in ecclesia gestarum*, the Latin prototype of his *Book of Martyrs*.

Bale's *Scriptorum* was an extraordinarily ambitious undertaking, representing in its final form the fruits of over a decade of research into the history of British authors. Bale's intention was to create a history of the English Church and people in the form of a biographical encyclopaedia, and to this end he had collected information on some nine hundred mythical and historical persons. His catalogue was, however, far from being an impartial work of scholarship; rather Bale offered a scheme of the past which served to validate events in England since 1529 as a return to the pure Christianity of the immediate post-Apostolic age, before the

---

[16] Appendix 1, no. 29. Hudson, *Ponet*, pp. 79–81. Further editions published 1573, 1576, and 1688. On the *Short Treatise* see Hudson, *Ponet*, pp. 109–216.

[17] Appendix 1, no 45. D. S. Bailey, *Thomas Becon and the Reformation of the Church in England* (Edinburgh, 1952), pp. 77–91. For Becon's other Latin works see ibid., p. 145 and appendix nos 30 and 38.

[18] L. P. Fairfield, *John Bale, Mythmaker for the English Reformation* (Purdue, 1976).

[19] Mozley, *Foxe and his Book*, pp. 37–61. William Haller, *Foxe's 'Book of Martyrs' and the Elect Nation* (London, 1963), pp. 48–81.

Roman pontificate had asserted its tyrannous hold.[20] The biographical sketches were interspersed with appendices dealing with political history and particularly the nefarious activities of papal agents in England. These sections on the papacy were also abstracted and published separately as the *Acta Romanorum Pontificum*, a work similar in style and purpose to Robert Barnes's *Lives of the Roman Pontiffs*. Barnes's book, first published in Wittenberg in 1536, was also reprinted by Oporinus during these years.[21]

Bale's historical writings were important too for their influence on John Foxe's intellectual development. Foxe and Bale had known each other in London during Edward's reign, at which time Foxe first began to pursue his historical writing. Foxe's debt to Bale is evident in his first publication abroad, the *Commentarii rerum in ecclesia gestarum*, an account of the life and doctrine of John Wyclif. This work, published soon after Foxe's arrival in Strasburg, was probably substantially complete before he departed for the Continent.[22] Once settled in Basle, Foxe embarked on a feverish programme of literary activity, writing and translating, in addition to his proof-reading and editorial work for Oporinus. From this period date a number of original Latin works, including *Christus triumphans*, an apocalyptical comedy, and *Ad inclytos Angliae proceres*, an appeal to the nobility of England to use their influence with the Queen to stop the persecution, which seems to have been inspired by news of the martyrdom of Cranmer, Ridley, and Latimer.[23]

Much of Foxe's energies, however, were devoted to the compilation of a history of the English martyrs, expanding the *Commentarii* of 1554 to take in more recent events. Although Foxe was ultimately to bear the major burdens of authorship, the martyrology was originally conceived as a collaborative venture. The moving spirit behind the project appears to have been Edmund Grindal. Writing to Foxe from Strasburg, where he was well placed to receive news and materials from England, Grindal

---

[20] Fairfield, *Bale*, pp. 96ff. See also Katharine Firth, *The Apocalyptic Tradition in Reformation Britain, 1530–1645* (Oxford, 1979), chs 2–3.

[21] Appendix 1, nos 33, 40 (Bale), and 11 (Barnes). Fairfield, *Bale*, pp. 103–5. A. G. Dickens and John Tonkin, *The Reformation in Historical Thought* (Oxford, 1985), pp. 63–5.

[22] Appendix 1, no 5. The *Commentarii* seems not to have sold well, since ten years later Rihel reissued copies with a new title page and dedication. [*Chronicon Ecclesiae* (1564). Copies Munich SB, Kiel UB.]

[23] Appendix 1, nos 17 and 22. On *Christus Triumphans* see J. H. Smith, *Two Latin Comedies by John Foxe the Martyrologist* (Ithica, 1973). See also R. Bauckham, *Tudor Apocalypse* (Sutton Courtenay, n.d.), pp. 75–83. Foxe's address to the nobility was reprinted in the martyrology of 1559 (below n. 25) and in subsequent editions of the *Acts and Monuments*. Mozley, *Foxe and his Book*, pp. 54–5.

suggested that he and his colleagues should compile the English version, while Foxe in Basle worked towards a simultaneous Latin edition.[24] In the event, the task proved more complicated than he had anticipated. New materials continued to arrive, and Grindal returned to England with the plan for an English martyrology unrealized. Foxe, however, persevered, delaying his return to England to see his Latin work through the press. It was published finally in 1559, a folio of some seven hundred pages, continuing the story begun with the Lollard martyrs in the *Commentarii* through the reigns of Henry VIII and Mary. Along with accounts of the death of the martyrs furnished from England, Foxe included a number of tracts already published separately, such as Philpot's account of the Convocation of 1553 and his own address to the nobility. It was, as far as possible, a full and lasting record of the trials to which the English Church had lately been subjected.[25]

Foxe's martyrology was one of a number of ventures on which the exiles collaborated in order to bring the fate of the English martyrs and their works to a wider public. Writing to Ridley in prison in 1555, Grindal recorded that he had received several of his prison writings; he proposed to have his treatise on the Eucharist translated into Latin ready for publication, but would not proceed until Ridley's fate was known, for fear of prejudicing his case. In the event, Ridley was put to death in October, and the treatise on the Eucharist, translated by William Whittingham, published the following year.[26] Other translations were entrusted to John Foxe, including an account of the examinations of John Philpot, and Cranmer's second treatise on the Eucharist.[27] Not all of these plans were brought to fruition. John Hooper had despatched a number of his writings to Bullinger in Zurich in the hope that he would see to their publication. But although the works found their way into Foxe's hands, no independent editions seem to have been published, although one was included in the martyrology. Perhaps in this case Foxe was deterred by the misgivings expressed by Grindal (and apparently shared by Bullinger and Martyr) that Hooper had not always expressed himself as carefully as they

---

[24] Letter of June 1557. *Remains of Archbishop Grindal*, PS (1843), pp. 226–7. See Mozley, *Foxe and his Book*, pp. 120–3.

[25] Appendix 1, no 39. Mozley, *Foxe and his Book*, pp. 122–8. 'Disputatio Synodalis Londini', *Rerum*, pp. 215–29; 'Ad Praepotentes Angliae proceres', pp. 239ff. See also n. 28 below.

[26] Appendix 1, no 13. Grindal to Ridley, 6 May 1555. *Works of Bishop Ridley*, PS (1843), p. 388.

[27] Appendix 1, no 25 (Philpot). See Strype, *Cranmer*, 3, p. 174. Apparently published separately, Foxe also included this translation in his martyrology: *Rerum* (1559), pp. 543–631. On his Cranmer translation see n. 29 below.

might have wished.[28] The publication of Cranmer's second Eucharistic treatise, his reply to Gardiner, also ran into difficulties. Foxe completed the translation, despite some problems with obscure passages, but then publication was held up by the delay in finding a printer, following a ban on the publication of controversial works imposed as a result of the outbreak of the Sacramentarian controversy in Germany. Even Oporinus was reluctant to proceed when advised by the town authorities to hold off, and although the work was passed to Froschover at Zurich he, too, never seems to have brought it out.[29]

These temporary difficulties in Switzerland may explain why Cranmer's first major writing on the Eucharist was published unusually in Emden, far away from the usual centres of Latin printing. Emden was a convenient location for the small vernacular pamphlets smuggled into England, but less so for the distribution of works intended for a European readership.[30] However, the more relaxed attitude displayed by the local authorities at this point was probably the principal motive for entrusting Cranmer's work to an Emden printer. The translation, by Sir John Cheke, was published now with a new preface, extolling the martyrs and the Reformation under Edward for which they died.[31] The appearance of this work in these circumstances was an event of special significance, almost as if the martyred Archbishop's writing was being presented as an official testament of the exiled English Church. The preface was endorsed by a list of the leading figures of the exile, ranged according to their ecclesiastical rank.[32]

With the accession of Elizabeth in November 1558 the exiles were

---

[28] Later Writings of Bishop Hooper, PS (1852), pp. 381–548. Hooper to Bullinger, 11 Dec. 1554. Original Letters, pp. 105–6. Grindal to Foxe, August 1556. Grindal, Remains, p. 223. 'De sacratissimae coenae Domini', included in Rerum (1559), pp. 309–403, but omitted in subsequent English editions of the Acts and Monuments. The dedicatory epistle to the second tract, 'De vera ratione inveniendae' is reprinted by Strype, Memorials, III, 2, pp. 267–73. See ibid., III, 1, pp. 283–4.

[29] Grindal to Foxe, May 1556, Jan. and June 1557. Grindal, Remains, pp. 220–2, 234–5.

[30] Of the Latin literature only this work and the Aetiologia of Robert Watson (App. 1, nos 14 and 15) were published in Emden. Watson, Cranmer's former steward, had escaped from prison in England only after making a highly equivocal declaration on the Mass. This tract is intended to defend his conduct. The fact that, in contrast, such a high proportion of the vernacular tracts were printed in north Germany (at Emden, Wesel, and Strasburg) must reflect the different markets at which the two classes of literature were aimed.

[31] Appendix 1, nos 20 and 21; reprinted in Writings and Disputations of Cranmer, PS (1844), appendix, pp. 1–99. Modern edition, including supplementary materials from Emden edition but omitting preface, Remains of Archbishop Cranmer, ed. H. Jenkyns, 4 vols (Oxford, 1833), 2, pp. 275–463.

[32] Cranmer, Writings, appendix, p. 9.

finally able to contemplate a return home. Not all left off their literary activities immediately. John Foxe, tied to Basle by the need to see his martyrology through the press, rapidly composed a celebratory address expressing the joy felt in Germany at the happy turn of events in England.[33] His friends Laurence Humphrey and John Bale also made their literary response to the new circumstances, Humphrey dedicating his tract *De religionis conservatione*, with its timely reflections on the reforming of religion, to the nobility and people of England, while Bale inserted into the latest copies of his *Scriptorum Brytanniae* a new dedication to Queen Elizabeth.[34] By the end of the year all three had returned to England, and the literary work of the exile was at an end.

The full significance of this exile literature cannot be explored in a brief introduction of this nature, but it may be appropriate to offer a few preliminary reflections. While it would no doubt be stretching a point to make all these works part of a co-ordinated campaign, the authors may be said broadly to have shared a common purpose, that is to present and justify the English Reformation to an international audience. Both the historical and theological works played their part in this scheme, present-ing a view of the Reformation in England which both anchored it historically and placed it in the mainstream of the European movement. The exiles often went to some pains to ensure that their writings presented a doctrinally coherent and orthodox face: in this respect Grindal's concern that Hooper and Philpot's prison writings be edited before publication to remove some unguarded expressions seems especially significant.[35] The exile authors were anxious above all to present a positive face of the English Reformation. There is little trace in these writings of the internal debates and divisions which so troubled the exile congregations during their sojourn abroad.[36]

The exiles' works seem to have found a ready audience. It would be rash to draw conclusions about contemporary patterns of dissemination from current locations of surviving copies, but it is clear that some of these works have survived in unusual numbers: these are among the sixteenth

---

[33] Appendix 1, no. 50. See Strype, *Annals* (1824), I, i, pp. 155–61.

[34] Appendix 1, nos 42 (Bale) and 49 (Humphrey). Other copies of the *Scriptorum* listed under no. 32 may also contain the new preface. On Humphrey's tract see Strype, *Annals*, I, i, pp. 161–2.

[35] Grindal, *Remains*, p. 223. See n. 28 above.

[36] Most famously in Frankfurt, but the English communities in Basle and Emden were also troubled by internal dissensions. *A brief discours off the troubles begonne at Franckfort 1554–1558 A.D.*, ed. E. Arber (London, 1908).

century's unrare books.[37] Their success should not though surprise us, because this was a period when European statesmen and church leaders were deeply interested in English affairs. The correspondence of the Reformers bears witness to the close attention with which they followed events in England following the death of Edward VI and the progress of the Catholic restoration.[38] Theodore Beza was sufficiently engaged to write a reply to the printed version of Northumberland's recantation, which had circulated widely on the Continent.[39] Later in the reign, Pole's diplomatic activity as mediator in the Franco-Imperial conflict helped keep English affairs to the forefront on the European stage.[40] The role played by the Marian exiles in the wider struggle between Catholic and Protestant in Europe, a struggle which in the 1550s would have appeared particularly tense and delicate, was one which the Reformers were not slow to acknowledge. Bullinger dedicated to the exiles his sermons on the Apocalypse published at Basle in 1557, and the hospitality proferred by the Swiss Reformers was a further tangible measure of their concern and regard.[41] The exiles responded in kind, both in their dedications and in the sincere expressions of gratitude which followed their return to England.[42]

The middle decades of the sixteenth century were years when, perhaps to an extent never again repeated, the Reformation in England was an

---

[37] See Appendix 1. Folio editions are inevitably represented by the greatest number of surviving copies, but many of the smaller books are also preserved in considerable numbers.

[38] See, for instance, pieces preserved in the Calvin correspondence. *Joannis Calvini Opera*, ed. G. Baum *et al.*, 14–17, *CR*, 42–5: e.g. nos 1761, 1768, 1778, 1856, 1940, 1953, 1992, etc.

[39] *Response a la confession du feu Jean de Northumberlande, n'agueres decapité en Angleterre* ([Geneva], 1554). *Index Aureliensis*, 4, p. 163. Loach, 'Marian Establishment', p. 144.

[40] Heinrich Lutz, 'Cardinal Reginald Pole and the path to Anglo-Papal Mediation at the Peace Conference of Marcq, 1553–55' in E. I. Kouri and Tom Scott, eds, *Politics and Society in Early Modern Europe* (London, 1987), pp. 329–52; Dermot Fenlon, *Heresy and Obedience in Tridentine Italy* (Cambridge, 1972), pp. 258–69. The polemical campaign waged against Pole by the Italian humanist Pier Paulo Vergerio also forms part of this context. In 1555 he published at Strasburg a new edition of Pole's *Pro ecclesiasticae unitate*, intending to discredit the religious talks in Germany. See also *Epistolae duae* (app. 1, no. 12), a short but vituperative polemical work denouncing Pole and contrasting his former policy of moderation with his treatment of the English Protestants.

[41] Bullinger, *In apocalypsim Jesu Christi . . . Conciones centum*, fol. a2: 'Ad omnes per Germaniam et Helvetiam, Galliae, Angliae, Italiae aliorumque regnorum vel nationum Christi nomine exules . . .'.

[42] Bale's *Acta Romanorum pontificum* (app. 1, no. 33) dedicated to the Reformers. Foxe dedicated his *Commentarii* (app. 1, no. 5) to the Duke of Württemberg and his *Locorum Communium* (app. 1, no. 23) to the students of the university of Basle. Becon's *Coenae sacrosanctae domini* was dedicated to William, son of Philip of Hesse: Mozley, *Foxe and his Book*, pp. 42, 53; Firth, *Apocalyptic Tradition*, pp. 79–80; Bailey, *Becon*, p. 90. For the exiles' correspondence with the Reformers following their return see *Zurich Letters*, PS (1842).

integral part of the wider European movement. The reign of Edward VI had been marked by the closest co-operation between the English Reformers and their foreign mentors, an association which the exile under Mary served to strengthen and continue. It is within this context that these Latin works should be viewed. For they helped to promote abroad a vision of a Reformed Protestant England which, though temporarily submerged, the exiles never seemed to doubt would one day be restored.

University of St Andrews

Appendix 1 Checklist of Latin Polemic Published by the Marian Exiles Abroad, 1553-1559[1]

1553

(1) <u>Narratio/ historica vi/cissitudinis, rerum/</u> quæ in inclyto Britanniæ Regno/ acciderunt, Anno Domini/ 1553. Mense Iulio.// Scripta a P.V.// 1553.

1553.
80. Col: A1–B8.
Copies: London BL*.

(2) John Ponet. De ecclesia ad regem Edwardum.
Zurich, 1553.
No copies known. Noted in *DNB*, 46, p. 79 (s.v. Ponet).

1554

(3) John Philpot. <u>Vera/ exposi/tio disputa/tionis/ institu/</u>tæ mandato <u>D. Mariae Reginae/</u> Angl. Franc. & Hibern. &c. in Synodo/

---

[1] I have included all works by English exiles on religious themes, along with works by foreign theologians who were part of the exile movement. Latin works by English authors have been omitted when they appeared purely literary in character (works by Cheke, Becon), as have works by the foreign exiles which relate to new controversies on the Continent, and thus have no relevance to the English context (such as Marten Micron's writings against Menno Simons).

Underlining indicates that this part of the title is capitalized in the original. An asterisk (*) indicates that I have inspected that copy.

In compiling the checklist of copies I have made use of Schaaber's *Checklist of Books of British Authors Published Abroad*, along with published library catalogues and, where possible, personal visits. But it is recognized that this list will be by no means complete.

Ecclesiastica, Londini in Comitijs re/gni ad 18. Octob. Anno/ 1553.// His accesit Reverendiss. in Christo patris ac Domini./ D. Archiepiscopi Cantuariens. epistola apologetica/ ex Anglico auto-grapho latino facta ... 1554.//

Impressum Romæ Coram castro S. Angeli [i.e. Cologne], 1554. *STC* 19891. Translated from the English by Valérand Poullain. 80. Col: A1–8, a1–d8.

Copies: London BL, Lam.*; Oxford Bod. (2), Mer., Queens, Cam-bridge UL, Emma.; Berlin SB.

(4)   Valérand Poullain. Liturgia/ sacra, seu ritus/ Ministerii in Ecclesia peregrinorum/ Francofordiæ ad Mœ/num.// Addita est summa doctrinæ seu fidei pro/fessio eiusdem Ecclesiæ.// Francofordiæ/ 1554.//

[Peter Brubach], Frankfurt, 1554.
80. Col: a1–f8 (f8 blank).

Copies: London BL*; Oxford BNC; Glasgow UL; Stuttgart LB; Zurich ZB.

(5)   John Foxe. Commentarii/ rerum in ecclesia ge/starum, maximar-umque, per/ totam Europam, persecutio/num, a Vuicleui tempor-ibus/ ad hanc usque aetate descripto./ Liber primus.// Autore Ionne Foxo Anglo.// ... Argentorati/ Excudebat Vuendelinus Rihelius/ Anno M.D.LIIII.

Rihel, Strasburg, 1554.
80. Col: a1–8, A1–Z8, Aa1–Dd8, Ee1–3.

Copies: London BL; Oxford Bod. BNC; Cambridge UL; St Andrews UL*; Munich SB; Wolfenbüttel HAB; Colmar CAC; Paris BN; Harvard UL; Yale UL; Ohio UL; Williamstown CL.

(6)   John Bale. Nova prae/fatio Anglica, in/ veterum librum Vin-tonien/sis, ante 20. annos de vera obedientia/ scriptum, & editam Hamburgi, an/no 36. Latino sermone, missa in hoc/ mercatu Lypsico verno ex Anglia, & bo/na fide conversa in Latinum spacio trium/ horarum// ... Lipsiae,/ In officina typographica/ Georgij Hanzsch.// 1554.//

G. Hantzsch, Leipzig, 1554.
80. 15 pp.

Copies: Berlin SB; Wolfenbüttel HAB.

(7)   Martin Bucer. Psalmorum libri quinque ad He/braicam veritatem traducti, et/ summa fide, parique diligentia a Martino Bucero

enarrati.// Eiusdem commentarii/ In librum Iudicum,/ &/ In
Sophoniam Prophetam.// Oliva Roberti Stephani./ M.D. LIIII.

R. Stephanus, [Geneva], 1554 (May).

fo. Col: *1–8, a1–z8, A1–P8.

Copies: London BL, Lam; Oxford Bod, AS, Bal., BNC, Cor. (imp),
Ch. Ch., Mer., Queens, Trin; Cambridge UL (2), Trin, Clare, Que,
Emma., Pemb., Magd., Caius; Edin UL; St Andrews UL*; Dublin
Trin; Augsburg SB; Berlin SB; Erlangen UB; Nuremberg SB;
Regensburg SB; Dresden LB; Zurich ZB; Vienna NB; Paris BN;
Basle OB; Geneva BP; Lausanne BCan; Sibiu BM; Stockholm KB;
Brown UL.

(8) [An aquittal of the Church of England]. Latin version recorded in
preface to translation by John Olde (Emden, 1555). 1554?
No copies found.

1555

(9) Valérand Poullain. Liturgia/ sacra, seu ritus Mini/sterii in ecclesia
peregri/norum Francofordiae/ ad Moenum.// Addita est summa
doctrinæ, seu fidei pro/fessio eiusdem Ecclesiæ.// Editio
Secunda.// Francofordiæ./ 1555.//

[Peter Brubach], Frankfurt, 1555.

8o. Col: A1–H8.

Copies: London BL* (2), Oxford Bod., Dublin Trin., Munich SB,
Wolfenbüttel HAB.

(10) Forma/ ac ratio tota eccle/siastici Ministerij, in peregrinorum, po/
tissimum vero Germanorum Ecclesia: in/stituta Londini in Anglia,
per Pientissi/mum Principem Angliæ &c. Regem E/duardum, eius
nominis Sextu': An/no post Christum natum 1550. Addito/ ad
calcem libelli Privilegio/ suæ Maiestatis.// Autore Ioanne a La/sco
Poloniæ Barone.// ...

[Ctematius, Emden & Egenolff, Frankfort, 1555]. *STC* 16571.

8o. Col: α1–ε8, ψ1–4, A1–Z8, Aa1–Pp8. 348ff.

Copies: London BL (2)*; Dutch Ch; Lamb.*; Oxford Bod., Cam-
bridge UL (imp), Caius, Emma.*, West., Edinburgh NL, UL (2);
Dublin Trin., Brussels KB*; Groningen UB; Utrecht UB; Paris BN;
Strasburg BNU; Geneva BPU; Bonn UL; Dilligen StUB; Göttingen
UB; Heidelberg UB; Munich SB*; Tübingen UB*; Wolfenbüttel
HAB; Copenhagen KB (2); Washington Fol, Huntington.

(11) Robert Barnes. <u>Vitae/ Romanorum ponti</u>/ficum, quos Papas vocamus, summa/ diligentia ac fide collectæ, per D./ <u>Robertum Barns</u>, S. Theo/logiæ Doctorem Anglum, Londini/ Anno abhinc XV pro Chri/sti nomine com/bustum.// <u>Eiusdem sententiae</u>,/ sive præcipui Christianæ religionis articuli . . .// <u>Basileae</u>.// [Oporinus], Basle [1555].
80. Col: α1–8, ψ1–4, a1–z8, A1–B8, C1–4, D1–8, E1–4.
Copies: London BL (2)*, Lam. (misf)*; Oxford Bod.; Cambridge UL; Dublin Trin.; Berlin SB; Cologne SUB; Gotha LB; Halle UB; Leipzig UB; Münster UB; Munich SB; Wolfenbüttel HAB; Zürich ZB; Paris BN; Vienna NB; Harvard; New York Union.

(12) <u>Episto/læ duæ, duorum/ amicorum, ex quibus</u>/ vana, flagitiosaque Pontificum Pau/li tertij, & Iulii tertij, & Cardinalis Po/li, & Stephani Gardineri pseudoepiscopi Vuintoniensis/ Angli, eorumque adulatorum sectatorumque/ ratio, magna ex parte potest/ intelligi.// <u>Cum Papae Privilegio</u>/ ad momentum horæ.// 1555.
80. Col: A1–8, B1–4.
Copies: London BL*; Cambridge St J.; Florence BN.

1556

(13) Nicolas Ridley. <u>D. Nicolai/ Ridleii episcopi Lon/dinensis De Coena</u>/ Dominica assertio,// <u>contra/ scelaratam illam trans</u>/substa'tiationis hæresim, quam e carcere author/ scripserat: unde etiam paulo post, id est XVI./ Octobr. die. M.D.LV. igni comburendus ex/trahebatur.// <u>Genevae</u>./ Apud Ioannem Crispinum/ M.D.LVI.//
Jean Crespin, Geneva, 1556. Translated from the English by William Whittingham.
80. Col: A1–G8, *1–**8.
Copies: London BL, Lam. (2)*; Oxford Bod., Bal., BNC, Ch. Ch. (2), Corp., Jesus, Queens, St J.; Univ., Worc., Cambridge UL (2), Trin., Caius, Emma., St J., Pemb., Jesus; Edinburgh NL, UL (2); Dublin Trin.; York Min.; Paris BN; Geneva NP; Maldon PL; Chicago New.

(14) <u>Aetiologi/a Roberti Vvatsoni</u>/ Angli, in qua explicatur, quare depre/hensus annum unum & menses pene/quatuor, propter Evangeliu'

incarce/ratus fuit: quena' inter ipsu' & eius An/tagonistas in carcere habita fuit disce/ptatio, de Transubstantiatione & reali/ Christi præsentia in Sacramento: &/ quo pacto corpore incolumi &/ illibata conscientia tandem/ expediuit eum/ Dominus.// . . .// Anno. M.D.LVI.

[Ctematius, Emden], 1556. *STC* 25111.
8o. Col: A1–H8, I1–4. 68ff.

Copies: London BL* (2); Cambridge UL*; Edinburgh UL; Norwich PL; York Minster; Halle UL; Munich SB (2)*; Zurich ZB.

(15) Aetiologi/a. Roberti Watsoni/ Anglia, in qua explicatur, quare depre/hensus annum unum & menses penequatuor, propter Evan-geliu' incarce/ratus fuit: quena' interipsu' & eius An/tagonistas in carcere habita fuit disce/ptatio, de Transubstantione & reali/ Christi praesentia in Sacramentis: &/ quo pacto corpore incolumi &/ illibata conscientia tandem/ expediuit eum/ Dominus.//

8o. Col: A1–H8, I1–4. 68ff. A variant edition.

Copies: Cambridge Trin.

(16) Liturgy. Ratio/ et forma/ publice orandi De/um, atque administ-stran/di sacramenta,/ et caet,// In Anglorum eccle/siam, quæ Genevæ colligitur, recepta: cum iu/dicio & comprobatione D. Iohannis Calvini.// Genevæ,/ apud Ioannem Crispinum,/ M.D.LVI.

Crespin, Geneva, 1556. *STC* 16565. Translation by William Whit-tingham.
8o. Col: A1–E8.

Copies: London BL*; Oxford Bod., Bal., Ch. Ch., Corpus, Jesus; Cambridge UL, Trin.; Edinburgh NL; Lincoln Cath.; Leiden UB*; Munich SB; Geneva NP; Boston PL; Harvard; New York Union.

(17) John Foxe. Christus Tri/umphans, comoe/dia apocaly/ptica;// Autore Ioanne Foxo Anglo.// Accessit,/ in Christum trium/ phantem, Autoris eiusdem Pa/negyricon.// Basileae, per Ioan/nem Oporinum.

Oporinus, Basle, 1556 (March).
8o. Col: A1–8, *1–4, B1–H8, J1–6.

Copies: London BL*; Oxford Bod. (imp), BNC; Cambridge UL, Trin.; Edinburgh UL; Munich SB; Zurich ZB; Harvard; Illinois UL; New York Union; Greenville Percy.

(18) John a Lasco. Epistolae/ tres lectu dignis/simæ,/ de recta et legi/ tima ecclesiarum Be/ne, instituendarum ratio/ne ac modo:// ad potentiss. Regem/ Poloniæ, Senatum, reliquosque/ Ordines:// D. Ioanne a Lasco Ba/rone Poloniæ, &c. autore.// Basileae, per Ioan/ nem Oporinum.//
Oporinus, Basle, 1556 (March).
80. Col: A1–G8.
Copies: Oxford Bod.* (2), Ch.Ch.; Manchester Ry; Leiden UB*; Utrecht UB; Munich SB; Harvard; New York Union.

(19) John a Lasco. Purgatio mini/strorum/ in ecclesiis pe/regrin. Francofurti,/ adversus eorum calumnias, qui ipso/rum doctrinam, de christi Do/mini in Coena sua præsentia, dis/sensionis accusant ab au/gustana Con/fessione.// Autore D. Ioanne a La/sco, Barone Polono.// Basileae,per Ioan/nem Oporinum.//
Oporinus, Basle, 1556 (Dec).
80. Col: a1–c8, d1–10.
Copies: London Lam*; Oxford Bod.*, Cambridge UL, Caius, Trin.; The Hague KB; Amsterdam UB; Utrecht UB; Munich SB.

1557

(20) Defensio/ veræ et catholicæ do/ctrinae de Sacramento corporis & sanguinis/ Christi Servatoris nostri, & quoru'dam/ in hac causa errorum co'futatio, verbo sanctissi/mo Domini nixa atq' fundata, & consensu anti/quissimorum Ecclesiæ scriptorum firmata, a Re/ verendiss. in Christo Patre ac Domino D./Thoma Cranmero/ Martyre, Archiepiscopo Can/tuariensi, Primate totius/ Angliæ, & Me/tropolitano,/ scripta,/ ab autorem in/ vinculis recognita/ & aucta.// Iesus Chrittus.// Embdæ, apud Gellium Ctematium./ M.D. LVII.//
Ctematius, Emden, 1557. STC 6005 (var.).
80. Col: A1–X8, Y1–4 (Y4 blank). 172ff.
Copies: London BL, Lambeth*; Oxford Bod., Bal., Corpus; Cambridge UL*; St J*, Edinburgh NL; Manchester Ry; St Andrews UL; Berlin SB; Munich SB*; Tübingen UB*; Stuttgart LB*; Amsterdam UL*; The Hague KB*; Copenhagen KB; Colmar ECA; Paris BN; St Gallen SB; Sibiu (Romania) BMB; Folger; Chicago New; Minneapolis UL.

(21)   Defensio/ veræ et catholicæ do/ctrinae de Sacramento corporis &
sanguinis/ Christi Servatoris nostri, & quoru'dam/ in hac causa
errorum co'futatio, verbo sanctissi/mo Domini nixa atq' fundata, &
consensu anti/quissimorum Ecclesiæ scriptoru' firmata, a Reve/-
rendiss. in Christo Patre & B. Martyre D./ Thoma Cranmero/
Archiepiscopo Cantuariensi,/ Primate totius Angliæ,/ & Me/tro-
politano,/ scripta, ab autore in vinculis recognita/ & aucta.// Iesus
Christus// M.D.LVII.

Ctematius, Emden, 1557. *STC* 6005. A variant edition.
8o. Col: A1–X8, Y1–4. 172ff.

Copies: London BL; Oxford Bod., All Souls, Exeter; Cambridge
Kings, Magd., St J. (2)*; Edinburgh NL, UL; Eton, Shrewsbury S;
York Min.; Harvard; Huntington; New York Union; Yale.

(22)   John Foxe. Ad inclytos ac/præpotentes An/gliae proceres,/
Ordines, & Status, totamque e/ius gentis Nobilitatem, pro/
afflictis fratri/bus/ supplicatio:// Autore Ioanne Foxo/ Anglo.//
Basileae, per Io/annem Oporinum.

Oporinus, Basle, 1557 (March).
8o. Col: a1–d8, e1–4.

Copies: London BL* (2), Lam*; Oxford Bod., BNC, Corpus; Cambridge UL; Munich SB; Wolfenbüttel HAB; Folger; Chicago New;
Harvard; Ohio UL.

(23)   John Foxe. Locorum Com/munium Tituli & Or/dines Centum
quinquaginda, ad seriem Præ/dicamentoru' decem descripti: in
quos, ceu/ certos nidos & capsulas, quæcunque sunt us/quam ex
Autoribus colligenda, le/ctores congerant stu/diosi: Autore Ioanne
Foxo Anglo.// . . . Basileae, apud Ioan/nem Oporinum.//

Oporinus, Basle, 1557 (March).
8o. Col: α1–4, a1–b8, (c1–z8, A1–R8, S1–4), T1–8. (Headed
pages, interleaved with blanks).

Copies: London BL*; Oxford Bod.; Cambridge UL; Munich SB,
UB (imp); Zurich ZB.

(24)   John Foxe. De Predicamentis Tabulae.

8o. Listed as a separate work in *Librorum per Oporinum Excusorum*
(1567), but probably a confusion with no. 23, above. See Mozley,
Foxe, p. 243.

(25)   John Foxe. Mira ac elegans cum primus Historia vel tragoedia
potius, de tota ratione examinationis et condemnationis J. Philpotti

Archidiaconi Wincestriae, nuper in Anglia exusti. Ab autore primum lingua sua congesta; nunc in Latinum versa. Interprete J.F.A.

1557? See Strype, *Cranmer* (1854), 3, p. 174. No copies found. Reprinted in *Rerum* (no. 39 below), pp. 543–631.

(26) Martin Bucer. <u>De Regno Chri</u>/sti Iesu servatoris nostri,/ Libri II.// <u>Ad Eduardum VI. Angliae</u>/ <u>Regem, annis abhinc sex scripti</u>:/ non solum Theologis atque Iurisperitis profutu/ri, verum etiam cunctis Rempub. bene & feliciter/ administraturis cognitu cumprimis/ necessarij.// <u>D. Martino Bucero</u>/ <u>Autore.</u>// ... <u>Basileae, per</u> <u>Ioan</u>/nem Oporinum.//

Oporinus, Basle, 1557 (Sept).

fo. Col: a1–6, a1–z4, A1–G4, H1–6 (H6 blank).

Copies: Oxford Bod. (2)*, Balliol, Magd., Queens; Cambridge UL (2), Cath., St J.; Edinburgh UL; The Hague KB; Leiden UB*; Augsburg SB; Coburg LB; Wolfenbüttel HAB (2); Basle OB; Bern StB; Zürich ZB; Strasburg BN; Copenhagen KB, UB; Debrecen Coll.

(27) Peter Martyr Vermigli. <u>Disputatio</u>/ <u>de Euchari</u>/stiae sacramento <u>ha</u>/<u>bita in celeberrima uni</u>/versitate Oxoniensi in Anglia, antea qui/dem illic excusa, iam vero denuo/ cum triplici Indice in lu/cem edita.// <u>Tiguri apud And. Gesne</u>/rum, anno M.D.LVII.//

Andreas Gesner, Zurich, 1557.

8o. Col: +1–8, A1–V8, Aa1–Cc8, Dd1–4.

Copies: Oxford Bod.*; Cambridge Emma.

(28) Peter Martyr Vermigli. <u>Petri Martyris</u>/ <u>Vermilii Florentini</u>/ <u>Viri</u> <u>doctissimi de sacra</u>/mento eucharistiæ in celeberrima An/gliæ schola Oxoniensi ha/bita tractatio.// <u>Tiguri apud And. Ges/-</u> <u>nerum, Anno M.D. LVII.</u>

Gesner, Zurich, 1557.

8o. Col: a1–b8, A1–V8.

Copies: Oxford Bod.*; Freiburg UL; Zurich ZB; Paris BN; Forence BNC.

(29) John Ponet. <u>Diallä</u>/<u>cticon viri bo</u>/<u>ni et literati, de veri</u>/tate, Natura atque Substantia Corpo/ris & Sanguinis Christi in/ Eucharistia.// ... Anno M.D.LVII.

[Rihel, Strasburg], 1557.

8o. Col:)(1–4, A1–O8, P1–4.

Copies: London BL*; Oxford Bod., Ch. Ch. (2); Cambridge UL; Edinburgh UL; Dublin Trin (2); Washington LCon.

(29a?) John Ponet. Axiomata Eucharistiae.
A different book? See *DNB*, 46, p. 79.

(30) Thomas Becon. Gnomotheca/ Solomonis, ad vi/<u>tam pie institu-endam</u>,/ dignosque Christiano homine mo/ses excole'dos longe utilissima: ex/ omnibus ipsius, qui quidem exta't,/ libris desumpta, atque in Locos dige/sta communes, per Thomam/ Beconum Anglum.// <u>Basileae, per Ioan</u>/nem Oporinum.

Oporinus, Basle, [1557].
8o. Col: a1–m8, n1–4.

Copies: Oxford Bod.*; Munich SB; Vienna NB; Colmar AC; Folger.

(30a) A number of other Latin works by Becon are listed by Bale, *Catalogus* (1557), p. 727: In Germania Latine congessit ... Introductionem ad pietatem; Miscellanea religionis; De authoritate verbi Dei, etc.

Whether these works were separately printed and published is not certain.

(31) John Bale. <u>Scriptorum il</u>/lustriu' maioris Britanniæ quam/ nunc Angliam & Scotiam vocant: mul/torumque aliorum, qui in eadem uixerunt & obierunt insula, Catalo/gus: a Iapheto per 3617 annos, usque ad annum hunc Domini 1556 ... in XII Centurias partitus.// Autore <u>Ioanne Baleo</u> Sudouolgio Anglo ...// <u>Basileae, apud</u> Ioan/nem Oporinum.//

Oporinus, Basle, 1557 (September). A first printing of no. 32, below.
fo. Col: t/p, a1–z4, A1–Z4, aa1–zz4, Aa1–Zz4, Aaa1–4.
Copies: London BL*.

(32) John Bale. <u>Scriptorum il</u>/lustriu' maioris Brytannie, quam/ nunc Angliam & Scotiam vocant: Ca/talogus: a Iapheto per 3618 annos, usque ad annu' hunc Domini 1557./ ... ix Centurias continens:// ... Autore <u>Ioanne Baleo</u> Sudouolgia Anglo ...// <u>Basileae, apud</u> Ioan/nem Oporinum.//

Oporinus, Basle, 1557 (September).
fo. Col: α1–6, β1–γ4, a1–z4, A1–Z4, aa1–zz4, Aa1–Zz4, Aaa1–4.

Copies: London BL (2); Oxford Bod. (3), AS, Bal., Corp., Ch. Ch., Eng., Hert., Magd., Mer., New, Queens, St J., Trin., Worc.; Cambridge UL (2), Trin., Caius, Kings (2), Corp., Jesus, Magd., Queens, St J., Emma., Pet., Clare, Cath.; Edinburgh NL, UL (2), New; Manchester UL (2); St Andrews UL*; Aberdeen UL; Glasgow UL; Exeter Cath.; The Hague KB; Leiden UB*; Utrecht UB; Berlin SB; Darmstadt LB, Erlangen UB, Frankfurt SUB, Göttingen UB, Hamburg SUB, Hannover KM; Karlsruhe LB; Lübeck SB; Munich SB; Mainz SB; Oldenburg LB; Stuttgart LB; Tübingen UB; Wolfenbüttel HAB; Weimar LB; Zürich ZB; Vienna NB, UB; Graz UB; St Gallen SB; Paris BN; Rome BA; Geneva UB; Wroclawin UB; Yale; Iowa UL; Baltimore PL; Princeton UL; New York PL; Penna BMC; Brown UL; Texas UL; Wisconsin UL.

Many copies with no. 43, below. See also no. 42.

1558

(33) John Bale. Acta Romano/<u>rum pontificum, a di</u>/spersione discipulorum Christi, usq'; ad/ tempora Pauli quarti, qui nunc in Eccle/sia tyrannizat: Ex Ioannis Balei Sudo/uolgii Angli maiore Catalogo Anglico/rum scriptorum desumpta, & in tres/ Classes, Libros vero se/ptem, divisa.// <u>Basileae.</u>//

Oporinus, Basle, 1558 (July).
8o. Col: *1–***8, a1–z8, A1–V8.

Copies: London BL, Lam.*; Oxford Bod., Exeter, Jes., Magd., Queens, Univ.; Cambridge UL, Emma., Pem., St J., Magd. (imp); Edinburgh UL; Aberdeen UL; Aberystwyth NL; The Hague KB; Berlin SB; Darmstadt LB; Detmold LB; Frankfurt SUB; Giessen UB; Göttingen UB; Halle UB; Munich SB; Nuremberg SB; Rostock UB; Weimar LB; Wolfenbüttel HAB; Zurich ZB; Paris BN; Sibiu BMB; Vienna NB; Chicago UL.

(34) Robert Barnes. <u>Senten/tiae ex doctori/bus collectae, per doctiss:</u> <u>virum R. Barni/ Anglum, sacrae theologiae</u>/ doctorem: Nunc longe quam antea emendatius edi/te ...// Authore Eberharto Haberkorn,/ Ursellanæ Ecclesiæ ministro./ Anno 1558.

Ursellis, excudebat Nicolaus Henricus, 1558.
8o. Col: *,)(, **1–8, A1–4, B1–Q8, R1–4.

Copies: Cambridge Caius (imp), Emma., Berlin SB; Frankfurt
SUB; Jena UB; Tübingen UB; Wiesbaden LB; Wolfenbüttel HAB;
Woclawin BU; Vienna NB.

(35) Simon Alexius [Pierre Alexandre]. <u>De/ origine/ novi Dei Mis</u>-
<u>sati/ci, quondam in Anglia</u>/ mortui, nunc denuo ab inferis excitati:
<u>Dialogi vii.</u>// <u>Simone Alexio Autore.</u>//

[Crespin, Geneva], 1558.
8o. Col: A1–4, B1–I8, K1–4.

Copies: Oxford Bod.*, Worc.; Cambridge Caius; Aberdeen UL;
Ghent UB; Paris BN.

(36) Pierre Alexandre. <u>De/ origine/ novi dei missati/ci, quondam in</u>
<u>anglia</u>/ mortui, nunc denuo ab inferis excitati:/ <u>dialogi vii.</u>// ...
<u>Simone Alexio Authore.</u>// Genevæ.

[Crespin], Geneva, [1558]. Variant of above.
8o. Col: A1–4, B1–I8, K1–4.

Copies: London BL, Lam. (2)*; Cambridge UL; Dublin Trin.;
Amsterdam FU; Utrecht UB.

(37) Peter Martyr Vermigli. <u>In epistolam S. Pau</u>/li Apostoli ad
Romanos, D. Petri/ Martyris Vermilii Florentini, Professoris/
divinarum literarum in schola Tigurina,/ commentarii doctissimi,
cum tra/ctatione perutili rerum & lo/corum, qui ad eam epi-
sto/lam pertinent.// <u>Basileæ/ apud Petrum Pernam.</u>/ M.D.LVIII.

Pernam, Basle, 1558.
fo. Col: α1–6, *1–4, a1–z6, A1–Z6, Aa1–Gg6, Hh1–4, α1–δ6
(δ6 blank).

Copies: Oxford Bod., Magd., New, Queens, Univ.; Cambridge
Corp. (imp), Pem.; Aberdeen UL; St Andrews UL (2)*; Tübingen
UB; Arrau AKB; Basle UB; Neuchâtel BP, PasB; St Gallen SB,
Zürich ZB, Deventer AB, Utrecht UB, Paris BN, Florence BNC,
Sarospatek RCL; Washington Con, St Louis Eden.

(38) Thomas Becon. <u>Antholia/ Lactantii/ Firmiani, Ele/gantissimas</u>
<u>sen</u>/tentias, easque tam pietate, quam doctri/na illustres, com-
plectens: recenter/ in locos digesta communes/ per Thomam
Be/conum.// <u>Lugduni/ apud Clementem Baudinum</u>/ 1558.

Clément Baudin, Lyons, 1558.
8o. Col: +1–8, *1–8, a1–q8.

Copies: Cambridge UL, St J.; Durham UL; Paris BN, Maz.;
Avignon MuC.

1559

(39) John Foxe. Rerum/ in ecclesia ge/starum, quæ postremis & peri-
cu/losis his temporibus evenerunt, maxi/marumq'; per Europam
persecutionum, act Sanctorum Dei/ Martyrum, cæterarumq';
rerum si quæ insignioris/ exempli sint, digesti per Regna & na-
tio/nes Commentarij.// Pars Prima .. // Autore Ioanne Foxo
Anglo.// Basileae, per Nicolaum/ Brylingerum, et Ioan/nem
Oporinum.//
Brilinger and Oporinus, Basle, 1559 (Aug).
fo. Col: A1–4, a1–z4, A1–Z8, aa1–qq4, rr1–8, ss1–zz4, Aa1–Ff4,
Gg1–6, Hh1–Jj4, Kk1–6, Ll1–Yy4.
Copies: London BL, Lam.*; Oxford Bod., AS, Bal., BNC, Ch. Ch.,
Jes., Keble, Pem.,Queens, Univ., Worc.; Cambridge UL, Trin.,
Emma., Queens, Pet., Sid., Corp., Magd.; Edinburgh NL, UL (2);
Manchester Ry; Dublin Trin.; Amsterdam UB; Deventer; Utrecht
UB; Göttingen UB; Munich SB (2); St Gallen SB; Zurich ZB;
Huntington; Harvard; Yale; Chicago New; Illinois UL; New York
PL, Union; Pennsylvania UL; Princeton UL; Williamstown CL.

(40) John Bale. Acta Romanorum pontificum, a dispersione disci-
pulorum Christi.
Basle, 1559.
8o.
Copies: Cologne SUB; Dresden LB; Gotha LB; Jena UB; Stuttgart
LB; Tübingen UB; Wolfenbüttel HAB; Rome BA; Vienna NB;
Yale.

(41) John Bale. Scriptorum Brytannia catalogus.
Basileae apud Ioannem Oporinum [1559].
fo.
Copies: London BL; Kassel LB; Boston CL; New York PL.

(42) John Bale. Scriptorum Il/lustriu' maioris Brytannie, quam/ nunc
Angliam & Scotiam vocant: Ca/talogus: a Iapheto per 3618 annos,
usque ad annu' hunc Domini 1557./ . . . IX Centurias continens://
Autore Ioanne Baleo Sudouolgia Anglo .. // Basileae, apud
Ioan/nem Oporinum.//

326

Oporinus, Basle, 1557 (September).

fo. Col: α1–5, [α2–6], β1–γ4, a1–z4, A1–Z4, aa1–zz4, Aa1–Zz4, Aaa1–4.

The edition of 1557 (no. 32) with a letter of dedication to Queen Elizabeth inserted.

Copies: London BL*.

(43) John Bale. <u>Scriptorum il</u>/lustrium maioris Brytanniæ po/sterior pars, quinque continens Cen/<u>turias ultimas, quas author, Ioannes</u>/ Baleus Sudouolgius, Anglus, ex Lelando Antiqua/rio, alijsque probis authoribus, non par/vo labore collegit.// . . . <u>Basileae per Ioan</u>/nem Oporinum.

Oporinus, Basle, 1559 (February).

fo. Col: α1–6, β1–4, a1–z4, A1–T4.
Second part of no. 32.

Copies: London BL (2)*, Lam.*; Oxford Bod. (3); Cambridge UL (2), Trin., Caius, Kings, Corp., Jesus, Magd., Queens, St J., Emma., Pet., Clare, Cath.; Edinburgh NL, UL (2), New; St Andrews UL*; Glasgow HM; Leiden UB*; Utrecht UB; Munich SB; Paris BN; Philadelphia LC.

(44) John Bale. <u>Scriptorum il</u>/lustriu' maioris Brytannie, quam/ nunc Angliam & Scotiam vocant: Ca/talogus: a Iapheto per 3620 annos, usque ad annu' hunc Domini 1559,/ ex Beroso, Gennadio . . . atque alijs authoribus collectus,/ & XIIII Centurias continens:// Autore <u>Ioanne Baleo</u> Sudouolgio Anglo . . . <u>Basileae, apud Ioan</u>/nem Oporinum.//

Oporinus, Basle, 1559.

fo. Col: α1–6, β1–γ4, a1–z4, A1–Z4, aa1–zz4, Aa1–Zz4, Aaa1–4.

Copies: London Lam.*; Canterbury CL.

(45) Thomas Becon. <u>Coenae Sa</u>/cro sanctae domini/ nostri Jesu Christi, & Missæ Papisti/cæ, Comparatio . . .// <u>Autore Thoma Beco</u>/no Anglo.// <u>Basileae, per Ioan</u>/nem Oporinum.//

Oporinus, Basle, 1559 (June).

8o. Col: α1–χ8, A1–Q8 (Q8 blank).

Copies: London BL*, Lam.*; Oxford Bod. (2), Ch. Ch., Linc., Worc.; Cambridge UL, Trin.; Edinburgh UL; Dublin Trin.; Exeter Cath.; York Min.; Ghent UB; Bonn UB; Berlin SB; Lübeck SB;

Munich SB; Oldenburg LB; Tübingen UB; Wolfenbüttel HAB; Colmar CAC; Salzburg BSB; Vienna NB; Wroclaw UB.

(46) Peter Martyr Vermigli. Defensio/ Doctrinæ veteris & Apostolicæ/ de sacrosancto Eucharistiæ Sacramento, D. Petri Martyris/ Vermilij, Florentini ... adversus Stephani Gardineri, quondam/ Vuintonien'. Episcopi, librum ...//

[Froschover, Zurich, 1559].
fo. Col: *1–6, a1–z6, A1–Z6, Aa1–Xx6, Yy1–4, Zz1–6.

Copies: London BL, Lam.*; Oxford Magd., Univ.; Cambridge UL, Trin., Caius, St J., Pet., Corp.; Edinburgh UL (3); Aberdeen UL; St Andrews UL; Groningen UB; Leiden UB*; Utrecht UB.

Leiden UB copy col: *1–6, aa1–6, bb1–4 (index), a1– etc.

(47) Peter Martyr Vermigli. Defensio/ D. Petri Marty/ris Vermilii Flor-entini/ Divinarum literarum in Scho/la Tigurina professoris, ad Riccardi Smythæi An/gli, olim Theologiæ professoris Oxoniensis/ duos libellos de Cælibatu sacerdo/tum, & Votis monasticis,/ Nunc primum in luce/ edita.// Basileae apud Petrum Pernam.// M.D.L.IX.

Pernam, Basle, 1559.
8o. Col: *1–4, a1–z8, A1–L8, M1–4.

Copies: London Lam.*; Oxford Bod., BNC, Ch. Ch.; Cambridge Trin., Sid., Corp.; Dublin Trin.; St Andrews UL; Utrecht UB; Ghent UB; Brown UL.

(48) Peter Martyr Vermigli. In Eposto/lam S. Pauli A/postoli ad Romanos D./ Petri Martyris Vermilii Floren/tini, Professoris divinarum literarum in schola Tigurina,/ commentarij doctissimi, ...// Tiguri M.D.LIX.//

[Gesner], Zurich, 1559.
8o. Col: α1–8, β1–4, γ1–8, δ1–2, a1–z8, A1–Z8, Aa1–Yy8, a1–e8, f1–4.

Copies: Cambridge Caius, Emma.; Edinburgh UL; St Andrews UL*; Dublin Trin.; Munich SB; Neuchâtel BV; Budapest Academy.

(49) Laurence Humphrey. De Religionis/ conservatione &/ reforma-tione/ vera:// Deque Primatu Regum &/ magistratuum, & obedientia/ illis ut summis in terra Chri/sti vicarijs præstanda,/ Liber:// Ad Nobilitatem, Clerum & po/pulum Anglicanum.//

Laurentio Hum/fredo autore.// Basileae, per Ioan/nem Oporinum.//

Oporinus, Basle, 1559 (Sept),
8o. Col: a1–g8.

Copies: London BL*; Cambridge UL (2), Caius, Emma.; Munich
SB; New York Union.

(50) John Foxe. Germaniæ ad/ Angliam,/ de Restituta E/vangelij luce,
Gra/tulatio.// Basileae, per Io/annem Oporinum./ 1559.

Oporinus, Basle, 1559 (Jan).
8o. Col: a1–d8 (d8 blank).

Copies: London Lam.*; Munich SB; Basle UB.

ERECTING THE DISCIPLINE IN PROVINCIAL ENGLAND: THE ORDER OF NORTHAMPTON, 1571

by W. J. SHEILS

> As that no Commonwealth can flourish or long indure without good
> lawes and sharpe execution of the same, so neither can the Kirk of
> God be brought to purity neither yet be retained in the same without
> the order of Ecclesiastical Discipline ... drunkenesse, excesse be it in
> apparel, or be it in eating and drinking, fornication, oppressing of the
> poore by exactions, deceiving of them in buying and selling by wrong
> met and measure, wanton words and licentious living tending to
> slander, doe openly appertaine to the Kirk of God to punish them, as
> God's word commands.

SUCH a declaration of the central role of discipline within the
Reformed tradition is a commonplace to all historians of the
Reformation and will be familiar to the editor of *The First Book of
Discipline*, from which the above quotation comes.[1] The head, the seventh
and entitled 'Of Ecclesiastical Discipline', conformed in its procedure to
the practice of established Calvinist congregations on the Continent in its
austere attitude to the unrepentant sinner as in its care for the repentant
individual who, on an appointed day before the whole kirk,

> in presence of all he may testifie his repentance, which before he pro-
> fessed. Which if he accept and with reverence confesse his sinne,
> doing the same and earnestly desiring the Congregation to pray to
> God with him for mercy, and to accept him within their societie
> notwithstanding the former offence; then the Kirk may and ought to
> receive him as a penitent. For the Kirk ought to be no more severe
> then God declares himselfe to be, who witnesses that in whatsoever
> houre a sinner unfainedly repents and turns from his wicked ay, that
> he will not remember one of his iniquities. And therefore ought the
> Kirk diligently to advert that it excommunicate not those whom God
> absolves.[2]

---

[1] *The First Book of Discipline*, ed. J. K. Cameron (Edinburgh, 1972), pp. 165–7.
[2] Ibid., p. 168.

Throughout the *Book of Discipline* the congregational responsibility for such pastoral discipline was stressed, and the exercise of such powers was vested in the ministry, that is the ministers, elders, and deacons, acting as executives of the wishes of the whole congregation.[3] And so it was to be understood in the Reformed tradition, which a number of the divines commissioned to write the *Book*, most particularly John Knox, had experienced during periods of exile or study on the Continent. Such experiences were, of course, shared by several English divines during the reign of Mary, and many of them came to admire the forms of church-manship they had witnessed in Strasburg, Frankfurt, or Geneva.[4] The English exiles, however, returned to an episcopal Church, which had seen briefly during Edward's reign some examples of Reformed episcopacy in action and had witnessed under Mary the sacrifice of martyrdom by those same bishops.[5] Whatever the experiences of the exiles, the vast majority were willing, if not completely convinced, to serve within an episcopal Church, and very few individuals chose to stay out of the formal church structures. The pastoral need for Protestant clergy was so great that this issue overrode both the wishes of those in authority and the personal qualms of individuals, so that a man like William Whittingham, who had been called to the ministry in Geneva and had never received episcopal ordination, could be presented to and accept the deanery of Durham.[6]

To a number of the returning exiles the Settlement of 1559 was the starting-point for further reform of the Church, if not entirely in the direction of the Continental Reformed Churches at least in the removal of the most objectional traces of popery within the liturgy and towards a more pastorally effective hierarchy. The wishes and the political needs of the Queen in dealing with her conservative subjects obstructed the first of these aims,[7] and the vexed question of ecclesiastical property rights and the financial exactions of the Crown and some magnates placed dif-ficulties in the way of the second.[8] Nevertheless, many of the returned

---

[3] *The First Book of Discipline*, ed. J. K. Cameron (Edinburgh, 1972), pp. 32–4.

[4] C. Garrett, *The Marian Exiles* (Cambridge, 1938).

[5] D. M. Loades, *The Oxford Martyrs* (London, 1970); R. Houlbrooke, 'The Protestant Episcopate 1547–1603: the pastoral contribution' in F. Heal and R. O'Day, eds, *Church and Society in England: Henry VIII to James I* (London, 1977), pp. 78–9.

[6] Garrett, *Marian Exiles*, pp. 327–30.

[7] N. L. Jones, *Faith by Statute: Parliament and the Settlement of Religion 1559* (London, 1982), esp. pp. 186–9; W. P. Haugaard, *Elizabeth and the English Reformation* (Cambridge, 1968), esp. pp. 109–11.

[8] F. M. Heal, *Of Prelates and Princes: a Study of the Economic and Social Position of the Tudor Episcopate* (Cambridge, 1980), pp. 202–36.

exiles, both those who had accepted senior posts in the Church and those who had stayed aloof, continued to look for advice and leadership from among the Continental divines and, in the early years of the reign, saw the English Church as part of a more general reform movement.[9]

Prominent among those who continued contact with the Continent was Percival Wiburn, a Cambridge graduate, whose career following his return from Geneva exemplifies the ambivalent and critical attitude which the more radical exiles, whom he himself chose to call 'the hotter sort of Protestants', adopted towards the Established Church. On his return, Wiburn was appointed junior dean and lecturer at St John's College, Cambridge, where he had been a scholar and later fellow[10] while Thomas Lever, who himself chose to remain somewhat aloof from the formal ministry as lecturer in Coventry in the early sixties, was Master. Wiburn's earlier career coincided with a period when St John's represented the vanguard of Cambridge Protestantism.[11] Significantly, in the context of future developments, Wiburn removed himself to Geneva in the spring of 1557, soon after the establishment of *The Forme of Prayers and Ministration of the Sacraments* for the English exiles there by John Knox. This document, and in particular the Confession of Faith which preceded it, laid particular emphasis on 'discipline' as a distinguishing mark of the Church, and Wiburn's time in the city coincided with Calvin's success in gaining this freedom of discipline for the Church in Geneva. His experience there most certainly informed the view of true churchmanship which he was eventually to introduce to Northampton. In the meantime, however, in 1560 Wiburn was ordained, but remained out of the pastoral ministry, retaining a fellowship at St John's and prebendal stalls at Norwich and Rochester cathedrals. He moved to London, but felt unable to comply with the subscription required of him to assume the important vicarage of St Sepulchre, Holborn. He remained in London with his family, preaching in an unofficial capacity, which was connived at by authority, while retaining his cathedral prebends,[12] and as such found himself involved in the Vestarian controversy, following Archbishop

[9] *Zurich Letters*, ed. H. Robinson, 2 vols, PS (1842–5) prints much correspondence between English and continental divines in this period.

[10] *DNB*, 21, p. 175.

[11] W. S. Hudson, *The Cambridge Connection and the Elizabethan Settlement of 1559* (Durham, N. Carolina, 1980), pp. 54–7; P. Collinson, *The Elizabethan Puritan Movement* (London, 1967), p. 51.

[12] Garrett, *Marian Exiles*, p. 331; G. Lewis, 'Calvinism in Geneva in the Time of Calvin and Beza 1541–1608' in M. Prestwich, ed., *International Calvinism 1541–1715* (Oxford, 1985), pp. 41, 44–50; J. Ridley, *John Knox* (Oxford, 1968), p. 264.

Parker's *Advertisements* requiring the London clergy to wear the surplice
and other aspects of clerical dress objectionable to the radicals. Wiburn,
with nineteen other leading divines, including John Foxe, the Dean of St
Paul's, three archdeacons in the London diocese, William Whittingham,
and two heads of Oxford colleges, appealed to the Ecclesiastical Commission on 20 March 1565 for more time for discussion before conformity
was enforced. A few clergy were moved against, but the crisis in the
capital came to a head in the following year when thirty-seven clergy of
London were suspended during Easter week 1566.[13]

The consequence of this crisis for Wiburn was to renew his contact
with the Continent. During the summer of 1566 he travelled to Geneva
and Zurich with a critical report on the state of the Church in England
which appears to have had a profound effect on Theodore Beza,
producing a lengthy account of the problems in England as perceived by a
leader of the Reformed tradition: 'Such, then, is the state of the Anglican
churches, which, as it appears to me, is very wretched, and altogether
beyond endurance'; and asking Heinrich Bullinger to despatch someone
from Zurich to England to attempt to solicit the Queen and the bishops,
and to lobby Parliament in the cause of further reform.[14] Wiburn's report,
a copy of which survives in the Zurich archives, comprised a comprehensive criticism of the Established Church under thirty-one heads: it
criticized the surviving number of popish clergy within the Church and
the fact that the call to the ministry depended upon episcopal ordination;
complained that clergy were required to acknowledge the royal supremacy and other externals of church order regarding rights and ceremonies,
but that no great difficulty was raised 'about any other points of doctrine';
pointed out the very restrictive attitude to clerical marriage in the royal
injunctions; noted the continued existence of the pre-Reformation
system of church courts, and the fact that many of the lawyers operating
therein were papists; and regretted the survival of so many superstitious
practices, such as feast-days, the sign of the cross in baptism, and the
wearing of vestments.[15] The list of defects represented the views of many
of the more radical of the returned exiles, but it is not clear on whose
authority Wiburn's mission to Europe was undertaken. It is clear that he
was not acting alone. The proposal to send Reformed divines to England
to plead the cause indicates that he was acting in concert with others,

[13] Collinson, *Elizabethan Puritan Movement*, pp. 67–83.
[14] *Zurich Letters*, 2, pp. 127–36, esp. p. 130.
[15] Ibid., pp. 358–61.

possibly including Thomas Lever.[16] Whatever the intention, the document was seen by hitherto sympathetic bishops like Edmund Grindal as a breach of faith and the source of the more hostile views of the English Church held among some Continental divines.[17] It ensured that Wiburn, unlike many of his fellow signatories to the petition of 1565, would remain outside the normal ecclesiastical structures.

Wiburn's movemens after his journey to the Continent are not clear, but he was brought to the attention of the Earl of Leicester, already a supporter of the more radical Protestants, and through him to the gentry of Northamptonshire, and it was almost certainly George Carleton of Overstone, a few miles north of the county town, who introduced Wiburn to Northampton itself.[18] This was in 1570.

At that date the Reformation appears to have made little progress in either the town or the countryside around, where a number of established Catholic families, like the Treshams and the Catesbys, were influential.[19] The town itself had a population of something over 3,000 in the mid-sixteenth century, and, in common with most other county towns, was governed by an oligarchic body comprising the mayor and ex-mayors, known as the Twenty-four, who were also responsible for nominating the members of the secondary chamber, the Common Council, representing the commonalty of the borough, known as the Forty-eight.[20] The town had an essentially service-based economy, with both textile and leather trades well represented, and a large number of shoemakers. The horse fair at the town was one of national importance, and the leather trades were probably also of more than local significance.[21] Despite this range of economic ties, and the relative proximity of the town to the universities, there is only modest evidence for early Protestant opinions at Northampton,[22] and, if anything, it was the survival of conservative practices that was remarked upon in the 1560s.[23] The most significant changes

[16] See the letters from Laurence Humphrey and Thomas Sampson in ibid., 1, pp. 151–5, 157–65.

[17] Ibid., pp. 168–9, 175–81.

[18] Collinson, *Elizabethan Puritan Movement*, pp. 142–3.

[19] G. Anstruther, *Vaux of Harrowden* (Newport, 1951); for the effect of recusancy on the Treshams see M. E. Finch, *Five Northamptonshire Families* = Northants Record Society, 19 (1956), pp. 72–92.

[20] *VCH Northamptonshire*, 3, p. 9, following C. A. Markham and J. C. Cox, eds, *The Borough Records of Northampton*, 2 vols (London and Northampton, 1898).

[21] W. G. Hoskins, *Provincial England* (London, 1963), p. 79.

[22] A. G. Dickens, 'Early Protestantism and the Church in Northamptonshire', *Northamptonshire Past and Present*, 8 (1983–4), pp. 27–40.

[23] Both the letter of the Earl of Leicester referred to at n. 42 below, and article 16 of the Order

brought about by the Reformation prior to 1570 were institutional ones; the town had been transferred from the large diocese of Lincoln to the more compact but impoverished see of Peterborough, which had been established in 1540, and the disruption resulting from this change had brought about uncertainty over relations between the traditional archdeaconry court and the consistory court of the new diocese, with harmful results for ecclesiastical discipline.[24] Within the town itself the parochial system was reorganized so that the nine pre-Reformation parishes were reduced to five, one of which, St Mary's, was itself to be absorbed by All Saints parish, in the centre of the town, by the end of the century. Further, All Saints itself became the 'town church', that most closely associated with the corporation, displacing St Giles. Three of the four main churches were Crown livings, and this gave the corporation the opportunity, which it took, to influence ecclesiastical patronage in the town.[25]

This local situation, which Wiburn found on his arrival in Northampton in 1570, needs to be set briefly in the context of national events. Cartwright's lectures at Cambridge had provided the native intellectual case for Presbyterianism, and had initiated a power struggle within the University which was to result in his removal from his professorship and departure for Geneva at the end of 1570.[26] In London some of Wiburn's earlier Puritan contacts around the personality of John Field were actively pursuing radical initiatives and were hopeful that Parliamentary pressure might bring further reform. Within London itself, Field was involved in a Presbyterian experiment, involving the election of elders, at Wandsworth,[27] and the sketchy details surviving from his correspondence provides us with a link between events in London and Northampton. One of Field's correspondents at this time, and his 'very friend', was a Mrs Catesby, probably Isabel Catesby of Whiston, who was soon to provide

---

refer to recent reports of conservative practices. See also Anstruther, *Vaux of Harrowden*, pp. 77–9.

[24] W. J. Sheils, 'Some problems of government in a new diocese: the bishop and the puritans in the diocese of Peterborough 1560–1630' in R. O'Day and F. Heal, eds, *Continuity and Change: Personnel and Administration of the Church in England 1500–1642* (Leicester, 1976), pp. 173–7. The upheavals resulted in the almost complete loss of court records from 1540 to 1570. W. J. Sheils, *The Puritans in the Diocese of Peterborough 1558–1610* = Northants Record Society, 30 (1979), p. 6.

[25] Ibid., p. 119. In addition to the parish churches, the hospital of St John was another useful source of patronage for the corporation: see the case of Arthur Wake in ibid., pp. 29–30.

[26] A. F. Scott-Pearson, *Thomas Cartwright and Elizabethan Puritanism* (Cambridge, 1925), pp. 102–6.

[27] Collinson, *Elizabethan Puritan Movement*, p. 138.

shelter and support to Wiburn.[28] The activities of some of his erstwhile companions in London, and the intellectual disputes in Cambridge, help to explain the timing of Wiburn's 'Order of Northampton' and to place it within the broad framework of radical activity at this time. We can now turn to the document itself, which, remarkably enough, was finalized on 5 June 1571 'by the consent of the Bysshop of Peterborough, the maior and brethrene of the Towne there, and others of the Queenes Majesties Justices of peace within the said Countie and Towne'.[29]

The Order, which comprised a system of church worship and discipline based firmly on Genevan lines, a regular exercise for the clergy of the area, and, perhaps most radical of all, a Confession of Faith to be made by all church members, was not without its opponents in a town which, hitherto, had shown little positive sign of 'zeal of the Gospel', and scurrilous pamphlets opposing Wiburn's policy were circulating in the town.[30] In this context, the support he received from the local gentry, the Justices mentioned in the Order, was probably crucial both in securing the support of the leading townsmen and, more surprisingly, in persuading the Bishop to agree. What was it that he agreed to?

The articles of the Order covered four main aspects of church life; the conduct of services, the administration of Communion, the practice of preaching, and the arrangements for discipline, as well as setting out general guide-lines for the clergy of the area. In their scope they were heavily influenced by the arrangements in Geneva.[31] In the conduct of

[28] Ibid., p. 136; *The Visitations of Northamptonshire made in 1564 and 1618–19*, ed. F. C. Metcalfe, Harleian Society (1887), pp. 105–6. Another branch of this family were Catholics and later implicated in the Gunpowder Plot.

[29] The Order is found in PRO, SP12/38/138, and has been printed in *Borough Records of Northampton*, 2, pp. 386–90; *VCH Northamptonshire*, 2, pp. 38–9; R. M. Serjeantson, *A History of the Church of All Saints, Northampton* (Northampton, 1901), pp. 104–8. Arrangements for the conduct of the exercise of the clergy and a Confession of Faith were also appended to the Order.

[30] Printed in *An Answer at Large to a most hereticall, trayterous, and Popisticall Byll, in English Verse, which was cast abroad in the streetes of Northampton . . .* (Northampton, 1881). The appearance of Reformers proved a divisive issue in many towns: see the cases of Rye and Gloucester: G. Mayhew, 'Religion, Faction and Politics in Reformation Rye: 1530–59' *Sussex Archaeological Collections*, 120 (1982), pp. 139–60 and P. Clark, 'The Ramoth-Gilead of the Good: Religion and Politics in Gloucester 1540–1690' in P. Clark, N. Tyacke, and A. G. R. Smith, eds, *The English Commonwealth* (Leicester, 1979), pp. 167–87. Similar conflicts occurred north of the border in Edinburgh: M. Lynch, *Edinburgh and the Reformation* (Edinburgh, 1981); and Calvin's own struggles in Geneva prior to 1557 provided a precedent, Lewis, 'Geneva 1541–1608', p. 41; R. Stauffer, 'Calvin' in Prestwich, ed., *International Calvinism*, pp. 20, 22–7.

[31] Lewis, 'Geneva 1541–1608', pp. 46–50; *Borough Records of Northampton*, 2, pp. 386–90. The articles of the Order are referred to by number in the following notes.

services, the trappings of the old Church, that is to say the organ and the practice of carrying the bell before corpses and having bidding prayers for the dead, which had continued in the town until the late sixties, were removed unexceptionally; more challenging, however, was the introduction of the Genevan practice of psalm singing on Sundays and on holy days before and after the morning services.[32] More radical still were the arrangements for the administration of the Eucharist, the service itself was moved from the chancel to the nave of the church, and the Sacrament was to be administered, in a fashion at odds with the *Book of Common Prayer*, by three ministers, one standing in the middle to offer the bread and the others at each end of the communion table to present the chalice. During the administration of the Communion, which seems unlikely to have been received kneeling, a further minister in the pulpit read portions of Scripture to the congregation, and at the end of the Communion the congregation were to sing a psalm.[33] This represented a radical innovation to the established order, but even more dramatic were the arrangements for the preparation for Communion. Here the existing parochial and urban structures were grafted to form a Reformed church order, though Communions were not held as frequently as in the Swiss churches, being quarterly. They were held in the parish churches and were announced on the four Sundays prior to the day so that the people could prepare. Two weeks before the day, the ministers and the church-wardens began a circuit of the parish making lists of the communicants and examining their lives. If any were found to be in discord, then they were to be presented to the mayor, the preacher, and other gentlemen, who gathered together to form a 'consistory' for the reconciliation, correction, or excommunication of offenders as appropriate. Importantly, at Northampton, the secular arm was involved at this stage, and this, of course, was a departure from Genevan or Scottish practice, but very much part of English Puritanism with its emphasis on magistracy and ministry working together. Following these examinations, the Communion proceeded in two separate services in each parish, one for servants and officers from 5 a.m. until 8 a.m., and one for householders and their families from 9 a.m. until noon. The minister of the parish then followed up the examination of the households in his care, reporting those who had not received the Communion to the mayor, who, with the minister, was

---

[32] Articles 1, 3, 15, 16.
[33] Articles 11, 14. It was claimed by Wiburn's supporters that this took place in addition to the order as set out in the *Book of Common Prayer*, and that nothing within that was omitted.

enjoined to use 'meanes of persuasion to induce them to their duties'. The Genevan influences need no underlining.[34]

As with the Reformed tradition, and in the view of the Puritans in England at the time, preaching was to have a central place in the ministry, and it was this role, a supra-parochial one, which Wiburn was to hold in the town, and which placed him at the head of the local ecclesiastical structure, not only within the town itself but, quite possibly, within the shire, where his authority would clearly conflict in some areas with that of the archdeacon. His chief work, however, was in preaching, and in this there was no inherent conflict. Each Sunday and holy day after the parochial services, which were to finish by 9 a.m., the people were exhorted to attend a sermon in the chief church, unless there was one in their own parish that day. In addition, a weekly lecture was established on Thursdays, and on Saturdays, between 9 and 11 a.m., an exercise for the ministers of town and country was established, presided over by the preacher and others in turn, and held in the presence of the people. Further than that, a quarterly assembly of all the clergy of the county was proposed, at which a sermon was preached.[35] The preacher, therefore, provided a civic focus to religious life,[36] but the act of preaching the Gospel was also enjoined on the parochial ministry, whose attendance at these exercises and assemblies was designed to fit them for that task. Preaching was an essential part of the quarterly Communions in the parish, and, if able to do so, the clergy were encouraged to preach at the parochial Sunday service. To supplement this activity, readings of the Scriptures were held in All Saints Church between 9 and 11 a.m., ending with the Confession of Faith which was enjoined on the people. Finally, in this regime of what would be described elsewhere as 'godly discipline', the youth of the town were examined and had expounded to them before their elders a portion of Calvin's *Catechism* for an hour after evening prayers in their parish churches on Sundays and holidays.[37] Such an extensive plan for exposition of and instruction in the Scriptures had not hitherto been adopted in England, and the desperate need for edification

---

[34] Articles 7–10; for frequency at Geneva see Stauffer, 'Calvin', p. 20.

[35] Articles 4, 12, 13.

[36] The 'civic' role of preachers in the context of other developments within urban communities is discussed in W. J. Sheils, 'Religion in Provincial Towns: Innovation and Tradition' in Heal and O'Day, eds, *Church and Society*, pp. 156–76; P. Collinson, 'The Protestant Town' in his *The Birthpangs of Protestant England* (London, 1988), pp. 43–9; and more generally in P. Clark and P. Slack, *English Towns in Transition 1500–1700* (Oxford, 1976), pp. 142–52.

[37] Article 6.

in the early years of Elizabeth's reign no doubt helped to persuade the Bishop of its desirability. What is more difficult to understand is Scambler's apparent willingness to go along with the judicial arrangements which accompanied this activity.

We have already seen how the mayor and others were given authority in the control of admission to the Eucharist, but this was only one small part of their responsibilities in the matter of discipline. After the Thursday sermon a court session was held which would not have been unfamiliar to the inhabitants of Geneva or the authors of the *Book of Discipline*. Its terms deserve quotation at length:

> The maior and his brethrene, assisted with the preacher, mynister, or other gentlemen, appointed by the Bisshoppe for the correction of discord made in the towne, as for notorious blasphemy, whoredome, drunkeness, rayling against religion, or the preachers thereof, skowlders, rybaulds, and suche lyke, which faults are eche Thursdaye presented unto them in writinge by certain sworne men, appointed for that service in each parish.

They showed the conjunction of secular and ecclesiastical discipline, recognized the right of the bishop to appoint those entrusted with correction, albeit apparently laymen, and implied in the appointment of sworn men in the parish some form of eldership.[38] How the Bishop could have been persuaded to give his support to such a scheme, which, though formally acknowledging his authority in these matters, for all practical purposes undermined his ability to control proceedings, is perhaps explained by the influence of political pressure from high quarters, and the problems created by the almost complete breakdown of normal ecclesiastical discipline in the early years of the new diocese.[39]

Even more surprising, however, was the Bishop's apparent willingness not only to support a local exercise or prophesying, not a contentious issue at that time, but to hand over the discipline of the clergy to a gathering of the clergy of the county, at least in the first instance. After the quarterly meeting of ministers they were required to withdraw to a place in the church, probably All Saints, and

> there pryvately to conferre amongst themselves of their manners and lyves, amongst whome yf any maye be founde in faulte, for the first

---

[38] Article 13.
[39] See below pp. 341–2 and Scambler's letter to Cecil, MS B.L. Lansd. 17, fol. 55.

tyme exhortation is made to hym amongest all the bretherne to amend, and so lykewyse to seconde, the thirde tyme by complaynt from all the bretherne, he is commytted unto the bysshopp for his correcion.[40]

This remarkable clause cut out the archdeaconry court altogether, and the effect of the whole document was to remove ecclesiastical discipline entirely from the purview of the church courts, save as a last resort in matters involving the clergy. Scambler, the Bishop, once he realized the full implication of the Order was swift to act in its suppression, and Wiburn was suspended from preaching. Having no official position within the framework of the Established Church, no further action was taken by the Bishop, but the preacher's supporters, including the mayor, enlisted the powerful influence of the Earl of Leicester, Scambler's patron, on their behalf.[41] At the end of January 1572 he wrote frankly to Scambler, reminding him that he himself had encouraged Wiburn, and giving the following testimony to the effect of the preacher's ministry:

> who hath taken not onelie greate paines theare among them nowe a good while, but such frute hath spronge by his doctrine and teaching in the hartes of the well disposed as (God be thanked therefore) it doth manifestlie appere no small nomber are increased to the true knowledge of Christ. And therebie finding the good taste thereof are loth to want that good and godlie instruction which from tyme to tyme he hath fed them with, and do seke by all the good meanes they may to have him remayne emong them with ther favour and countenance which heretofore he hath had, that he may procede under the same protection he hath had, especiallie at your Grace's handes.

Leicester went on to place particular emphasis on the value of the exercise in improving the standards of the clergy, and to stress the danger that might ensue if Wiburn were removed and the good he had already done dissipated thereby. Northampton had only recently been brought to the Gospel and its position in the town remained a precarious one. There followed the sort of critical harangue which bishops of the second rank, like Scambler, must have feared from their social superiors.

> Let him [Wiburn] not thus hang in suspense, as thoughe the gospell nor preachers had anie friend, as though theare weare no bysshopps,

---

[40] Article 17.
[41] Sheils, *Puritans*, p. 7.

or a bisshopp that had no care of his churche. Trie it yourself, be your owne Judge, you have aucthoritie, it is your charge, be not afraid to do that you ought and are bounde to do, for by this you shall please nobodie.[42]

Scambler replied, sticking to his earlier decision, and complained to Burghley of the interference of friends in high places.[43] A further letter followed from Leicester on 19 February, three weeks after his first, reminding the Bishop that Wiburn had only come to the town in response to episcopal invitation and that, having been called before the Ecclesiastial Commissioners, the preacher had been dismissed 'without any forbidding or restrainte'. If anything the Earl's tone was even sharper than before, reminding Scambler that

> where zealous and dilligent preachers have been placed who have sharplie and preciselie sought the reformation of the lycentious sort and procured the execution of some discipline sevearlie to be practiced, as well as to have doctrine taught and preached, that they have bene therefore the more violentlie and more hardlie pro-sequuted even to their utter discoragement. . . . In this predicament is Mr Wiborne.[44]

Leicester had clearly been sought by the local gentry to intervene on Wiburn's behalf, but Scambler was not to be moved, and the preacher was ordered to leave the town, retiring to the house of Isabel Catesby at Whiston, eight miles away.[45] The Order, therefore, was suppressed within a few months of its establishment, and this local incident was soon to be swallowed up in the controversy surrounding the publication of *An Admonition to the Parliament* and the campaign of Field and his associates to get support for the Presbyterians among MPs.[46] In formal terms, there-fore, the story of the Order of Northampton is one of failure to erect a Reformed Church discipline, but the circumstances of the attempt

---

[42] Magdalene College, Cambridge, Pepys Library, Papers of State, ii, pp. 647–8.

[43] National Register of Archives, Baskerville Transcripts, De Lisle and Dudley Papers, ii. no. 60.

[44] Magd. College, Pepys Library, Papers of State, ii, pp. 389–90.

[45] Sheils, *Puritans*, pp. 26, 34, 42, 121–2 for the continuing Puritan influence there. Wiburn retained his commitment to Reformed churchmanship, and in 1576 assisted in the estab-lishment of the Church in the Channel Isles, perhaps through Leicester's influence, Scott-Pearson, *Thomas Cartwright*, pp. 161–4.

[46] For *The Admonition* controversies in Parliament see J. E. Neale, *Elizabeth and Her Parliament*, 2 vols (London, 1965 edn), 1, pp. 293–8 and G. R. Elton, *The Parliament of England 1559–81* (Cambridge, 1986), pp. 209–16 for revision.

provide pointers both to the realities involved in bringing Protestantism to the provinces in early Elizabethan England, and to the future history of the Reformation in the locality.

It is clear that administrative upheaval and poor endowment created difficulties for diocesan authorities wishing to further the Reformation, and so the introduction of a well-known preacher to an important, but unestablished, post in the county town appeared to provide a valuable opportunity for evangelization.[47] That opportunity was perceived by a group of local gentry, many of whom had had experience of ecclesiastical affairs in the capital, where they would have heard and been influenced by Puritan preachers.[48] These gentry, perhaps with some support from Leicester, were able to prevail upon a hard-pressed bishop, whose cathedral was at one extremity of the diocese at some distance from the county town, to issue an invitation, and then, once the invitation was accepted, they prevailed upon the leadership of the urban community to provide support and welcome to an initiative which, in the ecclesiastical sphere, gave expression to, and further enforced, the sense of urban solidarity which they and the leaders of other towns were keen to see develop at that time.[49] This did not come about without opposition from sectors of the urban community unwilling to go along with such radical developments imposed in such a brief space of time, and it may well also have aroused opposition from some of the parochial clergy of the hinterland, who saw members of their congregations 'gadding' to the sermons and services in the town.[50] These people were presented to the church courts, whose officials were certainly angered by developments which fundamentally challenged their authority. It is difficult to understand how Scambler failed to foresee these developments, even in the confused state of affairs of the early seventies. Perhaps the example of Thomas Lever, who from 1561 had combined the non-pastoral post of preacher at Coventry with the jurisdictional one of archdeacon, seemed to provide a precedent for both the Bishop and Wiburn's supporters, but, if so, the terms of the Order went far beyond what Lever established, and made explicit the contradictions within the views of different groupings of

---

[47] Ever since Latimer's ministry in Bristol, G. R. Elton, *Policy and Police* (Cambridge, 1972), pp. 112–20, patrons had sought to use urban pulpits in this way.
[48] For the influence of the capital on local gentry see Sheils, *Puritans*, pp. 116–18.
[49] Clark and Slack, *English Towns in Transition*, pp. 149–52, explores the relationship between godly discipline and urban government.
[50] Sheils, *Puritans*, pp. 127–8, shows the effects of this by 1573; the visitation also revealed the extent and influence of the exercise on the parochial clergy of the area: ibid., pp. 27–31.

Puritans.[51] However desperate the need, the speed with which the Order was set up, and the formal nature of its articles, proved too much for the Bishop, and Wiburn, despite his influential supporters, was removed. In this way the episode illustrates the difficulties inherent in speedy reformation from above in early Elizabethan England.

A formal failure, but in a Church whose formal requirements, whether liturgical, theological, or jurisdictional, were still in the process of development and honoured as often in the breach as in the practice,[52] the official suppression of the Order is only part of the story, and, in terms of the subsequent history of religion in the area, the less important part. This is not the place to detail the subsequent story of the Reformation in Northampton,[53] but the events of 1571–2 left a significant mark on that story. Wiburn's removal to Whiston resulted in some of the townspeople taking themselves there to hear sermons and attend services. The exercise continued to flourish, and attracted and produced local clergy committed to the furtherance of Protestantism, who in 1574 provoked the first major confrontation between the Puritans and the Establishment in the provinces, with the result that five of them were deprived. Inhabitants of the town regularly appeared before the church courts for non-conformity, the corporation in the eighties exercised a moral and a sabbatarian jurisdiction on the townspeople, and continued to influence the appointment of local clergy. The sense of solidarity among this godly group, initiated in the Confession of Faith of 1571, was regularly expressed in their wills, and in the 1580s the classis based at Northampton continued to exercise an influence over the local clergy beyond its didactic purpose. When the Puritan vicar of All Saints was in trouble with the ecclesiastical authorities for refusing to subscribe to the Canons in 1605, the mayor and corporation complained that ceremonies were being enforced which had been 'omitted and grown out of use for nearly forty years', a direct reference back to the events of 1571–2.[54] The influence of the Order, therefore, was a durable one in the town and surrounding countryside, and the

---

[51] For Lever at Coventry see *Zurich Letters*, I, pp. 86–7; Collinson, *Elizabethan Puritan Movement*, p. 51.

[52] The precise character of religious practice in the early years of Elizabeth's reign was open to wide regional and local fluctuations which the appearance of several local studies since the mid-sixties has uncovered: see especially C. Haigh, *Reformation and Resistance in Tudor Lancashire* (Cambridge, 1974) and D. McCulloch, *Suffolk under the Tudors* (Oxford, 1986).

[53] This is done in Sheils, *Puritans*, pp. 122–7, upon which this paragraph is based.

[54] MS HMC Hatfield 17, p. 58.

reputation of Northampton as a Puritan centre was well known to the church authorities and within the wider Puritan movement: the author of the *Marprelate Tracts*, with characteristic bravado, challenged the Bishop in 1590 to 'send Mr Wiburn to Northampton that he may see some fruit of the seed he sowed there.'[55]

Consideration of the Order reminds us that, in the history of religion, outward signs do not always fully reveal inward graces, and that the measurement of the success or failure of evangelization is often elusive and not to be contained within formal ecclesiastical structures. The setting up of the Order shows the debt to a common Reformed tradition which many English Puritans of this generation shared with their Scottish counterparts;[56] its suppression reminds us of the very different social and political climate in which the Reformation was settled north and south of the border, but the motives behind it, that 'yll lyeff is corrected, Godds gloary sett fourthe, and the people brought in good obedience' are ones that would have commended themselves not only to the godly of Northampton, but also to the authors of *The First Book of Discipline* as, no doubt, to its modern editor.

University of York

[55] M. Marprelate, *An Epistle to the Terrible Priests of the Confocation House*, facsimile edn (Leeds, 1967), p. 28.
[56] Wiburn and Knox presumably met in Geneva, and he may also have had some earlier contact with Christopher Goodman.

PART III THE CHURCH IN SCOTLAND

ALEXANDER MYLN, BISHOP GEORGE BROWN, AND THE CHAPTER OF DUNKELD

by JOHN MACQUEEN

IT might seem reasonable to assume that Alexander Myln's *Vitae episcoporum Dunkeldensium*[1] was a humanist document. He begins with a paragraph called by Hannay[2] a dedication to Bishop Gavin Douglas and to the canons of Dunkeld who were promoted in the time of Bishop George Brown. If anyone in early sixteenth-century Scotland deserves the name humanist, Douglas is the man, and one would expect a work dedicated to him to adopt a corresponding style. The book, however, does not wholly live up to expectations. Myln was a lawyer devoted to documents, and his normal style is that of the early records which he consulted. The dedication is no more than a formal greeting to the Bishop and Myln's other colleagues on the residentiary Dunkeld chapter.

Towards the end of his book, apparently in an extended parenthesis, he places a series of pen-portraits,[3] some quite lengthy, of the same chapter (the bishop's cardinals, he calls them) and their vicars choral. This body, it is clear, he regards as exceptional, or at least exemplary, and primarily the creation not of Douglas, but of his predecessor, Bishop George Brown (1483–1515).[4] 'Watchful, in the first place, for the care of the Lord's flock committed to him, the bishop brought men of learning to Dunkeld and entrusted the more important offices to their charge.'

Brown's is the longest biography included. The pen-portraits are placed between this and the relatively brief account of Douglas's arrival in 1516. If the *Vitae* as a whole had been written during the latter episcopate, one might reasonably have expected a formal dedication to Douglas

---

[1] A. Myln, *Vitae Dunkeldensis ecclesiae episcoporum*, Bannatyne Club (1831) [hereafter Myln, *Vitae*].

[2] R. K. Hannay, *Rentale Dunkeldense* (Edinburgh, 1915), p. 338 [hereafter *Dunkeld Rentale*]. A translation of Myln, *Vitae*, from the election of Bishop Brown to the end of the work occupies pp. 302–34.

[3] Myln, *Vitae*, pp. 54–70; *Dunkeld Rentale*, pp. 320–31. For a good general account of medieval Scottish cathedral chapters see J. Dowden, *The Medieval Church in Scotland* (Glasgow, 1910), pp. 55–104; cf. Mark Dilworth, 'The Augustinian Chapter of St Andrews', *The Medieval Church of St Andrews*, ed. D. McRoberts (Glasgow, 1976), pp. 121–36.

[4] Dates for ecclesiastic officers are taken from D. E. R. Watt, *Fasti Ecclesiae Scoticanae medii Aevi ad annum 1638*, 2nd edn (St Andrews, 1969).

alone: compare, for instance, Hector Boece's presentation of *Murthla-censium et Aberdonensium episcoporum vitae* (Paris, 1522)[5] to Gavin Dunbar, Bishop of Aberdeen, 1518–32, or Ferrerius's of his *Historia abbatum de Kynlos*[6] to Robert Reid, commendator of Kinloss from 1526, and later (1541–58) Bishop of Orkney. The form in which the *Vitae* has survived suggests that the name of Gavin Douglas is a late addition or alteration, that Myln's first intention had been to have his book centre on Bishop Brown and his chapter, and that he intended to body out the initial list with the greater detail of the portraits at the end—that he wished to concentrate on the team, as it were, by whose efforts the affairs of Dunkeld diocese had reached a happy climax in the course of a distin-guished episcopate.

If this were his first intention, he later partially disguised it under circumstances which we may be able to reconstruct. Significant differ-ences exist between the names in the opening paragraph[7] and those included in the series of portraits. So far as canons are concerned, the first is the longer, with twenty-one names, as opposed to the seventeen of the second. There are some indications, too, that the second is the earlier in date; thus in place of Patrick Painter, Chancellor 1509–c.1517, it has George Brown (not the Bishop), Chancellor 1500–4. In place of Robert Shaw, Succentor 1507–42, it has his predecessor, David Balbirny, 1507–?1508. In place of Robert Boswell, who resigned the precentorship in 1500, when he exchanged it with Henry Wood for the deanship of the collegiate church of Restalrig, it has David Meldrum, Treasurer of Aberdeen in 1462, Official of Dunkeld, 1467–?1469, and Official of St Andrews 1479–1503. Boswell, who is only a canon in the opening para-graph, in the portraits is described as Succentor. He is said, in addition, to have improved the manse of Meldrum's prebend and also that of the Precentor, James Fenton. Myln does not mention Wood. In third place on the first list, however, and second in the portraits, he puts James Fenton, successor (1501–24) of Wood as Precentor.

In the first list the prebendary of Forgandenny is James Lyn, Dean of Strathearn, Fife, and Lothian (?1509–14); in the second it is Walter Brown, Succentor and Commissary of Dunkeld (1491–3), Official (1493–1505), and Rural Dean of the diocese until 1505, which was also the year of his death. Myln says that he was promoted by the resignation of Sir John

[5] New Spalding Club (1894).
[6] Bannatyne Club (1839).
[7] Myln, *Vitae*, pp. 1–2.

Myretoun to be pensioner of the precentorship ('per resignationem domini Johannis Myretoun promotus praecentoriae pensionarius'), but died before his predecessor. He also says that he himself had served as clerk and notary in Brown's court, and gives a vivid account of his sudden death by a fever: 'Sed in extrema hora, plausu manuum, vulgari nostro exclamavit ter "Wely, Wely, Wely"; et facto signo sanctae crucis, "in manus tuas" dicens, exspiravit.'

The place of Master David Wauchope, Prebendary of Ruffel, is taken in the portraits by his predecessor, Sir Thomas Lyne. Wauchope's succession is mentioned, but as if it were a very recent occurrence. Unfortunately I cannot give more than an approximate date for the transfer. Lyne was still Prebendary of Ruffel in 1501; Wauchope was in office by 1513/14.

It may be significant that neither list contains any mention of Alexander Wilson, Dean of Fife and Strathearn, 1505–9.

Some account of Myln's own career[8] at Dunkeld is necessary at this point. By 1500 he was acting as clerk to the Bishop and chapter. He served for a time as steward and was made Prebendary of Lundie. In 1505 he became Dean of Angus. In 1510 he was promoted to the richer prebend of Moneydie and became Master of Works on the new Tay bridge at Dunkeld, which the Bishop had begun to erect. In 1511 he gave over to Thomas Brown the episcopal accounts, for which he had hitherto himself been responsible. In 1513 he became Official of the diocese. In late 1516, or early 1517, he left Dunkeld to become Abbot of Cambuskenneth; much later, in 1532, he became first Lord President of the College of Justice, a post which he held until his death in 1548.

Myln concludes the *Vitae* with the sentence: 'The rest of his [Gavin Douglas's] good works, in matters spiritual and temporal, I leave his own canons at Dunkeld to record, as they have a better title (Reliqua bona ejus opera in spiritualibus et temporalibus suis et ecclesiae canonicis, uti majoribus, scribere relinquo).' This must have been written when he had already left, or was on the point of leaving, Dunkeld for Cambuskenneth and as a consequence no longer regarded himself as a member of the chapter. This fits in with the fact that he describes only the arrival of Douglas in Dunkeld during October 1516.

This dating, however, is difficult to reconcile with the first list where Myln describes himself as prebendary of Moneydie and Official. This presumably was written after 1513, but before his appointment to

---

[8] *Dunkeld Rentale*, pp. xiv–xvi.

Cambuskenneth—perhaps before the arrival of Gavin Douglas. The portraits in their original form seem to have been written earlier still, perhaps about the time of the death of Master Walter Brown in 1505, when Myln first became a canon.

It seems probable, in fact, that Myln worked occasionally on the composition of the *Vitae* during most of his carrer at Dunkeld. In a passage with some humanist overtones he states that his main objective was to know the origin and development of the see; he was driven to this by the beauty of the buildings and the high distinction of the chapter. Presumably at this point he gathered material for the early history and began to record the activities of Bishop Brown and his chapter. Although Myln knows something of Brown's earlier career (including his parentage and education, and the fact that he owed his bishopric to the influence of the Spanish Cardinal Rodrigo Borgia, the future Pope Alexander VI, to whose household he had belonged during his visit to Italy in 1483–4), little is included to which a date earlier than Myln's arrival in Dunkeld may safely be assigned. The career of Walter Brown as Official General and Rural Dean of the diocese, and the decision of the Bishop as a consequence of the good advice given him by Walter to divide (1505) the diocese into four rural deaneries, certainly forms part of the earliest stratum, as does the acquisition for the church of the lands of Fordel, Muckersie, Wester Kinvaid, Wester and Easter Louston, Clunie, Concraigie, and Cardney. To this same stratum probably belongs the account of the endowment by the Bishop of altars in his cathedral and at his birthplace, Dundee. The first of these is linked to the plague of 1500, and it is possible that the Dundee endowment was earlier—in effect, a commemoration of his election to the bishopric. The foundation of the parish church at Caputh is also connected with the plague, and it is said to be earlier than the establishment of a new parish church at Dowally, the restoration of the old one at Tibbermore, and the establishment of a perpetual chaplaincy at Buchquhane in the parish of the mensal church of Alyth. The account of these latter may therefore be later, as is almost certainly the long and moving account of the Bishop's death.

Myln often appears to write as an eyewitness or participant in the events described; he claims, for instance, that his relationship with Walter Brown was close, and the account already quoted of his death is scarcely explicable unless Myln was himself present. He is at pains to indicate any direct part which he played in diocesan legal actions. He describes how he administered extreme unction after hearing the confession of the dying Bishop, and includes a number of fascinating details about his last days.

The Bishop suffered from calculus ('quem lie felt vulgo dicebant'), and told him 'that the Lord had heard the petition, which had been always in his prayers, for continual torment in this world before death.' During his last summer, 'sometimes, for recreation, he would look out of his chamber window upon the work at the bridge.' He had always been active and would not now keep his bed; once when he had risen in the middle of the night, he dressed carefully, had his beard trimmed, and, exhibiting all the traditional contempt of the Lowland burgess (his father was Treasurer of Dundee) for the Highlander, said 'with reference to a man Mackay executed the day before, "Praise God I shall now die in a better fashion than that fellow who was hanged with beard unkempt."' During his anointing, while the appointed psalms were being said, his breathing became impeded, and 'he begged the chaplain to say the psalms more deliberately, a word or two at a time.'

Myln also regarded it as his duty to report what may be called good hearsay. During the plague of 1500, Bishop Brown designated, appointed, and blessed a cemetery at Caputh.

> He also visited certain afflicted in his church lands of Capeth and caused the sacraments of the church to be administered to them. On the following day he blessed water, in which he dipped a bone of St Columba, and sent it with the chancellor for the sick to drink. Many partook and were made whole. But one pert fellow answered the chancellor: 'Why sends the bishop water for us to drink? I had rather he had sent to me the best of his ale.' That man perished of the plague with the rest that did not receive the water of St Columba, and thirty of them were buried within the cemetery in a single grave.

Myln's source for the story was probably the Chancellor, Master George Brown (1500–4). Such details, it seems likely, were recorded, Boswell-like, more or less on the spot, and thereafter worked into the fabric of the *Vitae*. They are in themselves evidence that the book was written not at a single time, but in the course of some ten or twelve years.

Myln sees the monastic origins of Dunkeld as preparing the way for the later importance of the cathedral chapter. The monastery, he states, was founded in 729 by Constantine, King of the Picts, whom he calls Constantine III. The foundation he also associates with Adamnan (627–704), eighth successor of Columba as abbot of Iona. The chronological difficulties here are doubled by the fact that no Pictish king Constantine ruled at the beginning of the eighth century. Rather, he is to be identified with Constantine, son of Fergus, whose long reign extended from 789 to

820.[9] Under his name in Regnal List D, in one version of F, and in K, variants occur of the phrase 'Iste edificavit Dunkeldin'; in Regnal List I we have 'Iste primo edificauit ecclesiam Sancti Andree', a foundation which in D, F, and K is ascribed to Constantine's brother and successor, Oengus, son of Fergus (820–34). Myln refers to St Andrews ('sicut postea in ecclesia Beati Reguli, nunc Sancti Andreae') as a later foundation. He also states that the Dunkeld foundation post-dated that of Abernethy by 226 years, 9 months, and 6 days, or, alternatively, by 244 years. The same figures are to be found in Bower's *Scotichronicon* (iv, ch. 12);[10] later in the same chapter there is a reference to Constantine, son of Fergus, as founder of Dunkeld. It seems likely that *Scotichronicon* was one of Myln's sources for this paragraph.

He may well have had another, from which he learned the precise site of the old monastery in the bishop's east garden and the manse of the prebendary of Crieff ('in locis illis quae nunc occupatis, vos reverende pater, pro orto orientali, et vos Alexander pro mansione de Creif'), together with some details about the community. They were Culdees and, like the clergy of the Orthodox Church, had wives from whom, however, they kept apart whenever it was their turn to perform the Divine Office ('habentes tamen, secundum orientalis ecclesiae ritum, conjuges a quibus dum vicissim ministrarunt, abstinebant'). The same practice was afterwards followed at St Andrews. About 1127, David I (1124–53) erected the monastery into a cathedral church and replaced the Culdees with a college of secular canons. Gregory (c.1140–69), the first bishop named by Myln, was also abbot. Bishop Geoffrey de Liberatione (1236–49) made a new erection following the use of Sarum, and instituted generous provisions for the majority of the canons to become residentiary, as hitherto only few had been. As a consequence, it became possible for Gregorian chant to be used in the cathedral celebration of the Divine Office. (Here and elsewhere Myln regards the quality of its music as one of the distinguishing features of Dunkeld.)

It was by the provision of the manses already mentioned that the body of canons became residentiary. Since their institution, however, the manses themselves had not always been well maintained, and Myln regarded the efforts at improvement by the current chapter as cause for

---

[9] Marjorie O. Anderson, *Kings and Kingships in Early Scotland*, rev. edn (Edinburgh and London, 1980), p. 233. The regnal lists occupy pp. 264–89.

[10] *Joannis de Fordun Scotichronicon cum Supplementis et Continuatione Walteri Boweri*, ed. W. Goodall, 2 vols (Edinburgh, 1759). See also the edition of books iii and iv by J. and W. MacQueen (Aberdeen, 1989).

legitimate pride. The manse of the prebendary of Menmure, for instance, 'was completely ruinous and unoccupied'. Master Walter Leslie 'built an enclosure-wall of stone, within which he placed all the buildings and a well-sheltered garden. He always keeps his house in comfort and is most generous to the poor with money and food.' The Precentor, James Fentoun,

> took over a house which had long stood by the bank of the Tay as the precentor's manse, and to the front of the manse towards the yard he built a dwelling which would be sufficient for the precentor, if it were put in thorough order, and had it covered with small slates or *scalze*. He also adorned the canons' cloister. The rest of the building work at the manse has been due to Master Robert Boswell.

The Treasurer, Master Walter Small, the best penman of his time in every style of writing, 'found his manse a poor, old-fashioned Highland house and improved it till it was regarded as the best, after the dean's residence, of all the dwellings occupied by canons.' 'The prebendary of Inchmagrano, Master William Lindsay, vicar of Newtile, has put his manse into good repair: has, indeed, practically rebuilt it.' The manse of the prebendary of Ferdischawe stood at the end of the church of St George, and was built by the Bishop for the Prebendary, Sir John Stephenson, musician and organist, who set it in order, 'and the rest of the buildings belonging to the manse he erected from the foundations in a suitable style.'

The buildings of the cathedral church, together with his own palace, were the responsibility primarily of the bishop. In the sixth year of his episcopate, William Sinclair (1309–37) had hired the master builder Robert 'ad opus chori et ecclesiae, quem a fundamentis construxit'; in sign of his work the Bishop put above the eastern gable a cross virgate, borne as arms by his house and surname right up to the present day. The east end of the church, that is to say, was completed by this Bishop. John de Peebles (1378–90) added the glazed east window of the choir decorated with diverse images painted on clear glass. The construction of the nave was begun by Robert de Cardeny (1398–1437) on 27 April 1406, and during his episcopate it was completed as far as the second arches, *vulgariter le blyndstorijs*. At his own expense, he also decorated with glass the remaining windows of the choir. Up to his time the episcopal palace had been a Highland dwelling,[11] 'alpinatum more, ex domibus magnis super terram

---

[11] For the Highland house see John Dunbar, 'The medieval architecture of the Scottish

constructis'. In consequence of an attempt to surprise him there by night, he replaced it with the old tower-house, strongly fortified, with a hall on the first floor and vaulted larders and granaries beneath. Donald Macnachtan, Dean of Dunkeld, was perhaps elected bishop by the chapter in 1437; when he was still dean he glazed the window above the altar of the Blessed Virgin, which he had endowed, and decorated it with his own arms. John Ralston (1447–?52) arranged for cut-and-squared stones to be brought from the quarry of Burnbane for the completion of the nave, 'and as I, the writer of these presents have heard, he was so eager to get on with it that in company with one or other of the chiefs staying with him he was accustomed to carry a certain burden of stones beyond the quarry every day.' The nave was finally completed by Bishop Thomas Lauder (1452–75), who had all the windows glazed, covered the roof-beams, constructed the porch at the south door, and by the art of the sculptor placed figures there in a most becoming fashion ('et sculptoria arte ymagines ibidem quam decenter locavit'). He dedicated the church in 1464.

Lauder also built the chapter-house and bell-tower, of which the foundation stones were laid on 20 March 1457, and 5 March 1469, respectively. The task of bridge-building was regarded as peculiarly appropriate to a bishop (*pontifex*), and on 8 July 1461, he began the building of a bridge of stone and wood over the Tay near his palace. This was completed during his episcopate. His successor James Livingstone (1475–83) increased its height, 'adeo ut vulgo diceretur, Pontem Pontifex Perpetuavit'.

Little was left for Bishop Brown in construction work on the cathedral. He instituted and endowed a number of altars, and made substantial contributions to the general adornment of the church. He commissioned two great bells for the tower, the larger, Columba, named for the patron of the diocese, the smaller, George, for his own patron saint. A third, the largest, to be called Mary, he had to leave to his successors. In addition, he reconstructed the west side of his palace from the foundations and added a handsome oratory. His main work, however, was to build a stone bridge across the Tay, and he lived to see the first of three arches completed in 1513, and the piers for the other two laid before his death.

Highlands' in L. Maclean, ed., *The Middle Ages in the Highlands* (Inverness, 1981), pp. 48–9, 67 (hall-houses); 53–4, 68 (tower-houses). The old bishop's palace mentioned below appears to resemble the principal residence of the MacDonald Lords of the Isles on two small islands in Loch Finlaggan, Islay, see *Argyll. An Inventory of the Monuments* (Royal Commission on the Ancient and Historical Monuments of Scotland, 1984), pp. 275–81.

For Myln, it is clear, upkeep and improvement of church lands and buildings was important—in this paper I have indicated only some of the more important instances which he gives. But he does not restrict himself to such matters, nor is the esteem in which he holds the chapter based solely on their abilities as property managers. Almost from the beginning of his account of Bishop Brown, he stresses high standards of learning and morality and the spiritual duty of the clergy towards the people of the diocese. Sometimes this might take a very practical form. George Brown, the Chancellor, 'provided for a perpetual scholastic chaplain to celebrate in the church of St George and rule a grammar school; and this foundation, in honour of the Blessed Virgin of Consolation, will, if it be kept, supply the church with youths instructed in grammar.' George Hepburn, the Dean (1497–1527), 'besides a daily alms . . . provides each week a boll of meal for certain decrepit poor folk in the city. When there is a dearth in the country he orders porridge to be supplied every day, whether he is present or not, to the poor who come for it, to each in good measure.' Myln emphasizes that Hepburn was never absent from celebrations of the Divine Office—he was not an absentee—but nevertheless maintained contacts with some of the most progressive elements in the Scottish Church:

> When John Adamson, professor of sacred letters, that great and enlightened provincial of the Preachers in Scotland, brought about a thorough reformation of the order, the dean gave him great assistance. Adamson established their place at St Andrews (whence he deservedly enjoys his title as their 'founder') and endowed it for the sufficient maintenance of five friars.

A Highland diocese had its own peculiar problems. Troubles of various kinds were associated with the fact that the majority of the people of the diocese were Gaelic speakers, as it is fair to assume the majority of the canons were not. Through most of the fifteenth century, relations between the Church and the Gaelic speakers of Clandonnoquhy in particular remained delicate. During the episcopate of James Bruce (1441–7), Robert Reoch Makdonoquhy (Robert, son of Duncan, the clan's eponym) harried the ecclesiastical lands of the parish of Little Dunkeld. These were held in feu by the forester of Torwood, by whom Robert was mortally wounded in a skirmish, thus instituting a blood feud. Bishop Lauder (1452–75) preached to his Highland parishioners in person, made every attempt to impose spiritual discipline on them, but was compelled by their raids to capture and hang a number, notably the notorious

JOHN MACQUEEN

Makbre, with his sons and accomplices. He also imprisoned a Clandonnoquhy sorner, a professional beggar of a kind denounced in a poem from the *Book of the Dean of Lismore*,[12] but possessing inviolable status in Gaelic society. As a consequence, the son of the deceased chief already mentioned, Alexander Robertson of Struan (Alastair, son of Robert, son of Duncan), violently entered the cathedral while the Bishop was celebrating Mass on the feast of Pentecost, compelled him to take refuge in the rafters, and setting free his fellow clansman, departed. This incident was followed by a long and only partly successful legal action in retaliation.

The Lowland prejudices, already mentioned, of Bishop Brown were probably heightened by the close neighbourhood of Clandonnoquhy. In 1514, for instance, the hostile activities of the Laird of Struan, William, son of Patrick, son of Alastair, son of Robert, son of Duncan (grandson of the Alexander Robertson already mentioned), seem to have made it necessary for him to pass the autumn in the Carmelite friary of Tullylumb, near Perth, and afterwards to winter in the castle of Clunie. Despite this, in the course of his episcopate, the Bishop and his chapter made considerable efforts to serve the Gaelic-speaking community. Columba, the patron saint of Dunkeld, had himself, after all, been a Gaelic speaker.

Myln's comments sometimes incidentally highlight aspects of the Gaelic culture of the region. The Bishop noted that the population in the parishes of Little Dunkeld and Caputh had increased, 'and that in the upper parts of the parish of Capeth Irish [Gaelic] was spoken. He therefore built and endowed, in honour of St Anne, a parish church among the woods in his church land of Dowaly [Dowally], assigning a manse for the priest, as the formal writ fully testifies.' The church presumably was intended primarily for Gaels, and Myln had seen or retained in his own keeping the original deed of foundation. The Bishop also arranged that Friars Minors and Friars Preachers well acquainted with Gaelic should preach at least once a year in the upper parts of the diocese and hear confessions.

His Subdean, Master David Abercromby (1494–?1531), apparently

[12] Two poems in W. J. Watson, ed., *Scottish Verse from the Book of the Dean of Lismore*, (Scottish Gaelic Text Society, 1937) deal with sorners or thiggers, as they are sometimes called. The more general, a poem probably composed between 1476 and 1490 by a MacDonald bard, Giolla Coluim, occupies pp. 66–81; there are valuable notes, pp. 272–7. A direct satire on an individual sorner, Lachlann Galbraith, occupies pp. 14–21; it is by Sir Duncan Campbell of Glen Orchy, who was killed at Flodden. Both poems are thus approximately contemporary with the reference in the text.

belonged to a noble Highland house ('ex nobilium alpinatum familia originem duxit'), and was presumably Gaelic speaking, although Myln is not explicit as he is with others among the canons and vicars choral. Abercromby became Commissary and Rural Dean for the whole diocese.

> Clergy and laity alike cannot fail to be aware how many who kept concubines, were adulterers, or guilty of incest received correction from the sub-dean with the bishop's support. ... As he came of a noble highland house, persons guilty of incest, adultery and fornication, when summoned for correction, have been known to call themselves his kinsmen in the expectation of more indulgent dealings; but the sub-dean's answer has been that just for that reason he will, for the good of their souls, aim at making correction more severe. At this they denied community of blood, and offered to submit to the punishment inflicted upon the generality.

Sir Thomas Greig was appointed Rural Dean of Atholl and Drumalban,

> because of his knowledge of the local idiom [Gaelic, that is to say] and his rigorous correction of abuses ... he has succeeded, in fact, by wise chastisement in rooting out abominable sins in Athole and Drumalbane. ... There was a man in the district who seduced the populace, feigning to be dumb but pretending to reveal past and future by signs and nods. He reduced the fellow to confessing openly before bishop and clergy that he could speak, made him tell how he had been led astray by the devil, and, when he offered to abide by the commands of the church, contrived to bring about his reconciliation.

Sir Patrick Gardner, one of the vicars choral, became Vice-penitentiary as a result of his knowledge of Gaelic and his serious and estimable character.

The proper relationship between the two languages of Scotland was obviously a matter of some concern for the clergy of Dunkeld. It is perhaps significant that at the very time when Myln was writing his *Lives*, a vicar who held the charge of Fortingall in the same diocese, and was also Dean of the daughter diocese, Argyll, with its cathedral at Lismore, was engaged in compiling the manuscript Gaelic collection now known as the *Book of the Dean of Lismore*.[13] This, of course, is the great source of knowledge of the earlier stages of Gaelic literature in Scotland and, despite the title, was compiled primarily at Fortingall. There can be little

---

[13] See the Introduction to Watson, *Scottish Verse*.

question that the Dean and his associates were well acquainted with traditional Gaelic spelling, but despite this the manuscript is written in a slightly modified form of Lowland Scots orthography, intended, one presumes, to give easier access to Gaelic to those who had been educated in the system by now standard in the Lowlands and in the professions throughout the country. It is possible that the Dean's activities are more closely connected with the work of Abercromby, Greig, and Gardner than might otherwise be suspected.

As panegyric on the community and antiquities of Dunkeld, the *Vitae* comes well within the range of humanist rhetoric. Myln's legal training and consequent respect for early documentary sources did not permit him to use a consistently humanist Latin style, but he is eager to acknowledge the accomplishments of others. Patrick Painter is *orator lepidissimus*; Walter Small is *archiscriptor* (surely a humanist word?) and 'inter scriptores tempore suo in omni scribendi litera primus'. Sir Stephen Young, one of the vicars choral, is 'et chorista in cantu firmus [a play on *cantus firmus*, plainsong] et ordinario multum expertus'. Another, Master John Penicuik, is 'grammaticam, logicam, philosophiam, musicam, jusque canonicum doctus, choristarum columna, et horarum canonicarum sedulus observator'. Style and vocabulary here at least aspire to the humanist. The most convincing proof of Myln's humanism, however, is the fact that two humanists of undoubted pedigree, Boece and Ferrerius, attempted to imitate and outgo him by composing collections of panegyric ecclesiastical biographies linked to the establishments which each favoured.

University of Edinburgh

THE RELIGION OF EARLY SCOTTISH PROTESTANTS

by JAMES KIRK

IN Scotland as elsewhere, Protestant reform began as a clerical revolt within the Established Church. Without exception, the earliest leaders of reform in Scotland were disenchanted ecclesiastics, men whose backgrounds were essentially academic and clerical, men who possessed sufficient technical training and expertise to appreciate, before the sloganizing began, the significance (if not all the implications) of Luther's academic revolt in 1517, and the relevance of his challenging ideas on salvation and his attack on the 'treasury of merit'; not even the saints, he believed, had sufficient merit to save themselves. Luther, after all, was an Augustinian friar, priest, university teacher (as, for that matter, were Wyclif and Hus), and doctor of theology before his break with Rome. His thinking merited scrutiny, appraisal, and debate, even if only for refutation; and if nothing else, scholastic methodology had fostered theological speculation and critical discussion within an accepted framework of debate. Besides, Erasmus's initial reaction to Luther's *Ninety-Five Theses* was conciliatory: he considered Luther's beliefs would be approved by all men, apart from a few points on purgatory; and he was later to observe, in 1519, that Luther's detractors were intent on 'condemning passages in the writings of Luther which are deemed orthodox when they occur in the writings of Augustine and Bernard'.[1]

Such, indeed, was the diversity of doctrinal emphases and tensions within the Western Church that until Luther's doctrines were explicitly condemned as heretical by the papacy in 1520, he himself excommunicated by 1521, and his writings burned at Rome, Cologne, Ingolstadt, Louvain, and elsewhere, it was far from clear even among trained minds where the bounds of orthodoxy ended and those of heterodoxy began. The distinction between essential dogma and inessential belief was not easy to define. In academic circles, at least, a measure of speculative freedom existed, but prudence was still required in eschewing wayward views, as David Guild, regent in St Leonard's College, St Andrews, discovered in 1541, when John Major, as Dean of Divinity, with other members of faculty, investigated his seemingly heretical utterances on the

[1] R. H. Bainton, *Erasmus of Christendom* (London, 1969), p. 189.

Trinity, which he readily retracted; and much earlier, in 1521, Aberdeen University had consulted the faculty of theology in Paris about a Dominican friar's denial of the Immaculate Conception.[2]

In any event, within university schools, the philosophical realism of the *via antiqua*, embraced by the followers of Thomas Aquinas, vied with the newer nominalist school, or *via moderna*, embodying Ockham's sharp distinction between reason and faith; antipapalism might even find a haven within the conciliarist tradition; and 'Erasmian humanism' had tested how far the foundations and defences of the late medieval Church might be probed, both by applying the latest philological tools to understanding the biblical texts in Hebrew and Greek, and by exposing to ridicule contemporary ecclesiastical malpractice. Erasmus himself had protested how

> nowadays, if anyone differs from Thomas Aquinas, he is decried as a heretic; nay, he is a heretic if he demurs to any disputatious effusion which some sophist yesterday fabricated in the schools. Whatever they don't like, whatever they don't understand is heresy. To know Greek is heresy. Whatever they do not do themselves is heresy.[3]

The Inquisition might ban Spanish translations of Erasmus in 1537, and belatedly the Pope, who was once his friend, might universally forbid the reading of his works by 1559; but the damage had been done: the weaknesses in the medieval system had been exposed; and by then Scottish clerics, and laymen too (like their counterparts in other lands), were well versed in the substance and direction of Erasmian scholarship.

Support for the Dutchman was particularly pronounced at Aberdeen University, newly founded through Bishop Elphinstone's intellectual leadership as a Renaissance seat of learning, whose first principal, Hector Boece, once Erasmus's fellow-student at Montaigu, in Paris, under Standonck's principalship, had introduced Erasmian literature to the class-room at King's College: prayers from the *Colloquies* and Erasmus's *Paraphrases on the New Testament* were used by his students; and, through correspondence, Boece and Erasmus renewed their friendship. Besides, the king who had helped found this northern university had himself employed Erasmus as tutor in Italy to his eighteen-year-old son, the titular Archbishop of St Andrews. At Aberdeen, whose Bishop appreciated

---

[2] J. Herkless and R. K. Hannay, *The College of Saint Leonard* (Edinburgh, 1905), pp. 220–3; J. K. Farge, *Orthodoxy and Reform in Early Reformation France* (Leiden, 1985), p. 129.

[3] V. H. Green, *Luther and the Reformation* (London, 1964), p. 165.

Lorenzo Valla's outstanding classical scholarship, the humanist programme for moral and educational reform and for a renewal in Christian life along Erasmian lines, which Elphinstone initiated, survived his death in 1514. Nor did Erasmian influences at King's College cease with Boece's death in 1536, for his successor, William Hay, who as a student, with Boece, had attended Erasmus's biblical lectures in Paris, admired the humanist's scholarship, and possessed his own copy of the *Paraphrases*, designed as a popular exposition of Scripture to benefit, in Erasmus's words, the 'farmer, the tailor, the mason, prostitutes, pimps and Turks'. In addition, the grammarian at Aberdeen, John Vaus, was also a product of the Paris humanism which had nurtured Boece and Hay. By the troubled 1540s, however, Aberdeen's momentum was not maintained.[4]

Even so, that early Renaissance centre in Scotland did provide a humanist training for a new generation of students. Some, like John Adamson, Dominican prior in the town, sought religious reform within his Order; his successor, John Grierson, Bachelor of Sacred Letters, possessed three known works by Erasmus (The New Testament, his *Annotations on the New Testament*, and *Adagiorum Chiliades*), participated in the reforming provincial council of 1549, and by March 1559/60 (through persuasion or pressure) repented in St Andrews his former 'superstitioun and idolatrie', renounced papal headship, the doctrines of purgatory and transubstantiation, the use of images, prayers to the saints and for the departed, and the necessity of auricular confession and of clerical celibacy.[5] Other Aberdeen graduates, like John Davidson, favoured academic pursuits: after further theological training at Paris, he was recruited for the post of principal at Glasgow in 1556, as a scholar familiar with Greek and Hebrew, to promote humanist studies within the University under the chancellorship of Archbishop Beaton, who had acquired a later edition of Erasmus's *Annotations on the New Testament*, published at Basle in 1542. Again, in securing grammar-school masters to foster humanist study of the classics in the capital, Edinburgh favoured two Aberdeen graduates: Henry Henryson, convicted of heresy by 1534,

---

[4] J. Durkan and A. Ross, *Early Scottish Libraries* (Glasgow, 1961), pp. 32, 113, 155–7; L. J. Macfarlane, *William Elphinstone and the Kingdom of Scotland* (Aberdeen, 1985), pp. 37, 254; Bainton, *Erasmus*, p. 175.

[5] Durkan and Ross, *Libraries*, p. 108; J. Durkan and R. Pringle, 'St Andrews additions to Durkan and Ross: some unrecorded Scottish pre-Reformation ownership inscriptions in St Andrews University Library', *The Bibliotheck*, 9 (1978), no. 1, p. 16; D. Patrick, ed., *Statutes of the Scottish Church* (Edinburgh, 1907), p. 86; D. H. Fleming, ed., *Register of the Minster Elders and Deacons of the Christian Congregation of St Andrews* [hereafter *RStAKS*] (Edinburgh, 1889–90), I, pp. 16–18.

and Adam Mure, who had also studied at Paris. David Simson, another Aberdeen student (in theology), later moved from reformist Catholicism to Protestant reform, a path which John Davidson at Glasgow was to tread by 1559, and who in his debate with the Catholic Quintin Kennedy appealed to the testimony of Erasmus.[6]

In St Andrews University, too, humanist impulses and Erasmian evangelism are detectable in the creation of St Mary's College, licensed by papal bull in 1538, to reinvigorate Catholic teaching and refute heresy, and in repeated efforts to erect a trilingual college, as advocated by the nephew of Cardinal Beaton, Archibald Hay, first as regent in Paris and then as Principal of St Mary's. His dream was of a college not just for the study of the humanist disciplines of poetry, rhetoric, history, and ethics, but for advanced training in theology by promoting the biblical tongues. Chaldaic and Arabic, he argued, ought to be taught as well as Greek, Hebrew, and Latin.[7] More tangibly, in recommending the Scots humanist teacher at the College des Presles in Paris, John Douglas, for a post in St Andrews, Hay helped secure the services of a Paris bachelor of medicine (and probably also a doctor of theology) who, as Provost of St Mary's, chose the Protestant path at the Reformation and as a contributor to the Reformers' *Book of Discipline* in 1560 shared responsibility for the detailed discussion on reorganizing the universities.[8] Douglas's own arrival in St Andrews was followed with the appointment by 1556 of another Paris scholar, John Rutherford, to St Mary's (later to head St Salvator's), to teach philosophy, Greek, and Latin, a step which (despite his neo-Aristotelianism) helped strengthen the advance of the humanities within the University, for Rutherford (who also had medical interests) was well travelled in Europe, having

[6] J. Durkan and J. Kirk, *University of Glasgow, 1451–1577* (Glasgow, 1977), pp. 216–17, 232–4; Durkan and Ross, *Libraries*, p. 25; J. Durkan, 'The Beginnings of Humanism in Scotland', *InR*, 4 (1953), pp. 5–24; J. Durkan, 'The cultural background in sixteenth-century Scotland', *InR*, 10 (1959), pp. 382–439; J. Durkan, 'Early humanism and King's College', *Aberdeen University Review*, 163 (1980), pp. 259–79.
[7] J. K. Cameron, 'The Renaissance Tradition in the Reformed Church of Scotland', *SCH*, 14 (1977), pp. 251–69; J. K. Cameron, 'A Trilingual College for Scotland: the Founding of St Mary's College', *St Mary's College Bulletin*, 31 (1988), pp. 9–19; E. K. Cameron, 'Archibald Hay's "Elegantiae". Writings of a Scots Humanist at the College de Montaigue in the time of Budé and Beda' in J.-C. Margolin, ed., *Acta Conventus Neo-Latini Turonensis* (Paris, 1980), pp. 277–301.
[8] J. K. Cameron, 'Renaissance Tradition', p. 255; J. Durkan, 'Cultural Background', p. 463; Durkan and Kirk, *University of Glasgow*, p. 206; W. A. McNeill, 'Scottish Entries in the *Acta Rectoria Universitatis Parisiensis* 1519 to *c.*1633', *ScHR*, 43 (1964), pp. 66–83 at p. 73; J. K. Cameron, ed., *The First Book of Discipline* (Edinburgh, 1972), pp. 57ff.

lived in Bordeaux, Montaigne, Coimbra, Périgord, and Paris; and with the Reformation, he became a convert to Calvinism, owning copies of Calvin and Beza (and also Wolfgang Musculus, the reformer at Augsburg, on the Psalms).[9]

Apart from the contribution of universities (and grammar schools) and humanist-minded bishops (men like Elphinstone in Aberdeen, Robert Reid in Orkney, James Beaton in Glasgow, and John Hamilton in St Andrews) in promoting educational reform by encouraging the study of classical and Christian Antiquity, religious houses, too, could serve as centres of humanist culture: an outstanding example was the small Cistercian house of Kinloss, in Moray, where, as abbot, Robert Reid, the future Bishop of Orkney, had persuaded the Piedmontese humanist, Giovanni Ferrerio, to settle for a spell in the 1530s to teach the monks: the humanist scholarship of Agricola, Lefèvre, Erasmus, and Melanchthon was much in evidence, but instruction in theology was curiously slender. There, too, the bishop's nephew, Walter Reid (who succeeded as abbot by 1553) was trained in Greek as well as Latin by a monk of Kinloss, and ultimately chose the Protestant path at the Reformation.[10] By these various means, humanist values were diffused among scholarly clerics and educated laymen. In the process, the humanists' preoccupation with classical culture and scholarship, and their aim of introducing educational reform, created the conditions enabling reformers to challenge the Church's authority by a direct appeal to Scripture, whose text was available for study in Hebrew and Greek (and in English, too), and not just in the Latin Vulgate, as a consequence of humanist endeavour.

As the last pre-Reformation primate of the Scottish Church, papal legate and Chancellor of his university, Archbishop Hamilton, at least, recognized the need for ecclesiastical renewal and educational change: his reforming programme for the Church, initiated in a series of provincial councils between 1549 and 1559, attempted to remedy serious irregularities; the issuing of a *Catechism* under his authority in 1552 and a 'Godlie Exhortation' on the Eucharist (or 'Twopenny Faith') in 1559 aimed at popular instruction; and a reinvigoration of the academic education which priests (or, at any rate, some priests) received was the aim in Hamilton's continuing the foundation of St Mary's College in 1554. The

---

[9] T. McCrie, *Life of Andrew Melville* (Edinburgh, 1899), pp. 362–4; J. Durkan, 'John Rutherford and Montaigne: an early influence?', *BHR*, 41 (1979), pp. 115–22.

[10] J. Stuart, ed., *Records of the Monastery of Kinloss* (Edinburgh, 1872), pp. 66, 77; J. Durkan, 'Giovanni Ferrerio and religious humanism in sixteenth-century Scotland', *SCH*, 17 (1981), p. 183.

Archbishop himself possessed Erasmus's *Paraphrases on John's Gospel* (Basle, 1523) (a copy which had also belonged to Thomas Cunningham, Augustinian canon and Principal of St Leonard's from 1534 to 1539); and, in the *Catechism* which he and the council of 1552 had authorized, Hamilton was evidently prepared to countenance a belief that man is 'justifyit be faith', 'the faith that jutifeis a christin man according as sanct Paule sais to the Romanis'. Here was an apparent (orthodox) emphasis on justification by faith, a recognition that men were justified by Christ's merits imputed to them, and a neglect of the (usually accompanying) doctrine of merit, that the good works of the just merited an eternal reward. All this was plainly at odds with Tridentine orthodoxy (for in 1547 the Council had already condemned the idea that faith alone was needed for justification), but it was consistent with Erasmus's earlier proclivities when he had acknowledged that

> our salvation depends not on our desert, but on God's grace. I highly approve of Luther when he calls us away from frail confidence in ourselves to the most safe harbour of trust in evangelical grace, though I do not approve of his reasons. Our hope is in the mercy of God and the merits of Christ.[11]

All in all, by initiating his reforming policies in Church and college, Hamilton was acting in a manner consistent with the moderate programme of Catholic reform in Germany introduced by Archbishop Hermann von Wied in his provincial council at Cologne in 1536: and just as the canons of Cologne had ignored the papacy and the doctrine of transubstantiation, so, too, the reformist Scottish *Catechism* of 1552, compiled at Hamilton's behest, conspicuously failed to mention the pope, and in its exposition on the Eucharist which, it affirmed, contains Christ 'really and essentially', the emphasis placed on the commemorative and memorial aspect of 'the Communioun' would have found acceptance in some Protestant circles.[12] Even with the Reformation, Hamilton, in the Parliament of 1560, declined either to condemn or to consent to the new

---

[11] Patrick, *Statutes*, pp. 84–191; *The Catechism set forth by Archbishop Hamilton . . . together with the Two-Penny Faith, 1559*, ed. A. F. Mitchell (Edinburgh, 1882), fol. xciii v; *The Works of John Knox*, ed. D. Laing (Edinburgh, 1846–64), 6, pp. 676–8; R. G. Cant, *University of St Andrews* (Edinburgh, 1970), pp. 36–7; Durkan and Pringle, 'St Andrews additions', pp. 13, 16; H. Jedin, *History of the Council of Trent* (Edinburgh, 1957–61), 2, pp. 283–316; Bainton, *Erasmus*, p. 245 (cf. p. 229).

[12] J. K. Cameron, 'The Cologne Reformation and the Church of Scotland', *JEH*, 30 (1979), pp. 39–64 and '"Catholic Reform" in Germany and in the Pre-1560 Church in Scotland', *RSCHS*, 20 (1979), pp. 105–17; Mitchell, *Catechism*, fol. cxl.

Protestant Confession of Faith.[13] On the Continent, however, Trent (whose final session closed in 1563) brought to an end for obedient Catholics the phase of theological confusion and uncertainty. Not only so, the doctrinal conservatism which characterized that Council's proceedings signalled an end to any accommodation with Protestant practice. It also marked a swing away from the dominance of the biblical humanism espoused by Erasmus (whose death had occurred in 1536) and of a pronounced Augustinianism in favour of a revived Thomism, which the Dominicans so cherished.[14] In Scotland, however, these changing emphases were slower in emerging.

Besides Archbishop Hamilton, prominent though he was, other Scottish clerics promoted to the episcopate had more than a fleeting acquaintance with Erasmian scholarship and showed themselves supporters of humanist reform. The remarkable Renaissance library of Henry Sinclair, Dean of Glasgow from 1550, and Bishop of Ross from 1558, contained Erasmus's *Declarationes ad Censuras Lutitiae* (1532), his response to the Sorbonne's condemnation, his *Letters* (1538), the *Paraphrases on the New Testament* (1540), portions of his *Opera* (1540), and his *Annotations on the New Testament* (1541).[15] In the northern diocese of Caithness, Bishop Robert Stewart, who had favoured the English and Reforming causes in the 1540s, and who entered service in the Protestant Church at the Reformation, possessed a copy of the *Annotations on the New Testament* (1540); and another conforming bishop at the Reformation, Adam Bothwell of Orkney, a former canon of Glasgow, whose library was well stocked with humanist and patristic literature, also owned Erasmus's *Annotations*, with the Dutchman's sometimes controversial exegesis and elucidation of the biblical text.[16]

Certainly, the path from Erasmian humanism through reformist Catholicism to Protestant reform was one pursued by two Augustinian canons of St Andrews who shared the name John Duncanson, the one became Principal of St Leonard's College by 1556, and is presumably the John Duncanson who owned a copy of the canons of Hermann von

[13] *Calendar of Scottish Papers*, ed. J. Bain *et al.* (Edinburgh, 1898–1969), I, no. 885.
[14] L. B. Pascoe, 'The Council of Trent and Bible Study: humanism and scripture', *Catholic Historical Review*, 52 (1967), pp. 18–38; Jedin, *Trent*, 2, pp. 118ff.
[15] Durkan and Ross, *Libraries*, pp. 54–5; J. Durkan, 'Further additions to Durkan and Ross: some newly-discovered Scottish pre-Reformation provenances', *The Bibliotheck*, 10 (1980), no. 4, p. 91.
[16] Durkan and Ross, *Libraries*, p. 64; D. Shaw, 'Adam Bothwell, a Conserver of the Renaissance in Scotland', I. B. Cowan and D. Shaw, eds, *The Renaissance and Reformation in Scotland* (Edinburgh, 1983), pp. 141–69 at p. 152.

Wied's reforming provincial council of Cologne, the other, minister at Stirling by 1560, had a copy of Erasmus's *Annotations on the New Testament* (1540); Lord James Stewart, Prior of the Augustinian house in St Andrews, who rose to become a leader of the Protestant Lords of the Congregation, had also acquired early Erasmian literature, perhaps during his student years in Paris, as well as an edition of the *Paraphrases* of 1541.[17] Others, like William Gordon, last pre-Reformation Bishop of Aberdeen, with his copy of Erasmus's *Declarationes ... ad Censuras Lutetiae vulgatas* (1532), Henry Sinclair, Dean of Glasgow and Bishop of Ross, who died in 1565, or John Leslie, Sinclair's successor in Ross, with Erasmus's *Annotationes* remained firmly orthodox in religion, regardless of their reading Erasmus.[18] Some, too, however, like Gilbert Winram moved directly from Erasmian criticism to Lutheran belief: a student in St Leonard's College, St Andrews, where he enrolled in 1516, and owner of Erasmus's New Testament (1522), Winram became an early Lutheran convert, accompanying Patrick Hamilton, himself a devoted young humanist, to Marburg, where he died about 1530.[19] Another student, William Christison, who entered St Leonard's College, St Andrews in 1514 became Protestant minister in Lutheran Bergen, and on returning to Dundee, where he became the town's minister shortly after the Reformation, gifted to his old College a copy of Luther's work on Moses, published at Nuremberg in the 1550s.[20] Similarly, among the charges leading to Sir John Borthwick's condemnation for heresy in 1540 was his possession of suspect literature: 'diversos *Erasmi* et diversorum aliorum hereticorum condemnatorum, necnon, et librum *Vnio Dissidencium*', a work espousing the doctrine of justification by faith alone.[21] Not only so, the career of George Buchanan, a humanist of international repute (scholar at Paris, St Andrews, Bordeaux, and Coimbra), well illustrates how readily support for Catholic reform and Erasmian evangelism could lead to an approval of Lutheran heterodoxy and an attachment to Protestant reform.[22]

In all, the distaste shared by humanists and reformers for scholastic theology, their preoccupation with rediscovering the values and practice

[17] J. K. Cameron, 'Catholic Reform', p. 106; Durkan and Ross, *Libraries*, pp. 175; 148, 185.

[18] Durkan and Ross, *Libraries*, pp. 36, 53–5, 170.

[19] J. M. Anderson, ed., *Early Records of the University of St Andrews* [hereafter *RStAU*] (Edinburgh, 1926), pp. 212; 110; Durkan and Ross, *Libraries*, pp. 160–1; P. Lorimer, *Patrick Hamilton* (Edinburgh, 1857), p. 87; Durkan, 'Cultural background', p. 390.

[20] *RStAU*, p. 210; Durkan and Pringle, 'St Andrews additions', p. 15.

[21] *RStAKS*, 1, p. 98; Foxe, 5 (1858), p. 620.

[22] See pp. 383–4 below; J. Durkan, 'Native Influences on George Buchanan', in I. D. McFarlane, ed., *Acta Conventus Neo-Latini Sanctandreani* (New York, 1986), pp. 31–42.

of Christian Antiquity by studying the biblical texts in Hebrew and Greek and the writings of the Early Fathers in Greek and Latin, instead of relying on medieval glosses and commentaries, and their recognition of the textual errors and inadequacies in the Vulgate version of the Bible, on which the Catholic Church continued to rely, helped create among scholars a climate of reappraisal which invited fresh exegesis and new, or rediscovered, doctrinal insights. The novel emphasis on a reformation of doctrine, which Luther came to urge, proved far more threatening to the existing order than any call for a revitalized Church to be achieved through moral and educational reform, the sort of programme Archbishop Hamilton was later to espouse in an effort at eliminating abuse and lethargy. For those Scots who followed Luther's message, a reform of doctrine was the central issue. For a start, Luther's understanding of the doctrine of justification carried with it implications fatal to the sacrificial nature of the Mass and the mediating role of the priesthood; the Church's sacramental theology came under fire; a doctrinal revolution was the wholly unexpected sequel to what otherwise might have remained an unnoticed Wittenberg disputation.

In Scotland, whose king Pope Clement VII (somewhat prematurely) had congratulated in January 1525/6 for keeping the 'kingdom without injury from the perfidious Lutheran heresy although it is flourishing in the nearest country', there were already indications in academic circles of the invasion of Lutheran heresy and of incipient doctrinal turmoil. In Aberdeen, where Bishop Gavin Dunbar lamented how 'syndry strangearis and otheris within his diocesy of Aberdene has bukis of that heretik Luthyr, and favoris his arrorys and fals opinionys', the king's sheriffs were ordered in 1525 to confiscate the property of those who had Lutheran literature. At St Andrews, where Patrick Hamilton from Glasgow arrived in 1523, after studying at Paris and Louvain, academic disputations were held to refute Luther's doctrines: there Alexander Alane, an Augustinian canon in St Andrews Priory (before his own defection to Lutheranism by 1529), undertook to disprove the tenets in Luther's *Assertio omnium articulorum* by employing the arguments advanced in John Fisher's *Assertionis Lutheranae Confutatio*. At that stage, Alane took a contrary view to Patrick Hamilton, who, as a critic of scholastic teaching on grace and an exponent of Luther's opinion in St Andrews, sought refuge abroad in 1527, when accused of heresy, by reaching Wittenberg and then the Lutheran University of Marburg, where he defended his academic theses (the compilation known as *Patrick's Places*, or *Loci communes*), with support from Francis Lambert of Avignon, before returning home again to preach

'Luther's pravity', arguing for reform in doctrine, Sacraments, and ceremonies. In his theses, Hamilton had expounded the contrast between law and Gospel, between damnation and redemption, between justifying faith and good works which cannot win 'the inheritance of heaven or remission of sin'.[23]

If his humanist training at Paris and Louvain had led him to value Aristotle in the original Greek, and Plato too, at the expense of scholastic commentaries and the sophistry which he so abhorred, Hamilton had also witnessed in Paris the outcry against Luther, and Melanchthon's own attack on the 'prince of the Paris divines', John Major, the Scottish philosopher, whose commentaries on Peter Lombard Melanchthon likened to 'wagon-loads of trifling', and of whose theology he remarked: 'If he is a specimen of the Parisians, no wonder they are all the enemies of Luther.' Thereafter, Louvain, with its famous trilingual college which Erasmus himself had helped to promote, offered further scope for Hamilton's humanist pursuits. Yet it was ultimately Germany, and Lutheran Marburg, where William Tyndale and John Frith were also resident, which confirmed Hamilton's Protestant inclinations, already discernible in St Andrews by 1527. There, at any rate, after his flight, he affirmed his belief in salvation *sola gratia*, and in justification *sola fide*. With complete assurance, Hamilton proclaimed the message of salvation by directing men to Christ: 'faith maketh a man a member of Christ'; 'faith maketh a man the inheritor of heaven'; 'no works can make us righteous'; 'whosoever believeth or thinketh to be saved by his works, denieth that Christ is his Saviour.'[24]

The initial charge against Hamilton in 1527 of 'disputing, holding and maintaining divers heresies of Martin Luther and his followers, repugnant to the faith' (and of attacking the power of the keys), was reiterated on his return from Marburg in 1528. His home-coming to Kincavel, in West Lothian, was perhaps hastened by news of his father's death, but, regardless of his status as a cleric of St Andrews diocese, he chose a bride, following Luther's example, and his evangelical preaching in the area was soon drawn to the Archbishop's attention. Invited for conference to St Andrews, he 'taught and disputed openly in the university', Alane

---

[23] D. H. Fleming, *The Reformation in Scotland* (London, 1910), p. 210; J. Stuart, ed., *Extracts from the Council Register of the Burgh of Aberdeen, 1398–1570* (Aberdeen, 1844), p. 110; G. Wiedermann, 'Martin Luther versus John Fisher: some ideas concerning the debate on Lutheran theology at the University of St Andrews, 1525–30', *RSCHS*, 22 (1984), pp. 13–34; Lorimer, *Hamilton*, pp. 5, 28, 36–8, 50, 96, 114; Knox, *Works*, 1, pp. 15, 21–35.

[24] Lorimer, *Hamilton*, pp. 42–3, 93ff.; Foxe, 4 (1857), pp. 558ff., 569, 571.

observed, 'on all points on which he conceived a reformation to be necessary in the Church's doctrines, and in her administration of the sacraments and other rites.' At his trial, he affirmed his belief that the corruption of sin remains in children after baptism; no man by free will can do good; no man is free from sin; Christians know they are in a state of grace and are justified not by works, but by faith alone; good works do not make a man good, but a good man performs good works; ill works truly repented do not make an ill man; and faith, hope, and charity are so linked together that a man who has one has the rest. He also declined to condemn the disputed views that God is the cause of sin, in the sense that if God withdraws his grace, men cannot avoid sinning; that it is devilish to teach that by penance the remission of sins is purchased; that auricular confession is unnecessary for salvation; that there is no purgatory; that the holy patriarchs were in heaven before Christ's Passion; and that the pope is Antichrist, every priest having as much power as the pope. At his execution, too, he reiterated that it was 'lawful to all men that have souls to read the Word of God', unlawful to use images, futile to pray to Mary and the saints; that Christ is the only mediator, purgatory was unscriptural, Masses cannot purge souls—only the repentance of sins and faith in Christ may do that. In Hamilton's utterances and writings, which exhibit a firm adherence to the central theological themes of the Reformation, the teaching of Melanchthon and Lambert, as well as Luther, is all too apparent.[25]

What all this amounted to was little less than a revolt against the whole medieval system: it undermined the priestly domination of religion, discounted established teaching on salvation, challenged the efficacy of the Mass, placed the believing Christian on an even footing with the cleric, and, in so doing, recognized that religion belonged to the people. Yet Hamilton's theology was formulated within the context of an academic disputation; its immediate appeal was unlikely to extend beyond the confines of the class-room; after all, his opportunities for preaching to the public were severely limited; and his public execution was intended to suppress the circulation of deviant doctrine. But news of his burning, his protracted ordeal, his dignified profession of faith, and his steadfast adherence to his beliefs did reach a wider and more curious audience: so

[25] Lorimer, *Hamilton*, pp. 128, 143–50; A. F. Mitchell, *The Scottish Reformation* (Edinburgh, 1900), p. 290; Wiedermann, 'Luther versus Fisher', p. 21; Foxe, 4, pp. 559–60; J. Spottiswoode, *History of the Church of Scotland*, ed. M. Napier and M. Russell (Edinburgh, 1847–51), 1, pp. 124–5.

dramatic an event as his burning inevitably arrested attention and stimulated inquiry. Alane, who witnessed the spectacle, was profoundly moved; and he was unlikely to have been alone; for it was not John Knox but a bystander at the execution who is said to have remarked that 'the reik of Maister Patrik Hammyltoun hes infected as many as it blew upoun.' The whole episode even made international news: the University of Louvain congratulated the University of St Andrews for its commendable zeal in upholding Catholic doctrine; John Major from Paris applauded the Archbishop of St Andrews for his resolute action; and at Marburg, Lambert lamented the death of Scotland's 'first and now illustrious apostle'.[26]

Hamilton was the most striking example of an early evangelical, but he was by no means the only one. Others harboured Lutheran notions in one form or another. For a start, Hamilton's own immediate circle of family and friends displayed more than a fleeting affection for the new theology. Besides the academic audience reached through his university debates, which led, belatedly, to Alane's conversion by 1529, Hamilton privately discussed his controversial views with monks in his lodgings; and he later preached in the vicinity of Linlithgow. Two friends, John Hamilton from Linlithgow and Gilbert Winram from Edinburgh, were his companions at Lutheran Marburg in 1527 (and two further Scots registered in the University in 1533 and 1537);[27] and the degree to which familial ties facilitated the spread of religious opinions is illustrated in the charges of heresy directed against Hamilton's brother, sister, and, seemingly, his nephew. By the early 1530s, his brother, James Hamilton of Kincavill, the Sheriff of Linlithgow, was accused of denying free will and purgatory, of affirming the futility of prayers to the saints and for the dead, and repudiating the popes as successors of Peter. After making his peace with the Church, the Sheriff was charged once more in 1534, as 'a relapsed heretic and protector of heretics', with maintaining that God alone, and not the saints, should be adored, with possessing prohibited books in the vernacular, reciting the Lord's Prayer in the vernacular, and holding suspect opinions on purgatory and prayers for the dead. On fleeing to England, where he claimed to Thomas Cromwell that half the allegations were false, he was forfeited in his absence; but, as one who held he had been forced to leave his native land for proclaiming God's Word and censuring the usurped powers of the Bishop of Rome, he sought the

[26] Foxe, 4, p. 561; Knox, *Works*, 1, p. 42; Lorimer, *Hamilton*, p. 157.
[27] Lorimer, *Hamilton*, pp. 88, 232.

protection of Henry VIII, who, in turn, persuaded the Governor, Arran (himself inclined to Protestantism), to restore Hamilton's forfeited property; and although a papal pardon was secured before 1546, Hamilton survived not only to witness the Reformation victory of 1560, but also to gain the General Assembly's approval in 1563 for the doctrines he had held in 1534, namely, for believing his brother Patrick died 'a good Christian and catholick man'; that there was no purgatory; that the dead should not be prayed for; that man had no free will 'as the papists meane'; for saying the Lord's Prayer publicly in his native tongue; for possessing heretical literature; and for condemning the preaching of the Friars Preachers (or Dominicans).[28]

His sister, Katherine, the wife of the Captain of Dunbar (himself a Frenchman) was accused, also in 1534 at Holyrood, for affirming the heresy that her own works could not save her: at the scaffold she is said to have exclaimed before James V, 'I know perfectly that no kind of works can save me but only the works of Christ my Lord and Saviour.' Here was a simple and dignified profession of Luther's doctrine. The King, however, persuaded his kinswoman to recant; but she escaped to England where 'for holding our [English] ways', she remained reluctant to return home. Similarly, if correctly reported, Hamilton's nephew ('sister sone to the scherreffe of Linlithgow') was charged in 1534 with holding 'the opynions of Mertene Luter', which he was obliged to recant.[29]

The articulation (and no doubt popularization) of Luther's theology of grace, his denial of man's free will in determining his salvation, and his solution to the problems of sin and forgiveness, death, judgement, and resurrection through the transforming power of faith was already underway. Luther's central message removed much of the anguish and uncertainty in late medieval religion: it eliminated the burden of earning salvation and ended the need for saintly or priestly intercession; it replaced the seven Sacraments by a simpler two; it undercut the established penitential system and made redundant belief in purgatory and in

---

[28] *Letters of James V*, ed. D. Hay (Edinburgh, 1954), pp. 274–5; T. Thomson, ed., *Diurnal of Remarkable Occurrents* (Edinburgh, 1833), p. 19; Foxe, 4, p. 579; D. Calderwood, *History of the Kirk of Scotland*, ed. T. Thomson (Edinburgh, 1842–9), 1, pp. 108–9, 139; 2, p. 228; M. Livingstone *et al.*, ed., *Registrum Secreti Sigilli Regum Scotorum* [hereafter *RSS*] (Edinburgh, 1908–82), 2, nos 1585, 1699, 1928; *LP*, 7, no. 1184; 8, no. 734; 10, nos 50, 1256; 11, nos 248–9; 13, pt 2, no. 1280 (fol. 14b); 14, pt 1, no. 386; 15, no. 634; 18, pt 1, no. 222; T. Thomson and C. Innes, eds, *Acts of the Parliaments of Scotland* [hereafter *APS*] (London, 1814–75), 2, pp. 469, 472–3; T. Thomson, ed., *Book of the Universall Kirk of Scotland* [hereafter *BUK*] (Edinburgh, 1839–45), 1, pp. 35–6.

[29] Foxe 4, p. 579; *LP*, 14, pt 1, no. 625; *Diurnal*, p. 18.

the efficacy (and expense) of indulgences, and, in so far as the priesthood of believing Christians excluded dependence on a sacrificing priesthood, it undermined the clerical monopoly in religion. Luther's essential message was communicated by word of mouth, and by the secret circulation of evangelical literature which Parliament had sought to ban in 1525 (whose action the Lords of Council strengthened in 1527) and again in 1535. That Lutheran books were undoubtedly imported and read is attested not only by repeated legislation and by the Bishop of Aberdeen's complaint in 1525 on detecting 'bukis of that heretik Luthyr', but also by the report of the English agent in Antwerp in 1527 that Scottish merchants in both Antwerp and Bergen-op-Zoom were shipping home heretical works, including English New Testaments, especially to St Andrews and also to Edinburgh, and, yet again, by the heresy trials themselves, which sometimes exposed the harbouring or reading of suspect literature. At any rate, James Hamilton in 1534, Martin Balcasky, an Edinburgh merchant in 1538, James Watson, David Graham (apparently a custumar with ready access to imported books), Walter Cousland, and William Forrester, in Stirling in 1539, and John Borthwick, in 1540, were all charged with possessing prohibited or suspect works.[30]

Some literature written in languages other than English and Scots had an appeal limited to a scholarly readership: Robert Stewart (by 1541 Bishop of Caithness and later a convert to Protestantism) acquired an edition of Bugenhagen (1524) on the Psalms and Melanchthon's work on Romans, published in 1532 at Wittenberg (where at least a dozen Scots are known to have studied between 1519 and 1555). Other works of private devotion available in the vernacular, including English Bibles and *Patrick's Places*, which (with remarkable speed) Frith first published in 1529, obviously held a wider attraction for the literate and, at second hand, for those who gathered round a reader. Yet, the abilities of determined and even semi-educated minds to cope with foreign texts should not be underestimated: in 1550, Adam Wallace from Kyle, depicted as 'a simple poor man in appearance' possessing 'a Bible at his belt in French, Dutch and English', acknowledged 'I have not much Latin', but had 'read the Bible and word of God in three tongues, and have understood them so far as God gave me grace.' But well before then the circulation of English

[30] *APS*, 2, pp. 295, 431–2; *Aberdeen Burgh Records*, pp. 110–11; *LP*, 4, pt 2, no. 2903; *Letters of James V*, pp. 274–5; *RSS*, 2, no. 2936; R. Pitcairn, ed., *Criminal Trials in Scotland* (Edinburgh, 1833), 1, pt 1, pp. 216–18; T. Dickson *et al.*, ed., *Accounts of the Lord High Treasurer of Scotland* [hereafter *TA*] (Edinburgh, 1877ff.),7, p. 78; Foxe, 5, p. 620.

Bibles and New Testaments had made such headway in the 1530s that, as Norfolk observed to Thomas Cromwell in 1539, 'daily there are come to me gentlemen and clerks who flee out of Scotland, as they say, for reading the scriptures in English.'[31]

John Gau's *The Richt Vay to the Kingdom of Heuine*, printed at Malmö in 1533, is the first substantial exposition of Lutheran doctrine to appear in Scots. Translated from a Danish Lutheran text composed by Christiern Pedersen, *Den rette vey till Hiemmerigis Rige* (1531) (itself based on a German work by Urbanus Rhegius, who drew material from Luther's own writings), Gau's work was addressed to 'al chrissine breder and sister' who sought instruction in the Ten Commandments, the Creed, the Lord's Prayer, and the Angelic Salutation of the Virgin, at a time when so many were deceived by such 'blindnes' as the purchase of remissions from the pains of purgatory or intercessory prayers to saints. Not even Christ's mother could intercede: 'neyne sal put thair hop in the virgine Maria or trow that schw cane saiff ony man for prayerr or seruice dwne to hir.' Christ alone should be worshipped, for he had 'maid alanerlie perfit satisfactione for al our sinnis and wil marcifullie forgif ws thaime of his awne gracious guidnes.' Throughout, emphasis was placed on the need to trust in Christ for delivery from evil, 'and trowis this noth of the paip na cardinal na thair legatis na of ony oder mortal man' who might have worldly power yet lacked the 'power to saiff and to giff the ye euerlestand blis of hewine.' God's gift of faith teaches how men 'sal get grace marcie and forgiffine of thair sinnis' that they might 'risz wp agane fra deid and get the euerlestand liff thairefter.' Every man and woman should therefore learn and remember the Ten Commandments and the Creed and say the Lord's Prayer 'apone thair aune tung', while those with ability to read and understand should study the Bible itself. In keeping with Luther's insistence on Christ's Real Presence within the consecrated elements of bread and wine (and his rejection of transubstantiation and the sacrificial character of the Mass), *The Richt Vay* explained how 'the bodi and blwid of our lord Iesus is contenit veralie in the sacrament of the alter onder the forme of breid and vine.' The Church is defined simply as 'the congregacione of sanctis that is of al chrissine men and vemen' gathered throughout the world, in whom ('the haile chrissine kirk') resides the power of the keys to bind and loosen: 'the paip na the bischoips hesz na oder keyis of

---

[31] Durkan and Ross, *Libraries*, p. 63; Durkan, 'Cultural background', p. 428; W. A. Clebsch, *England's Earliest Protestants, 1520–1535* (New Haven, 1964), pp. 82–4; Foxe, 5, pp. 637–9; *LP*, 14, pt 1, no. 625.

Christ or of peter bot to prech godis word the law and the wangel the quhilk ii bindis and lowsis al conscience.' Indeed, the power belonged not to 'ane bischoip or ane prest or ane mwnk'. As Christ alone is head of the Church, 'na mortal sinful man quhedir he be pape or patriarch' can be other than a member. In a concluding letter to the Scottish nobles and barons, the false preaching of 'dremis and fablis and the tradicions of men' is contrasted with scriptural teaching, and illustrated by the experience of Patrick Hamilton, condemned as a heretic for confessing Christ.[32]

Another evangelical work designed to instruct and instil a sense of personal piety in times of persecution was John Johnsone's *An Confortable Exhortation of our mooste Holy Christen Faith and her Frutes written unto the Christen brethern in Scotland after the pure word of God*, probably printed at Malmö about 1533. Again, Luther's doctrine of salvation is reiterated, and Patrick Hamilton's fortitude and faithfulness in the face of persecution is recalled. Its object was to counsel believers to remain faithful, even to the point of suffering, in times of adversity and danger. Both authors (and their printers) evidently envisaged a ready market for their works in Scotland—and not without reason for, in 1534, the King himself revealed how 'divers tractatis and bukis translatit out of Latin in our Scottis toung be heretikis, favoraris, and of the sect of Luther' were circulating in 'Leith, Edinburgh, Dunde, Sanctandrois, Montros, Abirdene and Kircaldy', all east-coast ports with ample access to Scandinavia and Germany where Lutheranism abounded, and to England where translations of German works were prominent.[33]

Whatever the exact effect the distribution of these works had in Scotland, there are signs the message had reached receptive minds: the growing incidence of Lutheran heresy had prompted the authorities to make preparations in 1532 for 'the accusatioun of the Lutherianis'; by that date, too, David Strachan, a graduate, from the north-east had been convicted of heresy; in 1534 payment was made for 'xvj sergis to thame to turs that wes accusit of heresy'; and in 1537 steps were taken for 'serching of the heretiks in the West land'. At Holyrood Abbey in 1534, for favouring 'the

---

[32] J. Gau, *The Richt Vay to the Kingdom of Heuine*, ed. A. F. Mitchell (Edinburgh, 1888), pp. 3–4, 84–5, 101–2; 26; 8, 31, 35, 38; 5, 8, 27, 55–6, 59–62, 79–81, 104.

[33] J. K. Cameron, 'John Johnsone's *An confortable Exhortation of our Mooste Holy Christen Faith and her Frutes*: an early example of Scots Lutheran piety' in D. Baker, ed., *Reform and Reformation: England and the Continent c.1500–c.1750 = SCH.S*, 2 (1979), pp. 133–47; R. K. Hannay, ed., *Acts of the Lords of Council in Public Affairs, 1501–1554* [hereafter *ADC*] (Edinburgh, 1932), pp. 422–4: B. Hall, 'The Early Rise and Gradual Decline of Lutheranism in England (1520–1600)', in Baker, ed., *Reform*, p. 126.

opynions of Mertene Luter', three inhabitants of the port of Leith, with a chaplain from Leith, William Kirk, Edinburgh's grammar-school master, Henry Henryson, and an advocate, William Johnstone, appeared on charges of heresy (along with Patrick Hamilton's brother and sister): the schoolmaster was condemned, the advocate fled the country, the chaplain recanted, as reportedly did the three men from Leith (Adam Dayes, a shipwright, Henry Cairns, a skipper, and John Stewart), though one (Dayes) fled the country and was escheated, which suggests conviction, another (Cairns) was subsequently forfeited for heresy and fled 'to the easter seas', and the third died in exile. An unnamed 'woman of Leith', who in childbirth, it was said, had declined to invoke the Virgin's help, praying directly to Christ 'in whose help I trust', recanted her heresy.[34] At that point, too, Norman Gourlay, a St Andrews graduate of 1515, was executed for affirming that 'there was no such thing as purgatory, and that the pope was not a bishop but Antichrist, and had no jurisdiction in Scotland'—claims reminiscent of the Lollard tradition, but also consistent with Luther's soteriology and his fiery antipapalism. (Indeed, John Frith in exile had published an English rendering of Luther's *De Antichristo* at Antwerp in 1529, and his own *Disputacion of purgatorye* appeared from an Antwerp press in 1531.) The remaining culprit on trial in 1534, David Straiton, from the Mearns, also repudiated purgatory and placed his faith in 'the passion of Christ', in recognition that Christ's death was sufficient satisfaction for sin. Previously Stration had refused to pay his teinds or tithes (another feature of earlier Lollard protest) and took delight in having his nephew, a laird's son, read him passages from the New Testament (obviously in English) in a 'qwyet place'. Convicted of heresy, he refused to recant, and was executed.[35]

Despite the dearth of detail (in the absence of episcopal registers), these early prosecutions, convictions, and abjurations do reveal a curious blend of beliefs, ranging from old Lollard tenets to inchoate Protestant doctrine, as Reforming ideas permeated different sections of society, where some priests, merchants, tradesmen, lairds, and professional men found succour in their message. At any rate, it ought not to be discounted too readily that any recollection of Lollard protest which may have lingered as

---

[34] *TA*, 6, pp. 58; 8, 209, 313; Knox, *Works*, 1, pp. 56–8 and n. 1; *Criminal Trials*, 1, pt 1, p. 211; *Diurnal*, pp. 18–19; Calderwood, 1, p. 108; *RSS*, 2, nos 1583, 2988; *TA*, 6, pp. 175–6; 7, pp. 79, 233–4; Foxe, 4, p. 579.

[35] *RStAU*, pp. 101, 103–4, 206; Knox, *Works*, 1, pp. 8–10, 60; Foxe, 4, p. 579; Calderwood, 1, p. 108; Clebsch, *Protestants*, pp. 85–94; Knox, *Works*, 1, pp. 58–60; Foxe, 4, p. 579; Calderwood, 1, pp. 106–7; *TA*, 6, p. 176; 7, p. 77; *Diurnal*, pp. 18–19.

a folk memory in the popular (and retentive) mind—in Kyle or else-where—would be reinvigorated by Luther's startling challenge to the medieval system. By 1536 searches were under way in Dundee and Perth for two iconoclasts, John Blacat and George Luwett, 'suspectit of hangeing of the image of Sanct Francis'. To a repudiation that works justify, a disbelief in transubstantiation, purgatory, and the intercession of saints, a desire for the Scriptures in the native tongue, and criticism of teinds, there was added the violence of the image-breakers. The smashing of images startled and shocked communities accustomed to revere them as holy objects, linking the human with the divine; but to the iconoclasts, they contradicted the Second Commandment, and were symbols of false religion: their destruction also demonstrated a rebellion against the cult of Mary and the saints by people who felt tricked and betrayed by what was thought to be the Church's teaching.[36]

In Ayrshire—where some parishioners were spreading Lutheran errors 'both in public and in private', had copies of the English New Testament 'and other writings containing heretical opinions', and committed blasphemies against the Eucharist—the smashing of an image in the parish kirk of Ayr was attributed in 1533 to Walter Stewart, son of Lord Ochiltree (who was subsequently convicted of heresy); and, about the same time a statue of the Virgin, 'situated in the wall' of the friary of the Observantine Friars Minor in the burgh, was decapitated.[37] The mutila-tion of images by hanging, decapitation, or obliterating the faces of statues was also a measure of the intense hatred, aggression, frustration, resentment, and disappointment which lay behind the action of icono-clasts. The phenomenon itself also says something of the changing face (and pace) of theological reform: it marked a departure from Luther (who had opposed Karlstadt and the iconoclasts in Wittenberg) towards more radical influences associated with Bucer in Strasburg and Zwingli in Zurich.[38]

As yet, the isolated instances of reported image-breaking associated with the seaports of Ayr, Perth, and Dundee seem to have been the work of individuals rather than groups; they are unlikely to have been purely

[36] TA, 6, p. 307; C. M. N. Eire, War against the Idols (Cambridge, 1986); M. Aston, England's Iconoclasts (Cambridge, 1988); P. M. Crew, Calvinist Preaching and Iconoclasm in the Netherlands 1544–1569 (Cambridge, 1978).

[37] Calderwood, 1, p. 104; Criminal Trials, 1, pt 1, p. 335; RSS, 2, nos 2420, 2797. (Calderwood and Cr. Trials depict Walter Stewart as 'brother' to Andrew Lord Ochiltree but RSS describes him as 'son'.)

[38] Eire, Idols, pp. 55f.; Aston, Iconoclasts, pp. 39–40, 47.

spontaneous, but provoked by Protestant preaching or propaganda. Certainly, by the late 1530s, John Willock, a Dominican friar from Ayr, had fled because of heresy to England, where he preached against praying to saints and for the dead, and against purgatory. Another Dominican, John Macdowell, Prior of Wigtown, had left for England by 1535, where he gained the reputation of a blasphemer of saints for his preaching against the honouring of saints and images. The preaching in St Andrews of a third Dominican, Alexander Seton, confessor to James V, came under fire (while he was absent in Dundee) for his conspicuous failure to mention purgatory, pardons, pilgrimages, and prayers to the saints; and, as suspicions grew, Seton sought exile in England, where he was denounced in 1541 for preaching justification by faith alone and denying the efficacy of Masses and prayers for the dead, and man's free will. Nor need there be doubt that the views these friars expressed in England also circulated at home: in 1534, the provincial of the Dominicans and the Warden of the Franciscans appealed to the Lords of Council for help in preventing friars preach opinions associated with Lutheran heresy and in stopping 'the freris at are tholit pas furth of the realme in apostasy'.[39]

No effective remedy to the problem of apostasizing friars was evidently found: already, in 1532, Alexander Dick, depicted as an apostate, had left his Franciscan friary in Aberdeen for Dundee, where he was suspected of heresy; by 1535, a former Observant Franciscan, James Melville, who had earlier left for Germany, returned home in secular dress as an apostate, it was said, 'infected with Lutheranism which he attempts to spread among the ignorant people'; at that point, too, by the mid-1530s, John Mac-alpine, Dominican Prior of Perth and graduate of Cologne, left for England, was befriended by Thomas Cromwell, went on to Wittenberg University, and became Lutheran theologian at Copenhagen in 1542; John Craig, Dominican friar (later minister in Edinburgh and Aberdeen) was imprisoned for heresy in the 1530s; John Beveridge, Dominican friar, was burned for heresy at Edinburgh in 1539; James Hewat, Dominican friar in Perth and Dundee, is credited in the 1530s with helping to shape the religious outlook of James Wedderburn, the satirist, who fled to Dieppe, it was said, to escape the Church authorities; John Keillour, Dominican friar, was burned in 1539 after producing a play at Stirling on Christ's Passion, in which the clergy were charged with blinding the

[39] Foxe, 5, pp. 446, 448–51; J. Durkan, 'Some Local Heretics', *Transactions of the Dumfries and Galloway Nat. Hist. and Antiq. Soc.* [hereafter *TDGNHAS*], 36 (1959), p. 68; Knox, *Works*, 1, pp. 45–52; *ADC*, pp. 422–4.

379

people, and the rulers with persecuting Christ's followers; John Lyn, a Franciscan friar, 'left his hipocryticall habite', and was later found studying at Wittenberg in 1555; and by the early 1540s four Dominican friars were prominent preachers of Protestant doctrine: Thomas Gwilliam from Inverness preached on ecclesiastical abuses and promoted the English Bible; John Rough from Stirling, who was 'vehement against all impietie', spent four years in Ayr, inaugurated Knox to the ministry in St Andrews Castle, and in England approved the doctrines of Cranmer, Ridley, and Latimer and the second Edwardine Prayer Book, denied transubstantiation, disapproved of auricular confession, repudiated the papacy, and recognized the two dominical Sacraments only, for which heresies he was burned at Smithfield in 1557; John Roger, in Knox's estimation, was 'godly, learned and ane that had fructfully preached Christ Jesus to the conforte of many' in Angus and the Mearns, and Walter Thomson in Aberdeen.[40]

Also active, like the friars, as preachers were the Augustinian canons, among whose number were some defectors to Protestant thought: besides Alesius (whose Protestant career belonged to England, Germany, and Leipzig, where he died in 1565), Robert Richardson, formerly a Catholic reformer and author, as canon of Cambuskenneth, of a *Commentary on the Rule of St Augustine*, attributed his conversion to his English exile and association with Thomas Cromwell, who 'nexte God hathe brought me to the knowledge of the veritte'; his fellow canon from Cambuskenneth, Robert Logie, a teacher of the novices and reputed to have 'embraced the truthe', escaped, as a suspected heretic, by ship from Dundee to London in 1539; Thomas Cocklaw, canon of Cambuskenneth and curate of Tullibody, who helped Logie escape (and who had earlier studied with Richardson and Logie at St Victor's Abbey in Paris) in turn was condemned for heresy in 1539, after daringly taking a widow as his wife in marriage, and so fled to England; a canon of Inchcolm and vicar of Dollar, Thomas Forret, who preached each Sunday and 'showed the mysteries of the Scriptures to the vulgar people in English' was burned for heresy in 1539; William Forman, Premonstratensian canon of Holyrood,

[40] *ADC*, pp. 371–2, 426; *Letters of James V*, pp. 275–6, 287, 315–16; *LP*, 8, no. 469; J. Durkan, 'Scottish "Evangelicals" in the Patronage of Thomas Cromwell', *RSCHS*, 21 (1982), pp. 151–2; Spottiswoode, 3, p. 92; Knox, *Works*, 1, p. 62; Calderwood, 1, p. 142; Durkan, 'Cultural background', p. 428; *LP*, 18, pt 1, no. 155 (where the editor suggests the unnamed Blackfriar is Rough, but Gwilliam is at least as probable); Knox, *Works*, 1, pp. 95–7, 105, 184, 186, 188, 193; Foxe, 8, pp. 443–51; Knox, *Works*, 1, p. 119; D. McRoberts, ed., *Essays on the Scottish Reformation* (Glasgow, 1962), p. 205.

was repeatedly warded on suspicion of heresy; and another canon of Holyrood, Donald Makcarny, was accused in Glasgow in 1539 of various heretical tenets, which he abjured, and was absolved. Nor, for that matter, were the monks (though unaccustomed to preaching) wholly immune from Protestant heresy: John MacBrair, Cistercian monk from Glenluce, an associate of the Reforming Lockhart of Bar and Andrew Lord Ochiltree, was imprisoned at Hamilton in March 1549/50 for crimes of heresy, escaped to preach in England, and was present at Frankfort with Knox and the Marian exiles; and Andrew Charteris, Carthusian monk in Perth, fled, it is said, to England in 1538, went on to Germany, 'where he cast off his cowle', stayed at Wittenberg for a year, returned to Antwerp, and then to the province of Zealand, where he wrote to his brother in Dundee, denouncing 'bishops, preests, abbots, monkes, friers' as 'childrein of the divell', before setting off for Italy. Little or nothing is known of the doctrines these renegade friars, canons, and monks proclaimed.[41]

To this catalogue of churchmen sympathetic to Protestant teaching, there may be added the names of a few secular priests on record as heretics in the 1530s and 1540s, but of whose religious beliefs (apart from John Knox's) little has survived: in 1534 George Gilbert, a chaplain in Brechin diocese, who had visited Germany, was accused of heresy and of 'marying of ane woman in Rensbrig in Ducheland', but was rescued from episcopal custody by a 'gret nomer' of men (of whom thirteen were identified: two bear the same names as Angus men escheated in 1544; a third shared the surname of an Angus heretic; and a fourth, John Meldrum, vicar of Farnell, later conformed to the Reformation to serve as reader of that parish); Duncan Simson, chaplain in Stirling and associate of the heretic Thomas Forret, was burned for heresy in 1539; David Hutcheson, Provost of Roslin, was escheated after condemnation for heresy by 1540; Robert Richardson, a secular priest (apparently distinct from the Augustinian canon), preached to the Governor, Arran (during his Protestant phase) in 1543, and later, with the return of persecution, sought safety in England; John Knox, 'minister of the sacred altar', was a convert to Wishart's doctrines of 1545, associated with the Swiss Reformers; James Skea, a chaplain in Orkney, was condemned for 'his tenascite and pertinessite in halding of oppynionis concerning the faith' contrary to acts of parliament

---

[41] R. Richardson, *Commentary on the Rule of St Augustine*, ed. G. G. Coulton (Edinburgh, 1935); Durkan, 'Evangelicals', p. 136; Calderwood, 1, pp. 123–4; Foxe, 5, p. 622; *Criminal Trials*, 1, pt 1, p. 330; Durkan, 'Local Heretics', pp. 71, 73–7; J. K. Hewison, 'Sir John Macbriar', *TDGNHAS*, 9 (1924), pp. 158–68; *Criminal Trials*, 1, pt 1, p. 352; Calderwood, 1, p. 114.

(in 1541 forbidding dishonouring the Sacraments, Mary the saints and their images, impugning papal authority, or assisting suspected heretics), and in 1546 'for feare of burnyng for the word of God' he fled to England in the hope of gaining Somerset's patronage; and another Scot, John Melville, acquired the reputation in England by 1553 of being a 'very sedytious preacher'.[42]

Apart from clergy, laymen, too, had their part to play in popularizing the new opinions imparted by preachers and others: John Borthwick, the heretic of 1540, denounced papal pardons and indulgences, the treasury of merit, and the cult of the saints as devised by Satan to blot out the merits of Christ, the only remedy for salvation. Through his scriptural reading and exposition 'at the table, and sometymes in other prevy places', Adam Wallace, from Ayrshire, burned in 1550, rejected purgatory and claimed that 'to pray to Sanctes and for the dead is idolatrie and a vane superstitioun'. Again, during 1544 and 1545, the preaching mission of George Wishart (student of St Andrews, Louvain, and Cambridge) in places as far apart as Montrose, Dundee, Ayr, Kyle, Perth, Fife, Haddington, and elsewhere in East Lothian reinforced the view that saints should not be honoured with prayer, for the practice had no scriptural warrant, added to which there was no certainty that the saints could hear invocations. Purgatory was also exposed as an unscriptural invention.[43]

Wishart himself also produced an English translation of the first Swiss Confession of 1536, in which (like his disciple, Knox) he could still speak of the 'sacrament of the aulter'. This Confession, which helped shape Wishart's teaching, recognized man's free will to sin but not to do good, affirmed salvation through faith, and not through man's merits and works, reiterated the need for preaching, repudiated 'Romenishe heedes' who were pastors in name but not in deed, commended the early Fathers but criticized the 'Tradicions of men', and rejected ceremonialism associated with 'vessels, garmentes, waxe, lyghtes, alters, golde, sylver, in so moche as they serue to subuerte the trewe relygion of God: and chefely Idols and Images, that stande open to be worshyped, and geue offence and slaunder'; Anabaptism was denounced; and in the two Sacraments of baptism and the Lord's Supper—'Baptyme and Howslyne' (the Eucharist)—the symbols of water in baptism and bread and wine in Communion

[42] *ADC*, pp. 426–7, 437; *RSS*, 3, no. 686; Knox, *Works*, 1, pp. 58–9, 63; *RSS*, 2, nos 2903, 3612; *LP*, 18, pt 1, nos 354, 358, 361, 389–90, 478, 638, 696; pt 2, no. 392; W. Fraser, *Memorials of the Earls of Haddington* (Edinburgh, 1899), 1, p. xlii; *APS*, 2, p. 371; *RSS*, 4, no. 916; *Cal Scot Papers*, 1, no. 206; *APC*, 4, pp. 330, 429.
[43] Foxe, 5, pp. 610–11, 625–36; Knox, *Works*, 1, pp. 238–9; 125–71.

were understood not as mere 'naked sygnes', but as visible tokens of God's grace. Nor was the Lord's Supper purely symbolic and commemorative; it signified the spiritual presence of the body and blood of Christ in the souls of the faithful; 'any carnal or meruelous presence' contained in the bread and wine was emphatically denied. With Wishart's mission, therefore, the doctrines of the Swiss Reformers can be seen to compete with earlier Lutheran beliefs circulating in Scotland.[44]

That the Reformers' essential message did reach the ears and eyes of ordinary pious folk for whom religion provided the meaning to life and death is strikingly reinforced in a further series of prosecutions for heresy mainly among townsfolk in the late 1530s and early 1540s. To the escheat for heresy of James Melville in 1535 and the trial (and abjuration) of James Paterson, also in 1535, there may be added by 1538 the cases of some fourteen Dundonians convicted of heresy, and, by 1539, two burgesses of Dundee, a Perth burgess, four individuals in or near Stirling, an Edinburgh burgess, and three other individuals (one of whom was a pauper, and another clerk of the ship called 'the Barge'). By that date, too, Andrew Cunningham, son of the Master of Glencairn, and John Stewart, son of Henry Lord Methven, had also records of conviction for heresy.[45]

This, too, was the context in which George Buchanan, Erasmian Reformer, sceptic and satirist of ecclesiastical abuse, found himself drawn towards religious opinions decidedly at odds with orthodox belief. Identified with a group of heretics suspected of Lutheranism (of whose number in 1539 five were executed, nine recanted, and several were exiled), Buchanan on his own admission was imprisoned, but managed to escape: not only had he denounced the shortcomings of the Franciscan friars, at King James V's command, but he had condoned the eating of meat in Lent (and was encouraged in this view by a renegade Dominican prior who preached against fasting during Lent), was sympathetic to the view that priests should be permitted to marry, had questioned free will and auricular confession, had doubts about the Eucharist and whether the Mass was a sacrifice, and was inclined to Augustine's view of the Sacrament, which led to accusations that he was a Sacramentarian, believing in a figurative presence in the Sacrament. In all, the evidence strongly suggests Buchanan's connections with the five men from the Stirling area

---

[44] D. Laing, ed., *Miscellany of the Wodrow Society* (Edinburgh, 1844), pp. 19, 12–23.
[45] *RSS*, 2, no. 1611; *ADC*, p. 446; *TA*, 6, pp. 376–7; 7, pp. 74ff.; *RSS*, 2, nos 2648, 2686, 2704, 2733, 2742; *Cal. Scot. Papers*, 1, no. 71; *TA*, 7, p. 78; *RSS*, 2, nos 3016, 3033; *Criminal Trials*, 1, pt 1, p. 216; *RSS*, 2, nos 2923, 2975; *TA*, 7, pp. 77–9; *RSS*, 2, nos 2915, 2976, 2989; 2952, 3396.

executed for heresy in Edinburgh in 1539: they, too, were associated with
the vicar of Tullibody's scandalous marriage and ate meat in Lent; and as
the King's court spent Easter at Stirling in 1538, Buchanan was afforded
ample opportunity to forge such links.

In forming his opinions, Buchanan could draw, of course, on his earlier
experience of Lutheranism during his second period in Paris between
1525 and 1535. By his own disclosure, he 'came into contact with the
Lutheran sectaries who were already spreading their doctrines far and
wide'; his denunciation by the Franciscans at home also made him 'less
unfavourable to the Lutheran cause'; and his later career in France, Italy,
and Portugal (with visits to England, where he consulted Lutheran
literature) led him to deny transubstantiation, to doubt the Mass was a
sacrifice, to question the existence of purgatory, belief in miracles,
indulgences, and prayers for the dead, the necessity of confession (which
he considered 'human and not Devine') and the need to obey the Church's
prohibition of eating meat on certain days, to disapprove (as his English
experience had taught him) of the superstitious worship of images, and to
consider that the Babylon of the Apocalypse was Rome itself. He espoused
a belief in justification by faith alone, argued for direct access to God
rather than intercession through the saints, was familiar with the writings
of Bucer, Oecolampadius, and Calvin, became the friend of Beza, and
spent five years in the 1550s 'studying theology in order that he might pass
a more accurate judgment on the controversies which were then occupy-
ing most people's thoughts.'[46]

In courtly circles, too, as Buchanan would have appreciated, poems,
plays, and pageants might provide an opportunity for spreading dissident
opinions in religion, which the theologians could not have supported; and
the circulation of these unorthodox beliefs could prove as instructive to
receptive minds as the stinging satire of ecclesiastical abuse made satisfy-
ing entertainment.[47] Expressions of contempt for defective ecclesiastical
practice, so marked a feature of Lindsay's writings, could lead to dissatisfaction with aspects of prevailing doctrine. From 1530 onward, Sir David
Lindsay, in calling for ecclesiastical renewal, urged the prince to effect a
reform of churchmen and:

[46] J. A. Aitken, *The Trial of George Buchanan* (Edinburgh, 1939), pp. xiv–xxvii, 3ff., 19, 21, 37, 56, 60–2, 72, 81, 85, 105, 118–19, 143–4; Calderwood, 1, pp. 124–30; J. Durkan, 'Buchanan's Judaising Practices', *InR*, 15 (1964), pp. 186–7; I. D. McFarlane, *Buchanan* (London, 1981), pp. 70–2, 76, 98, 107 and n. 144, 110, 115, 136, 144.

[47] J. Row, *History of the Kirk of Scotland* (Edinburgh, 1842), pp. 6–8.

> Cause thame mak ministratioun
> Conforme to thare vocatioun,
> To Preche with vnfenzeit intentis,
> And trewly vse the Sacramentis,
> Efter Christis Institutionis,
> Leuyng thare vaine traditiounis,
> Quhilkis dois the syllie scheip Illude,
> Quhame for Crist Iesus sched his blude,
> As superstitious pylgramagis,
> Prayand to grawin Ymagis,
> Expres aganis the Lordis command.

The purity of the Early Church was contrasted with later degeneration, and the urgency of improving the moral and educational standards of church-men was proclaimed in Erasmian fashion. Accepted religious practices, including auricular confession, pilgrimages, penance, indulgences, and papal pardons, and the use of imagery and rosaries (for 'thame aye babland on our beidis') were trenchantly questioned, the pope, depicted as 'Prince of Purgatorie' was identified with Antichrist, human tradition contrasted with divine commandment, obligatory celibacy rejected, the superstitious elements in popular religion denounced as 'manifest abominatioun', and the reader's attention repeatedly directed to Christ's Passion:

> To the greit God Omnipotent
> Confes thy Syn, and sore repent,
> And traist in Christ, as wrytis Paule,
> Quhilk sched his blude to saif thy Saule:
> For nane can the absolve bot he,
> Nor tak away thy syn from the.

By the 1540s, too, Lindsay noted the Church's readiness to equate 'heresie' with the possession of 'Inglis Bukis', and parodied shortcomings among priests who failed to provide the spiritual succour which parishioners craved:

> And mekle Latyne he did mummill,
> I hard na thing but hummill bummill,
> He schew me nocht of Goddis word,
> Quhilk scharper is than ony sword,
> And deip in tyll our hart dois prent
> Our syn, quhairthrow we do repent.

*　　*　　*

> Nor schew he me of hellis pane,
> That I mycht feir, and vice refrane.
> He counsalit me nocht till abstene,
> And leid ane holy lyfe and clene.
> Of Christis blude, na thing he knew,
> Nor of his promisses full trew,
> That saifis all that wyll beleue,
> That Sathan sall vs neuer greue.
> He techit me nocht for tyll traist
> the confort of the haly Gaist.

Criticism directed at the Church's Latin services, considered unintelligible to the ordinary worshipper, contained some telling observations:

> Unlernit peple, on the holy day,
> Solemnitlye thay heir the Euangell soung,
> Nocht knawyng quhat *the* preist dois sing nor say,
> Bot as ane Bell quhen that thay heir it roung.
> Yit, wald the Preistis in to thare mother toung
> Pas to the Pulpitt, and that doctryne declare
> Tyll lawid pepyll, it wer more necessare.

The availability of the Scriptures in the native tongue, which the clergy still opposed, was considered by Lindsay essential for man's salvation.[48]

All this, of course, was the work of a brilliant satirist, but Lindsay's religious themes and imagery certainly mirrored, and presumably encouraged, growing disenchantment with the medieval system; his strictures often approximated to those of the religious Reformers themselves, and are amply substantiated from other evidence derived from heresy trials and popular literature. Besides, when religious revolt was in the air, in 1547, following the murder of the Cardinal, the revolutionaries recognized Lindsay as a friend of Reform and sought his counsel when appointing John Knox as their preacher.[49]

Not all critics, however, were as fortunate as Lindsay in escaping censure from Church or Crown. A Dominican friar was burned for heresy in 1539 after producing a play on Christ's Passion for the King at Stirling, in which the bishops and regular clergy were depicted as Pharisees who

---

[48] *The Works of Sir David Lindsay*, ed. D. Hamer (Edinburgh, 1931–6), I, p. 51 (cf. pp. 52–3, 143); pp. 127; 125; 218–19.

[49] *John Knox's History of the Reformation in Scotland*, ed. W. C. Dickinson (Edinburgh, 1949), I, p. 82.

blinded the people and persuaded princes 'to persecute such as profess Jesus Christ and his blessed Evangel'. Yet, despite the severity of that sentence, Reforming propaganda persisted. About 1539, Robert Alexander, an advocate and the Earl's former tutor, took the unusual step of setting to metre the testament of William, sixth Earl of Erroll, who had been 'speciallie weill versed in the New Testament' and trained 'in the schoole of Christ, for whose testimonie he suffered great injurie oft times'. This metrical version of a testament had evidently a Protestant appeal (though the Earl himself had died in 1541 before Protestantism had made substantial headway), and was deemed worthy of printing in 1571. John Stewart, son of Lord Methven, was depicted as a 'fervent professour of the truthe, and made manie ballats against the corruptiouns of the time, after the death of the Vicar of Dolar', executed for heresy in 1539. In that year, too, a young poet, Kennedy, from Glasgow diocese was burned for heresy, and comforted by a Franciscan, who shared the same fate, with the words 'our joy and consolation shall never end.' The religious issue was again to the forefront in the satirical verses composed by Alexander, fifth Earl of Glencairn, against Thomas Doughtie, founder of the Chapel of Our Lady at Loretto, in which attention was focused on Luther's example and the thirst 'to read the English New Testament'; and, consistent with Protestant polemics, the Catholic clergy were likened to 'devouring woolves into sheepe's skinnes', 'professors of hypocrisie', 'doctors of idolatrie', 'cankered corrupters of the creed', 'monsters with the Beast's marke', 'mainteaners of idols and false gods', whose offer to bring men to salvation 'quite excludeth Christ's passioun'. Far from being the work of a theologian, this was the genuine expression of a layman disillusioned by much contemporary religious practice. The evidence, then, seems irrefutable: religious songs and satirical poetry helped to spread the evangelical message.[50]

Even more significantly, by 1540 in Dundee, where Protestant opinions circulated, James Wedderburn, eldest son of a merchant in the burgh, who had studied at St Andrews and then had visited France, composed plays which were acted in Dundee: one a tragedy on John the Baptist (also the subject of Buchanan's more scholarly play, *Baptistes*, where John assumed the role of a Reformer), was performed at the west port, another, a comedy on Dionysius the Tyrant (of Syracuse), was acted in the burgh's playfield; in both, it was said, 'he nipped the abusses and superstitioun of the time'. His brother, David, was to acquire (after 1551)

[50] Ibid., 1, pp. 26–8; Calderwood, 1, pp. 132–5.

a 'Matthew Bible', prepared by the Marian martyr John Rogers (whose pseudonym was Thomas Matthew) and based on Tyndale's work, with glosses revealing a clear debt to Luther. A third brother, John, priest in Dundee, with experience of Germany (where he heard Luther and Melanchthon at Wittenberg), was mainly responsible (with assistance from James and youngest brother, Robert, vicar of Dundee) for the *Gude and Godlie Ballattis*, a collection of hymns, songs, and metrical psalms (partly derived from German Lutheran sources) published in the 1540s.[51]

In the songs and ballads set to popular tunes, emphasis was focused on the work of Christ, his suffering, death, and resurrection; their purpose was to foster personal faith and piety by demonstrating God's love and Christ's sacrifice, and man's utter inability to save himself. The notion of merit and good works as a means of securing salvation was repudiated in favour of salvation through faith alone:[52]

> Na kynde of outward deid,
> How haly that euer it be,
> May saue us at our neid,
> Nor zit vs Iustifie
>   Nor zit can mak vs remedie.
>
> Bot Christ we neid na thing,
> Quhair throw sauit we suld be;
> He is ane potent King,
> And will allanerlie,
>   Onlile be our remedie.

Beyond the warm, evangelical fervour imparted by the songs (which encouraged Scots almost subconsciously to sing themselves into Lutheranism), many verses vigorously attacked Roman doctrine and practice: God's Word 'is bot Heresie' to 'Doctouris of Idolatrie' who never had read the truth; the prelates were 'blinded from the veritie' by their very hypocricy; the 'cruell Kirkmen'—from popes and cardinals, archbishops, deans, and chancellors to chaplains and graduates in theology—were labelled false prophets who had 'baneist vs fra Christ'; the flock had been deluded by vanities, and Scripture mocked by the traditions of men; idolatry was vigorously condemned as 'contrair to Christis blude'; the pope was variously denounced as Antichrist, 'that Pagane full of pryde',

---

[51] Calderwood, 1, pp. 141–3; Durkan and Ross, *Libraries*, p. 158; A. F. Mitchell, ed., *A Compendious Book of Godly and Spiritual Songs* (Edinburgh, 1897), pp. xiv, xx, xxiv, xxviii, xliii–iv.
[52] *Compendious Book*, p. 64; cf. pp. 24, 63, 195.

and the 'creull beist' who devoured souls by his usurped authority in selling pardons for the remission of sins; the 'fals fyre of Purgatorie' was exposed; the futility of saintly intercession for saving souls was affirmed; canon law was depicted as false; cursings were of no avail and 'can hurt zou not'; the clergy's freedom to marry was recognized; pilgrimages, the worship of images, and 'the quhisperit sinnis, callit eir Confessioun' were repudiated as papal inventions; and the hocus-pocus in ceremonialism stood condemned:[53]

> Ze begylit vs with zour hudis,
> Schawand zour relykis and zour ruddis.
> To pluk fra vs pure men our guddis,
> Ze schaw vs the heid of Sanct Johne,
> With the arm of Sanct Geill;
> To rottin banis ze gart vs kneill,
> And sanit vs from neck to heill.
>   The nycht is neir gone
>
> *Requiem eternam* fast thay patter,
> Befoir the deide, with haly watter,
> The lawit folk trowis the heuin will clatter,
> Thay sing with sic deuotioun.
> Ze say that Seule ze sall gar Sanct,
> Bot and the money war neuer sa scant,
> Ane pennie of zour waige ze will not want.
>   The nycht is neir gone.

Disaffection with the Church's teaching and practice so expressed often in scurrilous rhymes extended to the Mass, denounced as idolatrous and 'ane wickit Inuentioun' unauthorized by Scripture, and the doctrine of transubstantiation was mercilessly challenged:[54]

> Knawing thair is na Christ bot ane,
> Quhilk rent was on the Rude with roddis,
> Quhy gif ze gloir to stock and stane,
> In wirschipping of vther Goddis?

---

[53] Ibid., pp. 56, 183, 190, 200; 89, 178, 182–3, 185, 202; 7, 72, 173, 203; 15, 175–6, 191, 204; 186, 197, 201; 191, 193, 209; 188, 196–7, 201, 207; 194.
[54] Ibid., pp. 209–11.

Thir Idolis, that on Altaris standis,
    Ar fenzeitnes,
Ze gat not God amang zour handis,
    Mumling zour Mes.

       *   *   *

Gif God was maid of bittis of breid,
Eit ze not oulklie sax or seuin,
As it had bene ane mortall feid,
Quhill ze had almaist heryit heuin;
Als mony Deuillis ze man deuoir,
    Quhill hell grow les;
Or doutles we dar not restoir
    Zow to zour Mes.

Gif God be transubstanciall
In breid, with *hoc est Corpus Meum*,
Quhy war ze sa vnnaturall,
As tak him in zour teith, and sla him,
Tripartit and deuydit him,
    At zour dum dres?
Bot God knawis how ze gydit him,
    Mumling zour Mes.

The whole medieval system—papacy, priesthood, and the Mass—was under fire; and the efficacy of the ballads in promoting popular Protestantism may be measured in the repeated (and fruitless) efforts by the authorities to suppress them. In an attempt to curb the circulation of 'sclanderous billis, writtingis, ballatis, and bukis that ar dalie maid, writtine, and prentit to the diffamatioune of all estatis baith sperituale and temporale', the Privy Council in June 1543 ordered printers to destroy their stocks and ensure they kept no 'works of condampnit heretics'. In 1549, it was the Church's turn, in a provincial council, to inquire about 'books of rhymes or popular songs containing calumnies and slanders defamatory of churchmen and church institutions, or infamous libels, or any kind of heresy'. Parliament itself intervened in 1552 to prohibit the printing of unapproved 'bukis, ballattis, sangis, blasphematiounis, rymes or Tragedeis outher in latine or Inglis toung'. But the problem persisted: in 1556 the Queen Regent, with Archbishop Hamilton's support, complained to the bailies of Edinburgh about 'certane odious ballettis and rymes laitlie sett furth be sum evil inclinit persones of youre town, quha hes alssua tane doun diveris imagis and contempnandlie brokin samyn, quhilk is ane thing verray sclanderous.' Even in the capital, circulation of sacred songs set to popular tunes could not be eradicated, and was liable to end in iconoclasm, directed in this instance at the images of the Trinity, Our Lady, and St Francis. That, of course, was a logical sequel to singing songs denouncing imagery, idolatry, and false religion. The new theology had been propagated as propaganda that ordinary folk could understand.[55]

If the incidence of iconoclasm in the 1530s (from the stray pieces of surviving evidence) suggests that image-breaking was then confined to individual and isolated acts of defiance, the impression for the 1540s is somewhat different: by then iconoclasm had become a violent protest by defiant groups, who disregarded the claims of clergy and magistracy, invaded ecclesiastical buildings, and smashed altars and images as an expression of their hostility to the cults which the images stood for, and perhaps to the ecclesiastical and social system which sustained them. In August 1543 iconoclastic rioting in Dundee, encouraged, even instigated, by the move to Protestantism of the Governor, Arran (who then favoured the abolition of papal jurisdiction and dissolution of the religious orders, and no longer believed in purgatory), was directed against the Dominican and Franciscan friaries, which were sacked by the mob, who destroyed 'the ornaments, vestments, images and candlesticks; carrying off the silvering of the altars', as well as food and clothing to render difficult continued habitation. Of eighteen named individuals prosecuted for oppressing the friars, the occupations of five are placed on record; all were craftsmen: a cooper, fuller, weaver, baker, and cutler; two other image-breakers were university graduates; in all, 190 men were charged with riot and treason.[56] In nearby Arbroath, the abbey was 'sacked' by Lord Gray in 1543, which led to the 'breiking and spulyeing of Sanct Vegeanis Kirk of Arbrotht and Oure Lady Chapell of the samin'; and in Fife, Lindores Abbey was attacked in 1543 and the monks expelled. Iconoclasm had become a revolutionary device: the expulsion of imagery had led, at least

---

[55] Scottish Record Office [hereafter SRO], CS7/1 Acts and Decreets of the Court of Session, fol. 368r; J. Robertson, ed., *Concilia Scotiae* (Edinburgh, 1866), 2, p. 294; *Statutes of the Scottish Church*, p. 127; *APS*, 2, pp. 488–9; J. D. Marwick, ed., *Extracts from the Records of Edinburgh* (Edinburgh, 1869–82), 2, pp. 251–2.

[56] R. Sadler, *Letters and Negotiations* (Edinburgh, 1720), pp. 147–8; *Diurnal*, p. 29; J. Bain, ed., *Hamilton Papers* (Edinburgh, 1890–2), 2, nos 11, 14, 30, 116; *LP*, 18, pt 2, nos 181, 425; Calderwood, 1, pp. 175–6; A. Maxwell, *Old Dundee* (Edinburgh, 1891), p. 395; *RSS*, 4, no. 2580.

for a spell, to the expulsion of the religious. Further north, by 1544, violence had erupted in Montrose and Aberdeen, with assaults on the Dominican friaries in both burghs, and two Aberdonians, with Protestant sympathies, were convicted of hanging (with others not caught) an image of St Francis.[57]

In Perth, action against the friars seems to have anticipated the troubles in Dundee and elsewhere. In May 1543 a group had broken into the Dominican friary 'with great violence and contemption' and carried away some of the friars' belongings. Other signs of religious disaffection and unrest were evident in the town: by 1543 several craftsmen had gathered in a conventicle for secret worship; they held disputations on Scripture, and dishonoured the Blessed Virgin Mary and communion of saints; on the Feast of All Saints, one burgess, fortified by his English Bible, interrupted a friar, who preached on the necessity for salvation of praying to saints for souls in purgatory, and declared his doctrine to be 'false and against the holie Scriptures'; a tumult ensued, and several members of the group desecrated an image of St Francis, which was hanged with a cord, a ram's horns nailed to its head, and a cow's rump for its tail (an idol of the Devil); they also happily ate a goose on the eve of All Saints' Day. Even in country areas, defiant challenges to the cult of the saints can be detected: in the township of Leny (near Callendar), in southern Perthshire, a culprit was charged in 1547 with 'casting down and breaking an image of Saint Magdalene' in the chapel there; at that point, too, the ecclesiastical capital came under attack when Henry Balnaves of Halhill (himself a lawyer), the Master of Rothes, James Kirkcaldy of Grange, and Peter Carmichael of Balmedie were charged with 'utheris rebellis' with 'the birnyng of Sanct Salvatouris college in Sanctandrois', and the 'destructioun and douncasting' of the Dominican and Franciscan kirk in the city; two Ayrshire lairds, John Lockhart of Bar and Charles Campbell of Bargour, were charged with repeated acts of violence between 1545 and 1548 in parish churches, religious houses, and chapels in Lanark, Renfrew, Kyle, Carrick, and Cunningham, by removing 'sundry Eucharistic chalices, Altars, and ornaments of the Mass', and breaking choral stalls and glazed windows— Ayr Town Council, it seems, had to deal with the consequences by arranging the removal of 'broken images' from the parish kirk in 1545; and Kilwinning Abbey, another victim of attack, sought protection by 1552 against 'heretics, raiders and sacrilegious men'. The chance survival

---

[57] *Diurnal*, p. 29; *Hamilton Papers*, 2, nos 11, 14; *LP*, 18, pt 2, no. 133; *RSS*, 3, no. 636; SRO, NP2/1 Admissions of Notaries, fol. 104; *Aberdeen Burgh Records 1398–1570*, pp. 206, 211.

of these incidents (in the absence of comprehensive records) presumably reveals only a measure of the dissension which then existed.[58]

Alarm, at any rate, expressed in Parliament in 1541, had produced a further spate of legislation, which gives some impression of the magnitude of the problem confronting the authorities: the Sacraments were to be honoured 'to the confusioun of all heresy'; the glorious Virgin Mary was to be 'reverendlie worschippit' and intercessory prayer addressed to her; the pope's authority was not to be impugned; 'negligence of divine service' was to be remedied by reforming kirks—and 'the misreule of kirkmen'; private conventicles for disputing Scripture were forbidden; no one was to associate with heretics or assist fugitive heretics—even those who had abjured their heresy were incapacitated from holding public office; informers were to be rewarded; and the 'ymagis of haly sanctis' were not to be broken, dishonoured, or irreverently treated. All this confirms the general trend of Protestant activity in the 1520s and 1530s directed at the Mass, the Sacraments as a means of salvation, auricular confession, free will, papal authority, the cult of Mary and the saints, and in favour of vernacular Scriptures (which Parliament conceded in 1543). As the individual read the Bible aloud in his own tongue, he heard God himself speak; he was pesonally confronted with God's words; the effect could be electrifying. In the north-east alone, some thirty landowners gained a pardon in 1544 for assorted crimes, which included disputing on Scripture, reading prohibited literature, and holding opinions forbidden by statute.[59]

By that date, too, the appearance of Sacramentarians who, it was noted, controverted Catholic teaching on Communion, indicates the emergence of some novel features in Protestant belief, decidedly not Lutheran, but Swiss, in their emphases. In particular, the debt to Zwingli seems clear enough: as early as 1525, in his *True and False Religion* Zwingli had argued that what was received at the Lord's Supper was not the body and blood of Christ, but the Sacrament of them, which led his opponents to condemn him as a 'sacramentarian'. A decade or so later, in 1539, the heretical vicar of Dollar is on record as teaching that 'as the bread entereth into your mouth, so sall Christ dwell in livelie faith into your hearts', a view straying from Roman orthodoxy to espouse what looks like the teaching of

---

[58] J. P. Lawson, ed., *The Book of Perth* (Edinburgh, 1847), p. 32; *RSS*, 3, no. 611; Foxe, 5, pp. 623–5; Knox, *Works*, 1, p. 117; *TA*, 8, p. 215; Calderwood, 1, pp. 171–5; Foxe, 5, pp. 623–5; *Criminal Trials*, 1, pt 1, pp. 335, 353; *RSS*, 3, nos 2515, 2368.

[59] *APS*, 2, pp. 370–1; *RSS*, 3, no. 820.

Zwingli and Oecolampadius. Other Scots evidently shared these thoughts. As 'diuers and sindrie personis' were understood to be 'sacramentaris haldand disputatioun of the effect and assence thairof quhilk tendis planelie to the enervatioun of the faith Catholik', the Lords of Council in June 1543 ordered that 'na man disput or hald openionis of the sacramentis nor of the affect or assence thairof utherwayis nor is ellis ressavit be the haly kirk' under pain of forfeiture. Not only that: 'dalie inquisitioun' was to be made of 'all sic personis sacramentaris and quhare thai ma be apprehendit', so that they might be detained by the justices, sheriffs, and provosts until the Government decided 'quhat salbe done with sic personis'. The problem was evidently considered an urgent one. Here, after all, was a radical belief which repudiated the teaching of both Rome and Wittenberg on the nature of Christ's presence in the Sacrament, and which argued for a symbolic understanding of the elements, and a purely spiritual union. Criticism of Zwinglian ideas was reiterated in 1547, when the clergy sought the Privy Council's assistance in rooting out not only the 'pestilencious hereseis of Luther, his sect and followaris' who remained unpunished, but also those who were 'becumin Sacramentis'; and the Church's provincial council of 1549 saw the need to proceed against 'heresiarchs, and sacramentarians, and chiefly against those who inveigh against the sacrament of the Eucharist' (and to suppress attacks on the seven Sacraments and views repudiating such beliefs as the saints reigned with Christ, the soul's immortality, reward for good works, purgatory, intercession of saints, images, fast and feast days, and the authority of the Church's councils). The attack on the Church's sacramental teaching on the Mass and transubstantiation (which could only have contributed to the concern expressed in 1552 that 'within these last few years', even in populous parishes, 'very few indeed' bothered to attend 'the sacrifice of holy mass') had moved from the subtlety of Luther's 'consubstantiation' to the stark and contrasting clarity of Zwingli's symbolism.[60]

Such a viewpoint, plainly ineradicable by the 1540s, must have been reinforced by the preaching tours of George Wishart in 1544 and 1545, where a Zwinglian influence is indicated, not least in his espousal of the

---

[60] R. C. Walton, *Zwingli's Theocracy* (Toronto, 1967), p. 213; W. P. Stephens, *The Theology of Huldrych Zwingli* (Oxford, 1986), pp. 218ff.; G. W. Locher, *Zwingli's Thought* (Leiden, 1981), pp. 220–8; Calderwood, 1, p. 128; SRO, CS7/1, Acts and Decreets, fol. 368r; *Concilia Scotiae*, 2, p. 294; *RPC*, 1, p. 63; *Statutes of the Scottish Church*, pp. 123–4, 138–9.

first Helvetic Confession. That apart, Wishart is on record (admittedly the late testimony of Petrie) as having fled from Montrose, where he had served as schoolmaster, in 1538, when accused of heresy by his bishop for teaching the New Testament in Greek; and he became exposed to Flemish, English, and Swiss Reforming influences. On his own admission, he 'once chanced to meet with a Jew, when I was sailing upon the water of Rhine', whose chief city, of course, was Cologne, which suggests some familiarity with both the Netherlands and Germany: indeed, Bishop Leslie remarked that Wishart had 'remained long in Germany'. At Bristol, he is reported in 1539 to have held, and taught, the radical tenet that 'Christ nother hath nor coulde merite for hym ne yett for us.' If his preaching was correctly reported, the inference is that Wishart believed (before he was obliged to recant) that Christ redeemed men not by the merits of his Passion, but by his ministry, a standpoint which hinted at Socinianism (which, if he ever entertained, he later eschewed in his translation of the Helvetic Confession).[61]

On returning home, Wishart is known to have taught the Ten Commandments, the Twelve Articles of Faith, and the Lord's Prayer in the vernacular, and to have preached on Paul's Epistle to the Romans (with its vindication of justification by faith). Under interrogation in 1546, he denied auricular confession was a Sacrament, but declined to enumerate the Sacraments, and simply professed those instituted by Christ; he denied free will and also the accusation that he was a 'soul sleeper'; he made scriptural warrant the test of sound doctrine and practice, affirmed the priesthood of believers, and argued that God 'cannot be comprehended in one place' because he is infinite; he was accused of believing that God could not 'be in so little space as betwixt the priest's hands', though he recognized God's presence in the congregation of believers, where the Word was truly preached and the Sacraments lawfully adminstered—the characteristically Protestant definition of the notes of the true Church. He also adhered to the Protestant argument in favour of Communion in both kinds. By quoting the sayings of a Jew, he seemed to approve that 'a piece of bread baken upon the ashes' was mistakenly worshipped by Catholics as God himself. At his execution, he repeatedly addressed his 'Christian brethren and sisters', and commended his spirit to the 'Saviour of the

[61] A. Petrie, *A Compendius History of the Catholik Church* (The Hague, 1662), p. 182; Foxe, 5, pp. 625–36; J. Leslie, *History of Scotland* (Edinburgh, 1830), p. 191; R. Ricart, *The Maire of Bristowe is Kalendar,*, ed. L. T. Smith (London, 1872), p. 55; *LP*, 14, pt 1, nos 184, 1095, 1219; *Wodrow Society Miscellany*, pp. 11–23.

world' in the certain hope that his 'soul shall sup with my Saviour Christ this night . . . for whom I suffer this.'[62]

The 'negative rule' to which Wishart appealed underlined the urgency for Protestant preaching and exposition of the Scriptures. Increasingly, in the 1540s, enterprising lairds undertook to promote Reformed preaching. Already, by 1544, the Earls of Lennox, Angus, Glencairn, and Cassillis were sufficiently attached to the English cause to 'cause the Word of God to be taught and preached', and their example was followed by others: in Kyle, Crawford of Lefnoris, a supporter of Wishart in 1544, declared himself 'zealous and bold in the cause of God'; Campbell of Kinyeancleuch, also accounted 'zealous', was ready to resort to force to gain Mauchine kirk for Wishart; Laurence Rankin of Shiel was converted by Wishart's preaching; and Lockhart of Bar, who had resorted to iconoclasm in the 1540s, sheltered the renegade Cistercian Macbriar, and later offered Knox his home for preaching in 1556. In the Lothians, Crichton of Brunstane, Douglas of Longniddry, Cockburn of Ormiston, and Sandilands the younger of Calder afforded Wishart protection, while the plotters against the Cardinal, Norman Leslie, Master of Rothes, James and William Kirkcaldy of Grange, David Monypenny of Pitmilly, Henry Balnaves of Halhill, with John Leslie of Parkhill and James Leslie, parson of Aberdour, were ready in 1547 'to succour all such of that realm as tender Goddis Word'; some were imprisoned at Cherbourg, and resisted efforts to make them attend Mass.[63] Another 'assured' Scot and propagandist for the English cause, James Henrison, by 1548 urged a return to 'the primitive church of Christ and his apostles' and an end to 'popish errors', a theme advanced also by the Highland cleric and English agent, John Eldar. As the advocates of Anglo-Scottish friendship were only too well aware, the genuine religious disaffection which undoubtedly existed could be directed towards supporting England's antipapal, and anti-French policies.[64]

Further support for the Reforming cause was forthcoming in Fife from James Melville of Carnbee, John Melville of Raith and his illegitimate son

[62] Foxe, 5, pp. 625–36; Knox, *Works*, 1, pp. 125–72.
[63] *LP*, 18, pt 1, no. 305; 19, pt 1, nos 143, 229, 243, 552; cf. *Cal. Scot. Papers*, 1, nos 26, 48; Knox, *History*, 1, pp. 61–2, 66–9, 107, 121; *Criminal Trials*, 1, pt 1, pp. 352–3; T. Rymer, *Foedera* (London, 1816–69), 15, p. 132.
[64] *Cal. Scot. Papers*, 1, no. 285; M. Merriman, 'James Henrisoun and "Great Britain": British Union and the Scottish Commonweal' in R. Mason, ed., *Scotland and England 1286–1815* (Edinburgh, 1987), pp. 85–112; J. Kirk, 'The Jacobean Church in the Highlands, 1567–1625', L. Maclean, ed., *The Seventeenth Century in the Highlands* (Inverness, 1986), p. 27.

John, and Alexander Whitelaw of New Grange. Robert, the fifth Lord Maxwell, who had introduced the act authorizing vernacular Bibles in 1543, led the Reforming, anti-Roman, and pro-English grouping in the south west, as did Hugh, the fourth Lord Somerville in Lanarkshire, while in the north-east the Earl Marischal and lairds convicted for disputing on Scripture and reading forbidden books continued to exhibit a record of promoting Protestantism. In Dundee itself, where Reforming opinions circulated, the Provost, John Scrimgeour of Dudhope, two bailies, and ten councillors pledged themselves in 1547 'to be faithful setters forth of God's word', at a point when the English garrisoned Broughty Ferry and fostered the spread of English Bibles and devotional literature; in St Andrews, too, as a result of Knox's preaching in 1547, James Balfour, later of Pittendreich, became attached to the Reforming cause (and suffered for it in the French galleys); and a citizen of St Andrews, George Winchester (whose son or kinsman, it seems, later served as deacon in the town's Reformed kirk session) was declared a heretic by 1550.[65] Besides, in towns and in the countryside, the phenomenon of conventicles created a fresh focus for Bible study and Protestant worship until preachers could be secured.

When preachers were forthcoming, little enough is known of the content of their sermons or of the specific theology they espoused. Gwilliam, it seems, preached on 'the abuses of the Church and in favour of setting forth the Bible and Testament in English' in 1543; John Rough, preaching in Ayr and St Andrews, was 'vehement against all impietie' in 1543, and his doctrine incurred the hatred of all who 'more favored darknes then light'; sir Robert Richardson received support from the Governor, Arran, 'in setting forth the Word of God' in 1543; and John Roger, it was said, profitably preached 'to the conforte of many in Anguss and Mearnes'. By 1550, Adam Wallace from Ayrshire, depicted as 'zelous in godlynes', was burned for affirming specific tenets of Reformed theology: he sought God's will and the assurance of his own salvation in the Bible, which he argued 'fyve thowsand within this realme' should read; he condemned the bishops as 'dum doggis and unsavery salt', open enemies 'to me and to the doctrin that I professe', which ought to be judged by Scripture alone; he had baptized his own child, found no biblical warrant for purgatory, the intercession of saints or prayers for the dead, which he considered 'mear inventionis of men, devised for covetousnes saik'; he denied that the consecrated bread and wine at the

---

[65] *Cal. Scot. Papers*, 1, nos 71, 74, 107, 129; *RSS*, 4, no. 911; *RStAKS*, 1, p. 342.

altar became the body and blood of Christ, stressed the memorial aspect of the Lord's Supper (following Wishart), and considered Christ's natural body 'cannot be in two places at once': he therefore repudiated the Mass as 'idolatry and abominable in the sight of God'.[66]

By the early 1550s, with the onset of Mary Tudor's rule, William Harlaw had returned home after service as a deacon in the English Church during Edward VI's reign to preach in Edinburgh, Dumfries, and Perth, and by 1559 with three other preachers was charged by the authorities with usurping the ministerial office, and of administering the Sacrament of the Altar in a manner different from that of the Catholic Church. As chaplain to the Earl of Argyll, John Douglas or Grant, a heretical Carmelite friar, undertook Reformed preaching in Leith and Edinburgh in the late 1550s as well as in Argyll itself; on the Earl's testimony, he preached against idolatry, hypocrisy, and 'all maner of abuses and corruptioun of Christes synceir religioun'; and he was one of the group charged in 1559 with speaking 'verrey sklanderouslie aganis the sacramentis, the authoritie of the kirk and utheris articles of the Catholique religeone'.[67]

In the north-east, between Perth and Aberdeen, all the signs suggest intensified Protestant preaching in the years immediately preceding 1560. At Dun, near Montrose, John Erskine, a supporter of Wishart in the 1540s, had invited Knox to stay for a month in 1555, where he 'daily exercised in doctrine'; he himself undertook to exhort in the privy kirks, and was ready to denounce Rome as the seat of the devil. Five miles to the south, Walter Miln, curate of Lunan for twenty years, was burned in St Andrews for heresy when over eighty years of age in 1558. Miln had been a friend of Reform from at least the 1540s, when he had fled to Germany, embraced 'the doctrine of the gospel' and returned home to set aside 'all papistry and compelled chastity' by marrying. Arrested at Dysart, in Fife, and tried in the ecclesiastical capital, he asked not to be addressed as 'one of the pope's knights', upheld a priest's right to marry, affirmed the two dominical Sacraments of baptism and the Lord's Supper, denied transubstantiation, and held the sacrifice of the Mass to be idolatrous and derogatory to Christ's sacrifice on the Cross, which 'will never be offered again, for then he ended all sacrifice'; he censured pilgrimages as un-

[66] LP, 18, pt 1, nos 155, 696; pt 2, no. 392; Knox, Works, 1, pp. 95–7, 119, 237–41; Foxe, 8, pp. 443ff.; 5, pp. 639–41.

[67] Calderwood, 1, pp. 303–4, 333, 343; Spottiswoode, 1, p. 183; R. Keith, History of the Affairs of Church and State in Scotland, ed. J. P. Lawson (Edinburgh, 1844–50), 1, pp. 150–1, 186; T. McCrie, Life of John Knox (Edinburgh, 1853), p. 360; Knox, Works, 1, pp. 256, 276–89; Leslie, History, pp. 266, 271.

scriptural, admitted to preaching secretly in houses, openly in the fields, and even 'on the sea, sailing in a ship', and condemned 'the lies of priests, monks, friars, priors, abbots, bishops and the rest of the sect of Antichrist'.[68]

In Dundee, Paul Methven, a former baker and native of Falkland, who had been brought up in England under Miles Coverdale and had married an Englishwoman, was active as a preacher by 1558. His preaching against 'the old idolatry' extended to other parts of Angus and across the estuary to Fife, where he was welcomed at the homes of lairds; he ministered the Sacraments at Lundie, and took part in the destruction of images. Along with Methven, Harlaw, and Willock, John Christison, a friar, was charged in 1559 with usurping ministerial office, preaching seditious doctrines, and administering Reformed Communion in the north-east. There, too, William Christison, who had studied in Lutheran Scandinavia, joined the Reformers by 1560 to become minister of Dundee; a former priest in the household of the Reforming Lord Innermeath, John Petrie or Patrick (afterwards minister in Kinneff and Arbuthnot) had once fled with Walter Miln to Germany in the 1540s, was then condemned as a heretic, and again charged in 1559 with broadcasting heretical doctrines and with introducing a new manner of administering the Sacraments; John Brabner, who undertook to preach in Angus, the Mearns, and Aberdeen, was considered by Robert Maule of Panmure, who supported his work, as 'ane vehement man, inculcatine the lawe and peane thearof', in contrast to Methven, depicted by Maule as 'ane mair myld man, preachine the Evangel of grace, and remissions of sinnes in the blud of Christ'. Others, like the vicar of Lintrathen, by May 1560 had adopted the English Books of Common Prayer and Homilies in worship.[69]

In Fife, a chaplain in Cupar, Thomas Jamieson (afterwards minister at Largo and Newburn), was charged in 1558 for preaching against the Mass in St Andrews, where Robert Hamilton, a regent in St Mary's College at the Reformation, had undertaken to exhort in the privy kirks, was a member of the Congregation in 1559, and offered his services as a minister by 1560. As a leading intellectual and ecclesiastical centre,

---

[68] Knox, *History*, I, pp. 64, 119–21, 148, 153, 190; J. Stuart, ed., *Miscellany of the Spalding Club*, 4 (Aberdeen, 1849), p. 103; Foxe, 5, pp. 644–7; R. Lindesay of Pitscottie, *The Historie and Cronicles of Scotland*, ed. A. J. G. Mackay (Edinburgh, 1899–1911), 2, pp. 130–6.

[69] Knox, *History*, I, pp. 148, 159, 161; Pitscottie, 2, pp. 136–7; 132; *Cal. Scot. Papers*, I, no. 1163, p. 680; *Accounts of the Collectors of Thirds of Benefices 1561–1572*, ed. G. Donaldson (Edinburgh, 1949), p. 234; McCrie, *Knox*, pp. 360, 465; *Registrum de Panmure*, ed. H. Maule (Edinburgh, 1874), I, p. xxxii; *Spalding Club Miscellany*, 4, pp. 120–2.

St Andrews from 1559 had for its minister the assorted services of an Augustinian canon, Adam Heriot, who left for Aberdeen, John Knox, when advised to withdraw from Edinburgh in 1559, and the English radical, Christopher Goodman, fresh from Geneva and from a brief ministry in Ayr, esteemed as a 'fervent preichar of the word of god'. By that point, too, David Fergusson, from Dundee, a former glover, was settled as minister of Dunfermline. Earlier, in 1558, he had been charged with misusing Scripture, disputing erroneous doctrines, and eating meat at Lent; and by 1562 had placed on record the familiar Protestant beliefs that assurance of salvation proceeded not from men's merits or worthiness 'as the blasphemous Papistes do affirme', but from the mercy of God in Christ; that the Mass was idolatrous, blasphemous, and derogatory to Christ's sacrifice; that transubstantiation was 'magical' and unscriptural; that the worship of images was forbidden by scripture; that the Early Fathers may be followed only so far as they followed Christ; that the Roman Church was no true Church but 'that spirituall Babylone', and that the pope was Antichrist. For Fergusson, Christ's presence in the Sacrament was to be understood by believers not as 'carnally nor magically inclosed in a bit of conjured bread', but as a spiritual reality 'effectually working in their hartes that thing which his bodylie presence could not do'; the bread and wine did not become Christ's body and blood, but neither were they 'bare signes or figures onely', for as believers received the elements, 'so verilie are we partakers of Christes body by faith, whereby we are nourished to lyfe everlastinge; and this partaking requireth neither transubstantiation, impanation, nor carnall presence, but requireth the elevation of our spirites by faith to heaven, there to be partakers of Christ, not with carnal teith, but with faith affectual'. Here was a high Calvinist exposition of Communion, consistent with the Scots Confession of Faith, and reminiscent of Calvin's own verdict that 'the flesh and blood of Christ feed our souls just as bread and wine maintain and support our corporeal life.'[70]

Like Fergusson, though not the author of any known work, John Willock hit out against the Mass. Already in 1555, at the home of Erskine of Dun, he had heard Knox argue how it was unlawful for a Christian to present himself at Mass; returning from Emden in 1558 he preached in

[70] Pitscottie, 2, pp. 138–9, 161; Knox, History, 1, pp. 148, 294–5; BUK, 1, p. 2; RStAKS, 1, pp. 339; 3–4, 27; TA, 10, pp. 369–70; Tracts by David Fergusson, ed. J. Lee (Edinburgh, 1860), pp. xiv, 29, 40, 45–7; 37; 11, 32, 50; 30–5; J. Calvin, Institutes of the Christian Religion, ed. H. Beveridge (Edinburgh, 1846), 4: 17: 10.

Dundee and Edinburgh, and was summoned in December 1558 to appear before the Archbishop of St Andrews, and then, in May 1559, to stand trial with others at Stirling for ministering Reformed Communion. At Ayr, he preached in St John's Kirk in March 1559 'with intolerabill exclamatiouns, cryand out on the Messe, persuadand the haill peple' by citing the testimony of Scripture and the Early Fathers (so a Catholic observer noted). His audience, significantly enough, included the Earl of Glencairn, Robert Lord Boyd, Andrew Lord Ochiltree, Campbell of Loudoun, Wallace of Craigie, Campbell of Cessnock, Lockhart of Bar, Wallace of Carnel, Crawford of Kerse, Mure of Rowallan, Dunbar of Blantyre, Fullerton of Dreghorn, Campbell of Kinyeancleuch, Cathcart of Carleton, Shaw of Sornbeg, and Corrie of Kelwood, all friends of Reform. In correspondence with Abbot Quintin Kennedy in 1559, Willock, it is true, committed to paper a few thoughts on 'the Papis Mess', which he predictably denounced as unscriptural, 'playn ydolatrie and vayn supersititioun', but he failed to appear for the arranged disputation with Kennedy; and it was left to John Davidson, the Protestant Principal of Glasgow University, to respond to the abbot's *Compendius Tractive* of 1558, which depicted 'the Sacramentis, Predestinatioun, Fre Wyll, and Justificatioun', as the central controverted issues. In his *Answer*, published in 1563, Davidson denied Kennedy's claim that the Church was judge of Scripture, and understood Communion neither in terms of transubstantiation nor as 'ane baire signe', but as 'ane sacramentall signe, with the quhilk God exhebitis to the receaver worthely that thing quhilk is signifeit be the same signe.' Much of this recalls the wording in Calvin's *Institutes*, where the Genevan had taught how the

> sacred communion of flesh and blood by which Christ transfuses his life into us ... he testifies and seals in the Supper, and that not by presenting a vain or empty sign, but by there exerting an efficacy of the Spirit by which he fulfils what he promises. And truly the thing there signified he exhibits and offers to all who sit down at that spiritual feast, although it is beneficially received by believers only.[71]

It is only with John Knox, however, that something approaching a coherent picture of Protestant doctrine in Scotland presents itself, for Knox's advantage over his associates lies very largely in the preservation of

[71] Knox, *History*, 1, pp. 120, 125, 148, 177; *Wodrow Soc. Miscellany*, 1, pp. 55; 265–77; 133; 181–258; McCrie, *Knox*, p. 125; Leslie, *History*, pp. 266, 271, 293, 295; Calvin, *Institutes*, 4: 17: 10; cf. 4: 17: 21.

his writings, though even for Knox no corpus of his sermons has survived. Influenced by Thomas Gwilliam, the renegade Blackfriar, from whom he first 'receaved anie taste of the truthe', and then by George Wishart, Knox in his first sermon at St Andrews in 1547 preached on the apocalyptic theme of the four monarchies from Daniel, and uncompromisingly distinguished Christ's true Kirk, and its notes, from the Roman Church, which bore the marks of the beast, that 'synagogue of Sathan', whose head the pope, that 'man of sin', the 'whore of Babylon', was identified with Antichrist. He expounded how the doctrine of justification in Scripture was by faith alone, and how Christ's sacrifice redeemed men from sin. Like Henry Balnaves in 1548, he repudiated pilgrimages, pardons, abstinence from meat, obligatory celibacy, and 'other such baggage' as 'works of man's invention', and was not only contemptuously dismissive of the Mass as a means of helping souls in purgatory, but proclaimed the Mass to be 'abominable idolatry, blasphemous to the death of Christ, and a profanation of the Lord's Supper'; urged that the Sacraments of the New Testament be 'ministered as they were instituted by Christ Jesus, and practised by his Apostles'; condemned prayer for the dead as 'vain' and prayers to the dead as 'idolatry'; repudiated a belief in purgatory, for the faithful rest in heaven and 'the reprobate' perish in hell; and he also affirmed that earlier Protestant (and Lollard) tenet that teinds did not necessarily belong to kirkmen (a theme which Sir James Hamilton and others had articulated in 1536 when they had urged the clergy at a provincial council in Edinburgh to 'give up "crospresandes and the owmest claycht"' and allow 'that every man should pay his own teind "syklyk as he payis to his landislord"').[72]

At Rouen, Knox revised Balnaves's work on justification, and with first-hand knowledge of English, Swiss, French, and even German Protestantism, as a traveller to Dieppe and resident at Frankfurt-on-Main and at Geneva in 1554, he arrived home in 1555 to demonstrate the dangers of idolatry, and to argue that believers should abstain from 'that idol', the Mass. He preached at the homes of influential lairds—Dun, Calder, Bar, Carnell, Kinyeancleuch, Ochiltree, Gadgirth, and Finlayston, the Earl of Glencairn's home—as well as in Ayr and Edinburgh. At Finlayston, in Renfrewshire, 'after doctrine' Knox ministered the Sacrament of the Lord's Supper to the Earl, his wife, and 'certain of his friends'; at Calder in West Lothian, where some inhabitants from Edin-

---

[72] Calderwood, 1, p. 156; Knox, *History*, 1, pp. 67–9, 84–6; Knox, *Works*, 3, pp. 506, 519; *LP*, 10, no. 536.

burgh and its environs assembled, he demonstrated 'the right use of the Lord's Table, which before they had never practised'; and at Dun in 1556 he was again requested to minister 'the Table of the Lord Jesus' to the 'most part' of the gentry in Angus.[73] Knox's action (which, of course, was accompanied by preaching the Word) was less startling to contemporaries than to some modern writers, who have pointlessly remarked that for Knox, unlike Calvin, it was 'the sacraments that form the Church',[74] forgetful of Knox's priority for the Word (without which the Sacraments would be meaningless) and unmindful (in a way in which Knox was not) that Calvin himself had observed (irrespective of advice to Huguenots) that 'wherever we see the word of God sincerely preached and heard, wherever we see the sacraments administered according to the Institution of Christ, there we cannot have any doubt that the Church of God has some existence.'[75] These, after all, were the characteristic notes enabling Reformers to discern the true Church from the church malignant. And the logical sequel to Knox's emphasis, first, on proclaiming the Word, and then on counselling abstention from Mass, was the administering of Reformed Communion to those assembled in the 'privy kirks'. Indeed, in his 'Letter of Wholesome Counsel' in 1556, Knox had commended these 'assemblies of brethren' of one household or more, which made up 'the congregacion' (in effect privy kirks) for scriptural study and understanding through 'readyng, exhorting, and in makyng common prayers'. In these gatherings, the members of 'the bodie of Christ' had each a part to play as 'no member is of sufficiency to susteyne and feade it selfe without the helpe and support of another'; Knox therefore urged weekly meetings so that 'by hearing, readyng, and conferryng the Scriptures in the asssemblie, the hole body of the Scriptures of God shall become familiar' and the biblical meaning grasped by the group of ordinary pious Christians. Exposition of the Word in its entirety, imparted in this manner, was thus for Knox the means of confirming Protestants 'in theis dangerous and perilous dayes to behold the face of Chryst Jesus his loving spous and church, frome Abell to him selfe, and frome him self to thys day, in all ages to be one.'[76]

For Knox, salvation was understood to be no longer dependent on repeated infusions of grace imparted through the Sacraments, which

---

[73] Knox, *History*, 1, pp. 120–1.
[74] J. S. McEwen, *The Faith of John Knox* (London, 1961), p. 57; D. Shaw, 'Zwinglian Influences on the Scottish Reformation', *RSCHS*, 22 (1985), p. 132.
[75] Calvin, *Institutes*, 4: 1: 9.
[76] Knox, *Works*, 4, pp. 137–9.

helped make men just, but the outcome of God's grace proclaimed in the Word and unmerited by man's action: through the Bible, the believer was confronted with the Word of salvation, and with the message of justification by faith alone. Indeed, from Patrick Hamilton to John Knox at the heart of the Protestant message was the conviction that man could not earn his salvation or co-operate with God in achieving it; man's justification was purely an act of God's grace, of his love and forgiveness, and of Christ's passion and sacrifice which could not be repeated or re-enacted as an offering to God in a Sacrament. The Word, it seemed, took precedence over the Sacraments.

If, as was so for many Reformers, Knox's earlier insights into Protestant theology were soteriological and specifically related to justification, his understanding of predestination lay within the context of God's sovereign will and its relationship to man's redemption, which, of course, rested not on good works, but on trusting God, who, by his free grace, mediated through Christ, elected men to salvation. In 1557, Knox advised 'his brethren in Scotland', that

> salvatioun doith not proceid of our workis, nether yit that it was apoyntit till us in tyme, but that befoir the foundatioun of the warld was laid, did God elect us in Chryst Jesus, . . . and did predestinat us, and frelie chois us to be his inheritouris with Chryst, according to the gud pleasure of his will.

Besides, in his sole doctrinal treatise of any length, Knox considered 'the doctrine of God's eternal Predestination is so necessarie to the Church of God that, without the same, can Faith neither be truely taught, nether surely established.' Christ's death for man's redemption was itself decreed in God's eternal counsel before the foundations of the world were laid; so, too, those whom God had chosen were 'elected in Christe Jesus before all tymes, that in tyme be called, and by the power of the Holie Spirit do give obedience to the caller'; faith confirms election, and assurance derives from faith; the reprobate, who were 'left' justly to perish in their perdition (which might indicate no more than God's preterition), were also understood to be 'rejected' by God's 'irrevocable sentence' and ordained to 'destruction' by 'tormentes and fier inextinguible'.[77]

All in all, the preachers' assorted backgrounds and their varied styles in proclaiming the Gospel strongly suggest a measure of diversity in the doctrines they articulated, as they undertook the task of broadcasting the

[77] Knox, *Works*, 4, p. 273; 5, pp. 25, 142; 96; 42, 54, 62; 38, 61.

message of the Reformation. Amid the competing tenets of belief, one pattern, at any rate, is readily discernible: by the 1540s, the early Lutheran concentration on the doctrines of grace and justification, so characteristic of the 1520s and 1530s, had been widened immeasurably, under the Swiss Reforming infuences of Zurich, Berne, Basle, and Geneva (mediated in part through England), to embrace a wholesale Reformation of the Church in doctrine, worship, and morality by restoring Christianity to the model of the New Testament. This, indeed, was the professed aim of the 'first oration and petition of the Protestants of Scotland' to the Queen Regent in 1558, which argued for reforms in worship, doctrine, and in the lives of churchmen, and for the restoration of 'the grave and godly face of the primitive Church'.[78]

In achieving Reformation by resorting to revolution in defiance of the Crown, the Protestant Lords of the Congregation displayed uncompromising determination in their crusade to remove all the manifestations of idolatry; the suppression of idolatry and false religion certainly figured in their 'common band' or covenant of 1557; and their radical plans resulted in widespread iconoclasm; churches were systematically purged of Catholic symbolism; removing the symbols, of course, was the prelude to removing both Rome and the Mass; smashing images, it was hoped, reinforced the process of smashing beliefs. Nor was this all. The destruction of statues, altars and altar-pieces, ornaments, wood carvings, and (where they existed) stained-glass windows, the burning of mass books and paintings, and the damage inflicted on the buildings of religious orders are testimony not only to the violence (and thoroughness) of the iconoclasts, but to how readily unrest, rioting, and disorder could deteriorate into an armed struggle against the higher powers, as the Congregation resorted to force to defend the 'Evangel' and their preachers against the regime of Mary of Guise.[79]

The revolutionary outbreak of iconoclasm, which preceded Knox's return from Geneva in 1559, was certainly under way by 1558, when Paul Methven's preaching in Angus and Fife (where he ministered the Sacraments) was followed by the breaking of images and obliteration of 'the popis reliegieoun'. In so far as seeing was believing, the destruction of imagery was designed to denounce, and to eliminate from men's minds, the sacrifice of the Mass (and the repetition of Masses at altars) and contact with Mary and the saints, as intercessors, through their images. As

---

[78] Knox, *History*, 1, pp. 150–2.
[79] Spottiswoode, 1, pp. 372–3; Knox, *History*, 1, pp. 136–7, 178–9, 206–7, 314–16; 2, pp. 55–6.

Methven's followers seem to have appreciated, to rid churches of imagery was to rid them of Rome. In Edinburgh, the earlier theft of several images from St Giles's Kirk in 1556 was followed in 1558 with the disappearance of an image of St Giles 'privatly in the night', just before the customary St Giles's Day procession, which Mary of Guise was due to attend. The provincial council had recently met in the capital, and, in its aftermath, some heretics had been ordained to recant their errors. The occasion was ready made for a defiant act of protest; and that, it seems, (despite some modern reappraisals) is just what occurred: another image of St Giles, borrowed from the Franciscans for the celebrations, was unceremoniously 'pulled downe and broken by some brethren of the towne', it was said, who 'could not suffer such manifest idolatrie'—a statement supported, in essence, by Knox whose account adds (without corroboration) that 'the great idol called St Giles' was drowned in the Nor' Loch and then burned, 'which raised no small trouble in the town'. At any rate, by June 1559, anticipating further trouble, the Town Council prudently arranged for the safe custody of its relic—'the arme of Sanct Geill'—before 'the cuming of the Congregatioun'.[80]

There was good reason for its action. As a whole, the Protestant preachers had expounded 'how odious was idolatry in God's presence; what commandment he had given for the destruction of the monuments thereof; what idolatry and what abomination was in the mass.' In May 1559, Knox's inflammatory sermon, 'vehement against idolatry' at Perth had unleashed a whirlwind of destruction, which neither preacher nor magistrate could contain. A Catholic commentator considered Knox, Lord Ruthven, the provost, and bailies had 'encouraged' the 'multitude of the people and craftismen' to pull down all the altars, images and tabernacles (or altar-pieces) in the parish kirk and burn them. Knox's 'dear brethren' or 'rascal multitude' (as he later called them) proceeded to overthrow the Charterhouse, and Dominican and Franciscan friaries, including nearby Tullilum, whose buildings they purged and 'made bare', so rendering difficult continued occupation. As the Congregation mobilized, the familiar tactics were repeated in St Andrews, all of whose kirks and chapels were purged, and the friaries suppressed. Iconoclasm spread like wildfire to engulf the Abbeys of Lindores and Balmerino, and 'the parish kirkis within Fyfe'. Scone Abbey was 'sackit and burned', and the decision was taken 'to make reformatioun in all uther borrows townis

[80] Pitscottie, 2, p. 137; Knox, *History*, 1, pp. 148; 125, 127–9; *Edinburgh Burgh Records*, 2, pp. 251–2; 3, pp. 42–3; *Wodrow Soc. Miscellany*, p. 54; Leslie, *History*, p. 266.

in the southe and west pairtis of Scotlande'. In Stirling and Linlithgow the
kirks were purged and the friaries overthrown; and in Edinburgh and its
environs the activities of iconoclasts in rooting out altars and images from
churches and colleges, and in suppressing the friaries, helped prepare the
way for a public Protestant ministry in the capital. In the kirks of Glasgow,
too, the altars and 'monuments of idolatrye' were removed, on the orders
of the Lords of the Congregation, who instructed their followers to 'tak
guid heyd that neither the dasks, windocks, nor durris be ony ways hurt or
broken, either glassin wark or iron wark.' Similar instructions for the
removal of all 'monuments of idolatry' (and forbidding further damage to
the fabric) were issued for Dunkeld cathedral, though in rural Aberdeen-
shire, not only were the images cast out of the kirk at Echt, but the building itself was burned in 1559, while in Aberdeen the friaries were
despoiled, and churches purged in characteristic fashion.[81]

Plainly, as a means of inculcating Protestant belief, eradicating
Catholic worship, and engineering revolutionary religious change,
iconoclasm had helped force the pace of Reformation. Spurred on by
preachers, Reforming laymen did the rest: earls like Argyll—whose
example in 'destroying the false faith and false worship and in burning
images and idols and in casting down and smashing altars and places
where false sacrifices were offered' was extolled by his Gaelic preacher,
John Carswell—Lord James Stewart (later Earl of Moray), who 'plucked
down the images in divers churches' and 'changed the monks' coats to
other apparel', and Glencairn, who saw himself in battle with the Devil
and idolatry, and was committed to advance 'trew preaching' and 'to
remove superstition and all sortes of externall idolatrie'; lairds who associated themselves with the party of revolution; and inhabitants from such
burghs as Dundee, Perth, St Andrews, Brechin, Montrose, Stirling, Ayr,
and Edinburgh, who gained Protestant ministers by 1559. In burghs like St
Andrews, too, by the spring of 1560 Catholic priests were encouraged to
recant their former beliefs before the Reformed congregation by
renouncing

the Pape, quhai is the verray Antichriste and suppressour of Godis
glorie, with all diabolic inventioneis as be purgatorie, the mess,

[81] Knox, *History*, 1, pp. 161–3, 176, 182, 190–2, 203; *Wodrow Soc. Miscellany*, pp. 57–62; Pitscottie, 2, pp. 145–60; Leslie, *History*, pp. 271–5; Durkan and Kirk, *University of Glasgow*, p. 23;
J. H. Burton, *History of Scotland* (Edinburgh, 1897), 3, p. 354n.; Keith, *History*, 1, p. cxxii;
Aberdeen Burgh Records, 1, pp. 315, 323–4, 326; *CalSP Foreign Elizabeth*, ed. J. Stevenson, 2
(1865), no. 485, p. 226.

invocatioun of sanctis and prayaris to them, worschipping of images, prayeris in strange language, and multipliing of them to certane numer, and all ceremonies useit in Papistrie, as be hallowing of candellis, watter, salt, and bread, with all there conjurationes.

That, at any rate, was the negative side of Protestantism, and these were the practices the iconoclasts hoped to obliterate.[82] In all, it is a measure of the Reformers' achievement that whereas the Privy Council in 1546 had condemned the rioters who 'invaid, distroy, cast doun' and plunder abbeys, kirks, friaries, nunneries, and chapels, its successor, in 1561, is said to have decreed 'that all places and monuments of idolatry should be destroyed', in response to a petition from the General Assembly.[83]

By that stage, too, it was Swiss doctrines on the theory of the Church and its Sacraments which prevailed at the Reformation in 1560. These were expressed in the Reformed Confession of Faith, approved by Parliament in 1560, and in the *First Book of Discipline*, prepared at Parliament's behest in 1560 and accepted by the General Assembly of the Kirk. Here was a positive, creative expression of Protestantism. The earlier articles of the Confession (a document hastily produced by six leading ministers) on the central themes of Christian understanding—God, the Trinity, man's creation, fall, and redemption, the Incarnation, Christ's Passion, Resurrection and Ascension, his return for 'the final judgement'—were affirmations of the early Creeds, and scarcely controversial in themselves. Atonement through Christ who 'redeemed us when we were enemies to him' and sanctification through the Holy Ghost 'without all respect of any merit proceeding from us, be it before or be it after our regeneration' were duly proclaimed; a more polemical note was struck on the subject of good works, which were performed not by man's free will (and merited no eternal reward), but were done in faith as the fruit of election when Christ's spirit 'takes possession in the heart of any man', and evil works were defined as contraventions of God's commandments, which specifically covered the worship of 'idols' and other inventions of man 'which God from the beginning has ever rejected'.[84]

Justification by faith alone, familiar as it must have been to all Protestants, was assumed rather than explicitly defined (though the doctrine permeates the document); and predestination, biblical as it was, appeared

[82] R. L. Thomson, ed., *Foirm na n-Urrnuidheadh* (Edinburgh, 1970), pp. 176–7; *Cal. Scot. Papers*, 1, nos 469, 493–4; G. Donaldson, *All the Queen's Men* (London, 1983), pp. 161–4; *RStAKS*, 1, p. 13; cf. pp. 6–18.
[83] *RPC*, 1, p. 28; Knox, *History*, 1, p. 364; cf. pp. 360, 362 n. 5.
[84] Knox, *Works*, 2, pp. 97–107.

almost casually without systematic exposition in passages on the 'elect' and 'reprobate' (consistent perhaps with Calvin's counsel to treat the doctrine sensitively). Even so, election in Christ, it is stated plainly enough, took place 'before the foundations of the world were laid', and not only were the righteous or elect chosen to 'inherit that blessed immortality promised from the beginning', but 'contrariwise' the stubborn and unfaithful, or reprobate, were assigned to be 'cast in the dungeon of utter darkness, where their worm shall not die neither yet their fire shall be extinguished.' This suggests a belief in a double decree: a belief not only in God's decree of merciful election, but also in an accompanying retributive decree of damnation (that is, double pre-destination). In other words, the teaching here amounted to more than the mere abandonment of the reprobate; it pointed to their destruction after judgement.[85] Such a statement, at any rate, does little to sustain the claim of one recent writer who remarked that the Confession 'does not go beyond single predestination'.[86] As it turns out, on this issue Knox, the Genevans, and the Confession were in much closer agreement than is sometimes imagined.

— In defining the Church, the emphasis (typically Protestant) was on the invisible Church, the company of the elect through all ages and of all nations, whose members were known only to God; but as a visible congregation, a 'particular church such as was in Corinth', the true Church had to be distinguished from the false, 'the kirk malignant', not by 'antiquity, title usurped, lineal descent, place appointed, nor multitude of men approving an error', but by true preaching of the Word, right administration of Christ's Sacraments, and ecclesiastical discipline correctly administered. The Church, the Confession taught, remains subject to Scripture, whose interpretation belongs not to individuals, churches, or councils, which can err, but to the Spirit of God. The two dominical Sacraments of baptism and the Lord's Supper distinguish God's people from those outside his league; they also 'exercise the faith of his children'; and they serve 'to seal in their hearts the assurance of his promise', the union of the elect with Christ. Nor are the Sacraments 'naked and bare signs'. In baptism (which 'appertains as well to the infants of the faithful as unto them that be of age and discretion'), 'we are ingrafted into Christ', and in the Supper, 'Christ Jesus is so joined with us

---

[85] Calvin, *Institutes*, 3: 23: 14; Knox, *Works*, 2, pp. 100, 103; cf. pp. 109, 120.
[86] W. I. P. Hazlett, 'The Scots Confession 1560: Context, Complexion and Critique', *ARG*, 78 (1987), p. 312.

that he becomes the very nourishment of our souls.' Roman transubstantiation was condemned, the sacrifice of the Mass, offered to God for the
sins of the living and the dead, was denounced as blasphemous and
derogatory to Christ, and the Calvinist interpretation of the Sacrament
commended in the Confession (whereby the faithful are nourished by
Christ's body and blood in heaven, so that 'he remaineth in them and they
in him', through operation of the Holy Ghost) was manifestly at variance
both with Lutheran 'consubstantiation' and the mere memorialism of
Zurich and the Sacramentarians. To the Christian magistrate was assigned
'the conservation and purgation of religion', the maintainance of true
religion, and suppression of idolatry and superstition, and obedience to
his rule was enjoined so far as he fulfilled that 'which appertains to his
charge', though the Christian's duty to 'repress tyranny' and to 'defend the
oppressed' was stoutly upheld.[87]

-- In the *Book of Discipline*, also prepared in 1560, the first short chapter
was devoted to doctrine, the second to the Sacraments, and the third to
the abolition of idolatry, though the rest of the document was primarily
concerned with the organization of the Reformed Church. Emphasis
there was placed on proclaiming the Word, suppressing doctrines incon-
sistent with the biblical message, and discarding such human inventions as
vows of chastity and celibacy, distinctive religious attire, the 'superstitious
observance' of fast and feast days, prayers for the dead, and saints' days
'commanded by men', which had no assurance in Scripture. The two
Sacraments were understood as seals confirming spiritual promises. In
baptism, the element of water alone was approved, and Roman ceremonialism—'oyle, salt, waxe, spittle, conjuration and crossing'— was
repudiated as 'inventions devised by men' detracting from 'Christs perfect
ordinance'; at the Lord's Supper, 'sitting at a table' was judged 'most convenient to that holy action', and the wine, 'the cup of the Lords bloud',
was restored to communicants whom priests in the past had denied 'the
one part of that holy sacrament'.[88]

A Reformed Confession had received Parliament's sanction, a Protestant Church, adopting a Calvinist polity, had assumed the task of
supplanting the old Church, whose beliefs and practices increasingly had
come under scrutiny in the four decades preceding the Reformation of
1560. As Reformers intensified their work of evangelization, the new faith

---

[87] Knox, *Works*, 2, pp. 108–19; 106; J. Kirk, 'The Influence of Calvinism on the Scottish
Reformation', *RSCHS*, 18 (1974), pp. 159–61.
[88] J. K. Cameron, ed., *The First Book of Discipline* (Edinburgh, 1972), pp. 87–95.

found invigorating expression in the Kirk's distinctive forms of worship, as it sought to communicate with the whole people of Scotland. The religion of early Scottish Protestants, hitherto at odds with the Establishment, and promulgated within a movement of defiant protest, faced at the Reformation the prospect of becoming the Established Faith, defended by the magistracy, with all the accompanying gains and losses, opportunities and setbacks which that relationship encompassed.

University of Glasgow

'THE FACE OF ANE PERFYT REFORMED KYRK': ST ANDREWS AND THE EARLY SCOTTISH REFORMATION*

by JANE E. A. DAWSON

WITH supreme self-confidence the St Andrews kirk-session declared on 31 May 1564:

> Seing it hes pleased the gudnes of the Eternall, our God, of his meir mercy, to deliver and reduce us furth of the bondage and yok of Antecrist, to the lycht of the Ewangell of Jesus Crist be plenteows prechyng of the same; so that the face of ane perfyt reformed kyrk hes beyn seyn wythin this cite be the space of fyve yearis, the sacramentis deuly ministrat, all thingis done in the kyrk be comly ordor establesched, disciplyn used and resavit wythowtyn contempt or ony plane contradiccione of ony person'.[1]

They had reason to salute their own achievement. By the mid-1560s St Andrews exhibited the features of a fully Reformed church and was an example for other Scottish Protestants as they struggled to establish their faith. Above all, it provided a model for the whole of Scotland of the Reformed ideal worked out in practice. It had to face few of the constraints imposed by political necessity which inhibited the progress of reform in the rest of the country, and in these early years St Andrews came closer than most other burghs to the practical implementation of the Reformed ideal. Both its success and the limits of its achievement provide a microcosm of the strengths and weaknesses of the whole Scottish Reformation. The session's boast reflected the way in which the congregation of its parish kirk of Holy Trinity demonstrated the three characteristics or 'marks' of the church listed in the Scottish Confession of Faith and the *First Book of Discipline*: the preaching of the Word, the

---

* I have benefited from reading Achim Guessgen's unpublished dissertation, 'Die Reformation in St. Andrews (1546–1573) in vergleichender Perspektive zu den mitteleuropaischen Stadtreformationen' (University of Giessen, 1987), which the author has been kind enough to allow me to consult.
[1] D. H. Fleming, ed., *Register of the Minister, Elders and Deacons of the Christian Congregation of St Andrews, 1559–1600*, SHS, 2 vols (Edinburgh, 1889–90) [hereafter *RStAKS*], 1, p. 198.

right administration of the sacraments, and the exercise of ecclesiastical discipline.[2]

St Andrews was a burgh of about 2,500 inhabitants on the north-east coast of Fife. It had a small but busy port, which traded with Scandinavia, the Baltic, and the Low Countries.[3] As the seat of John Hamilton, the Archbishop of St Andrews and Catholic primate of Scotland, the burgh was the country's ecclesiastical capital. It also contained Scotland's oldest and most prestigious university, with its colleges of St Salvator, St Leonard, and the new foundation of St Mary.[4] The great cathedral dominated the town physically and brought a steady flow of pilgrims up its broad streets through the magnificent western front to see the relics of St Andrew, the patron saint of Scotland. Serving the cathedral was the equally famous Augustinian priory, which was the richest ecclesiastical foundation in the land.[5] Its Prior was Lord James Stewart, the half-brother of Mary Queen of Scots. Both the Dominicans and the Observant Franciscans also had houses in the burgh. St Andrews itself was governed by its Burgh Council, headed by the Provost, usually one of the Learmonth family.[6] The combination of the Augustinian priory, the University, and the archbishop's seat brought St Andrews such a concentration of ecclesiastical power and prestige that it dominated the pre-Reformation Church in Scotland. It was the ecclesiastical capital in practice as well as in theory, and provided the religious leadership for the country.

St Andrews retained its unique position within the Scottish Church even after the Reformation. By a striking and unexpected transformation it remained Scotland's religious capital, though it performed a very different function from its earlier role as the centre of the medieval church hierarchy. It was always intended that St Andrews should act like other Scottish burghs as one of the regional centres which would provide the 'best reformed kirk' for its locality and the seat of the Superintendent of Fife. However, its influence transcended the local and regional, and St

[2] J. K. Cameron, ed., *The First Book of Discipline* (Edinburgh, 1972), pp. 15–17, 32–9, 87f., 165f.; G. Henderson, ed., *Confession of Faith* (Edinburgh, 1937); W. I. P. Hazlett, 'The Scots Confession, 1560: Context, Complexion and Critique', *ARG*, 78 (1987), pp. 287–320.

[3] G. Parker, 'The "Kirk by Law Established" and the Origins of "The Taming of Scotland"; St Andrews, 1559–1600' in L. Leneman, ed., *Perspectives in Scottish Social History* (Aberdeen, 1988), pp. 1–2, 24–5.

[4] R. G. Cant, *The University of St Andrews*, rev. edn (Edinburgh, 1970), pp. 45ff. and *The College of St Salvator* (Edinburgh, 1950); J. Herkless and R. K. Hannay, *The College of St Leonard* (Edinburgh, 1905).

[5] D. McRoberts, *The Medieval Church of St Andrews* (Glasgow, 1976), pp. 63–136.

[6] M. Lynch, ed., *The Early Modern Town in Scotland* (London, 1987), pp. 1–35.

Andrews continued to provide religious leadership for the whole nation. This was primarily because it achieved the most successful Reformation in the country. Within the first year of the Reformation St Andrews had indeed established 'the face of ane perfyt reformed kirk'.

The great transformation of the burgh from the seat of Scotland's Catholic primate to her foremost Reformed community happened very quickly. Unlike many of their Protestant contemporaries throughout Europe, the good 'citiners' of St Andrews could recall precisely when they had been delivered from the 'bondage and yoke of Antichrist'.[7] They literally awoke on Sunday 11 June 1559 in a town full of Catholic churches and went to bed that night with a Protestant burgh and a Reformed parish church. They understood the Reformation to mean the dramatic events of one day, which they themselves had witnessed, and which changed their lives. However much one can trace the antecedents of reform within the burgh and the University, it is important to remember that the break with the past had been dramatic and decisive, an event rather than a process, and one witnessed and participated in by the burgh's inhabitants. It was not surprising that such an upheaval should be widely attributed to direct divine intervention. This view seemed to be confirmed nine months later, when the Lords of the Congregation were in full retreat, and the town seemed on the brink of capture by French soldiers. Then an English fleet miraculously appeared on the horizon through the mid-winter storms and saved the day, the burgh, and ultimately the Protestant cause in Scotland.[8]

The events of the 'Reformation Day' in St Andrews are clear, although there is some uncertainty over the precise date and whether they were spread over three days or accomplished on one. It happened at the beginning of the revolt against the French Regent, Mary of Guise, which developed into the Wars of the Congregation. After the dramatic events of the Reformation of Perth and the Regent's violent reaction to them, the Earl of Argyll and Lord James Stewart finally broke with Mary of Guise

---

[7] J. K. Cameron, 'The Uproar of Religioun', *Alumnus Chronicle of St Andrews University*, 50 (1959), pp. 20–3; *John Knox's History of the Reformation in Scotland*, ed. W. Croft Dickinson, 2 vols (Edinburgh, 1949), I, pp. 179–81; letter from Knox to Anne Locke, 23 June 1559, *The Works of John Knox*, ed. D. Laing, 6 vols (Edinburgh, 1846–64), 6, pp. 21–7; *Historie of the Estate of Scotland from July 1558 to April 1560* in D. Laing, ed., *Miscellany of the Wodrow Society* (Edinburgh, 1844), I, p. 59; Croft to Privy Council, 20 June 1559, *Calendar of State Papers Foreign, Elizabeth*, ed. J. Stevenson *et al.*, 23 vols (London, 1863–1950), 1559–60, I, p. 321.

[8] Knox, *History*, I, pp. 280–1; Knox to Railton, 29 Jan. 1560, *Works*, 6, pp. 105–7; *RStAKS*, p. 12n. *Historie*, p. 78. The ships were sighted on 23 Jan. 1560, T. Glasgow, 'The Navy in the First Elizabethan Undeclared War, 1559–60', *Mariners Mirror*, 54 (1968), pp. 23–37.

and joined the Congregation.[9] They then made their way with a small group of their household men to St Andrews, where they hoped to make changes quietly and with the minimum fuss. Once they heard that the Archbishop of St Andrews was coming 'to supper' on Saturday 10 June they sent out urgent letters to their friends, because Hamilton intended 'to bring in ane power of Frenche men sa to mak impediment to sic things as we wald sett fordwart to ye glory of God.' They asked the Earl of Menteith, Lord Ruthven, William Murray of Tullibardine, and Colin Campbell of Glenorchy, 'to cum to us with all possible dili[gence] wele accompaignit', but warned them, 'to be veray circumspect in your fordwart commyng and walk warily.'[10] Whether the men from Perth, Breadalbane, and Strathearn arrived in time to help with the Reformation in St Andrews, or were part of the host who saved the day for the Congregation at Cuparmuir later in the week, is not clear. However, the fact that reinforcements could be summoned at short notice was important and probably helped to give Argyll and Lord James as much confidence as John Knox's brave words. Knox had arrived in St Andrews from the south, having preached his way up the coast of the East Neuk of Fife and reformed the churches along the way. He had been greeted by a threatening message from Archbishop Hamilton who had declared, 'That in case John Knox presented himself to the preaching place . . . he should gar him to be saluted with a dozen culverins, whereof the most part should light upon his nose.'[11]

Supported by Argyll and Lord James, and knowing that help was on its way, a defiant Knox began Sunday 11 June by preaching in the parish church of Holy Trinity. He chose as his text the Gospel story of the cleansing of the Temple. There followed the forcible and violent removal of all the 'idols' and images from the burgh's parish and cathedral churches. In addition, the two houses of friars, the Dominicans and the Observant Franciscans, were completely destroyed. The friars were regarded as the

---

[9] Knox, *History*, 1, pp. 181–2 and notes; D. McRoberts, ed., *Essays on the Scottish Reformation, 1513–1625* (Glasgow, 1962), pp. 430–1 and n. 73. M. B. Verschuur, 'The Outbreak of the Scottish Reformation at Perth, 11 May 1559', *Scotia* (1987), pp. 41–53.

[10] The hitherto unknown letter found in the Breadalbane Papers (SRO, GD.112/39/1 no. 5) from Argyll and Lord James to the Lords Menteith and Ruthven and the Lairds of Tullibardine and Glenorchy, written from St Andrews on 10 June 1559, was probably one of several sent out to supporters of the Congregation. Menteith, Ruthven, and Tullibardine had all been at Perth during its Reformation and the subsequent negotiations with the Regent (Knox, *History*, 1, p. 180) and Glenorchy might have joined them in Perth to await just such a summons.

[11] Knox, *History*, 1, p. 181.

main enemy of the Reformers and, as had recently happened in Perth, their houses were deliberately and ruthlessly removed. This was the only part of the process which aimed at the full-scale destruction of property and was intended to intimidate and subdue the friars. It was also specifically designed to neutralize the threat they represented and prevent any future activity by depriving them of the bases from which to work.[12]

The destruction was thorough, efficient, and executed in an orderly manner and under tight control by the Lords of the Congregation. There was much breaking and burning of images but none of heads. Despite the violence to property, no life was lost in St Andrews, and it seems probable that even the friars avoided the beatings to which their brethren had been subjected in Perth. Those who opposed the iconoclasm recognized overwhelming force and did not seek to resist it. However, the Reformation of St Andrews was not simply imposed upon the burgh from outside through the presence of a large body of troops to enforce the change. All the evidence suggests that the destruction was supported or permitted by those who wielded authority within the burgh. The soldiers of the Congregation were led by the Commendator Prior of St Andrews, Lord James Stewart, and the well-known Protestant magnate, the Earl of Argyll. Their presence provided the military force to carry the project through, and an important link with the national Protestant cause which had just emerged into the open to challenge the Regent. These Lords of the Congregation had the active co-operation of the secular authorities of St Andrews, the Provost and baillies who supervised and directed the events of that day. The university authorities also favoured the 'cleansing'.[13] There was no organized resistance within the burgh, for the Archbishop's conspicuous absence had left the way open for the iconoclasts. His own position was in any case ambiguous, as the Duke of Châtelherault, the Archbishop's elder brother, was a prominent Lord of the Congregation.[14] The absence of

---

[12] M. Verschuur, 'The Perth Charterhouse in the Sixteenth Century', *InR*, 39 (1988), pp. 1–11; 'Outbreak', p. 47. For St Andrews see D. McRoberts, 'Material Destruction caused by the Scottish Reformation' in McRoberts, ed., *Essays*, pp. 415–62; McRoberts, *Medieval House*, p. 119.

[13] For the development of reforming ideas within the University see J. K. Cameron, 'Aspects of the Lutheran Contributions to the Scottish Reformation, 1528–1552', *RSCHS*, 22 (1984), pp. 1–12; 'Catholic Reform in Germany and in the Pre-Reformation Church in Scotland', *RSCHS*, 20 (1978–80), pp. 105–17; 'The Cologne Reformation and the Church of Scotland', *JEH*, 30 (1979), pp. 39–64; 'John Johnstone's "An Confortable Exhortation of our mooste holy Christen faith and her frutes": an early example of Scots Lutheran Piety', in D. Baker, ed., *Reform and Reformation*, *SCH*, 2 (1979), pp. 133–47; G. Wiedermann, 'Martin Luther versus John Fisher: some ideas concerning the debate on Lutheran theology at the University of St Andrews, 1525–30', *RSCHS*, 22 (1984), pp. 13–34.

[14] Archbishop Hamilton's behaviour at this critical juncture has not been satisfactorily

opposition made it easier to turn the destruction into a symbolic ritual of iconoclasm and prevent any degeneration into mob rioting.[15] The preparation and orderliness also permitted the removal into 'safe keeping' of anything with intrinsic value, such as jewels and precious metals.

The abrupt and destructive break with the past enabled the Reformers to put their ideals straight into practice. In St Andrews there was no gradual change or series of compromises, but a swift transition from one style of religion to another. Whatever else the people of St Andrews understood about the events of June 1559, they knew that the Reformers intended a fundamental religious reconstruction. What actually happened to their churches was more significant for them than any national decision or legislation at the 'Reformation Parliament' of August 1560. 'Reformation' was something they experienced directly; it was a dramatic and conclusive event. They were in little doubt that the new ways were intended to be very different from the old ones, and that a fresh start had been made possible by the calculated destruction.

The most obvious effect of the 'cleansing' was to emphasize the importance of the parish church. Regular worship at the friaries ceased when they were destroyed and was discontinued at the cathedral. The University, incorporated within its own parish of St Leonards, maintained its separate arrangements in the college chapels. The attention of the burgh was now focused entirely upon the Church of Holy Trinity in the centre of the town which was sufficiently large and spacious to serve the whole parish. With adequate accommodation in the parish church there was no need to use the cathedral which was allowed to fall into disrepair and ruin.[16]

On the 'Reformation day' the objective had been to remove all those items within Holy Trinity which in the Protestant view encouraged idolatry or interfered in any way with the true worship of God. This produced an overnight transformation of the interior of the church. All the pictures and statues of the Virgin and the saints were destroyed, even the representation of Calvary on the Rood, along with its great screen. It was hoped that the temptation to worship any image would likewise be expunged from men's hearts. The Reformers also strove to be rid of the

---

explained, J. Herkless and R. K. Hannay, *The Archbishops of St Andrews*, 5 vols (Edinburgh, 1915), 5, pp. 105f.; E. Finnie, 'The House of Hamilton', *InR*, 36 (1985), pp. 3–28.

[15] J. Phillips, *The Reformation of Images* (Berkeley, Calif., 1973); M. Aston, *England's Iconoclasts* (Oxford, 1988); N. Z. Davis, *Society and Culture in Early Modern France* (London, 1975), ch. 7.

[16] McRoberts, *Essays*, p. 431 and n. 75, 443.

whole cult of the saints and not just their pictures: with Christ as the only mediator and intercessor there was simply no room for them.

The most serious form of idolatry identified by the Reformers was to be found in the Catholic Mass. The Mass itself, its trappings, and its physical setting had to be taken away. As well as the high altar there were over thirty side altars dedicated to different saints in Holy Trinity.[17] These side altars had been endowed as chantries, where masses were said for the living and the dead. The Reformers' rejection of the doctrine of purgatory and their assertion of justification by faith alone made chantries redund- ant as well as unwelcome. The great 'cleansing' removed most of the familiar interior furnishings and fittings of the medieval church. What remained were bare walls, probably whitewashed to cover any murals, the pulpit and lectern, a table for the Lord's Supper, and some pews. For the Reformers, this stripped and stark interior furnished the most appropriate background for Christian worship.[18]

They had destroyed the rich, varied, and complex visual setting and apparatus of the medieval Catholic liturgy, with all its colours, gilding, and lifelike representation to catch and hold the eye. The destruction was not only a ritual cleansing and purification of the church, it was also a positive reordering of the church interior. This was not simply an attempt to remove distractions to worship, but also to offer an alternative. The unadorned walls were intentionally plain to present a stark backdrop which would concentrate attention upon a new type of drama. With no other competing visual distractions the actions of the congregation itself were placed centre stage. The plain background was deliberately created to spotlight the new form of dramatic religious action and permit it to be seen and recognized. By destroying the old style of church interior the Reformers were attempting to redirect the whole way in which people worshipped.

It is difficult to imagine the shock experienced by the citizens of St Andrews when they saw the new interior of Holy Trinity. It would have brought home to them that the Reformed church now had a 'public face', that it was the religion of the burgh, and that it was completely and self- consciously different from the Catholic church it replaced. All would instantly be aware of the magnitude of the change. Those who had been

[17] W. Rankin, *The Parish Church of Holy Trinity, St Andrews* (Edinburgh, 1955), pp. 54–99, 138; on idolatry, *Book of Discipline*, pp. 88, 94–5.
[18] G. Donaldson, 'Reformation to Covenant' in D. Forrester and D. Murray, eds, *Studies in the History of Worship in Scotland* (Edinburgh, 1984), pp. 33–51; W. MacMillan, *The Worship of the Scottish Reformed Church, 1550–1638* (London, 1931).

secretly practising their Protestantism within their own homes, privately reading their Bibles and saying their prayers, would rejoice at the event. They would understand and welcome the new church interior, but, like their fellow citizens, they would still be experiencing it for the first time. The church would feel familiar only to those who had lived and worshipped in the Protestant communities abroad. In those early months everyone in St Andrews would be able to see the new forms of public worship displayed in their intended setting.

The dramatic visual impact of Reformed worship has tended to be obscured by the familiar emphasis upon Protestantism as the religion of the Word. Yet it was almost certainly the first clear impression gained by the majority of the population of St Andrews. They saw before they heard or properly understood. The Protestants substituted the corporate actions of the whole congregation, played in the middle of an empty stage, for the dramatic ritual of Catholic liturgy, with its magnificent setting and accoutrements. Even the 'props' were changed from the ornate gold and silver communion plate to the wooden and pewter vessels of everyday use.[19] The focus was directed entirely upon the human players themselves. The people of the burgh were being invited to look closely at what they, as a congregation, did in their worship.

It was no accident that the Reformers chose to describe themselves as displaying the 'face' of the Reformed Kirk in St Andrews. The Church was a living corporate body which could be recognized by sight. Every time it gathered for worship in the local church it was visibly constituted, and it had a 'public face'.[20] This corporate body had its own personality, which was embodied in the local congregation. Only by coming together in the church for worship could this body of the Church grow, develop, and exercise its corporate priesthood. It required nurture and nourishment in the same way as an individual, and these it received through the Word and Sacraments. The Scottish Reformers' down-to-earth emphasis upon the specific and concrete nature of the local church underlined the human element in its creation and continuation. They gloried in the human face of the Kirk and its precise physical and geographical existence. Their celebration of the human element alongside the divine explains their acceptance of discipline, the 'sinews' which bound the congregation

---

[19] MacMillan, *Worship*, ch. 20.

[20] The public face of the Church was important: *Book of Discipline*, pp. 6, 87, 180; Knox, *History*, I, pp. 148f. The strong emphasis upon the local nature of the congregation did not mean that the wider aspects of the 'universall church' were ignored at either the national or the international level, *Book of Discipline*, pp. 34, 68.

together, as an equal mark of the Church together with Word and Sacraments, the gifts of divine grace.

The fellowship of the congregation was a visible, almost tangible, entity. The Reformers insisted that Word, Sacraments, and discipline, as well as the important dramas of human life, the 'rites of passage', must all happen 'in the face of the congregation'.[21] A baby had actually to be brought to the church by its father for baptism, usually at the Sunday service. The child was then presented to the congregation, who could see and accept their new member. A marriage should also take place within the church and in front of witnesses. Private baptisms and marriages were discouraged.[22] Burials were not specifically congregational acts, as the Reformers attempted to remove all traces of ritual and, in their view, the superstitions which had surrounded these occasions in the Catholic past. However, the services associated with discipline were full of visual and physical gestures. At his reconciliation, the penitent was embraced by the ministers and elders, and he literally returned to the middle of the congregation.[23] The Communion required all the members of the congregation to come within touching distance when they sat together at the Lord's Table and distributed the sacramental elements to each other.[24] In this sense Reformed worship was just as visual and tangible as its Catholic predecessor, but with the stress upon the human and down-to-earth quality of its actions.

The necessity to attend church in person, the close physical proximity, and the congregational participation in worship all focused attention upon the actions performed by the people of the congregation. It underlined that the Church was a real body, which could be seen and recognized by the rest of the world. If the Church was something which could be heard, touched, and seen by everyone, then its life on earth could also be assessed and judged by the rest of the world. The earthy insistence that the corporate body of the Church was a physical reality brought with it a pronounced emphasis upon discipline. It held the members of the congregation together, and so created the one corporate body of the visible Church. Since that body was real and easily identifiable, its conduct was under constant scrutiny. The very concrete and specific

[21] Donaldson, 'Reformation to Covenant', pp. 33, 38.
[22] *Book of Discipline*, pp. 91, 170, 182–3; Donaldson, 'Reformation to Covenant', pp. 38–9; *RStAKS*, pp. 194–5.
[23] *Book of Discipline*, pp. 34, 172; *RStAKS*, pp. 205–6; Donaldson, 'Reformation to Covenant', p. 39.
[24] *Book of Discipline*, pp. 90–3, and 91, n. 9, 92 n. 13.

JANE E. A. DAWSON

nature of the Reformers' concept of the Church and its embodiment in individual local congregations encouraged the great stress upon the value of discipline.[25]

The true exercise of ecclesiastical discipline ensured that the local congregations could maintain their cohesion and purity and be seen to do so. Each individual who was part of the visible Church should live an upright life and uphold the purity of the whole. In this way, the entire body was strengthened and edified internally and preserved its good reputation in the external world. The purity of the congregation was vital, because the corporate body of the Church was not simply a human body, it was also a divine one. The Church was the body of Christ, and must be preserved from any stain so that it remained a holy recepticle for the divine presence.

The gathering together of the faithful was at the heart of the Protestant view of the Church and its worship. Both the preaching of the Word and the administration of the Sacraments, the twin pillars of Reformed worship, were congregational acts. Preaching, by definition, was not an individual activity, and the members of the congregation were essential, though passive, participants. Action by the congregation was required in a more emphatic manner in the celebration of the Lord's Supper. The Reformers demanded a very different form of physical presence from the one posited in the Catholic doctrine of transubstantiation. They insisted upon the visible and physical presence of the congregation gathered for worship. The practice of the priest celebrating Mass on his own was anathema to the Reformers, who believed that without the presence and participation of the faithful there could be no Lord's Supper. The Communion was a communal action performed by the whole congregation acting as a corporate priest.[26]

By shifting the emphasis from the single priest to all the people they also removed the precise visual focus in the Lord's Supper. Instead of an altar or robed priest to catch the eye and become the apex of the triangle of worship, the Reformers introduced the circle or square of communicants seated around the communion table. They rejected the implication of a single mystical and timeless moment signalled by the elevation of the Host and the ringing of the bell. By giving equal emphasis to all parts of the Communion service, they tried to avoid any single sharp

[25] *Book of Discipline*, pp. 87f., 180; Hazlett, 'Scots Confession', pp. 310–11.
[26] R. S. Wallace, *Calvin's Doctrine of the Word and Sacrament* (Edinburgh, 1953), chs 12–13, 16–18; D. Shaw, 'Zwinglian Influences on the Scottish Reformation', *RSCHS*, 22 (1985), pp. 119–39; G. Burnet, *The Holy Communion in the Reformed Church of Scotland, 1560–1960* (Edinburgh, 1960).

422

point of attention in either time or place. Both the bread and the wine were distributed to the congregation, who came to the table in groups rather than as individuals, and were served by minister and layman alike. The Reformers wanted to expunge all traces of a magical instant of transformation produced by a sacerdotal priest.

Every effort was made to avoid the localization of the divine presence in the Lord's Supper.[27] Obviously bowing, kneeling, or crossing oneself was inappropriate, as such gestures had to be directed towards a physical object or location, and there could be no exact visible focus during the Communion service. The adoration of God should take place in the heart, and its only outward signs were the orderliness, dignity, and respect in which the whole service was conducted. God could not be recognized by the physical senses in any crude or direct fashion. He was perceived in the heart and soul of the believer through faith. Through the operation of the Holy Spirit, Christ was really and truly present in spiritual form in the Lord's Supper, and joined to the believer in a sacramental union.

The overarching purpose of all the changes in the church interior was to remove the attention from a single moment and location and permit the spiritual presence of Christ to be recognized in a spiritual setting. Although the Reformers rejected the view that God was present in physical objects, they still wanted and needed some form of physical and sensual focus to their worship. That was provided by the gathering of the faithful who were physically present within the walls of the church.

The 'Reformation Day' and the great cleansing of the church signalled the break with the past practices and demonstrated the full reordering of worship which the Protestants intended to undertake. As they well knew, this was just the start of the task of awakening and instructing the burgh in true Christianity. The Reformers started both logically and chronologically with the preaching of the Word.[28] As the kirk-session had declared, the Church was created and also sustained by plenteous preaching. It had been a sermon which had preceded the great cleansing of the churches. Preaching remained central to the Reformation in the town and became the very core of worship, because Communion was relatively infrequent. Within a short time St Andrews enjoyed a sermon at least twice a week, and was provided with a series of very highly qualified and renowned preachers. After the services of Adam Heriot and John Knox in the initial eighteen months, the first settled minister was Christopher

[27] Wallace, *Calvin*, pp. 208, 210.
[28] *Book of Discipline*, p. 87.

Goodman, himself a celebrated preacher. He was assisted in the provision of the weekly sermons by members of the University.[29] The burgh became so used to having a distinguished preacher in its pulpit that when Goodman left in 1565 it requested that Knox be sent to replace him.[30] As the main function of preaching was to bring the Word to the people, it was decided to adopt the practice of expounding each of the books of the Bible from start to finish. This method was used to explain one of the most difficult and, to the Reformers, most important books, the Revelation of St John. Goodman's sermons on the Apocalypse were delivered at some point between 1563 and 1565. They made such a profound impression upon one young student, John Napier of Merchiston, that he studied its meaning for the rest of his life, producing his major commentary in 1593 and its more famous by-product, the invention of logarithms.[31]

The orderly exposition of the Scriptures was assisted by the 'exercise', the weekly meeting for biblical discussion and interpretation. This was taking place in St Andrews by 1562 at the latest, when attendance became compulsory for students at the University.[32] The Word was not only interpreted in sermon and exercise: it was read aloud during Sunday and weekday services, and private reading and study of the Bible were also encouraged. The Geneva Bible itself was probably the version utilized in St Andrews, since Goodman had been one of its principal translators, and John Knox had assisted in the project. In 1560 it was the most satisfactory available version of the Scriptures in English. It had a clear, easy-to-follow text, newly divided into verses, and its copious notes, summaries, pictures, and tables provided the reader with a complete biblical manual and concordance in one volume. Although relatively expensive, particularly in the folio edition, it seems probable that there were a number of copies circulating in the burgh where Goodman was minister.[33]

Sunday worship comprised two services before and after noon. There

[29] Book of Discipline, pp. 180f.; RStAKS, pp. 344–5; Donaldson, 'Reformation to Covenant', p. 37.
[30] T. Thomson, ed., The Booke of the Universall Kirk, Acts and Proceedings of the General Assemblies of the Kirk of Scotland, 1560–1618, Bannatyne and Maitland Clubs (Edinburgh, 1839–45), I, p. 72. In 1577 the kirk-session took order to ensure that St Andrews should not be 'defrauded' of preaching, RStAKS, p. 428.
[31] John Napier, A Plaine Discovery of the whole Revelation of Saint John (Edinburgh, 1593), fol. A6r; RStAKS, p. 829; Book of Discipline, p. 185 and n. 20.
[32] Book of Discipline, pp. 42f., 187f., and n. 30; A. I. Dunlop, ed., Acta Facultatis Artium Universitatis Sanctiandree, 1413–1588, SHS (Edinburgh, 1964), p. 416.
[33] Book of Discipline, pp. 184–5; L. Berry, ed., Geneva Bible: facsimile edition (Madison, Wisconsin, 1969), pp. 1–24.

was the reader's service with prayers and psalm-singing before noon, as well as the sermon and Scripture reading.[34] Congregational participation was essential to the Reformed ideal of worship. The use of metrical psalms and hymns was an important way of involving the congregation in the service, and provided another example of the attempts by the Reformers to change previous attitudes. They wished to cut sacred music away from its past and place it in a new setting. The increasingly elaborate polyphonic music of the choir in the chancel, which had been such a feature of the medieval Church, and had flourished in Holy Trinity, was far removed from the congregation in every sense. In its place, the reformers wanted simple tunes which everyone could sing. Understanding the words, which were nearly always taken from Scripture, was vitally important.[35] St Andrews consciously led the way in this departure from musical tradition. Lord James Stewart commissioned David Peebles, a canon of St Andrews, and 'ane of the principall musitians in all this land in hys tyme', to produce a complete Psalter with tunes. After some prodding by Thomas Wood, who carefully and beautifully copied the scores, the work was completed, providing the congregation of Holy Trinity with music for psalms and holy songs in four parts.[36] As the 'Gude and Godly Ballads' had already demonstrated, songs and communal singing were an excellent medium for spreading the Protestant message throughout Scotland. They also provided an easy way for those who could not read to learn passages from Scripture, especially the Psalms, which in time became the prayers and occasionally the battle hymns of the Lord for the Scots.[37]

As well as morning service, the members of the congregation were expected to attend the catechizing on Sunday afternoon. It is difficult to overestimate the long-term impact of weekly catechizing. The Reformers were well aware that to achieve a national renewal they needed to inculcate in the young a new way of approaching religion. Whether they ultimately produced a new faith cannot be determined with certainty, but they eventually remoulded the religious perceptions of the Scottish people. By 1570 the citizens of St Andrews could recite the Creed, the

[34] McMillan, *Worship*, chs 10–11; Donaldson, 'Reformation to Covenant', p. 37; *Book of Discipline*, p. 182.

[35] McMillan, *Worship*, chs 5–7; M. Patrick, *Four Centuries of Scottish Psalmody* (London, 1949), chs 1–6.

[36] Patrick, *Psalmody*, ch. 6; D. Laing, 'An Account of the Scottish Psalter of A.D. 1566', *Proceedings of Society of Antiquaries of Scotland*, 7 (1866–8), pp. 445–58; K. Elliot, 'Scottish Music of the Early Reformed Church', *Transactions of the Scottish Ecclesiological Society*, 15 (1961), pp. 18–41.

[37] W. S. Reid, 'The Battle Hymns of the Lord: Calvinist Psalmody of the Sixteenth Century', *Sixteenth Century Essays and Studies*, 2 (1971), pp. 36–54.

Commandments, and the Lord's Prayer, and give a personal account of their faith.[38] Of greater social significance was the alteration in the rhythms of burgh life by the rejection of the old Christian calendar, with its festivals and saints' days. The Reformers completely changed the timing of public religious exercises, giving central place to the Sunday preaching and instruction and the additional weekday sermon. The removal of the great communal celebrations of Christmas and Easter and the many holy days probably constituted the greatest change in the burgh's religious and social life throughout the sixteenth century.[39]

Following after and closely linked to the preaching of the Word came the second mark of the Church, the proper administration of the Sacraments. One of the purposes of the 'cleansing' was to provide the correct setting for the Sacraments and the right backdrop, which would emphasize the essential difference from the old practices. Both baptism and the Lord's Supper, the only Sacraments recognized by the Reformed Church, were celebrated in the body of the kirk, the nave, which had always been regarded as belonging to the congregation. This was to demonstrate that they were congregational acts.

If possible, the whole of the burgh should attend the church in person. However, for the individual, simple physical attendance was not sufficient to benefit from Protestant worship. The members of the congregation needed to be aware of what was happening. Without understanding, there could be no true participation, especially in the Communion. Christ could only be received in the Sacraments through faith, and for faith to exist a basic understanding was required. This basic understanding was to be acquired through the preaching of the Word and catechizing. An examination was made to ensure that for those attending the Lord's Supper understanding had been achieved and faith could be present. The speed and efficiency with which a system of pre-Communion examination by the elders was organized in St Andrews was remarkable.[40] A token system was in operation by May 1560, whereby all those who had satisfied their examiners were given a lead token to present at the time of Communion. Those without a token were not admitted to the Lord's Table. There is later evidence that the burgh was divided into four quarters for examination, and that those who did not attend Communion were

[38] *STAKSR*, pp. 340–1; Donaldson, 'Reformation to Covenant', p. 39. The Book of Common Order contained a translation of Calvin's Catechism: *Book of Discipline*, pp. 40, 130–1, 182.
[39] Cf. P. Collinson, *The Birthpangs of Protestant England* (London, 1988), p. 54.
[40] *RStAKS*, pp. lvi, 34–5 and n. 2, 196, 254, 436; *Book of Discipline*, pp. 183–4; *Booke of the Universall Kirk*, 1, pp. 30, 58.

summoned before the kirk-session. In St Andrews, the Lord's Supper was celebrated four times a year as laid down by the *First Book of Discipline*.

Although not a Sacrament, the divine ordinance of marriage was also to be celebrated in the presence of the congregation. The Reformers in St Andrews made strenuous and largely successful efforts to ensure that there was only one binding and legitimate marriage service and that it took place in church after the sermon. They fought a long battle to reduce the importance of traditional practices of betrothal and hand-fasting, and particularly to stop couples living together after these initial promises, but before a full marriage in church.[41] The order for all these services and the rites for Christian burial were taken from the Form of Prayers devised for use by the English exile church in Geneva, which was adopted as the Book of Common Order for the Scottish Church. Both Knox and Goodman had been ministers to that Genevan congregation and had helped to write the service book, which was in use in St Andrews from an early date.[42]

In its demonstration of the third mark of the Church, the exercise of ecclesiastical discipline, the Reformed church of St Andrews gave Scotland its greatest lead and inspiration. Although the Word was preached and the Sacraments duly administered in many places thoughout the country, very few could boast proper ecclesiastical discipline. Its existence indicated a church that was genuinely settled and established. It demonstrated that the corporate body of the congregation was alive and growing.[43] St Andrews was in a unique position, and its peculiar advantages allowed it to offer an example to the rest of Scotland. It was small enough to be amenable to tight control, and sufficiently distant from the court and centre of government to be able to manage its own affairs without undue external interference. Its tradition as the ecclesiastical capital made it important enough to attract attention, while its University added the gravity of learning to what was being accomplished. Yet these advantages would have been useless without the remarkable unanimity of the various authorities within the burgh, who were all willing to support the establishment of a Reformed community.

The Provost, baillies, and Burgh Council, along with a large number of the leading citizens (over three hundred) had supported the Lords of the

---

[41] *Book of Discipline*, pp. 44–5, 191–9; problems with hand-fasting, *RStAKS*, pp. xl–xli, 29, 145, 248–9, 280, 330; Parker, '"Kirk by Law Established"', p. 20, appendix 1.
[42] *Book of Discipline*, pp. 45–6, 199–201; W. D. Maxwell, *John Knox's Genevan Service Book* (Edinburgh, 1931).
[43] A. Ross, 'Reformation and Repression', in McRoberts, ed., *Essays*, pp. 392–401.

Congregation and had signed the Band of 13 July 1559.[44] The University was controlled by Reformers and lent its official backing.[45] The Augustinian priory was similarly a major source of support with its Prior, Lord James, and Sub-Prior, John Winram, who subsequently became the Superintendent of Fife, and providing fifteen ministers and five readers and exhorters for the new church.[46] As well as the burgh government, many of the local Fife lairds were also enthusiasts for reform and had attended the Reformation Parliament in August 1560.[47]

The most obvious focus for opposition, John Hamilton, the Archbishop, remained quiescent in the early 1560s, and although later very active in the Queen's party it was primarily as a political agent. Hamilton's ambivalence in these early years and his family links with the Lords of the Congregation were a considerable assistance to the Protestants within St Andrews, because it hamstrung the Catholic opposition. It was left without leadership from the Archbishop, but still hopeful that he might provide it. Within the burgh itself there was no serious or organized opposition to the establishment and exercise of ecclesiastical discipline by the new kirk-session. The Reformers could look for and receive the enthusiastic support of the Burgh Council in its attempts to enforce its decrees. The *First Book of Discipline* had dealt with the subject in its seventh head, and there it had emphasized the preservation of high standards of public morality. The other and related aspect of discipline lay in the regulation of matters of belief and the maintenance of the purity of the Church, particularly in relation to the Sacraments.[48]

Defending the true doctrine of the Church and ensuring uniformity of belief within St Andrews was achieved in a variety of ways. Preaching and catechizing were the main positive methods, and should they fail, the sanctions of the kirk-session could be used. In the first few years of its existence the kirk-session was also concerned to ensure that those who had been heavily identified with the Catholic Church in St Andrews should publicly recant. The selection of those to make a recantation provides an interesting indication of where the opposition to reform was

---

[44] *RStAKS*, pp. viii, 6–10.

[45] J. K. Cameron, 'The Church and the Universities in Scotland in the era of the Reformation', *The Church in a Changing Society* (Uppsala, 1978), pp. 217–22; Dunlop, *Acta*, p. 415n.

[46] Of the 32 to 39 canons at the Priory in 1560, 21 served in the Reformed Church, McRoberts, *Medieval Church*, pp. 132–3.

[47] G. Donaldson, *All the Queen's Men* (London, 1983), pp. 9–30.

[48] *Book of Discipline*, pp. 32–4, 165–73. J. K. Cameron, 'Scottish Calvinism and the Principle of Intolerance', in B. A. Gerrish, ed., *Reformatio Perennis: Essays on Calvin and the Reformation* (Pittsburgh, 1981), pp. 113–28.

thought to lie. The absentees from the list are also suggestive, the most obvious being John Winram himself, who had been the most prominent churchman in the burgh after the Archbishop, but who had joined the Reformers. The lack of a recantation from Winram did not go unnoticed and attracted some unfavourable comment. Andrew Wardlaw refused to take orders from Winram 'that fals, dissaitfull, gredy and dissimlbit smayk, for he wes ane of tham that maist oppressed, smored and held down the Word of God, and now he is cumin to it, and professis the same for gredines of gayr, lurkand and watchand quhill he may se ane other tym.'[49]

All those who did recant publicly were priests, and they fall into two groups. The first were those who staffed the town church of Holy Trinity and had been under the control of the Burgh Council before the Reformation. It was not surprising that they should be required to make a formal acknowledgement of the religious changes in the place where they worked.[50] The other category comprised priests, who were regarded as a continuing threat, and so pressurized into publicly accepting the new religion. This obviously applied to the Provincial General of the Observant Friars, John Grierson, who was a figure of national significance. His confession of faith, sincere or not, was a considerable psychological victory for the new Protestant regime.[51] Though of only local significance, John Wilson and John Kipper also fall into this category. Kipper voiced his opposition in such a pointed manner that he was imprisoned in the castle.[52] It is probable that other priests who were regarded as troublemakers were ejected from the burgh. Not satisfied with simply getting rid of Thomas Methven, the burgh sent letters after him to dog his trail.[53] An exile order could be employed to remove major elements of opposition from the burgh, and helps to explain the remarkable grip in which ecclesiastical discipline held St Andrews from 1559. Banishment was a practical option for those who would have preferred the full vigour of the law against 'mass-mongers', but were not in a position to implement the death sentence. They could order exile instead, which was a less drastic sentence of 'legal death'.[54]

With the full support of the Provost and Burgh Council, the kirk-session could guarantee that its decrees would be enforced. Throughout

---

[49] *RStAKS*, pp. xxviii–xxix, 86; Ross, 'Reformation', p. 394 and n. 95.
[50] *RStAKS*, pp. xii–xx, 10–15, 169–71, 191, 297, 318–20, 322–3, 352–3, 375–6.
[51] Ibid., pp. 16–18; McRoberts, *Essays*, pp. 197–9, 400.
[52] Ross, 'Reformation', p. 400; *RStAKS*, pp. xvi, 81–2; (Wilson), pp. xii, 11–13.
[53] *RStAKS*, pp. xvi–xvii, lxi–xii, 77, 135–9, 317–18, 609; Ross, 'Reformation', p. 397.
[54] *RStAKS*, pp. 173–4.

the period, baillies sat as elders in the kirk-session and could use their civil authority to ensure compliance with the decrees of the session.[55] This solidarity between ecclesiastical and civil authorities made it extremely difficult to sustain dissent or organize opposition to the Reformed Church. There was plenty of offensive and abusive talk, which expressed dissatisfaction with the Kirk, but no serious attempt to oppose or overturn it.[56] In that sense, the session were correct in their assertion that discipline had been used and received without contempt or plain contradiction by anyone in the burgh.

The occasion for the statement, the process against John Bicarton, underlined the session's hold upon the town. Bicarton was an important craftsman who fell foul of the minister and session of St Andrews by refusing to present his child for baptism.[57] It was an unusual case, because Bicarton had fought for the Lords of the Congregation and was widely regarded as a committed Protestant. He was a full member of the Church and had been admitted to Communion. He challenged the sacrament of baptism as not based on Scripture, refused the pre-Communion examination, and would not submit himself to the kirk-session. It is not clear whether this was a theological dispute over infant baptism, as Bicarton's views were not recorded at any length. He refused to appear again before the kirk-session despite three summones and a further public admonition, and so eventually he was excommunicated. The final sanction of ecclesiastical discipline was very rarely used against citizens of St Andrews. Bicarton's case demonstrated just how devastating it could be. At his reconciliation seven months later Bicarton explained that he had 'sustenit gret damneg and disays in guddis and body . . . and subject instantly to ane disays and maledy.'[58]

The whole process of Bicarton's excommunication and reconciliation, and the rarity of its use within the burgh revealed the contrast which the Reformers wished to establish between Catholic practice and their own. It had taken a full two months to move from the original offence, through the long summonses, to the final sentence of excommunication. Both the sentence and the act of reconciliation involved the whole congregation and were full of visual signs. At his reconciliation, Bicarton asked the congregation for their forgiveness, and then shook hands and was

[55] In 1562 adulterers were handed over to 'the bailies present to be civile correctit and punist according to the ordour resavit in this citie', *RStAKS*, pp. lvii, 141.
[56] Ibid., pp. 33–6.
[57] Ibid., pp. lvi, 194–206.
[58] Ibid., p. 206.

embraced by the minister and elders in front of all. This underlined the restorative side of discipline, the return to full congregational unity and the healing of the corporate body of the visible Church. Long before the 'Order of Excommunication' had been published, St Andrews had devised its own form to demonstrate the difference between Catholic 'cursing' and the separation from the body and the fellowship of the Reformed congregation.[59]

The maintenance of public morality was the second and related strand of ecclesiastical discipline. Almost inevitably this was dominated by cases of sexual misdemeanour. It is notoriously difficult to judge the 'success' rate of the kirk-session in this area of its work. On a superficial level St Andrews was 'tamed' by this discipline, and the public behaviour of its citizens was changed. The tight control enforced by the session maintained strict outward conformity and ensured that the 'public face' of the burgh was sufficiently moral to uphold its status as a fully Reformed community.[60]

The kirk-session of St Andrews was never simply concerned with its own burgh. It also performed the role of 'best reformed kirk' for the surrounding area, and was the seat of the Superintendent of Fife framers of the *First Book of Discipline* were well aware of the difficulties facing the new Church and sought to bring their undoubted strength in the urban centres to aid the superintendents and to influence the surrounding rural areas. The startling success which the session had achieved in turning St Andrews into a reformed burgh, and the organization which worked so efficiently within a small urban community could not produce the same results for the whole region. The widening of the area brought with it a decrease in control.

The workings of the Superintendent's Court in Fife reveal in microcosm the problems which faced the Reformers when they sought to establish their Church throughout the country.[62] The Court was composed of the Superintendent, John Winram, and the St Andrews kirk-session, and its records form part of the minutes of the session. Its business was

---

[59] *Book of Discipline*, pp. 168–70. The 'Order of Excommunication' of 1569: Knox, *Works*, 6, pp. 390, 460, 462f.; *Booke of the Universall Kirke*, 1, p. 37.

[60] For the 'taming', Parker, '"Kirk by Law Established"', pp. 1–32.

[61] *Book of Discipline*, pp. 49f., 68–9, 97f., 115f.; (Superintendent of Fife), p. 119. Winram's election, 13 April 1561, *RStAKS*, pp. 72–5; J. K. Cameron, 'The Office of Superintendent in the "First Book of Discipline"', B. Vogler, ed., *Miscellanea Historiae Ecclesiasticae*, 8 (Brussels, 1987), pp. 239–50.

[62] For a recent survey, M. Lynch, 'Calvinism in Scotland, 1559–1638' in M. Prestwich, ed., *International Calvinism* (Oxford, 1985), pp. 225–55.

conducted during the normal weekly meetings of the session after the local cases.[63] Between 1561 and 1572 it dealt with 124 cases and made 12 decrees. St Andrews provided competent personnel and a functioning organization for the Superintendent, and so gave him a firm base. It also by its nature created a major problem for him, because his Court was only intended to operate when he was present in St Andrews.[64] The members of the kirk-session could hardly be expected to be on continual visitation with the Superintendent, and this practical need to return to the burgh made it impossible for Winram (or his fellow Superintendents) to accomplish the Herculean task of visitation for three-quarters of each year, as laid down in the *First Book of Discipline*. This did not prevent Winram's slackness in visitation being frequently criticized in the General Assembly.[65]

As well as a practical need to return to St Andrews, a psychological pull also operated. Cases were brought into St Andrews in the hope that they could be resolved in its safe, Reformed environment. The defensive movement inwards towards a secure centre is understandable in these troubled years immediately after the Reformation. Although St Andrews could offer a safe haven, it could not extend the social and political control which it exercised within the burgh to the surrounding area. The harmonious co-operation of secular and ecclesiastical authority which dominated St Andrews and made prolonged defiance of the kirk-session difficult could not cover the kingdom of Fife. The surrounding region was not particularly hostile to the Reformation as it contained a large number of sympathetic lairds, but, as in the rest of the country, the Protestants lacked the absolute control which could be achieved within the burgh. Without total local control or complete commitment from the central authority of the monarchy, the Reformation of the rural parishes was bound to be a slow and painstaking process. Within the Superintendent of Fife's jurisdiction, the dignity and authority of his court were usually sufficient to overawe or coerce ordinary people, but they conspicuously failed when those of higher social standing were involved. Robert Stewart, Lord Rosyth, had no hesitation in preventing the Superintendent's Court from investigating his wife's behaviour. As the register

[63] *RStAKS*, pp. xxviii, 107, 184, 231, 346–7, 370; (the oath of the elders and deacons), pp. 369–70.
[64] On 22 June 1569 the Superintendent did empower the session to act in his absence, but this seems an isolated incident, ibid., p. 321, and in one case where he was personally involved the case was conducted by the session, pp. 82–9.
[65] For example, Dec. 1563: *Book of the Universall Kirk*, 1, pp. 39, 43.

succinctly phrased it, 'the proces ceassed because the Lard of Rosyt wald nocht consent to ony persut at instance of his Lady.'[66]

The cases which did come before the Court, and the decrees which the Superintendent promulgated, reveal a very different religious situation in the Fife hinterland from that found in St Andrews. A number of parishes were without a competent minister, exhorter, or even a reader, there were only a few active kirk-sessions, and considerable confusion about even the basic tenets of the Reformed Kirk and its organization.[67] The decree which explained that those who had been excommunicated should not be chosen as elders of the kirk does not suggest a deep understanding of Reformed practice or ecclesiology.[68]

It was one of the major functions and a main justification of the super-intendent's position that he should 'plant' kirks. In these landward areas the marks of the true Church were barely visible. There was little preach-ing, because few men were qualified to do so, and it was part of the super-intendent's job to preach assiduously while on visitation. He also tried to ensure that the sacraments were duly administered, and was again hampered by the shortage of ministers and ignorance concerning the Reformed faith. The third mark of ecclesiastical discipline was even more elusive. For the majority of the parishes in Fife at the outset, discipline was to be found in the Superintendent's Court or not at all. With so few functioning kirk-sessions, that court became the court of first instance for cases discovered or reported to the Supterintendent on visitation.

The most obvious and urgent need for Fife and the Reformed Church as a whole was to find qualified ministers and establish them in the rural parishes of Scotland. St Andrews with its University and highly developed Reformed community was an obvious 'factory' for such men. In the second half of the sixteenth century it did indeed produce a large number of ministers for the Reformed Kirk, but its performance in the early years was not as substantial as it might have been. In the first regular General Assembly twenty-one people from St Andrews, the largest single group, were designated fit for the ministry.[69] Many found it difficult to leave St

[66] *RStAKS*, p. 175.

[67] The main problem facing the Kirk was the lack of a properly trained and funded ministry, *Book of Discipline*, pp. 17–22, 96–107.

[68] Professor Cameron and Mr Smart discovered a damaged manuscript in St Andrews University Library which contains a list of ecclesiastical decrees. Some of these emanated from the General Assembly, but others appear to have a more local provenance, possibly from the superintendent of Fife's synod, STAUL MS 30451, fol. 3v for decree forbidding excommunicants to become elders.

[69] *Book of the Universall Kirk*, 1, p. 4.

Andrews: some had good reason because they held important teaching posts within the University and were training the next generation of ministers.[70] Those who did leave the burgh tended to remain in Fife. For these men, the vigorous religious life of St Andrews was a constant temptation to non-residency, one of the evils of the Catholic Church most vehemently denounced by the Reformers. Many of the ministers found it comfortable to retreat inside the safe and supportive environment of St Andrews, their holy city upon a hill, and extremely difficult to remain in the valley of their rural cure simply looking towards the burgh for inspiration. Instead of acting like a centrifugal force, pushing the Reformed religion out into the surrounding region, St Andrews was tending to act as a centripetal force, sucking into itself and holding in its reforming achievement. In this way the very success and strength of the Reformed burgh of St Andrews proved to be a weakness for the regional and the national movement.

However much St Andrews might seem to its admirers to be a miniature Geneva, it could not perform the same role as the great Swiss city. Unlike the Swiss cantons or the German imperial cities, control over the town did not automatically bring with it control over the hinterland. In this context there was a crucial difference between the political systems found in Scotland and in Switzerland and the Holy Roman Empire. The decentralization of Stewart government could not hide the fact that Scotland was a national monarchy. It did help to disguise the limits placed upon local autonomy, especially in the unique circumstances enjoyed by St Andrews in the early years of the Reformation. Ultimately, national leadership had to come from the political centre, because that was the only authority which could hope to secure overall control. However influential a single burgh might be, it was incapable of assuming the leadership necessary to implement religious change throughout Scotland. The constraints of the political system ensured that St Andrews could inspire and assist, but it could never lead.

The remarkable Reformation achieved within the burgh could not be replicated outside its walls. It could not even extend its absolute local control throughout the surrounding region of Fife. On its own, St Andrews could never be the power-house of the Scottish Reformation.

[70] For example, John Rutherford, Provost of St Salvator's, or James Wylkie, later Provost of St Leonards. There was also the old problem of appropriated parishes in the General Assembly of June 1565. St Salvator's was in trouble for not providing a preacher for their church at Kilmany; *Book of the Universall Kirk*, I, pp. 62–3.

With its Reformed University it was able to help in curing the fundamental weakness of the new Church: the chronic shortage of trained ministers to staff the parishes of Scotland. The best which St Andrews could, and did, do was to provide a perfect example of a Reformed community in practice. It demonstrated that the Reformation was a dramatic religious event which could change the life of a community. Its contribution was to inspire the country by allowing the rest of Scotland to see and so be able to recognize and emulate 'the face of ane perfyt reformed kyrk'.

University of St Andrews

BIBLIOGRAPHY OF THE WRITINGS OF JAMES K. CAMERON

by JAMES KIRK

1953   'Henry of Langenstein: A Letter on Behalf of a Council of Peace',
'John Gerson: On the Unity of the Church', 'Dietrich of Niem:
Ways of Uniting and Reforming the Church', 'John Major: A Dis-
putation on the Authority of a Council', ed. and tr. in Matthew
Spinka, ed., *Advocates of Reform: From Wyclif to Erasmus = The
Library of Christian Classics*, 14 (The Westminster Press, Phila-
delphia and SCM Press, London), pp. 106–84.

1954   'Conciliarism in Theory and Practice, 1378–1418' [Abstract of
Doctoral Thesis 1952–3] *The Hartford Seminary Foundation Bulletin*,
16, pp. 34–7.

1959   'James Cargill (*c.*1565–1616)', *Aberdeen University Review*, 38,
pp. 148–51.
'The Uproar of Religion', *The Alumnus Chronicle of the University of
St Andrews*, 50, pp. 20–3.
REVIEW
Calvin: Commentaries, ed. J. Haroutunian = *The Library of Christian
Classics*, 23 (London, 1958), *The Expository Times*, 70, p. 237.

1960   REVIEW
Owen Chadwick, ed., *Western Asceticism = The Library of Christian
Classics*, 12 (London, 1958), *The Expository Times*, 71, no. 6,
pp. 68–9.

1961   REVIEWS
Institutes of the Christian Religion by John Calvin, ed. John T. McNeill
and tr. Ford Lewis Battles, 2 vols = *The Library of Christian Classics*,
20 and 21 (London, 1961), *The Expository Times*, 73, no. 3,
pp. 72–3.
Paul T. Fuhrmann, *An Introduction to the Great Creeds of the
Church* (Philadelphia, 1960), *The Scottish Journal of Theology*, 14,
pp. 311–12.

1962   'Theological Education in St Andrews', *St Mary's College Bulletin*, 4
(St Andrews), pp. 8–13.
'A St Andrews manuscript of poems by John Johnston', *Aberdeen
University Review*, 39, pp. 230–2.

REVIEWS

J. H. Burleigh, *A Church History of Scotland* (London, 1960), *JEH*, 13, pp. 108–9.

H. Jackson Forstman, *Word and Spirit*, *Calvin's Doctrine of Biblical Authority* (Stanford, 1962), *The Expository Times*, 73, no. 12, pp. 367–8.

1963   'Further information on the life and likeness of George Buchanan', *ScHR*, 42, pp. 135–42.

Letters of John Johnston c.1565–1611 and Robert Howie c.1565–c.1645 = *St Andrews University Publications*, 54 (Oliver and Boyd, Edinburgh, 1963).

REVIEWS

Lectures on Romans by Martin Luther, ed. and tr. William Pauck = *The Library of Christian Classics*, 15 (London, 1961), *The Expository Times*, 74, no. 5, p. 187.

Luther: Early Theological Works, ed. and tr. James Atkinson = *The Library of Christian Classics*, 16 (London, 1962), *The Expository Times*, 74, no. 7, pp. 204–5.

1964   REVIEW

'A Review Article on the Eldership', J. M. Barkely, *The Eldership in Irish Presbyterianism* (privately printed, Belfast, 1963) and *The Magazine of the Coleraine Ruling Elders Fellowship*, 1 'Spotlight on the Eldership', *Biblical Theology*, 14, pp. 7–16.

1965   'George Buchanan (1506–1582)', *The Alumnus Chronicle of the University of St Andrews*, 56 (1965), pp. 17–19.

REVIEW

Annie I. Dunlop, *Acta Facultatis Artium Universitatis Sanctiandree 1413–1588* = *St Andrews University Publications*, no. 56 (Edinburgh, 1964), *ZKG*, 3/4, pp. 391–2.

1966

REVIEWS

Irvonwy Morgan, *The Godly Preachers of the Elizabethan Church* (London, 1965), *The Expository Times*, 77, no. 4 (1966), p. 125.

D. S. Chambers, *Cardinal Bainbridge in the Court of Rome 1509–1514* (Oxford, 1965), *ZKG*, 1/2, pp. 169–70.

Duncan Shaw, *The General Assemblies of the Church of Scotland 1560–1600* (Edinburgh, 1964), *JTS*, ns 17, pp. 232–5.

1967 'The Church of Scotland in the Age of Reason', *Studies on Voltaire and the Eighteenth Century*, 58 (Geneva, 1967), pp. 1939–51.
REVIEW
T. H. L. Parker, ed., *English Reformers* = *The Library of Christian Classics*, 26 (London, 1966) and Arthur C. Cochrane, *Reformed Confessions of the Sixteenth Century* (London, 1966), *The Expository Times*, 78, no. 8, p. 238.

1968 'The St Andrews Lutherans', *St Mary's College Bulletin*, 10, pp. 17–23.
REVIEWS
Kevin T. Kelly, *Conscience: Dictator or Guide? A Study of Seventeenth-century English Protestant Moral Theology* (London, 1967), *JEH*, 19, pp. 262–3.
Ian A. Dunlop, *William Carstairs and the Kirk by Law Established* (Edinburgh, 1967), *The Scottish Journal of Theology*, 21, pp. 105–6.

1969 REVIEW
Jasper Ridley, *John Knox* (Oxford, 1968), *ScHR*, 48, pp. 184–6.

1970 *Bibliographie de la Réforme 1450–1648, Septième Fascicule Écosse: Ouvrages parus de 1940 à 1960.* Commission Internationale d'Histoire Ecclésiastique Comparée (E. J. Brill, Leiden, 1970), pp. 1–18.

1972 Ed. with Introduction and Commentary, *The First Book of Discipline* (The Saint Andrew Press, Edinburgh, 1972).

1973 'Europe's influence in the making of the Kirk', *The Scotsman*, 15, p. 14.

1974 'The Swiss and the Covenant' in G. W. S. Barrow, ed., *The Scottish Tradition: Essays in Honour of Ronald Gordon Cant* (Edinburgh, 1974), pp. 155–63.

1975 With R. N. Smart, 'A Scottish Form of the Emblème de la Réligion Reformée: the post-Reformation seal of St Mary's College in the University of St Andrews', *Proceedings of the Society of Antiquaries of Scotland*, 105, 1972–1974 (1975), pp. 248–54.
'Scotland' in Derek Baker, ed., *The Bibliography of the Reform 1450–1648, relating to the United Kingdom and Ireland for the Years 1955–70* (Oxford, 1975), pp. 181–217.

1976 REVIEW
Gordan Donaldson, *Scotland Church and Nation through Sixteen*

Centuries, rev. edn (Edinburgh, 1972) and Gordan Donaldson, *The Scottish Reformation* (Cambridge, 1960; repr. 1972), *ScHR*, 55, pp. 77–9.

1977   'The Renaissance Tradition in the Reformed Church of Scotland' in Derek Baker, ed., *Renaissance and Renewal in Christian History*, *SCH*, 14, pp. 251–69.

1978   'The Church and the Universities in Scotland in the era of the Reformation' in *The Church in a Changing Society: Conflict—Reconciliation or Adjustment?* (Uppsala, 1978), pp. 217–22.

1979   'The Cologne Reformation and the Church of Scotland', *JEH*, 30, pp. 39–64.
'John Johnsone's *An confortable exhortation of our mooste holy Christen faith and her frutes*: an early example of Scots Lutheran piety' in Derek Baker, ed., *Reform and Reformation: England and the Continent c.1500–c.1750 = SCH.S*, 2, pp. 133–47.
'The Correspondence of John Johnston and Robert Howie' in P. Tuynan, G. C. Kuiper, and E. Kessler, eds, *Acta Conventus Neo-Latini Amstelodamensis* (Munich, 1979), pp. 197–205.
'Catholic Reform in Germany and the pre-1560 Church in Scotland', *RSCHS*, 20, pp. 105–17.
REVIEW
G. R. Potter, *Zwingli* (Cambridge, 1977) and G. R. Potter, *Huldrich Zwingli* (London, 1978), *ScHR*, 58, pp. 96–8.

1980   'The British Itinerary of Johann Peter Hainzel von Degerstein by Caspar Waser', *Zwingliana*, 15, Heft 3/4 (Zurich, 1980), pp. 259–95.
'The Refoundation of the University in 1579', *The Alumnus Chronicle of the University of St Andrews*, 71 (1980), pp. 3–10.
'Andrew Melville in St Andrews', *St Mary's College Bulletin*, 22, pp. 14–25.
'Andrew Melville: Humanist, Educational Reformer, Theologian and Churchman', *Kate Kennedy Annual 1980*, pp. 7–9.
REVIEWS
Andrew L. Drummond and James Bulloch, *The Church in Late Victorian Scotland, 1874–1900* (Edinburgh, 1978), *JTS*, pp. 262–3.
W. Croft Dickinson, *Scotland from the Earliest Times to 1603*, 3rd edn rev. and ed. A. A. M. Duncan (Oxford, 1977), *JEH*, 31, p. 255.

1981   'Scottish Calvinism and the Principle of Intolerance' in B. Gerrish and R. Benedetto, eds, *Reformatio Perennis: Essays in Honor of Ford Lewis Battles* (Pittsburg, Pa., 1981), pp. 113–28.

'Thomas Chalmers (1780–1847)' in David Daiches, ed., *A Companion to Scottish Culture* (London, 1981), pp. 59–60.

'The Church after 1560' in David Daiches, ed., *A Companion to Scottish Culture* (London, 1981), pp. 65–6.

'Andrew Melville (1542–1622)' in David Daiches, ed., *A Companion to Scottish Culture* (London, 1981), pp. 247–8.

REVIEW

Arthur H. Williamson, *Scottish National Consciousness in the Age of James VI* (Edinburgh, 1979), *JEH*, 32, pp. 103–4.

1982 'Edinburgh, Universität', *TRE*, 9, pp. 288–91.

'Theological controversy: a factor in the origins of the Scottish Enlightenment' in R. H. Campbell and Andrew S. Skinner, eds, *The Origins and Nature of the Scottish Enlightenment* (Edinburgh, 1982), pp. 116–30.

REVIEWS

Jenny Wormald, *Court, Kirk and Community: Scotland 1470–1625* (London, 1981), *JEH*, 33, pp. 652–3.

Maurice Lee, Jr., *Government by Pen: Scotland under James VI and I* (Illinois and London, 1980), *JEH*, 33, p. 504.

1983 REVIEWS

Ian B. Cowan, *The Scottish Reformation: Church and Society in Sixteenth Century Scotland* (New York, 1982), *AHR*, 88, pp. 988–9.

Richard L. Greaves, *Theology and Revolution in the Scottish Reformation: Studies in the Thought of John Knox* (Grand Rapids, 1980), *The Journal of Religion*, 63, pp. 421–2.

Anne Hudson, *English Wycliffite Sermons* (Oxford, 1983), *The Scottish Journal of Theology*, 37, pp. 548–50.

1984 'Aspects of the Lutheran Contribution to the Scottish Reformation', *RSCHS*, 22, pp. 1–12.

REVIEWS

Bernard M. G. Reardon, *Religious Thought in the Reformation* (London, 1981), *The Scottish Journal of Theology*, 37, pp. 267–8.

Paul D. L. Avis, *The Church in the Theology of the Reformers* (London, 1981), ibid., pp. 270–2.

Peter N. Newman, ed., *Seven-Headed Luther: Essays in Commemoration of a Quincentenary 1483–1983* (Oxford, 1983), *The Expository Times*, 95, no. 6, p. 188.

1985 'The Piety of Samuel Rutherford (c.1621–1661): a neglected feature of seventeenth-century Scottish Calvinism', *Nederlands Archief voor Kerkgeschiedenis*, 65, pp. 153–9.

REVIEWS

George Yule, ed., *Luther: Theologian for Catholics and Protestants* (Edinburgh, 1985), *The Expository Times*, 97, no. 3, pp. 91–2.

James Atkinson, *Martin Luther, Prophet to the Catholic Church* (Exeter, 1983), *Religious Studies*, 21, pp. 263–6.

1986 'Faith and Faction—Conflicting Loyalties in the Scottish Reformation' in Michael Hurst, ed., *States, Countries, Provinces* (London, 1986), pp. 72–90.

'Some Continental visitors to Scotland in the late sixteenth and early seventeenth centuries' in T. C. Smout, ed., *Scotland and Europe 1200–1850* (Edinburgh, 1986), pp. 45–61.

1987 'The Office of Superintendent in the *First Book of Discipline*' in B. Vogler, ed., *Miscellanea Historiae Ecclesiasticae*, 8 = *Bibliothèque de la Révue d'Histoire Ecclésiastique* (Louvain, 1987), pp. 239–50.

'Leaves from the lost *Album amicorum* of Sir John Scot of Scotsarvit', *Scottish Studies*, 28, pp. 35–48.

REVIEWS

Alistair McGrath, *The Intellectual Origins of the European Reformation* (Oxford, 1987), *The Expository Times*, 99, no. 2, pp. 58–9.

'The Church Superintendent'—review article of Gordan Donaldson, *Scottish Church History* (Edinburgh, 1986) and David G. Mullan, *Episcopacy in Scotland: the History of an Idea 1560–1638* (Edinburgh, 1986), *The Times Literary Supplement* (16 January 1987), p. 68.

Carlos M. N. Eire, *War Against the Idols: the Reformation of Worship from Erasmus to Calvin* (Cambridge, 1986), *The Durham University Journal*, 79, ns 48, pp. 421–2.

T. H. L. Parker, *Commentaries on Romans 1532–1542* (Edinburgh, 1986), *The Expository Times*, 98, no. 10, p. 314.

Stephen Haliczer, ed. and tr., *Inquisition and Society in Early Modern Europe* (London, 1987), *The Durham University Journal*, 80, ns 49, p. 136.

1988 'A Trilingual College for Scotland: the founding of St Mary's College', *St Mary's College Bulletin*, 31 , pp. 9–19.

REVIEWS

'Men of the Enlightenment'—review article of Richard B. Sher,

Church and University in the Scottish Enlightenment; the Moderate Literati of Edinburgh (Edinburgh, 1985) and Norbert Waszek, *Man's Social Nature: a Topic of the Scottish Enlightenment in its Historical Setting* (Frankfurt-on-Main, 1986), *Scottish Economic and Social History*, 8, pp. 91–3.

Walther von Loewenich, *Martin Luther: the Man and his Work*, tr. L. W. Denef (Minneapolis, 1986) and Bernhard Lohse, *Martin Luther: an Introduction to His Life and Work*, tr. R. C. Schultz (Edinburgh, 1986), *The Expository Times*, 99, no. 5, pp. 153–4.

Dorothea McEwan, *Das Wirken des Voralberger Reformators Bartolomäus Bernhardi: Der Lutherfreund und einer der ersten verheirateten Priester der Lutheraner kommt zu Wort* (Dorbirn, 1986), *German History*, 6, pp. 185–6.

Jörn Sieglerschmidt, *Territorialstaat und Kirchenregiment: Studien zur Rechtsdogmatik des Kirchenpatronatsrecht im 15. und 16. Jahrhundert* (Cologne and Vienna, 1987), *German History*, 6, p. 309.

R. Emmet McLaughlin, *Caspar Schwenckfeld, Reluctant Radical: His Life to 1540* (New Haven, 1986), *German History*, 6, p. 311.

1989   'John Knox (*ca.* 1514–1572)', *TRE*, 19, 1/2, pp. 281–7.
REVIEW
W. P. Stephens, *The Theology of Huldrich Zwingli*, *The Heythrop Journal*, 30, pp. 368–71.

1990   'Humanism in the Low Countries' in Anthony Goodman and Angus MacKay, eds, *The Impact of Humanism on Western Europe* (London, 1990), pp. 137–63.
'Godly Nurture and Admonition in the Lord: Ecclesiastical Discipline in the Reformed Tradition' in Leif Grane and Kai Horby, eds, *Die dänische Reformation vor ihrem internationalen Hintergrund* (Göttingen, 1990), pp. 264–76.
'Humanism and Religious Life' in John MacQueen, ed, *Humanism in Renaissance Scotland* (Edinburgh, 1990), pp. 161–77.

1991   'The conciliarism of John Mair: a note on *A Disputation on the Authority of a Council*' in Diana Wood, ed., *The Church and Sovereignty: Essays in Honour of Michael Wilks = SCH.S*, 9, pp. 429–35.
'Some students from the Netherlands at the University of St Andrews in the late sixteenth and early seventeenth centuries' in C. G. F. de Jong and J. van Sluis, eds, *Gericht verleden. Kerkhistorische opstellen aangeboden aan Prof. Dr. W. Nijenhuis ter gelegenheld van zijn 75ste verjaardag* (Amsterdam, 1991), pp. 1–25.

443